PHP 8 Objects, Patterns, and Practice

Mastering OO Enhancements, Design Patterns, and Essential Development Tools

Sixth Edition

Matt Zandstra

Apress®

PHP 8 Objects, Patterns, and Practice: Mastering OO Enhancements, Design Patterns, and Essential Development Tools

Matt Zandstra
Brighton, UK

ISBN-13 (pbk): 978-1-4842-6790-5   ISBN-13 (electronic): 978-1-4842-6791-2
https://doi.org/10.1007/978-1-4842-6791-2

Managing Director, Apress Media LLC: Welmoed Spahr
Acquisitions Editor: Steve Anglin
Development Editor: Matthew Moodie
Coordinating Editor: Mark Powers

Cover designed by eStudioCalamar

Cover image by Devin Avery on Unsplash (www.unsplash.com)

Distributed to the book trade worldwide by Apress Media, LLC, 1 New York Plaza, New York, NY 10004, U.S.A. Phone 1-800-SPRINGER, fax (201) 348-4505, e-mail orders-ny@springer-sbm.com, or visit www.springeronline.com. Apress Media, LLC is a California LLC and the sole member (owner) is Springer Science + Business Media Finance Inc (SSBM Finance Inc). SSBM Finance Inc is a **Delaware** corporation.

For information on translations, please e-mail booktranslations@springernature.com; for reprint, paperback, or audio rights, please e-mail bookpermissions@springernature.com.

Apress titles may be purchased in bulk for academic, corporate, or promotional use. eBook versions and licenses are also available for most titles. For more information, reference our Print and eBook Bulk Sales web page at http://www.apress.com/bulk-sales.

Any source code or other supplementary material referenced by the author in this book is available to readers on GitHub via the book's product page, located at www.apress.com/9781484267905. For more detailed information, please visit http://www.apress.com/source-code.

Printed on acid-free paper

To Louise. Still the whole point.

Table of Contents

About the Author

Matt Zandstra has worked as a web programmer, consultant, and writer for over two decades. He is the author of *SAMS Teach Yourself PHP in 24 Hours* (three editions) and is a contributor to *DHTML Unleashed*. He has written articles for *Linux Magazine*, Zend, IBM DeveloperWorks, and *php|architect* magazine, among others. Matt was a senior developer/tech lead at Yahoo! and API tech lead at LoveCrafts. Matt works as a consultant advising companies on their architectures and system management and also develops systems primarily with PHP and Java. Matt also writes fiction.

About the Technical Reviewer

Paul Tregoing has worked in ops and development in a variety of environments for nearly 20 years. He worked at Yahoo! for 5 years as a senior developer on the frontpage team; there he generated his first PHP using Perl. Other employers include Bloomberg, Schlumberger, and the British Antarctic Survey, where he became intimate with thousands of penguins.

He now works as a freelance engineer for various clients, small and large, building multitiered web apps using PHP, JavaScript, and many other technologies. Paul is a voracious consumer of science fiction and fantasy and harbors not-so-secret ambitions to try his hand at writing in the near future. He lives in Cambridge, United Kingdom, with his wife and children.

About the Technical Reviewer

Acknowledgments

As always, I have benefited from the support of many people while working on this edition. But as always, I must also look back to the book's origins. I tried out some of this book's underlying concepts in a talk in Brighton, back when we were all first marveling at the shiny possibilities of PHP 5. Thanks to Andy Budd, who hosted the talk, and to the vibrant Brighton developer community. Thanks also to Jessey White-Cinis, who was at that meeting and who put me in touch with Martin Streicher at Apress.

Once again, this time around, the Apress team has provided enormous support, feedback, and encouragement. I am lucky to have benefited from such professionalism.

I'm very lucky to have had my friend and colleague, Paul Tregoing, working on this edition as Technical Reviewer. The fact that PHP itself was under active development throughout the writing of this book demanded extra vigilance. Code examples that were perfectly valid in early drafts were rendered incorrect by the language's fast evolution. Once again, this edition has greatly benefited from Paul's knowledge, insight, and attention to detail—many thanks Paul!

Thanks and love to my wife, Louise. The production of this book has coincided with three pandemic lockdowns, so thanks are also due to our children, Holly and Jake, for many much-needed distractions—often provided during Zoom meetings conducted in my office space (the corner of the kitchen table).

Thanks to Steven Metsker for his kind permission to reimplement in PHP a simplified version of the parser API he presented in his book, *Building Parsers with Java* (Addison-Wesley Professional, 2001).

I write to music, and, in previous editions of this book, I remembered the great DJ, John Peel, champion of the underground and the eclectic. The soundtrack for this edition was largely provided by BBC Radio 3's contemporary music show, *Late Junction*, played on a loop. Thanks to them for keeping things weird.

Introduction

When I first conceived of this book, object-oriented design in PHP was an esoteric topic. The intervening years have not only seen the inexorable rise of PHP as an object-oriented language but also the march of the framework. Frameworks are incredibly useful, of course. They manage the guts and the glue of many (perhaps, these days, most) web applications. What's more, they often exemplify precisely the principles of design that this book explores.

There is, though, a danger for developers here, as there is in all useful APIs. This is the fear that one might find oneself relegated to userland, forced to wait for remote gurus to fix bugs or add features at their whim. It's a short step from this standpoint to a kind of exile in which one is left regarding the innards of a framework as advanced magic and one's own work as not much more than a minor adornment stuck up on top of a mighty unknowable infrastructure.

Although I'm an inveterate reinventor of wheels, the thrust of my argument is not that we should all throw away our frameworks and build MVC applications from scratch (at least not always). It is rather that, as developers, we should understand the problems that frameworks solve and the strategies they use to solve them. We should be able to evaluate frameworks not only functionally but in terms of the design decisions their creators have made and to judge the quality of their implementations. And yes, when the conditions are right, we should go ahead and build our own spare and focused applications and, over time, compile our own libraries of reusable code.

I hope this book goes some way toward helping PHP developers apply design-oriented insights to their platforms and libraries and provides some of the conceptual tools needed when it's time to go it alone.

PART I

Objects

## CHAPTER 1

PHP: Design and Management

In July 2004, PHP 5.0 was released. This version introduced a suite of radical enhancements. Perhaps first among these was radically improved support for object-oriented programming. This stimulated much interest in objects and design within the PHP community. In fact, this was an intensification of a process that began when version 4 first made object-oriented programming with PHP a serious reality.

In this chapter, I look at some of the needs that coding with objects can address. I very briefly summarize some aspects of the evolution of patterns and related practices.

I also outline the topics covered by this book. I will look at the following:

- *The evolution of disaster*: A project goes bad

- *Design and PHP*: How object-oriented design techniques took root in the PHP community

- *This book*: Objects, Patterns, Practice

The Problem

The problem is that PHP is just too easy. It tempts you to try out your ideas and flatters you with good results. You write much of your code straight into your web pages, because PHP is designed to support that. You add utility functions (such as database access code) to files that can be included from page to page, and before you know it, you have a working web application.

You are well on the road to ruin. You don't realize this, of course, because your site looks fantastic. It performs well, your clients are happy, and your users are spending money.

© Matt Zandstra 2021
M. Zandstra, *PHP 8 Objects, Patterns, and Practice*, https://doi.org/10.1007/978-1-4842-6791-2_1

Trouble strikes when you go back to the code to begin a new phase. Now you have a larger team, some more users, and a bigger budget. Yet, without warning, things begin to go wrong. It's as if your project has been poisoned.

Your new programmer is struggling to understand code that is second nature to you, although perhaps a little byzantine in its twists and turns. She is taking longer than you expected to reach full strength as a team member.

A simple change, estimated at a day, takes three days when you discover that you must update 20 or more web pages as a result.

One of your coders saves his version of a file over major changes you made to the same code some time earlier. The loss is not discovered for three days, by which time you have amended your own local copy. It takes a day to sort out the mess, holding up a third developer who was also working on the file.

Because of the application's popularity, you need to shift the code to a new server. The project has to be installed by hand, and you discover that file paths, database names, and passwords are hard-coded into many source files. You halt work during the move because you don't want to overwrite the configuration changes the migration requires. The estimated two hours becomes eight as it is revealed that someone did something clever involving the Apache module ModRewrite, and the application now requires this to operate properly.

You finally launch phase 2. All is well for a day and a half. The first bug report comes in as you are about to leave the office. The client phones minutes later to complain. Her report is similar to the first, but a little more scrutiny reveals that it is a different bug causing similar behavior. You remember the simple change back at the start of the phase that necessitated extensive modifications throughout the rest of the project.

You realize that not all of the required modifications are in place. This is either because they were omitted to start with or because the files in question were overwritten in merge collisions. You hurriedly make the modifications needed to fix the bugs. You're in too much of a hurry to test the changes, but they are a simple matter of copy and paste, so what can go wrong?

The next morning, you arrive at the office to find that a shopping basket module has been down all night. The last-minute changes you made omitted a leading quotation mark, rendering the code unusable. Of course, while you were asleep, potential customers in other time zones were wide awake and ready to spend money at your store. You fix the problem, mollify the client, and gather the team for another day's firefighting.

This everyday tale of coding folk may seem a little over the top, but I have seen all these things happen over and over again. Many PHP projects start their life small and evolve into monsters.

Because the presentation layer also contains application logic, duplication creeps in early as database queries, authentication checks, form processing, and more are copied from page to page. Every time a change is required to one of these blocks of code, it must be made everywhere that the code is found, or bugs will surely follow.

Lack of documentation makes the code hard to read, and lack of testing allows obscure bugs to go undiscovered until deployment. The changing nature of a client's business often means that code evolves away from its original purpose until it is performing tasks for which it is fundamentally unsuited. Because such code has often evolved as a seething, intermingled lump, it is hard, if not impossible, to switch out and rewrite parts of it to suit the new purpose.

Now, none of this is bad news if you are a freelance PHP consultant. Assessing and fixing a system like this can fund expensive espresso drinks and DVD box sets for six months or more. More seriously, though, problems of this sort can mean the difference between a business's success and failure.

PHP and Other Languages

PHP's phenomenal popularity meant that its boundaries were tested early and hard. As you will see in the next chapter, PHP started life as a set of macros for managing personal home pages. With the advent of PHP 3 and, to a greater extent, PHP 4, the language rapidly became the successful power behind large enterprise websites. In many ways, however, the legacy of PHP's beginnings carried through into script design and project management. In some quarters, PHP retained an unfair reputation as a hobbyist language, best suited for presentation tasks.

About this time (around the turn of the millennium), new ideas were gaining currency in other coding communities. An interest in object-oriented design galvanized the Java community. Since Java is an object-oriented language, you may think that this is a redundancy. Java provides a grain that is easier to work with than against, of course, but using classes and objects does not in itself determine a particular design approach.

The concept of the design pattern as a way of describing a problem, together with the essence of its solution, was first discussed in the 1970s. Perhaps aptly, the idea originated in the field of architecture, not computer science, in a seminal work by Christopher

Alexander: *A Pattern Language* (Oxford University Press, 1977). By the early 1990s, object-oriented programmers were using the same technique to name and describe problems of software design. The seminal book on design patterns, *Design Patterns: Elements of Reusable Object-Oriented Software* (Addison-Wesley Professional, 1995), by Erich Gamma, Richard Helm, Ralph Johnson, and John Vlissides (henceforth referred to in this book by their affectionate nickname, the *Gang of Four*), is still indispensable today. The patterns it contains are a required first step for anyone starting out in this field, which is why most of the patterns in this book are drawn from it.

The Java language itself deployed many core patterns in its API, but it wasn't until the late 1990s that design patterns seeped into the consciousness of the coding community at large. Patterns quickly infected the computer sections of Main Street bookstores, and the first flame wars began on mailing lists and in forums.

Whether you think that patterns are a powerful way of communicating craft knowledge or largely hot air (and, given the title of this book, you can probably guess where I stand on that issue), it is hard to deny that the emphasis on software design they have encouraged is beneficial in itself.

Related topics also grew in prominence. Among them was Extreme Programming (XP), championed by Kent Beck. XP is an approach to projects that encourages flexible, design-oriented, highly focused planning and execution.

Prominent among XP's principles is an insistence that testing is crucial to a project's success. Tests should be automated, run often, and preferably designed before their target code is written.

XP also dictates that projects should be broken down into small (very small) iterations. Both code and requirements should be scrutinized at all times. Architecture and design should be a shared and constant issue, leading to the frequent revision of code.

If XP was the militant wing of the design movement, then the moderate tendency is well represented by one of the best books about programming that I have ever read: *The Pragmatic Programmer: From Journeyman to Master* by Andrew Hunt and David Thomas (Addison-Wesley Professional, 1999).

XP was deemed a tad cultish by some, but it grew out of two decades of object-oriented practice at the highest level, and its principles were widely cannibalized. In particular, code revision, known as refactoring, was taken up as a powerful adjunct to patterns. Refactoring has evolved since the 1980s, but it was codified in Martin Fowler's catalog of refactorings, *Refactoring: Improving the Design of Existing Code* (Addison-Wesley Professional), which was published in 1999 and defined the field.

Testing, too, became a hot issue with the rise to prominence of XP and patterns. The importance of automated tests was further underlined by the release of the powerful JUnit test platform, which became a key weapon in the Java programmer's armory. A landmark article on the subject, "Test Infected: Programmers Love Writing Tests" by Kent Beck and Erich Gamma (`http://junit.sourceforge.net/doc/testinfected/testing.htm`), gives an excellent introduction to the topic and remains hugely influential.

PHP 4 was released at about this time, bringing with it improvements in efficiency and, crucially, enhanced support for objects. These enhancements made fully object-oriented projects a possibility. Programmers embraced this feature, somewhat to the surprise of Zend founders Zeev Suraski and Andi Gutmans, who had joined Rasmus Lerdorf to manage PHP development. As you shall see in the next chapter, PHP's object support was by no means perfect. But with discipline and careful use of syntax, one could really begin to think in objects and PHP at the same time.

Nevertheless, design disasters such as the one depicted at the start of this chapter remained common. Design culture was some way off and almost nonexistent in books about PHP. Online, however, the interest was clear. Leon Atkinson wrote a piece about PHP and patterns for Zend in 2001, and Harry Fuecks launched his journal at `www.phppatterns.com` (now defunct) in 2002. Pattern-based framework projects such as BinaryCloud began to emerge, as well as tools for automated testing and documentation.

The release of the first PHP 5 beta in 2003 ensured the future of PHP as a language for object-oriented programming. Zend Engine 2 provided greatly improved object support. Equally important, it sent a signal that objects and object-oriented design were now central to the PHP project.

Over the years, PHP 5 continued to evolve and improve, incorporating important new features such as namespaces and closures. During this time, it secured its reputation as the best choice for server-side web programming.

PHP 7, released in December 2015, represented a continuation of this trend. In particular, it provided support for both parameter and return type declarations—two features that many developers (together with previous editions of this book) had been clamoring for over the years. There were many other features and improvements including anonymous classes, improved memory usage, and boosted speed. Over the years, the language grew steadily more robust, cleaner, and more fun to work with from the perspective of an object-oriented coder.

In December 2020, almost exactly five years after the release of PHP 7, PHP 8 is due for release. While some of the implementation details may change (and have changed a little during the writing of this book), the features are already available at the time of this writing (August 2020). I cover many of them in detail here. They include improvements to type declarations, streamlined property assignment, and many other new features. The headline addition is, perhaps, support for attributes (often called annotations in other languages).

About This Book

This book does not attempt to break new ground in the field of object-oriented design; in that respect, it perches precariously on the shoulders of giants. Instead, I examine, in the context of PHP, some well-established design principles and some key patterns (particularly those inscribed in *Design Patterns*, the classic Gang of Four book). Finally, I move beyond the strict limits of code to look at tools and techniques that can help to ensure the success of a project. Aside from this introduction and a brief conclusion, the book is divided into three main parts: objects, patterns, and practice.

Objects

I begin Part 1 with a quick look at the history of PHP and objects, charting their shift from afterthought in PHP 3 to core feature in PHP 5.

You can still be an experienced and successful PHP programmer with little or no knowledge of objects. For this reason, I start from first principles to explain objects, classes, and inheritance. Even at this early stage, I look at some of the object enhancements that PHP 5, PHP 7, and PHP 8 introduced.

The basics established, I delve deeper into our topic, examining PHP's more advanced object-oriented features. I also devote a chapter to the tools that PHP provides to help you work with objects and classes.

It is not enough, however, to know how to declare a class, and to use it to instantiate an object. You must first choose the right participants for your system and decide the best ways for them to interact. These choices are much harder to describe and to learn than the bald facts about object tools and syntax. I finish Part 1 with an introduction to object-oriented design with PHP.

Patterns

A pattern describes a problem in software design and provides the kernel of a solution. "Solution" here does not mean the kind of cut-and-paste code that you might find in a cookbook (excellent though cookbooks are as resources for the programmer). Instead, a design pattern describes an approach that can be taken to solve a problem. A sample implementation may be given, but it is less important than the concept that it serves to illustrate.

Part 2 begins by defining design patterns and describing their structure. I also look at some of the reasons behind their popularity.

Patterns tend to promote and follow certain core design principles. An understanding of these can help in analyzing a pattern's motivation and can usefully be applied to all programming. I discuss some of these principles. I also examine the Unified Modeling Language (UML), a platform-independent way of describing classes and their interactions.

Although this book is not a pattern catalog, I examine some of the most famous and useful patterns. I describe the problem that each pattern addresses, analyze the solution, and present an implementation example in PHP.

Practice

Even a beautifully balanced architecture will fail if it is not managed correctly. In Part 3, I look at the tools available to help you create a framework that ensures the success of your project. If the rest of the book is about the practice of design and programming, Part 3 is about the practice of managing your code. The tools that I examine can form a support structure for a project, helping to track bugs as they occur, promoting collaboration among programmers, and providing ease of installation and clarity of code.

I have already discussed the power of the automated test. I kick off Part 3 with an introductory chapter that gives an overview of problems and solutions in this area.

Many programmers are guilty of giving in to the impulse to do everything themselves. Composer, together with Packagist, its main repository, offers access to thousands of dependency managed packages that can be stitched into projects with ease. I look at the trade-offs between implementing a feature yourself and deploying a Composer package.

While I'm on the topic of Composer, I look at the installation mechanism that makes the deployment of a package as simple as a single command.

Code is about collaboration. This fact can be rewarding. It can also be a complete nightmare. Git is a version control system that enables many programmers to work together on the same codebase without overwriting one another's work. It lets you grab snapshots of your project at any stage in development, see who has made which changes, and split the project into mergeable branches. Git will save your project one day.

When people and libraries collaborate, they often bring different conventions and styles to the party. While this is healthy, it can also undermine interoperability. Words like *conform* and *comply* give me the shivers, but it is undeniable that the creativity of the Internet is underpinned by standards. By obeying certain conventions, we are freed to play in an unimaginably vast sandbox. So, in a new chapter, I explore PHP standards, how they can help us, and how and why we should, yes, *comply*.

Two facts seem inevitable. First, bugs often recur in the same region of code, making some work days an exercise in déjà vu. Second, often improvements break as much as, or more than, they fix. Automated testing can address both of these issues, providing an early warning system for problems in your code. I introduce PHPUnit, a powerful implementation of the so-called xUnit test platform designed first for Smalltalk but ported now to many languages, notably Java. I look in particular at PHPUnit's features and more generally at the benefits, and some of the costs, of testing.

Applications are messy. They may need files to be installed in nonstandard locations or want to set up databases or need to patch server configuration. In short, applications need *stuff* to be done during installation. Phing is a faithful port of a Java tool called Ant. Phing and Ant interpret a build file and process your source files in any way you tell them to. This usually means copying them from a source directory to various target locations around your system, but, as your needs get more complex, Phing scales effortlessly to meet them.

Some companies enforce development platforms—but in many cases, teams end up running an array of different operating systems. Contractors arrive wielding PC laptops (hello Paul Tregoing, fifth and current edition tech editor), some team members evangelize endlessly for their favorite Linux distro (that's me and my Fedora), and many hold out for yet another sexy-looking PowerBook (the coffee bar and meeting room use of which doesn't at all make you look like just another node in a hipster Borg army). All of these will run a LAMP stack with varying degrees of ease. Ideally, though, developers should run their code in environments that closely resemble the ultimate production system. I examine Vagrant, an application which uses virtualization so that team members can keep their idiosyncratic development platforms but run project code on a production-like system.

10

Testing and build are all very well, but you have to install and run your tests and keep on doing so in order to reap the benefits. It's easy to become complacent and let things slide if you don't automate your builds and tests. I look at some tools and techniques that are lumped together in the category "continuous integration" that will help you do just that.

What's New in the Sixth Edition

PHP is a living language, and as such it's under constant review and development. This new edition, too, has been reviewed and thoroughly updated to take account of changes and new opportunities.

I cover new features such as attributes and the many enhancements to type declarations. Examples use PHP 8 features where appropriate, so be aware that you will often need to run code against the PHP 8 interpreter—or be ready to do some work to downgrade.

Summary

This is a book about object-oriented design and programming. It is also about tools for managing a PHP codebase from collaboration through to deployment.

These two themes address the same problem from different but complementary angles. The primary aim is to build systems that achieve their objectives and lend themselves well to collaborative development.

A secondary goal lies in the aesthetics of software systems. As programmers, we build machines that have shape and action. We invest many hours of our working day, and many days of our lives, writing these shapes into being. We want the tools we build, whether individual classes and objects, software components, or end products, to form an elegant whole. The process of version control, testing, documentation, and build does more than support this objective: it is part of the shape we want to achieve. Just as we want clean and clever code, we want a codebase that is designed well for developers and users alike. The mechanics of sharing, reading, and deploying the project should be as important as the code itself.

CHAPTER 2

PHP and Objects

Objects were not always a key part of the PHP project. In fact, they were once described as an afterthought by PHP's designers.

As afterthoughts go, this one has proved remarkably resilient. In this chapter, I introduce this book's coverage of objects by summarizing the development of PHP's object-oriented features.

We will look at the following:

- *PHP/FI 2.0*: PHP, but not as we know it.

- *PHP 3*: Objects make their first appearance.

- *PHP 4*: Object-oriented programming grows up.

- *PHP 5*: Objects at the heart of the language.

- *PHP 7*: Closing the gap.

- *PHP 8*: The consolidation continues.

The Accidental Success of PHP Objects

With PHP's extensive object support and so many object-oriented PHP libraries and applications in circulation, the rise of the object in PHP may seem like the culmination of a natural and inevitable process. In fact, nothing could be further from the truth.

In the Beginning: PHP/FI

The genesis of PHP as we know it today lies with two tools developed by Rasmus Lerdorf using Perl. PHP stood for Personal Home Page Tools. FI stood for Form Interpreter. Together, they comprised macros for sending SQL statements to databases, processing forms, and flow control.

© Matt Zandstra 2021
M. Zandstra, *PHP 8 Objects, Patterns, and Practice*, https://doi.org/10.1007/978-1-4842-6791-2_2

These tools were rewritten in C and combined under the name PHP/FI 2.0. The language at this stage looked different from the syntax we recognize today, but not *that* different. There was support for variables, associative arrays, and functions. Objects, however, were not even on the horizon.

Syntactic Sugar: PHP 3

In fact, even as PHP 3 was in the planning stage, objects were off the agenda. The principal architects of PHP 3 were Zeev Suraski and Andi Gutmans. PHP 3 was a complete rewrite of PHP/FI 2.0, but objects were not deemed a necessary part of the new syntax.

According to Zeev Suraski, support for classes was added almost as an afterthought (on August 27, 1997, to be precise). Classes and objects were actually just another way to define and access associative arrays.

Of course, the addition of methods and inheritance made classes much more than glorified associative arrays, but there were still severe limitations on what you might do with your classes. In particular, you could not access a parent class's overridden methods (don't worry if you don't know what this means yet; I will explain later). Another disadvantage that I will examine in the next section was the less than optimal way that objects were passed around in PHP scripts.

That objects were a marginal issue at this time is underlined by their lack of prominence in official documentation. The manual devoted one sentence and a code example to objects. The example did not illustrate inheritance or properties.

PHP 4 and the Quiet Revolution

If PHP 4 was yet another groundbreaking step for the language, most of the core changes took place beneath the surface. The Zend Engine (its name derived from *Zee*v and A*nd*i) was written from scratch to power the language. The Zend Engine is one of the main components that drive PHP. Any PHP function you might care to call is in fact part of the high-level extension layer. These do the busywork they were named for, like talking to database APIs or juggling strings for you. Beneath that, the Zend Engine manages memory, delegates control to other components, and translates the familiar PHP syntax you work with every day into runnable bytecode. It is the Zend Engine that we have to thank for core language features like classes.

From our *objective* perspective, the fact that PHP 4 made it possible to override parent methods and access them from child classes was a major benefit.

A major drawback remained, however. Assigning an object to a variable, passing it to a function, or returning it from a method resulted in a copy being made. Consider an assignment like this:

```
$my_obj = new  User('bob');
$other  = $my_obj;
```

This resulted in the existence of two User objects rather than two references to the same User object. In most object-oriented languages, you would expect assignment by reference rather than by value. This means that you would pass and assign handles that point to objects rather than copy the objects themselves. The default pass-by-value behavior resulted in many obscure bugs as programmers unwittingly modified objects in one part of a script, expecting the changes to be seen via references elsewhere. Throughout this book, you will see many examples in which I maintain multiple references to the same object.

Luckily, there was a way of enforcing pass by reference, but it meant remembering to use a clumsy construction.

Here's how you would assign by reference:

```
$other =& $my_obj;
// $other and $my_obj point to same object
```

This enforces pass by reference:

```
function setSchool(& $school)
{
    // $school is now a reference to not a copy of passed object
}
```

And here is return by reference:

```
function & getSchool()
{
    // returning a reference not a copy
    return  $this->school;
}
```

Although this worked fine, it was easy to forget to add the ampersand, and that meant it was all too easy for bugs to creep into object-oriented code. These were particularly hard to track down, because they rarely caused any reported errors, just plausible but broken behavior.

Coverage of syntax in general, and objects in particular, was extended in the PHP manual, and object-oriented coding began to bubble up to the mainstream. Objects in PHP were not uncontroversial (then, as now, no doubt), and threads like "Do I need objects?" were common flame-bait in mailing lists. Indeed, the Zend site played host to articles that encouraged object-oriented programming side by side with others that sounded a warning note. Pass-by-reference issues and controversy notwithstanding, many coders just got on and peppered their code with ampersand characters. Object-oriented PHP grew in popularity. Zeev Suraski wrote this in an article for DevX.com (`www.devx.com/webdev/Article/10007/0/page/1`):

> *One of the biggest twists in PHP's history was that despite the very limited functionality, and despite a host of problems and limitations, object-oriented programming in PHP thrived and became the most popular para-digm for the growing numbers of off-the-shelf PHP applications. This trend, which was mostly unexpected, caught PHP in a suboptimal situation. It became apparent that objects were not behaving like objects in other OO languages, and were instead behaving like [associative] arrays.*

As noted in the previous chapter, interest in object-oriented design became obvious in sites and articles online. PHP's official software repository, PEAR, itself embraced object-oriented programming. With hindsight, it's easy to think of PHP's adoption of object-oriented support as a reluctant capitulation to an inevitable force. It's important to remember that although object-oriented programming has been around since the 1960s, it really gained ground in the mid-1990s. Java, the great popularizer, was not released until 1995. A superset of C, a procedural language, C++ has been around since 1979. After a long evolution, it arguably made the leap to the big time during the 1990s. Perl 5 was released in 1994, another revolution within a formerly procedural language that made it possible for its users to think in objects (although some argue that Perl's object-oriented support also felt like something of an afterthought). For a small procedural language, PHP developed its object support remarkably fast, showing a real responsiveness to the requirements of its users.

Change Embraced: PHP 5

PHP 5 represented an explicit endorsement of objects and object-oriented programming. That is not to say that objects were the only way to work with PHP (this book does not say that either, by the way). Objects were, however, recognized as a powerful and important means for developing enterprise systems, and PHP fully supported them in its core design.

Arguably, one significant effect of the enhancements in PHP 5 was the adoption of the language by larger Internet companies. Both Yahoo! and Facebook, for example, started using PHP extensively within their platforms. With version 5, PHP became one of the standard languages for development and enterprise on the Internet.

Objects had moved from afterthought to language driver. Perhaps the most important change was the new apparent pass-by-reference behavior which replaced the evils of object copying. That was only the beginning, however. Throughout this book, and particularly in this part of it, we will encounter many more enhancements, including private and protected methods and properties, the static keyword, namespaces, type hints (now called type declarations), and exceptions. PHP 5 was around for a long time (about 12 years), and important new features were released incrementally.

Note   It is worth noting that PHP did not strictly speaking move to pass by reference with the introduction of PHP 5, and this has not changed. Instead, by default, when an object is assigned, passed to a method, or returned from one, an identifier to that object is *copied*. So, unless you pin matters down and enforce pass by reference with the ampersand character, you are still performing a copy operation. In practical terms, however, there is usually little difference between this kind of copying and pass by reference since you reference the same target object with your copied identifier as you did with your original.

PHP 5.3, for example, brought namespaces. These let you create a named scope for classes and functions, so that you are less likely to run into duplicate names as you include libraries and expand your system. They also rescue you from ugly but necessary naming conventions such as this:

```
class megaquiz_util_Conf
{

}
```

Class names such as this are one way of preventing clashes between packages, but they can make for tortuous code.

We have also seen support for closures, generators, traits, and late static bindings.

PHP 7: Closing the Gap

Programmers are a demanding lot. For many lovers of design patterns, there were two key features that PHP still lacked. These were scalar type declarations and enforced return types. With PHP 5, it was possible to enforce the type of an argument passed to a function or method, so long as you only needed to require an object, an array, or, later, callable code. Scalar values (like integers, strings, and floats) could not be enforced at all. Furthermore, if you wanted to declare a method or a function's return type, you were altogether out of luck.

As you will see, object-oriented design often uses a method declaration as a kind of contract. The method demands certain inputs, and, reciprocally, it promises to give you a particular type of data back. PHP 5 programmers were forced to rely on comments, convention, and manual type checking to maintain contracts of this kind in many cases. Developers and commentators often complained about this. Here is a quote from the Fourth Edition of this book:

> there is still no commitment to provide support for hinted return types. This would allow you to declare in a method or function's declaration the object type that it returns. This would then be enforced by the PHP engine. Hinted return types would further improve PHP's support for pattern principles (principles such as "code to an interface, not an implementation"). I hope one day to revise this book to cover that feature!

I'm pleased to write that the day did arrive! PHP 7 introduced scalar type declarations (previously known as type hints) and return type declarations. What's more, PHP 7.4 took type safety even further by introducing typed properties. Naturally, all of that is covered in this edition.

PHP 7 also provided other nice-to-haves, including anonymous classes and some namespace enhancements.

PHP 8: The Consolidation Continues

PHP has always been a great magpie, borrowing shiny proven features from other languages. PHP 8 introduces many new features including attributes, often known in other languages as *annotations*. These handy tags can be used to provide additional contextual information about classes, methods, properties, and constants in a system. Furthermore, PHP 8 has continued to extend its support for type declarations. Particularly interesting in this area is the union type declaration. This allows you to declare that the type of a property or parameter should be constrained to one of several specified types. You can lock down your types at the same time as taking advantage of PHP's type flexibility. The very definition of having your cake and eating it!

Advocacy and Agnosticism: The Object Debate

Objects and object-oriented design seem to stir passions on both sides of the enthusiasm divide. Many excellent programmers have produced excellent code for years without using objects, and PHP continues to be a superb platform for procedural web programming.

This book naturally displays an object-oriented bias throughout, a bias that reflects my object-infected outlook. Because this book *is* a celebration of objects, and an introduction to object-oriented design, it is inevitable that the emphasis is unashamedly object oriented. Nothing in this book is intended, however, to suggest that objects are the one true path to coding success with PHP.

Whether a developer chose to work with PHP as an object-oriented language was once a matter of preference. This is still true to the extent that one can create perfectly acceptable working systems using functions and global code. Some great tools (e.g., WordPress) are still procedural in their underlying architecture (though even these may make extensive use of objects these days). It is, however, becoming increasingly hard to work as a PHP programmer without using and understanding PHP's support for objects, not least because the third-party libraries you are likely to rely upon in your projects will themselves likely be object oriented.

Still, as you read, it is worth bearing in mind the famous Perl motto, "There's more than one way to do it." This is especially true of smaller scripts, where quickly getting a working example up and running is more important than building a structure that will scale well into a larger system (scratch projects of this sort are often known as "spikes").

Code is a flexible medium. The trick is to know when your quick proof of concept is becoming the root of a larger development and to call a halt before lasting design decisions are made for you by the sheer weight of your code. Now that you have decided to take a design-oriented approach to your growing project, I hope that this book provides the help that you need to get started building object-oriented architectures.

Summary

This short chapter placed objects in their context in the PHP language. The future for PHP is very much bound up with object-oriented design. In the next few chapters, I take a snapshot of PHP's current support for object features and introduce some design issues.

CHAPTER 3

Object Basics

Objects and classes lie at the heart of this book, and, since the introduction of PHP 5 over a decade ago, they have lain at the heart of PHP, too. In this chapter, I establish the groundwork for more in-depth coverage of objects and design by examining PHP's core object-oriented features. If you are new to object-oriented programming, you should read this chapter carefully.

This chapter will cover the following topics:

- *Classes and objects*: Declaring classes and instantiating objects

- *Constructor methods*: Automating the setup of your objects

- *Primitive and class types*: Why type matters

- *Inheritance*: Why we need inheritance and how to use it

- *Visibility*: Streamlining your object interfaces and protecting your methods and properties from meddling

Classes and Objects

The first barrier to understanding object-oriented programming is the strange and wonderful relationship between the class and the object. For many people, it is this relationship that represents the first moment of revelation, the first flash of object-oriented excitement. So let's not skimp on the fundamentals.

A First Class

Classes are often described in terms of objects. This is interesting, because objects are often described in terms of classes. This circularity can make the first steps in object-oriented programming hard going. Because it's classes that shape objects, we should begin by defining a class.

© Matt Zandstra 2021
M. Zandstra, *PHP 8 Objects, Patterns, and Practice*, https://doi.org/10.1007/978-1-4842-6791-2_3

In short, a class is a code template used to generate one or more objects. You declare a class with the `class` keyword and an arbitrary class name. Class names can be any combination of numbers and letters, although they must not begin with a number. They can also contain underscore characters. The code associated with a class must be enclosed within braces. Here, I combine these elements to build a class:

```
// listing 03.01

class ShopProduct
{
    // class body
}
```

The `ShopProduct` class in the example is already a legal class, although it is not terribly useful yet. I have done something quite significant, however. I have defined a type; that is, I have created a category of data that I can use in my scripts. The power of this should become clearer as you work through the chapter.

A First Object (or Two)

If a class is a template for generating objects, it follows that an object is data that has been structured according to the template defined in a class. An object is said to be an instance of its class. It is of the type defined by the class.

I use the `ShopProduct` class as a mold for generating `ShopProduct` objects. To do this, I need the `new` operator. The `new` operator is used in conjunction with the name of a class, like this:

```
// listing 03.02
$product1 = new ShopProduct();
$product2 = new ShopProduct();
```

The `new` operator is invoked with a class name as its only operand and returns an instance of that class; in our example, it generates a `ShopProduct` object.

I have used the `ShopProduct` class as a template to generate two `ShopProduct` objects. Although they are functionally identical (i.e., empty), `$product1` and `$product2` are different objects of the same type generated from a single class.

If you are still confused, try this analogy. Think of a class as a cast in a machine that makes plastic ducks. Our objects are the ducks that this machine generates. The type of thing generated is determined by the mold from which it is pressed. The ducks look identical in every way, but they are distinct entities. In other words, they are different instances of the same type. The ducks may even have their own serial numbers to prove their identities. Every object that is created in a PHP script is also given its own unique identifier. (Note that the identifier is unique for the life of the object; that is, PHP reuses identifiers, even within a process.) I can demonstrate this by printing out the $product1 and $product2 objects:

```
// listing 03.03
var_dump($product1);
var_dump($product2);
```

Executing these functions produces the following output:

```
object(popp\ch03\batch01\ShopProduct)#235 (0) {

}

object(popp\ch03\batch01\ShopProduct)#234 (0) {

}
```

Note   In ancient versions of PHP (up to version 5.1), you could print an object directly. This casted the object to a string containing the object's ID. From PHP 5.2 onward, the language no longer supported this magic, and any attempt to treat an object as a string now causes an error unless a method named __toString() is defined in the object's class. I look at methods later in this chapter, and I cover __toString() in Chapter 4.

By passing the objects to var_dump(), I extract useful information including, after the hash sign, each object's internal identifier.

In order to make these objects more interesting, I can amend the ShopProduct class to support special data fields called properties.

Setting Properties in a Class

Classes can define special variables called properties. A property, also known as a member variable, holds data that can vary from object to object. So in the case of ShopProduct objects, you may wish to manipulate title and price fields, for example.

A property in a class looks similar to a standard variable except that, in declaring a property, you must precede the property variable with a visibility keyword. This can be public, protected, or private, and it determines the location in your code from which the property can be accessed. Public properties are accessible outside the class, for example, and private properties can only be accessed by code within the class.

I will return to these keywords and the issue of visibility later in this chapter. For now, I will declare some properties using the public keyword:

```
// listing 03.04

class ShopProduct
{
    public $title = "default product";
    public $producerMainName = "main name";
    public $producerFirstName = "first name";
    public $price = 0;
}
```

As you can see, I set up four properties, assigning a default value to each of them. Any objects I instantiate from the ShopProduct class will now be prepopulated with default data. The public keyword in each property declaration ensures that I can access the property from outside of the object context.

You can access property variables on an object-by-object basis using the characters '->' (the object operator) in conjunction with an object variable and property name, like this:

```
// listing 03.05
$product1 = new ShopProduct();
print $product1->title;
```

```
default product
```

Because the properties are defined as `public`, you can assign values to them just as you can read them, replacing any default value set in the class:

```
// listing 03.06
$product1 = new ShopProduct();
$product2 = new ShopProduct();
$product1->title = "My Antonia";
$product2->title = "Catch 22";
```

By declaring and setting the `$title` property in the `ShopProduct` class, I ensure that all `ShopProduct` objects have this property when first created. This means code that uses this class can work with `ShopProduct` objects based on that assumption. Because I can reset it, though, the value of `$title` may vary from object to object.

Note   Code that uses a class, function, or method is often described as the class's, function's, or method's *client* or as *client code*. You will see this term frequently in the coming chapters.

In fact, PHP does not force us to declare all our properties in the class. You could add properties dynamically to an object, like this:

```
// listing 03.07
$product1->arbitraryAddition = "treehouse";
```

However, this method of assigning properties to objects is not considered good practice in object-oriented programming.

Why is it bad practice to set properties dynamically? When you create a class, you define a type. You inform the world that your class (and any object instantiated from it) consists of a particular set of fields and functions. If your `ShopProduct` class defines a `$title` property, then any code that works with `ShopProduct` objects can proceed on the assumption that a `$title` property will be available. There can be no guarantees about properties that have been dynamically set, though.

My objects are still cumbersome at this stage. When I need to work with an object's properties, I must currently do so from outside the object. I reach in to set and get

property information. Setting multiple properties on multiple objects will soon become
a chore:

```
// listing 03.08
$product1 = new ShopProduct();
$product1->title = "My Antonia";
$product1->producerMainName  = "Cather";
$product1->producerFirstName = "Willa";
$product1->price = 5.99;
```

I work once again with the ShopProduct class, overriding all the default property
values one by one until I have set all product details. Now that I have set some data, I can
also access it:

```
// listing 03.09
print "author: {$product1->producerFirstName} "
    . "{$product1->producerMainName}\n";
```

This outputs the following:

```
author: Willa Cather
```

There are a number of problems with this approach to setting property values.
Because PHP lets you set properties dynamically, you will not get warned if you misspell
or forget a property name. For example, assume I want to type this line:

```
// listing 03.10
$product1->producerFirstName = "Shirley";
$product1->producerMainName = "Jackson";
```

Unfortunately, I mistakenly type it like this:

```
// listing 03.11
$product1->producerFirstName = "Shirley";
$product1->producerSecondName = "Jackson";
```

As far as the PHP engine is concerned, this code is perfectly legal, and I would not be
warned. When I come to print the author's name, though, I will get unexpected results.

Another problem is that my class is altogether too relaxed. I am not forced to set
a title, a price, or producer names. Client code can be sure that these properties exist,

but is likely to be confronted with default values as often as not. Ideally, I would like to encourage anyone who instantiates a ShopProduct object to set meaningful property values.

Finally, I have to jump through hoops to do something that I will probably want to do quite often. As we have seen, printing the full author name is a tiresome process.

It would be nice to have the object handle such drudgery on my behalf.

All of these problems can be addressed by giving the ShopProduct object its own set of functions that can be used to manipulate property data from within the object context.

Working with Methods

Just as properties allow your objects to store data, methods allow your objects to perform tasks. Methods are special functions declared within a class. As you might expect, a method declaration resembles a function declaration. The function keyword precedes a method name, followed by an optional list of argument variables in parentheses. The method body is enclosed by braces:

```
// listing 03.12

public function myMethod($argument, $another)
{
    // ...
}
```

Unlike functions, methods must be declared in the body of a class. They can also accept a number of qualifiers, including a visibility keyword. Like properties, methods can be declared public, protected, or private. By declaring a method public, you ensure that it can be invoked from outside of the current object. If you omit the visibility keyword in your method declaration, the method will be declared public implicitly. It is considered good practice, however, to declare visibility explicitly for all methods (I will return to method modifiers later in the chapter).

Note   In Chapter 15, I cover rules for best practices in code. The coding style standard PSR-12 requires that visibility is declared for all methods.

```
// listing 03.13

class ShopProduct
{
    public $title = "default product";
    public $producerMainName = "main name";
    public $producerFirstName = "first name";
    public $price = 0;

    public function getProducer()
    {
        return $this->producerFirstName . " "
            . $this->producerMainName;

    }
}
```

In most circumstances, you will invoke a method using an object variable in conjunction with the object operator, ->, and the method name. You must use parentheses in your method call as you would if you were calling a function (even if you are not passing any arguments to the method):

```
// listing 03.14

$product1 = new ShopProduct();
$product1->title = "My Antonia";
$product1->producerMainName = "Cather";
$product1->producerFirstName = "Willa";
$product1->price = 5.99;

print "author: {$product1->getProducer()}\n";
```

This outputs the following:

```
author: Willa Cather
```

I add the getProducer() method to the ShopProduct class. Notice that I declare getProducer() public, which means it can be called from outside the class.

I introduce a feature in this method's body. The $this pseudo-variable is the mechanism by which a class can refer to an object instance. If you find this concept hard to swallow, try replacing $this with the phrase "the current instance." Consider the following statement:

`$this->producerFirstName`

This translates to the following:

the $producerFirstName property of the current instance

So the getProducer() method combines and returns the $producerFirstName and $producerMainName properties, saving me from the chore of performing this task every time I need to quote the full producer name.

This has improved the class a little. I am still stuck with a great deal of unwanted flexibility, though. I rely on the client coder to change a ShopProduct object's properties from their default values. This is problematic in two ways. First, it takes five lines to properly initialize a ShopProduct object, and no coder will thank you for that. Second, I have no way of ensuring that any of the properties are set when a ShopProduct object is initialized.

What I need is a method that is called automatically when an object is instantiated from a class.

Creating a Constructor Method

A constructor method is invoked when an object is created. You can use it to set things up, ensuring that essential properties are assigned values and any necessary preliminary work is completed.

Note   In versions previous to PHP 5, a constructor method took on the name of the class that enclosed it. So the ShopProduct class would use a ShopProduct() method as its constructor. This was deprecated as of PHP 7 and no longer works at all as of PHP 8. Name your constructor method __construct().

Note that the method name begins with two underscore characters. You will see this naming convention for many other special methods in PHP classes. Here, I define a constructor for the ShopProduct class:

Note   Built-in methods which begin this way are known as *magic methods* because they are automatically invoked in specific circumstances. You can read more about them in the PHP manual at www.php.net/manual/en/language.oop5.magic.php. Although it is not illegal to do so, because double underscores have such a specific connotation, it is a good idea to avoid using them in your own custom methods.

```php
// listing 03.15
class ShopProduct
{
    public $title;
    public $producerMainName;
    public $producerFirstName;
    public $price = 0;

    public function __construct(
        $title,
        $firstName,
        $mainName,
        $price
    ) {
        $this->title = $title;
        $this->producerFirstName = $firstName;
        $this->producerMainName = $mainName;
        $this->price = $price;
    }

    public function getProducer()
    {
        return $this->producerFirstName . " "
            . $this->producerMainName;
    }
}
```

Once again, I gather functionality into the class, saving effort and duplication in the code that uses it. The __construct() method is invoked when an object is created using the new operator:

```
// listing 03.16
$product1 = new ShopProduct(
    "My Antonia",
    "Willa",
    "Cather", 5.99
);
print "author: {$product1->getProducer()}\n";
```

This produces the following:

```
author: Willa Cather
```

Any arguments supplied are passed to the constructor. So in my example, I pass the title, the first name, the main name, and the product price to the constructor. The constructor method uses the pseudo-variable $this to assign values to each of the object's properties.

Note   A ShopProduct object is now easier to instantiate and safer to use. Instantiation and setup are completed in a single statement. Any code that uses a ShopProduct object can be reasonably sure that all its properties are initialized.

You can leave a property uninitialized without error. But any attempt to access that property will then result in a fatal error.

Constructor Property Promotion

While we have made the ShopProduct class safer and, from a client perspective, more convenient, we have also introduced quite a lot of boilerplate. Take a look back at the class as it stands. In order to instantiate an object with four properties, we need a total of three sets of references to the data. First of all, we declare the properties, then we provide constructor arguments to hold the data, and then we bring it all together when we assign the method arguments to the properties. PHP 8 provides a feature called *constructor property promotion* which offers a welcome shortcut. By including a visibility keyword

for your constructor arguments, you can combine them with property declarations *and*
assign to them at the same time. Here is a new version of ShopProduct:

```
// listing 03.17
class ShopProduct
{
    public function __construct(
        public $title,
        public $producerFirstName,
        public $producerMainName,
        public $price
    ) {
    }

    public function getProducer()
    {
        return $this->producerFirstName . " "
            . $this->producerMainName;
    }
}
```

Both declaration of and assignment to the properties in the constructor method
signature are handled implicitly. By reducing repetition, this also reduces the chance of
bugs creeping into code. By making the class more compact, it makes it easier for those
reading source code to focus on the logic.

Note   Constructor property promotion was introduced in PHP 8. If your project is still
running PHP 7, then you should hold off from taking advantage of the new syntax.

Predictability is an important aspect of object-oriented programming. You should
design your classes so that users of objects can be sure of their features. One way
you can make an object safe is to render predictable the types of data it holds in its
properties. One might ensure that a $name property is always made up of character data,
for example. But how can you achieve this if property data is passed in from outside the
class? In the next section, I examine a mechanism you can use to enforce object types in
method declarations.

Default Arguments and Named Arguments

Over time, method argument lists can grow long and unwieldy. This can make working with a class increasingly difficult as it becomes hard to keep track of the arguments its methods demand. We can make things easier for client coders by providing default values in method definitions. Let's say, for example, that we need a title for our ShopProduct object but would accept empty string values for the producer names and a zero value for the price. As things stand with ShopProduct, the calling code would need to provide all this data:

```
// listing 03.18
$product1 = new ShopProduct("Shop Catalogue", "", "", 0);
```

We can streamline this instantiation by providing default values for our arguments. In the next example, I do just that:

```
// listing 03.19
class ShopProduct
{
    public function __construct(
    public $title,
    public $producerFirstName = "",
    public $producerMainName = "",
    public $price = 0
    ) {
    }
    // ...
}
```

These assignments are only activated if the calling code does not provide values in its call. Now, a call to the constructor need only specify one value: the title.

```
// listing 03.20
$product1 = new ShopProduct("Shop Catalogue");
```

Default argument values can make working with methods more convenient, but, as is so often the way, they can also cause unintended complications. What would happen to my nice compact constructor call if I wanted to provide a price but would still like the producer names to fall back to their defaults? Prior to PHP 8, I would be stuck. I would have to provide the empty producer names in order to specify the price. That brings us full circle. And I would also need to work out what kind of values the constructor expects for empty producer name values. Should I pass empty strings? Or null values? Far from saving work, my support for default values may well have sown confusion.

Luckily, PHP 8 provides named arguments. In my method call, I can now specify each argument name ahead of the value I wish to pass. PHP will then associate the value with the correct argument in the method signature regardless of the order in the calling code.

```
// listing 03.21
$product1 = new ShopProduct(
    price: 0.7,
    title: "Shop Catalogue"
);
```

Note the syntax here: I tell PHP I want to set the $price argument to 0.7 by first specifying the argument name, price, then a colon, and then the value I want to provide. Because I have used named arguments, their order in the call is no longer relevant, and I no longer need to provide the empty producer name values.

Arguments and Types

A type determines the way data can be managed in your scripts. You use the string type to display character data, for example, and manipulate such data with string functions. Integers are used in mathematical expressions, Booleans are used in test expressions, and so on. These categories are known as primitive types. On a higher level, though, a class defines a type. A ShopProduct object, therefore, belongs to the primitive type object, but it also belongs to the ShopProduct class type. In this section, I will look at types of both kinds in relation to class methods.

Method and function definitions do not necessarily require that an argument should be of a particular type. This is both a curse and a blessing. The fact that an argument can be of any type offers you flexibility. You can build methods that respond intelligently to different data types, tailoring functionality to changing circumstances. This flexibility can also cause ambiguity to creep into code when a method body expects an argument to hold one type but gets another.

Primitive Types

PHP is a loosely typed language. This means that there is no necessity for a variable to be declared to hold a particular data type. The variable $number could hold the value 2 and the string "two" within the same scope. In strongly typed languages, such as C or Java, you must declare the type of a variable before assigning a value to it, and, of course, the value must be of the specified type.

This does not mean that PHP has no concept of type. Every value that can be assigned to a variable has a type. You can determine the type of a variable's value using one of PHP's type-checking functions. Table 3-1 lists the primitive types recognized in PHP and their corresponding test functions. Each function accepts a variable or value and returns true if this argument is of the relevant type.

Table 3-1. *Primitive Types and Checking Functions in PHP*

Type-Checking Function	Type	Description
is_bool()	Boolean	One of the two special values true or false
is_integer()	Integer	A whole number. Alias of is_int() and is_long()
is_float()	Float	A floating-point number (a number with a decimal point). Alias of is_double()
is_string()	String	Character data
is_object()	Object	An object
is_resource()	Resource	A handle for identifying and working with external resources such as databases or files
is_array()	Array	An array
is_null()	Null	An unassigned value

Checking the type of a variable can be particularly important when you work with method and function arguments.

Primitive Types: An Example

You need to keep a close eye on type in your code. Here's an example of one of the many type-related problems that you could encounter.

Imagine that you are extracting configuration settings from an XML file. The
XML element tells your application whether
it should attempt to resolve IP addresses to domain names, a useful but relatively
expensive process.

Here is some sample XML:

```
// listing 03.22
<settings>
    <resolvedomains>false</resolvedomains>
</settings>
```

The string "false" is extracted by your application and passed as a flag to a method
called outputAddresses(), which displays IP address data. Here is outputAddresses():

```
// listing 03.23

class AddressManager
{
    private $addresses = ["209.131.36.159", "216.58.213.174"];

    public function outputAddresses($resolve)
    {
        foreach ($this->addresses as $address) {
            print $address;
            if ($resolve) {
                print " (" . gethostbyaddr($address) . ")";
            }
            print "\n";
        }
    }
}
```

Of course, the AddressManager class could do with some improvement. It's not
very useful to hard-code IP addresses into a class, for example. Nevertheless, the
outputAddresses() method loops through the $addresses array property, printing each
element. If the $resolve argument variable itself resolves to true, the method outputs
the domain name, as well as the IP address.

Here's one approach that uses the settings XML configuration element in conjunction with the AddressManager class. See if you can spot how it is flawed:

```
// listing 03.24
$settings = simplexml_load_file(__DIR__ . "/resolve.xml");
$manager = new AddressManager();
$manager->outputAddresses((string)$settings->resolvedomains);
```

The code fragment uses the SimpleXML API to acquire a value for the resolvedomains element. In this example, I know that this value is the text element "false", and I cast it to a string as the SimpleXML documentation suggests I should.

This code will not behave as you might expect. In passing the string "false" to the outputAddresses() method, I misunderstand the implicit assumption the method makes about the argument. The method is expecting a Boolean value (i.e., true or false). The string "false" will, in fact, resolve to true in a test. This is because PHP will helpfully cast a nonempty string value to the Boolean true for you in a test context. Consider this code:

```
if ("false") {
    // ...
}
```

It is actually equivalent to this:

```
if (true) {
    // ...
}
```

There are a number of approaches you might take to fix this.

You could make the outputAddresses() method more forgiving, so that it recognizes a string and applies some basic rules to convert it to a Boolean equivalent:

```
// listing 03.25
public function outputAddresses($resolve)
{
    if (is_string($resolve)) {
        $resolve = (preg_match("/^(false|no|off)$/i", $resolve)) ? false : true;
    }
    // ...
}
```

There are good design reasons for avoiding an approach like this, however. Generally speaking, it is better to provide a clear and strict interface for a method or function than it is to offer a fuzzily forgiving one. Fuzzy and forgiving functions and methods can promote confusion and thereby breed bugs.

You could take another approach: Leave the outputAddresses() method as it is and include a comment containing clear instructions that the $resolve argument should contain a Boolean value. This approach essentially tells the coder to read the small print or reap the consequences:

```
// listing 03.26

/**
 * Outputs the list of addresses.
 * If $resolve is true then each address will be resolved
 * @param    $resolve    boolean    Resolve the address?
 */
public function outputAddresses($resolve)
{
    // ...
}
```

This is a reasonable approach, assuming your client coders are diligent readers of documentation (or use clever editors that recognize annotations of this sort).

Finally, you could make outputAddresses() strict about the type of data it is prepared to find in the $resolve argument. For primitive types like Boolean, there was really only one way to do this prior to the release of PHP 7. You would have to write code to examine incoming data and take some kind of action if it does not match the required type:

```
// listing 03.27
public function outputAddresses($resolve)
{
    if (! is_bool($resolve)) {
        // do something drastic
    }
}
```

This approach can be used to force client code to provide the correct data type in the $resolve argument or to issue a warning.

Note   In the next section, "Type Declarations: Object Types," I will describe a much better way of constraining the type of arguments passed to methods and functions.

Converting a string argument on the client's behalf would be friendly but would probably present other problems. In providing a conversion mechanism, you second-guess the context and intent of the client. By enforcing the Boolean data type, on the other hand, you leave the client to decide whether to map strings to Boolean values and determine which word should map to true or false. The outputAddresses() method, meanwhile, concentrates on the task it is designed to perform. This emphasis on performing a specific task in deliberate ignorance of the wider context is an important principle in object-oriented programming, and I will return to it frequently throughout the book.

In fact, your strategies for dealing with argument types will depend on the seriousness of any potential bugs on the one hand and the benefits of flexibility on the other. PHP casts most primitive values for you, depending on context. Numbers in strings are converted to their integer or floating-point equivalents when used in a mathematical expression, for example. So your code might be naturally forgiving of type errors.

On the whole, however, it is best to err on the side of strictness when it comes to both object and primitive types. Luckily, PHP 8 provides more tools than ever before to enforce type safety.

Some Other Type-Checking Functions

We have seen variable handling functions that check for primitive types. While we are checking on the contents of our variables, it is worth mentioning a few functions that go beyond checking primitive types to provide more general information about ways that data held in a variable might be used. I list these in Table 3-2.

Table 3-2. *Pseudo-type-Checking Functions*

Function	Description
is_countable()	An array or an object that can be passed to the count() function
is_iterable()	A traversable data structure—that is, one that can be looped through using foreach
is_callable()	Code that can be invoked—often an anonymous function or a function name
is_numeric()	Either an int, a long, or a string which can be resolved to a number

The functions described in Table 3-2 do not check for specific types so much as ways you can treat the values you test. If is_callable() returns true for a variable, for example, you know that you can treat it like a function or method and invoke it. Similarly, you can loop through a value that passes the is_iterable() test—even though it may be a special kind of object rather than an array.

Type Declarations: Object Types

Just as an argument variable can contain any primitive type, by default it can contain an object of any type. This flexibility has its uses, but can present problems in the context of a method definition.

Imagine a method designed to work with a ShopProduct object:

```
// listing 03.28
class ShopProductWriter
{
    public function write($shopProduct)
    {
        $str  = $shopProduct->title . ": "
            . $shopProduct->getProducer()
            . " (" . $shopProduct->price . ")\n";
        print $str;
    }
}
```

You can test this class like this:

```
// listing 03.29
$product1 = new ShopProduct("My Antonia", "Willa", "Cather", 5.99);
$writer = new ShopProductWriter();
$writer->write($product1);
```

This outputs the following:

```
My Antonia: Willa Cather (5.99)
```

The ShopProductWriter class contains a single method, write(). The write() method accepts a ShopProduct object and uses its properties and methods to construct and print a summary string. I used the name of the argument variable, $shopProduct, as a signal that the method expects a ShopProduct object, but I did not enforce this. That means I could be passed an unexpected object or primitive type and be none the wiser until I begin trying to work with the $shopProduct argument. By that time, my code may already have acted on the assumption that it has been passed a genuine ShopProduct object.

Note   You might wonder why I didn't add the write() method directly to ShopProduct. The reason lies with areas of responsibility. The ShopProduct class is responsible for managing product data; the ShopProductWriter is responsible for writing it. You will begin to see why this division of labor can be useful as you read this chapter.

To address this problem, PHP 5 introduced class type declarations (known then as type hints). To add a class type declaration to a method argument, you simply place a class name in front of the method argument you need to constrain. So I can amend the write() method thus:

```
// listing 03.30
public function write(ShopProduct $shopProduct)
{
    // ...
}
```

Now the write() method will only accept the $shopProduct argument if it contains an object of type ShopProduct.

Here is a basic class:

```
// listing 03.31
class Wrong
{
}
```

And here is a snippet that tries to call write() with a Wrong object:

```
// listing 03.32
$writer = new ShopProductWriter();
$writer->write(new Wrong());
```

Because the write() method contains a class type declaration, passing it a Wrong object causes a fatal error.

```
TypeError: popp\ch03\batch08\ShopProductWriter::write(): Argument #1
($shopProduct) must be of type
popp\ch03\batch04\ShopProduct, popp\ch03\batch08\Wrong given, called in
/var/popp/src/ch03/batch08/Runner.php on ...
```

Note   In the TypeError example output, you might have noticed that the classes referenced included much additional information. The Wrong class is quoted as popp\ch03\batch08\ Wrong, for example. These are examples of *namespaces*, and you will encounter them in great detail in Chapter 4.

This saves me from having to test the type of the argument before I work with it. It also makes the method signature much clearer for the client coder. She can see the requirements of the write() method at a glance. She does not have to worry about some obscure bug arising from a type error because the declaration is rigidly enforced.

Even though this automated type checking is a great way of preventing bugs, it is important to understand that type declarations are checked at runtime. This means that a class declaration will only report an error at the moment that an unwanted object is passed to the method. If a call to write() is buried in a conditional clause that only runs on Christmas morning, you may find yourself working the holiday if you haven't checked your code carefully.

Type Declarations: Primitive Types

Up until the release of PHP 7, it was only possible to constrain objects and a couple of other types (callable and array). PHP 7 at last introduced scalar type declarations. This allows you to enforce the Boolean, string, integer, and float types in your argument list.

Armed with scalar type declarations, I can add some constraints to the ShopProduct class:

```
// listing 03.33
class ShopProduct
{
    public $title;
    public $producerMainName;
    public $producerFirstName;
    public $price = 0;

    public function __construct(
        string $title,
        string $firstName,
        string $mainName,
        float $price
    ) {
        $this->title = $title;
        $this->producerFirstName = $firstName;
        $this->producerMainName = $mainName;
        $this->price = $price;
    }

    // ...
}
```

With the constructor method shored up in this way, I can be sure that the $title, $firstName, and $mainName arguments will always contain string data and that $price will contain a float. I can demonstrate this by instantiating ShopProduct with the wrong information:

```
// listing 03.34
// will fail
$product = new ShopProduct("title", "first", "main", []);
```

I attempt to instantiate a ShopProduct object. I pass three strings to the constructor, but I fail at the final hurdle by passing in an empty array instead of the required float. Thanks to type declarations, PHP won't let me get away with that:

```
TypeError: popp\ch03\batch09\ShopProduct:: construct(): Argument #4
($price) must be of type float, array given, called in...
```

By default, PHP will implicitly cast arguments to the required type, where possible. This is an example of the tension between safety and flexibility we encountered earlier. The new implementation of the ShopProduct class, for example, will quietly turn a string into a float for us. So, this instantiation would not fail:

```
// listing 03.35
$product = new ShopProduct("title", "first", "main", "4.22");
```

Behind the scenes, the string "4.22" becomes the float 4.22. So far, so useful. But think back to the problem we encountered with the AddressManager class. The string "false" was quietly resolving to the Boolean true. By default, this will still happen if I use a bool type declaration in the AddressManager::outputAddresses() method like this:

```
// listing 03.36
public function outputAddresses(bool $resolve)
{
    // ...
}
```

Now consider a call that passes along a string like this:

```
// listing 03.37
$manager->outputAddresses("false");
```

Because of implicit casting, it is functionally identical to one that passes the Boolean value true.

You can make scalar type declarations strict, although only on a file-by-file basis. Here, I turn on strict type declarations and call outputAddresses() with a string once again:

```
// listing 03.38
declare(strict_types=1);

        $manager->outputAddresses("false");
```

Because I declare strict typing, this call causes a TypeError to be thrown:

```
TypeError: popp\ch03\batch09\AddressManager::outputAddresses(): Argument #1
($resolve) must be of type bool, string given, called in...
```

Note   A strict_types declaration applies to the file from which a call is made, and not to the file in which a function or method is implemented. So it's up to client code to enforce strictness.

You may need to make an argument optional, but nonetheless constrain its type if it is provided. You can do this by providing a default value:

```
// listing 03.39
class ConfReader
{

    public function getValues(array $default = [])
    {
        $values = [];

        // do something to get values

        // merge the provided defaults (it will always be an array)
        $values = array_merge($default, $values);
        return $values;
    }
}
```

mixed Types

The mixed type declaration introduced in PHP 8.0 might be seen as an example of syntactic sugar—that is, it does not do very much in itself. There is no *functional* difference between this:

```
// listing 03.40
class Storage
{
    public function add(string $key, $value)
```

```
    {
        // do something with $key and $value
    }
}
```

and this:

```
// listing 03.41

class Storage
{
    public function add(string $key, mixed $value)
    {
        // do something with $key and $value
    }
}
```

In the second version, I declared that the $value argument to add() would accept mixed—in other words, any type from array, bool, callable, int, float, null, object, resource, or string. So declaring a mixed $value is the same as leaving $value without a type declaration in an argument list. So why bother with the mixed declaration at all? In essence, you are declaring that the argument *intentionally* accepts any value. A bare argument might be intended to accept any value—or it may have been left without a type declaration because the code author was lazy. mixed removes doubt and uncertainty, and for that reason it is useful.

To sum up, in Table 3-3, I list the type declarations supported by PHP.

Table 3-3. *Type Declarations*

Type Declaration	Since	Description
array	5.1	An array. Can default to null or an array
int	7.0	An integer. Can default to null or an integer
float	7.0	A floating-point number (a number with a decimal point). An integer will be accepted—even with strict mode enabled. Can default to null, a float, or an integer
callable	5.4	Callable code (such as an anonymous function). Can default to null
bool	7.0	A Boolean. Can default to null or a Boolean
string	5.0	Character data. Can default to null or a string
self	5.0	A reference to the containing class
[a class type]	5.0	The type of a class or interface. Can default to null
iterable	7.1	Can be traversed with foreach (not necessarily an array—could implement Traversable)
object	7.2	An object
mixed	8.0	Explicit notification that the value can be of any type

Union Types

There is quite a gulf between the all-inclusive mixed declaration and the relative strictness of type declarations. What do you do if you need to constrain an argument to two, three, or more named types? Until PHP 8, the only way you could achieve this was by testing for type within the body of a method. Let's return to the Storage class with a new requirement. The add() should only accept a string or a Boolean value as its $value method. Here is an implementation that checks type within the method body:

```
// listing 03.42

class Storage
{
    public function add(string $key, $value)
    {
```

47

```
        if (! is_bool($value) && ! is_string($value)) {
            error_log("value must be string or Boolean - given: " .
            gettype($value));
            return false;
        }
        // do something with $key and $value
    }
}
```

Note   In fact, rather than return `false`, we would likely throw an exception. You can read more about exceptions in Chapter 4.

Although this manual checking gets the job done, it is unwieldy and hard to read. Luckily, PHP 8 introduced a new feature: union types which allow you to combine two or more types separated by a pipe symbol to make a composite type declaration.

Here is my reimplementation of Storage:

```
// listing 03.43

class Storage
{
    public function add(string $key, string|bool $value)
    {
        // do something with $key and $value
    }
}
```

If I now attempt to set `$value` to anything other than a float or a Boolean, I will trip a now-familiar `TypeError`.

If I wanted to make `add()` a little more forgiving, I can also use a union type to allow a null value.

```
// listing 03.44

class Storage
{
    public function add(string $key, string|bool|null $value)
```

```
    {
        // do something with $key and $value
    }

}
```

Union type declarations will work just as well with object type declarations. This example will accept either an object of type ShopProduct or a null value:

```
// listing 03.45
public function setShopProduct(ShopProduct|null $product)
{
    // do something with $product
}
```

Because many methods accept or return false as an alternative value, PHP 8 supports the false pseudo-type in the context of unions. So, in this example, I will accept either a ShopProduct object or false:

```
// listing 03.46
    public function setShopProduct2(ShopProduct|false $product)
    {
        // do something with $product
    }

}
```

This is more useful than the union ShopProduct|bool because I do not want to accept true in any scenario.

Note   Union types were added in PHP 8.

Nullable Types

Where a union type accepts null as one of two options, there is an equivalent argument you can use. The nullable type consists of a type declaration preceded by a question mark. So this version of Storage will accept either a string or null:

```
// listing 03.47

class Storage
{
    public function add(string $key, ?string $value)
    {
        // do something with $key and $value
    }
}
```

When I described class type declarations, I implied that types and classes are synonymous. There is a key difference between the two, however. When you define a class, you also define a type, but a type can describe an entire family of classes. The mechanism by which different classes can be grouped together under a type is called inheritance. I discuss inheritance in the next section.

Return Type Declarations

Just as we can declare the type of an argument, so we can use return type declarations to constrain the types that our methods return. A return type declaration is placed directly after a method or function's closing parenthesis and takes the form of a colon character followed by the type. The same set of types are supported when declaring a return type as when declaring argument types. So here I constrain the return type of getPlayLength():

```
// listing 03.48
public function getPlayLength(): int
{
    return $this->playLength;
}
```

If this method fails to return an integer value when called, PHP will generate an error:

```
TypeError: popp\ch03\batch15\CdProduct::getPlayLength(): Return value must
be of type int, none returned
```

Because the return value is enforced in this way, any code that calls this method can treat its return value as an integer with assurance.

Return type declarations support nullable and union types. Let's enforce a union type:

```
// listing 03.49
public function getPrice(): int|float
{
    return ($this->price - $this->discount);
}
```

As of PHP 8, there is one type that is supported by return type declarations and not by argument type declarations. You can declare that a method will never return a value with the void pseudo-type. So, for example, because the setDiscount() method is designed to set rather than provide a value, I use a void return type declaration here:

```
// listing 03.50
public function setDiscount(int|float $num): void
{
    $this->discount = $num;
}
```

Inheritance

Inheritance is the means by which one or more classes can be derived from a base class.

A class that inherits from another is said to be a subclass of it. This relationship is often described in terms of parents and children. A child class is derived from and inherits characteristics from the parent. These characteristics consist of both properties and methods. The child class will typically add new functionality to that provided by its parent (also known as a superclass); for this reason, a child class is said to extend its parent.

Before I dive into the syntax of inheritance, I'll examine the problems it can help you to solve.

The Inheritance Problem

Look again at the ShopProduct class. At the moment, it is nicely generic. It can handle all sorts of products:

```
// listing 03.51

$product1 = new ShopProduct("My Antonia", "Willa", "Cather", 5.99);
$product2 = new ShopProduct(
    "Exile on Coldharbour Lane", "The",
    "Alabama 3",
    10.99
);
print "author: " . $product1->getProducer() . "\n";
print "artist: " . $product2->getProducer() . "\n";
```

Here's the output:

```
author: Willa Cather
artist: The Alabama 3
```

Separating the producer name into two parts works well with both books and CDs. I want to be able to sort on "Alabama 3" and "Cather", not on "The" and "Willa". Laziness is an excellent design strategy, so there is no need to worry about using ShopProduct for more than one kind of product at this stage.

If I add some new requirements to my example, however, things rapidly become more complicated. Imagine, for example, that you need to represent data specific to books and CDs. For CDs, you must store the total playing time; for books, the total number of pages. There could be any number of other differences, but this will serve to illustrate the issue.

How can I extend my example to accommodate these changes? Two options immediately present themselves. First, I could throw all the data into the ShopProduct class. Second, I could split ShopProduct into two separate classes.

Let's examine the first approach. Here, I combine CD- and book-related data in a single class:

```
// listing 03.52
class ShopProduct
{
    public $numPages;
    public $playLength;
    public $title;
    public $producerMainName;
    public $producerFirstName;
    public $price;

    public function __construct(
        string $title,
        string $firstName,
        string $mainName,
        float $price,
        int $numPages = 0,
        int $playLength = 0
    ) {
        $this->title            = $title;
        $this->producerFirstName = $firstName;
        $this->producerMainName  = $mainName;
        $this->price            = $price;
        $this->numPages          = $numPages;
        $this->playLength        = $playLength;
    }

    public function getNumberOfPages(): int
    {
        return $this->numPages;
    }

    public function getPlayLength(): int
    {
        return $this->playLength;
    }
```

```
    public function getProducer(): string
    {
        return $this->producerFirstName . " "
            . $this->producerMainName;
    }
}
```

I have provided method access to the $numPages and $playLength properties to illustrate the divergent forces at work here. An object instantiated from this class will include a redundant method and, for a CD, must be instantiated using an unnecessary constructor argument: a CD will store information and functionality relating to book pages, and a book will support play-length data. This is probably something you could live with right now. But what would happen if I added more product types, each with its own methods, and then added more methods for each type? Our class would become increasingly complex and hard to manage.

So forcing fields that don't belong together into a single class leads to bloated objects with redundant properties and methods.

The problem doesn't end with data, either. I run into difficulties with functionality as well. Consider a method that summarizes a product. The sales department has requested a clear summary line for use in invoices. They want me to include the playing time for CDs and a page count for books, so I will be forced to provide different implementations for each type. I could try using a flag to keep track of the object's format.

Here's an example:

```
// listing 03.53

public function getSummaryLine(): string
{
    $base  = "{$this->title} ( {$this->producerMainName}, ";
    $base .= "{$this->producerFirstName} )";
    if ($this->type == 'book') {
        $base .= ": page count - {$this->numPages}";
    } elseif ($this->type == 'cd') {
        $base .= ": playing time - {$this->playLength}";
    }
    return $base;
}
```

In order to set the $type property, I could test the $numPages argument to the constructor. Still, once again, the ShopProduct class has become more complex than necessary. As I add more differences to my formats, or add new formats, these functional differences will become even harder to manage. Perhaps I should try another approach to this problem.

As ShopProduct is beginning to feel like two classes in one, I could accept this and create two types rather than one. Here's how I might do it:

```php
// listing 03.54
class CdProduct
{
    public $playLength;
    public $title;
    public $producerMainName;
    public $producerFirstName;
    public $price;

    public function __construct(
        string $title,
        string $firstName,
        string $mainName,
        float $price,
        int $playLength
    ) {
        $this->title             = $title;
        $this->producerFirstName = $firstName;
        $this->producerMainName  = $mainName;
        $this->price             = $price;
        $this->playLength        = $playLength;
    }

    public function getPlayLength(): int
    {
        return $this->playLength;
    }
}
```

```php
    public function getSummaryLine(): string
    {
        $base  = "{$this->title} ( {$this->producerMainName}, ";
        $base .= "{$this->producerFirstName} )";
        $base .= ": playing time - {$this->playLength}";
        return $base;
    }

    public function getProducer(): string
    {
        return $this->producerFirstName . " "
            . $this->producerMainName;
    }
}

// listing 03.55
class BookProduct
{
    public $numPages;
    public $title;
    public $producerMainName;
    public $producerFirstName;
    public $price;

    public function __construct(
        string $title,
        string $firstName,
        string $mainName,
        float $price,
        int $numPages
    ) {
        $this->title            = $title;
        $this->producerFirstName = $firstName;
        $this->producerMainName  = $mainName;
        $this->price            = $price;
        $this->numPages         = $numPages;
    }
```

```php
public function getNumberOfPages(): int
{
    return $this->numPages;
}

public function getSummaryLine(): string
{
    $base  = "{$this->title} ( {$this->producerMainName}, ";
    $base .= "{$this->producerFirstName} )";
    $base .= ": page count - {$this->numPages}";
    return $base;
}

public function getProducer(): string
{
    return $this->producerFirstName . " "
        . $this->producerMainName;
}
}
```

I have addressed the complexity issue, but at a cost. I can now create a
getSummaryLine() method for each format without having to test a flag. Neither class
maintains fields or methods that are not relevant to it.

The cost lies in duplication. The getProducerName() method is exactly the same in
each class. Each constructor sets a number of identical properties in the same way. This
is another unpleasant odor you should train yourself to sniff out.

If I need the getProducer() methods to behave identically for each class, any
changes I make to one implementation will need to be made for the other. Without care,
the classes will soon slip out of synchronization.

Even if I am confident that I can maintain the duplication, my worries are not over. I
now have two types rather than one.

Remember the ShopProductWriter class? Its write() method is designed to work
with a single type: ShopProduct. How can I amend this to work as before? I could remove
the class type declaration from the method signature, but then I must trust to luck that

write() is passed an object of the correct type. I could add my own type-checking code to the body of the method:

```
// listing 03.56
class ShopProductWriter
{
    public function write($shopProduct): void
    {
        if (
            ! ($shopProduct instanceof CdProduct) &&
            ! ($shopProduct instanceof BookProduct)
        ) {
            die("wrong type supplied");
        }
        $str  = "{$shopProduct->title}: "
            . $shopProduct->getProducer()
            . " ({$shopProduct->price})\n";
        print $str;
    }
}
```

Notice the instanceof operator in the example; instanceof resolves to true if the object in the left-hand operand is of the type represented by the right-hand operand.

Once again, I have been forced to include a new layer of complexity. Not only do I have to test the $shopProduct argument against two types in the write() method, but I have to trust that each type will continue to support the same fields and methods as the other. It was all much neater when I simply demanded a single type because I could use a class type declaration and because I could be confident that the ShopProduct class supported a particular interface.

The CD and book aspects of the ShopProduct class don't work well together but can't live apart, it seems. I want to work with books and CDs as a single type while providing a separate implementation for each format. I want to provide common functionality in one place to avoid duplication, but allow each format to handle some method calls differently. I need to use inheritance.

Working with Inheritance

The first step in building an inheritance tree is to find the elements of the base class that don't fit together or that need to be handled differently.

I know that the getPlayLength() and getNumberOfPages() methods do not belong together. I also know that I need to create different implementations for the getSummaryLine() method.

Let's use these differences as the basis for two derived classes:

```php
// listing 03.57
class ShopProduct
{
    public $numPages;
    public $playLength;
    public $title;
    public $producerMainName;
    public $producerFirstName;
    public $price;

    public function __construct(
        string $title,
        string $firstName,
        string $mainName,
        float $price,
        int $numPages = 0,
        int $playLength = 0
    ) {
        $this->title             = $title;
        $this->producerFirstName = $firstName;
        $this->producerMainName  = $mainName;
        $this->price             = $price;
        $this->numPages          = $numPages;
        $this->playLength        = $playLength;
    }
```

```php
    public function getProducer(): string
    {
        return $this->producerFirstName . " "
            . $this->producerMainName;
    }

    public function getSummaryLine(): string
    {
        $base  = "{$this->title} ( {$this->producerMainName}, ";
        $base .= "{$this->producerFirstName} )";
        return $base;
    }
}

// listing 03.58
class CdProduct extends ShopProduct
{
    public function getPlayLength(): int
    {
        return $this->playLength;
    }

    public function getSummaryLine(): string
    {
        $base  = "{$this->title} ( {$this->producerMainName}, ";
        $base .= "{$this->producerFirstName} )";
        $base .= ": playing time - {$this->playLength}";
        return $base;
    }
}

// listing 03.59
class BookProduct extends ShopProduct
{
    public function getNumberOfPages(): int
    {
        return $this->numPages;
    }
```

```
public function getSummaryLine(): string
{
    $base  = "{$this->title} ( {$this->producerMainName}, ";
    $base .= "{$this->producerFirstName} )";
    $base .= ": page count - {$this->numPages}"; return $base;
}
}
```

To create a child class, you must use the extends keyword in the class declaration. In the example, I created two new classes, BookProduct and CdProduct. Both extend the ShopProduct class.

Because the derived classes do not define constructors, the parent class's constructor is automatically invoked when they are instantiated. The child classes inherit access to all the parent's public and protected methods (though not to private methods or properties). This means that you can call the getProducer() method on an object instantiated from the CdProduct class, even though getProducer() is defined in the ShopProduct class:

```
// listing 03.60
$product2 = new CdProduct(
    "Exile on Coldharbour Lane",
    "The",
    "Alabama 3",
    10.99,
    0,
    60.33
);
print "artist: {$product2->getProducer()}\n";
```

So both the child classes inherit the behavior of the common parent. You can treat a BookProduct object as if it were a ShopProduct object. You can pass a BookProduct or CdProduct object to the ShopProductWriter class's write() method, and all will work as expected.

Notice that both the CdProduct and BookProduct classes override the getSummaryLine() method, providing their own implementation. Derived classes can extend but also alter the functionality of their parents.

The superclass's implementation of this method might seem redundant because it is overridden by both its children. Nevertheless, it provides basic functionality that new child classes might use. The method's presence also provides a guarantee to client code that all ShopProduct objects will provide a getSummaryLine() method. Later on, you will see how it is possible to make this promise in a base class without providing any implementation at all. Each child ShopProduct class inherits its parent's properties. Both BookProduct and CdProduct access the $title property in their versions of getSummaryLine().

Inheritance can be a difficult concept to grasp at first. By defining a class that extends another, you ensure that an object instantiated from it is defined by the characteristics of first the child and then the parent class. Another way of thinking about this is in terms of searching. When I invoke $product2->getProducer(), there is no such method to be found in the CdProduct class, and the invocation falls through to the default implementation in ShopProduct. When I invoke $product2->getSummaryLine(), on the other hand, the getSummaryLine() method is found in CdProduct and invoked.

The same is true of property accesses. When I access $title in the BookProduct class's getSummaryLine() method, the property is not found in the BookProduct class. It is acquired instead from the parent class, from ShopProduct. The $title property applies equally to both subclasses, and therefore it belongs in the superclass.

A quick look at the ShopProduct constructor, however, shows that I am still managing data in the base class that should be handled by its children. The BookProduct class should handle the $numPages argument and property, and the CdProduct class should handle the $playLength argument and property. To make this work, I will define constructor methods in each of the child classes.

Constructors and Inheritance

When you define a constructor in a child class, you become responsible for passing any arguments on to the parent. If you fail to do this, you can end up with a partially constructed object.

To invoke a method in a parent class, you must first find a way of referring to the class itself: a handle. PHP provides us with the parent keyword for this purpose.

To refer to a method in the context of a class rather than an object, you use :: rather than ->:

```
parent::__construct()
```

Note   I cover the scope resolution operator (::) in more detail in Chapter 4.

The preceding snippet means "Invoke the __construct() method of the parent class."
Here, I amend my example so that each class handles only the data that is appropriate to it:

```
// listing 03.61
class ShopProduct
{
    public $title;
    public $producerMainName;
    public $producerFirstName;
    public $price;

    public function __construct(
        $title,
        $firstName,
        $mainName,
        $price
    ) {
        $this->title            = $title;
        $this->producerFirstName = $firstName;
        $this->producerMainName  = $mainName;
        $this->price            = $price;
    }

    public function getProducer(): string
    {
        return $this->producerFirstName . " "
            . $this->producerMainName;
    }

    public function getSummaryLine(): string
    {
        $base  = "{$this->title} ( {$this->producerMainName}, ";
        $base .= "{$this->producerFirstName} )"; return $base;
    }
}
```

```php
// listing 03.62
class BookProduct extends ShopProduct
{
    public $numPages;

    public function __construct(
        string $title,
        string $firstName,
        string $mainName,
        float $price,
        int $numPages
    ) {
        parent:: __construct(
            $title,
            $firstName,
            $mainName,
            $price
        );
        $this->numPages = $numPages;
    }

    public function getNumberOfPages(): int
    {
        return $this->numPages;
    }

    public function getSummaryLine(): string
    {
        $base  = "{$this->title} ( $this->producerMainName, ";
        $base .= "$this->producerFirstName )";
        $base .= ": page count - {$this->numPages}";
        return $base;
    }
}
```

```
// listing 03.63
class CdProduct extends ShopProduct
{
    public $playLength;

    public function __construct(
        string $title,
        string $firstName,
        string $mainName,
        float $price,
        int $playLength
    ) {
        parent:: __construct(
            $title,
            $firstName,
            $mainName,
            $price
        );
        $this->playLength = $playLength;
    }

    public function getPlayLength(): int
    {
        return $this->playLength;
    }

    public function getSummaryLine(): string
    {
        $base  = "{$this->title} ( {$this->producerMainName}, ";
        $base .= "{$this->producerFirstName} )";
        $base .= ": playing time - {$this->playLength}";
        return $base;
    }
}
```

Each child class invokes the constructor of its parent before setting its own properties. The base class now knows only about its own data. Child classes are generally specializations of their parents. As a rule of thumb, you should avoid giving parent classes any special knowledge about their children.

Note   Prior to PHP 5, constructors took on the name of the enclosing class. The new unified constructors use the name `__construct()`. Using the old syntax, a call to a parent constructor would tie you to that particular class: `parent::ShopProduct();`. The old constructor syntax was deprecated in PHP 7.0 and removed altogether in PHP 8.

Invoking an Overridden Method

The parent keyword can be used with any method that overrides its counterpart in a parent class. When you override a method, you may not wish to obliterate the functionality of the parent, but rather to extend it. You can achieve this by calling the parent class's method in the current object's context. If you look again at the getSummaryLine() method implementations, you will see that they duplicate a lot of code. It would be better to use rather than reproduce the functionality already developed in the ShopProduct class:

```
// listing 03.64
// ShopProduct

    public function getSummaryLine(): string
    {
        $base  = "{$this->title} ( {$this->producerMainName}, ";
        $base .= "{$this->producerFirstName} )";
        return $base;
    }

// listing 03.65
// BookProduct
```

```
public function getSummaryLine(): string
{
    $base  = parent::getSummaryLine();
    $base .= ": page count - $this->numPages";
    return $base;
}
```

I set up the core functionality for the getSummaryLine() method in the ShopProduct base class.

Rather than reproduce this in the CdProduct and BookProduct subclasses, I simply call the parent method before proceeding to add more data to the summary string.

Now that you have seen the basics of inheritance, I will reexamine property and method visibility in light of the full picture.

Public, Private, and Protected: Managing Access to Your Classes

So far, I have declared all properties public. Public access was the default setting for methods and for properties if you used the old var keyword in your property declaration.

Note   var was deprecated in PHP 5 and will likely be completely removed from the language in future.

As we have seen, elements in your classes can be declared public, private, or protected:

- Public properties and methods can be accessed from any context.

- A private method or property can only be accessed from within the enclosing class. Even subclasses have no access.

- A protected method or property can only be accessed from within either the enclosing class or from a subclass. No external code is granted access.

So how is this useful to us? Visibility keywords allow you to expose only those aspects of a class that are required by a client. This sets a clear interface for your object.

By preventing a client from accessing certain properties, access control can also help prevent bugs in your code. Imagine, for example, that you want to allow ShopProduct objects to support a discount. You could add a $discount property and a setDiscount() method:

```
// listing 03.66

// ShopProduct class

    public $discount = 0;
//...

    public function setDiscount(int $num): void
    {
        $this->discount = $num;
    }
```

Armed with a mechanism for setting a discount, you can create a getPrice() method that takes account of the discount that has been applied:

```
// listing 03.67

public function getPrice(): int|float
{
    return ($this->price - $this->discount);
}
```

At this point, you have a problem. You only want to expose the adjusted price to the world, but a client can easily bypass the getPrice() method and access the $price property:

```
print "The price is {$product1->price}\n";
```

This will print the raw price and not the discount-adjusted price you wish to present. You can put a stop to this straightaway by making the $price property private. This will prevent direct access, forcing clients to use the getPrice() method. Any attempt from outside the ShopProduct class to access the $price property will fail. As far as the wider world is concerned, this property has ceased to exist.

Setting properties to private can be an overzealous strategy. A private property cannot be accessed by a child class. Imagine that our business rules state that books alone should be ineligible for discounts. You could override the getPrice() method so that it returns the $price property, applying no discount:

```
// listing 03.68
// BookProduct

    public function getPrice(): int|float
    {
        return $this->price;
    }
```

As the private $price property is declared in the ShopProduct class and not BookProduct, the attempt to access it here will fail. The solution to this problem is to declare the $price variable as protected, thereby granting access to descendant classes. Remember that a protected property or method cannot be accessed from outside the class hierarchy in which it was declared. It can only be accessed from within its originating class or from within children of the originating class.

As a general rule, err on the side of privacy. Make properties private or protected at first and relax your restriction only as needed. Many (if not most) methods in your classes will be public, but once again, if in doubt, lock it down. A method that provides local functionality for other methods in your class has no relevance to your class's users. Make it private or protected.

Accessor Methods

Even when client programmers need to work with values held by your class, it is often a good idea to deny direct access to properties, providing methods instead that relay the needed values. Such methods are known as accessors or getters and setters.

You have already seen one benefit afforded by accessor methods. You can use an accessor to filter a property value according to circumstances, as was illustrated by the getPrice() method.

You can also use a setter method to enforce a property type. Type declarations can be used to constrain method arguments, but a property can contain data of any type. Remember the ShopProductWriter class that uses a ShopProduct object to output list data? I can develop this further, so that it writes any number of ShopProduct objects at one time:

```
// listing 03.69
class ShopProductWriter
{
    public $products = [];

    public function addProduct(ShopProduct $shopProduct): void
    {
        $this->products[] = $shopProduct;
    }

    public function write(): void
    {
        $str = "";
        foreach ($this->products as $shopProduct) {
            $str .= "{$shopProduct->title}: ";
            $str .= $shopProduct->getProducer();
            $str .= " ({$shopProduct->getPrice()})\n";
        }
        print $str;
    }
}
```

The ShopProductWriter class is now much more useful. It can hold many
ShopProduct objects and write data for them all in one go. I must trust my client coders
to respect the intentions of the class, though. Despite the fact that I have provided an
addProduct() method, I have not prevented programmers from manipulating the
$products property directly. Not only could someone add the wrong kind of object to
the $products array property, but he could even overwrite the entire array and replace it
with a primitive value. I can prevent this by making the $products property private:

```
// listing 03.70

class ShopProductWriter
{
    private $products = [];

    //...
```

It's now impossible for external code to damage the $products property. All access must be via the addProduct() method, and the class type declaration I use in the method declaration ensures that only ShopProduct objects can be added to the array property.

Typed Properties

So, by combining type declarations in method signatures with property visibility declarations, you can control the property types in your classes. Here is another example: a Point class in which I use type declarations and property visibility to manage the property types:

```
// listing 03.71
class Point
{
    private $x = 0;
    private $y = 0;

    public function setVals(int $x, int $y)
    {
        $this->x = $x;
        $this->y = $y;
    }

    public function getX(): int
    {
        return $this->x;
    }

    public function getY(): int
    {
        return $this->y;
    }
}
```

Because the $x and $y properties are private, they can only be set via the setVals() method—and because setVals() will only accept integer values, you can be sure that $x and $y always contain integers.

Of course, because these properties are set private, the only way they can be accessed is through *getter* or *accessor* methods.

We were stuck with this method of fixing the types of properties up until PHP version 7.4 which introduced typed properties. This allows us to declare types for our properties. Here is a version of Point that takes advantage of this:

```
// listing 03.72
class Point
{
    public int $x = 0;
    public int $y = 0;
}
```

I have made the properties $x and $y public and used type declaration to constrain their types. Because of this, I can choose, if I want, to get rid of the setVals() method without sacrificing control. I also no longer need the getX() and getY() methods. Point is now an exceptionally simple class, but, even with both its properties public, it offers the world guarantees about the data it holds.

Let's try to set a string on one of those properties:

```
// listing 03.73
$point = new Point();
$point->x = "a";
```

PHP won't let us get away with that:

```
TypeError: Cannot assign string to property popp\ch03\batch11\Point::$x of
type int
```

Note   Union types can also be used in type property declarations.

The ShopProduct Classes

Let's close this chapter by amending the ShopProduct class and its children to lock down access control and to incorporate some of the other features we have covered:

```
// listing 03.74
class ShopProduct
{
    private int|float $discount = 0;

    public function __construct(
        private string $title,
        private string $producerFirstName,
        private string $producerMainName,
        protected int|float $price
    ) {
    }

    public function getProducerFirstName(): string
    {
        return $this->producerFirstName;
    }

    public function getProducerMainName(): string
    {
        return $this->producerMainName;
    }

    public function setDiscount(int|float $num): void
    {
        $this->discount = $num;
    }

    public function getDiscount(): int
    {
        return $this->discount;
    }

    public function getTitle(): string
    {
        return $this->title;
    }
```

```
    public function getPrice(): int|float
    {
        return ($this->price - $this->discount);
    }

    public function getProducer(): string
    {
        return $this->producerFirstName . " "
            . $this->producerMainName;
    }

    public function getSummaryLine(): string
    {
        $base  = "{$this->title} ( {$this->producerMainName}, ";
        $base .= "{$this->producerFirstName} )";
        return $base;
    }
}
```

In addition to closing down access to most of the properties by setting their visibility to private (or protected in the case of $discount), I have reintroduced constructor property promotion so that I can combine my property declarations with my constructor signature. I also used a property type declaration for $discount—demonstrating PHP 8's new type union feature at the same time. I have constrained $discount so that it can be assigned *either* an int or a float value. This constraint might seem redundant, since $discount is declared private and the type declaration in the setDiscount() method—another union—will enforce the same condition. However, it is good practice to declare types for your properties partly because this acts as a kind of enforced inline documentation and partly because it will prevent us from accidentally playing fast and loose with $discount during further development of ShopProduct.

```
// listing 03.75
class CdProduct extends ShopProduct
{
    public function __construct(
        string $title,
        string $firstName,
```

```
        string $mainName,
        int|float $price,
        private int $playLength
    ) {
        parent:: __construct(
            $title,
            $firstName,
            $mainName,
            $price
        );
    }

    public function getPlayLength(): int
    {
        return $this->playLength;
    }

    public function getSummaryLine(): string
    {
        $base  = "{$this->title} ( {$this->producerMainName}, ";
        $base .= "{$this->producerFirstName} )";
        $base .= ": playing time - {$this->playLength}";
        return $base;
    }
}
```

Again, I am using property promotion in the constructor's signature. This time, it is for one argument alone: $playLength. Because I am passing on the remainder of the constructor arguments to the parent class, I do not set visibility for them. I use them instead within the body of the constructor.

```
// listing 03.76
class BookProduct extends ShopProduct
{
    public function __construct(
        string $title,
        string $firstName,
```

```
        string $mainName,
        int|float $price,
        private int $numPages
    ) {
        parent:: construct(
            $title,
            $firstName,
            $mainName,
            $price
        );
    }

    public function getNumberOfPages(): int
    {
        return $this->numPages;
    }

    public function getSummaryLine(): string
    {
        $base  = parent::getSummaryLine();
        $base .= ": page count - $this->numPages";
        return $base;
    }

    public function getPrice(): int|float
    {
        return $this->price;
    }
}
```

So, all properties are either private or protected in this version of the ShopProduct family. I have added a number of accessor methods to round things off.

Summary

This chapter covered a lot of ground, taking a class from an empty implementation through to a fully featured inheritance hierarchy. You took in some design issues, particularly with regard to type and inheritance. You saw PHP's support for visibility and explored some of its uses. In the next chapter, I will show you more of PHP's object-oriented features.

Advanced Features

You have already seen how class type hinting and access control give you more control over a class's interface. In this chapter, I will delve deeper into PHP's object-oriented features.

This chapter will cover several subjects:

- *Static methods and properties*: Accessing data and functionality through classes rather than objects

- *Abstract classes and interfaces*: Separating design from implementation

- *Traits*: Sharing implementation between class hierarchies

- *Error handling*: Introducing exceptions

- *Final classes and methods*: Limiting inheritance

- *Interceptor methods*: Automating delegation

- *Destructor methods*: Cleaning up after your objects

- *Cloning objects*: Making object copies

- *Resolving objects to strings*: Creating a summary method

- *Callbacks*: Adding functionality to components with anonymous functions and classes

Static Methods and Properties

All of the examples in the previous chapter worked with objects. I characterized classes as templates from which objects are produced and objects as active instances of classes—the things whose methods you invoke and whose properties you access. I implied that, in object-oriented programming, the real work is done by instances of classes. Classes, after all, are merely templates for objects.

© Matt Zandstra 2021
M. Zandstra, *PHP 8 Objects, Patterns, and Practice*, https://doi.org/10.1007/978-1-4842-6791-2_4

In fact, it is not that simple. You can access both methods and properties in the context of a class rather than that of an object. Such methods and properties are "static" and must be declared as such by using the static keyword:

```
// listing 04.01
class StaticExample
{
    public static int $aNum = 0;
    public static function sayHello(): void
    {
        print "hello";
    }
}
```

Static methods are functions with class scope. They cannot themselves access any normal properties in the class because these would belong to an object; however, they can access static properties. If you change a static property, all instances of that class are able to access the new value.

Because you access a static element via a class and not an instance, you do not need a variable that references an object. Instead, you use the class name in conjunction with ::, as in this example:

```
// listing 04.02
print StaticExample::$aNum;
StaticExample::sayHello();
```

This syntax should be familiar from the previous chapter. I used :: in conjunction with parent to access an overridden method. Now, as then, I am accessing class rather than object data. Class code can use the parent keyword to access a superclass without using its class name. To access a static method or property from within the same class (rather than from a child), I would use the self keyword. self is to classes what the $this pseudo-variable is to objects. So from outside the StaticExample class, I access the $aNum property using its class name:

```
StaticExample::$aNum;
```

From within a class, I can use the self keyword:

```
// listing 04.03
class StaticExample2
{
    public static int $aNum = 0;
    public static function sayHello(): void
    {
        self::$aNum++;
        print "hello (" . self::$aNum . ")\n";
    }
}
```

Note   Making a method call using parent is the only circumstance in which you should use a static reference to a nonstatic method.

Unless you are accessing an overridden method, you should only ever use > :: to access a method or > property that has been explicitly declared static.

In documentation, however, you will often see static syntax used to refer to a method or property. This does not mean that the item in question is necessarily static, just that it belongs to a certain class. The write() method of the ShopProductWriter class might be referred to as ShopProductWriter::write(), for example, even though the write() method is not static. You will see this syntax here when that level of specificity is appropriate.

By definition, static methods and properties are invoked on classes and not objects. For this reason, they are often referred to as class variables and properties. As a consequence of this class orientation, you cannot use the $this pseudo-variable inside a static method.

So, why would you use a static method or property? Static elements have a number of characteristics that can be useful. First, they are available from anywhere in your script (assuming that you have access to the class). This means you can access functionality without needing to pass an instance of the class from object to object or, worse, storing an instance in a global variable. Second, a static property is available to every instance of a class, so you can set values that you want to be available to all members of a type. Finally, the fact that you don't need an instance to access a static property or method can save you from instantiating an object purely to get at a simple function.

To illustrate this, I will build a static method for the ShopProduct class that automates the instantiation of ShopProduct objects. Using SQLite, I might define a products table like this:

```
// listing 04.04
CREATE TABLE products (
    id INTEGER PRIMARY KEY AUTOINCREMENT,
    type TEXT,
    firstname TEXT,
    mainname TEXT,
    title TEXT,
    price float,
    numpages int,
    playlength int,
    discount int )
```

Now I want to build a getInstance() method that accepts a row ID and PDO object, uses them to acquire a database row, and then returns a ShopProduct object. I can add these methods to the ShopProduct class I created in the previous chapter. As you probably know, *PDO* stands for *PHP Data Object*. The PDO class provides a common interface to different database applications:

```
// listing 04.05

// ShopProduct class...

    private int $id = 0;
    // ...

    public function setID(int $id): void
    {
        $this->id = $id;
    }
    // ...

    public static function getInstance(int $id, \PDO $pdo): ShopProduct
    {
        $stmt = $pdo->prepare("select * from products where id=?");
        $result = $stmt->execute([$id]);
```

```
    $row = $stmt->fetch();
    if (empty($row)) {
        return null;
    }

    if ($row['type'] == "book") {
        $product = new BookProduct(
            $row['title'],
            $row['firstname'],
            $row['mainname'],
            (float) $row['price'],
            (int) $row['numpages']
        );
    } elseif ($row['type'] == "cd") {
        $product = new CdProduct(
            $row['title'],
            $row['firstname'],
            $row['mainname'],
            (float) $row['price'],
            (int) $row['playlength']
        );
    } else {
        $firstname = (is_null($row['firstname'])) ? "" :
        $row['firstname'];
        $product = new ShopProduct(
            $row['title'],
            $firstname,
            $row['mainname'],
            (float) $row['price']
        );
    }
    $product->setId((int) $row['id']);
    $product->setDiscount((int) $row['discount']);
    return $product;
}
```

As you can see, the getInstance() method returns a ShopProduct object and, based on a type flag, is smart enough to work out the precise specialization it should instantiate. I have omitted any error handling to keep the example compact. In a real-world version of this, for example, I would not be so trusting as to assume that the provided PDO object was initialized to talk to the correct database. In fact, I probably wrap the PDO with a class that would guarantee this behavior. You can read more about object-oriented coding and databases in Chapter 13.

This method is more useful in a class context than an object context. It lets you convert raw data from the database into an object easily, without requiring that you have a ShopProduct object to start with. The method does not use any instance properties or methods, so there is no reason why it should not be declared static. Given a valid PDO object, I can invoke the method from anywhere in an application:

```
// listing 04.06
$dsn = "sqlite:/tmp/products.sqlite3";
$pdo = new \PDO($dsn, null, null);
$pdo->setAttribute(\PDO::ATTR_ERRMODE, \PDO::ERRMODE_EXCEPTION);
$obj = ShopProduct::getInstance(1, $pdo);
```

Methods like this act as "factories" in that they take raw materials (such as row data or configuration information) and use them to produce objects. The term *factory* is applied to code designed to generate object instances. You will encounter factory examples again in future chapters.

In some ways, of course, this example poses as many problems as it solves. Although I make the ShopProduct::getInstance() method accessible from anywhere in a system without the need for a ShopProduct instance, I also demand that client code provides a PDO object. Where is this to be found? And is it really good practice for a parent class to have such intimate knowledge of its children? (Hint: No, it is not.) Problems of this kind—where to acquire key objects and values and how much classes should know about one another—are very common in object-oriented programming. I examine various approaches to object generation in Chapter 9.

Constant Properties

Some properties should not be changed. The Answer to Life, the Universe, and Everything is 42, and you want it to stay that way. Error and status flags will often be hard-coded into your classes. Although they should be publicly and statically available, client code should not be able to change them.

PHP allows you to define constant properties within a class. Like global constants, class constants cannot be changed once they are set. A constant property is declared with the const keyword. Constants are not prefixed with a dollar sign like regular properties. By convention, they are often named using only uppercase characters:

```
// listing 04.07
class ShopProduct
{
    public const AVAILABLE    = 0;
    public const OUT_OF_STOCK = 1;
```

Constant properties can contain only primitive values. You cannot assign an object to a constant. Like static properties, constant properties are accessed through the class and not an instance. Just as you define a constant without a dollar sign, no leading symbol is required when you refer to one:

```
// listing 04.08
print ShopProduct::AVAILABLE;
```

Note   Support for constant visibility modifiers was introduced in PHP 7.1. They work in just the same way as visibility modifiers do for properties.

Attempting to set a value on a constant once it has been declared will cause a parse error.

You should use constants when your property needs to be available across all instances of a class, as well as when the property value needs to be fixed and unchanging.

Abstract Classes

An abstract class cannot be instantiated. Instead, it defines (and, optionally, partially implements) the interface for any class that might extend it.

You define an abstract class with the abstract keyword. Here, I redefine the ShopProductWriter class I created in the previous chapter, this time as an abstract class:

```
// listing 04.09
abstract class ShopProductWriter
{
    protected array $products = [];

    public function addProduct(ShopProduct $shopProduct): void
    {
        $this->products[] = $shopProduct;
    }
}
```

You can create methods and properties as normal, but any attempt to instantiate an abstract object in this way will cause an error:

```
// listing 04.10
$writer = new ShopProductWriter();
```

You can see the error in this output:

```
Error: Cannot instantiate abstract class
popp\ch04\batch03\ShopProductWriter
```

In most cases, an abstract class will contain at least one abstract method. These are declared, once again, with the abstract keyword. An abstract method cannot have an implementation. You declare it in the normal way but end the declaration with a semicolon rather than a method body. Here, I add an abstract write() method to the ShopProductWriter class:

```
// listing 04.11
abstract class ShopProductWriter
{
    protected array $products = [];
```

```
    public function addProduct(ShopProduct $shopProduct): void
    {
        $this->products[] = $shopProduct;
    }

    abstract public function write(): void;
}
```

In creating an abstract method, you ensure that an implementation will be available in all concrete child classes, but you leave the details of that implementation undefined.

Assume I were to create a class derived from ShopProductWriter that does not implement the write() method, as in this example:

```
// listing 04.12

class ErroredWriter extends ShopProductWriter
{
}
```

I would face the following error:

```
Fatal error: Class popp\ch04\batch03\ErroredWriter contains 1 abstract
method and must therefore be declared abstract or implement the remaining
methods (popp\ch04\batch03\ShopProductWriter::write) in...
```

So any class that extends an abstract class must implement all abstract methods or itself be declared abstract. An extending class is responsible for more than simply implementing an abstract method. In doing so, it must reproduce the method signature. This means that the access control of the implementing method cannot be stricter than that of the abstract method. The implementing method should also require the same number of arguments as the abstract method, reproducing any class type declarations.

Here are two implementations of ShopProductWriter—first, XmlProductWriter:

```
// listing 04.13
class XmlProductWriter extends ShopProductWriter
{

    public function write(): void
    {
        $writer = new \XMLWriter();
        $writer->openMemory();
```

```
        $writer->startDocument('1.0', 'UTF-8');
        $writer->startElement("products");
        foreach ($this->products as $shopProduct) {
            $writer->startElement("product");
            $writer->writeAttribute("title", $shopProduct->getTitle());
            $writer->startElement("summary");
            $writer->text($shopProduct->getSummaryLine());
            $writer->endElement(); // summary
            $writer->endElement(); // product
        }
        $writer->endElement(); // products
        $writer->endDocument();
        print $writer->flush();
    }
}
```

This is the more basic TextProductWriter:

```
// listing 04.14
class TextProductWriter extends ShopProductWriter
{
    public function write(): void
    {
        $str = "PRODUCTS:\n";
        foreach ($this->products as $shopProduct) {
            $str .= $shopProduct->getSummaryLine() . "\n";
        }
        print $str;
    }
}
```

So, I have created two classes, each with its own implementation of the write()
method. The first outputs XML and the second outputs text. A method that requires a
ShopProductWriter object will not know which of these two classes it is receiving, but it
can be absolutely certain that a write() method is implemented. Note that I don't test
the type of $products before treating it as an array. This is because this property is both
declared an array and initialized in the ShopProductWriter class.

Interfaces

Although abstract classes let you provide some measure of implementation, interfaces are pure templates. An interface can only define functionality; it can never implement it. An interface is declared with the `interface` keyword. It can contain properties and method declarations but not method bodies.

Here's an interface:

```
// listing 04.15
interface Chargeable
{
    public function getPrice(): float;
}
```

As you can see, an interface looks very much like a class. Any class that incorporates this interface commits to implementing all the methods it defines, or it must be declared abstract.

A class can implement an interface using the `implements` keyword in its declaration. Once you have done this, the process of implementing an interface is the same as extending an abstract class that contains only abstract methods. Now I will make the ShopProduct class implement `Chargeable`:

```
// listing 04.16
class ShopProduct implements Chargeable
{
    // ...
    protected float $price;
    // ...

    public function getPrice(): float
    {
        return $this->price;
    }
    // ...
}
```

ShopProduct already had a getPrice() method, so why might it be useful to implement the Chargeable interface? Once again, the answer has to do with types. An implementing class takes on the type of the class it extends and the interface that it implements.

This means that the CdProduct class belongs to the following:

```
CdProduct
ShopProduct
Chargeable
```

This can be exploited by client code. To know an object's type is to know its capabilities. Consider this method:

```
// listing 04.17
public function cdInfo(CdProduct $prod): int
{
    // we know we can call getPlayLength()
    $length = $prod->getPlayLength();
    // ...
}
```

The method knows that the $prod object has a getPlayLength() method in addition to all the methods defined in the ShopProduct class and Chargeable interface.

Passed the same object, however, a method with a more generic type requirement— ShopProduct rather than CdProduct—can only know that the provided object contains ShopProduct methods.

```
// listing 04.18
public function addProduct(ShopProduct $prod)
{
    // even if $prod is a CdProduct object
    // we don't *know* this -- so we can't
    // presume to use getPlayLength()
    // ...
}
```

Without further testing, the method will know nothing of the getPlayLength() method.

Passed the same CdProduct object, a method which required a Chargeable object knows nothing at all of the ShopProduct or CdProduct types:

```
// listing 04.19
public function addChargeableItem(Chargeable $item)
{
    // all we know about $item is that it
    // is a Chargeable object -- the fact that it
    // is also a CdProduct object is irrelevant.
    // We can only be sure of getPrice()
    //
    //...
}
```

This method is only concerned with whether the $item argument contains a getPrice() method.

Because any class can implement an interface (in fact, a class can implement any number of interfaces), interfaces effectively join types that are otherwise unrelated. I might define an entirely new class that implements Chargeable:

```
// listing 04.20
class Shipping implements Chargeable
{
    public function __construct(private float $price)
    {
    }

    public function getPrice(): float
    {
        return $this->price;
    }
}
```

I can pass a Shipping object to the addChargeableItem() method just as I can pass it a ShopProduct object.

The important thing to a client working with a Chargeable object is that it can call a getPrice() method. Any other available methods are associated with other types, whether through the object's own class, a superclass, or another interface. These are irrelevant to the client.

A class can both extend a superclass and implement any number of interfaces. The extends clause should precede the implements clause:

```
// listing 04.21
class Consultancy extends TimedService implements Bookable, Chargeable
{
    // ...
}
```

Notice that the Consultancy class implements more than one interface. Multiple interfaces follow the implements keyword in a comma-separated list.

PHP only supports inheritance from a single parent, so the extends keyword can precede a single class name only.

Traits

As we have seen, interfaces help you manage the fact that, like Java, PHP does not support multiple inheritance. In other words, a class in PHP can only extend a single parent. However, you can make a class promise to implement as many interfaces as you like; for each interface it implements, the class takes on the corresponding type.

So interfaces provide types without implementation. But what if you want to share an implementation across inheritance hierarchies? PHP 5.4 introduced traits, and these let you do just that.

A trait is a class-like structure that cannot itself be instantiated but can be incorporated into classes. Any methods defined in a trait become available as part of any class that uses it. A trait changes the structure of a class, but doesn't change its type. Think of traits as includes for classes.

Let's look at why a trait might be useful.

A Problem for Traits to Solve

Here is a version of the ShopProduct class with a calculateTax() method:

```
// listing 04.22

class ShopProduct
{
    private int $taxrate = 20;

// ...

    public function calculateTax(float $price): float
    {
        return (($this->taxrate / 100) * $price);
    }
}
```

The calculateTax() method accepts a $price argument and calculates a sales tax amount based on the private $taxrate property.

Of course, a subclass gains access to calculateTax(). But what about entirely different class hierarchies? Imagine a class named UtilityService, which inherits from another class, Service. If UtilityService needs to use an identical routine, I might find myself duplicating calculateTax() in its entirety. Here is service:

```
// listing 04.23

abstract class Service
{
    // service oriented stuff
}
```

And here is UtilityService:

```
// listing 04.24

class UtilityService extends Service
{
    private int $taxrate = 20;
```

```
    public function calculateTax(float $price): float
    {
        return ( ( $this->taxrate / 100 ) * $price );
    }
}
```

Because UtilityService and ShopProduct do not share any common base classes, they cannot easily share the calculateTax() implementation. We are forced, therefore, to copy and paste our implementation from one class to another.

Defining and Using a Trait

One of the core object-oriented design goals I will cover in this book is the removal of duplication. As you will see in Chapter 11, one solution to this kind of duplication is to factor it out into a reusable strategy class. Traits provide another approach—less elegant, perhaps, but certainly effective.

Here, I declare a single trait that defines a calculateTax() method, and then I include it in both ShopProduct and UtilityService:

```
// listing 04.25
trait PriceUtilities
{
    private $taxrate = 20;

    public function calculateTax(float $price): float
    {
        return (($this->taxrate / 100) * $price);
    }

    // other utilities
}
```

I declare the PriceUtilities trait with the trait keyword. The body of a trait looks very similar to that of a class. It is simply a set of methods and properties collected within braces. Once I have declared it, I can access the PriceUtilities trait from within my classes. I do this with the use keyword followed by the name of the trait I wish to incorporate. So having declared and implemented the `calculateTax()` method in a single place, I go ahead and incorporate it into the ShopProduct class.

```
// listing 04.26
use popp\ch04\batch06_1\PriceUtilities;

class ShopProduct
{
    use PriceUtilities;
}
```

Also, of course, I add it to the UtilityService class:

```
// listing 04.27
class UtilityService extends Service
{
    use PriceUtilities;
}
```

Now, when I invoke these classes, I know that they share the PriceUtilities implementation without duplication. If I were to find a bug in PriceUtilities, I could fix it in a single place.

```
// listing 04.28
$p = new ShopProduct();
print $p->calculateTax(100) . "\n";

$u = new UtilityService();
print $u->calculateTax(100) . "\n";
```

Using More Than One Trait

You can include multiple traits in a class by listing each one after the use keyword, separated by commas. In this example, I define and apply a new trait, IdentityTrait, keeping my original PriceUtilities trait:

```
// listing 04.29
trait IdentityTrait
{
    public function generateId(): string
    {
        return uniqid();
    }
}
```

By applying both PriceUtilities and IdentityTrait with the use keyword, I make the calculateTax() and the generateId() methods available to the ShopProduct class. This means the class offers both the calculateTax() and generateId() methods.

```
// listing 04.30
class ShopProduct
{
    use PriceUtilities;
    use IdentityTrait;
}
```

Note   The IdentityTrait trait provides the generateId() method. In fact, a database often generates identifiers for objects, but you might switch in a local implementation for testing purposes. You can find out more about objects, databases, and unique identifiers in Chapter 13, which covers the Identity Map pattern. You can learn more about testing and mocking in Chapter 18.

Now I can call both the generateId() and calculateTax() methods on a ShopProduct class.

```
// listing 04.31
$p = new ShopProduct();
print $p->calculateTax(100) . "\n";
print $p->generateId() . "\n";
```

Combining Traits and Interfaces

Although traits are useful, they don't change the type of the class to which they are applied. So when you apply the IdentityTrait trait to multiple classes, they won't share a type that could be hinted for in a method signature.

Luckily, traits play well with interfaces. I can define an interface that requires a generateId() method and then declare that ShopProduct implements it:

```
// listing 04.32
interface IdentityObject
{
    public function generateId(): string;
}
```

If I want ShopProduct to fulfill the IdentityObject type, I must now make it implement the IdentityObject interface.

```
// listing 04.33
class ShopProduct implements IdentityObject
{
    use PriceUtilities;
    use IdentityTrait;
}
```

As before, ShopProduct uses the IdentityTrait trait. However, the method this imports, generateId(), now also fulfills a commitment to the IdentityObject interface. This means that we can pass ShopProduct objects to methods and functions that use type hinting to demand IdentityObject instances, like this:

```
// listing 04.34
public static function storeIdentityObject(IdentityObject $idobj)
{
    // do something with the IdentityObject
}
```

Managing Method Name Conflicts with insteadof

The ability to combine traits is a nice feature, but sooner or later conflicts are inevitable. Consider what would happen, for example, if I were to use two traits that provide a calculateTax() method:

```
// listing 04.35
trait TaxTools
{
    public function calculateTax(float $price): float
    {
        return 222;
    }
}
```

Because I have included two traits that contain calculateTax() methods, PHP is unable to work out which should override the other. The result is a fatal error:

```
Fatal error: Trait method popp\ch04\batch06_3\TaxTools::calculateTax has
not been applied as
popp\ch04\batch06_3\UtilityService::calculateTax, because of collision with
popp\ch04\batch06_3\PriceUtilities::calculateTax in...
```

To fix this problem, I can use the insteadof keyword. Here's how:

```
// listing 04.36
class UtilityService extends Service
{
    use PriceUtilities;
    use TaxTools {
        TaxTools::calculateTax insteadof PriceUtilities;
    }
}
```

In order to apply further directives to a use statement, I must first add a body. I do this with opening and closing braces. Within this block, I use the insteadof operator. This requires a fully qualified method reference (i.e., one that identifies both the trait and the method names, separated by a scope resolution operator) on the left-hand side.

On the right-hand side, insteadof requires the name of the trait whose equivalent method should be overridden:

```
TaxTools::calculateTax insteadof PriceUtilities;
```

The preceding snippet means "Use the calculateTax() method of TaxTools instead of the method of the same name in PriceUtilities."

So when I run this code:

```
// listing 04.37
$u = new UtilityService();
print $u->calculateTax(100) . "\n";
```

I get the dummy output I planted in TaxTools::calculateTax():

```
222
```

Aliasing Overridden Trait Methods

We have seen that you can use insteadof to disambiguate between methods. What do you do, though, if you want to then access the overridden method? The as operator allows you to alias trait methods. Once again, the as operator requires a full reference to a method on its left-hand side. On the right-hand side of the operator, you should put the name of the alias. So here, for example, I reinstate the calculateTax() method of the PriceUtilities trait using the new name basicTax():

```
// listing 04.38
class UtilityService extends Service
{
    use PriceUtilities;
    use TaxTools {
        TaxTools::calculateTax insteadof PriceUtilities;
        PriceUtilities::calculateTax as basicTax;
    }
}
```

Now the UtilityService class has acquired two methods: the TaxTools version of calculateTax() and the PriceUtilities version aliased to basicTax(). Let's run these methods:

```
// listing 04.39
$u = new UtilityService();
print $u->calculateTax(100) . "\n";
print $u->basicTax(100) . "\n";
```

This gives the following output:

```
222
20
```

So PriceUtilities::calculateTax() has been resurrected as part of the UtilityService class under the name basicTax().

Note   Where a method name clashes between traits, it is not enough to alias one of the method names in the use block. You must first determine which method supersedes the other using the insteadof operator. Then you can reassign the discarded method a new name with the as operator.

Incidentally, you can also use method name aliasing where there is no name clash. You might, for example, want to use a trait method to implement an abstract method signature declared in a parent class or in an interface.

Using Static Methods in Traits

Most of the examples you have seen so far could use static methods because they do not store instance data. There's nothing complicated about placing a static method in a trait. Here, I change the PriceUtilities::$taxrate property and the PriceUtilities::calculateTax() methods so that they are static:

```
// listing 04.40
trait PriceUtilities
{
    private static int $taxrate = 20;
```

```
public static function calculateTax(float $price): float
{
    return ((self::$taxrate / 100) * $price);
}

// other utilities
}
```

Here is UtilityService back to its minimal form:

```
// listing 04.41
class UtilityService extends Service
{
    use PriceUtilities;
}
```

All it does is use the PriceUtilities trait. There is a key difference, though, when it comes to calling the calculateTax() method:

```
// listing 04.42
print UtilityService::calculateTax(100) . "\n";
```

I must now call the method on the class rather than on an object. As you might expect, this script outputs the following:

20

So, static methods are declared in traits and accessed via the host class in the normal way.

Accessing Host Class Properties

You might assume that static methods are really the only way to go as far as traits are concerned. Even trait methods that are not declared static are essentially static in nature, right? Well, wrong, in fact, you can access properties and methods in a host class:

```
// listing 04.43
trait PriceUtilities
{
    public function calculateTax(float $price): float
```

```
    {
        // is this good design?
        return (($this->taxrate / 100)  *  $price);
    }

    // other utilities
}
```

In the preceding code, I amend the PriceUtilities trait so that it accesses a property in its host class. Here is a host—PriceUtilities—amended to declare the property:

```
// listing 04.44
class UtilityService extends Service
{
    use PriceUtilities;

    public $taxrate = 20;
}
```

If you think that this is a bad design, you're right. It's a spectacularly bad design. Although it's useful for the trait to access data set by its host class, there is nothing to require the UtilityService class to actually provide a $taxrate property. Remember that traits should be usable across many different classes. What is the guarantee or even the likelihood that any host classes will declare a $taxrate?

On the other hand, it would be great to be able to establish a contract that says, essentially, "If you use this trait, then you must provide it certain resources."

In fact, you can achieve exactly this effect. Traits support abstract methods.

Defining Abstract Methods in Traits

You can define abstract methods in a trait in just the same way you would in a class. When a trait is used by a class, it takes on the commitment to implement any abstract methods it declares.

Note Prior to PHP 8, method signatures for abstract methods defined in traits were not always fully enforced. This meant that in some circumstances argument and return types might vary in the implementing class from those set down in the abstract method declaration. This loophole has now been shut.

Armed with this knowledge, I can reimplement my previous example so that the trait forces any class that uses it to provide tax rate information:

```
// listing 04.45
trait PriceUtilities
{
    public function calculateTax(float $price): float
    {
        // better design.. we know getTaxRate() is implemented
        return (($this->getTaxRate() / 100) * $price);
    }

    abstract public function getTaxRate(): float;
    // other utilities
}
```

By declaring an abstract getTaxRate() method in the PriceUtilities trait, I force the UtilityService class to provide an implementation.

```
// listing 04.46
class UtilityService extends Service
{
    use PriceUtilities;

    public function getTaxRate(): float
    {
        return 20;
    }
}
```

Thanks to the abstract declaration in the trait, if I had not provided a getTaxRate() method, I would have been rewarded with a fatal error.

Changing Access Rights to Trait Methods

You can, of course, declare a trait method public, private, or protected. However, you can also change this access from within the class that uses the trait. You have already seen that the as operator can be used to alias a method name. If you use an access modifier on the right-hand side of this operator, it will change the method's access level rather than its name.

Imagine, for example, you would like to use calculateTax() from within UtilityService, but not make it available to implementing code. Here's how you would change the use statement:

```
// listing 04.47
class UtilityService extends Service
{
    use PriceUtilities {
        PriceUtilities::calculateTax as private;
    }

    public function __construct(private float $price)
    {
    }

    public function getTaxRate(): float
    {
        return 20;
    }

    public function getFinalPrice(): float
    {
        return ($this->price + $this->calculateTax($this->price));
    }
}
```

I deploy the as operator in conjunction with the private keyword in order to set private access to calculateTax(). This means I can access the method from getFinalPrice(). Here's an external attempt to access calculateTax():

```
// listing 04.48
$u = new UtilityService(100);
print $u->calculateTax() . "\n";
```

Unfortunately, this code will generate an error:

```
Error: Call to private method popp\ch04\batch06_9\
UtilityService::calculateTax() from context ...
```

Late Static Bindings: The static Keyword

Now that you've seen abstract classes, traits, and interfaces, it's time to return briefly to static methods. You saw that a static method can be used as a factory, a way of generating instances of the containing class. If you're as lazy a coder as me, you might chafe at the duplication in an example like this:

```
// listing 04.49
abstract class DomainObject
{

}

// listing 04.50
class User extends DomainObject
{
    public static function create(): User
    {
        return new User();
    }
}

// listing 04.51
class Document extends DomainObject
{
    public static function create(): Document
    {
        return new Document();
    }
}
```

I create a superclass named DomainObject. In a real-world project, of course, this would contain functionality common to its extending classes. Then I create two child classes, User and Document. I would like my concrete classes to have static create() methods.

Note   Why would I use a static factory method when a constructor performs the work of creating an object already? In Chapter 13, I'll describe a pattern called Identity Map. An Identity Map component generates and manages a new object only if an object with the same distinguishing characteristics is not already under management. If the target object already exists, it is returned. A factory method like create() would make a good client for a component of this sort.

This code works fine, but it has an annoying amount of duplication. I don't want to have to create boilerplate code like this for every DomainObject child class that I create. Instead, I'll try pushing the create() method up to the superclass:

```
// listing 04.52
abstract class DomainObject
{
    public static function create(): DomainObject
    {
        return new self();
    }
}
```

Well, that *looks* neat. I now have common code in one place, and I've used self as a reference to the class. But I have made an assumption about the self keyword. In fact, it does not act for classes exactly the same way that $this does for objects. self does not refer to the calling context; it refers to the context of resolution. So if I run the previous example, I get this:

```
Error: Cannot instantiate abstract class
popp\ch04\batch06\DomainObject
```

So self resolves to DomainObject, the place where create() is defined, and not to Document, the class on which it was called. Until PHP 5.3, this was a serious limitation, which spawned many rather clumsy workarounds. PHP 5.3 introduced a concept called *late static bindings*. The most obvious manifestation of this feature is the keyword:

static. static is similar to self, except that it refers to the *invoked* rather than the *containing* class. In this case, it means that calling Document::create() results in a new Document object and not a doomed attempt to instantiate a DomainObject object.

So now I can take advantage of my inheritance relationship in a static context:

```
// listing 04.53
abstract class DomainObject
{
    public static function create(): DomainObject
    {
        return new static();
    }
}
```

```
// listing 04.54
class User extends DomainObject
{
}
```

```
// listing 04.55
class Document extends DomainObject
{
}
```

Now if we call create() on one of the child classes, we should no longer cause an error—and get back an object related to the class we *called* and not to the class that houses create().

```
// listing 04.56
print_r(Document::create());
```

Here is the output.

```
popp\ch04\batch07\Document Object
(
)
```

The static keyword can be used for more than just instantiation. Like self and parent, static can be used as an identifier for static method calls, even from a nonstatic context. Let's say I want to include the concept of a group for my DomainObject classes.

By default, in my new classification, all classes fall into category "default," but I'd like to be able to override this for some branches of my inheritance hierarchy:

```
// listing 04.57
abstract class DomainObject
{
    private string $group;

    public function __construct()
    {
        $this->group = static::getGroup();
    }

    public static function create(): DomainObject
    {
        return new static();
    }

    public static function getGroup(): string
    {
        return "default";
    }
}

// listing 04.58
class User extends DomainObject
{
}

// listing 04.59
class Document extends DomainObject
{
    public static function getGroup(): string
    {
        return "document";
    }
}
```

```
// listing 04.60
class SpreadSheet extends Document
{
}
```

```
// listing 04.61
print_r(User::create());
print_r(SpreadSheet::create());
```

I introduced a constructor to the DomainObject class. It uses the static keyword to invoke a static method: getGroup(). DomainObject provides the default implementation, but Document overrides it. I also created a new class, SpreadSheet, that extends Document. Here's the output:

```
popp\ch04\batch07\User Object (
    [group:popp\ch04\batch07\DomainObject:private] => default
)
popp\ch04\batch07\SpreadSheet Object (
    [group:popp\ch04\batch07\DomainObject:private] => document
)
```

For the User class, not much clever needs to happen. The DomainObject constructor calls getGroup() and finds it locally. In the case of SpreadSheet, though, the search begins at the invoked class, SpreadSheet itself. It provides no implementation, so the getGroup() method in the Document class is invoked. Before PHP 5.3 and late static binding, I would have been stuck with the self keyword here, which would only look for getGroup() in the DomainObject class.

Handling Errors

Things go wrong. Files are misplaced, database servers are left uninitialized, URLs are changed, XML files are mangled, permissions are poorly set, and disk quotas are exceeded. The list goes on and on. In the fight to anticipate every problem, a simple method can sometimes sink under the weight of its own error-handling code.

Here is a simple Conf class that stores, retrieves, and sets data in an XML configuration file:

```
// listing 04.62
class Conf
{
    private \SimpleXMLElement $xml;
    private \SimpleXMLElement $lastmatch;

    public function __construct(private string $file)
    {
        $this->xml = simplexml_load_file($file);
    }

    public function write(): void
    {
        file_put_contents($this->file, $this->xml->asXML());
    }

    public function get(string $str): ?string
    {
        $matches = $this->xml->xpath("/conf/item[@name=\"$str\"]");
        if (count($matches)) {
            $this->lastmatch = $matches[0];
            return (string)$matches[0];
        }
        return null;
    }

    public function set(string $key, string $value): void
    {
        if (! is_null($this->get($key))) {
            $this->lastmatch[0] = $value;
            return;
        }
        $conf = $this->xml->conf;
        $this->xml->addChild('item', $value)->addAttribute('name', $key);
    }
}
```

The Conf class uses the SimpleXml extension to access name value pairs. Here's the kind of format with which it is designed to work:

```
<?xml version="1.0" ?>
<conf>
    <item name="user">bob</item>
    <item name="pass">newpass</item>
    <item name="host">localhost</item>
</conf>
```

The Conf class's constructor accepts a file path, which it passes to simplexml_load_file(). It stores the resulting SimpleXmlElement object in a property called $xml. The get() method uses XPath to locate an item element with the given name attribute, returning its value. set() either changes the value of an existing item or creates a new one. Finally, the write() method saves the new configuration data back to the file.

Like much example code, the Conf class is highly simplified. In particular, it has no strategy for handling nonexistent or unwriteable files. It is also optimistic in outlook. It assumes that the XML document will be well formed and will contain the expected elements.

Testing for these error conditions is relatively trivial, but I must still decide how to respond to them should they arise. There are generally two options.

First, I could end execution. This is simple but drastic. My humble class would then take responsibility for bringing an entire script crashing down around it. Although methods such as __construct() and write() are well placed to detect errors, they do not have the information to decide how to handle them.

Rather than handle the error in my class, then, I could return an error flag of some kind. This could be a Boolean or an integer value such as 0 or -1. Some classes will also set an error string or flag, so that the client code can request more information after a failure.

Many PEAR packages combine these two approaches by returning an error object (an instance of PEAR_Error), which acts as a notification that an error has occurred and contains the error message within it. This approach is now deprecated, but plenty of classes have not been upgraded, not least because client code often depends on the old behavior.

The problem here is that you pollute your return value. You have to rely on the client coder to test for the return type every time your error-prone method is called. This can be risky. Trust no one!

When you return an error value to calling code, there is no guarantee that the client will be any better equipped than your method to decide how to handle the error.

If this is the case, then the problem begins all over again. The client method will have to determine how to respond to the error condition, maybe even implementing a different error-reporting strategy.

Exceptions

PHP 5 introduced exceptions to PHP, a radically different way of handling error conditions. Different for PHP, that is. You will find them hauntingly familiar if you have Java or C++ experience. Exceptions address all of the issues that I have raised so far in this section.

An exception is a special object instantiated from the built-in Exception class (or from a derived class).

Objects of type Exception are designed to hold and report error information.

The Exception class constructor accepts two optional arguments, a message string and an error code. The class provides some useful methods for analyzing error conditions. These are described in Table 4-1.

The Exception class is fantastically useful for providing error notification and debugging information (the getTrace() and getTraceAsString() methods are particularly helpful in this regard). In fact, it is almost identical to the PEAR_Error class that was discussed earlier. There is much more to an exception than the information it holds, though.

Table 4-1. *The Exception Class's Public Methods*

Method	Description
getMessage()	Get the message string that was passed to the constructor
getCode()	Get the code integer that was passed to the constructor
getFile()	Get the file in which the exception was generated
getLine()	Get the line number at which the exception was generated
getPrevious()	Get a nested Exception object
getTrace()	Get a multidimensional array tracing the method calls that led to the exception, including method, class, file, and argument data
getTraceAsString()	Get a string version of the data returned by getTrace()
__toString()	Called automatically when the Exception object is used in string context. Returns a string describing the exception details

Throwing an Exception

The throw keyword is used in conjunction with an Exception object. It halts execution of the current method and passes responsibility for handling the error back to the calling code. Here, I amend the __construct() method to use the throw statement:

```
// listing 04.63
public function __construct(private string $file)
{
    if (! file_exists($file)) {
        throw new \Exception("file '{$file}' does not exist");
    }
    $this->xml = simplexml_load_file($file);
}
```

The write() method can use a similar construct:

```
// listing 04.64
public function write(): void
{
    if (! is_writeable($this->file)) {
        throw new \Exception("file '{$this->file}' is not writeable");
    }
    print "{$this->file} is apparently writeable\n";
    file_put_contents($this->file, $this->xml->asXML());
}
```

```
// listing 04.65
try {
    $conf = new Conf("/tmp/conf01.xml");
    //$conf = new Conf( "/root/unwriteable.xml" );
    //$conf = new Conf( "nonexistent/not_there.xml" );
    print "user: " . $conf->get('user') . "\n";
    print "host: " . $conf->get('host') . "\n";
    $conf->set("pass", "newpass");
    $conf->write();
```

```
} catch (\Exception $e) {
    // handle error in some way
}
```

As you can see, the catch block superficially resembles a method declaration. When an exception is thrown, the catch block in the invoking scope is called. The Exception object is automatically passed in as the argument variable.

Just as execution is halted within the throwing method when an exception is thrown, so it is within the try block—control passes directly to the catch block. There, you can perform any error recovery tasks available to you. If you can, avoid falling back on a die statement. By invoking die, you make testing harder and might prevent other code in your system from performing necessary cleanup operations. If you cannot recover from an error, you can always throw a new exception:

```
// listing 04.66
} catch (\Exception $e) {
    // handle error in some way
    // or
    throw new \Exception("Conf error: " . $e->getMessage());
}
```

Alternatively, you can just rethrow the exception you have been given:

```
// listing 04.67
try {
    $conf = new Conf("nonexistent/not_there.xml");
} catch (\Exception $e) {
    // handle error...
    // or rethrow
    throw $e;
}
```

If you have no need of the Exception object itself in your error handling, you can, as of PHP 8, omit the exception argument altogether and just specify the type:

```
// listing 04.68
try {
    $conf = new Conf("nonexistent/not_there.xml");
```

```
} catch (\Exception) {
    // handle error without using the Exception object
}
```

Subclassing Exception

You can create classes that extend the Exception class as you would with any user-defined class. There are two reasons why you might want to do this. First, you can extend the class's functionality. Second, the fact that a derived class defines a new class type can aid error handling in itself.

You can, in fact, define as many catch blocks as you need for a try statement. The particular catch block invoked will depend on the type of the thrown exception and the class type hint in the argument list. Here are some simple classes that extend Exception:

```
// listing 04.69
class XmlException extends \Exception
{
    public function construct(private \LibXmlError $error)
    {
        $shortfile = basename($error->file);
        $msg = "[{$shortfile}, line {$error->line}, col {$error->column}]
        {$error->message}";
        $this->error = $error;
        parent:: __construct($msg, $error->code);
    }

    public function getLibXmlError(): \LibXmlError
    {
        return $this->error;
    }
}

// listing 04.70
class FileException extends \Exception
{
}
```

115

```
// listing 04.71
class ConfException extends \Exception
{
}
```

The LibXmlError class is generated behind the scenes when SimpleXml encounters a broken XML file. It has $message and $code properties, and it resembles the Exception class. I take advantage of this similarity and use the LibXmlError object in the XmlException class. The FileException and ConfException classes do nothing more than subclass Exception. I can now use these classes in my code and amend both construct() and write():

```
// listing 04.72

// Conf class...

    public function __construct(private string $file)
    {
        if (! file_exists($file)) {
            throw new FileException("file '$file' does not exist");
        }
        $this->xml = simplexml_load_file($file, null, LIBXML_NOERROR);
        if (! is_object($this->xml)) {
            throw new XmlException(libxml_get_last_error());
        }
        $matches = $this->xml->xpath("/conf");
        if (! count($matches)) {
            throw new ConfException("could not find root element: conf");
        }
    }

    public function write(): void
    {
        if (! is_writeable($this->file)) {
            throw new FileException("file '{$this->file}' is not writeable");
        }
        file_put_contents($this->file, $this->xml->asXML());
    }
```

__construct() throws either an XmlException, a FileException, or a ConfException, depending on the kind of error it encounters. Note that I pass the option flag LIBXML_NOERROR to simplexml_load_file(). This suppresses warnings, leaving me free to handle them with my XmlException class after the fact. If I encounter a malformed XML file, I know that an error has occurred because simplexml_load_file() won't have returned an object. I can then access the error using libxml_get_last_error().

The write() method throws a FileException if the $file property points to an unwriteable entity.

So, I have established that __construct() might throw one of three possible exceptions. How can I take advantage of this? Here's some code that instantiates a Conf object:

```
// listing 04.73
class Runner
{
    public static function init()
    {
        try {
            $conf = new Conf(__DIR__ . "/conf.broken.xml");
            print "user: " . $conf->get('user') . "\n";
            print "host: " . $conf->get('host') . "\n";
            $conf->set("pass", "newpass");
            $conf->write();
        } catch (FileException $e) {
            // permissions issue or non-existent file throw $e;
        } catch (XmlException $e) {
            // broken xml
        } catch (ConfException $e) {
            // wrong kind of XML file
        } catch (\Exception $e) {
            // backstop: should not be called
        }
    }
}
```

I provide a catch block for each class type. The block invoked depends on the exception type thrown. The first to match will be executed, so remember to place the most generic type at the end and the most specialized at the start. For example, if you were to place the catch block for Exception ahead of the block for XmlException and ConfException, neither of these would ever be invoked. This is because both of these classes belong to the Exception type and would therefore match the first test.

The first catch block (FileException) is invoked if there is a problem with the configuration file (if the file is nonexistent or unwriteable). The second block (XmlException) is invoked if an error occurs in parsing the XML file (e.g., if an element is not closed). The third block (ConfException) is invoked if a valid XML file does not contain the expected root conf element. The final block (Exception) should not be reached because my methods only generate the three exceptions, which are explicitly handled. It is often a good idea to have a "backstop" block like this, in case you add new exceptions to the code during development.

Note   If you do provide a "backstop" catch block, you should ensure that you actually do something about the exception in most instances—failing silently can cause bugs which are hard to diagnose.

The benefit of these fine-grained catch blocks is that they allow you to apply different recovery or failure mechanisms to different errors. For example, you may decide to end execution, log the error and continue, or explicitly rethrow an error.

Another trick you can play here is to throw a new exception that wraps the current one. This allows you to stake a claim to the error and add your own contextual information while retaining the data encapsulated by the exception you have caught. You can read more about this technique in Chapter 15.

So what happens if an exception is not caught by client code? It is implicitly rethrown, and the client's own calling code is given the opportunity to catch it. This process continues either until the exception is caught or until it can no longer be thrown. At this point, a fatal error occurs. Here's what would happen if I did not catch one of the exceptions in my example:

```
PHP Fatal error: Uncaught exception 'FileException' with message

'file 'nonexistent/not_there.xml' does not exist' in ...
```

So, when you throw an exception, you force the client to take responsibility for handling it. This is not an abdication of responsibility. An exception should be thrown when a method has detected an error, but does not have the contextual information to be able to handle it intelligently. The write() method in my example knows when the attempt to write will fail, and it knows why, but it does not know what to do about it. This is as it should be. If I were to make the Conf class more knowledgeable than it currently is, it would lose focus and become less reusable.

Cleaning Up After try/catch Blocks with finally

The way that code flow is affected by exceptions can cause unexpected problems. For example, cleanup code or other essential housekeeping may not be performed after an exception is generated within a try block. As you have seen, if an exception is generated within a try block, the flow moves directly to the relevant catch block. Code that closes database connections or file handles may not get called, and status information might not be updated.

Imagine, for example, that Runner::init() keeps a log of its actions. It logs the start of the initialization process, any errors encountered, and then it logs the end of the initialization process. Here, I provide a typically simplified example of this kind of logging:

```
// listing 04.74
public static function init(): void
{
    try {
        $fh = fopen("/tmp/log.txt", "a"); fputs($fh, "start\n");
        $conf = new Conf(dirname( FILE ) . "/conf.broken.xml");
        print "user: " . $conf->get('user') . "\n";
        print "host: " . $conf->get('host') . "\n";
        $conf->set("pass", "newpass");
        $conf->write();
        fputs($fh, "end\n");
        fclose($fh);
    } catch (FileException $e) {
        // permissions issue or non-existent file
        fputs($fh, "file exception\n");
        throw $e;
```

```
    } catch (XmlException $e) {
        fputs($fh, "xml exception\n");
        // broken xml
    } catch (ConfException $e) {
        fputs($fh, "conf exception\n");
        // wrong kind of XML file
    } catch (\Exception $e) {
        fputs($fh, "general  exception\n");
        // backstop: should not be called
    }
}
```

I open a file, log.txt; I write to it; and then I call my configuration code. If an exception is encountered in this process, I log this fact in the relevant catch block. I end the try block by writing to the log and closing its file handle.

Of course, this last step will never be reached if an exception is encountered. The flow passes straight to the relevant catch block, and the rest of the try block is never run. Here is the log output when an XML exception is generated:

```
start
xml exception
```

As you can see, the logging began, and the file exception was noted, but the portion of code that registers the end of logging was never reached, and so the log was not updated with that.

You might think that the solution would be to place the final logging step outside of the try/catch block altogether. This would not work reliably. If a generated exception is caught, and the try block allows execution to continue, then the flow will move beyond the try/catch construct. However, a catch block could rethrow the exception, or it might end script execution altogether.

To help programmers deal with problems like this, PHP 5.5 introduced a new keyword: finally. If you're familiar with Java, it's likely you'll have seen this before. Although catch blocks are only conditionally run when matching exceptions are thrown, a finally block is always run, whether or not an exception is generated within the try block.

CHAPTER 4   ADVANCED FEATURES

I can fix this problem by moving my log write and code to close to a `finally` block:

```
// listing 04.75
public static function init2(): void
{
    $fh = fopen("/tmp/log.txt", "a");
    try {
        fputs($fh, "start\n");
        $conf = new Conf(dirname( FILE ) . "/conf.not-there.xml");
        print "user: " . $conf->get('user') . "\n";
        print "host: " . $conf->get('host') . "\n";
        $conf->set("pass", "newpass");
        $conf->write();
    } catch (FileException $e) {
        // permissions issue or non-existent file
        fputs($fh, "file exception\n");
        //throw $e;
    } catch (XmlException $e) {
        fputs($fh, "xml exception\n");
        // broken xml
    } catch (ConfException $e) {
        fputs($fh, "conf exception\n");
        // wrong kind of XML file
    } catch (Exception $e) {
        fputs($fh, "general exception\n");
        // backstop: should not be called
    }  finally  {
        fputs($fh, "end\n");
        fclose($fh);
    }
}
```

Because the log write and the `fclose()` invocation are wrapped in a `finally` block, these statements will be run even if, as is the case when a `FileException` is caught, the exception is rethrown.

Here, now, is the log text when a FileException is generated:

```
start
file exception
end
```

Note   A finally block will be run if an invoked catch block rethrows an exception or returns a value. However, calling die() or exit() in a try or catch block will end script execution, and the finally block will not be run.

Final Classes and Methods

Inheritance allows for enormous flexibility within a class hierarchy. You can override a class or method so that a call in a client method will achieve radically different effects, according to which class instance it has been passed. Sometimes, though, a class or method should remain fixed and unchanging. If you have achieved the definitive functionality for your class or method, and you feel that overriding it can only damage the ultimate perfection of your work, you may need the final keyword.

final puts a stop to inheritance. A final class cannot be subclassed. Less drastically, a final method cannot be overridden.

Here's a final class:

```
// listing 04.76
final class Checkout
{
    // ...
}
```

Here's an attempt to subclass the Checkout class:

```
// listing 04.77
class IllegalCheckout extends Checkout
{
    // ...
}
```

This produces an error:

```
Fatal error: Class popp\ch04\batch13\IllegalCheckout may not inherit
from final class (popp\ch04\batch13\Checkout) in ...
```

I could relax matters somewhat by declaring a method in Checkout final, rather than the whole class. The final keyword should be placed in front of any other modifiers such as protected or static, like this:

```
// listing 04.78
class Checkout
{
    final public function totalize(): void
    {
        // calculate bill
    }
}
```

I can now subclass Checkout, but any attempt to override totalize() will cause a fatal error:

```
// listing 04.79
class IllegalCheckout extends Checkout
{
    final public function totalize(): void
    {
        // change bill calculation
    }
}
```

```
Fatal error: Cannot override final method popp\ch04\batch14\
Checkout::totalize() in /var/popp/src/ch04/batch14/IllegalCheckout.php on
line 9
```

Good object-oriented code tends to emphasize the well-defined interface. Behind the interface, though, implementations will often vary. Different classes or combinations of classes conform to common interfaces but behave differently in different circumstances. By declaring a class or method final, you limit this flexibility. There will be times when this is desirable, and you will see some of them later in the book.

However, you should think carefully before declaring something final. Are there really no circumstances in which overriding would be useful? You could always change your mind later on, of course, but this might not be so easy if you are distributing a library for others to use. Use final with care.

The Internal Error Class

Back when exceptions were first introduced, the world of trying and catching applied primarily to code written in PHP and not the core engine. Internally generated errors maintained their own logic. This could get messy if you wanted to manage core errors in the same way as code-generated exceptions. PHP 7 has made a start on addressing this issue with the Error class. This implements Throwable—the same built-in interface that the Exception class implements, and therefore it can be treated in the same way. This also means the methods described in Table 4-1 are honored. Error is subclassed for individual error types. Here's how you might catch a parse error generated by an eval statement:

```
// listing 04.80
try {
    eval("illegal code");
} catch (\Error $e) {
    print get_class($e) . "\n";
    print $e->getMessage();
} catch (\Exception $e) {
    // do something with an Exception
}
```

Here's the output:

```
ParseError
syntax error, unexpected identifier "code"
```

So you can match some types of internal errors in catch blocks, either by specifying the Error superclass or by specifying a more specific subclass. Table 4-2 shows the current Error subclasses.

Table 4-2. *The Built-in Error Classes Introduced by PHP 7*

Error	Description
ArgumentCountError	Thrown when too few arguments are passed to a user-defined method or function
ArithmeticError	Thrown for math-related errors—particularly those related to bitwise arithmetic
AssertionError	Thrown when the assert() language construct (used in debugging) fails
CompileError	Thrown when PHP code is malformed and cannot be compiled for running
DivisionByZeroError	Thrown when an attempt is made to divide a number by zero
ParseError	Thrown when a runtime attempt to parse PHP (e.g., using eval()) fails
TypeError	Thrown when an argument of the wrong type is passed to a method, a method returns a value of the wrong type, or an incorrect number of arguments are passed to a method

Working with Interceptors

PHP provides built-in interceptor methods that can intercept messages sent to undefined methods and properties. This is also known as *overloading*, but as that term means something quite different in Java and C++, I think it is better to talk in terms of interception.

PHP supports various built-in interceptor or "magic" methods. Like __construct(), these are invoked for you when the right conditions are met. Table 4-3 describes some of these methods.

Table 4-3. *The Interceptor Methods*

Method	Description
__get($property)	Invoked when an undefined property is accessed
__set($property, $value)	Invoked when a value is assigned to an undefined property
__isset($property)	Invoked when isset() is called on an undefined property
__unset($property)	Invoked when unset() is called on an undefined property
__call($method, $arg_array)	Invoked when an undefined nonstatic method is called
__callStatic($method, $arg_array)	Invoked when an undefined static method is called

Note   You can read more about interceptor or magic methods at the PHP manual page: www.php.net/manual/en/language.oop5.magic.php.

The __get() and __set() methods are designed for working with properties that have not been declared in a class (or its parents).

__get() is invoked when client code attempts to read an undeclared property. It is called automatically with a single string argument containing the name of the property that the client is attempting to access. Whatever you return from the __get() method will be sent back to the client as if the target property exists with that value. Here's a quick example:

```
// listing 04.81
class Person
{
    public function __get(string $property): mixed
    {
        $method = "get{$property}";
        if (method_exists($this, $method)) {
            return $this->$method();
        }
    }
```

```
public function getName(): string
{
    return "Bob";
}

public function getAge(): int
{
    return 44;
}
}
```

When a client attempts to access an undefined property, the __get() method is invoked. I have implemented __get() to take the property name and construct a new string, prepending the word "get". I pass this string to a function called method_exists(), which accepts an object and a method name and tests for method existence. If the method does exist, I invoke it and pass its return value to the client. Assume the client requests a $name property:

```
// listing 04.82
$p = new Person();
print $p->name;
```

In this case, the getName() method is invoked behind the scenes:

```
Bob
```

If the method does not exist, I do nothing. The property that the user is attempting to access will resolve to null.

The __isset() method works in a similar way to __get(). It is invoked after the client calls isset() on an undefined property. Here's how I might extend Person:

```
// listing 04.83
public function __isset(string $property): bool
{
    $method = "get{$property}";
    return (method_exists($this, $method));
}
```

Now a cautious user can test a property before working with it:

```
// listing 04.84
$p = new Person();
if (isset($p->name)) {
    print $p->name;
}
```

The __set() method is invoked when client code attempts to assign to an undefined property. It is passed two arguments: the name of the property and the value the client is attempting to set. You can then decide how to work with these arguments. Here, I further amend the Person class:

```
// listing 04.85
class Person
{
    private ?string $myname;
    private ?int $myage;

    public function __set(string $property, mixed $value): void
    {
        $method = "set{$property}";
        if (method_exists($this, $method)) {
            $this->$method($value);
        }
    }

    public function setName(?string $name): void
    {
        $this->myname = $name;
        if (! is_null($name)) {
            $this->myname = strtoupper($this->myname);
        }
    }
}
```

```
    public function setAge(?int $age): void
    {
        $this->myage = $age;
    }
}
```

In this example, I work with "setter" methods rather than "getters." If a user attempts to assign to an undefined property, the __set() method is invoked with the property name and the assigned value. I test for the existence of the appropriate method and invoke it if it exists. In this way, I can filter the assigned value.

Note   Remember that methods and properties in PHP documentation are frequently spoken of in static terms in order to identify them with their classes. So you might talk about the Person::$name property, even though the property is not declared static and would in fact be accessed via an object.

So if I create a Person object and then attempt to set a property called Person::$name, the __set() method is invoked because this class does not define a $name property. The method is passed the string "name" and the value that the client assigned. How the value is then used depends on the implementation of __set(). In this example, I construct a method name out of the property argument combined with the string "set". The setName() method is found and duly invoked. This transforms the incoming value and stores it in a real property:

```
// listing 04.86
$p = new Person();
$p->name = "bob";
// the $myname property becomes 'BOB'
```

As you might expect, __unset() mirrors __set(). When unset() is called on an undefined property, __unset() is invoked with the name of the property. You can then do what you like with the information. This example passes null to a method resolved using the same technique that you saw used by __set():

```
// listing 04.87
public function __unset(string $property): void
{
    $method = "set{$property}";
    if (method_exists($this, $method)) {
        $this->$method(null);
    }
}
```

The __call() method is probably the most useful of all the interceptor methods. It is invoked when an undefined method is called by client code. __call() is invoked with the method name and an array holding all arguments passed by the client. Any value that you return from the __call() method is returned to the client as if it were returned by the method invoked.

The __call() method can be useful for delegation. Delegation is the mechanism by which one object passes method invocations on to a second. It is similar to inheritance, in that a child class passes on a method call to its parent implementation. With inheritance, the relationship between child and parent is fixed, so the ability to switch the receiving object at runtime means that delegation can be more flexible than inheritance. An example clarifies things a little. Here is a simple class for formatting information from the Person class:

```
// listing 04.88
class PersonWriter
{

    public function writeName(Person $p): void
    {
        print $p->getName() . "\n";
    }

    public function writeAge(Person $p): void
    {
        print $p->getAge() . "\n";
    }
}
```

I could, of course, subclass this to output `Person` data in various ways. Here is an implementation of the `Person` class that uses both a `PersonWriter` object and the `__call()` method:

```
// listing 04.89
class Person
{

    public function __construct(private PersonWriter $writer)
    {
    }

    public function __call(string $method, array $args): mixed
    {
    if (method_exists($this->writer, $method)) {
        return $this->writer->$method($this);
    }
    }
}

    public function getName(): string
    {
        return "Bob";
    }

    public function getAge(): int
    {
        return 44;
    }
}
```

The `Person` class here demands a `PersonWriter` object as a constructor argument and stores it in a property variable. In the `__call()` method, I use the provided `$method` argument, testing for a method of the same name in the `PersonWriter` object I have stored. If I encounter such a method, I delegate the method call to the `PersonWriter` object, passing my current instance to it (in the `$this` pseudo-variable). Consider what happens if the client makes this call to `Person`:

```
// listing 04.90
$person = new Person(new PersonWriter());
$person->writeName();
```

In this case, the __call() method is invoked. I find a method called writeName()
in my PersonWriter object and invoke it. This saves me from manually invoking the
delegated method like this:

```
// listing 04.91
public function writeName(): void
{
    $this->writer->writeName($this);
}
```

Using interceptor methods, the Person class magically gains two new methods.
Although automated delegation can save a lot of legwork, there can be a cost in clarity.
If you rely too much on delegation, you present the world with a dynamic interface that
resists reflection (the runtime examination of class facets) and is not always clear to the
client coder at first glance. This is because the logic that governs the interaction between
a delegating class and its target can be obscure—buried in methods like __call() rather
than signaled up front by inheritance relationships or method type hints, as is the case
for similar relationships. The interceptor methods have their place, but they should be
used with care, and classes that rely on them should document this fact very clearly.

I will return to the topics of delegation and reflection later in the book.

The __get() and __set() interceptor methods can also be used to manage
composite properties. This can be a convenience for the client programmer. Imagine, for
example, an Address class that manages a house number and a street name. Ultimately,
this object data will be written to database fields, so the separation of number and
street is sensible. But if house numbers and street names are commonly acquired in
undifferentiated lumps, then you might want to help the class's user. Here is a class that
manages a composite property, Address::$streetaddress:

```
// listing 04.92
class Address
{
    private string $number;
    private string $street;
```

```php
public function __construct(string $maybenumber, string $maybestreet =
null)
{
    if (is_null($maybestreet)) {
        $this->streetaddress = $maybenumber;
    } else {
        $this->number = $maybenumber;
        $this->street = $maybestreet;
    }
}

public function __set(string $property, mixed $value): void
{
    if ($property === "streetaddress") {
        if (preg_match("/^(\d+.*?)[\s,]+(.+)$/", $value, $matches)) {
            $this->number = $matches[1];
            $this->street = $matches[2];
        } else {
            throw new \Exception("unable to parse street address:
            '{$value}'");
        }
    }
}

public function __get(string $property): mixed
{
    if ($property === "streetaddress") {
        return $this->number . " " . $this->street;
    }
}
}
```

When a user attempts to set the (nonexistent) Address::$streetaddress property (via the class constructor), the interceptor method __set() is invoked. There, I test for the property name, streetaddress. Before I can set the $number and $street properties, I must first ensure that the provided value can be parsed and then go ahead and extract the fields. For this example, I have set simple rules. An address can be parsed if it begins with a number and has spaces or commas ahead of a second part. Thanks to back references, if the check passes, I already have the data I'm looking for in the $matches array, and I assign values to the $number and $street properties. If the parse fails, I throw an exception. So when a string such as 441b Bakers Street is assigned to Address::$streetaddress, it's actually the $number and $street properties that get populated. I can demonstrate this with print_r():

```
// listing 04.93
$address = new Address("441b Bakers Street"); print_r($address);

popp\ch04\batch16\Address Object
(
    [number:popp\ch04\batch16\Address:private] => 441b
    [street:popp\ch04\batch16\Address:private] => Bakers Street
)
```

The __get() method is much more straightforward, of course. Whenever the Address::$streetaddress property is accessed, __get() is invoked. In my implementation of this interceptor, I test for streetaddress, and, if I find a match, I return a concatenation of the $number and $street properties.

Note   __get(), __set(), and __call() are also automatically invoked when a client attempts to access an inaccessible method or property (i.e., methods or properties which are set to private or protected and are therefore hidden from the calling context).

Defining Destructor Methods

You have seen that the __construct() method is automatically invoked when an object is instantiated. PHP 5 also introduced the __destruct() method. This is invoked just before an object is garbage-collected; that is, before it is expunged from memory. You can use this method to perform any final cleaning up that might be necessary.

Imagine, for example, a class that saves itself to a database when so ordered. I could use the __destruct() method to ensure that an instance saves its data when it is deleted:

```
// listing 04.94
class Person
{
    private int $id;

    public function __construct(protected string $name, private int $age)
    {
        $this->name = $name;
        $this->age  = $age;
    }

    public function setId(int $id): void
    {
        $this->id = $id;
    }

    public function __destruct()
    {
        if (! empty($this->id)) {
            // save Person data
            print "saving person\n";
        }
    }
}
```

The __destruct() method is invoked whenever you call the unset() function on an object or when no further references to the object exist in the process. So if I create and destroy a Person object, you can see the __destruct() method come into play:

```
// listing 04.95
$person = new Person("bob", 44);
$person->setId(343);
unset($person);
```

Here is the output:

```
saving person
```

Although tricks like this are fun, it's worth sounding a note of caution. __call(), __
destruct(), and their colleagues are sometimes called *magic methods*. As you will know
if you have ever read a fantasy novel, magic is not always a good thing. Magic is arbitrary
and unexpected. Magic bends the rules. Magic incurs hidden costs.

In the case of __destruct(), for example, you can end up saddling clients with
unwelcome surprises. Think about the Person class—it performs a database write in
its __destruct() method. Now imagine a novice developer idly putting the Person
class through its paces. He doesn't spot the __destruct() method, and he sets about
instantiating a set of Person objects. Passing values to the constructor, he assigns the
CEO's secret and faintly obscene nickname to the $name property and then sets $age at
150. He runs his test script a few times, trying out colorful name and age combinations.

The next morning, his manager asks him to step into a meeting room to explain why
the database contains insulting Person data. The moral? Do not trust magic.

Copying Objects with __clone()

In PHP 4, copying an object was a simple matter of assigning from one variable to
another:

```
// listing 04.96
class CopyMe
{
}
```

```
// listing 04.97
```

```
$first = new CopyMe();
$second = $first;
```

```
// PHP 4: $second and $first are 2 distinct objects
// PHP 5 plus: $second and $first refer to one object
```

This "simple matter" was a source of many bugs, as object copies were accidentally spawned when variables were assigned, methods were called, and objects were returned. This was made worse by the fact that there was no way of testing two variables to see whether they referred to the same object. Equivalence tests would tell you whether all fields were the same (==) or whether both variables were objects (===), but not whether they pointed to the same object.

In PHP, a variable that *seems* to contain an object in fact contains an identifier that references the underlying data structure. When such a variable is assigned or passed in to a method, the identifier it contains is copied. However, each copy continues to point to the same object. This means that, in my previous example, $first and $second contain identifiers pointing to the same object rather than two copies of the object. Although this is generally what you want when working with objects, there will be occasions when you need to get a copy of an object.

PHP provides the clone keyword for just this purpose. clone operates on an object instance, producing a by-value copy:

```
// listing 04.98

$first = new CopyMe();
$second = clone $first;

// PHP 5 plus: $second and $first are 2 distinct objects
```

The issues surrounding object copying only start here. Consider the Person class that I implemented in the previous section. A default copy of a Person object would contain the identifier (the $id property), which in a full implementation I would use to locate the correct row in a database. If I allow this property to be copied, a client coder can end up with two distinct objects representing the same data entity (database row), which may not be what she wanted when she made her copy.

Luckily, you can control what is copied when clone is invoked on an object. You do this by implementing a special method called __clone() (note the leading two underscores that are characteristic of magic methods). __clone() is called automatically when the clone keyword is invoked on an object.

When you implement __clone(), it is important to understand the context in which the method runs. __clone() is run on the *copied* object and not the original. Here, I add __clone() to yet another version of the Person class:

```
// listing 04.99
class Person
{
    private int $id = 0;

    public function __construct(private string $name, private $age)
    {
    }

    public function setId(int $id): void
    {
        $this->id = $id;
    }

    public function __clone(): void
    {
        $this->id = 0;
    }
}
```

When clone is invoked on a Person object, a new shallow copy is made, and *its* __ clone() method is invoked. This means that anything I do in __clone() overwrites the default copy I already made. In this case, I ensure that the copied object's $id property is set to zero:

```
// listing 04.100
$person = new Person("bob", 44);
$person->setId(343);
$person2 = clone $person;
```

A shallow copy ensures that primitive properties are copied from the old object to the new. Object properties have their identifiers copied but not their underlying data, though, which may not be what you want or expect when cloning an object. Say that I give the Person object an Account object property. This object holds a balance that I want copied to the cloned object. What I don't want, though, is for both Person objects to hold references to the *same* account:

```
// listing 04.101
class Account
{
    public function __construct(public float $balance)
    {
    }
}

// listing 04.102
class Person
{
    private int $id;

    public function __construct(private string $name, private int $age,
    public Account $account)
    {
    }

    public function setId(int $id): void
    {
        $this->id = $id;
    }

    public function __clone(): void
    {
        $this->id = 0;
    }
}

// listing 04.103
$person = new Person("bob", 44, new Account(200));
$person->setId(343);
$person2 = clone $person;

// give $person some money
$person->account->balance += 10;
// $person2 sees the credit too
print $person2->account->balance;
```

139

This gives the following output:

```
210
```

$person holds a reference to an Account object that I have kept publicly accessible for the sake of brevity (as you know, I would usually restrict access to a property, providing an accessor method, if necessary). When the clone is created, it holds a reference to the same Account object that $person references. I demonstrate this by adding to the $person object's Account and confirming the increased balance via $person2.

If I do not want an object property to be shared after a clone operation, then it is up to me to clone it explicitly in the __clone() method:

```
// listing 04.104
public function __clone(): void
{
    $this->id = 0;
    $this->account = clone $this->account;
}
```

Defining String Values for Your Objects

Another Java-inspired feature introduced by PHP 5 was the __toString() method. Before PHP 5.2, when you printed an object, it would resolve to a string like this:

```
// listing 04.105
class StringThing
{
}
```

```
// listing 04.106
$st = new StringThing();
print $st;
```

Since PHP 5.2, this code will produce an error like this:

```
Object of class popp\ch04\batch22\StringThing could not be converted to
string ...
```

By implementing a __toString() method, you can control how your objects represent themselves when accessed in string context (or explicitly cast to a string). __toString() should be written to return a string value. The method is invoked automatically when your object is passed to print or echo, and its return value is substituted. Here, I add a __toString() version to a minimal Person class:

```
// listing 04.107
class Person
{
    public function getName(): string
    {
        return "Bob";
    }

    public function getAge(): int
    {
        return 44;
    }

    public function __toString(): string
    {
        $desc  = $this->getName() . " (age ";
        $desc .= $this->getAge() . ")"; return $desc;
    }
}
```

Now when I print a Person object, the object will resolve to this:

```
// listing 04.108
$person = new Person();
print $person;

Bob (age 44)
```

The __toString() method is particularly useful for logging and error reporting, as well as for classes whose main task is to convey information. The Exception class, for example, summarizes exception data in its __toString() method.

As of PHP 8, any class that implements a __toString() method is implicitly declared as implementing the built-in Stringable interface. That means you can use a union type declaration to constrain arguments and properties. Here's an example:

```
// listing 04.109
public static function printThing(string|\Stringable $str): void
{
    print $str;
}
```

We could pass a string *or* our Person object to the printThing() method, and it would happily accept either, secure in the knowledge that it could work with whatever we passed along in any string-like fashion it chose.

Callbacks, Anonymous Functions, and Closures

Although not strictly an object-oriented feature, anonymous functions are useful enough to mention here because you may encounter them in object-oriented applications that utilize callbacks.

Note   A *callback* is a block of executable code that can be stored in a variable or passed to methods and functions for later invocation.

To kick things off, here are a couple of classes:

```
// listing 04.110
class Product
{
    public function __construct(public string $name, public float $price)
    {
    }
}
```

```
// listing 04.111
class ProcessSale
{
    private array $callbacks;

    public function registerCallback(callable $callback): void
    {
        $this->callbacks[] = $callback;
    }

    public function sale(Product $product): void
    {
        print "{$product->name}: processing \n";
        foreach ($this->callbacks as $callback) {
            call_user_func($callback, $product);
        }
    }
}
```

This code is designed to run my various callbacks. It consists of two classes, Product and ProcessSale. Product simply stores $name and $price properties. I've made these public for the purposes of brevity. Remember, in the real world, you'd probably want to make your properties private or protected and provide accessor methods if necessary.

ProcessSale consists of two methods. The first, registerCallback(), accepts a callable type and adds it to the $callbacks array property. The second method, sale(), accepts a Product object, outputs a message about it, and then loops through the $callbacks array property.

It passes each element to call_user_func(), which calls the code, passing it a reference to the product. All of the following examples will work with the framework.

Why are callbacks useful? They allow you to plug functionality into a component at runtime that is not directly related to that component's core task. By making a component callback-aware, you give others the power to extend your code in contexts you don't yet know about.

Imagine, for example, that a future user of ProcessSale wants to create a log of sales. If the user has access to the class, she might add logging code directly to the sale() method. This isn't always a good idea, though. If she is not the maintainer of the package that provides ProcessSale, then her amendments will be overwritten the next time the package is upgraded. Even if she is the maintainer of the component, adding many incidental tasks to the sale() method will begin to overwhelm its core responsibility and potentially make it less usable across projects. I will return to these themes in the next section.

Luckily, though, I made ProcessSale callback-aware. Here, I create a callback that simulates logging:

```
// listing 04.112
$logger = function ($product) {
    print "    logging ({$product->name})\n";
};

$processor = new ProcessSale();
$processor->registerCallback($logger);

$processor->sale(new Product("shoes", 6));
print "\n";
$processor->sale(new Product("coffee", 6));
```

Here, I create an anonymous function. That is, I use the function keyword inline and without a function name. Note that because this is an inline statement, a semicolon is required at the end of the code block. My anonymous function can be stored in a variable and passed to functions and methods as a parameter. That's just what I do, assigning the function to the $logger variable and passing that to the ProcessSale::r egisterCallback() method. Finally, I create a couple of products and pass them to the sale() method. The sale is then processed (in reality, a simple message is printed about the product), and any callbacks are executed. Here is the code in action:

```
shoes: processing
    logging (shoes)

coffee: processing
    logging (coffee)
```

PHP 7.4 introduced a new way of declaring anonymous functions. Arrow functions are functionally very similar to the anonymous functions you've already encountered. The syntax is much more compact, however. Instead of the function keyword, they are defined by fn, then parentheses for an argument list, and finally, in place of braces, an arrow operator (=>) followed by a single expression. This compact form makes arrow functions very handy for building small callbacks for custom sorts and the like. Here, I replace the $logger anonymous function with an exact equivalent using an arrow function:

```
// listing 04.113

$logger = fn($product) => print "    logging ({$product->name})\n";
```

The arrow function is much more compact, but, because you define only a single expression, it is best used for relatively simple tasks.

Of course, callbacks needn't be anonymous. You can use the name of a function, or even an object reference and a method, as a callback. Here, I do just that:

```
// listing 04.114
class Mailer
{
    public function doMail(Product $product): void
    {
        print "    mailing ({$product->name})\n";
    }
}
```

```
// listing 04.115
$processor = new ProcessSale();
$processor->registerCallback([new  Mailer(), "doMail"]);

$processor->sale(new Product("shoes", 6));
print "\n";
$processor->sale(new Product("coffee", 6));
```

I create a class: Mailer. Its single method, doMail(), accepts a Product object and outputs a message about it. When I call registerCallback(), I pass it an array. The first element is a Mailer object, and the second is a string that matches the name of the method I want invoked.

Remember that registerCallback() uses a type declaration to enforce a callable argument. PHP is smart enough to recognize an array of this sort as callable. A valid callback in array form should have an object as its first element and the name of a method as its second element. I pass that test here, and here is my output:

```
shoes: processing
    mailing (shoes)
```

```
coffee: processing
    mailing (coffee)
```

You can have a method return an anonymous function—something like this:

```
// listing 04.116
class Totalizer
{
    public static function warnAmount(): callable
    {
        return function (Product $product) {
            if ($product->price > 5) {
                print "    reached high price: {$product->price}\n";
            }
        };
    }
}
```

```
// listing 04.117
$processor = new ProcessSale();
$processor->registerCallback(Totalizer::warnAmount());

$processor->sale(new Product("shoes", 6));
print "\n";
$processor->sale(new Product("coffee", 6));
```

Apart from the convenience of using the warnAmount() method as a factory for the anonymous function, I have not added much of interest here. But this structure allows me to do much more than just generate an anonymous function. It allows me to take advantage of closures. Anonymous functions can reference variables declared in the anonymous functions' parent scope. This is a hard concept to grasp at times. It's as if the anonymous function continues to remember the context in which it was created. Imagine that I want `Totalizer::warnAmount()` to do two things. First of all, I'd like it to accept an arbitrary target amount. Second, I want it to keep a tally of prices as products are sold. When the total exceeds the target amount, the function will perform an action (in this case, as you might have guessed, it will simply write a message).

I can make my anonymous function track variables from its wider scope with a `use` clause:

```
// listing 04.118
class Totalizer2
{
    public static function warnAmount($amt): callable
    {
        $count = 0;
        return function ($product) use ($amt, &$count) {
            $count += $product->price;
            print "    count: $count\n";
            if ($count > $amt) {
                print "    high price reached: {$count}\n";
            }
        };
    }
}
```

```
// listing 04.119
$processor = new ProcessSale();
$processor->registerCallback(Totalizer2::warnAmount(8));

$processor->sale(new Product("shoes", 6));
print "\n";
$processor->sale(new Product("coffee", 6));
```

The anonymous function returned by `Totalizer2::warnAmount()` specifies two variables in its `use` clause. The first is `$amt`. This is the argument that `warnAmount()` accepted. The second closure variable is `$count`. `$count` is declared in the body of `warnAmount()` and set initially to zero. Notice that I prepend an ampersand to the `$count` variable in the `use` clause. This means the variable will be accessed by reference rather than by value in the anonymous function. In the body of the anonymous function, I increment $count by the product's value and then test the new total against $amt. If the target value has been reached, I output a notification.

Here is the code in action:

```
shoes: processing
   count: 6

coffee:  processing
   count: 12
   high price reached: 12
```

This demonstrates that the callback is keeping track of $count between invocations. Both $count and $amt remain associated with the function because they were present to the context of its declaration and because they were specified in its use clause.

Arrow functions also generate closures (like anonymous functions, they resolve to an instance of the built-in Closure class). Unlike anonymous functions, which require an explicit association with closure variables, they automatically get a by-value copy of all variables in scope. Here is an example:

```
// listing 04.120
$markup = 3;
$counter = fn(Product $product) => print "($product->name) marked up
price: " .
          ($product->price + $markup) . "\n";
$processor = new ProcessSale();
$processor->registerCallback($counter);

$processor->sale(new Product("shoes", 6));

print "\n";
$processor->sale(new Product("coffee", 6));
```

I am able to access $markup within the anonymous function I pass to ProcessSale::sale(). However, because the function only has access by value, any manipulation I perform within the function will not affect the source variable.

PHP 7.1 introduced a new way of managing closures in object context. The `Closure::fromCallable()` method allows you to generate a closure which gives calling code access to an object's classes and properties. Here is a version of the `Totalizer` series that uses object properties to achieve the same result as the last example:

```
// listing 04.121

class Totalizer3
{
    private float $count = 0;
    private float $amt = 0;

    public function warnAmount(int $amt): callable
    {
        $this->amt = $amt;
        return \Closure::fromCallable([$this, "processPrice"]);
    }

    private function processPrice(Product $product): void
    {
        $this->count += $product->price;
        print "    count: {$this->count}\n";
        if ($this->count > $this->amt) {
            print "    high price reached: {$this->count}\n";
        }
    }
}
```

The `warnAmount()` method is not static in this example. That is because, thanks to `Closure::fromCallable()`, I return a callback to the `processPrice()` method that has access to the wider object. I set the $amt property and return a callable method reference. `processPrice()`, when called, increments a $count property and issues a warning when the $amt property value is reached. If `processPrice()` were a public method I could have simply returned [$this, "processPrice"]. As we have seen, PHP is clever enough to work out that such a two-element array should resolve as callable. There are two good reasons why I might want to use `Closure::fromCallable()`, however. Firstly, I can give controlled access to private or protected methods without having to expose them to the whole world—offering enhanced functionality while controlling access. Secondly, I get a performance boost because there is an overhead involved in working out whether the return value is truly callable.

Here, I use Totalizer3 with the unchanged ProcessSale class:

```
// listing 04.122
$totalizer3 = new Totalizer3();
$processor = new ProcessSale();
$processor->registerCallback($totalizer3->warnAmount(8));

$processor->sale(new Product("shoes", 6));
print "\n";
$processor->sale(new Product("coffee", 6));
```

Anonymous Classes

PHP 7 introduced anonymous classes. These are useful when you need to create and derive an instance from a small class, when the parent class in question is simple and specific to the local context.

Let's return to our PersonWriter example. I'll start off by creating an interface this time:

```
// listing 04.123
interface PersonWriter
{
    public function write(Person $person): void;
}
```

Now, here's a version of the Person class that can use a PersonWriter object:

```
// listing 04.124
class Person
{
    public function output(PersonWriter $writer): void
    {
        $writer->write($this);
    }
```

```
public function getName(): string
{
    return "Bob";
}

public function getAge(): int
{
    return 44;
}
}
```

The output() method accepts a PersonWriter instance and then passes an instance of the current class to its write() method. In this way, the Person class is nicely insulated from the implementation of the writer.

Moving on to client code, if we need a writer to print name and age values for a Person object, we might go ahead and create a class in the usual way. But it's such a trivial implementation that we could equally create a class and pass it to Person at the same time:

```
// listing 04.125
$person = new Person();
$person->output(
    new class implements PersonWriter {
        public function write(Person $person): void
        {
            print $person->getName() . " " . $person->getAge() . "\n";
        }
    }
);
```

As you can see, you can declare an anonymous class with the keywords new class. You can then add any extends and implements clauses required before creating the class block.

Anonymous classes do not support closures. In other words, variables declared in a wider scope cannot be accessed within the class. However, you *can* pass values to an anonymous class's constructor. Let's create a slightly more complex PersonWriter:

```
// listing 04.126
$person = new Person();
$person->output(
    new class ("/tmp/persondump") implements PersonWriter {
        private $path;

        public function __construct(string $path)
        {
            $this->path = $path;
        }

        public function write(Person $person): void
        {
            file_put_contents($this->path, $person->getName() . " " .
            $person->getAge() . "\n");
        }
    }
);
```

I passed a path argument to the constructor. This value was stored in the $path property and eventually used by the write() method.

Of course, if your anonymous class begins to grow in size and complexity, it becomes more sensible to create a named class in a class file. This is especially true if you find yourself duplicating your anonymous class in more than one place.

Summary

In this chapter, we came to grips with PHP's advanced object-oriented features. Some of these will become familiar as you work through the book. In particular, I will return frequently to abstract classes, exceptions, and static methods.

In the next chapter, I take a step back from built-in object features and look at classes and functions designed to help you work with objects.

CHAPTER 5

Object Tools

As we have seen, PHP supports object-oriented programming through language constructs such as classes and methods. The language also provides wider support through functions and classes designed to help you work with objects.

In this chapter, we will look at some tools and techniques that you can use to organize, test, and manipulate objects and classes.

This chapter will cover the following tools and techniques:

- *Namespaces*: Organize your code into discrete package-like compartments

- *Include paths*: Setting central accessible locations for your library code

- *Class and object functions*: Functions for testing objects, classes, properties, and methods

- *The Reflection API*: A powerful suite of built-in classes that provide unprecedented access to class information at runtime

- *Attributes*: PHP's implementation of *annotations*—a mechanism by which classes, methods, properties, and parameters can be enhanced with rich information using tags in source code

PHP and Packages

A package is a set of related classes and functions, usually grouped together in some way. Packages can be used to separate parts of a system from one another. Some programming languages formally recognize packages and provide them with distinct namespaces. PHP has no native concept of a package, but as of PHP 5.3, it introduced namespaces. I'll look at this feature in the next section. I'll also take a look at the old way of organizing classes into package-like structures.

153

© Matt Zandstra 2021
M. Zandstra, *PHP 8 Objects, Patterns, and Practice*, https://doi.org/10.1007/978-1-4842-6791-2_5

PHP Packages and Namespaces

Although PHP does not intrinsically support the concept of a package, developers have traditionally used both naming schemes and the file system to organize their code into package-like structures.

Until PHP 5.3, developers were forced to name their files in a shared context. In other words, if you named a class ShoppingBasket, it would become instantly available across your system. This caused two major problems. First, and most damaging, was the possibility of naming collisions. You might think that this is unlikely. After all, all you have to do is remember to give all your classes unique names, right? The trouble is, we all rely increasingly on library code. This is a good thing, of course, because it promotes code reuse. But assume your project does this:

```
// listing 05.01
require_once __DIR__ . "/../useful/Outputter.php";

class Outputter
{
    // output data
}
```

Now assume you incorporate the included file at useful/Outputter.php:

```
// listing 05.02
class Outputter
{
    //
}
```

Well, you can guess what will happen, right? This happens:

```
PHP Fatal error: Cannot declare class Outputter because the name is
already in use in /var/popp/src/ch05/batch01/useful/Outputter.php on
line 4
```

Back before the introduction of namespaces, there was a conventional workaround to this problem. The answer was to prepend package names to class names, so that class names were guaranteed to be unique:

```
// listing 05.03

// my/Outputer.php

require_once __DIR__ . "/../useful/Outputter.php";

class my_Outputter
{
    // output data
}

// listing 05.04

// useful/Outputter.php

class useful_Outputter
{
    //
}
```

The problem here was that, as projects got more involved, class names grew longer and longer. It was not an enormous problem, but it resulted in issues with code readability and made it harder to hold class names in your head while you worked. Many cumulative coding hours were lost to typos.

If you're maintaining legacy code, you may well still see code that follows this convention. For that reason, I'll return briefly to the old way of handling packages later in this chapter.

Namespaces to the Rescue

PHP 5.3 introduced namespaces. In essence, a namespace is a bucket in which you can place your classes, functions, and variables. Within a namespace, you can access these items without qualification. From outside, you must either import the namespace or reference it in order to access the items it contains.

Confused? An example should help. Here, I rewrite the previous example using namespaces:

```
// listing 05.05
namespace my;

require_once __DIR__ . "/../useful/Outputter.php";

class Outputter
{
    // output data
}
```

```
// listing 05.06

namespace useful;

class Outputter
{
    //
}
```

Notice the namespace keyword. As you might expect, this keyword establishes a namespace. If you are using this feature, then the namespace declaration must be the first statement in its file. I have created two namespaces: my and useful. Typically, though, you'll want to have deeper namespaces. You'll start with an organization or project identifier. Then you'll want to further qualify this by package. PHP lets you declare nested namespaces. To do this, you simply use a backslash character to divide each level:

```
// listing 05.07
namespace popp\ch05\batch04\util;

class Debug
{
    public static function helloWorld(): void
    {
        print "hello from Debug\n";
    }
}
```

You will typically use a name related to a product or organization to define a repository. I might use one of my domains: getinstance.com, for example. Because a domain name is unique to its owner, this is a trick that Java developers typically use for their package names. They invert domain names so that they run from the most generic to the most specific. Alternatively, I might use the namespace I have chosen for code examples in this book: popp, for the book name. Once I've identified my repository, I might go on to define packages. In this case, I use the chapter and then a numbered batch. This allows me to organize groups of examples into discrete buckets. So at this point in the chapter, I am at popp\ch05\batch04. Finally, I can further organize code by category. I've gone with util.

So how would I call the method? In fact, it depends where you're doing the calling from. If you are calling the method from within the namespace, you can go ahead and call the method directly:

```
// listing 05.08
Debug::helloWorld();
```

This is known as an unqualified name. Because I'm already in the popp\ch05\batch04\util namespace, I don't have to prepend any kind of path to the class name. If I were accessing the class from outside of a namespaced context, I could do this:

```
// listing 05.09
\popp\ch05\batch04\Debug::helloworld();
```

What output would I get from the following code?

```
// listing 05.10
namespace main;

    popp\ch05\batch04\Debug::helloworld();
```

That's a trick question. In fact, this is my output:

```
PHP Fatal error: Class 'popp\ch05\batch04\Debug' not found in...
```

That's because I'm using a relative namespace here. PHP is looking below the namespace main for popp\ ch05\batch04\util and not finding it. Just as you can make absolute URLs and file paths by starting off with a separator, so you can with namespaces. This version of the example fixes the previous error:

```
// listing 05.11
namespace main;

    \popp\ch05\batch04\Debug::helloworld();
```

That leading backslash tells PHP to begin its search at the root, and not from the current namespace.

But aren't namespaces supposed to help you cut down on typing? The Debug class declaration is shorter, certainly, but those calls are just as wordy as they would have been with the old naming convention. You can get around this with the use keyword. This allows you to alias other namespaces within the current namespace. Here's an example:

```
// listing 05.12
namespace main;

use popp\ch05\batch04\util;

    util\Debug::helloWorld();
```

The popp\ch05\batch04\util namespace is imported and implicitly aliased to util. Notice that I didn't begin with a leading backslash character. The argument to use is searched from root space and not from the current namespace. If I don't want to reference a namespace at all, I can import the Debug class itself:

```
// listing 05.13
namespace main;

use popp\ch05\batch04\util\Debug;

    Debug::helloWorld();
```

This is the convention that is most often used. But what would happen if I already had a Debug class in the calling namespace? Here is such a class:

```
// listing 05.14
namespace popp\ch05\batch04;
```

```
class Debug
{
    public static function helloWorld(): void
    {
        print "hello from popp\\ch05\\batch04\\Debug\n";
    }
}
```

And here is some calling code from the popp\ch05\batch04 namespace which references both Debug classes:

```
// listing 05.15
namespace popp\ch05\batch04;

use popp\ch05\batch04\util\Debug;
use popp\ch05\batch04\Debug;

Debug::helloWorld();
```

As you might expect, this causes a fatal error:

```
PHP Fatal error: Cannot use popp\ch05\batch04\Debug as Debug because the
name is already in use in...
```

So I seem to have come full circle, arriving back at class name collisions. Luckily, there's an answer for this problem. I can make my alias explicit:

```
// listing 05.16
namespace popp\ch05\batch04;

use popp\ch05\batch04\util\Debug;
use popp\ch05\batch04\Debug as CoreDebug;

CoreDebug::helloWorld();
```

By using the as clause to use, I am able to change the Debug alias to coreDebug.

If you are writing code in a namespace and you want to access a class, trait, or interface that resides in root (non-namespaced) space (e.g., PHP's core classes such as Exception, Error, Closure), you can simply precede the name with a backslash. Here's a class declared in root space:

```
// listing 05.17
class TreeLister
{
    public static function helloWorld(): void
    {
        print "hello from root namespace\n";
    }
}
```

And here's some namespaced code:

```
// listing 05.18
namespace popp\ch05\batch04\util;

class TreeLister
{
    public static function helloWorld(): void
    {
        print "hello from " . __NAMESPACE__ . "\n";
    }
}
```

```
// listing 05.19
namespace popp\ch05\batch04;

use popp\ch05\batch04\util\TreeLister;

        TreeLister::helloWorld();   // access local
        \TreeLister::helloWorld(); // access from root
```

The namespaced code declares its own TreeLister class. The client code uses the local version, specifying the full path with a use statement. A name qualified with a single backslash accesses a similarly named class in the root namespace.

Here's the output from the previous fragment:

```
hello from popp\ch05\batch04\util
hello from root namespace
```

This output is worth showing because it demonstrates the operation of the __NAMESPACE__ constant. This will output the current namespace, and it's useful in debugging.

You can declare more than one namespace in the same file using the syntax you have already seen. You can also use an alternative syntax that uses braces with the namespace keyword:

```
// listing 05.20
namespace com\getinstance\util {

    class Debug
    {
        public static function helloWorld(): void
        {
            print "hello from Debug\n";
        }
    }
}

namespace other {

    \com\getinstance\util\Debug::helloWorld();
}
```

If you must combine multiple namespaces in the same file, then this is the recommended practice. Usually, however, it's considered best practice to define namespaces on a per-file basis.

Note   You can't use both the brace and line namespace syntaxes in the same file. You must choose one and stick to it throughout.

Using the File System to Simulate Packages

Whichever version of PHP you use, you should organize classes using the file system, which affords a kind of package structure. For example, you might create util and business directories and include class files with the require_once() statement, like this:

```
// listing 05.21
require_once('business/Customer.php');
require_once('util/WebTools.php');
```

You could also use include_once() with the same effect. The only difference between the include() and require() statements lies in their handling of errors. A file invoked using require() will bring down your entire process when you meet an error. The same error encountered via a call to include() will merely generate a warning and end execution of the included file, leaving the calling code to continue. This makes require() and require_once() the safe choice for including library files, and include() and include_once() useful for operations like templating.

Note   require() and require_once() are actually statements, not functions. This means that you can omit the brackets when using them. Personally, I prefer to use brackets anyway, but if you follow suit, be prepared to be bored by pedants eager to explain your mistake.

Figure 5-1 shows the util and business packages from the point of view of the Nautilus file manager.

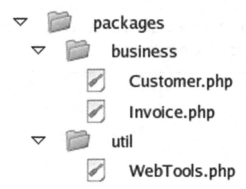

Figure 5-1. *PHP packages organized using the file system*

Note   `require_once()` accepts a path to a file and includes it evaluated in the current script. The statement will only incorporate its target if it has not already been incorporated elsewhere. This one-shot approach is particularly useful when accessing library code because it prevents the accidental redefinition of classes and functions. This can happen when the same file is included by different parts of your script in a single process using a statement like `require()` or `include()`.

It is customary to use `require()` and `require_once()` in preference to the similar `include()` and `include_once()` functions. This is because a fatal error encountered in a file accessed with the `require()` functions takes down the entire script. The same error encountered in a file accessed using the `include()` functions will cause the execution of the included file to cease, but will only generate a warning in the calling script. The former, more drastic behavior, is safer.

There is an overhead associated with the use of `require_once()` when compared with `require()`. If you need to squeeze every last millisecond out of your system, you may like to consider using `require()` instead. As is so often the case, this is a trade-off between efficiency and convenience.

As far as PHP is concerned, there is nothing special about this structure. You are simply placing library scripts in different directories. It does lend itself to clean organization and can be used in parallel with either namespaces or a naming convention.

Naming the PEAR Way

Back before namespaces were introduced, developers were forced to resort to conventions in order to avoid class name collisions. The most common of these, as we have seen, was the fake namespacing maintained by PEAR developers.

Note   PEAR stands for the PHP Extension and Application Repository. It is an officially maintained archive of packages and tools that add to PHP's functionality. Core PEAR packages are included in the PHP distribution, and others can be added using a simple command-line tool. You can browse the PEAR packages at `http://pear.php.net`.

PEAR uses the file system to define its packages as I have described. Before namespaces were introduced, every class was named according to its package path, with each directory name separated by an underscore character.

For example, PEAR includes a package called XML, which has an RPC subpackage. The RPC package contains a file called `Server.php`. The class defined inside `Server.php` is not called `Server`, as you might expect. Without namespaces, that would sooner or later clash with another `Server` class elsewhere in the PEAR project or in a user's code. Instead, the class is named `XML_RPC_Server`. This approach made for unattractive class names. It did, however, make code easy to read because a class name always described its own context.

Include Paths

When you organize your components, there are two perspectives that you should bear in mind. I have covered the first, where files and directories are placed on the file system. But you should also consider the way that components access one another. I have glossed over the issue of include paths so far in this section.

When you include a file, you could refer to it using a relative path from the current working directory or an absolute path on the file system.

Note   Although it is important to understand the way that include paths work and the issues involved in requiring files, it is also important to bear in mind that many modern systems no longer rely upon require statements at the class level. Instead, they use a combination of autoload and namespaces. I will cover autoload later and then look in more detail at practical autoload recommendations and tools in Chapters 15 and 16.

The examples you have seen so far have occasionally specified a fixed relationship the requiring and required files:

```
// listing 05.22
require_once __DIR__ . "/../useful/Outputter.php";
```

This works quite nicely, except that it hard-codes the relationship between files. There must always be a `useful` directory alongside the calling class's containing directory.

Perhaps the worst approach is the tortuous relative path:

```
// listing 05.23
require_once('../../projectlib/business/User.php');
```

This is problematic because the path specified here is not relative to the file that contains this `require_once` statement, but to a configured calling context (often, but not always, the current working directory). Paths like this are a recipe for confusion (and in my experience almost always a sign that a system will need considerable improvement in other areas, too).

You could use an absolute path, of course:

```
// listing 05.24
require_once('/home/john/projectlib/business/User.php');
```

This will work for a single instance—but it's brittle. By specifying paths in this much detail, you freeze the library file into a particular context. Whenever you install the project on a new server, all `require` statements will need changing to account for a new file path. This can make libraries hard to relocate and impractical to share among projects without making copies. In either case, you lose the package idea in all the additional directories. Is it the `business` package, or is it the `projectlib/business` package?

If you must manually include files in your code, the neatest approach is to decouple the invoking code from the library. You have already seen a structure like this:

```
// listing 05.25
require_once('business/User.php');
```

In previous examples that used a path like this, we implicitly assumed a relative path. `business/User.php`, in other words, was functionally identical to `./business/User.php`. But what if the preceding require statement could be made to work from any directory on a system? You can do this with the include path. This is a list of directories that PHP searches when attempting to require a file. You can add to this list by altering the `include_path` directive. `include_path` is usually set in PHP's central configuration file, `php.ini`. It defines a list of directories separated by colons on Unix-like systems and semicolons on Windows systems:

```
include_path = ".:/usr/local/lib/php-libraries"
```

If you're using Apache, you can also set include_path in the server application's configuration file (usually called httpd.conf) or a per-directory Apache configuration file (usually called .htaccess) with this syntax:

```
php_value include_path value .:/usr/local/lib/php-libraries
```

Note   .htaccess files are particularly useful in web space provided by some hosting companies, which provide very limited access to the server environment.

When you use a file system function such as fopen() or require() with a nonabsolute path that does not exist relative to the current working directory, the directories in the include path are searched automatically, beginning with the first in the list (in the case of fopen(), you must include a flag in its argument list to enable this feature). When the target file is encountered, the search ends, and the file function completes its task.

So by placing a package directory in an include directory, you need only refer to packages and files in your require() statements.

You may need to add a directory to the include_path so that you can maintain your own library directory. To do this, you can edit the php.ini file (remember that, for the PHP server module, you will need to restart your server for the changes to take effect).

If you do not have the privileges necessary to work with the php.ini file, you can set the include path from within your scripts using the set_include_path() function. set_include_path() accepts an include path (as it would appear in php.ini) and changes the include_path setting for the current process only. The php.ini file probably already defines a useful value for include_path, so rather than overwrite it, you can access it using the get_include_path() function and append your own directory. Here's how you can add a directory to the current include path:

```
set_include_path(get_include_path() . PATH_SEPARATOR . "/home/john/
phplib/");
```

The PATH_SEPARATOR constant will resolve to a colon on a Unix system and a semicolon on a Windows platform. So, for reasons of portability, its use is considered best practice.

Autoload

Although it's neat to use require_once in conjunction with the include path, many developers are doing away with require statements altogether at a high level and relying instead on autoload.

Note   Previous editions of this book discussed a built-in function called __autoload() which provided a cruder version of the functionality discussed in this section. This function was deprecated as of PHP 7.2.0 and removed in PHP 8.

To do this, you should organize your classes so that each sits in its own file. Each class file should bear a fixed relationship to the name of the class it contains, so you might define a ShopProduct class in a file named ShopProduct.php with directories corresponding to elements of the class's namespace.

PHP 5 introduced autoload functionality to help automate the inclusion of class files. The default support is pretty basic but still useful. It can be enabled by calling a function named spl_autoload_register() with no arguments. Then, if autoload functionality has been activated in this way, when you attempt to instantiate an unknown class, PHP will invoke a built-in function called spl_autoload(). This will use the provided class name (converted to lowercase) to search your include path for files named either <classname>.php or <classname>.inc (where <classname> is the name of the unknown class).

Here's a simple example:

```
// listing 05.26
spl_autoload_register();
$writer = new Writer();
```

Assuming I have not already included a file containing a Writer object, this instantiation looks bound to fail. However, because I have set up autoloading, PHP will attempt to include a file named writer.php or writer.inc and will then try the instantiation a second time. If one of these files exists, and contains a class named Writer, then all will be well.

This default behavior supports namespaces, substituting directory names for each package:

```
// listing 05.27
spl_autoload_register();
$writer = new util\Writer();
```

The preceding code will find a file named writer.php (note the lowercase name) in a directory named util.

What if I happen to name my class files case-dependently? That is, what if I name them with the capital letters preserved? If I had placed the Writer class in a file named Writer.php, then the default implementation would have failed to find it.

Luckily, I can register my own custom function to handle different sets of conventions. In order to take advantage of this, I must pass a reference to a custom function to spl_autoload_register(). My autoload function should require a single argument. Then, if the PHP engine encounters an attempt to instantiate an unknown class, it will invoke this function, passing it the unknown class name as a string. It is up to the autoload function to define a strategy for locating and then including the missing class file. Once the autoload function has been invoked, PHP will attempt to instantiate the class once again.

Here's a simple autoload function, together with a class to load:

```
// listing 05.28
class Blah
{
    public function wave(): void
    {
        print "saying hi from root";
    }
}

// listing 05.29
$basic = function (string $classname) {
    $file = __DIR__ . "/" . "{$classname}.php";
    if (file_exists($file)) {
        require_once($file);
    }
};
```

```
\spl_autoload_register($basic);

$blah = new Blah();
$blah->wave();
```

Having failed to instantiate Blah initially, the PHP engine will see that I have registered an autoload function with the spl_autoload_register() function and pass it the string, "Blah". My implementation simply attempts to include the file Blah.php. This will only work, of course, if the file is in the same directory as the file in which the autoload function was declared. In a real-world example, I would have to combine include path configuration with my autoload logic (this is precisely what Composer's autoload implementation does).

If I want to provide old school support, I might automate PEAR package includes:

```
// listing 05.30

class util_Blah
{
    public function wave(): void
    {
        print "saying hi from underscore file";
    }
}
```

```
// listing 05.31

$underscores = function (string $classname) {
    $path = str_replace('_', DIRECTORY_SEPARATOR, $classname);
    $path = __DIR__ . "/$path";
    if (file_exists("{$path}.php")) {
        require_once("{$path}.php");
    }
};

\spl_autoload_register($underscores);

$blah = new util_Blah();
$blah->wave();
```

As you can see, the autoload function matches underscores in the supplied $classname and replaces each with the DIRECTORY_SEPARATOR character (/ on Unix systems). I attempt to include the class file (util/Blah.php). If the class file exists, and the class it contains has been named correctly, the object should be instantiated without an error. Of course, this does require the programmer to observe a naming convention that forbids the underscore character in a class name, except where it divides up packages.

What about namespaces? We've seen that the default autoload functionality supports namespaces. But if we override that default, it's up to us to provide namespace support. This is just a matter of matching and replacing backslash characters:

```
// listing 05.32
namespace util;

class LocalPath
{

    public function wave(): void
    {
        print "hello from " . get_class();
    }
}

// listing 05.33
$namespaces = function (string $path) {
    if (preg_match('/\\\\/', $path)) {
        $path = str_replace('\\', DIRECTORY_SEPARATOR, $path);
    }
    if (file_exists("{$path}.php")) {
        require_once("{$path}.php");
    }
};

\spl_autoload_register($namespaces);
$obj = new util\LocalPath();
$obj->wave();
```

The value that is passed to the autoload function is always normalized to a fully qualified name, without a leading backslash, so there is no need to worry about aliasing or relative namespaces at the point of instantiation.

Note that this solution is by no means perfect. The file_exists() function does not take account of the include path, so it will not accurately reflect all circumstances in which require_once will operate perfectly well. There are various solutions to this. You might roll your own path-aware version of file_exists() or attempt to require the file in a try clause (catching Error in this case and not Exception). Luckily, however, PHP provides the stream_resolve_include_path() function. This will return a string representing the absolute filename of a provided path or, crucially for our purposes, false if the file cannot be found in the include path.

```
// listing 05.34
$namespaces = function (string $path) {
    if (preg_match('/\\\\/', $path)) {
        $path = str_replace('\\', DIRECTORY_SEPARATOR, $path);
    }

    if (\stream_resolve_include_path("{$path}.php") !== false) {
        require_once("{$path}.php");
    }
};

\spl_autoload_register($namespaces);
$obj = new util\LocalPath();
$obj->wave();
```

What if I wanted to support *both* PEAR-style class names *and* namespaces? I could combine my autoload implementations into a single custom function. Or, I could use the fact that spl_autoload_register() stacks its autoload functions:

```
// listing 05.35
$underscores = function (string $classname) {
    $path = str_replace('_', DIRECTORY_SEPARATOR, $classname);
    $path = __DIR__ . "/$path";
    if (\stream_resolve_include_path("{$path}.php") !== false) {
        require_once("{$path}.php");
    }
};
```

```
$namespaces = function (string $path) {
    if (preg_match('/\\\\/',  $path)) {
        $path = str_replace('\\', DIRECTORY_SEPARATOR, $path);
    }
    if (\stream_resolve_include_path("{$path}.php") !== false) {
        require_once("{$path}.php");
    }
};

\spl_autoload_register($namespaces);
\spl_autoload_register($underscores);

$blah = new util_Blah();
$blah->wave();

$obj = new util\LocalPath();
$obj->wave();
```

When it encounters an unknown class, the PHP engine will invoke the autoload
functions in turn (according to the order in which they were registered), stopping when
instantiation is possible or when all options have been exhausted.

There is obviously an overhead to this kind of stacking, so why does PHP support it?
In a real-world project, you'd likely combine the namespace and underscore strategies
into a single function. However, components in large systems and in third-party libraries
may need to register their own autoload mechanisms. Stacking allows multiple parts of
a system to register autoload strategies independently, without overwriting one another.
In fact, a library that only needs an autoload mechanism briefly can pass the name of its
custom autoload function (or any kind of callable such as an anonymous function) to
spl_autoload_unregister() to clean up after itself!

The Class and Object Functions

PHP provides a powerful set of functions for testing classes and objects. Why is this
useful? After all, you probably wrote most of the classes you are using in your script.

In fact, you don't always know at runtime about the classes that you are using. You
may have designed a system to work transparently with third-party bolt-on classes, for

example. In this case, you will typically instantiate an object given only a class name. PHP allows you to use strings to refer to classes dynamically, like this:

```
// listing 05.36
namespace tasks;

class Task
{
    public function doSpeak()
    {
        print "hello\n";
    }
}
```

```
// listing 05.37
$classname = "Task";
require_once("tasks/{$classname}.php");
$classname = "tasks\\$classname";
$myObj = new $classname();
$myObj->doSpeak();
```

This script might acquire the string I assign to $classname from a configuration file or by comparing a web request with the contents of a directory. You can then use the string to load a class file and instantiate an object. Notice that I've constructed a namespace qualification in this fragment.

Typically, you would do something like this when you want your system to be able to run user-created plug-ins. Before you do anything as risky as that in a real project, you would have to check that the class exists, that it has the methods you are expecting, and so on.

Note   Even with safeguards in place, you should be extremely wary of dynamically installing third-party plug-in code. You should never automatically run code uploaded by users. Any plug-in so installed would typically execute with the same privileges as your core code, so a malicious plug-in author could wreak havoc on your system.

This isn't to say that plug-ins aren't a fine idea. Allowing third-party developers to enhance a core system can offer great flexibility. To ensure greater security, you might support a directory for plug-ins, but require that the code files be installed by a system's administrator, either directly or from within a password-protected management environment. The administrator would either personally check the plug-in code before installation or would source plug-ins from a reputable repository. This is the way that the popular blogging platform, WordPress, handles plug-ins.

Some class functions have been superseded by the more powerful Reflection API, which I will examine later in the chapter. Their simplicity and ease of use make them a first port of call in some instances, however.

Looking for Classes

The class_exists() function accepts a string representing the class to check for and returns a Boolean true value if the class exists and false otherwise.

Using this function, I can make the previous fragment a little safer:

```
// listing 05.38
$base = __DIR__;
$classname = "Task";
$path = "{$base}/tasks/{$classname}.php";
if (! file_exists($path)) {
    throw new \Exception("No such file as {$path}");
}
require_once($path);
$qclassname = "tasks\\$classname";
if (! class_exists($qclassname)) {
    throw new Exception("No such class as $qclassname");
}
$myObj = new $qclassname();
$myObj->doSpeak();
```

Of course, you can't be sure that the class in question does not require constructor arguments. For that level of safety, you would have to turn to the Reflection API, covered later in the chapter. Nevertheless, `class_exists()` does allow you to check that the class exists before you work with it.

Note   Remember, as stated previously, you should always be wary of any data provided by outside sources. Test it and treat it before using it in any way. In the case of a file path, you should escape or remove dots and directory separators to prevent an unscrupulous user from changing directories and including unexpected files. However, when I describe ways of building systems that are easily extensible, these techniques generally cover a deployment's owner (with the write privileges that implies), and not her external users.

You can also get an array of all classes defined in your script process using the `get_declared_classes()` function:

```
// listing 05.39
print_r(get_declared_classes());
```

This will list user-defined and built-in classes. Remember that it only returns the classes declared at the time of the function call. You may run `require()` or `require_once()` later on and thereby add to the number of classes in your script.

Learning About an Object or Class

As you know, you can constrain the object types of method arguments using class type hinting. Even with this tool, you can't always be certain of an object's type.

There are a number of basic tools available to check the type of an object. First of all, you can check the class of an object with the `get_class()` function. This accepts any object as an argument and returns its class name as a string:

```
// listing 05.40
$product = self::getProduct();
if (get_class($product) === 'popp\ch05\batch05\CdProduct') {
    print "\$product is a CdProduct object\n";
}
```

In the fragment, I acquire *something* from the getProduct() function. To be absolutely certain that it is a CdProduct object, I use the get_class() method.

Note   I covered the CdProduct and BookProduct classes in Chapter 3.

Here's the getProduct() function:

```
// listing 05.41
public static function getProduct()
{
    return new CdProduct(
        "Exile on Coldharbour Lane",
        "The",
        "Alabama 3",
        10.99,
        60.33
    );
}
```

getProduct() simply instantiates and returns a CdProduct object. I will make good use of this function in this section.

The get_class() function is a very specific tool. You often want a more general confirmation of a class's type. You may want to know that an object belongs to the ShopProduct family, but you don't care whether its actual class is BookProduct or CdProduct. To this end, PHP provides the instanceof operator.

Note   PHP 4 did not support instanceof. Instead, it provided the is_a() function, which was deprecated in PHP 5.0 but restored to the fold with PHP 5.3.

The instanceof operator works with two operands, the object to test on the left of the keyword and the class or interface name on the right. It resolves to true if the object is an instance of the given type:

```
// listing 05.42
$product = self::getProduct();
if ($product instanceof \popp\ch05\batch05\CdProduct) {
    print "\$product is an instance of CdProduct\n";
}
```

Getting a Fully Qualified String Reference to a Class

Namespaces have cleaned up much that was ugly about object-oriented PHP. We no longer have to tolerate ridiculously long class names or risk naming collisions (legacy code aside). On the other hand, with aliasing and with relative namespace references, it can be a chore to resolve some class paths so that they are fully qualified.

Here are some examples of hard-to-resolve class names:

```
// listing 05.43
namespace mypackage;

use util as u;
use util\db\Querier as q;

class Local
{
}

// Resolve these:

// Aliased namespace
//  u\Writer;

// Aliased class
//  q;

// Class referenced in local context
//  Local
```

It's not too hard to work out how these class references resolve, but it would be a pain to write code to capture every possibility. Given u\Writer, for example, an automated resolver would need to know that u is aliased to util and is not a namespace in its own right. Helpfully, PHP 5.5 introduced the ClassName::class syntax. In other words, given

CHAPTER 5   OBJECT TOOLS

a class reference, you can append a scope resolution operator and the `class` keyword to get the fully qualified class name:

```
// listing 05.44
print u\Writer::class . "\n";
print q::class . "\n";
print Local::class . "\n";
```

The preceding snippet outputs this:

```
util\Writer
util\db\Querier
mypackage\Local
```

As of PHP 8, you can also call `::class` on an object. So, for example, given an instance of `ShopProduct`, I can get the full class name like this:

```
// listing 05.45
$bookp = new BookProduct(
    "Catch 22",
    "Joseph",
    "Heller",
    11.99,
    300
);
print $bookp::class;
```

Running this outputs

```
popp\ch04\batch02\BookProduct
```

Note that this convenient syntax does not offer new functionality—you have already encountered the `get_class()` function which achieves the same result.

Learning About Methods

You can acquire a list of all the methods in a class using the `get_class_methods()` function. This requires a class name and returns an array containing the names of all the methods in the class:

```
// listing 05.46
print_r(get_class_methods('\\popp\\ch04\\batch02\\BookProduct'));
```

Assuming the BookProduct class exists, you might see something like this:

```
Array
(
    [0] => __construct
    [1] => getNumberOfPages
    [2] => getSummaryLine
    [3] => getPrice
    [4] => setID
    [5] => getProducerFirstName
    [6] => getProducerMainName
    [7] => setDiscount
    [8] => getDiscount
    [9] => getTitle
    [10] => getProducer
    [11] => getInstance
)
```

In the example, I pass a string containing a class name to get_class_methods()
and dump the returned array with the print_r() function. I could alternatively have
passed an *object* to get_class_methods() with the same result. Only the names of public
methods will be included in the returned list.

As you have seen, you can store a method name in a string variable and invoke it
dynamically together with an object, like this:

```
// listing 05.47
$product = self::getProduct();
$method = "getTitle";    // define a method name
print $product->$method(); // invoke the method
```

Of course, this can be dangerous. What happens if the method does not exist? As you
might expect, your script will fail with an error. You have already encountered one way of
testing that a method exists:

```
// listing 05.48
if (in_array($method, get_class_methods($product))) {
    print $product->$method(); // invoke the method
}
```

I check that the method name exists in the array returned by get_class_methods() before invoking it.

PHP provides more specialized tools for this purpose. You can check method names to some extent with two functions: is_callable() and method_exists(). is_callable() is the more sophisticated of the two functions. It accepts a string variable representing a function name as its first argument and returns true if the function exists and can be called. To apply the same test to a method, you should pass it an array in place of the function name. The array must contain an object or class name as its first element and the method name to check as its second element. The function will return true if the method exists in the class:

```
// listing 05.49
if (is_callable([$product, $method])) {
    print $product->$method(); // invoke the method
}
```

is_callable() optionally accepts a second argument, a Boolean. If you set this to true, the function will only check the syntax of the given method or function name, not for its actual existence. It also accepts an optional third argument which should be a variable. If provided, this will be populated with a string representation of your provided callable.

Here, I call is_callable() with that optional third argument which I then output:

```
// listing 05.50
if (is_callable([$product, $method], false, $callableName)) {
    print $callableName;
}
```

And here is my output:

```
popp\ch05\batch05\CdProduct::getTitle
```

Such functionality may come in handy for the purposes of documentation or logging.

The method_exists() function requires an object (or a class name) and a method name and returns true if the given method exists in the object's class:

```
// listing 05.51
if (method_exists($product, $method)) {
    print $product->$method(); // invoke the method
}
```

Caution   Remember that the fact that a method exists does not mean that it will be callable. method_exists() returns true for private and protected methods, as well as for public ones.

Learning About Properties

Just as you can query the methods of a class, so can you query its fields. The get_class_vars() function requires a class name and returns an associative array. The returned array contains field names as its keys and field values as its values. Let's apply this test to the CdProduct object. For the purposes of illustration, we add a public property to the class, CdProduct::$coverUrl:

```
// listing 05.52
print_r(get_class_vars('\\popp\\ch05\\batch05\\CdProduct'));
```

Only the public property is shown:

```
Array (
    [coverUrl] => cover url
)
```

Learning About Inheritance

The class functions also allow us to chart inheritance relationships. We can find the parent of a class, for example, with get_parent_class(). This function requires either an object or a class name, and it returns the name of the superclass, if any. If no such class exists—that is, if the class we are testing does not have a parent—then the function returns false.

```
// listing 05.53
print get_parent_class('\\popp\\ch04\\batch02\\BookProduct');
```

As you might expect, this yields the parent class: ShopProduct.

We can also test whether a class is a descendant of another using the is_subclass_ of() function. This requires a child object (or the name of a class) and the name of the parent class. The function returns true if the second argument is a superclass of the first argument:

```
// listing 05.54
$product = self::getBookProduct(); // acquire an object

if (is_subclass_of($product, '\\popp\\ch04\\batch02\\ShopProduct')) {
    print "BookProduct is a subclass of ShopProduct\n";
}
```

is_subclass_of() will tell you only about class inheritance relationships. It will not tell you that a class implements an interface. For that, you should use the instanceof operator. Or, you can use a function that is part of the SPL (Standard PHP Library). class_implements() accepts a class name or an object reference and returns an array of interface names:

```
// listing 05.55
if (in_array('someInterface', class_implements($product))) {
    print "BookProduct is an interface of someInterface\n";
}
```

Method Invocation

You have already encountered an example in which I used a string to invoke a method dynamically:

```
// listing 05.56
$product = self::getProduct();
$method = "getTitle";   // define a method name
print $product->$method(); // invoke the method
```

PHP also provides the call_user_func() method to achieve the same end. call_user_func() can invoke any kind of callable (such as a function name or an anonymous function). Here, I invoke a function, by passing along the function name in a string:

```
$returnVal = call_user_func("myFunction");
```

To invoke a method, I can pass along an array. The first element of this should be an object, and the second should be the name of the method to invoke:

```
$returnVal = call_user_func([$myObj, "methodName"]);
```

Any further arguments passed into call_user_func() will be treated as the arguments to the target function or method and passed in the same order, like this:

```
// listing 05.57
$product = self::getBookProduct(); // Acquire a BookProduct object
call_user_func([$product, 'setDiscount'], 20);
```

This dynamic call is, of course, equivalent to this:

```
$product->setDiscount(20);
```

The call_user_func() method won't change your life greatly because you can equally use a string directly in place of the method name, like this:

```
// listing 05.58
$method = "setDiscount";
$product->$method(20);
```

Much more impressive, though, is the related call_user_func_array() function. This operates in the same way as call_user_func(), as far as selecting the target method or function is concerned. Crucially, though, it accepts any arguments required by the target method as an array.

Note Beware—arguments passed to a function or method using call_user_func() are not passed by reference.

So why is this useful? Occasionally, you are given arguments in array form. Unless you know in advance the number of arguments you are dealing with, it can be difficult to pass them on. In Chapter 4, I looked at the interceptor methods that can be used to create delegator classes. Here's a simple example of a __call() method:

```
// listing 05.59
public function __call(string $method, array $args): mixed
{
    if (method_exists($this->thirdpartyShop, $method)) {
        return $this->thirdpartyShop->$method();
    }
}
```

As you have seen, the __call() method is invoked when an undefined method is called by client code. In this example, I maintain an object in a property called $thirdpartyShop. If I find a method in the stored object that matches the $method argument, I invoke it. I blithely assume that the target method does not require any arguments, which is where my problems begin. When I write the __call() method, I have no way of telling how large the $args array may be from invocation to invocation. If I pass $args directly to the delegate method, I will pass a single array argument, and not the separate arguments it may be expecting. call_user_func_array() solves the problem perfectly:

```
// listing 05.60
public function __call(string $method, array $args): mixed
{
    if (method_exists($this->thirdpartyShop, $method)) {
        return call_user_func_array(
            [
                $this->thirdpartyShop,
                $method
            ],
            $args
        );
    }
}
```

The Reflection API

PHP's Reflection API is to PHP what the `java.lang.reflect` package is to Java. It consists of built-in classes for analyzing properties, methods, and classes. It's similar in some respects to existing object functions, such as `get_class_vars()`, but is more flexible and provides much greater detail. It's also designed to work with PHP's object-oriented features, such as access control, interfaces, and abstract classes, in a way that the older, more limited class functions are not.

Getting Started

The Reflection API can be used to examine more than just classes. For example, the `ReflectionFunction` class provides information about a given function, and `ReflectionExtension` yields insight about an extension compiled into the language. Table 5-1 lists some of the classes in the API.

Table 5-1. *Key classes in the Reflection API*

Class	Description
Reflection	Provides a static `export()` method for summarizing class information
ReflectionAttribute	Contextual information about classes, properties, constants, or parameters
ReflectionClass	Class information and tools
ReflectionClassConstant	Information about a constant
ReflectionException	An error class
ReflectionExtension	PHP extension information
ReflectionFunction	Function information and tools
ReflectionGenerator	Information about a generator
ReflectionMethod	Class method information and tools
ReflectionNamedType	Information about a function's or method's return type (union return types are described with `ReflectionUnionType`)

(*continued*)

Table 5-1. (*continued*)

Class	Description
ReflectionObject	Object information and tools (inherits from ReflectionClass
ReflectionParameter	Method argument information
ReflectionProperty	Class property information
ReflectionType	Information about a function's or method's return type
ReflectionUnionType	A collection of ReflectionType objects for a union type declaration
ReflectionZendExtension	PHP Zend extension information

Between them, the classes in the Reflection API provide unprecedented runtime access to information about the objects, functions, and extensions in your scripts.

The Reflection API's power and reach mean you should usually use it in preference to the class and object functions. You will soon find it indispensable as a tool for testing classes. You might want to generate class diagrams or documentation, for example, or you might want to save object information to a database, examining an object's accessor (getter and setter) methods to extract field names. Building a framework that invokes methods in module classes according to a naming scheme is another use of Reflection.

Time to Roll Up Your Sleeves

You have already encountered some functions for examining the attributes of classes. These are useful but often limited. Here's a tool that *is* up to the job. ReflectionClass provides methods that reveal information about every aspect of a given class, whether it's a user-defined or internal class. The constructor of ReflectionClass accepts a class or interface name (or an object instance) as its sole argument:

```
// listing 05.61
$prodclass = new \ReflectionClass(CdProduct::class);
print $prodclass;
```

Once you've created a ReflectionClass object, you can instantly dump all sorts of information about the class, simply by accessing it in string context. Here's an abridged extract from the output generated when I print my ReflectionClass instance for ShopProduct:

```
Class [ <user> class popp\ch04\batch02\CdProduct extends popp\ch04\batch02\
ShopProduct ] {
  @@ /var/popp/src/ch04/batch02/CdProduct.php 6-37

  - Constants [2] {
    Constant [ public int AVAILABLE ] { 0 }
    Constant [ public int OUT_OF_STOCK ] { 1 }
}

  - Static properties [0] {
}

  - Static methods [1] {
    Method [ <user, inherits popp\ch04\batch02\ShopProduct> static public
    method getInstance ] {
      @@ /var/popp/src/ch04/batch02/ShopProduct.php 93 - 130

      - Parameters [2] {
        Parameter #0 [ <required> int $id ]
        Parameter #1 [ <required> PDO $pdo ]
      }
      - Return [ popp\ch04\batch02\ShopProduct ]
    }
  }

  - Properties [3] {
    Property [ private $playLength = 0 ]
    Property [ public $status = NULL ]
    Property [ protected int|float $price ]
  }
...
```

Note   A utility method, Reflection::export(), was once the standard way to dump ReflectionClass information. This was deprecated in PHP 7.4 and removed entirely in PHP 8.0

As you can see, ReflectionClass provides remarkable access to information about a class. The string output provides summary information about almost every aspect of CdProduct, including the access control status of properties and methods, the arguments required by every method, and the location of every method within the script document. Compare that with a more established debugging function. The var_dump() function is a general-purpose tool for summarizing data. You must instantiate an object before you can extract a summary, and even then it provides nothing like the detail made available by ReflectionClass:

```
// listing 05.62
$cd = new CdProduct("cd1", "bob", "bobbleson", 4, 50);
var_dump($cd);
```

Here's the output:

```
object(popp\ch04\batch02\CdProduct)#15 (8) {
  ["playLength":"popp\ch04\batch02\CdProduct":private]=>
  int(50)
  ["status"]=>
  NULL
  ["title":"popp\ch04\batch02\ShopProduct":private]=>
  string(3) "cd1"
  ["producerMainName":"popp\ch04\batch02\ShopProduct":private]=>
  string(9) "bobbleson"
  ["producerFirstName":"popp\ch04\batch02\ShopProduct":private]=>
  string(3) "bob"
  ["price":protected]=>
  float(4)
  ["discount":"popp\ch04\batch02\ShopProduct":private]=>
  int(0)
```

```
["id":"popp\ch04\batch02\ShopProduct":private]=>
int(0)
}
```

var_dump() and its cousin print_r() are fantastically convenient tools for exposing the data in your scripts. For classes and functions, the Reflection API takes things to a whole new level, though.

Examining a Class

A crude dump of a ReflectionClass instance can provide a great deal of useful information for debugging, but we can use the API in more specialized ways. Let's work directly with the Reflection classes.

You've already seen how to instantiate a ReflectionClass object:

```
// listing 05.63
$prodclass = new \ReflectionClass(CdProduct::class);
```

Next, I will use the ReflectionClass object to investigate CdProduct within a script. What kind of class is it? Can an instance be created? Here's a function to answer these questions:

```
// listing 05.64
// class ClassInfo

public static function getData(\ReflectionClass $class): string
{
    $details = "";
    $name = $class->getName();

    $details .= ($class->isUserDefined())  ?
    "$name is user defined\n"       : "" ;
    $details .= ($class->isInternal())     ?
    "$name is built-in\n"           : "" ;
    $details .= ($class->isInterface())    ?
    "$name is interface\n"          : "" ;
    $details  .=  ($class->isAbstract())   ?
    "$name is an abstract class\n" : "" ;
```

```
    $details .= ($class->isFinal())         ?
    "$name is a final class\n"     : "" ;
    $details .= ($class->isInstantiable()) ?
    "$name can be instantiated\n"  : "$name can not be instantiated\n" ;
    $details .= ($class->isCloneable())     ?
    "$name can be cloned\n"        : "$name can not be cloned\n" ;
    return $details;
}

// listing 05.65
$prodclass = new \ReflectionClass(CdProduct::class);
print ClassInfo::getData($prodclass);
```

I create a ReflectionClass object, assigning it to a variable called $prodclass by
passing the CdProduct class name to ReflectionClass's constructor. $prodclass is then
passed to a method named ClassInfo::classData() that demonstrates some of the
methods that can be used to query a class.

The methods should be self-explanatory, but here's a brief description of some of
them:

- ReflectionClass::getName() returns the name of the class being
  examined.

- The ReflectionClass::isUserDefined() method returns
  true if the class has been declared in PHP code, and
  ReflectionClass::isInternal() yields true if the class is built-in.

- You can test whether a class is abstract with
  ReflectionClass::isAbstract() and whether it's an interface with
  ReflectionClass::isInterface().

- If you want to get an instance of the class, you can test the feasibility
  of that with ReflectionClass::isInstantiable().

- You can check whether a class is cloneable with the
  ReflectionClass::isCloneable() method.

- You can even examine a user-defined class's source code. The
  ReflectionClass object provides access to its class's filename and to
  the start and finish lines of the class in the file.

Here's a quick-and-dirty method that uses `ReflectionClass` to access the source of a class:

```
// listing 05.66
class ReflectionUtil
{
    public static function getClassSource(\ReflectionClass $class): string
    {
        $path  = $class->getFileName();
        $lines = @file($path);
        $from  = $class->getStartLine();
        $to    = $class->getEndLine();
        $len   = $to - $from + 1;
        return implode(array_slice($lines, $from - 1, $len));
    }
}

// listing 05.67
print ReflectionUtil::getClassSource(
    new \ReflectionClass(CdProduct::class)
);
```

`ReflectionUtil` is a simple class with a single static method, `ReflectionUtil::get ClassSource()`. That method takes a `ReflectionClass` object as its only argument and returns the referenced class's source code. `ReflectionClass::getFileName()` provides the path to the class's file as an absolute path, so the code should be able to go right ahead and open it. `file()` obtains an array of all the lines in the file. `ReflectionClass::getSta rtLine()` provides the class's start line; `ReflectionClass::getEndLine()` finds the final line. From there, it's simply a matter of using `array_slice()` to extract the lines of interest.

To keep things brief, this code omits error handling (by placing the character @ in front of the call to `file()`). In a real-world application, you'd want to check arguments and result codes.

Examining Methods

Just as `ReflectionClass` is used to examine a class, a `ReflectionMethod` object examines a method.

You can get an array of ReflectionMethod objects from ReflectionClas s::getMethods(). Alternatively, if you need to work with a specific method, ReflectionClass::getMethod() accepts a method name and returns the relevant ReflectionMethod object.

You can also instantiate ReflectionMethod directly, passing it either a class/method string, the class name and method name, or an object and a method name.

Here is what those variations might look like:

```
// listing 05.68
$cd = new CdProduct("cd1", "bob", "bobbleson", 4, 50);
$classname = CdProduct::class;

$rmethod1 = new \ReflectionMethod("{$classname}:: construct");
// class/method string
$rmethod2 = new \ReflectionMethod($classname, " construct");
// class name and method name
$rmethod3 = new \ReflectionMethod($cd, " construct");
// object and method name
```

Here, we use ReflectionClass::getMethods() to put the ReflectionMethod class through its paces:

```
// listing 05.69
$prodclass = new \ReflectionClass(CdProduct::class);
$methods = $prodclass->getMethods();

foreach ($methods as $method) {
    print ClassInfo::methodData($method);
    print "\n----\n";
}
```

```
// listing 05.70

// class ClassInfo

public static function methodData(\ReflectionMethod $method): string
{
    $details = "";
    $name = $method->getName();
```

```
$details .= ($method->isUserDefined())     ?
"$name is user defined\n"       : ""  ;
$details .= ($method->isInternal())        ? "$name is built-in\n" : "" ;
$details .= ($method->isAbstract())        ?
"$name is an abstract class\n"      : ""  ;
$details .= ($method->isPublic())          ? "$name is public\n" : "" ;
$details .= ($method->isProtected())       ?
"$name is protected\n"      : ""  ;
$details .= ($method->isPrivate())         ? "$name is private\n" : "" ;
$details .= ($method->isStatic())          ? "$name is static\n"  : "" ;
$details .= ($method->isFinal())           ? "$name is final\n"   : "" ;
$details .= ($method->isConstructor())     ?
"$name is the constructor\n"        : ""  ;
$details .= ($method->returnsReference()) ?
"$name returns a reference (as opposed to a value)\n"       : ""  ;

    return $details;
}
```

The code uses `ReflectionClass::getMethods()` to get an array of `ReflectionMethod` objects and then loops through the array, passing each object to `methodData()`.

The names of the methods used in `methodData()` reflect their intent: the code checks whether the method is user-defined, built-in, abstract, public, protected, static, or final. You can also check whether the method is the constructor for its class and whether or not it returns a reference.

There's one caveat: `ReflectionMethod::returnsReference()` doesn't return `true` if the tested method simply returns an object, even though objects are passed and assigned by reference in PHP 5. Instead, `ReflectionMethod::returnsReference()` returns true only if the method in question has been explicitly declared to return a reference (by placing an ampersand character in front of the method name).

As you might expect, you can access a method's source code using a technique similar to the one used previously with `ReflectionClass`:

```
// listing 05.71

// class ReflectionUtil
public static function getMethodSource(\ReflectionMethod $method): string
{
    $path  = $method->getFileName();
    $lines = @file($path);
    $from  = $method->getStartLine();
    $to    = $method->getEndLine();
    $len   = $to - $from + 1;
    return implode(array_slice($lines, $from - 1, $len));
}
```

```
// listing 05.72
$class = new \ReflectionClass(CdProduct::class);
$method = $class->getMethod('getSummaryLine');
print ReflectionUtil::getMethodSource($method);
```

Because ReflectionMethod provides us with getFileName(), getStartLine(), and getEndLine() methods, it's a simple matter to extract the method's source code.

Examining Method Arguments

Now that method signatures can constrain the types of object arguments, the ability to examine the arguments declared in a method signature becomes immensely useful. The Reflection API provides the ReflectionParameter class just for this purpose. To get a ReflectionParameter object, you need the help of a ReflectionMethod object. The Re flectionMethod::getParameters() method returns an array of ReflectionParameter objects.

You can also instantiate a ReflectionParameter object directly in the usual way. The constructor to ReflectionParameter requires a callable argument and either an integer representing the parameter number (indexed by zero) or a string representing the argument name.

So, all four of these instantiations are equivalent. Each establishes a ReflectionParameter object for the second argument to the constructor of the CdProduct class.

```
// listing 05.73
$classname = CdProduct::class;

$rparam1 = new \ReflectionParameter([$classname, "__construct"], 1);
$rparam2 = new \ReflectionParameter([$classname, "__construct"],
"firstName");

$cd = new CdProduct("cd1", "bob", "bobbleson", 4, 50);
$rparam3 = new \ReflectionParameter([$cd, "__construct"], 1);
$rparam4 = new \ReflectionParameter([$cd, "__construct"], "firstName");
```

ReflectionParameter can tell you the name of an argument and whether the variable is passed by reference (i.e., with a preceding ampersand in the method declaration). It can also tell you the class required by argument hinting and whether the method will accept a null value for the argument.

Here are some of ReflectionParameter's methods in action:

```
// listing 05.74
$class = new \ReflectionClass(CdProduct::class);

$method = $class->getMethod("__construct");
$params = $method->getParameters();

foreach ($params as $param) {
    print ClassInfo::argData($param) . "\n";
}
```

```
// listing 05.75

// class ClassInfo
public static function argData(\ReflectionParameter $arg): string
{
    $details = "";
    $declaringclass = $arg->getDeclaringClass();
    $name = $arg->getName();

    $position = $arg->getPosition();
    $details .= "\$$name has position $position\n";
```

```
    if ($arg->hasType()) {
        $type = $arg->getType();
        $typenames = [];
        if ($type instanceof \ReflectionUnionType) {
            $types = $type->getTypes();
            foreach ($types as $utype) {
                    $typenames[] = $utype->getName();
            }
        } else {
            $typenames[] = $type->getName();
        }
        $typename = implode("|",  $typenames);
        $details .= "\$$name should be type {$typename}\n";
    }

    if ($arg->isPassedByReference()) {
        $details .= "\${$name} is passed by reference\n";
    }

    if ($arg->isDefaultValueAvailable()) {
        $def = $arg->getDefaultValue();
        $details .= "\${$name} has default: $def\n";
    }
    if ($arg->allowsNull()) {
        $details .= "\${$name} can be null\n";
    }

    return $details;
}
```

Using the `ReflectionClass::getMethod()` method, the code acquires a `ReflectionMethod` object. It then uses `ReflectionMethod::getParameters()` to get an array of `ReflectionParameter` objects. The `argData()` function uses the `ReflectionParameter` object it was passed to acquire information about the argument.

First, it gets the argument's variable name with `ReflectionParameter::getName()`. The `ReflectionParameter::getType()` method returns a `ReflectionType` object if a type was specified or a `ReflectionUnionType` class if the specified type is a union type. From whichever of these is returned, a string representing the required type is constructed. The code then checks whether the argument is a reference with `isPassedByReference()`; and, finally, it looks for the availability of a default value, which it then adds to the return string.

Using the Reflection API

With the basics of the Reflection API under your belt, you can now put the API to work.

Imagine that you're creating a class that calls `Module` objects dynamically. That is, it can accept plug-ins written by third parties that can be slotted into the application without the need for any hard-coding. To achieve this, you might define an `execute()` method in the `Module` interface or abstract base class, forcing all child classes to define an implementation. You could allow the users of your system to list `Module` classes in an external XML configuration file. Your system can use this information to aggregate a number of `Module` objects before calling `execute()` on each one.

What happens, however, if each `Module` requires *different* information to do its job? In that case, the XML file can provide property keys and values for each `Module`, and the creator of each `Module` can provide setter methods for each property name. Given that foundation, it's up to your code to ensure that the correct setter method is called for the correct property name.

Here's some groundwork for the `Module` interface and a couple of implementing classes:

```
// listing 05.76
class Person
{
    public $name;

    public function __construct(string $name)
    {
        $this->name = $name;
    }
}
```

197

```
// listing 05.77
interface Module
{
    public function execute(): void;
}

// listing 05.78
class FtpModule implements Module
{
    public function setHost(string $host): void
    {
        print "FtpModule::setHost(): $host\n";
    }

    public function setUser(string|int $user): void
    {
        print "FtpModule::setUser(): $user\n";
    }

    public function execute(): void
    {
        // do things
    }
}

// listing 05.79
class PersonModule implements Module
{
    public function setPerson(Person $person): void
    {
        print "PersonModule::setPerson(): {$person->name}\n";
    }

    public function execute(): void
    {
        // do things
    }
}
```

Here, `PersonModule` and `FtpModule` both provide empty implementations of the `execute()` method. Each class also implements setter methods that do nothing but report that they were invoked. The system lays down the convention that all setter methods must expect a single argument: either a string or an object that can be instantiated with a single string argument. The `PersonModule::setPerson()` method expects a `Person` object, so I include a `Person` class in my example.

To work with `PersonModule` and `FtpModule`, the next step is to create a `ModuleRunner` class. It will use a multidimensional array indexed by module name to represent configuration information provided in the XML file. Here's that code:

```
// listing 05.80
class ModuleRunner
{
    private array $configData = [
        PersonModule::class => ['person' => 'bob'],
        FtpModule::class    => [
            'host' => 'example.com',
            'user' => 'anon'
        ]
    ];

    private array $modules = [];

    // ...
}
```

The `ModuleRunner::$configData` property contains references to the two `Module` classes. For each module element, the code maintains a subarray containing a set of properties. `ModuleRunner`'s `init()` method is responsible for creating the correct `Module` objects, as shown here:

```
// listing 05.81

// class ModuleRunner
public function init(): void
{
    $interface = new \ReflectionClass(Module::class);
    foreach ($this->configData as $modulename => $params) {
        $module_class = new \ReflectionClass($modulename);
```

```
        if (! $module_class->isSubclassOf($interface)) {
            throw new Exception("unknown module type: $modulename");
        }
        $module = $module_class->newInstance();
        foreach ($module_class->getMethods() as $method) {
            $this->handleMethod($module, $method, $params);
            // we cover handleMethod() in a future listing!
        }
        array_push($this->modules, $module);
    }
}

// listing 05.82
$test = new ModuleRunner();
$test->init();
```

The init() method loops through the ModuleRunner::$configData array, and for each module element, it attempts to create a ReflectionClass object. An exception is generated when ReflectionClass's constructor is invoked with the name of a nonexistent class, so in a real-world context, I would include more error handling here. I use the ReflectionClass::isSubclassOf() method to ensure that the module class belongs to the Module type.

Before you can invoke the execute() method of each Module, an instance has to be created. That's the purpose of ReflectionClass::newInstance(). That method accepts any number of arguments, which it passes on to the relevant class's constructor method. If all's well, it returns an instance of the class (for production code, be sure to code defensively: check that the constructor method for each Module object doesn't require arguments before creating an instance).

ReflectionClass::getMethods() returns an array of all ReflectionMethod objects available for the class. For each element in the array, the code invokes the ModuleRunner::handleMethod() method. It then passes it a Module instance, the ReflectionMethod object, and an array of properties to associate with the Module. handleMethod() verifies and invokes the Module object's setter methods:

```
// listing 05.83

// class ModuleRunner
public function handleMethod(Module $module, \ReflectionMethod $method,
array $params):
bool
{
    $name = $method->getName();
    $args = $method->getParameters();

    if (count($args) != 1 || substr($name, 0, 3) != "set") {
        return  false;
    }
    $property = strtolower(substr($name, 3));

    if (! isset($params[$property])) {
        return false;
    }

    if (! $args[0]->hasType()) {
        $method->invoke($module, $params[$property]);
        return true;
    }

    $arg_type = $args[0]->getType();

    if (! ($arg_type instanceof \ReflectionUnionType) && class_exists(
$arg_type->getName())) {
        $method->invoke(
            $module,
            (new \ReflectionClass($arg_type->getName()))->newInstance(
            $params[$property])
        );
    } else {
        $method->invoke($module, $params[$property]);
    }
    return true;
}
```

`handleMethod()` first checks that the method is a valid setter. In the code, a valid setter method must be named `setXXXX()` and must declare one—and only one—argument.

Assuming that the argument checks out, the code then extracts a property name from the method name by removing `set` from the beginning of the method name and converting the resulting substring to lowercase characters. That string is used to test the `$params` array argument. This array contains the user-supplied properties that are to be associated with the `Module` object. If the `$params` array doesn't contain the property, the code gives up and returns `false`.

If the property name extracted from the module method matches an element in the `$params` array, I can go ahead and invoke the correct setter method. To do that, the code must check the type of the first (and only) required argument of the setter method. If the parameter has a type declaration (`ReflectionParameter::hasType()`) and the specified type resolves to a class, then we know that the method expects an object. Otherwise, we assume that it expects a primitive.

To call the setter method, I need a new Reflection API method. `ReflectionMethod::invoke()` requires an object (or `null` for a static method) and any number of method arguments to pass on to the method it represents. `ReflectionMethod::invoke()` throws an exception if the provided object does not match its method. I call this method in one of two ways. If the setter method doesn't require an object argument, I call `ReflectionMethod::invoke()` with the user-supplied property string. If the method requires an object (which I can test for using `class_exists` with the type name), I use the property string to instantiate an object of the correct type. This is then passed to the setter.

The example assumes that the required object can be instantiated with a single string argument to its constructor. It's best, of course, to check this before calling `ReflectionClass::newInstance()`.

By the time that the `ModuleRunner::init()` method has run its course, the object has a store of `Module` objects, all primed with data. The class can now be given a method to loop through the `Module` objects, calling `execute()` on each one.

Attributes

Many languages provide a mechanism by which special tags in source files can be made available to the code. These are often known as *annotations*. Although there have been some userland implementations in PHP packages (notably, e.g., the Doctrine database library and Symfony routing component) until PHP 8, there was no support for this feature at a language level. This has changed with the introduction of *attributes*.

Essentially, an attribute is a special tag that allows you to add additional information to a class, method, property, parameter, or constant. This information becomes available to a system through reflection.

So what can you use annotations for? Typically, a method might provide more information about the way that it expects to be used. Client code might scan a class to discover methods that should be automatically run, for example. I'll mention other use cases as we go.

Let's declare and access an annotation:

```
// listing 05.84
namespace popp\ch05\batch09;

#[info]
class Person
{
}
```

So an annotation is declared with a string token enclosed by #[and]. In this case, I have gone with #[info]. In many code examples, I exclude a namespace declaration because the code will run equally well within a declared namespace or main. In this case, though, it is worth noting the namespace. I'll return to this point.

Now to access the annotation:

```
// listing 05.85
$rpers = new \ReflectionClass(Person::class);
$attrs = $rpers->getAttributes();
foreach ($attrs as $attr) {
    print $attr->getName() . "\n";
}
```

I instantiate a ReflectionClass object so that I can examine Person. Then I call the getAttributes() method. This returns an array of ReflectionAttribute objects. ReflectionAttribute::getName() returns the name of the attribute I declared.

Here is the output:

```
popp\ch05\batch09\info
```

So, in my output, the annotation is namespaced. The popp\ch05\batch09 portion of the name is implicit. I can reference an annotation according to the same rules and aliases we use to reference a class. So declaring [#info] within the popp\ch05\batch09 namespace is equivalent to declaring [#\popp\ch05\batch09\info] elsewhere. In fact, as you'll see, you can even declare a class that can be instantiated for any attribute you reference.

Annotations can be applied to various aspects of PHP. Table 5-2 lists features that can be annotated along with corresponding Reflection classes.

Table 5-2. *PHP features that are amenable to annotation*

Feature	Acquisition
Class	ReflectionClass::getAttributes()
Property	ReflectionProperty::getAttributes()
Function/Method	ReflectionFunction::getAttributes()
Constant	ReflectionConstant::getAttributes()

Here is an example of an attribute applied to a method:

```
// listing 05.86
#[moreinfo]
public function setName(string $name): void
{
    $this->name = $name;
}
```

Now to access it. You should find the process pretty familiar:

```
// listing 05.87
$rpers = new \ReflectionClass(Person::class);
$rmeth = $rpers->getMethod("setName");
$attrs = $rmeth->getAttributes();
foreach ($attrs as $attr) {
    print $attr->getName() . "\n";
}
```

The output should be familiar now, as well. We display a fully namespaced path to moreinfo.

popp\ch05\batch09\moreinfo

There is already some use in what you've seen so far. We might include an attribute as a flag of some kind. For example, a Debug attribute could be associated with methods that should only be invoked during development. There is still more to attributes, however. We can define a type and provide further information through arguments. This opens up new possibilities. In a routing library, I might assert the URL endpoint a method should map to. In an event system, an attribute might signal that a class or method should be associated with a particular event.

In this example, I define an attribute that includes two arguments:

```
// listing 05.88
#[ApiInfo("The 3 digit company identifier", "A five character department tag")]
public function setInfo(int $companyid, string $department): void
{
    $this->companyid = $companyid;
    $this->department = $department;
}
```

Once I have acquired a ReflectionAttribute object, I can access the arguments using the getArguments() method.

```
// listing 05.89
$rpers = new \ReflectionClass(Person::class);
$rmeth = $rpers->getMethod("setInfo");
$attrs = $rmeth->getAttributes();
foreach ($attrs as $attr) {
    print $attr->getName() . "\n";
    foreach ($attr->getArguments() as $arg) {
        print "  - $arg\n";
    }
}
```

Here is the output:

```
popp\ch05\batch09\ApiInfo
  - The 3 digit company identifier
  - A five character department tag
```

As I mentioned, you can explicitly map an attribute to a class. Here is a simple ApiInfo class:

```
// listing 05.90
namespace popp\ch05\batch09;

use Attribute;
#[Attribute]

class ApiInfo
{
    public function __construct(public string $compinfo, public string
    $depinfo)
    {
    }
}
```

In order to properly make the association between the attribute and my class, I must remember to use Attribute and also apply the built-in [#Attribute] to the class.

At the time of instantiation, any arguments to the associated attribute are automatically passed along to the corresponding class's constructor. In this case, I simply assign the data to corresponding properties. In a real-world application, I would probably perform some additional processing or provide associated functionality to justify the declaration of a class.

It is important to understand that the attribute class is not automatically invoked. We must do that through ReflectionAttribute::newInstance(). Here, I adapt my client code to work with the new class:

```
// listing 05.91
$rpers = new \ReflectionClass(Person::class);
$rmeth = $rpers->getMethod("setInfo");
$attrs = $rmeth->getAttributes();
```

```
foreach ($attrs as  $attr) {
    print $attr->getName() . "\n";
    $attrobj = $attr->newInstance();
    print "  - " . $attrobj->compinfo . "\n";
    print "  - " . $attrobj->depinfo . "\n";
}
```

Although I'm accessing the attribute data through the ApiInfo object, the effect here is identical. I call ReflectionAttribute::newInstance(), and then I access the populated properties.

Wait, though! That last example has a deep and potentially fatal flaw. Multiple attributes can be added to a method. We cannot be sure, therefore, that every attribute assigned to the setInfo() method is an instance of ApiInfo. Those property accesses to ApiInfo::$compinfo and ApiInfo::$depinfo are bound to fail for any attribute that is not of type ApiInfo.

Luckily, we can apply a filter to getAttributes():

```
// listing 05.92
$rpers = new \ReflectionClass(Person::class);
$rmeth = $rpers->getMethod("setInfo");
$attrs = $rmeth->getAttributes(ApiInfo::class);
```

Now, only exact matches for ApiInfo::class will be returned—rendering the rest of the code safe. We could relax things a little further like this:

```
// listing 05.93
$rpers = new \ReflectionClass(Person::class);
$rmeth = $rpers->getMethod("setInfo");
$attrs = $rmeth->getAttributes(ApiInfo::class, \ReflectionAttribute::IS_
INSTANCEOF);
```

By passing along a second parameter, ReflectionAttribute::IS_INSTANCEOF, to Re flectionAttribute::getAttributes(), I loosen the filter to match the specified class and any extending or implementing child classes or interfaces.

Table 5-3 lists the methods of ReflectionAttribute we have encountered.

Table 5-3. *Some ReflectionAttribute methods*

Method	Description
getName()	Returns a fully namespaced type for the attribute
getArguments()	Returns an array of all arguments associated with the referenced attribute
newInstance()	Instantiates and returns an instance of the attribute class, having passed any arguments to the constructor

Note   In Chapter 9, I work through a much more sophisticated example of attribute usage.

Summary

In this chapter, I covered some of the techniques and tools that you can use to manage your libraries and classes. I explored PHP's namespace feature. You saw that we can combine include paths, namespaces, autoload, and the file system to provide a flexible organization for classes.

We also examined PHP's object and class functions, before taking things to the next level with the powerful Reflection API. We used the Reflection classes to build a simple example that illustrates one of the potential uses that Reflection has to offer. Finally, we combined the Reflection classes with attributes: a major feature new to PHP 8.

CHAPTER 6

Objects and Design

Now that we have seen the mechanics of PHP's object support in some detail, we will step back from the details and consider how best to use the tools that we have encountered. In this chapter, I introduce you to some of the issues surrounding objects and design. I will also look at the UML, a powerful graphical language for describing object-oriented systems.

This chapter will cover the following topics:

- *Design basics*: What I mean by design and how object-oriented design differs from procedural code

- *Class scope*: How to decide what to include in a class

- *Encapsulation*: Hiding implementation and data behind a class's interface

- *Polymorphism*: Using a common supertype to allow the transparent substitution of specialized subtypes at runtime

- *The UML*: Using diagrams to describe object-oriented architectures

Defining Code Design

One sense of code design concerns the definition of a system: the determination of a system's requirements, scope, and objectives. What does the system need to do? For whom does it need to do it? What are the outputs of the system? Do they meet the stated need? On a lower level, design can be taken to mean the process by which you define the participants of a system and organize their relationships. This chapter is concerned with the second sense: the definition and disposition of classes and objects.

So what is a participant? An object-oriented system is made up of classes. It is important to decide the nature of these players in your system. Classes are made up, in part, of methods; so in defining your classes, you must decide which methods belong

© Matt Zandstra 2021
M. Zandstra, *PHP 8 Objects, Patterns, and Practice*, https://doi.org/10.1007/978-1-4842-6791-2_6

together. As you will see, though, classes are often combined in inheritance relationships to conform to common interfaces. It is these interfaces, or types, that should be your first port of call in designing your system.

There are other relationships that you can define for your classes. You can create classes that are composed of other types or that manage lists of other type instances. You can design classes that simply use other objects. The potential for such relationships of composition or use is built into your classes (e.g., through the use of type declarations in method signatures), but the actual object relationships take place at runtime, which can add flexibility to your design. You will see how to model these relationships in this chapter, and we'll explore them further throughout the book.

As part of the design process, you must decide when an operation should belong to a type and when it should belong to another class used by the type. Everywhere you turn, you are presented with choices, decisions that might lead to clarity and elegance or might mire you in compromise.

In this chapter, I will examine some issues that might influence a few of these choices.

Object-Oriented and Procedural Programming

How does object-oriented design differ from the more traditional procedural code? It is tempting to say that the primary distinction is that object-oriented code has objects in it. This is neither true nor useful. In PHP, you will often find procedural code using objects. You may also come across classes that contain tracts of procedural code. The presence of classes does not guarantee object-oriented design, even in a language such as Java, which forces you to do most things inside a class.

One core difference between object-oriented and procedural code can be found in the way that responsibility is distributed. Procedural code takes the form of a sequential series of commands and function calls. The controlling code tends to take responsibility for handling differing conditions. This top-down control can result in the development of duplications and dependencies across a project. Object-oriented code tries to minimize these dependencies by moving responsibility for handling tasks away from client code and toward the objects in the system.

In this section, I'll set up a simple problem and then analyze it in terms of both object-oriented and procedural code to illustrate these points. My project is to build a quick tool for reading from and writing to configuration files. In order to maintain focus on the structures of the code, I will omit implementation details in these examples.

I'll begin with a procedural approach to this problem. To start with, I will read and write text in this format:

```
key:value
```

I need only two functions for this purpose:

```
// listing 06.01
function readParams(string $source): array
{
    $params = [];
    // read text parameters from $source
    return $params;
}

function writeParams(array $params, string $source): void
{
    // write text parameters to $source
}
```

The readParams function requires the name of a source file. It attempts to open it and reads each line, looking for key/value pairs. It builds up an associative array as it goes. Finally, it returns the array to the controlling code. writeParams() accepts an associative array and the path to a source file. It loops through the associative array, writing each key/value pair to the file. Here's some client code that works with the functions:

```
// listing 06.02
$file = "/tmp/params.txt";
$params = [
    "key1" => "val1",
    "key2" => "val2",
    "key3" => "val3",
];
writeParams($params, $file);
$output = readParams($file);
print_r($output);
```

This code is relatively compact and should be easy to maintain. The writeParams() function is called to create param.txt and to write to it with something like this:

```
key1:val1
key2:val2
key3:val3
```

The readParams() function parses the same format.

In many projects, scope grows and evolves. Let's fake this by introducing a new requirement. The code must now also handle an XML structure that looks like this:

```
<params>
    <param>
        <key>my key</key>
        <val>my val</val>
    </param>
</params>
```

The parameter file should be read in XML mode if the parameter file ends in .xml. Although this is not difficult to accommodate, it threatens to make my code much harder to maintain. I really have two options at this stage. I can check the file extension in the controlling code, or I can test inside my read and write functions. Here, I go for the latter approach:

```
// listing 06.03
function readParams(string $source): array
{
    $params = [];
    if (preg_match("/\.xml$/i", $source)) {
        // read XML parameters from $source
    } else {
        // read text parameters from $source
    }
    return $params;
}
```

```
function writeParams(array $params, string $source): void
{
    if (preg_match("/\.xml$/i", $source)) {
        // write XML parameters to $source
    } else {
        // write text parameters to $source
    }
}
```

Note   Illustrative code always involves a difficult balancing act. It needs to be clear enough to make its point, which often means sacrificing error checking and fitness for its ostensible purpose. In other words, the example here is really intended to illustrate issues of design and duplication rather than the best way to parse and write file data. For this reason, I omit implementation where it is not relevant to the issue at hand.

As you can see, I have had to use the test for the XML extension in each of the functions. It is this repetition that might cause us problems down the line. If I were to be asked to include yet another parameter format, I would need to remember to keep the readParams() and writeParams() functions in line with one another.

Now I'll address the same problem with some simple classes. First, I create an abstract base class that will define the interface for the type:

```
// listing 06.04
abstract class ParamHandler
{
    protected array $params = [];

    public function __construct(protected string $source)
    {
    }

    public function addParam(string $key, string $val): void
    {
        $this->params[$key] = $val;
    }
```

```
    public function getAllParams(): array
    {
        return $this->params;
    }

    public static function getInstance(string $filename): ParamHandler
    {
        if (preg_match("/\.xml$/i",  $filename))  {
            return new XmlParamHandler($filename);
        }
        return new TextParamHandler($filename);
    }

    abstract public function write(): void;
    abstract public function read(): void;
}
```

I define the addParam() method to allow the user to add parameters to the protected $params property and getAllParams() to provide access to a copy of the array.

I also create a static getInstance() method that tests the file extension and returns a particular subclass according to the results. Crucially, I define two abstract methods, read() and write(), ensuring that any subclasses will support this interface.

Note   Placing a static method for generating child objects in the parent class is convenient. Such a design decision has its own consequences, however. The ParamHandler type is now essentially limited to working with the concrete classes in this central conditional statement. What happens if you need to handle another format? Of course, if you are the maintainer of ParamHandler, you can always amend the getInstance() method. If you are a client coder, however, changing this library class may not be so easy (in fact, changing it won't be hard, but you face the prospect of having to reapply your patch every time you reinstall the package that provides it). I will discuss issues of object creation in Chapter 9.

Now, I'll define the subclasses, once again omitting the details of implementation to keep the example clean:

```
// listing 06.05
class XmlParamHandler extends ParamHandler
{

    public function write(): void
    {
        // write XML
        // using $this->params
    }

    public function read(): void
    {
        // read XML
        // and populate $this->params
    }
}

// listing 06.06
class TextParamHandler extends ParamHandler
{

    public function write(): void
    {
        // write text
        // using $this->params
    }

    public function read(): void
    {
        // read text
        // and populate $this->params
    }
}
```

These classes simply provide implementations of the write() and read() methods.
Each class will write and read according to the appropriate format.

Client code will write to both text and XML formats entirely transparently, according to the file extension:

```
// listing 06.07
$test = ParamHandler::getInstance(__DIR__ . "/params.xml");
$test->addParam("key1", "val1");
$test->addParam("key2", "val2");
$test->addParam("key3", "val3");
$test->write(); // writing in XML format
```

We can also read from either file format:

```
// listing 06.08
$test = ParamHandler::getInstance(__DIR__ . "/params.txt");
$test->read(); // reading in text format
$params = $test->getAllParams();
print_r($params);
```

So, what can we learn from these two approaches?

Responsibility

The controlling code in the procedural example takes responsibility for deciding about format—not once, but twice. The conditional code is tidied away into functions, certainly, but this merely disguises the fact of a single flow, making decisions as it goes. Calls to readParams() and to writeParams() take place in different contexts, so we are forced to repeat the file extension test in each function (or to perform variations on this test).

In the object-oriented version, this choice about file format is made in the static getInstance() method, which tests the file extension only once, serving up the correct subclass. The client code takes no responsibility for implementation. It uses the provided object with no knowledge of, or interest in, the particular subclass it belongs to. It knows only that it is working with a ParamHandler object and that it will support write() and read(). While the procedural code busies itself about details, the object-oriented code works only with an interface, unconcerned about the details of implementation. Because responsibility for implementation lies with the objects and not with the client code, it would be easy to switch in support for new formats transparently.

Cohesion

Cohesion is the extent to which proximate procedures are related to one another. Ideally, you should create components that share a clear responsibility. If your code spreads related routines widely, you will find them harder to maintain as you have to hunt around to make changes.

Our `ParamHandler` classes collect related procedures into a common context. The methods for working with XML share a context in which they can share data and where changes to one method can easily be reflected in another if necessary (e.g., if you needed to change an XML element name). The `ParamHandler` classes can therefore be said to have high cohesion.

The procedural example, on the other hand, separates related procedures. The code for working with XML is spread across functions.

Coupling

Tight coupling occurs when discrete parts of a system's code are tightly bound up with one another so that a change in one part necessitates changes in the others. Tight coupling is by no means unique to procedural code, though the sequential nature of such code makes it prone to the problem.

You can see this kind of coupling in the procedural example. The `writeParams()` and `readParams()` functions run the same test on a file extension to determine how they should work with data. Any change in logic you make to one will have to be implemented in the other. If you were to add a new format, for example, you would have to bring the functions into line with one another, so that they both implement a new file extension test in the same way. This problem can only get worse as you add new parameter-related functions.

The object-oriented example decouples the individual subclasses from one another and from the client code. If you were required to add a new parameter format, you could simply create a new subclass, amending a single test in the static `getInstance()` method.

Orthogonality

The killer combination of components with tightly defined responsibilities that are also independent from the wider system is sometimes referred to as *orthogonality*. Andrew Hunt and David Thomas discuss this subject in their book, *The Pragmatic Programmer, 20th Anniversary Edition* (Addison-Wesley, 2019).

Orthogonality, it is argued, promotes reuse in that components can be plugged into new systems without needing any special configuration. Such components will have clear inputs and outputs, independent of any wider context. Orthogonal code makes change easier because the impact of altering an implementation will be localized to the component being altered. Finally, orthogonal code is safer. The effects of bugs should be limited in scope. An error in highly interdependent code can easily cause knock-on effects in the wider system.

There is nothing automatic about loose coupling and high cohesion in a class context. We could, after all, embed our entire procedural example into one misguided class. So how can we achieve this balance in our code? I usually start by considering the classes that should live in my system.

Choosing Your Classes

It can be surprisingly difficult to define the boundaries of your classes, especially as they will evolve with any system that you build.

It can seem straightforward when you are modeling the real world. Object-oriented systems often feature software representations of real things—Person, Invoice, and Shop classes abound. This would seem to suggest that defining a class is a matter of finding the *things* in your system and then giving them agency through methods. This is not a bad starting point, but it does have its dangers. If you see a class as a noun, a subject for any number of verbs, then you may find it bloating as ongoing development and requirement changes call for it to do more and more things.

Let's consider the ShopProduct example that we created in Chapter 3. Our system exists to offer products to a customer, so defining a ShopProduct class is an obvious choice. But is that the only decision we need to make? We provide methods such as getTitle() and getPrice() for accessing product data. When we are asked to provide a mechanism for outputting summary information for invoices and delivery notes, it seems to make sense to define a write() method. When the client asks us to provide the product summaries in different formats, we look again at our class. We duly create writeXML() and writeHTML() methods in addition to the write() method. Or we add conditional code to write() to output different formats, according to an option flag.

Either way, the problem here is that the ShopProduct class is now trying to do too much. It is struggling to manage strategies for display, as well as for managing product data.

How *should* you think about defining classes? The best approach is to think of a class as having a primary responsibility and to make that responsibility as singular and focused as possible. Put the responsibility into words. It has been said that you should be able to describe a class's responsibility in 25 words or less, rarely using the words "and" or "or." If your sentence gets too long or mired in clauses, it is probably time to consider defining new classes along the lines of some of the responsibilities you have described.

So, ShopProduct classes are responsible for managing product data. If we add methods for writing to different formats, we begin to add a new area of responsibility: product display. As you saw in Chapter 3, we actually defined two types based on these separate responsibilities. The ShopProduct type remained responsible for product data, and the ShopProductWriter type took on responsibility for displaying product information. Individual subclasses refined these responsibilities.

Note   Very few design rules are entirely inflexible. You will sometimes see code for saving object data in an otherwise unrelated class, for example. Although this would seem to violate the rule that a class should have a singular responsibility, it can be the most convenient place for the functionality to live because a method has to have full access to an instance's fields. Using local methods for persistence can also save us from creating a parallel hierarchy of persistence classes mirroring our savable classes and thereby introducing unavoidable coupling. We deal with other strategies for object persistence in Chapter 12. Avoid religious adherence to design rules; they are not a substitute for analyzing the problem before you. Try to remain alive to the reasoning behind the rule and emphasize that over the rule itself.

Polymorphism

Polymorphism, or class switching, is a common feature of object-oriented systems. You have encountered it several times already in this book.

Polymorphism is the maintenance of multiple implementations behind a common interface. This sounds complicated, but in fact it should be very familiar to you by now. The need for polymorphism is often signaled by the presence of extensive conditional statements in your code.

When I first created the ShopProduct class in Chapter 3, I experimented with a single class which managed functionality for books and CDs, in addition to generic products. In order to provide summary information, I relied on a conditional statement:

```
// listing 06.09
public function getSummaryLine(): string
{
    $base = "{$this->title} ( {$this->producerMainName}, ";
    $base .= "{$this->producerFirstName} )";
    if ($this->type == 'book') {
        $base .= ": page count - {$this->numPages}";
    } elseif ($this->type == 'cd') {
        $base .= ": playing time - {$this->playLength}";
    }
    return $base;
}
```

These statements suggested the shape for the two subclasses: CdProduct and BookProduct.

By the same token, the conditional statements in my procedural parameter example contained the seeds of the object-oriented structure I finally arrived at. I repeated the same condition in two parts of the script:

```
// listing 06.10
function readParams(string $source): array
{
    $params = [];
    if (preg_match("/\.xml$/i", $source)) {
        // read XML parameters from $source
    } else {
        // read text parameters from $source
    }
    return $params;
}
```

```
function writeParams(array $params, string $source): void
{
    if (preg_match("/\.xml$/i", $source)) {
        // write XML parameters to $source
    } else {
        // write text parameters to $source
    }
}
```

Each clause suggested one of the subclasses I finally produced: XmlParamHandler and TextParamHandler. These extended the abstract base class ParamHandler's write() and read() methods:

```
// listing 06.11
// could return XmlParamHandler or TextParamHandler
$test = ParamHandler::getInstance($file);

$test->read(); // could be XmlParamHandler::read() or
TextParamHandler::read()
$test->addParam("newkey1", "newval1");
$test->write(); // could be XmlParamHandler::write() or
TextParamHandler::write()
```

It is important to note that polymorphism doesn't banish conditionals. Methods such as ParamHandler::getInstance() will often determine which objects to return based on switch or if statements. These tend to centralize the conditional code into one place, though.

As you have seen, PHP enforces the interfaces defined by abstract classes. This is helpful because we can be sure that a concrete child class will support exactly the same method signatures as those defined by an abstract parent. This includes type declarations and access controls. Client code can, therefore, treat all children of a common superclass interchangeably (as long as it only relies on only functionality defined in the parent).

Encapsulation

Encapsulation simply means the hiding of data and functionality from a client. And once again, it is a key object-oriented concept.

On the simplest level, you encapsulate data by declaring properties `private` or `protected`. By hiding a property from client code, you enforce an interface and prevent the accidental corruption of an object's data.

Polymorphism illustrates another kind of encapsulation. By placing different implementations behind a common interface, you hide these underlying strategies from the client. This means that any changes that are made behind this interface are transparent to the wider system. You can add new classes or change the code in a class without causing errors. The interface is what matters, not the mechanisms working beneath it. The more independent these mechanisms are kept, the less chance that changes or repairs will have a knock-on effect in your projects.

Encapsulation is, in some ways, the key to object-oriented programming. Your objective should be to make each part as independent as possible from its peers. Classes and methods should receive as much information as is necessary to perform their allotted tasks, which should be limited in scope and clearly identified.

The introduction of the `private`, `protected`, and `public` keywords have made encapsulation easier. Encapsulation is also a state of mind, though. PHP 4 provided no formal support for hiding data. Privacy had to be signaled using documentation and naming conventions. An underscore, for example, is a common way of signaling a private property:

```
var $_touchezpas;
```

Code had to be checked closely, of course, because privacy was not strictly enforced. Interestingly, though, errors were rare because the structure and style of the code made it pretty clear which properties wanted to be left alone.

By the same token, even after PHP 5 arrived, we could break the rules and discover the exact subtype of an object that we were using in a class-switching context simply by using the `instanceof` operator:

```
// listing 06.12
public function workWithProducts(ShopProduct $prod)
{
    if ($prod instanceof CdProduct) {
        // do cd thing
    } elseif ($prod instanceof BookProduct) {
        // do book thing
    }
}
```

You may have a very good reason to do this, but, in general, it carries a slightly uncertain odor. By querying the specific subtype in the example, I am setting up a dependency. Although the specifics of the subtype were hidden by polymorphism, it would have been possible to have changed the ShopProduct inheritance hierarchy entirely with no ill effects. This code ends that. Now, if I need to rationalize the CdProduct and BookProduct classes, I may create unexpected side effects in the workWithProducts() method.

There are two lessons to take away from this example. First, encapsulation helps you to create orthogonal code. Second, the extent to which encapsulation is enforceable is beside the point. Encapsulation is a technique that should be observed equally by classes and their clients.

Forget How to Do It

If you are like me, the mention of a problem will set your mind racing, looking for mechanisms that might provide a solution. You might select functions that will address an issue, revisit clever regular expressions, and track down Composer packages. You probably have some pasteable code in an old project that does something somewhat similar. At the design stage, you can profit by setting all that aside for a while. Empty your head of procedures and mechanisms.

Think only about the key participants of your system: the types it will need and their interfaces. Of course, your knowledge of process will inform your thinking. A class that opens a file will need a path, database code will need to manage table names and passwords, and so on. Let the structures and relationships in your code lead you, though. You will find that the implementation falls into place easily behind a well-defined interface. You then have the flexibility to switch out, improve, or extend an implementation should you need to, without affecting the wider system.

In order to emphasize interface, think in terms of abstract base classes or interfaces rather than concrete children. In my parameter-fetching code, for example, the interface is the most important aspect of the design. I want a type that reads and writes name/value pairs. It is this responsibility that is important about the type, not the actual persistence medium or the means of storing and retrieving data. I design the system around the abstract ParamHandler class and only add in the concrete strategies for actually reading and writing parameters later on. In this way, I build both polymorphism and encapsulation into my system from the start. The structure lends itself to class switching.

Having said that, of course, I knew from the start that there would be text and XML implementations of `ParamHandler`, and there is no question that this influenced my interface. There is always a certain amount of mental juggling to do when designing interfaces.

In *Design Patterns: Elements of Reusable Object-Oriented Software* (Addison-Wesley Professional, 1995), the Gang of Four summed up this principle with the phrase, "Program to an interface, not an implementation." It is a good one to add to your coder's handbook.

Four Signposts

Very few people get it absolutely right at the design stage. Most of us amend our code as requirements change or as we gain a deeper understanding of the nature of the problem we are addressing.

As you amend your code, it can easily drift beyond your control. A method is added here and a new class there, and gradually your system begins to decay. As you have seen already, your code can point the way to its own improvement. These pointers in code are sometimes referred to as code smells—that is, features in code that *may* suggest particular fixes or at least call you to look again at your design. In this section, I distill some of the points already made into four signs that you should watch out for as you code.

Code Duplication

Duplication is one of the great evils in code. If you get a strange sense of déjà vu as you write a routine, chances are you have a problem.

Take a look at the instances of repetition in your system. Perhaps they belong together. Duplication generally means tight coupling. If you change something fundamental about one routine, will the similar routines need amendment? If this is the case, they probably belong in the same class.

The Class Who Knew Too Much

It can be a pain passing parameters around from method to method. Why not simply reduce the pain by using a global variable? With a global, everyone can get at the data.

Global variables have their place, but they do need to be viewed with some level of suspicion. That's quite a high level of suspicion, by the way. By using a global variable, or by giving a class any kind of knowledge about its wider domain, you anchor it into its context, making it less reusable and dependent on code beyond its control. Remember, you want to decouple your classes and routines and not create interdependence. Try to limit a class's knowledge of its context. I will look at some strategies for doing this later in the book.

The Jack of All Trades

Is your class trying to do too many things at once? If so, see if you can list the responsibilities of the class. You may find that one of them will form the basis of a good class itself.

Leaving an overzealous class unchanged can cause particular problems if you create subclasses. Which responsibility are you extending with the subclass? What would you do if you needed a subclass for more than one responsibility? You are likely to end up with too many subclasses or an overreliance on conditional code.

Conditional Statements

You will use if and switch statements with perfectly good reason throughout your projects. Sometimes, though, such structures can be a cry for polymorphism.

If you find that you are testing for certain conditions frequently within a class, especially if you find these tests mirrored across more than one method, this could be a sign that your one class should be two or more. See whether the structure of the conditional code suggests responsibilities that could be expressed in classes. The new classes should implement a shared abstract base class. Chances are that you will then have to work out how to pass the right class to client code. I will cover some patterns for creating objects in Chapter 9.

The UML

So far in this book, I have let the code speak for itself, and I have used short examples to illustrate concepts such as inheritance and polymorphism. This is useful because PHP is a common currency here: it's a language we have in common, if you have read this far.

As our examples grow in size and complexity, though, using code alone to illustrate the broad sweep of design becomes somewhat absurd. It is hard to see an overview in a few lines of code.

UML stands for Unified Modeling Language. The initials are correctly used with the definite article. This isn't just *a* unified modeling language, it is *the* Unified Modeling Language.

Perhaps this magisterial tone derives from the circumstances of the language's forging. According to Martin Fowler (*UML Distilled*, Addison-Wesley Professional, 1999), the UML emerged as a standard only after long years of intellectual and bureaucratic sparring among the great and good of the object-oriented design community.

The result of this struggle is a powerful graphical syntax for describing object-oriented systems. We will only scratch the surface in this section, but you will soon find that a little UML (sorry, a little of *the* UML) goes a long way.

Class diagrams in particular can describe structures and patterns so that their meaning shines through. This luminous clarity is often harder to find in code fragments and bullet points.

Class Diagrams

Although class diagrams are only one aspect of the UML, they are perhaps the most ubiquitous. Because they are particularly useful for describing object-oriented relationships, I will primarily use these in this book.

Representing Classes

As you might expect, classes are the main constituents of class diagrams. A class is represented by a named box (see Figure 6-1).

Figure 6-1. *A class*

The class is divided into three sections, with the name displayed in the first. These dividing lines are optional when we present no more information than the class name. In designing a class diagram, we may find that the level of detail in Figure 6-1 is enough for some classes. We are not obligated to represent every field and method or even every class in a class diagram.

Abstract classes are represented either by italicizing the class name (see Figure 6-2) or by adding {abstract} to the class name (see Figure 6-3). The first method is the more common of the two, but the second is more useful when you are making notes.

Figure 6-2. *An abstract class*

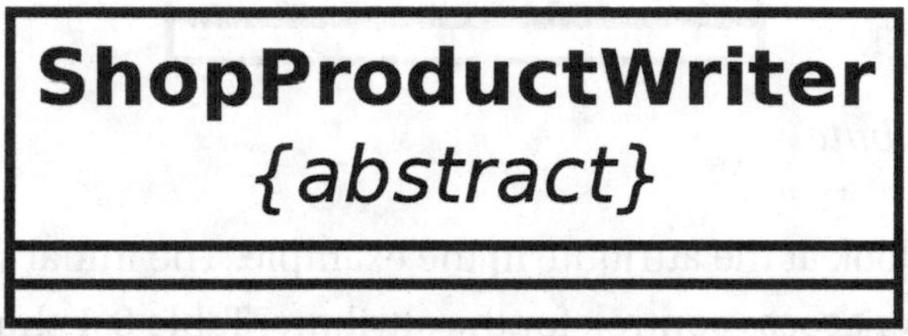

Figure 6-3. *An abstract class defined using a constraint*

Note   The {abstract} syntax is an example of a constraint. Constraints are used in class diagrams to describe the way in which specific elements should be used. There is no special structure for the text between the braces; it should simply provide a short clarification of any conditions that may apply to the element.

Interfaces are defined in the same way as classes, except that they must include a stereotype (i.e., an extension to the UML), as shown in Figure 6-4.

Figure 6-4. *An interface*

Attributes

Broadly speaking, attributes describe a class's properties. Attributes are listed in the section directly beneath the class name (see Figure 6-5).

Figure 6-5. *An attribute*

Let's take a close look at the attribute in the example. The initial symbol represents the level of visibility, or access control, for the attribute. Table 6-1 shows the three symbols available.

Table 6-1. *Visibility Symbols*

Symbol	Visibility	Explanation
+	Public	Available to all code
-	Private	Available to the current class only
#	Protected	Available to the current class and its subclasses only

The visibility symbol is followed by the name of the attribute. In this case, I am describing the ShopProduct::$price property. A colon is used to separate the attribute name from its type (and optionally, a default value can be supplied at the end, delimited by an equals sign).

Once again, you need only include as much detail as is necessary for clarity.

Operations

Operations describe methods; or, more properly, they describe the calls that can be made on an instance of a class. Figure 6-6 shows two operations in the ShopProduct class.

```
ShopProduct
#price: int = 0
+setDiscount(amount:int)
+getTitle(): String
```

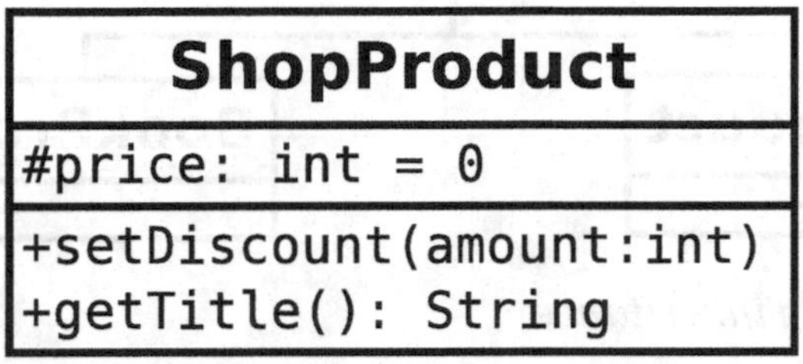

Figure 6-6. *Operations*

As you can see, operations use a similar syntax to that used by attributes. The visibility symbol precedes the method name. A list of parameters is enclosed in parentheses. The method's return type, if any, is delineated by a colon. Parameters are separated by commas and follow the attribute syntax, with the attribute name separated from its type by a colon.

As you might expect, this syntax is relatively flexible. You can omit the visibility flag and the return type. Parameters are often represented by their type alone, as the argument name is not usually significant.

Describing Inheritance and Implementation

The UML describes the inheritance relationship as generalization. This relationship is signified by a line leading from the subclass to its parent. The line is tipped with an empty closed arrow.

Figure 6-7 shows the relationship between the ShopProduct class and its child classes.

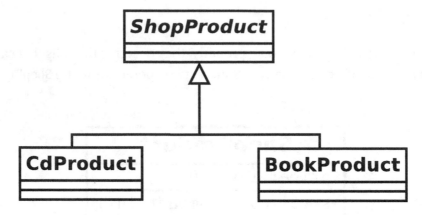

Figure 6-7. *Describing inheritance*

The UML describes the relationship between an interface and the classes that implement it as realization. So, if the ShopProduct class were to implement the Chargeable interface, we could add it to our class diagram, as in Figure 6-8.

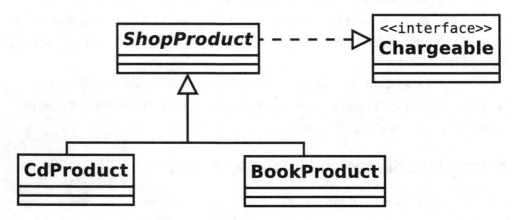

Figure 6-8. *Describing interface implementation*

Associations

Inheritance is only one of a number of relationships in an object-oriented system. An association occurs when a class property is declared to hold a reference to an instance (or instances) of another class.

In Figure 6-9, we model two classes and create an association between them.

Figure 6-9. *A class association*

At this stage, we are vague about the nature of this relationship. We have only specified that a Teacher object will have a reference to one or more Pupil objects, or vice versa. This relationship may or may not be reciprocal.

You can use arrows to describe the direction of the association. If the Teacher class has an instance of the Pupil class but not the other way round, then you should make your association an arrow leading from the Teacher to the Pupil class. This association, which is called unidirectional, is shown in Figure 6-10.

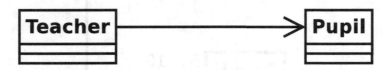

Figure 6-10. *A unidirectional association*

If each class has a reference to the other, you can use a double-headed arrow to describe a bidirectional relationship, as in Figure 6-11.

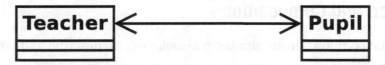

Figure 6-11. *A bidirectional association*

You can also specify the number of instances of a class that are referenced by another in an association (this is also known as "cardinality" of an association). You do this by placing a number or range beside each class. You can also use an asterisk (*) to stand for any number. In Figure 6-12, there can be one Teacher object and zero or more Pupil objects.

Figure 6-12. *Defining multiplicity for an association*

In Figure 6-13, there can be one Teacher object and between five and ten Pupil objects in the association.

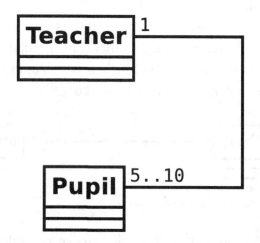

Figure 6-13. *Defining multiplicity for an association*

Aggregation and Composition

Aggregation and composition are similar to association. All describe a situation in which a class holds a permanent reference to one or more instances of another. With aggregation and composition, though, the referenced instances form an intrinsic part of the referring object.

In the case of aggregation, the contained objects are a core part of the container, but they can also be contained by other objects at the same time. The aggregation relationship is illustrated by a line that begins with an unfilled diamond.

In Figure 6-14, I define two classes: SchoolClass and Pupil. The SchoolClass class aggregates Pupil.

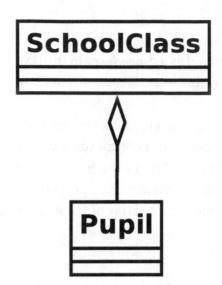

Figure 6-14. *Aggregation*

Pupils make up a class, but the same `Pupil` object can be referred to by different `SchoolClass` instances at the same time. If I were to disband a school class, I would not necessarily delete the pupil, who may attend other classes.

Composition represents an even stronger relationship than this. In composition, the contained object can be referenced by its container only. It should be deleted when the container is deleted. Composition relationships are depicted in the same way as aggregation relationships, except that the diamond should be filled (see Figure 6-15).

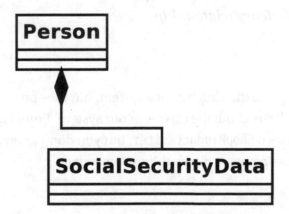

Figure 6-15. *Composition*

A `Person` class maintains a reference to a `SocialSecurityData` object. The contained instance can belong only to the containing `Person` object.

233

Describing Use

The use relationship is described as a *dependency* in the UML. It is the most transient of the relationships discussed in this section because it does not describe a permanent link between classes.

A used class may be passed as an argument or acquired as a result of a method call.

The Report class in Figure 6-16 uses a ShopProductWriter object. The use relationship is shown by the broken line and open arrow that connects the two. It does not, however, maintain this reference as a property in the same way that a ShopProductWriter object maintains an array of ShopProduct objects.

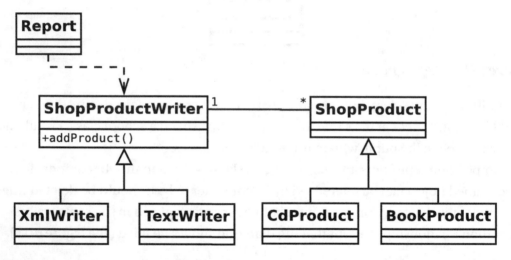

Figure 6-16. *A dependency relationship*

Using Notes

Class diagrams can capture the structure of a system, but they provide no sense of process. Figure 6-16 tells us about the classes in our system. From Figure 6-16, you know that a Report object uses a ShopProductWriter, but you don't know the mechanics of this. In Figure 6-17, I use a note to clarify things somewhat.

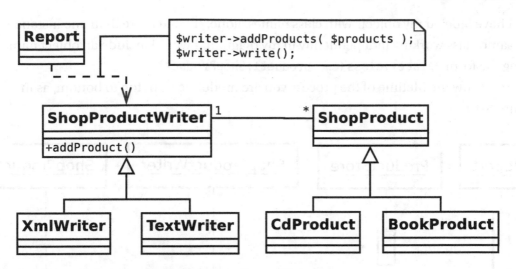

Figure 6-17. *Using a note to clarify a dependency*

As you can see, a note consists of a box with a folded corner. It will often contain scraps of pseudo-code.

This clarifies Figure 6-16; you can now see that the Report object uses a ShopProductWriter to output product data. This is hardly a revelation, but use relationships are not always so obvious. In some cases, even a note might not provide enough information. Luckily, you can model the interactions of objects in your system, as well as the structure of your classes.

Sequence Diagrams

A sequence diagram is object based rather than class based. It is used to model a process in a system step by step.

Let's build up a simple diagram, modeling the means by which a Report object writes product data. A sequence diagram presents the participants of a system from left to right (see Figure 6-18).

Figure 6-18. *Objects in a sequence diagram*

I have labeled my objects with class names alone. If I had more than one instance of the same class working independently in my diagram, I would include an object name using the format, label:class (e.g., product1:ShopProduct).

You show the lifetime of the process you are modeling from top to bottom, as in Figure 6-19.

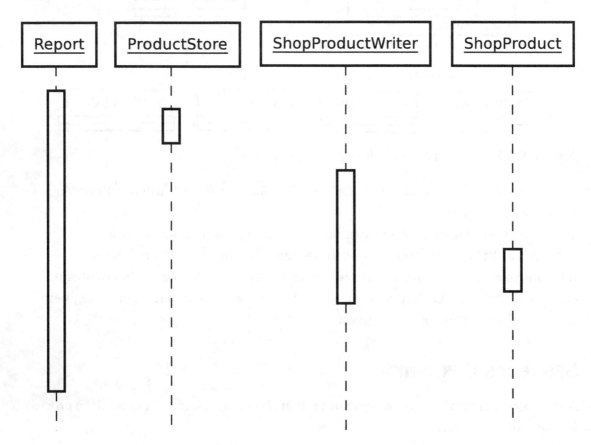

Figure 6-19. *Object lifelines in a sequence diagram*

The vertical broken lines represent the lifetime of the objects in the system. The larger boxes that follow the lifelines represent the focus of a process. If you read Figure 6-19 from top to bottom, you can see how the process moves among objects in the system. This is hard to read without showing the messages that are passed between the objects. I add these in Figure 6-20.

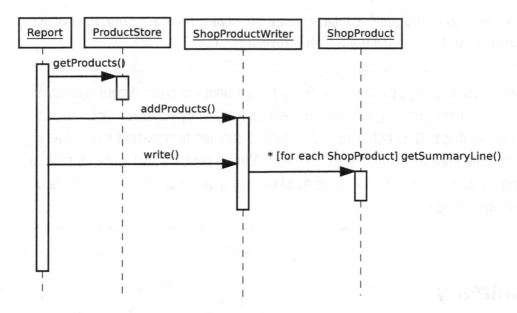

Figure 6-20. *The complete sequence diagram*

The arrows represent the messages sent from one object to another. Return values are often left implicit (although they can be represented by a broken line, passing from the invoked object to the message originator). Each message is labeled using the relevant method call. You can be quite flexible with your labeling, although there is some syntax. Square brackets represent a condition:

```
[okToPrint]
write()
```

This snippet means that the write() invocation should only be made if the correct condition is met. An asterisk is used to indicate a repetition; optionally, further clarification can be in square brackets:

```
*[for each ShopProduct]
write()
```

You can interpret Figure 6-20 from top to bottom. First, a Report object acquires a list of ShopProduct objects from a ProductStore object. It passes these to a ShopProductWriter object, which stores references to them (though we can only infer this from the diagram). The ShopProductWriter object calls ShopProduct::getSummaryLine() for every ShopProduct object it references, adding the result to its output.

As you can see, sequence diagrams can model processes, freezing slices of dynamic interaction and presenting them with surprising clarity.

Note   Look at Figures 6-16 and 6-20. Notice how the class diagram illustrates polymorphism, showing the classes derived from `ShopProductWriter` and `ShopProduct`. Now notice how this detail becomes transparent when we model the communication among objects. Where possible, we want objects to work with the most general types available, so that we can hide the details of implementation.

Summary

In this chapter, I went beyond the nuts and bolts of object-oriented programming to look at some key design issues. I examined features such as encapsulation, loose coupling, and cohesion that are essential aspects of a flexible and reusable object-oriented system. I went on to look at the UML, laying groundwork that will be essential in working with patterns later in the book.

PART II

Patterns

## CHAPTER 7

What Are Design Patterns? Why Use Them?

Most problems we encounter as programmers have been handled time and again by others in our community. Design patterns can provide us with the means to mine that wisdom. Once a pattern becomes a common currency, it enriches our language, making it easy to share design ideas and their consequences. Design patterns simply distill common problems, define tested solutions, and describe likely outcomes. Many books and articles focus on the details of computer languages, such as the available functions, classes and methods, and so on. Pattern catalogs concentrate instead on how you can move on from these basics (the "what") to an understanding of the problems and potential solutions in your projects (the "why" and "how").

In this chapter, I introduce you to design patterns and look at some of the reasons for their popularity. This chapter will cover the following:

- *Pattern basics*: What are design patterns?

- *Pattern structure*: What are the key elements of a design pattern?

- *Pattern benefits*: Why are patterns worth your time?

What Are Design Patterns?

In the world of software, a pattern is a tangible manifestation of an organization's tribal memory.

—Grady Booch in *Core J2EE Patterns*

© Matt Zandstra 2021
M. Zandstra, *PHP 8 Objects, Patterns, and Practice*, https://doi.org/10.1007/978-1-4842-6791-2_7

[A pattern is] a solution to a problem in a context.

—*The Gang of Four, Design Patterns: Elements of Reusable Object-
Oriented Software*

As these quotations imply, a design pattern provides analysis of a particular problem
and describes good practice for its solution.

Problems tend to recur, and as web programmers, we must solve them time and time
again. How should we handle an incoming request? How can we translate this data into
instructions for our system? How should we acquire data? Present results? Over time,
we answer these questions with a greater or lesser degree of elegance and evolve an
informal set of techniques that we use and reuse in our projects. These techniques are
patterns of design.

Design patterns inscribe and formalize these problems and solutions, making hard-
won experience available to the wider programming community. Patterns are (or should
be) essentially bottom-up and not top-down. They are rooted in practice and not theory.
That is not to say that there isn't a strong theoretical element to design patterns (as we
will see in the next chapter), but patterns are based on real-world techniques used by
real programmers. Renowned pattern-hatcher Martin Fowler says that he discovers
patterns; he does not invent them. For this reason, many patterns will engender a sense
of déjà vu as you recognize techniques you have used yourself.

A catalog of patterns is not a cookbook. Recipes can be followed slavishly; code can
be copied and slotted into a project with minor changes. You do not always need even
to understand all the code used in a recipe. Design patterns inscribe *approaches* to
particular problems. The details of implementation may vary enormously according to
the wider context. This context might include the programming language you are using,
the nature of your application, the size of your project, and the specifics of the problem.

Let's say, for example, that your project requires that you create a templating system.
Given the name of a template file, you must parse it and build a tree of objects to
represent the tags you encounter.

You start off with a default parser that scans the text for trigger tokens. When it
finds a match, it hands off responsibility for the hunt to another parser object, which is
specialized for reading the internals of tags. This continues examining template data
until it either fails, finishes, or finds another trigger. If it finds a trigger, it, too, must
hand off responsibility to a specialist—perhaps an argument parser. Collectively, these
components form what is known as a recursive descent parser.

So these are your participants: a `MainParser`, a `TagParser`, and an `ArgumentParser`. You create a `ParserFactory` class to create and return these objects.

Of course, nothing is easy, and you're informed late in the game that you must support more than one syntax in your templates. Now, you need to create a parallel set of parsers according to the syntax: an `OtherTagParser`, an `OtherArgumentParser`, and so on.

This is your problem: you need to generate a different set of objects according to the circumstance, and you want this to be more or less transparent to other components in the system. It just so happens that the Gang of Four defines the following problem in their book's summary page for the pattern Abstract Factory, "Provide an interface for creating families of related or dependent objects without specifying their concrete classes."

That fits nicely. It is the nature of our problem that determines and shapes our use of this pattern. There is nothing cut and paste about the solution either, as you can see in Chapter 9, in which I cover Abstract Factory.

The very act of naming a pattern is valuable; it contributes to the kind of common vocabulary that has arisen naturally over the years in older crafts and professions. Such shorthand greatly aids collaborative design as alternative approaches and their various consequences are weighed and tested. When you discuss your alternative parser families, for example, you can simply tell colleagues that the system creates each set of objects using the Abstract Factory pattern. They will nod sagely, either immediately enlightened or making a mental note to look it up later. The point is that this bundle of concepts and consequences has a handle, which makes for a useful shorthand, as I'll illustrate later in this chapter.

Finally, it is illegal, according to international law, to write about patterns without quoting Christopher Alexander, an architecture academic whose work heavily influenced the original object-oriented pattern advocates. He states in *A Pattern Language* (Oxford University Press, 1977):

> *Each pattern describes a problem which occurs over and over again in our environment, and then describes the core of the solution to that problem, in such a way that you can use this solution a million times over, without ever doing it the same way twice.*

It is significant that this definition (which applies to architectural problems and solutions) begins with the problem and its wider setting and then proceeds to a solution. There has been some criticism in recent years that design patterns have been overused, especially by inexperienced programmers. This is often a sign that solutions have been applied where the problem and context are not present. Patterns are more than a particular organization of classes and objects, cooperating in a particular way. Patterns are structured to define the conditions in which solutions should be applied and to discuss the effects of the solution.

In this book, I will focus on a particularly influential strand in the patterns field: the form described in *Design Patterns: Elements of Reusable Object-Oriented Software* by the Gang of Four (Addison-Wesley Professional, 1995). It concentrates on patterns in object-oriented software development and inscribes some of the classic patterns that are present in most modern object-oriented projects.

The Gang of Four book is important because it inscribes key patterns and because it describes the design principles that inform and motivate these patterns. We will look at some of these principles in the next chapter.

Note   The patterns described by the Gang of Four and in this book are really instances of a pattern language. A pattern language is a catalog of problems and solutions organized together so that they complement one another, forming an interrelated whole. There are pattern languages for other problem spaces, such as visual design and project management (and architecture, of course). When I discuss design patterns here, I refer to problems and solutions in object-oriented software development.

A Design Pattern Overview

At heart, a design pattern consists of four parts: the name, the problem, the solution, and the consequences.

Name

Names matter. They enrich the language of programmers; a few short words can stand in for quite complex problems and solutions. They must balance brevity and description. The Gang of Four claims, "Finding good names has been one of the hardest parts of developing our catalog."

Martin Fowler agrees: "Pattern names are crucial, because part of the purpose of patterns is to create a vocabulary that allows developers to communicate more effectively" (*Patterns of Enterprise Application Architecture*, Addison-Wesley Professional, 2002).

In *Patterns of Enterprise Application Architecture*, Martin Fowler refines a database access pattern I first encountered in *Core J2EE Patterns* by Deepak Alur, Dan Malks, and John Crupi (Prentice Hall, 2001). Fowler defines two patterns that describe specializations of the older pattern. The logic of his approach is clearly correct (one of the new patterns models domain objects, while the other models database tables, a distinction that was vague in the earlier work). Nonetheless, it was hard to train myself to think in terms of the new patterns. I had been using the name of the original in design sessions and documents for so long that it had become part of my language.

The Problem

No matter how elegant the solution (and some are very elegant indeed), the problem and its context are the grounds of a pattern. Recognizing a problem is harder than applying any one of the solutions in a pattern catalog. This is one reason that some pattern solutions can be misapplied or overused.

Patterns describe a problem space with great care. The problem is described in brief and then contextualized, often with a typical example and one or more diagrams. It is broken down into its specifics, its various manifestations. Any warning signs that might help in identifying the problem are described.

The Solution

The solution is summarized initially in conjunction with the problem. It is also described in detail, often using UML class and interaction diagrams. The pattern usually includes a code example.

Although code may be presented, the solution is never cut and paste. The pattern describes an approach to a problem. There may be hundreds of nuances in its implementation. Think about instructions for sowing a food crop. If you simply follow a set of steps blindly, you are likely to go hungry come harvest time. More useful would be a pattern-based approach that covers the various conditions that may apply. The basic solution to the problem (making your crop grow) will always be the same (prepare soil, plant seeds, irrigate, harvest crop), but the actual steps you take will depend on all sorts of factors, such as your soil type, your location, the orientation of your land, local pests, and so on.

Martin Fowler refers to solutions in patterns as "half-baked." That is, the coder must take away the concept and finish it for himself.

Consequences

Every design decision you make will have wider consequences. This should include the satisfactory resolution of the problem in question, of course. A solution, once deployed, may be ideally suited to work with other patterns. There may also be dangers to watch for.

The Gang of Four Format

As I write, I have five pattern catalogs on the desk in front of me. A quick look at the patterns in each confirms that none of them use the same structure. Some are formal; some are fine-grained, with many subsections; and others are discursive.

There are a number of well-defined pattern structures, including the original form developed by Christopher Alexander (the Alexandrian form) and the narrative approach favored by the Portland Pattern Repository (the Portland form). Because the Gang of Four book is so influential, and because we will cover many of the patterns they describe, let's examine a few of the sections they include in their patterns:

- *Intent*: A brief statement of the pattern's purpose. You should be able to see the point of the pattern at a glance.

- *Motivation*: The problem described, often in terms of a typical situation. The anecdotal approach can help make the pattern easy to grasp.

- *Applicability*: An examination of the different situations in which you might apply the pattern. While the motivation describes a typical problem, this section defines specific situations and weighs the merits of the solution in the context of each.

- *Structure/interaction*: These sections may contain UML class and interaction diagrams describing the relationships among classes and objects in the solution.

- *Implementation*: This section looks at the details of the solution. It examines any issues that may come up when applying the technique and provides tips for deployment.

- *Sample code*: I always skip ahead to this section. I find that a simple code example often provides a way into a pattern. The example is often chopped down to the basics in order to lay the solution bare. It could be in any object-oriented language. Of course, in this book, it will always be PHP.

- *Known uses*: These describe real systems in which the pattern (problem, context, and solution) occurs. Some people say that for a pattern to be genuine, it must be found in at least three publicly available contexts. This is sometimes called the "rule of three."

- *Related patterns*: Some patterns imply others. In applying one solution, you can create the context in which another becomes useful. This section examines these synergies. It may also discuss patterns that have similarities to the problem or the solution, as well as any antecedents (i.e., patterns defined elsewhere on which the current pattern builds).

Why Use Design Patterns?

So what benefits can patterns bring? Given that a pattern is a problem defined and a solution described, the answer should be obvious. Patterns can help you to solve common problems. There is more to patterns, of course.

A Design Pattern Defines a Problem

How many times have you reached a stage in a project and found that there is no going forward? Chances are you must backtrack some way before starting out again.

By defining common problems, patterns can help you to improve your design. Sometimes, the first step to a solution is recognizing that you have a problem.

A Design Pattern Defines a Solution

Having defined and recognized the problem (and made certain that it is the right problem), a pattern gives you access to a solution, together with an analysis of the consequences of its use. Although a pattern does not absolve you of the responsibility to consider the implications of a design decision, you can at least be certain that you are using a tried-and-tested technique.

Design Patterns Are Language Independent

Patterns define objects and solutions in object-oriented terms. This means that many patterns apply equally in more than one language. When I first started using patterns, I read code examples in C++ and Smalltalk and then deployed my solutions in Java. Others transfer with modifications to the pattern's applicability or consequences, but remain valid. Either way, patterns can help you as you move between languages. Equally, an application that is built on good object-oriented design principles can be relatively easy to port between languages (although there are always issues that must be addressed).

Patterns Define a Vocabulary

By providing developers with names for techniques, patterns make communication richer. Imagine a design meeting. I have already described my Abstract Factory solution, and now I need to describe my strategy for managing the data the system compiles. I describe my plans to Bob:

> *Me*: I'm thinking of using a Composite.
>
> *Bob*: I don't think you've thought that through.

Okay, Bob didn't agree with me. He never does. But he knew what I was talking about and therefore why my idea sucked. Let's play that scene through again without a design vocabulary.

> *Me*: I intend to use a tree of objects that share the same type. The type's interface will provide methods for adding child objects of its own type. In this way, we can build up complex combinations of implementing objects at runtime.
>
> *Bob*: Huh?

Patterns, or the techniques they describe, tend to interoperate. The Composite pattern lends itself to collaboration with the Visitor pattern, for example:

> *Me*: And then we can use Visitors to summarize the data.

> *Bob*: You're missing the point.

Ignore Bob. I won't describe the tortuous nonpattern version of this; I will cover Composite in Chapter 10 and Visitor in Chapter 11.

The point is that, without a pattern language, we would still use these techniques. They *precede* their naming and organization. If patterns did not exist, they would evolve on their own, anyway. Any tool that is used sufficiently will eventually acquire a name.

Patterns Are Tried and Tested

So if patterns document good practice, is naming the only truly original thing about pattern catalogs? In some senses, that would seem to be true. Patterns represent best practice in an object-oriented context. To some highly experienced programmers, this may seem an exercise in repackaging the obvious. To the rest of us, patterns provide access to problems and solutions we would otherwise have to discover the hard way.

Patterns make design accessible. As pattern catalogs emerge for more and more specializations, even the highly experienced can find benefits as they move into new aspects of their fields. A GUI programmer can gain fast access to common problems and solutions in enterprise programming, for example. A web programmer can quickly chart strategies for avoiding the pitfalls that lurk in tablet and smartphone projects.

Patterns Are Designed for Collaboration

By their nature, patterns should be generative and composable. This means that you should be able to apply one pattern and thereby create conditions suitable for the application of another. In other words, in using a pattern, you may find other doors opened for you.

Pattern catalogs are usually designed with this kind of collaboration in mind, and the potential for pattern composition is always documented in the pattern itself.

Design Patterns Promote Good Design

Design patterns demonstrate and apply principles of object-oriented design. So, a study of design patterns can yield more than a specific solution in a context. You can come away with a new perspective on the ways that objects and classes can be combined to achieve an objective.

Design Patterns Are Used by Popular Frameworks

This book is primarily about designing from the ground up. The patterns and principles covered here should enable you to design your own core frameworks with the needs of your projects in mind. However, laziness is also a virtue, and you may wish to work with (or you may inherit code that already uses) a framework such as Zend, Laravel, or Symfony. A good understanding of core design patterns will help you as you engage with these framework APIs.

PHP and Design Patterns

There is little in this chapter that is specific to PHP, which is characteristic of our topic to some extent. Many patterns apply to many object-capable languages with few or no implementation issues.

This is not always the case, of course. Some enterprise patterns work well in languages in which an application process continues to run between server requests. PHP does not work that way. A new script execution is kicked off for every request. This means that some patterns need to be treated with more care.

Front Controller, for example, often requires some serious initialization time. This is fine when the initialization takes place once at application startup, but it's more of an issue when it must take place for every request. That is not to say that we can't use the pattern; I have deployed it with very good results in the past. We must simply ensure that we take account of PHP-related issues when we discuss the pattern. PHP forms the context for all the patterns that this book examines.

I referred to object-capable languages earlier in this section. You could code in PHP without defining any classes at all. With a few notable exceptions, however, objects and object-oriented design lie at the heart of most PHP projects and libraries.

Summary

In this chapter, I introduced design patterns, showed you their structure (using the Gang of Four form), and suggested some reasons why you might want to use design patterns in your scripts.

It is important to remember that design patterns are not snap-on solutions that can be combined like components to build a project. They are suggested approaches to common problems. These solutions embody some key design principles. It is these that we will examine in the next chapter.

## CHAPTER 8

Some Pattern Principles

Although design patterns simply describe solutions to problems, they tend to emphasize solutions that promote reusability and flexibility. To achieve this, they manifest some key object-oriented design principles. We will encounter some of them in this chapter and in more detail throughout the rest of the book.

This chapter will cover the following topics:

- *Composition*: How to use object aggregation to achieve greater flexibility than you could with inheritance alone

- *Decoupling*: How to reduce dependency between elements in a system

- *The power of the interface*: Patterns and polymorphism

- *Pattern categories*: The types of patterns that this book will cover

The Pattern Revelation

I first started working with objects in the Java language. As you might expect, it took a while before some concepts clicked. When it did happen, though, it happened very fast, almost with the force of revelation. The elegance of inheritance and encapsulation bowled me over. I could sense that this was a different way of defining and building systems. I *got* polymorphism, working with a type and switching implementations at runtime. It seemed to me that this understanding would solve most of my design problems and help me design beautiful and elegant systems.

All the books on my desk at the time focused on language features and the very many APIs available to the Java programmer. Beyond a brief definition of polymorphism, there was little attempt to examine design strategies.

M. Zandstra, *PHP 8 Objects, Patterns, and Practice*, https://doi.org/10.1007/978-1-4842-6791-2_8

Language features alone do not engender object-oriented design. Although my projects fulfilled their functional requirements, the kind of design that inheritance, encapsulation, and polymorphism had seemed to offer continued to elude me.

My inheritance hierarchies grew wider and deeper as I attempted to build a new class for every eventuality. The structure of my systems made it hard to convey messages from one tier to another without giving intermediate classes too much awareness of their surroundings, binding them into the application and making them unusable in new contexts.

It wasn't until I discovered *Design Patterns: Elements of Reusable Object-Oriented Software* (Addison-Wesley Professional, 1995), otherwise known as *the Gang of Four book*, that I realized I had missed an entire design dimension. By that time, I had already discovered some of the core patterns for myself, but others contributed to a new way of thinking.

I found that I had overprivileged inheritance in my designs, trying to build too much functionality into my classes. But where else can functionality go in an object-oriented system?

I found the answer in composition. Software components can be defined at runtime by combining objects in flexible relationships. The Gang of Four boiled this down into a principle: "favor composition over inheritance." The patterns described ways in which objects could be combined at runtime to achieve a level of flexibility impossible in an inheritance tree alone.

Composition and Inheritance

Inheritance is a powerful way of designing for changing circumstances or contexts. It can limit flexibility, however, especially when classes take on multiple responsibilities.

The Problem

As you know, child classes inherit the methods and properties of their parents (as long as they are protected or public elements). You can use this fact to design child classes that provide specialized functionality.

Figure 8-1 presents a simple example using the UML.

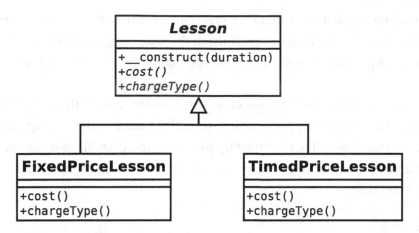

Figure 8-1. *A parent class and two child classes*

The abstract Lesson class in Figure 8-1 models a lesson in a college. It defines abstract cost() and chargeType() methods. The diagram shows two implementing classes, FixedPriceLesson and TimedPriceLesson, which provide distinct charging mechanisms for lessons.

Using this inheritance scheme, I can switch between lesson implementations. Client code will know only that it is dealing with a Lesson object, so the details of cost will be transparent.

What happens, though, if I introduce a new set of specializations? I need to handle lectures and seminars. Because these organize enrollment and lesson notes in different ways, they require separate classes. Now I have two forces that operate upon my design. I need to handle pricing strategies and separate lectures and seminars.

Figure 8-2 shows a brute-force solution.

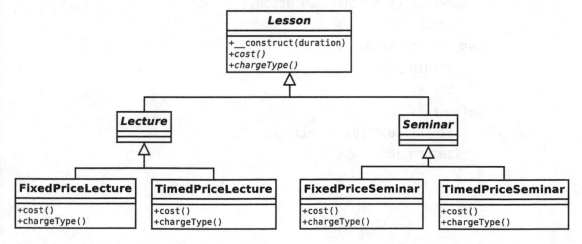

Figure 8-2. *A poor inheritance structure*

255

Figure 8-2 shows a hierarchy that is clearly faulty. I can no longer use the inheritance tree to manage my pricing mechanisms without duplicating great swathes of functionality. The pricing strategies are mirrored across the Lecture and Seminar class families.

At this stage, I might consider using conditional statements in the Lesson superclass, removing those unfortunate duplications. Essentially, I remove the pricing logic from the inheritance tree altogether, moving it up into the superclass. This is the reverse of the usual refactoring, where you replace a conditional with polymorphism. Here is an amended Lesson class:

```
// listing 08.01
abstract class Lesson
{
    public const FIXED = 1;
    public const TIMED = 2;

    public function __construct(protected int $duration, private int
    $costtype = 1)
    {
    }

    public function cost(): int
    {
        switch ($this->costtype) {
            case self::TIMED:
                return (5 * $this->duration);
                break;
            case self::FIXED:
                return 30;
                break;
            default:
                $this->costtype = self::FIXED;
                return 30;
        }
    }
}
```

```
    public function chargeType(): string
    {
        switch ($this->costtype) {
            case self::TIMED:
                return "hourly rate";
                break;
            case self::FIXED:
                return "fixed rate";
                break;
            default:
                $this->costtype = self::FIXED;
                return "fixed rate";
        }
    }

    // more lesson methods...
}

// listing 08.02
class Lecture extends Lesson
{
    // Lecture-specific implementations ...
}

// listing 08.03
class Seminar extends Lesson
{
    // Seminar-specific implementations ...
}
```

Here's how I might work with these classes:

```
// listing 08.04
$lecture = new Lecture(5, Lesson::FIXED);
print "{$lecture->cost()} ({$lecture->chargeType()})\n";

$seminar = new Seminar(3, Lesson::TIMED);
print "{$seminar->cost()} ({$seminar->chargeType()})\n";
```

And here's the output:

```
30 (fixed rate)
15 (hourly rate)
```

You can see the new class diagram in Figure 8-3.

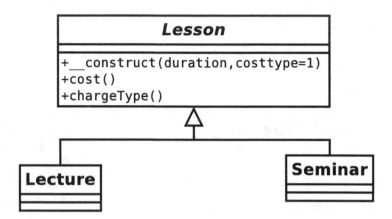

Figure 8-3. *Inheritance hierarchy improved by removing cost calculations from subclasses*

I have made the class structure much more manageable, but at a cost. Using conditionals in this code is a retrograde step. Usually, you would try to replace a conditional statement with polymorphism. Here, I have done the opposite. As you can see, this has forced me to duplicate the conditional statement across the chargeType() and cost() methods.

I seem doomed to duplicate code.

Using Composition

I can use the Strategy pattern to compose my way out of trouble. Strategy is used to move a set of algorithms into a separate type. By moving cost calculations, I can simplify the Lesson type. You can see this in Figure 8-4.

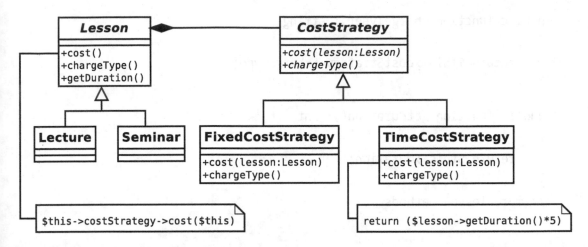

Figure 8-4. *Moving algorithms into a separate type*

I create an abstract class, CostStrategy, which defines the abstract methods, cost()
and chargeType(). The cost() method requires an instance of Lesson, which it will
use to generate cost data. I provide two concrete subclasses for CostStrategy. Lesson
objects work only with the CostStrategy type, not a specific implementation, so I can
add new cost algorithms at any time by subclassing CostStrategy. This would require
no changes at all to any Lesson classes.

Here's a simplified version of the new Lesson class illustrated in Figure 8-4:

```
// listing 08.05
abstract class Lesson
{

    public function __construct(private int $duration, private CostStrategy
    $costStrategy)
    {
    }

    public function cost(): int
    {
        return $this->costStrategy->cost($this);
    }
}
```

259

```
    public function chargeType(): string
    {
        return $this->costStrategy->chargeType();
    }

    public function getDuration(): int
    {
        return $this->duration;
    }
    // more lesson methods...
}

// listing 08.06
class Lecture extends Lesson
{
    // Lecture-specific implementations ...
}

// listing 08.07
class Seminar extends Lesson
{
    // Seminar-specific implementations ...
}
```

The Lesson class requires a CostStrategy object, which it stores as a property. The Lesson::cost() method simply invokes CostStrategy::cost(). Equally, Lesson::chargeType() invokes CostStrategy::chargeType(). This explicit invocation of another object's method in order to fulfill a request is known as delegation. In my example, the CostStrategy object is the delegate of Lesson. The Lesson class washes its hands of responsibility for cost calculations and passes on the task to a CostStrategy implementation. Here, it is caught in the act of delegation:

```
// listing 08.08
public function cost(): int
{
    return $this->costStrategy->cost($this);
}
```

Here is the CostStrategy class, together with its implementing children:

```
// listing 08.09
abstract class CostStrategy
{
    abstract public function cost(Lesson $lesson): int;
    abstract public function chargeType(): string;
}
```

```
// listing 08.10
class TimedCostStrategy extends CostStrategy
{
    public function cost(Lesson $lesson): int
    {
        return ($lesson->getDuration() * 5);
    }

    public function chargeType(): string
    {
        return "hourly rate";
    }
}
```

```
// listing 08.11
class FixedCostStrategy extends CostStrategy
{
    public function cost(Lesson $lesson): int
    {
        return 30;
    }
    public function chargeType(): string
    {
        return "fixed rate";
    }
}
```

I can change the way that any `Lesson` object calculates cost by passing it a different `CostStrategy` object at runtime. This approach then makes for highly flexible code. Rather than building functionality into my code structures statically, I can combine and recombine objects dynamically:

```
// listing 08.12
$lessons[] = new Seminar(4, new TimedCostStrategy());
$lessons[] = new Lecture(4, new FixedCostStrategy());

foreach ($lessons as $lesson) {
    print "lesson charge {$lesson->cost()}. ";
    print "Charge type: {$lesson->chargeType()}\n";
}

lesson charge 20. Charge type: hourly rate
lesson charge 30. Charge type: fixed rate
```

As you can see, one effect of this structure is that I have focused the responsibilities of my classes. `CostStrategy` objects are responsible solely for calculating cost, and `Lesson` objects manage lesson data.

So, composition can make your code more flexible because objects can be combined to handle tasks dynamically in many more ways than you can anticipate in an inheritance hierarchy alone. There can be a penalty with regard to readability, though. Because composition tends to result in more types, with relationships that aren't fixed with the same predictability as they are in inheritance relationships, it can be slightly harder to digest the relationships in a system.

Decoupling

You saw in Chapter 6 that it makes sense to build independent components. A system with highly interdependent classes can be hard to maintain. A change in one location can require a cascade of related changes across the system.

The Problem

Reusability is one of the key objectives of object-oriented design, and tight coupling is its enemy. You can diagnose tight coupling when you see that a change to one component of a system necessitates many changes elsewhere. You should aspire to create independent components, so that you can make changes without a domino effect of unintended consequences. When you alter a component, the extent to which it is independent is related to the likelihood that your changes will cause other parts of your system to fail.

You saw an example of tight coupling in Figure 8-2. Because the cost logic was mirrored across the Lecture and Seminar types, a change to TimedPriceLecture would necessitate a parallel change to the same logic in TimedPriceSeminar. By updating one class and not the other, I would break my system—without any warning from the PHP engine. My first solution, using a conditional statement, produced a similar dependency between the cost() and chargeType() methods.

By applying the Strategy pattern, I distilled my cost algorithms into the CostStrategy type, locating them behind a common interface and implementing each only once.

Coupling of another sort can occur when many classes in a system are embedded explicitly into a platform or environment. Let's say that you are building a system that works with a MySQL database, for example. You might use methods such as mysqli::query() to speak to the database server.

Should you be required to deploy the system on a server that does not support MySQL, you *could* convert your entire project to use SQLite. You would be forced to make changes throughout your code, though, and face the prospect of maintaining two parallel versions of your application.

The problem here is not the system's dependency on an external platform. Such a dependency is inevitable. You need to work with code that speaks to a database. The problem comes when such code is scattered throughout a project. Talking to databases is not the primary responsibility of most classes in a system, so the best strategy is to extract such code and group it together behind a common interface. In this way, you promote the independence of your classes. At the same time, by concentrating your gateway code in one place, you make it much easier to switch to a new platform without disturbing your wider system. This process, the hiding of implementation behind a clean interface, is known as *encapsulation*. The Doctrine database library solves this problem with the DBAL (database abstraction layer) project. This provides a single point of access for multiple databases.

The DriverManager class provides a static method called getConnection() that accepts a parameter array. According to the makeup of this array, it returns a particular implementation of an interface called Doctrine\DBAL\Driver. You can see the class structure in Figure 8-5.

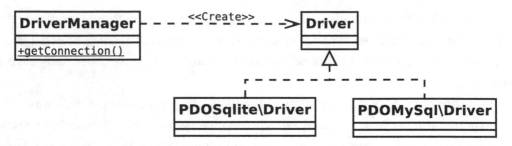

Figure 8-5. *The DBAL package decouples client code from database objects*

Note   Static attributes and operations should be underlined in the UML.

The DBAL package, then, lets you decouple your application code from the specifics of your database platform. You should be able to run a single system with MySQL, SQLite, MSSQL, and others without changing a line of code (apart from your configuring parameters, of course).

Loosening Your Coupling

To handle database code flexibly, you should decouple the application logic from the specifics of the database platform it uses. You will see lots of opportunities for this kind of separation of components in your own projects.

Imagine, for example, that the Lesson system must incorporate a registration component to add new lessons to the system. As part of the registration procedure, an administrator should be notified when a lesson is added. The system's users can't agree whether this notification should be sent by mail or by text message. In fact, they're so argumentative that you suspect they might want to switch to a new mode of communication in the future. What's more, they want to be notified of all sorts of things, so that a change to the notification mode in one place will mean a similar alteration in many other places.

If you've hard-coded calls to a Mailer class or a Texter class, then your system is tightly coupled to a particular notification mode, just as it would be tightly coupled to a database platform by the use of a specialized database API.

Here is some code that hides the implementation details of a notifier from the system that uses it:

```
// listing 08.13
class RegistrationMgr
{
    public function register(Lesson $lesson): void
    {
        // do something with this Lesson

        // now tell someone
        $notifier = Notifier::getNotifier();
        $notifier->inform("new lesson: cost ({$lesson->cost()})");
    }
}
```

```
// listing 08.14
abstract class Notifier
{
    public static function getNotifier(): Notifier
    {
        // acquire concrete class according to
        // configuration or other logic

        if (rand(1, 2) === 1) {
            return new MailNotifier();
        } else {
            return new TextNotifier();
        }
    }

    abstract public function inform($message): void;
}
```

```
// listing 08.15
class MailNotifier extends Notifier
{
    public function inform($message): void
    {
        print "MAIL notification: {$message}\n";
    }
}
```

```
// listing 08.16
class TextNotifier extends Notifier
{
    public function inform($message): void
    {
        print "TEXT notification: {$message}\n";
    }
}
```

I create RegistrationMgr, a sample client for my Notifier classes. The Notifier class is abstract, but it does implement a static method, getNotifier(), which fetches a concrete Notifier object (TextNotifier or MailNotifier). In a real project, the choice of Notifier would be determined by a flexible mechanism, such as a configuration file. Here, I cheat and make the choice randomly. MailNotifier and TextNotifier do nothing more than print out the message they are passed along with an identifier to show which one has been called.

Notice how the knowledge of which concrete Notifier should be used has been focused in the Notifier::getNotifier() method. I could send notifier messages from a hundred different parts of my system, and a change in Notifier would only have to be made in that one method.

Here is some code that calls the RegistrationMgr:

```
// listing 08.17
$lessons1 = new Seminar(4, new TimedCostStrategy());
$lessons2 = new Lecture(4, new FixedCostStrategy());
$mgr = new  RegistrationMgr();
$mgr->register($lessons1);
$mgr->register($lessons2);
```

And here's the output from a typical run:

```
TEXT notification: new lesson: cost (20)
MAIL notification: new lesson: cost (30)
```

Figure 8-6 shows these classes.

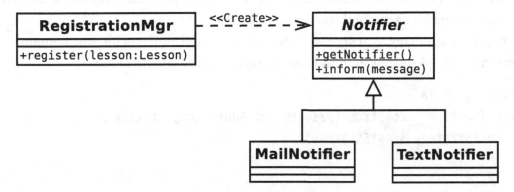

Figure 8-6. *The Notifier class separates client code from Notifier implementations*

Notice how similar the structure in Figure 8-6 is to that formed by the Doctrine components shown in Figure 8-5.

Code to an Interface, Not to an Implementation

This principle is one of the all-pervading themes of this book. You saw in Chapter 6 (and in the last section) that you can hide different implementations behind the common interface defined in a superclass. Client code can then require an object of the superclass's type rather than that of an implementing class, unconcerned by the specific implementation it is actually getting.

Parallel conditional statements, like the ones I rooted out from Lesson::cost() and Lesson::chargeType(), are a common sign that polymorphism is needed. They make code hard to maintain because a change in one conditional expression necessitates a change in its siblings. Conditional statements are occasionally said to implement a "simulated inheritance."

By placing the cost algorithms in separate classes that implement CostStrategy, I remove duplication. I also make it much easier should I need to add new cost strategies in the future.

From the perspective of client code, it is often a good idea to require abstract or general types in your methods' parameters. By requiring more specific types, you could limit the flexibility of your code at runtime.

Having said that, of course, the level of generality you choose in your argument hints is a matter of judgment. Make your choice too general, and your method may become less safe. If you require the specific functionality of a subtype, then accepting a differently equipped sibling into a method could be risky.

Still, make your choice of argument hint too restricted, and you lose the benefits of polymorphism. Take a look at this altered extract from the Lesson class:

```
// listing 08.18
public function __construct(private int $duration, private
FixedCostStrategy $costStrategy)
{
}
```

There are two issues arising from the design decision in this example. First, the Lesson object is now tied to a specific cost strategy, which closes down my ability to compose dynamic components. Second, the explicit reference to the FixedPriceStrategy class forces me to maintain that particular implementation.

By requiring a common interface, I can combine a Lesson object with any CostStrategy implementation:

```
// listing 08.19
public function __construct(private int $duration, private CostStrategy
$costStrategy)
{
}
```

I have, in other words, decoupled my Lesson class from the specifics of cost calculation. All that matters is the interface and the guarantee that the provided object will honor it.

Of course, coding to an interface can often simply defer the question of how to instantiate your objects. When I say that a Lesson object can be combined with any CostStrategy interface at runtime, I beg the question, "But where does the CostStrategy object come from?"

When you create an abstract superclass, there is always the issue of how its children should be instantiated. Which child do you choose and according to which condition? This subject forms a category of its own in the Gang of Four pattern catalog, and I will examine this further in the next chapter.

The Concept That Varies

It's easy to interpret a design decision once it has been made, but how do you decide where to start?

The Gang of Four recommends that you "encapsulate the concept that varies." In terms of my lesson example, the varying concept is the cost algorithm. Not only is the cost calculation one of two possible strategies in the example, but it is obviously a candidate for expansion: special offers, overseas student rates, introductory discounts, all sorts of possibilities present themselves.

I quickly established that subclassing for this variation was inappropriate, and I resorted to a conditional statement. By bringing my variation into the same class, I underlined its suitability for encapsulation.

The Gang of Four recommends that you actively seek varying elements in your classes and assess their suitability for encapsulation in a new type. Each alternative in a suspect conditional may be extracted to form a class that extends a common abstract parent. This new type can then be used by the class or classes from which it was extracted. This has the following effects:

- Focusing responsibility

- Promoting flexibility through composition

- Making inheritance hierarchies more compact and focused

- Reducing duplication

So how do you spot variation? One sign is the misuse of inheritance. This might include inheritance deployed according to multiple forces at one time (e.g., lecture/seminar and fixed/timed cost). It might also include subclassing on an algorithm where the algorithm is incidental to the core responsibility of the type. The other sign of variation suitable for encapsulation is, as you have seen, a conditional expression.

Patternitis

One problem for which there is no pattern is the unnecessary or inappropriate use of patterns. This has earned patterns a bad name in some quarters. Because pattern solutions are neat, it is tempting to apply them wherever you see fit, whether they truly fulfill a need or not.

The eXtreme Programming (XP) methodology offers a couple of principles that might apply here. The first is, "You aren't going to need it" (often abbreviated to YAGNI). This is generally applied to application features, but it also makes sense for patterns.

When I build large environments in PHP, I tend to split my application into layers, separating application logic from presentation and persistence layers. I use all sorts of core and enterprise patterns in conjunction with one another.

When I am asked to build a feedback form for a small business website, however, I may simply use procedural code in a single-page script. I do not need enormous amounts of flexibility; I won't be building on the initial release. I don't need to use patterns that address problems in larger systems. Instead, I apply the second XP principle: "Do the simplest thing that works."

When you work with a pattern catalog, the structure and process of the solution are what stick in the mind, consolidated by the code example. Before applying a pattern, though, pay close attention to the problem, or "when to use it," section and then read up on the pattern's consequences. In some contexts, the cure may be worse than the disease.

The Patterns

This book is not a pattern catalog. Nevertheless, in the coming chapters, I will introduce a few of the key patterns in use at the moment, providing PHP implementations and discussing them in the broad context of PHP programming.

The patterns described will be drawn from key catalogs, including *Design Patterns: Elements of Reusable Object-Oriented Software* (Addison-Wesley Professional, 1995), *Patterns of Enterprise Application Architecture* by Martin Fowler (Addison-Wesley Professional, 2002), and *Core J2EE Patterns: Best Practices and Design Strategies* (Prentice Hall, 2001) by Alur et al. I use the Gang of Four's categorization as a starting point, dividing patterns into five categories, as follows.

Patterns for Generating Objects

These patterns are concerned with the instantiation of objects. This is an important category given the principle, "Code to an interface." If you are working with abstract parent classes in your design, then you must develop strategies for instantiating objects from concrete subclasses. It is these objects that will be passed around your system.

Patterns for Organizing Objects and Classes

These patterns help you to organize the compositional relationships of your objects. More simply, these patterns show how you combine objects and classes.

Task-Oriented Patterns

These patterns describe the mechanisms by which classes and objects cooperate to achieve objectives.

Enterprise Patterns

I look at some patterns that describe typical Internet programming problems and solutions. Drawn largely from *Patterns of Enterprise Application Architecture* and *Core J2EE Patterns: Best Practices and Design Strategies*, the patterns deal with presentation and application logic.

Database Patterns

This section provides an examination of patterns that help with storing and retrieving data and with mapping objects to and from databases.

Summary

In this chapter, I examined some of the principles that underpin many design patterns. I looked at the use of composition to enable object combination and recombination at runtime, resulting in more flexible structures than would be available using inheritance alone. I also introduced you to decoupling, the practice of extracting software components from their context to make them more generally applicable. Finally, I reviewed the importance of interface as a means of decoupling clients from the details of implementation.

In the coming chapters, I will examine some design patterns in detail.

CHAPTER 9

Generating Objects

Creating objects is a messy business. So, many object-oriented designs deal with nice, clean abstract classes, taking advantage of the impressive flexibility afforded by polymorphism (the switching of concrete implementations at runtime). To achieve this flexibility, though, I must devise strategies for object generation. This is the topic I will look at in this chapter.

This chapter will cover the following patterns:

- *The Singleton pattern*: A special class that generates one—and only one—object instance

- *The Factory Method pattern*: Building an inheritance hierarchy of creator classes

- *The Abstract Factory pattern*: Grouping the creation of functionally related products

- *The Prototype pattern*: Using `clone` to generate objects

- *The Service Locator pattern*: Asking your system for objects

- *The Dependency Injection pattern*: Letting your system give you objects

Problems and Solutions in Generating Objects

Object creation can be a weak point in object-oriented design. In the previous chapter, you saw the principle, "Code to an interface, not to an implementation." To this end, you are encouraged to work with abstract supertypes in your classes. This makes code more flexible, allowing you to use objects instantiated from different concrete subclasses at runtime. This has the side effect that object instantiation is deferred.

© Matt Zandstra 2021
M. Zandstra, *PHP 8 Objects, Patterns, and Practice*, https://doi.org/10.1007/978-1-4842-6791-2_9

Here's an abstract class that accepts a name string and instantiates a particular object:

```
// listing 09.01
abstract class Employee
{

    public function __construct(protected string $name)
    {
    }

    abstract public function fire(): void;
}
```

This is a concrete class that extends Employee:

```
// listing 09.02
class Minion extends Employee
{
    public function fire(): void
    {
        print "{$this->name}: I'll clear my desk\n";
    }
}
```

Now, here's a client class that works with Minion objects:

```
// listing 09.03
class NastyBoss
{
    private array $employees = [];
    public function addEmployee(string $employeeName): void
    {
        $this->employees[] = new Minion($employeeName);
    }

    public function projectFails(): void
    {
        if (count($this->employees) > 0) {
```

```
        $emp = array_pop($this->employees);
        $emp->fire();
    }
  }
}
```

Time to put the code through its paces:

```
// listing 09.04
$boss = new NastyBoss();
$boss->addEmployee("harry");
$boss->addEmployee("bob");
$boss->addEmployee("mary");
$boss->projectFails();
```

Here is the output:

```
mary: I'll clear my desk
```

As you can see, I define an abstract base class, Employee, with a downtrodden implementation, Minion. Given a name string, the NastyBoss::addEmployee() method instantiates a new Minion object. Whenever a NastyBoss object runs into trouble (via the NastyBoss::projectFails() method), it looks for a Minion to fire.

By instantiating a Minion object directly in the NastyBoss class, we limit flexibility. If a NastyBoss object could work with *any* instance of the Employee type, we could make our code amenable to variation at runtime as we add more Employee specializations. You should find the polymorphism in Figure 9-1 familiar.

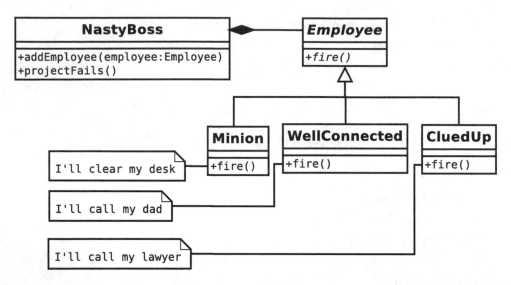

Figure 9-1. *Working with an abstract type enables polymorphism*

If the NastyBoss class does not instantiate a Minion object, where does it come from? Authors often duck out of this problem by constraining an argument type in a method declaration and then conveniently omitting to show the instantiation in anything other than a test context:

```
// listing 09.05
class NastyBoss
{
    private array $employees = [];

    public function addEmployee(Employee $employee): void
    {
        $this->employees[] = $employee;
    }

    public function projectFails(): void
    {
        if (count($this->employees)) {
            $emp = array_pop($this->employees);
            $emp->fire();
        }
    }
}
```

```
// listing 09.06
class CluedUp extends Employee
{
    public function fire(): void
    {
        print "{$this->name}: I'll call my lawyer\n";
    }
}

// listing 09.07
$boss = new NastyBoss();
$boss->addEmployee(new Minion("harry"));
$boss->addEmployee(new CluedUp("bob"));
$boss->addEmployee(new Minion("mary"));
$boss->projectFails();
$boss->projectFails();
$boss->projectFails();

mary: I'll clear my desk
bob: I'll call my lawyer
harry: I'll clear my desk
```

Although this version of the NastyBoss class works with the Employee type, and therefore benefits from polymorphism, I still haven't defined a strategy for object creation. Instantiating objects is a dirty business, but it has to be done. This chapter is about classes and objects that work with concrete classes, so that the rest of your classes do not have to.

If there is a principle to be found here, it is "delegate object instantiation." I did this implicitly in the previous example by demanding that an Employee object be passed to the NastyBoss::addEmployee() method. I could, however, equally delegate to a separate class or method that takes responsibility for generating Employee objects. Here, I add a static method to the Employee class that implements a strategy for object creation:

```
// listing 09.08
abstract class Employee
{
    private static $types = ['Minion', 'CluedUp', 'WellConnected'];
```

```
    public static function recruit(string $name): Employee
    {
        $num = rand(1, count(self::$types)) - 1;
        $class = __NAMESPACE __ . "\\" . self::$types[$num];
        return new $class($name);
    }

    public function __construct(protected string $name)
    {
    }

    abstract public function fire(): void;
}

// listing 09.09
class WellConnected extends Employee
{
    public function fire(): void
    {
        print "{$this->name}: I'll call my dad\n";
    }
}
```

As you can see, this takes a name string and uses it to instantiate a particular Employee subtype at random. I can now delegate the details of instantiation to the Employee class's recruit() method:

```
// listing 09.10
$boss = new NastyBoss();
$boss->addEmployee(Employee::recruit("harry"));
$boss->addEmployee(Employee::recruit("bob"));
$boss->addEmployee(Employee::recruit("mary"));
```

You saw a simple example of such a class in Chapter 4. I placed a static method in the ShopProduct class called getInstance().

Note   I use the term "factory" frequently in this chapter. A factory is a class or method with responsibility for generating objects.

---

getInstance() is responsible for generating the correct ShopProduct subclass based on a database query. The ShopProduct class, therefore, has a dual role. It defines the ShopProduct type, but it also acts as a factory for concrete ShopProduct objects:

```
// listing 09.11
public static function getInstance(int $id, \PDO $pdo): ShopProduct
{
    $stmt = $pdo->prepare("select * from products where id=?");
    $result = $stmt->execute([$id]);
    $row = $stmt->fetch();
    if (empty($row)) {
        return null;
    }
    if ($row['type'] == "book") {
        // instantiate a BookProduct object
    } elseif ($row['type'] == "cd") {
        // instantiate a CdProduct object
    } else {
        // instantiate a ShopProduct object
    }
    $product->setId((int) $row['id']);
    $product->setDiscount((int) $row['discount']);
    return $product;
}
```

The getInstance() method uses a large if/else statement to determine which subclass to instantiate. Conditionals like this are quite common in factory code. Although you should attempt to excise large conditional statements from your projects, doing so often has the effect of pushing the conditional back to the moment at which an object is generated. This is not generally a serious problem because you remove parallel conditionals from your code in pushing the decision-making back to this point.

In this chapter, then, I will examine some of the key Gang of Four patterns for generating objects.

The Singleton Pattern

The global variable is one of the great bugbears of the object-oriented programmer. The reasons should be familiar to you by now. Global variables tie classes into their context, undermining encapsulation (see Chapters 6 and 8 for more on this). A class that relies on global variables becomes impossible to pull out of one application and use in another, without first ensuring that the new application itself defines the same global variables.

Although this is undesirable, the unprotected nature of global variables can be a greater problem. Once you start relying on global variables, it is perhaps just a matter of time before one of your libraries declares a global that clashes with another declared elsewhere. You have seen already that, if you are not using namespaces, PHP is vulnerable to class name clashes. But this is much worse. PHP will not warn you when globals collide. The first you will know about it is when your script begins to behave oddly. Worse still, you may not notice any issues at all in your development environment. By using globals, though, you potentially leave your users exposed to new and interesting conflicts when they attempt to deploy your library alongside others.

Globals remain a temptation, however. This is because there are times when the sin inherent in global access seems a price worth paying in order to give all of your classes access to an object.

As I hinted, namespaces provide some protection from this. You can at least scope variables to a package, which means that third-party libraries are less likely to clash with your own system. Even so, the risk of collision exists within the namespace itself.

Note   In addition to variables, constants and functions are also scoped to namespaces. When a variable, constant, or function is invoked without an explicit namespace, PHP first looks for it locally and then in the global namespace.

The Problem

Well-designed systems generally pass object instances around via method calls. Each class retains its independence from the wider context, collaborating with other parts of the system via clear lines of communication. Sometimes, though, you find that this forces you to use some classes as conduits for objects that do not concern them, introducing dependencies in the name of good design.

Imagine a Preferences class that holds application-level information. We might use a Preferences object to store data such as DSN strings (Data Source Names are strings that hold the information needed to connect to a database), URL roots, file paths, and so on. This is the sort of information that will vary from installation to installation. The object may also be used as a notice board, a central location for messages that could be set or retrieved by otherwise unrelated objects in a system.

Passing a Preferences object around from object to object may not always be a good idea. Many classes that do not otherwise use the object could be forced to accept it simply so that they could pass it on to the objects that they work with. This is just another kind of coupling.

You also need to be sure that all objects in your system are working with the *same* Preferences object. You do not want objects setting values on one object, while others read from an entirely different one.

Let's distill the forces in this problem:

- A Preferences object should be available to any object in your system.

- A Preferences object should not be stored in a global variable, which can be overwritten.

- There should be no more than one Preferences object in play in the system. This means that *object Y* can set a property in the Preferences object, and *object Z* can retrieve the same property, without either one talking to the other directly (assuming both have access to the Preferences object).

Implementation

To address this problem, I can start by asserting control over object instantiation. Here, I create a class that cannot be instantiated from outside of itself. That may sound difficult, but it's simply a matter of defining a private constructor:

```
// listing 09.12
class Preferences
{
    private array $props = [];
```

```
    private function __construct()
    {
    }

    public function setProperty(string $key, string $val): void
    {
        $this->props[$key] = $val;
    }

    public function getProperty(string $key): string
    {
        return $this->props[$key];
    }
}
```

Of course, at this point, the Preferences class is entirely unusable. I have taken access restriction to an absurd level. Because the constructor is declared private, no client code can instantiate an object from it. The setProperty() and getProperty() methods are therefore redundant.

Here, I use a static method and a static property to mediate object instantiation:

```
// listing 09.13
class Preferences
{
    private array $props = [];
    private static Preferences $instance;
    private function __construct()
    {
    }

    public static function getInstance(): Preferences
    {
        if (empty(self::$instance)) {
            self::$instance = new Preferences();
        }
        return self::$instance;
    }
```

```php
    public function setProperty(string $key, string $val): void
    {
        $this->props[$key] = $val;
    }

    public function getProperty(string $key): string
    {
        return $this->props[$key];
    }
}
```

The $instance property is private and static, so it cannot be accessed from outside the class. The getInstance() method has access, though. Because getInstance() is public and static, it can be called via the class from anywhere in a script:

```php
// listing 09.14
$pref = Preferences::getInstance();
$pref->setProperty("name", "matt");

unset($pref); // remove the reference

$pref2 = Preferences::getInstance();
print $pref2->getProperty("name") . "\n"; // demonstrate value is not lost
```

The output is the single value we added to the Preferences object initially, available through a separate access:

```
matt
```

A static method cannot access object properties because it is, by definition, invoked in a class and not an object context. It can, however, access a static property. When getInstance() is called, I check the Preferences::$instance property. If it is empty, then I create an instance of the Preferences class and store it in the property. Then I return the instance to the calling code. Because the static getInstance() method is part of the Preferences class, I have no problem instantiating a Preferences object, even though the constructor is private.

Figure 9-2 shows the Singleton pattern.

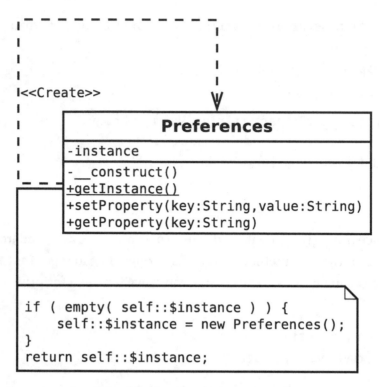

Figure 9-2. *An example of the Singleton pattern*

Consequences

So, how does the Singleton approach compare to using a global variable? First, the bad news. Both Singletons and global variables are prone to misuse. Because Singletons can be accessed from anywhere in a system, they can serve to create dependencies that can be hard to debug. Change a Singleton, and classes that use it may be affected. Dependencies are not a problem in themselves. After all, we create a dependency every time we declare that a method requires an argument of a particular type. The problem is that the global nature of the Singleton lets a programmer bypass the lines of communication defined by class interfaces. When a Singleton is used, the dependency is hidden away inside a method and not declared in its signature. This can make it harder to trace the relationships within a system. Singleton classes should therefore be deployed sparingly and with care.

Nevertheless, I think that moderate use of the Singleton pattern can improve the design of a system, saving you from horrible contortions as you pass objects unnecessarily around your system.

Singletons represent an improvement over global variables in an object-oriented context. You cannot overwrite a Singleton with the wrong kind of data. Furthermore, you can group operations and bundles of data together within a Singleton class, making it a much superior option to an associative array or a set of scalar variables.

Factory Method Pattern

Object-oriented design emphasizes the abstract class over the implementation. That is, it works with generalizations rather than specializations. The Factory Method pattern addresses the problem of how to create object instances when your code focuses on abstract types. The answer? Let specialist classes handle instantiation.

The Problem

Imagine a personal organizer project that manages Appointment objects, among other object types. Your business group has forged a relationship with another company, and you must communicate appointment data to it using a format called BloggsCal. The business group warns you that you may face yet more formats as time wears on, though.

Staying at the level of interface alone, you can identify two participants right away. You need a data encoder that converts your Appointment objects into a proprietary format. Let's call that class ApptEncoder. You need a manager class that will retrieve an encoder and maybe work with it to communicate with a third party. You might call that CommsManager. Using the terminology of the pattern, the CommsManager is the creator, and the ApptEncoder is the product. You can see this structure in Figure 9-3.

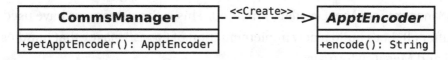

Figure 9-3. *Abstract creator and product classes*

How do you get your hands on a real concrete ApptEncoder, though?

You could demand that an ApptEncoder be passed to the CommsManager, but that simply defers your problem, and you want the buck to stop about here. Here, I instantiate a BloggsApptEncoder object directly within the CommsManager class:

```
// listing 09.15
abstract class ApptEncoder
{
    abstract public function encode(): string;
}

// listing 09.16
class BloggsApptEncoder extends ApptEncoder
{
    public function encode(): string
    {
        return "Appointment data encoded in BloggsCal format\n";
    }
}

// listing 09.17
class CommsManager
{
    public function getApptEncoder(): ApptEncoder
    {
        return new BloggsApptEncoder();
    }
}
```

The CommsManager class is responsible for generating BloggsApptEncoder objects. When the sands of corporate allegiance inevitably shift, and we are asked to convert our system to work with a new format called MegaCal, we can simply add a conditional into the CommsManager::getApptEncoder() method. This is the strategy we have used in the past, after all. Let's build a new implementation of CommsManager that handles both BloggsCal and MegaCal formats:

```
// listing 09.18
class CommsManager
{
    public const BLOGGS = 1;
    public const MEGA = 2;
    public function __construct(private int $mode)
```

```
    {
    }

    public function getApptEncoder(): ApptEncoder
    {
        switch ($this->mode) {
            case (self::MEGA):
                return new MegaApptEncoder();
            default:
                return new  BloggsApptEncoder();
        }
    }

}


// listing 09.19
class MegaApptEncoder extends ApptEncoder
{
    public function encode(): string
    {
        return "Appointment data encoded in MegaCal format\n";
    }
}

// listing 09.20
$man = new CommsManager(CommsManager::MEGA);
print (get_class($man->getApptEncoder())) . "\n";
$man = new CommsManager(CommsManager::BLOGGS);
print (get_class($man->getApptEncoder())) . "\n";
```

I use constant flags to define two modes in which the script might be run: MEGA and BLOGGS. I use a switch statement in the getApptEncoder() method to test the $mode property and instantiate the appropriate implementation of ApptEncoder.

There is little wrong with this approach. Conditionals are sometimes considered examples of bad "code smells," but object creation often requires a conditional at some point. You should be less sanguine if you see duplicate conditionals creeping into your code. The CommsManager class provides functionality for communicating calendar data.

Imagine that the protocols you work with require you to provide header and footer data to delineate each appointment. I can extend the previous example to support a getHeaderText() method:

```
// listing 09.21
class CommsManager
{
    public const BLOGGS = 1;
    public const MEGA = 2;

    public function __construct(private int $mode)
    {
    }

    public function getApptEncoder(): ApptEncoder
    {
        switch ($this->mode) {
            case (self::MEGA):
                return new MegaApptEncoder();
            default:
                return new BloggsApptEncoder();
        }
    }

    public function getHeaderText(): string
    {
        switch ($this->mode) {
            case (self::MEGA):
                return "MegaCal header\n";
            default:
                return "BloggsCal header\n";
        }
    }
}
```

As you can see, the need to support header output has forced me to duplicate the protocol conditional test. This will become unwieldy as I add new protocols, especially if I also add a getFooterText() method.

So, let's summarize the problem so far:

- I do not know until runtime the kind of object I need to produce (`BloggsApptEncoder` or `MegaApptEncoder`).

- I need to be able to add new product types with relative ease (SyncML support is just a new business deal away!).

- Each product type is associated with a context that requires other customized operations (e.g., `getHeaderText()`, `getFooterText()`).

Additionally, I am using conditional statements, and you have seen already that these are naturally replaceable by polymorphism. The Factory Method pattern enables you to use inheritance and polymorphism to encapsulate the creation of concrete products. In other words, you create a `CommsManager` subclass for each protocol, each one implementing the `getApptEncoder()` method.

Implementation

The Factory Method pattern splits creator classes from the products they are designed to generate. The creator is a factory class that defines a method for generating a product object. If no default implementation is provided, it is left to creator child classes to perform the instantiation. Typically, each creator subclass instantiates a parallel product child class.

I can redesignate `CommsManager` as an abstract class. That way, I keep a flexible superclass and put all my protocol-specific code in the concrete subclasses. You can see this alteration in Figure 9-4.

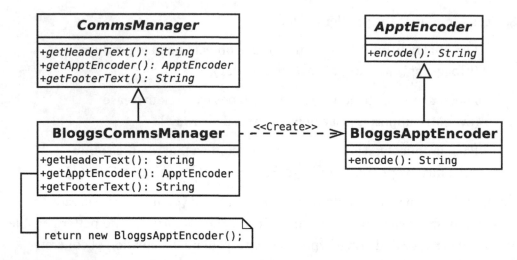

Figure 9-4. *Concrete creator and product classes*

Here's some simplified code:

```
// listing 09.22
abstract class ApptEncoder
{
    abstract public function encode(): string;
}

// listing 09.23
class BloggsApptEncoder extends ApptEncoder
{
    public function encode(): string
    {
        return "Appointment data encoded in BloggsCal format\n";
    }
}

// listing 09.24
abstract class CommsManager
{
    abstract public function getHeaderText(): string;
    abstract public function getApptEncoder(): ApptEncoder;
    abstract public function getFooterText(): string;
}
```

```
// listing 09.25
class BloggsCommsManager extends CommsManager
{
    public function getHeaderText(): string
    {
        return "BloggsCal header\n";
    }

    public function getApptEncoder(): ApptEncoder
    {
        return new BloggsApptEncoder();
    }

    public function getFooterText(): string
    {
        return "BloggsCal footer\n";
    }
}
```

```
// listing 09.26
$mgr = new BloggsCommsManager();
print $mgr->getHeaderText();
print $mgr->getApptEncoder()->encode();
print $mgr->getFooterText();
```

Here is the output:

```
BloggsCal header
Appointment data encoded in BloggsCal format
BloggsCal footer
```

So, when I am required to implement MegaCal, supporting it is simply a matter of writing a new implementation for my abstract classes. Figure 9-5 shows the MegaCal classes.

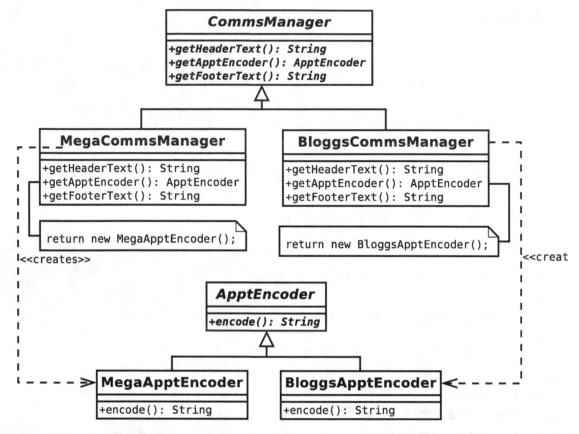

Figure 9-5. *Extending the design to support a new protocol*

Consequences

Notice that the creator classes mirror the product hierarchy. This is a common consequence of the Factory Method pattern and disliked by some as a special kind of code duplication. Another issue is the possibility that the pattern could encourage unnecessary subclassing. If your only reason for subclassing a creator is to deploy the Factory Method pattern, you may need to think again (that's why I introduced the header and footer constraints to the example here).

I have focused only on appointments in my example. If I extend it somewhat to include to-do items and contacts, I face a new problem. I need a structure that will handle sets of related implementations at one time.

The Factory Method pattern is often used with the Abstract Factory pattern, as you will see in the next section.

Abstract Factory Pattern

In large applications, you may need factories that produce related sets of classes. The Abstract Factory pattern addresses this problem.

The Problem

Let's look again at the organizer example. I manage encoding in two formats, BloggsCal and MegaCal. I can grow this structure horizontally by adding more encoding formats, but how can I grow vertically, adding encoders for different types of PIM objects? In fact, I have been working toward this pattern already.

In Figure 9-6, you can see the parallel families with which I will want to work. These are appointments (Appt), things to do (Ttd), and contacts (Contact).

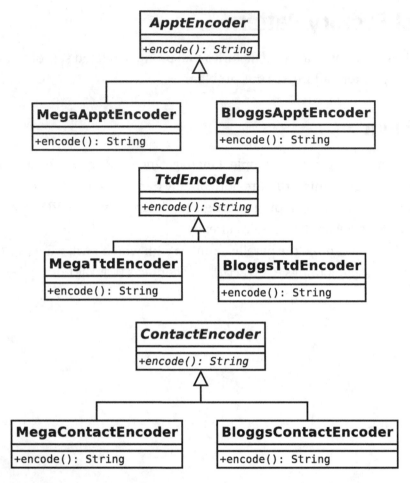

Figure 9-6. *Three product families*

The BloggsCal classes are unrelated to one another by inheritance (although they could implement a common interface), but they are functionally parallel. If the system is currently working with BloggsTtdEncoder, it should also be working with BloggsContactEncoder.

To see how I enforce this, you can begin with the interface, as I did with the Factory Method pattern (see Figure 9-7).

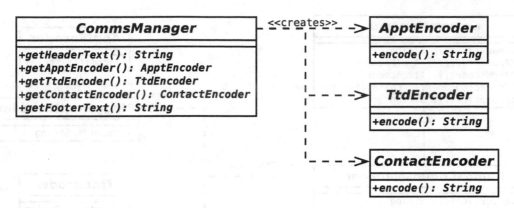

Figure 9-7. An abstract creator and its abstract products

Implementation

The abstract CommsManager class defines the interface for generating each of the three products (ApptEncoder, TtdEncoder, and ContactEncoder). You need to implement a concrete creator in order to actually generate the concrete products for a particular family. I illustrate that for the BloggsCal format in Figure 9-8.

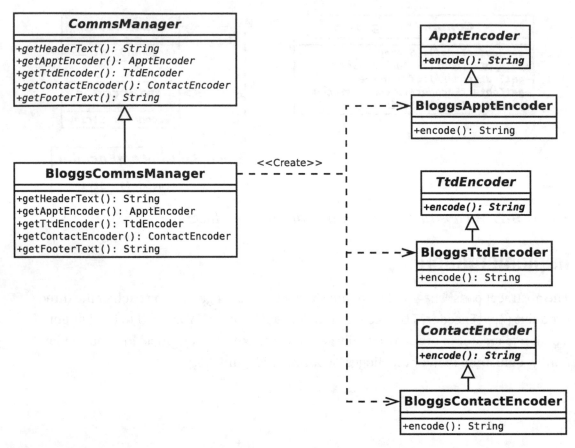

Figure 9-8. *Adding a concrete creator and some concrete products*

Here is a code version of CommsManager and BloggsCommsManager:

```
// listing 09.27
abstract class CommsManager
{
    abstract public function getHeaderText(): string;
    abstract public function getApptEncoder(): ApptEncoder;
    abstract public function getTtdEncoder(): TtdEncoder;
    abstract public function getContactEncoder(): ContactEncoder;
    abstract public function getFooterText(): string;
}
```

```
// listing 09.28
class BloggsCommsManager extends CommsManager
{
    public function getHeaderText(): string
    {
        return "BloggsCal header\n";
    }

    public function getApptEncoder(): ApptEncoder
    {
        return new BloggsApptEncoder();
    }
    public function getTtdEncoder(): TtdEncoder
    {
        return new BloggsTtdEncoder();
    }

    public function getContactEncoder(): ContactEncoder
    {
        return new BloggsContactEncoder();
    }

    public function getFooterText(): string
    {
        return "BloggsCal footer\n";
    }
}
```

Notice that I use the Factory Method pattern in this example. getContactEncoder() is abstract in CommsManager and implemented in BloggsCommsManager. Design patterns tend to work together in this way, one pattern creating the context that lends itself to another. In Figure 9-9, I add support for the MegaCal format.

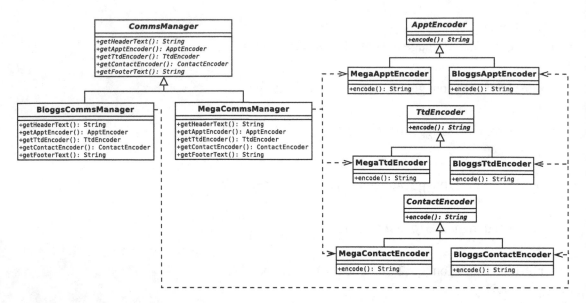

Figure 9-9. *Adding concrete creators and some concrete products*

Consequences

So, let's look at what this pattern buys:

- First, I decouple my system from the details of implementation.
  I can add or remove any number of encoding formats in my example
  without causing a knock-on effect.

- I enforce the grouping of functionally related elements of my system.
  So, by using `BloggsCommsManager`, I am guaranteed that I will work
  only with BloggsCal-related classes.

- Adding new products can be a pain. Not only do I have to create
  concrete implementations of the new product, but I also have
  to amend the abstract creator and every one of its concrete
  implementers in order to support it.

Many implementations of the Abstract Factory pattern use the Factory Method
pattern. This may be because most examples are written in Java or C++. PHP, however,
does not have to enforce a return type for a method (though it now can), which affords us
some flexibility that we might leverage.

Rather than create separate methods for each Factory Method, you can create a
single `make()` method that uses a flag argument to determine which object to return:

```
// listing 09.29
interface Encoder
{
    public function encode(): string;
}

// listing 09.30
abstract class CommsManager
{
    public const APPT    = 1;
    public const TTD     = 2;
    public const CONTACT = 3;
    abstract public function getHeaderText(): string;
    abstract public function make(int $flag_int): Encoder;
    abstract public function getFooterText(): string;
}

// listing 09.31
class BloggsCommsManager extends CommsManager
{
    public function getHeaderText(): string
    {
        return "BloggsCal header\n";
    }

    public function make(int $flag_int): Encoder
    {
        switch ($flag_int) {
            case self::APPT:
                return  new  BloggsApptEncoder();
            case self::CONTACT:
                return new BloggsContactEncoder();
            case self::TTD:
                return new BloggsTtdEncoder();
        }
    }
```

```
    public function getFooterText(): string
    {
        return "BloggsCal footer\n";
    }
}
```

As you can see, I have made the class interface more compact. I've done this at a considerable cost, though. In using a factory method, I define a clear interface and force all concrete factory objects to honor it. In using a single make() method, I must remember to support all product objects in all the concrete creators. I also introduce parallel conditionals, as each concrete creator must implement the same flag tests. A client class cannot be certain that concrete creators generate all the products because the internals of make() are a matter of choice in each case.

On the other hand, I can build more flexible creators. The base creator class can provide a make() method that guarantees a default implementation of each product family. Concrete children could then modify this behavior selectively. It would be up to implementing creator classes to call the default make() method after providing their own implementation.

You will see another variation on the Abstract Factory pattern in the next section.

Prototype

The emergence of parallel inheritance hierarchies can be a problem with the Factory Method pattern. This is a kind of coupling that makes some programmers uncomfortable. Every time you add a product family, you are forced to create an associated concrete creator (e.g., the BloggsCal encoders are matched by BloggsCommsManager). In a system that grows fast enough to encompass many products, maintaining this kind of relationship can quickly become tiresome.

One way of avoiding this dependency is to use PHP's clone keyword to duplicate existing concrete products. The concrete product classes themselves then become the basis of their own generation. This is the Prototype pattern. It enables you to replace inheritance with composition. This in turn promotes runtime flexibility and reduces the number of classes you must create.

The Problem

Imagine a Civilization-style web game in which units operate on a grid of tiles. Each tile can represent sea, plains, or forests. The terrain type constrains the movement and combat abilities of units occupying the tile. You might have a TerrainFactory object that serves up Sea, Forest, and Plains objects. You decide that you will allow the user to choose among radically different environments, so the Sea object is an abstract superclass implemented by MarsSea and EarthSea. Forest and Plains objects are similarly implemented. The forces here lend themselves to the Abstract Factory pattern. You have distinct product hierarchies (Sea, Plains, Forests), with strong family relationships cutting across inheritance (Earth, Mars). Figure 9-10 presents a class diagram that shows how you might deploy the Abstract Factory and Factory Method patterns to work with these products.

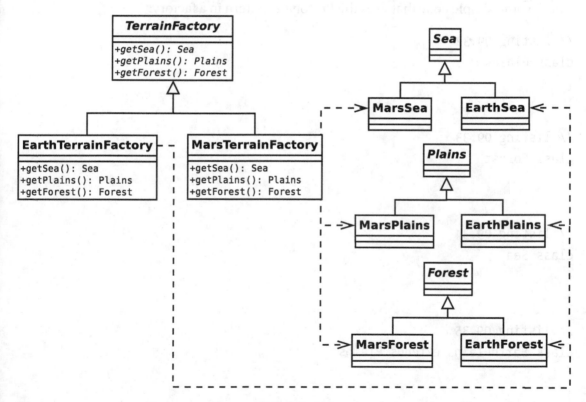

Figure 9-10. *Handling terrains with the Abstract Factory method*

As you can see, I rely on inheritance to group the terrain family for the products that a factory will generate. This is a workable solution, but it requires a large inheritance hierarchy, and it is relatively inflexible. When you do not want parallel inheritance hierarchies, and when you need to maximize runtime flexibility, the Prototype pattern can be used in a powerful variation on the Abstract Factory pattern.

Implementation

When you work with the Abstract Factory/Factory Method patterns, you must decide, at some point, which concrete creator you wish to use, probably by checking some kind of preference flag. As you must do this anyway, why not simply create a factory class that stores concrete products and then populate this during initialization? You can cut down on a couple of classes this way and, as you shall see, take advantage of other benefits. Here's some simple code that uses the Prototype pattern in a factory:

```
// listing 09.32
class Plains
{
}

// listing 09.33
class Forest
{
}

// listing 09.34
class Sea
{
}

// listing 09.35
class EarthPlains extends Plains
{
}
```

```php
// listing 09.36
class EarthSea extends Sea
{
}

// listing 09.37
class EarthForest extends Forest
{
}

// listing 09.38
class MarsSea extends Sea
{
}

// listing 09.39
class MarsForest extends Forest
{
}

// listing 09.40
class MarsPlains extends Plains
{
}

// listing 09.41
class TerrainFactory
{
    public function __construct(private Sea $sea, private Plains $plains,
    private Forest $forest)
    {
    }

    public function getSea(): Sea
    {
        return clone $this->sea;
    }
}
```

```
    public function getPlains(): Plains
    {
        return clone $this->plains;
    }

    public function getForest(): Forest
    {
        return clone $this->forest;
    }
}

// listing 09.42
$factory = new TerrainFactory(
    new EarthSea(),
    new EarthPlains(),
    new EarthForest()
);
print_r($factory->getSea());
print_r($factory->getPlains());
print_r($factory->getForest());
```

Here is the output:

```
popp\ch09\batch11\EarthSea Object
(
)

popp\ch09\batch11\EarthPlains Object
(
)

popp\ch09\batch11\EarthForest Object
(
)
```

As you can see, I load up a concrete TerrainFactory with instances of product objects. When a client calls getSea(), I return a clone of the Sea object that I cached during initialization. This structure buys me additional flexibility. Want to play a game on a new planet with Earth-like seas and forests, but Mars-like plains? No need to write a new creator class—you can simply change the mix of classes you add to TerrainFactory:

```
// listing 09.43
$factory = new TerrainFactory(
    new EarthSea(),
    new MarsPlains(),
    new EarthForest()
);
```

So the Prototype pattern allows you to take advantage of the flexibility afforded by composition. We get more than that, though. Because you are storing and cloning objects at runtime, you reproduce object state when you generate new products. Imagine that Sea objects have a $navigability property. The property influences the amount of movement energy a sea tile saps from a vessel and can be set to adjust the difficulty level of a game:

```
// listing 09.44
class Sea
{
    public function __construct(private int $navigability)
    {
    }
}
```

Now when I initialize the TerrainFactory object, I can add a Sea object with a navigability modifier. This will then hold true for all Sea objects served by TerrainFactory:

```
// listing 09.45
$factory = new TerrainFactory(
    new EarthSea(-1),
    new EarthPlains(),
    new EarthForest()
);
```

This flexibility is also apparent when the object you wish to generate is composed of other objects.

Note   I covered object cloning in Chapter 4. The clone keyword generates a shallow copy of any object to which it is applied. This means that the product object will have the same properties as the source. If any of the source's properties are objects, then these will not be copied into the product. Instead, the product will reference the *same* object properties. It is up to you to change this default and to customize object copying in any other way, by implementing a __clone() method. This is called automatically when the clone keyword is used.

Perhaps all Sea objects can contain Resource objects (FishResource, OilResource, etc.). According to a preference flag, we might give all Sea objects a FishResource by default. Remember that if your products reference other objects, you should implement a __clone() method to ensure that you make a deep copy:

```
// listing 09.46
class Contained
{
}
```

```
// listing 09.47
class Container
{
    public Contained $contained;

    public function __construct()
    {
        $this->contained = new Contained();
    }

    public function __clone()
    {
        // Ensure that cloned object holds a
        // clone of self::$contained and not
        // a reference to it

        $this->contained = clone $this->contained;
    }
}
```

Pushing to the Edge: Service Locator

I promised that this chapter would deal with the logic of object creation, doing away with the sneaky buck-passing of many object-oriented examples. Yet some patterns here have slyly dodged the decision-making part of object creation, if not the creation itself.

The Singleton pattern is not guilty. The logic for object creation is built-in and unambiguous. The Abstract Factory pattern groups the creation of product families into distinct concrete creators. How do we decide which concrete creator to use, though? The Prototype pattern presents us with a similar problem. Both these patterns handle the creation of objects, but they defer the decision as to which object or group of objects should be created.

The particular concrete creator that a system chooses is often decided according to the value of a configuration switch of some kind. This could be located in a database, a configuration file, or a server file (such as Apache's directory-level configuration file, usually called .htaccess), or it could even be hard-coded as a PHP variable or property. Because PHP applications must be reconfigured for every request or CLI call, you need script initialization to be as painless as possible. For this reason, I often opt to hard-code configuration flags in PHP code. This can be done by hand or by writing a script that autogenerates a class file. Here's a crude class that includes a flag for calendar protocol types:

```
// listing 09.48
class Settings
{
    public static string $COMMSTYPE = 'Mega';
}
```

Now that I have a flag (however inelegant), I can create a class that uses it to decide which CommsManager to serve on request. It is quite common to see a Singleton used in conjunction with the Abstract Factory pattern, so let's do that:

```
// listing 09.49
class AppConfig
{
    private static ?AppConfig $instance = null;
    private CommsManager $commsManager;
```

```
    private function __construct()
    {
        // will run once only
        $this->init();
    }

    private function init(): void
    {
        switch (Settings::$COMMSTYPE) {
            case 'Mega':
                $this->commsManager = new MegaCommsManager();
                break;
            default:
                $this->commsManager = new BloggsCommsManager();
        }
    }

    public static function getInstance(): AppConfig
    {
        if (is_null(self::$instance)) {
            self::$instance = new self();
        }
        return self::$instance;
    }

    public function getCommsManager(): CommsManager
    {
        return $this->commsManager;
    }
}
```

The AppConfig class is a standard Singleton. For that reason, I can get an AppConfig instance anywhere in the system, and I will always get the same one. The init() method is invoked by the class's constructor and is therefore only run once in a process. It tests the Settings::$COMMSTYPE property, instantiating a concrete CommsManager object according to its value. Now my script can get a CommsManager object and work with it without ever knowing about its concrete implementations or the concrete classes it generates:

```
$commsMgr = AppConfig::getInstance()->getCommsManager();
$commsMgr->getApptEncoder()->encode();
```

Because `AppConfig` manages the work of finding and creating components for us, it is an instance of what's known as the Service Locator pattern. It's neat but it does introduce a more benign dependency than direct instantiation. Any classes using its service must explicitly invoke this monolith, binding them to the wider system. For this reason, some prefer another approach.

Splendid Isolation: Dependency Injection

In the previous section, I used a flag and a conditional statement within a factory to determine which of two `CommsManager` classes to serve up. The solution was not as flexible as it might have been. The classes on offer were hard-coded within a single locator, with a choice of two components built-in to a conditional. That inflexibility was a facet of my demonstration code, though, rather than a problem with Service Locator, per se. I could have used any number of strategies to locate, instantiate, and return objects on behalf of client code. The real reason Service Locator is often treated with suspicion, however, is the fact that a component must explicitly invoke the locator. This feels a little, well, global. And object-oriented developers are rightly suspicious of all things global.

The Problem

Whenever you use the new operator, you close down the possibility of polymorphism within that scope. Imagine a method that deploys a hard-coded `BloggsApptEncoder` object, for example:

```
// listing 09.50
class AppointmentMaker
{
    public function makeAppointment(): string
    {
        $encoder = new BloggsApptEncoder();
        return $encoder->encode();
    }
}
```

This might work for our initial needs, but it will not allow any other `ApptEncoder` implementation to be switched in at runtime. That limits the ways in which the class can be used, and it makes the class harder to test.

Note   Unit tests are usually designed to focus on specific classes and methods in isolation from a wider system. If the class under test includes a directly instantiated object, then all sorts of code extraneous to the test may be executed—possibly causing errors and unexpected side effects. If, on the other hand, a class under test acquires objects it works with in some way other than direct instantiation, it can be provided with fake—*mock* or *stub*—objects for the purposes of testing. I cover testing detail in Chapter 18.

Direct instantiations make code hard to test. Much of this chapter addresses precisely this kind of inflexibility. But, as I pointed out in the previous section, I have skated over the fact that, even if we use the Prototype or Abstract Factory patterns, instantiation has to happen *somewhere*. Here again is a fragment of code that creates a Prototype object:

```
// listing 09.51
$factory = new TerrainFactory(
    new EarthSea(),
    new EarthPlains(),
    new EarthForest()
);
```

The Prototype `TerrainFactory` class called here is a step in the right direction—it demands generic types: `Sea`, `Plains`, and `Forest`. The class leaves it up to the client code to determine which implementations should be provided. But how is this done?

Implementation

Much of our code calls out to factories. As we have seen, this model is known as the Service Locator pattern. A method delegates responsibility to a provider which it trusts to find and serve up an instance of the desired type. The Prototype example inverts this; it simply expects the instantiating code to provide implementations at call time. There's no magic here—it's simply a matter of requiring types in a constructor's signature, instead of creating them directly within the method. A variation on this is to provide setter methods, so that clients can pass in objects before invoking a method that uses them.

So let's fix up `AppointmentMaker` in this way:

```
// listing 09.52
class AppointmentMaker2
{
    public function __construct(private ApptEncoder $encoder)
    {
    }

    public function makeAppointment(): string
    {
        return $this->encoder->encode();
    }
}
```

`AppointmentMaker2` has given up control—it no longer creates the `BloggsApptEncoder`, and we have gained flexibility. What about the logic for the actual creation of `ApptEncoder` objects, though? Where do the dreaded new statements live? We need an assembler component to take on the job. A common strategy here uses a configuration file to figure out which implementations should be instantiated. There are tools to help us with this, but this book is all about doing it ourselves, so let's build a very naive implementation. I'll start with a crude XML format which describes the relationships between abstract classes and their preferred implementations.

```
// listing 09.53
<objects>

    <class name="popp\ch09\batch06\ApptEncoder">
    <instance inst="popp\ch09\batch06\BloggsApptEncoder" />
    </class>

</objects>
```

This asserts that where we ask for an ApptEncoder, our tool should generate a BloggsApptEncoder. Of course, we have to create the assembler.

```
// listing 09.54
class ObjectAssembler
{
    private array $components = [];

    public function __construct(string $conf)
    {
        $this->configure($conf);
    }
    private function configure(string $conf): void
    {
        $data = simplexml_load_file($conf);
        foreach ($data->class as $class) {
            $name = (string)$class['name'];
            $resolvedname = $name;
            if (isset($class->instance)) {
                if (isset($class->instance[0]['inst'])) {
                    $resolvedname = (string)$class->instance[0]['inst'];
                }
            }
            $this->components[$name] = function () use ($resolvedname) {
                $rclass = new \ReflectionClass($resolvedname);
                return $rclass->newInstance();
            };
        }
    }

    public function getComponent(string $class): object
    {
        if (isset($this->components[$class])) {
            $inst = $this->components[$class]();
```

```
    } else {
        $rclass = new \ReflectionClass($class);
        $inst = $rclass->newInstance();
    }
    return $inst;
    }
}
```

This is a little dense at first reading, so let's work through it briefly. Most of the real action takes place in configure(). The method accepts a path which is passed on from the constructor. It uses the simplexml extension to parse the configuration XML. In a real project, of course, we'd add more error handling here and throughout. For now, I'm pretty trusting of the XML I'm parsing.

For every <class> element, I extract the fully qualified class name and store it in the $name variable. I also create a $resolvedname variable which will hold the name of the concrete class we will generate. Assuming an <instance> element is found (and in later examples, you will see that it will not always be present), I assign the correct value to $resolvedname.

I don't want to create an object unless and until it's needed, so I create an anonymous function which will do the creation when called upon and add it to the $components property.

The getComponent() method takes a given class name and resolves it to an instance. It does this in one of two ways. If the provided class name is a key in the $components array, then I extract and run the corresponding anonymous function. If, on the other hand, I can find no record of the provided class, I can still gamely attempt to create an instance. Finally, I return the result.

Let's put this code through its paces:

```
// listing 09.55
$assembler = new ObjectAssembler("src/ch09/batch14_1/objects.xml");
$encoder = $assembler->getComponent(ApptEncoder::class);
$apptmaker = new AppointmentMaker2($encoder);
$out = $apptmaker->makeAppointment();
print $out;
```

Because ApptEncoder::class resolves to popp\ch09\batch06\ApptEncoder—the key established in the objects.xml file—a BloggsApptEncoder object is instantiated and returned. You can see that demonstrated by the output from this fragment:

Appointment data encoded in BloggsCal format

As you have seen, code is clever enough to create a concrete object even if it isn't in the configuration file.

```
// listing 09.56
$assembler = new ObjectAssembler("src/ch09/batch14_1/objects.xml");
$encoder = $assembler->getComponent(MegaApptEncoder::class);
$apptmaker = new AppointmentMaker2($encoder);
$out = $apptmaker->makeAppointment();
print $out;
```

There is no MegaApptEncoder key in the configuration file, but, because the MegaApptEncoder class exists and is instantiable, the ObjectAssembler class is able to create and return an instance.

But what about objects with constructors that require arguments? We can achieve that without much more work. Remember the most recent TerrainFactory class? It demands a Sea, a Plains, and a Forest object. Here, I amend my XML format to accommodate this requirement.

```
// listing 09.57
<objects>

    <class name="popp\ch09\batch11\TerrainFactory">
        <arg num="0" inst="popp\ch09\batch11\EarthSea" />
        <arg num="1" inst="popp\ch09\batch11\MarsPlains" />
        <arg num="2" inst="popp\ch09\batch11\Forest" />
    </class>

    <class name="popp\ch09\batch11\Forest">
        <instance inst="popp\ch09\batch11\EarthForest" />
    </class>
```

```
<class name="popp\ch09\batch14\AppointmentMaker2">
    <arg num="0" inst="popp\ch09\batch06\BloggsApptEncoder" />
</class>
```

```
</objects>
```

I've described two classes from this chapter: TerrainFactory and AppointmentMaker2. I want TerrainFactory to be instantiated with an EarthSea object, a MarsPlains object, and an EarthForest object. I would also like AppointmentMaker2 to be passed a BloggsApptEncoder object. Because TerrainFactory and AppointmentMaker2 are already concrete classes, I do not need to provide <instance> elements in either case.

While EarthSea and MarsPlains are concrete classes, note that Forest is abstract. This is a neat piece of logical recursion. Although Forest cannot itself be instantiated, there is a corresponding <class> element which defines a concrete instance. Do you think a new version of ObjectAssembler will be able to cope with these requirements?

```php
// listing 09.58
class ObjectAssembler
{
    private array $components = [];

    public function __construct(string $conf)
    {
        $this->configure($conf);
    }

    private function configure(string $conf): void
    {
        $data = simplexml_load_file($conf);
        foreach ($data->class as $class) {
            $args = [];
            $name = (string)$class['name'];
            $resolvedname = $name;
            foreach ($class->arg as $arg) {
                $argclass = (string)$arg['inst'];
                $args[(int)$arg['num']] = $argclass;
            }
```

```php
            if (isset($class->instance)) {
                if (isset($class->instance[0]['inst'])) {
                    $resolvedname = (string)$class->instance[0]['inst'];
                }
            }
            ksort($args);
            $this->components[$name] = function () use ($resolvedname,
            $args) {
                $expandedargs = [];
                foreach ($args as $arg) {
                    $expandedargs[] = $this->getComponent($arg);
                }
                $rclass = new \ReflectionClass($resolvedname);
                return $rclass->newInstanceArgs($expandedargs);
            };
        }
    }

    public function getComponent(string $class): object
    {
        if (isset($this->components[$class])) {
            $inst = $this->components[$class]();
        } else {
            $rclass = new \ReflectionClass($class);
            $inst = $rclass->newInstance();
        }
        return $inst;
    }
}
```

Let's take a closer look at what is new here.

Firstly, in the configure() method, I now loop through any <arg> elements in each <class> element and build up a list of class names.

```
// listing 09.59
foreach ($class->arg as $arg) {
    $argclass = (string)$arg['inst'];
    $args[(int)$arg['num']] = $argclass;
}
```

Then, in the anonymous builder function, I really don't have to do much to expand each of these elements into object instances for passing into my class's constructor. I have already created the getComponent() method for this purpose, after all.

```
// listing 09.60
ksort($args);
$this->components[$name] = function () use ($resolvedname, $args) {
    $expandedargs = [];
    foreach ($args as $arg) {
        $expandedargs[] = $this->getComponent($arg);
    }
    $rclass = new \ReflectionClass($resolvedname);
    return $rclass->newInstanceArgs($expandedargs);
};
```

Note   If you are considering building a Dependency Injection assembler/container, you should look at a couple of options: Pimple (notwithstanding its unpleasant name) and Symfony DI. You can find out more about Pimple at http://pimple. sensiolabs.org/; you can learn more about the Symfony DI component at http://symfony.com/doc/current/components/dependency_ injection/introduction.html.

So we can now maintain the flexibility of our components and handle instantiation dynamically. Let's try out the ObjectAssembler class:

```
// listing 09.61
$assembler = new ObjectAssembler("src/ch09/batch14/objects.xml");
$apptmaker = $assembler->getComponent(AppointmentMaker2::class);
$out = $apptmaker->makeAppointment();
print $out;
```

Once we have an `ObjectAssembler`, object acquisition takes up a single statement. The `AppointmentMaker2` class is free of its previous hard-coded dependency on an `ApptEncoder` instance. A developer can now use the configuration file to control what classes are used at runtime, as well as to test `AppointmentMaker2` in isolation from the wider system.

Dependency Injection with Attributes

We can also use the attributes feature introduced with PHP 8 to shift some of this logic from the configuration file to the classes themselves, and we can do this without sacrificing the functionality we have already defined.

Note I covered attributes in Chapter 5.

Here is another XML file. I'm not introducing any new features here. In fact, the configuration file is taking responsibility for *less* logic.

```
// listing 09.62
<objects>

    <class name="popp\ch09\batch06\ApptEncoder">
        <instance inst="popp\ch09\batch06\BloggsApptEncoder" />
    </class>

    <class name="popp\ch09\batch11\Sea">
        <instance inst="popp\ch09\batch11\EarthSea" />
    </class>
    <class name="popp\ch09\batch11\Plains">
        <instance inst="popp\ch09\batch11\MarsPlains" />
    </class>

    <class name="popp\ch09\batch11\Forest">
        <instance inst="popp\ch09\batch11\EarthForest" />
    </class>
</objects>
```

I want to generate a new version of TerrainFactory. If the definition for this is not evident in the configuration file, then where might I find it? The answer lies in the TerrainFactory class itself:

```
// listing 09.63
class TerrainFactory
{
    #[InjectConstructor(Sea::class, Plains::class, Forest::class)]
    public function __construct(private Sea $sea, private Plains $plains,
    private Forest $forest)
    {
    }

    public function getSea(): Sea
    {
        return clone $this->sea;
    }

    public function getPlains(): Plains
    {
        return clone $this->plains;
    }

    public function getForest(): Forest
    {
        return clone $this->forest;
    }
}
```

This is just the Prototype TerrainConstructor class you have already seen but with the crucial addition of the InjectConstructor attribute. This requires a boilerplate class definition:

```
// listing 09.64
use Attribute;

#[Attribute]
```

```
public class InjectConstructor
{
    function __construct()
    {
    }
}
```

So, the InjectConstructor attribute defines my required behavior. I want my dependency injection example to provide concrete instances of the Sea, Plains, and Forest abstract classes. Time once again for the hardworking ObjectAssembler class to step up.

```
// listing 09.65
class ObjectAssembler
{
    private array $components = [];

    public function __construct(string $conf)
    {
        $this->configure($conf);
    }

    private function configure(string $conf): void
    {
        $data = simplexml_load_file($conf);
        foreach ($data->class as $class) {
            $args = [];
            $name = (string)$class['name'];
            $resolvedname = $name;
            foreach ($class->arg as $arg) {
                $argclass = (string)$arg['inst'];
                $args[(int)$arg['num']] = $argclass;
            }
            if (isset($class->instance)) {
                if (isset($class->instance[0]['inst'])) {
                    $resolvedname = (string)$class->instance[0]['inst'];
                }
            }
```

```
        ksort($args);
        $this->components[$name] = function () use ($resolvedname,
        $args) {
            $expandedargs = [];
            foreach ($args as $arg) {
                $expandedargs[] = $this->getComponent($arg);
            }
            $rclass = new \ReflectionClass($resolvedname);
            return $rclass->newInstanceArgs($expandedargs);
        };
    }
}

public function getComponent(string $class): object
{
    // create $inst -- our object instance
    // and a list of \ReflectionMethod objects

    if (isset($this->components[$class])) {
        // instance found in config
        $inst = $this->components[$class]();
        $rclass = new \ReflectionClass($inst::class);
        $methods = $rclass->getMethods();
    } else {

        $rclass = new \ReflectionClass($class);
        $methods = $rclass->getMethods();
        $injectconstructor = null;
        foreach ($methods as $method) {
            foreach ($method->getAttributes(InjectConstructor::class)
            as $attribute) {
                $injectconstructor = $attribute;
                break;
            }
        }
```

```
            if (is_null($injectconstructor)) {
                $inst = $rclass->newInstance();
            } else {
                $constructorargs = [];
                foreach ($injectconstructor->getArguments() as $arg) {
                    $constructorargs[] = $this->getComponent($arg);
                }
                $inst = $rclass->newInstanceArgs($constructorargs);
            }
        }
        return $inst;
    }

}
```

Perhaps this seems even more daunting now. Once again, though, I have not added
that much. Let's break it down. The additions are all to be found in getComponent().
If I find the provided class key—the $class argument variable—in the $components
array property, I simply rely on the corresponding anonymous function to take care
of instantiation. If not, then the logic may be found in attributes. To check this, I loop
through all methods in the target class looking for an InjectConstructor attribute.
If I find one, then I treat the related method as a constructor. I expand each of the
attribute arguments into an object instance in its own right and then pass the finished
list to ReflectionClass::newInstanceArgs(). If, on the other hand, I don't find the
InjectConstructor attribute, I simply instantiate without arguments using ReflectionC
lass::newInstance().

Note that throughout this example I create an array named $methods which contains
the ReflectionMethod objects for the class. This array is redundant here, but we will
soon find a use for it!

Here is that logic again, extracted from the ObjectAssembler::getComponent()
method:

// listing 09.66

```
$rclass = new \ReflectionClass($class);
$methods = $rclass->getMethods();
$injectconstructor = null;
```

```
foreach ($methods as $method) {
    foreach ($method->getAttributes(InjectConstructor::class) as $attribute) {
        $injectconstructor = $attribute;
        break;
    }
}
if (is_null($injectconstructor)) {
    $inst = $rclass->newInstance();
} else {
    $constructorargs = [];
    foreach ($injectconstructor->getArguments() as $arg) {
        $constructorargs[] = $this->getComponent($arg);
    }
    $inst = $rclass->newInstanceArgs($constructorargs);
}
```

Note the use of recursion here. In order to expand the attribute argument to an object, I pass the class name back to getComponent().

Now, in theory, I can generate a magically populated TerrainFactory object.

```
// listing 09.67
$assembler = new ObjectAssembler("src/ch09/batch15/objects.xml");
$terrainfactory = $assembler->getComponent(TerrainFactory::class);
$plains = $terrainfactory->getPlains(); // MarsPlains
```

When the ObjectAssembler object is called with the TerrainFactory name, the method, ObjectAssembler::getcomponent(), first looks in its $components array for a matching configuration element. In this case, it does not find one. So then it loops through the methods in TerrainFactory and lights upon the InjectConstructor attribute. This has three arguments. For each of these, it recursively calls getComponent(). In each of these cases, it *does* find a configuration element which provides a class from which an argument can be instantiated.

Note   This example code does not check for circular recursion. At the very least, a production version of this should prevent recursive calls to getComponent() from running to too many levels.

Finally, let's round things out with a new attribute. Inject is similar to InjectConstructor except that it should be applied to standard methods. These will be called after the target object is instantiated. Here is the attribute in use:

```
// listing 09.68
class AppointmentMaker
{
    private ApptEncoder $encoder;

    #[Inject(ApptEncoder::class)]
    public function setApptEncoder(ApptEncoder $encoder)
    {
        $this->encoder = $encoder;
    }

    public function makeAppointment(): string
    {
        return $this->encoder->encode();
    }
}
```

The directive here is that the AppointmentMaker class should be provided with an ApptEncoder object after instantiation.

Here is the boilerplate Inject class which corresponds to the attribute:

```
// listing 09.69
use Attribute;
#[Attribute]
class Inject
{
    public function __construct()
    {
    }
}
```

As with InjectConstructor, it really does not do anything useful except fill the namespace. Time to add support for Inject to ObjectAssembler:

```
// listing 09.70
public function getComponent(string $class): object
{
    // create $inst -- our object instance
    // and a list of \ReflectionMethod objects

    $this->injectMethods($inst, $methods);
    return $inst;
}

public function injectMethods(object $inst, array $methods)
{
    foreach ($methods as $method) {
        foreach ($method->getAttributes(Inject::class) as $attribute) {
            $args = [];
            foreach ($attribute->getArguments() as $argstring) {
                $args[] = $this->getComponent($argstring);
            }
            $method->invokeArgs($inst, $args);
        }
    }
}
```

I have omitted most of getComponent() since it does not change here. The only addition is a call to a new method: injectMethods(). This accepts the new instantiated object and an array of ReflectionMethod objects. It then performs a familiar dance, looping through any methods with Inject attributes, acquiring the attribute arguments, and passing each back to getComponent(). Once an argument list has been compiled, the method is invoked on the instance.

Here is some client code:

```
// listing 09.71
$assembler = new ObjectAssembler("src/ch09/batch15/objects.xml");
$apptmaker = $assembler->getComponent(AppointmentMaker::class);
$output = $apptmaker->makeAppointment();
print $output;
```

So, when I call getComponent(), it creates an AppointmentMaker instance according to the flow we have explored. It then calls injectMethods() which finds a method with an Inject attribute in the AppointmentMaker class. The attribute's argument specifies ApptEncoder. This class key is passed to getComponent() in a recursive call. Because our configuration file specifies BloggsApptEncoder as the resolution for ApptEncoder, this object is instantiated and passed to the setter method.

Once again, this is demonstrated by the output which is

```
Appointment data encoded in BloggsCal format
```

Here is the whole of ObjectAssembler. It comprises a limited proof of concept dependency injection class in not much more than 80 lines!

```
// listing 09.72
class ObjectAssembler
{
    private array $components = [];

    public function __construct(string $conf)
    {
        $this->configure($conf);
    }

    private function configure(string $conf): void
    {
        $data = simplexml_load_file($conf);
        foreach ($data->class as $class) {
            $args = [];
            $name = (string)$class['name'];
            $resolvedname = $name;
            foreach ($class->arg as $arg) {
                $argclass = (string)$arg['inst'];
                $args[(int)$arg['num']] = $argclass;
            }
            if (isset($class->instance)) {
                if (isset($class->instance[0]['inst'])) {
                    $resolvedname = (string)$class->instance[0]['inst'];
                }
            }
```

```php
        ksort($args);
        $this->components[$name] = function () use ($resolvedname,
        $args) {
            $expandedargs = [];
            foreach ($args as $arg) {
                $expandedargs[] = $this->getComponent($arg);
            }
            $rclass = new \ReflectionClass($resolvedname);
            return $rclass->newInstanceArgs($expandedargs);
        };
    }
}

public function getComponent(string $class): object
{
    // create $inst -- our object instance
    // and a list of \ReflectionMethod objects

    if (isset($this->components[$class])) {
        // instance found in config
      $inst = $this->components[$class]();
      $rclass = new \ReflectionClass($inst::class);
      $methods = $rclass->getMethods();
    } else {

        $rclass = new \ReflectionClass($class);
        $methods = $rclass->getMethods();
        $injectconstructor = null;
        foreach ($methods as $method) {
            foreach ($method->getAttributes(InjectConstructor::class)
            as $attribute) {
                $injectconstructor = $attribute;
                break;

            }

        }
```

```
        if (is_null($injectconstructor)) {
            $inst = $rclass->newInstance();
        } else {
            $constructorargs = [];
            foreach ($injectconstructor->getArguments() as $arg) {
                $constructorargs[] = $this->getComponent($arg);
            }
            $inst = $rclass->newInstanceArgs($constructorargs);
        }
    }

    $this->injectMethods($inst, $methods);
    return $inst;
}

public function injectMethods(object $inst, array $methods)
{
    foreach ($methods as $method) {
        foreach ($method->getAttributes(Inject::class) as $attribute) {
            $args = [];
            foreach ($attribute->getArguments() as $argstring) {
                $args[] = $this->getComponent($argstring);
            }
            $method->invokeArgs($inst, $args);
        }
    }
}
}
```

Consequences

So, now we've seen two options for object creation. The AppConfig class was an instance
of Service Locator (i.e., a class with the ability to find components or services on behalf
of its client). Using dependency injection certainly makes for more elegant client code.
The AppointmentMaker2 class is blissfully unaware of strategies for object creation. It
simply does its job. This is the ideal for a class, of course. We want to design classes that

can focus on their responsibilities, isolated as far as possible from the wider system. However, this purity does come at a price. The object assembler component hides a lot of magic. We must treat it as a black box and trust it to conjure up objects on our behalf. This is fine, so long as the magic works. Unexpected behavior can be hard to debug.

The Service Locator pattern, on the other hand, is simpler, though it embeds your components into a wider system. It is not the case that, used well, a Service Locator makes testing harder. Nor does it make a system inflexible. A Service Locator can be configured to serve up arbitrary components for testing or according to configuration. But a hard-coded call to a Service Locator makes a component dependent upon it. Because the call is made from within the body of a method, the relationship between the client and the target component (which is provided by the Service Locator) is also somewhat obscured. This relationship is made explicit in the Dependency Injection example because it is declared in the constructor method's signature.

So, which approach should we choose? To some extent, it's a matter of preference. For my own part, I tend to prefer to start with the simplest solution and then to refactor to greater complexity, if needed. For that reason, I usually opt for Service Locator. I can create a Registry class in a few lines of code and increase its flexibility according to the requirements. My components are a little more knowing than I would like, but since I rarely move classes from one system to another, I have not suffered too much from the embedding effect. When I have moved a system-based class into a stand-alone library, I have not found it particularly hard to refactor the Service Locator dependency away.

Dependency Injection offers purity, but it requires another kind of embedding. You must buy in to the magic of the assembler. If you are already working within a framework which offers this functionality, there is no reason not to avail yourself of it. The Symfony Dependency Injection component, for example, provides a hybrid solution of Service Locator (known as the "service container") and Dependency Injection. The service container manages the instantiation of objects according to the configuration (or code, if you prefer) and provides a simple interface for clients to obtain those objects. The service container even allows the use of factories for object creation. On the other hand, if you are rolling your own, or using components from various frameworks, you may wish to keep things simple at the cost of some elegance.

Summary

This chapter covered some of the tricks that you can use to generate objects. I began by examining the Singleton pattern, which provides global access to a single instance. Next, I looked at the Factory Method pattern, which applies the principle of polymorphism to object generation. And I combined Factory Method with the Abstract Factory pattern to generate creator classes that instantiate sets of related objects. I also looked at the Prototype pattern and saw how object cloning can allow composition to be used in object generation. Finally, I examined two strategies for object creation: Service Locator and Dependency Injection.

CHAPTER 10

Patterns for Flexible Object Programming

With strategies for generating objects covered, we're free now to look at some strategies for structuring classes and objects. I will focus in particular on the principle that composition provides greater flexibility than inheritance. The patterns I examine in this chapter are once again drawn from the Gang of Four catalog.

This chapter will cover a trio of patterns:

- *The Composite pattern*: Composing structures in which groups of objects can be used as if they were individual objects

- *The Decorator pattern*: A flexible mechanism for combining objects at runtime to extend functionality

- *The Facade pattern*: Creating a simple interface to complex or variable systems

Structuring Classes to Allow Flexible Objects

Way back in Chapter 3, I said that beginners often confuse objects and classes. This was only half true. In fact, most of the rest of us occasionally scratch our heads over UML class diagrams, attempting to reconcile the static inheritance structures they show with the dynamic object relationships their objects will enter into off the page.

Remember the pattern principle, "Favor composition over inheritance"? This principle distills this tension between the organization of classes and objects. In order to build flexibility into our projects, we structure our classes so that their objects can be composed into useful structures at runtime.

© Matt Zandstra 2021
M. Zandstra, *PHP 8 Objects, Patterns, and Practice*, https://doi.org/10.1007/978-1-4842-6791-2_10

This is a common theme running through the first two patterns of this chapter. Inheritance is an important feature in both, but part of its importance lies in providing the mechanism by which composition can be used to represent structures and extend functionality.

The Composite Pattern

The Composite pattern is perhaps the most extreme example of inheritance deployed in the service of composition. It is a simple and yet breathtakingly elegant design. It is also fantastically useful. Be warned, though; it is so neat, you might be tempted to overuse this strategy.

The Composite pattern is a simple way of aggregating and then managing groups of similar objects so that an individual object is indistinguishable to a client from a collection of objects. The pattern is, in fact, very simple, but it is also often confusing. One reason for this is the similarity in structure of the classes in the pattern to the organization of its objects. Inheritance hierarchies are trees, beginning with the superclass at the root and branching out into specialized subclasses. The inheritance tree of *classes* laid down by the Composite pattern is designed to allow the easy generation and traversal of a tree of *objects*.

If you are not already familiar with this pattern, you have every right to feel confused at this point. Let's try an analogy to illustrate the way that single entities can be treated in the same way as collections of things. Given broadly irreducible ingredients such as cereals and meat (or soya if you prefer), we can make a food product—a sausage, for example. We then act on the result as a single entity. Just as we eat, cook, buy, or sell meat, we can eat, cook, buy, or sell the sausage that the meat in part composes. We might take the sausage and combine it with the other composite ingredients to make a pie, thereby rolling a composite into a larger composite. We behave in the same way to the collection as we do to the parts. The Composite pattern helps us to model this relationship between collections and components in our code.

The Problem

Managing groups of objects can be quite a complex task, especially if the objects in question might also contain objects of their own. This kind of problem is very common in coding. Think of invoices, with line items that summarize additional products or services, or things-to-do lists with items that themselves contain multiple subtasks. In content management, we can't move for trees of sections, pages, articles, or media components. Managing these structures from the outside can quickly become daunting.

Let's return to a previous scenario. I am designing a system based on a game called Civilization. A player can move units around hundreds of tiles that make up a map. Individual counters can be grouped together to move, fight, and defend themselves as a unit. Here, I define a couple of unit types:

```
// listing 10.01
abstract class Unit
{
    abstract public function bombardStrength(): int;
}

class Archer extends Unit
{
    public function bombardStrength(): int
    {
        return 4;
    }
}

class LaserCannonUnit extends Unit
{
    public function bombardStrength(): int
    {
        return 44;
    }
}
```

The Unit class defines an abstract bombardStrength() method, which sets the attack strength of a unit bombarding an adjacent tile. I implement this in both the Archer and LaserCannonUnit classes. These classes would also contain information about movement and defensive capabilities, but I'll keep things simple. I could define a separate class to group units together, like this:

```
// listing  10.02
class Army
{
    private array $units = [];

    public function addUnit(Unit $unit): void
    {
        array_push($this->units, $unit);
    }

    public function bombardStrength(): int
    {
        $ret = 0;
        foreach ($this->units as $unit) {
            $ret += $unit->bombardStrength();
        }
        return $ret;
    }
}
```

```
// listing 10.03
$unit1 = new Archer();
$unit2 = new LaserCannonUnit();
$army = new Army();
$army->addUnit($unit1);
$army->addUnit($unit2);
print $army->bombardStrength();
```

The Army class has an addUnit() method that accepts a Unit object. Unit objects are stored in an array property called $units. I calculate the combined strength of my army in the bombardStrength() method. This simply iterates through the aggregated Unit objects, calling the bombardStrength() method of each one. Here is the output:

48

This model is perfectly acceptable, as long as the problem remains as simple as this. What happens, though, if I were to add some new requirements? Let's say that an army should be able to combine with other armies. Each army should retain its own identity so that it can disentangle itself from the whole at a later date. The Arch Duke's brave forces might share common cause today with General Soames's assault upon the exposed flank of the enemy, but a domestic rebellion may send his army scurrying home at any time. For this reason, I can't just decant the units from each army into a new force.

I could amend the Army class to accept Army objects as well as Unit objects:

```
// listing 10.04
public function addArmy(Army $army): void
{
    array_push($this->armies, $army);
}
```

Then I'd need to amend the bombardStrength() method to iterate through all armies as well as units:

```
// listing 10.05
public function bombardStrength(): int
{
    $ret = 0;
    foreach ($this->units as $unit) {
        $ret += $unit->bombardStrength();
    }

    foreach ($this->armies as $army) {
        $ret += $army->bombardStrength();
    }

    return $ret;
}
```

This additional complexity is not too problematic at the moment. Remember, though, I would need to do something similar in methods like defensiveStrength(), movementRange(), and so on. My game is going to be richly featured. Already the business group is calling for troop carriers that can hold up to ten units to improve their movement range on certain terrains. Clearly, a troop carrier is similar to an army in that it groups units. It also has its own characteristics. I could further amend the Army class to handle TroopCarrier objects, but I know that there will be a need for still more unit groupings. It is clear that I need a more flexible model.

Let's look again at the model I have been building. All the classes I created shared the need for a bombardStrength() method. In effect, a client does not need to distinguish between an army, a unit, or a troop carrier. They are functionally identical. They need to move, attack, and defend. Those objects that contain others need to provide methods for adding and removing them. These similarities lead us to an inevitable conclusion. Because container objects share an interface with the objects that they contain, they are naturally suited to share a type family.

Implementation

The Composite pattern defines a single inheritance hierarchy that lays down two distinct sets of responsibilities. We have already seen both of these in our example. Classes in the pattern must support a common set of operations as their primary responsibility. For us, that means the bombardStrength() method. Classes must also support methods for adding and removing child objects.

Figure 10-1 shows a class diagram that illustrates the Composite pattern as applied to our problem.

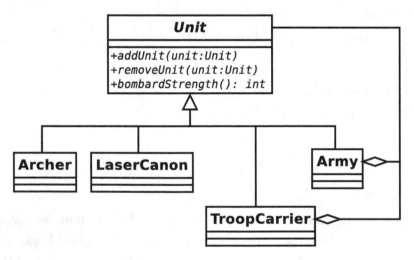

Figure 10-1. *The Composite pattern*

As you can see, all the units in this model extend the Unit class. A client can be sure, then, that any Unit object will support the bombardStrength() method. So, an Army can be treated in exactly the same way as an Archer.

The Army and TroopCarrier classes are *composites*: they are designed to hold Unit objects. The Archer and LaserCannon classes are *leaves*, designed to support unit operations, but not to hold other Unit objects. There is actually an issue as to whether leaves should honor the same interface as composites, as they do in Figure 10-1. The diagram shows TroopCarrier and Army aggregating other units, even though the leaf classes are also bound to implement addUnit(). I will return to this question shortly. Here is the abstract Unit class:

```
// listing 10.06
abstract class Unit
{
    abstract public function addUnit(Unit $unit): void;
    abstract public function removeUnit(Unit $unit): void;
    abstract public function bombardStrength(): int;
}
```

As you can see, I lay down the basic functionality for all Unit objects here. Now, let's see how a composite object might implement these abstract methods:

```
// listing 10.07
class Army extends Unit
{
    private array $units = [];

    public function addUnit(Unit $unit): void
    {
        if (in_array($unit, $this->units, true)) {
            return;
        }

        $this->units[] = $unit;
    }
```

```php
    public function removeUnit(Unit $unit): void
    {
        $idx = array_search($unit, $this->units, true);
        if (is_int($idx)) {
            array_splice($this->units, $idx, 1, []);
        }
    }

    public function bombardStrength(): int
    {
        $ret = 0;
        foreach ($this->units as $unit) {
            $ret += $unit->bombardStrength();
        }
        return $ret;
    }
}
```

The addUnit() method checks whether I have already added the same Unit object before storing it in the private $units array property. removeUnit() uses a similar check to remove a given Unit object from the property.

Note   In checking whether I have already added a particular object to the addUnit() method, I use in_array() with a third Boolean true argument. This tightens the strictness of in_array() such that it will only match references to the same object. The third argument to array_search() works in the same way, returning an array index only if the provided search value is an equivalent object reference to one found in the array.

Army objects, then, can store Units of any kind, including other Army objects, or leaves such as Archer or LaserCannonUnit. Because all units are guaranteed to support bombardStrength(), our Army::bombardStrength() method simply iterates through all the child Unit objects stored in the $units property, calling the same method on each.

One problematic aspect of the Composite pattern is the implementation of add and remove functionality. The classic pattern places add() and remove() methods in the abstract superclass. This ensures that all classes in the pattern share a common interface. As you can see here, though, it also means that leaf classes must provide an implementation:

```
// listing 10.08
class UnitException extends \Exception
{
}
```

```
// listing 10.09
class Archer extends Unit
{
    public function addUnit(Unit $unit): void
    {
        throw new UnitException(get_class($this) . " is a leaf");
    }

    public function removeUnit(Unit $unit): void
    {
        throw new UnitException(get_class($this) . " is a leaf");
    }

    public function bombardStrength(): int
    {
        return 4;
    }
}
```

I do not want to make it possible to add a Unit object to an Archer object, so I throw exceptions if addUnit() or removeUnit() are called. I will need to do this for all leaf objects, so I could perhaps improve my design by replacing the abstract addUnit()/ removeUnit() methods in Unit with default implementations:

```
// listing 10.10
abstract class Unit
{
    public function addUnit(Unit $unit): void
    {
        throw new UnitException(get_class($this) . " is a leaf");
    }
```

```php
    public function removeUnit(Unit $unit): void
    {
        throw new UnitException(get_class($this) . " is a leaf");
    }

    abstract public function bombardStrength(): int;
}

// listing 10.11
class Archer extends Unit
{
    public function bombardStrength(): int
    {
        return 4;
    }
}
```

This removes duplication in leaf classes, but has the drawback that a composite is not forced at compile time to provide an implementation of addUnit() and removeUnit(), which could cause problems down the line.

I will look in more detail at some of the problems presented by the Composite pattern in the next section. Let's end this section by examining some of its benefits:

- *Flexibility*: Because everything in the Composite pattern shares a common supertype, it is very easy to add new composite or leaf objects to the design without changing a program's wider context.

- *Simplicity*: A client using a Composite structure has a straightforward interface. There is no need for a client to distinguish between an object that is composed of others and a leaf object (except when adding new components). A call to Army::bombardStrength() may cause a cascade of delegated calls behind the scenes; but to the client, the process and result are exactly equivalent to those associated with calling Archer::bombardStrength().

- *Implicit reach*: Objects in the Composite pattern are organized in a tree. Each composite holds references to its children. An operation on a particular part of the tree, therefore, can have a wide effect. We might remove a single Army object from its Army parent and add it to another. This simple act is wrought on one object, but it has the effect of changing the status of the Army object's referenced Unit objects and of their own children.

- *Explicit reach*: Tree structures are easy to traverse. They can be iterated in order to gain information or to perform transformations. We will look at a particularly powerful technique for this in the next chapter when we deal with the Visitor pattern.

Often, you really see the benefit of a pattern only from the client's perspective, so here are a couple of armies:

```
// listing 10.12
// create an army
$main_army = new Army();

// add some units
$main_army->addUnit(new Archer());
$main_army->addUnit(new LaserCannonUnit());

// create a new army
$sub_army = new Army();

// add some units
$sub_army->addUnit(new Archer());
$sub_army->addUnit(new Archer());
$sub_army->addUnit(new Archer());

// add the second army to the first
$main_army->addUnit($sub_army);

// all the calculations handled behind the scenes
print "attacking with strength: {$main_army->bombardStrength()}\n";
```

I create a new Army object and add some primitive Unit objects. I repeat the process for a second Army object that I then add to the first. When I call Unit::bombardStrength() on the first Army object, all the complexity of the structure that I have built up is entirely hidden. Here is my output:

```
attacking with strength: 60
```

Consequences

If you're anything like me, you would have heard alarm bells ringing when you saw the code extract for the Archer class. Why do we put up with these redundant addUnit() and removeUnit() methods in leaf classes that do not need to support them? An answer of sorts lies in the transparency of the Unit type.

If a client is passed a Unit object, it knows that the addUnit() method will be present. The Composite pattern principle that primitive (leaf) classes have the same interface as composites is upheld. This does not actually help you much because you still do not know how safe you might be calling addUnit() on any Unit object you might come across.

If I move these add/remove methods down so that they are available only to composite classes, then passing a Unit object to a method leaves me with the problem that I do not know by default whether or not it supports addUnit(). Nevertheless, leaving booby-trapped methods lying around in leaf classes makes me uncomfortable. It adds no value and confuses a system's design because the interface effectively lies about its own functionality.

You can split composite classes off into their own CompositeUnit subtype quite easily. First of all, I excise the add/remove behavior from Unit:

```
// listing 10.13
abstract class Unit
{
    public function getComposite(): ?CompositeUnit
    {
        return null;
    }

    abstract public function bombardStrength(): int;
}
```

Notice the new getComposite() method. I will return to this in a little while. Now, I need a new abstract class to hold addUnit() and removeUnit(). I can even provide default implementations:

```php
// listing 10.14
abstract class CompositeUnit extends Unit
{
    private array $units = [];

    public function getComposite(): ?CompositeUnit
    {
        return $this;
    }

    public function addUnit(Unit $unit): void
    {
        if (in_array($unit, $this->units, true)) {
            return;
        }

        $this->units[] = $unit;
    }

    public function removeUnit(Unit $unit): void
    {
        $idx = array_search($unit, $this->units, true);
        if (is_int($idx)) {
            array_splice($this->units, $idx, 1, []);
        }
    }

    public function getUnits(): array
    {
        return $this->units;
    }
}
```

The CompositeUnit class is declared abstract, even though it does not itself declare an abstract method. It does, however, extend Unit, and it does not implement the abstract bombardStrength() method. Army (and any other composite classes) can now extend CompositeUnit. The classes in my example are now organized as in Figure 10-2.

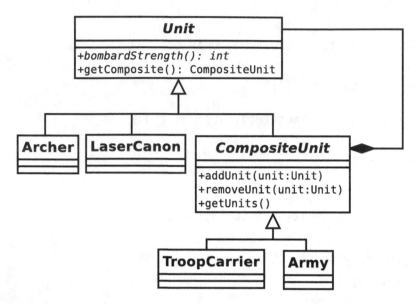

Figure 10-2. *Moving add/remove methods out of the base class*

The annoying, useless implementations of add/remove methods in the leaf classes are gone, but the client must still check to see whether it has a CompositeUnit before it can use addUnit().

This is where the getComposite() method comes into its own. By default, this method returns a null value. Only in a CompositeUnit class does it return CompositeUnit. So if a call to this method returns an object, we should be able to call addUnit() on it. Here's a client that uses this technique:

```
// listing 10.15
class UnitScript
{
    public static function joinExisting(
        Unit $newUnit,
        Unit $occupyingUnit
    ): CompositeUnit {
        $comp = $occupyingUnit->getComposite();
        if (! is_null($comp)) {
            $comp->addUnit($newUnit);
        } else {
            $comp = new Army();
            $comp->addUnit($occupyingUnit);
```

```
        $comp->addUnit($newUnit);
    }
    return $comp;
    }
}
```

The joinExisting() method accepts two Unit objects. The first is a newcomer to a tile, and the second is a prior occupier. If the second Unit is a CompositeUnit, then the first will attempt to join it. If not, then a new Army will be created to cover both units. I have no way of knowing at first whether the $occupyingUnit argument contains a CompositeUnit. A call to getComposite() settles the matter, though. If getComposite() returns an object, I can add the new Unit object to it directly. If not, I create the new Army object and add both.

I could simplify this model further by having the Unit::getComposite() method return an Army object prepopulated with the current Unit. Or I could return to the previous model (which did not distinguish structurally between composite and leaf objects) and have Unit::addUnit() do the same thing: create an Army object and add both Unit objects to it. This is neat, but it presupposes that you know in advance the type of composite you would like to use to aggregate your units. Your business logic will determine the kinds of assumptions you can make when you design methods like getComposite() and addUnit().

These contortions are symptomatic of a drawback to the Composite pattern. Simplicity is achieved by ensuring that all classes are derived from a common base. The benefit of simplicity is sometimes bought at a cost to type safety. The more complex your model becomes, the more manual type checking you are likely to have to do. Let's say that I have a Cavalry object. If the rules of the game state that you cannot put a horse on a troop carrier, I have no automatic way of enforcing this with the Composite pattern:

```
// listing 10.16
class TroopCarrier extends CompositeUnit
{
    public function addUnit(Unit $unit): void
    {
        if ($unit instanceof Cavalry) {
            throw new UnitException("Can't get a horse on the vehicle");
        }
```

```
        parent::addUnit($unit);
    }

    public function bombardStrength(): int
    {
        return 0;
    }
}
```

I am forced to use the `instanceof` operator to test the type of the object passed to `addUnit()`. If you have too many special cases of this kind, the drawbacks of the pattern begin to outweigh its benefits. Composite works best when most of the components are interchangeable.

Another issue to bear in mind is the cost of some Composite operations. The `Army::bombardStrength()` method is typical in that it sets off a cascade of calls to the same method down the tree. For a large tree with lots of subarmies, a single call can cause an avalanche behind the scenes. `bombardStrength()` is not itself very expensive, but what would happen if some leaves performed a complex calculation to arrive at their return values? One way around this problem is to cache the result of a method call of this sort in the parent object, so that subsequent invocations are less expensive. You need to be careful, though, to ensure that the cached value does not grow stale. You should devise strategies to wipe any caches whenever any operations take place on the tree. This may require that you give child objects references to their parents.

Finally, a note about persistence. The Composite pattern is elegant, but it doesn't lend itself neatly to storage in a relational database. This is because, by default, you access the entire structure only through a cascade of references. To construct a Composite structure from a database in the natural way, you would have to make multiple expensive queries. You can get around this problem by assigning an ID to the whole tree, so that all components can be drawn from the database in one go. Having acquired all the objects, however, you would still have the task of recreating the parent/child references, which themselves would have to be stored in the database. This is not difficult, but it is somewhat messy.

Although Composites sit uneasily with relational databases, they lend themselves very well indeed to storage in XML or JSON and, therefore, in various NoSQL stores such as MongoDB, CouchDB, and Elasticsearch. This is because in both cases elements are often themselves composed of trees of subelements.

Composite in Summary

So the Composite pattern is useful when you need to treat a collection of things in the same way as you would an individual, either because the collection is intrinsically like a component (armies and archers) or because the context gives the collection the same characteristics as the component (line items in an invoice). Composites are arranged in trees, so an operation on the whole can affect the parts, and data from the parts is transparently available via the whole. The Composite pattern makes such operations and queries transparent to the client. Trees are easy to traverse (as we shall see in the next chapter). It is easy to add new component types to Composite structures.

On the downside, Composites rely on the similarity of their parts. As soon as we introduce complex rules as to which composite object can hold which set of components, our code can become hard to manage. Composites do not lend themselves well to storage in relational databases.

The Decorator Pattern

While the Composite pattern helps us to create a flexible representation of aggregated components, the Decorator pattern uses a similar structure to help us to modify the functionality of concrete components. Once again, the key to this pattern lies in the importance of composition at runtime. Inheritance is a neat way of building on characteristics laid down by a parent class. This neatness can lead you to hard-code variation into your inheritance hierarchies, often causing inflexibility.

The Problem

Building all your functionality into an inheritance structure can result in an explosion of classes in a system. Even worse, as you try to apply similar modifications to different branches of your inheritance tree, you are likely to see duplication emerge.

Let's return to our game. Here, I define a Tile class and a derived type:

```
// listing 10.17
abstract class Tile
{
    abstract public function getWealthFactor(): int;
}
```

```
// listing 10.18
class Plains extends Tile
{
    private int $wealthfactor = 2;

    public function getWealthFactor(): int
    {
        return $this->wealthfactor;
    }
}
```

A tile represents a square on which my units might be found. Each tile has certain characteristics. In this example, I have defined a getWealthFactor() method that affects the revenue a particular square might generate if owned by a player. As you can see, Plains objects have a wealth factor of 2. Obviously, tiles manage other data. They might also hold a reference to image information, so that the board can be drawn. Once again, I'll keep things simple here.

I need to modify the behavior of the Plains object to handle the effects of natural resources and human abuse. I wish to model the occurrence of diamonds on the landscape and the damage caused by pollution. One approach might be to inherit from the Plains object:

```
// listing 10.19
class DiamondPlains extends Plains
{
    public function getWealthFactor(): int
    {
        return parent::getWealthFactor() + 2;
    }
}

// listing 10.20
class PollutedPlains extends Plains
{
    public function getWealthFactor(): int
```

```
    {
        return parent::getWealthFactor() - 4;
    }
}
```

I can now acquire a polluted tile very easily:

```
// listing 10.21
$tile = new PollutedPlains();
print $tile->getWealthFactor();
```

Here is the output:

```
-2
```

You can see the class diagram for this example in Figure 10-3.

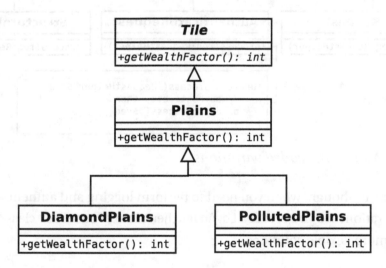

Figure 10-3. *Building variation into an inheritance tree*

This structure is obviously inflexible. I can get plains with diamonds. I can get polluted plains. But can I get them both? Clearly not, unless I am willing to perpetrate the horror that is PollutedDiamondPlains. This situation can only get worse when I introduce the Forest class, which can also have diamonds and pollution.

This is an extreme example, of course, but the point is made. Relying entirely on inheritance to define your functionality can lead to a multiplicity of classes and a tendency toward duplication.

Let's take a more commonplace example at this point. Serious web applications often have to perform a range of actions on a request before a task is initiated to form a response. You might need to authenticate the user, for example, and to log the request. Perhaps you should process the request to build a data structure from raw input. Finally, you must perform your core processing. You are presented with the same problem.

You can extend the functionality of a base ProcessRequest class with additional processing in a derived LogRequest class, in a StructureRequest class, and in an AuthenticateRequest class. You can see this class hierarchy in Figure 10-4.

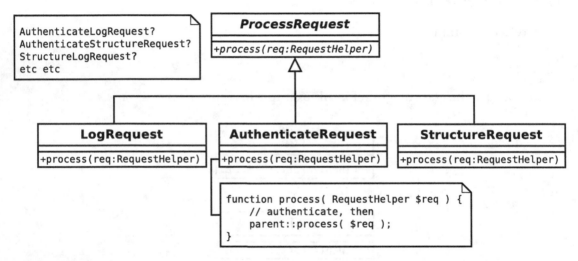

Figure 10-4. *More hard-coded variations*

What happens, though, when you need to perform logging and authentication, but not data preparation? Do you create a LogAndAuthenticateProcessor class? Clearly, it is time to find a more flexible solution.

Implementation

Rather than use only inheritance to solve the problem of varying functionality, the Decorator pattern uses composition and delegation. In essence, Decorator classes manage a reference to instance of another class of their own type. A Decorator will implement an operation so that it calls the same operation on the object to which it has a reference before (or after) performing its own actions. In this way, it is possible to build a pipeline of Decorator objects at runtime.

Let's rewrite our game example to illustrate this:

```
// listing 10.22
abstract class Tile
{
    abstract public function getWealthFactor(): int;
}
```

```
// listing 10.23
class Plains extends Tile
{
    private int $wealthfactor = 2;

    public function getWealthFactor(): int
    {
        return $this->wealthfactor;
    }
}
```

```
// listing 10.24
abstract class TileDecorator extends Tile
{
    protected Tile $tile;

    public function construct(Tile $tile)
    {
        $this->tile = $tile;
    }
}
```

Here, I have declared Tile and Plains classes as before, but I have also introduced a new class: TileDecorator. This does not implement getWealthFactor(), so it must be declared abstract. I define a constructor that requires a Tile object, which it stores in a property called $tile. I make this property protected so that child classes can gain access to it. Now I'll redefine the Pollution and Diamond classes:

```
// listing 10.25

class DiamondDecorator extends TileDecorator
{
    public function getWealthFactor(): int
    {
        return $this->tile->getWealthFactor() + 2;
    }
}
```

```
// listing 10.26

class PollutionDecorator extends TileDecorator
{
    public function getWealthFactor(): int
    {
        return $this->tile->getWealthFactor() - 4;
    }
}
```

Each of these classes extends TileDecorator. This means that they have a reference to a Tile object. When getWealthFactor() is invoked, each of these classes invokes the same method on its Tile reference before making its own adjustment.

By using composition and delegation like this, you make it easy to combine objects at runtime. Because all the objects in the pattern extend Tile, the client does not need to know which combination it is working with. It can be sure that a getWealthFactor() method is available for any Tile object, whether it is decorating another behind the scenes or not:

```
// listing 10.27
$tile = new Plains();
print $tile->getWealthFactor(); // 2
```

Plains is a component. It simply returns 2:

```
// listing 10.28
$tile = new DiamondDecorator(new Plains());
print $tile->getWealthFactor(); // 4
```

DiamondDecorator has a reference to a Plains object. It invokes getWealthFactor() before adding its own weighting of 2:

```
// listing 10.29
$tile = new PollutionDecorator(new DiamondDecorator(new Plains()));
print $tile->getWealthFactor(); // 0
```

PollutionDecorator has a reference to a DiamondDecorator object, which has its own Tile reference.

You can see the class diagram for this example in Figure 10-5.

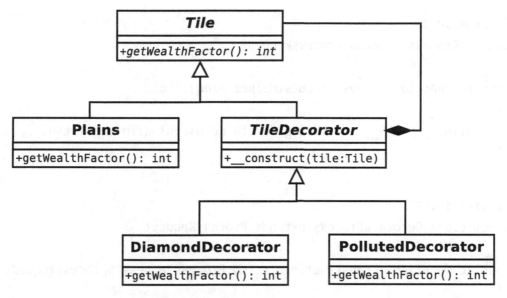

Figure 10-5. *The Decorator pattern*

This model is very extensible. You can add new decorators and components very easily. With lots of decorators, you can build very flexible structures at runtime. The component class, Plains in this case, can be significantly modified in many ways without the need to build the totality of the modifications into the class hierarchy. In plain English, this means you can have a polluted Plains object that has diamonds, without having to create a PollutedDiamondPlains object.

The Decorator pattern builds up pipelines that are very useful for creating filters. The java.io package makes great use of decorator classes. The client coder can combine decorator objects with core components to add filtering, buffering, compression, and so on to core methods like read(). My web request example can also be developed into a configurable pipeline. Here's a simple implementation that uses the Decorator pattern:

```
// listing 10.30
class RequestHelper
{
}
```

```
// listing 10.31
abstract class ProcessRequest
{
    abstract public function process(RequestHelper $req): void;
}
```

```
// listing 10.32
class MainProcess extends ProcessRequest
{
    public function process(RequestHelper $req): void
    {
        print __CLASS__ . ": doing something useful with request\n";
    }
}
```

```
// listing 10.33
abstract class DecorateProcess extends ProcessRequest
{
    public function __construct(protected ProcessRequest $processrequest)
    {
    }
}
```

As before, we define an abstract superclass (ProcessRequest), a concrete component (MainProcess), and an abstract decorator (DecorateProcess). MainProcess::process() does nothing but report that it has been called. DecorateProcess stores a ProcessRequest object on behalf of its children. Here are some simple concrete decorator classes:

```
// listing 10.34
class LogRequest extends DecorateProcess
{
    public function process(RequestHelper $req): void
    {
        print __CLASS__ . ": logging request\n";
        $this->processrequest->process($req);
    }
}

// listing 10.35
class AuthenticateRequest extends DecorateProcess
{
    public function process(RequestHelper $req): void
    {
        print __CLASS__ . ": authenticating request\n";
        $this->processrequest->process($req);
    }
}

// listing 10.36
class StructureRequest extends DecorateProcess
{
    public function process(RequestHelper $req): void
    {
        print __CLASS__ . ": structuring request data\n";
        $this->processrequest->process($req);
    }
}
```

Each process() method outputs a message before calling the referenced
ProcessRequest object's own process() method. You can now combine objects
instantiated from these classes at runtime to build filters that perform different actions
on a request and in different orders. Here's some code to combine objects from all these
concrete classes into a single filter:

```
// listing 10.37
$process = new AuthenticateRequest(
    new StructureRequest(
        new LogRequest(
            new MainProcess()
        )
    )
);
$process->process(new  RequestHelper());
```

This code gives the following output:

```
popp\ch10\batch07\AuthenticateRequest: authenticating request
popp\ch10\batch07\StructureRequest: structuring request data
popp\ch10\batch07\LogRequest: logging request
popp\ch10\batch07\MainProcess: doing something useful with request
```

Note   This example is, in fact, also an instance of an enterprise pattern called Intercepting Filter. Intercepting Filter is described in *Core J2EE Patterns: Best Practices and Design Strategies (Prentice Hall, 2001)* by Alur et al.

Consequences

Like the Composite pattern, Decorator can be confusing. It is important to remember that both composition and inheritance are coming into play at the same time. So LogRequest inherits its interface from ProcessRequest, but it is acting as a wrapper around another ProcessRequest object.

Because a decorator object forms a wrapper around a child object, it helps to keep the interface as sparse as possible. If you build a heavily featured base class, then decorators are forced to delegate to all public methods in their contained object. This can be done in the abstract decorator class, but it still introduces the kind of coupling that can lead to bugs.

Some programmers create decorators that do not share a common type with the objects they modify. As long as they fulfill the same interface as these objects, this strategy can work well. You get the benefit of being able to use the built-in interceptor methods to automate delegation (implementing `call()` to catch calls to nonexistent methods and invoking the same method on the child object automatically). However, by doing this, you also lose the safety afforded by class type checking. In our examples so far, client code can demand a `Tile` or a `ProcessRequest` object in its argument list and be certain of its interface, whether or not the object in question is heavily decorated.

The Facade Pattern

You may have had occasion to stitch third-party systems into your own projects in the past. Whether or not the code is object oriented, it will often be daunting, large, and complex. Your own code, too, may become a challenge to the client programmer who needs only to access a few features. The `Facade` pattern is a way of providing a simple, clear interface to complex systems.

The Problem

Systems tend to evolve large amounts of code that is really only useful within the system itself. Just as classes define clear public interfaces and hide their guts away from the rest of the world, so should well-designed systems. However, it is not always clear which parts of a system are designed to be used by client code and which are best hidden.

As you work with subsystems (like web forums or gallery applications), you may find yourself making calls deep into the logic of the code. If the subsystem code is subject to change over time, and your code interacts with it at many different points, you may find yourself with a serious maintenance problem as the subsystem evolves.

Similarly, when you build your own systems, it is a good idea to organize distinct parts into separate tiers. Typically, you may have a tier responsible for application logic, another for database interaction, another for presentation, and so on. You should aspire to keep these tiers as independent of one another as you can, so that a change in one area of your project will have minimal repercussions elsewhere. If code from one tier is tightly integrated into code from another, then this objective is hard to meet.

Here is some deliberately confusing procedural code that makes a song-and-dance routine of the simple process of getting log information from a file and turning it into object data:

```
// listing 10.38

function getProductFileLines(string $file): array
{
    return file($file);
}

function getProductObjectFromId(string $id, string $productname): Product
{
    // some kind of database lookup
    return new Product($id, $productname);
}

function getNameFromLine(string $line): string
{
    if (preg_match("/.*-(.*)\s\d+/", $line, $array)) {
        return str_replace('_', ' ', $array[1]);
    }
    return '';
}

function getIDFromLine($line): int|string
{
    if (preg_match("/^(\d{1,3})-/", $line, $array)) {
        return $array[1];
    }
    return -1;
}

class Product
{
    public string $id;
    public string $name;
```

```
public function __construct(string $id, string $name)
{
    $this->id = $id;
    $this->name = $name;
}
```
}

Let's imagine that the internals of this code are more complicated than they actually are and that I am stuck with using it rather than rewriting it from scratch. For example, assume I have to turn a file that contains lines like these into an array of objects:

```
234-ladies_jumper 55
532-gents_hat 44
```

To do so, I must call all of these functions (note that, for the sake of brevity, I don't extract the final number, which represents a price):

```
// listing 10.39
$lines = getProductFileLines(__DIR__ . '/test2.txt');
$objects = [];
foreach ($lines as $line) {
    $id = getIDFromLine($line);
    $name = getNameFromLine($line);
    $objects[$id] = getProductObjectFromID($id, $name);
}

print_r($objects);
```

Here is the output:

```
Array
(
    [234] => Product Object
    (
        [id] => 234
        [name] => ladies jumper
    )
```

```
[532] => Product Object
(
    [id] => 532
    [name] => gents hat
)
```
)

If I call these functions directly like this throughout my project, my code will become tightly wound into the subsystem it is using. This could cause problems if the subsystem changes or if I decide to switch it out entirely. I really need to introduce a gateway between the system and the rest of our code.

Implementation

Here is a simple class that provides an interface to the procedural code you encountered in the previous section:

```
// listing 10.40
class ProductFacade
{
    private array $products = [];

    public function __construct(private string $file)
    {
        $this->compile();
    }

    private function compile(): void
    {
        $lines = getProductFileLines($this->file);
        foreach ($lines as $line) {
            $id = getIDFromLine($line);
            $name = getNameFromLine($line);
            $this->products[$id] = getProductObjectFromID($id, $name);
        }
    }
}
```

```
public function getProducts(): array
{
    return $this->products;
}

public function getProduct(string $id): ?\Product
{
    if (isset($this->products[$id])) {
        return $this->products[$id];
    }
    return null;
}

}
```

From the point of view of the client code, access to `Product` objects from a log file is much simplified:

```
// listing 10.41
$facade = new ProductFacade(__DIR__ . '/test2.txt');
$object = $facade->getProduct("234");
```

Consequences

A Facade is really a very simple concept. It is just a matter of creating a single point of entry for a tier or subsystem. This has a number of benefits. It helps to decouple distinct areas in a project from one another. It is useful and convenient for client coders to have access to simple methods that achieve clear ends. It reduces errors by focusing the use of a subsystem in one place; changes to the subsystem should cause failure in a predictable location. Errors are also minimized by Facade classes in complex subsystems where client code might otherwise use internal functions incorrectly.

Despite the simplicity of the Facade pattern, it is all too easy to forget to use it, especially if you are familiar with the subsystem you are working with. There is a balance to be struck, of course. On the one hand, the benefit of creating simple interfaces to complex systems should be clear. On the other hand, one could abstract systems with reckless abandon and then abstract the abstractions. If you are making significant simplifications for the clear benefit of client code, and/or shielding it from systems that might change, then you are probably right to implement the Facade pattern.

Summary

In this chapter, I looked at a few of the ways that classes and objects can be organized in a system. In particular, I focused on the principle that composition can be used to engender flexibility where inheritance fails. In both the `Composite` and `Decorator` patterns, inheritance is used to promote composition and to define a common interface that provides guarantees for client code.

You also saw delegation used effectively in these patterns. Finally, I looked at the simple but powerful `Facade` pattern. `Facade` is one of those patterns that many people have been using for years without having a name to give it. `Facade` lets you provide a clean point of entry to a tier or subsystem. In PHP, the `Facade` pattern is also used to create object wrappers that encapsulate blocks of procedural code.

CHAPTER 11

Performing and Representing Tasks

In this chapter, we get active. I look at patterns that help you to get things done, whether interpreting a mini-language or encapsulating an algorithm.

This chapter will walk you through several patterns:

- *The Interpreter pattern*: Building a mini-language interpreter that can be used to create scriptable applications

- *The Strategy pattern*: Identifying algorithms in a system and encapsulating them into their own types

- *The Observer pattern*: Creating hooks for alerting disparate objects about system events

- *The Visitor pattern*: Applying an operation to all the nodes in a tree of objects

- *The Command pattern*: Creating command objects that can be saved and passed around

- *The Null Object pattern*: Using nonoperational objects in place of null values

The Interpreter Pattern

Languages are written in other languages (at least at first). PHP itself, for example, is written in C. By the same token, odd as it may sound, you can define and run your own languages using PHP. Of course, any language you might create will be slow and somewhat limited. Nonetheless, mini-languages can be very useful, as you will see in this chapter.

© Matt Zandstra 2021
M. Zandstra, *PHP 8 Objects, Patterns, and Practice*, https://doi.org/10.1007/978-1-4842-6791-2_11

The Problem

When you create web (or command-line) interfaces in PHP, you give the user access to functionality. The trade-off in interface design is between power and ease of use. As a rule, the more power you give your user, the more cluttered and confusing your interface becomes. Good interface design can help a lot here, of course. But if 90% of users are using the same 30% of your features, the costs of piling on the functionality may outweigh the benefits. You may wish to consider simplifying your system for most users. But what of the power users, that 10% who use your system's advanced features? Perhaps you can accommodate them in a different way. By offering such users a domain language (often called a DSL—Domain-Specific Language), you might actually extend the power of your application.

Of course, you have a programming language at hand right away. It's called PHP. Here's how you could allow your users to script your system:

```
// listing 11.01
$form_input = $_REQUEST['form_input'];
// contains: "print file_get_contents('/etc/passwd');"
eval($form_input);
```

This approach to making an application scriptable is clearly insane. Just in case the reasons are not blatantly obvious, they boil down to two issues: security and complexity. The security issue is well addressed in the example. By allowing users to execute PHP via your script, you are effectively giving them access to the server the script runs on. The complexity issue is just as big a drawback. No matter how clear your code is, the average user is unlikely to extend it easily and certainly not from the browser window.

A mini-language, though, can address both these problems. You can design flexibility into the language, reduce the possibility that the user can do damage, and keep things focused.

Imagine an application for authoring quizzes. Producers design questions and establish rules for marking the answers submitted by contestants. It is a requirement that quizzes must be marked without human intervention, even though some answers can be typed into a text field by users.

Here's a question:

```
How many members in the Design Patterns gang?
```

You can accept "four" or "4" as correct answers. You might create a web interface that allows a producer to use a regular expression for marking responses:

```
^4|four$
```

Most producers are not hired for their knowledge of regular expressions, however. To make everyone's life easier, you might implement a more user-friendly mechanism for marking responses:

```
$input equals "4" or $input equals "four"
```

You propose a language that supports variables, an operator called equals, and Boolean logic (or and and). Programmers love naming things, so let's call it MarkLogic. It should be easy to extend, as you envisage lots of requests for richer features. Let's leave aside the issue of parsing input for now and concentrate on a mechanism for plugging these elements together at runtime to produce an answer. This, as you might expect, is where the Interpreter pattern comes in.

Implementation

A language contains expressions (i.e., things that resolve to a value). As you can see in Table 11-1, even a tiny language like MarkLogic needs to keep track of a lot of elements.

Table 11-1. *Elements of the MarkLogic Grammar*

Description	EBNF Meta-identifier	Class Name	Example
Variable	variable	VariableExpression	$input
String literal	stringLiteral	LiteralExpression	"four"
Boolean and	andExpr	BooleanAndExpression	$input equals '4' and $other equals '6'
Boolean or	orExpr	BooleanOrExpression	$input equals '4' or $other equals '6'
Equality test	eqExpr	BooleanEqualsExpression	$input equals '4'

Table 11-1 lists EBNF names. So what is EBNF all about? EBNF is a syntactic meta-language that you can use to describe a language grammar. EBNF stands for Extended Backus-Naur Form. It consists of a series of lines (called productions), each one consisting of a name and a description that takes the form of references to other productions and to terminals (i.e., elements that are not themselves made up of references to other productions). Here is one way of describing my grammar using EBNF:

```
Expr     = operand { orExpr | andExpr }
Operand  = ( '(' expr ')' | ? string literal ? | variable ) { eqExpr }
orExpr   = 'or' operand
andExpr  = 'and' operand
eqExpr   = 'equals' operand
variable = '$' , ? word ?
```

Some symbols have special meanings (that should be familiar from regular expression notation): | (more properly a definition separator) can be loosely thought of as *or* for, for example. You can group identifiers using brackets. So in the example, an expression (expr) consists of an operand followed by zero or more of either orExpr or andExpr. An operand can be a bracketed expr (i.e., an expr wrapped in literal "(" and ")" characters), a quoted string (I have omitted the production for this), or a variable followed by zero or more instances of eqExpr. Once you get the hang of referring from one production to another, EBNF becomes quite easy to read.

In Figure 11-1, I represent the elements of my grammar as classes.

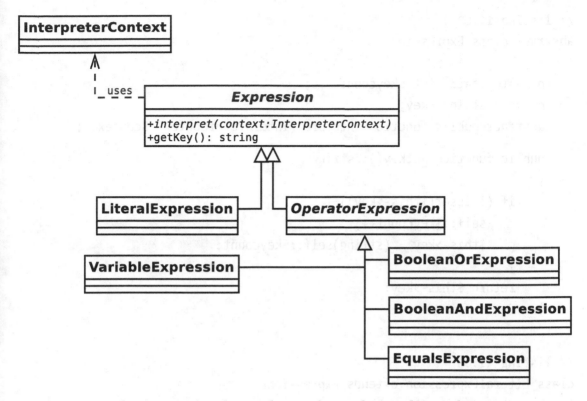

Figure 11-1. *The Interpreter classes that make up the MarkLogic language*

As you can see, BooleanAndExpression and its siblings inherit from
OperatorExpression. This is because these classes all perform their operations upon
other Expression objects. VariableExpression and LiteralExpression work directly
with values.

All Expression objects implement an interpret() method that is defined
in the abstract base class, Expression. The interpret() method expects an
InterpreterContext object that is used as a shared data store. Each Expression object
can store data in the InterpreterContext object. The InterpreterContext will then be
passed along to other Expression objects. So that data can be retrieved easily from the
InterpreterContext, the Expression base class implements a getKey() method that
returns a unique handle. Let's see how this works in practice with an implementation of
Expression:

```php
// listing 11.02
abstract class Expression
{
    private static int $keycount = 0;
    private string $key;
    abstract public function interpret(InterpreterContext $context);

    public function getKey(): string
    {
        if (! isset($this->key)) {
            self::$keycount++;
            $this->key = (string)self::$keycount;
        }
        return $this->key;
    }
}

// listing 11.03
class LiteralExpression extends Expression
{
    private mixed $value;

    public function __construct(mixed $value)
    {
        $this->value = $value;
    }

    public function interpret(InterpreterContext $context): void
    {
        $context->replace($this, $this->value);
    }
}

// listing 11.04
class InterpreterContext
{
    private array $expressionstore = [];
```

```php
    public function replace(Expression $exp, mixed $value): void
    {
        $this->expressionstore[$exp->getKey()] = $value;
    }

    public function lookup(Expression $exp): mixed
    {
        return $this->expressionstore[$exp->getKey()];
    }
}

// listing 11.05
$context = new InterpreterContext();
$literal = new LiteralExpression('four');
$literal->interpret($context);
print $context->lookup($literal) . "\n";
```

Here's the output:

four

I'll begin with the InterpreterContext class. As you can see, it is really only a front
end for an associative array, $expressionstore, which I use to hold data. The replace()
method accepts an Expression object as key and a value of any type and then adds the
pair to $expressionstore. It also provides a lookup() method for retrieving data.

The Expression class defines the abstract interpret() method and a concrete getKey()
method that uses a static counter value to generate, store, and return a string identifier.

This method is used by InterpreterContext::lookup() and
InterpreterContext::replace() to index data.

The LiteralExpression class defines a constructor that accepts a value argument.
The interpret() method requires an InterpreterContext object. I simply call
replace() using getKey() to define the key for retrieval and the $value property.
This will become a familiar pattern as you examine the other Expression classes. The
interpret() method always inscribes its results upon the InterpreterContext object.

I include some client code as well, instantiating both an InterpreterContext object
and a LiteralExpression object (with a value of "four"). I pass the InterpreterContext
object to LiteralExpression::interpret(). The interpret() method stores the
key/value pair in InterpreterContext, from where I retrieve the value by calling lookup().

Here's the remaining terminal class. VariableExpression is a little more complicated:

```php
// listing 11.06
class VariableExpression extends Expression
{
    public function __construct(private string $name, private mixed $val =
    null)
    {
    }

    public function interpret(InterpreterContext $context): void
    {
        if (! is_null($this->val)) {
            $context->replace($this, $this->val);
            $this->val = null;
        }
    }

    public function setValue(mixed $value): void
    {
        $this->val = $value;
    }

    public function getKey(): string
    {
        return $this->name;
    }
}

// listing 11.07
$context = new InterpreterContext();
$myvar = new VariableExpression('input', 'four');
$myvar->interpret($context);
print $context->lookup($myvar) . "\n";
// output: four
```

```
$newvar = new VariableExpression('input');
$newvar->interpret($context);
print $context->lookup($newvar) . "\n";
// output: four

$myvar->setValue("five");
$myvar->interpret($context);
print $context->lookup($myvar) . "\n";
// output: five
print $context->lookup($newvar) . "\n";
// output: five
```

The VariableExpression class accepts both name and value arguments for storage in property variables. I provide the setValue() method, so that client code can change the value at any time.

The interpret() method checks whether or not the $val property has a nonnull value. If the $val property has a value, it sets it on the InterpreterContext. I then set the $val property to null. This is in case interpret() is called again after another identically named instance of VariableExpression has changed the value in the InterpreterContext object. This is quite a limited variable, accepting only string values. If you intend to extend your language, you should consider having it work with other Expression objects, so that it can contain the results of tests and operations. For now, though, VariableExpression will do the work I need of it. Notice that I have overridden the getKey() method, so that variable values are linked to the variable name and not to an arbitrary static ID.

Operator expressions in the language all work with two other Expression objects in order to get their job done. It makes sense, therefore, to have them extend a common superclass. Here is the OperatorExpression class:

```
// listing 11.08
abstract class OperatorExpression extends Expression
{
    public function __construct(protected Expression $l_op, protected
    Expression $r_op)
    {
    }
```

```
public function interpret(InterpreterContext $context): void
{
    $this->l_op->interpret($context);
    $this->r_op->interpret($context);
    $result_l = $context->lookup($this->l_op);
    $result_r = $context->lookup($this->r_op);
    $this->doInterpret($context, $result_l, $result_r);
}

abstract protected function doInterpret(
    InterpreterContext $context,
    $result_l,
    $result_r
): void;
}
```

OperatorExpression is an abstract class. It implements interpret(), but it also defines the abstract dointerpret() method.

The constructor demands two Expression objects, $l_op and $r_op, which it stores in properties.

The interpret() method begins by invoking interpret() on both its operand properties (if you have read the previous chapter, you might notice that I am creating an instance of the Composite pattern here). Once the operands have been run, interpret() still needs to acquire the values that this yields. It does this by calling InterpreterContext::lookup() for each property. It then calls dointerpret(), leaving it up to child classes to decide what to do with the results of these operations.

Note   dointerpret() is an instance of the Template Method pattern. In this pattern, a parent class both defines and calls an abstract method, leaving it up to child classes to provide an implementation. This can streamline the development of concrete classes, as shared functionality is handled by the superclass, leaving the children to concentrate on clean, narrow objectives.

Here's the BooleanEqualsExpression class, which tests two Expression objects for equality:

```
// listing 11.09
class BooleanEqualsExpression extends OperatorExpression
{
    protected function doInterpret(
        InterpreterContext $context,
        mixed $result_l,
        mixed $result_r
    ): void {
        $context->replace($this, $result_l == $result_r);
    }
}
```

BooleanEqualsExpression only implements the dointerpret() method, which tests the equality of the operand results it has been passed by the interpret() method, placing the result in the InterpreterContext object.

To wrap up the Expression classes, here are BooleanOrExpression and BooleanAndExpression:

```
// listing 11.10
class BooleanOrExpression extends OperatorExpression
{
    protected function doInterpret(
        InterpreterContext $context,
        mixed $result_l,
        mixed $result_r
    ): void {
        $context->replace($this, $result_l || $result_r);
    }
}

// listing 11.11
class BooleanAndExpression extends OperatorExpression
{
    protected function doInterpret(
        InterpreterContext $context,
```

```
        mixed $result_l,
        mixed $result_r
    ): void {
        $context->replace($this, $result_l && $result_r);
    }
}
```

Instead of testing for equality, the BooleanOrExpression class applies a logical or operation and stores the result of that via the InterpreterContext::replace() method. BooleanAndExpression, of course, applies a logical and operation.

I now have enough code to execute the mini-language fragment I quoted earlier. Here it is again:

```
$input equals "4" or $input equals "four"
```

Here's how I can build this statement up with my Expression classes:

```
// listing 11.12
$context = new InterpreterContext();
$input = new VariableExpression('input');
$statement = new BooleanOrExpression(
    new BooleanEqualsExpression($input, new LiteralExpression('four')),
    new BooleanEqualsExpression($input, new LiteralExpression('4'))
);
```

I instantiate a variable called "input" but hold off on providing a value for it. I then create a BooleanOrExpression object that will compare the results from two BooleanEqualsExpression objects. The first of these objects compares the VariableExpression object stored in $input with a LiteralExpression containing the string "four"; the second compares $input with a LiteralExpression object containing the string "4".

Now, with my statement prepared, I am ready to provide a value for the input variable and run the code:

```
// listing 11.13
foreach ([ "four", "4", "52" ] as $val) {
    $input->setValue($val);
    print "$val:\n";
    $statement->interpret($context);
```

```
if ($context->lookup($statement)) {
    print "top marks\n\n";
} else {
    print "dunce hat on\n\n";
}
}
```

In fact, I run the code three times, with three different values. The first time through, I set the temporary variable $val to "four", assigning it to the input VariableExpression object using its setValue() method. I then call interpret() on the topmost Expression object (the BooleanOrExpression object that contains references to all other expressions in the statement). Here are the internals of this invocation, step by step:

- $statement calls interpret() on its $l_op property (the first BooleanEqualsExpression object).

- The first BooleanEqualsExpression object calls interpret() on *its* $l_op property (a reference to the input VariableExpression object, which is currently set to "four").

- The input VariableExpression object writes its current value to the provided InterpreterContext object by calling InterpreterContext ::replace().

- The first BooleanEqualsExpression object calls interpret() on its $r_op property (a LiteralExpression object charged with the value "four").

- The LiteralExpression object registers its key and its value with InterpreterContext.

- The first BooleanEqualsExpression object retrieves the values for $l_op ("four") and $r_op ("four") from the InterpreterContext object.

- The first BooleanEqualsExpression object compares these two values for equality and then registers the result (true) and its key with the InterpreterContext object.

- Back at the top of the tree, the $statement object (BooleanOrExpression) calls interpret() on its $r_op property. This resolves to a value (false, in this case) in the same way the $l_op property did.

- The $statement object retrieves values for each of its operands from the InterpreterContext object and compares them using ||. It is comparing true and false, so the result is true. This final result is stored in the InterpreterContext object.

And all that is only for the first iteration through the loop. Here is the final output:

```
four:
top marks 4:
top marks 52:
dunce hat on
```

You may need to read through this section a few times before the process clicks. The old issue of object vs. class trees might confuse you, here. Expression classes are arranged in an inheritance hierarchy, just as Expression objects are composed into a tree at runtime. As you read back through the code, keep this distinction in mind.

Figure 11-2 shows the complete class diagram for the example.

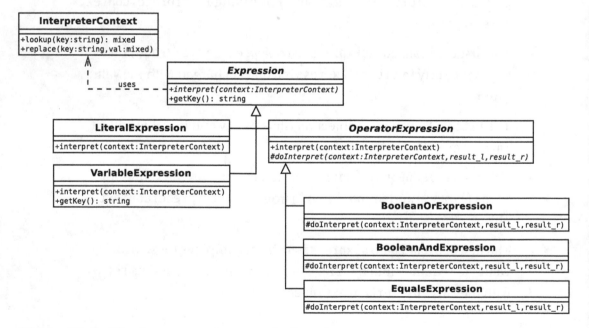

Figure 11-2. *The Interpreter pattern deployed*

Interpreter Issues

Once you set up the core classes for an Interpreter pattern implementation, it becomes easy to extend. The price you pay is in the sheer number of classes you could end up creating. For this reason, Interpreter is best applied to relatively small languages. If you have a need for a general-purpose programming language, you would do better to look for a third-party tool to use.

Because Interpreter classes often perform very similar tasks, it is worth keeping an eye on the classes you create with a view to factoring out duplication.

Many people approaching the Interpreter pattern for the first time are disappointed, after some initial excitement, to discover that it does not address parsing. This means that you are not yet in a position to offer your users a nice, friendly language. Appendix B contains some rough code to illustrate one strategy for parsing a mini-language.

The Strategy Pattern

Classes often try to do too much. It's understandable: you create a class that performs a few related actions; and, as you code, some of these actions need to be varied according to the circumstances. At the same time, your class needs to be split into subclasses. Before you know it, your design is being pulled apart by competing forces.

The Problem

Since I have recently built a marking language, I'm sticking with the quiz example. Quizzes need questions, so you build a Question class, giving it a mark() method. All is well until you need to support different marking mechanisms.

Imagine that you are asked to support the simple MarkLogic language, marking by straight match and regular expression. Your first thought might be to subclass for these differences, as in Figure 11-3.

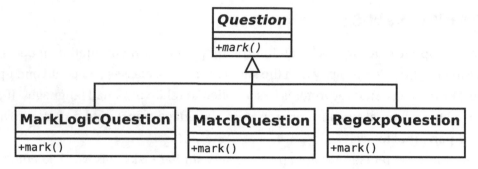

Figure 11-3. *Defining subclasses according to marking strategies*

This would serve you well, as long as marking remains the only aspect of the class that varies. Imagine, though, that you are called on to support different kinds of questions: those that are text based and those that support rich media. This presents you with a problem when it comes to incorporating these forces in one inheritance tree, as you can see in Figure 11-4.

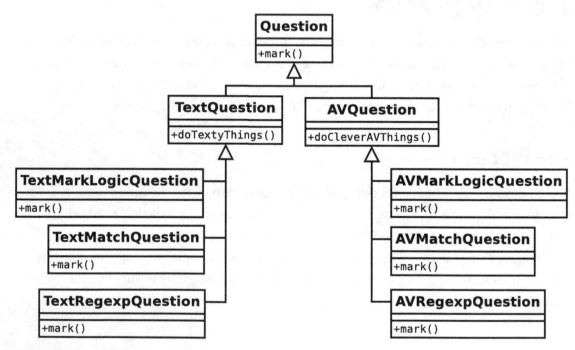

Figure 11-4. *Defining subclasses according to two forces*

Not only have the number of classes in the hierarchy ballooned, but you also necessarily introduce repetition. Your marking logic is reproduced across each branch of the inheritance hierarchy.

Whenever you find yourself repeating an algorithm across siblings in an inheritance tree (whether through subclassing or repeated conditional statements), consider abstracting these behaviors into their own type.

Implementation

As with all the best patterns, Strategy is simple and powerful. When classes must support multiple implementations of an interface (e.g., multiple marking mechanisms), the best approach is often to extract these implementations and place them in their own type rather than to extend the original class to handle them.

So, in the example, your approach to marking might be placed in a Marker type. Figure 11-5 shows the new structure.

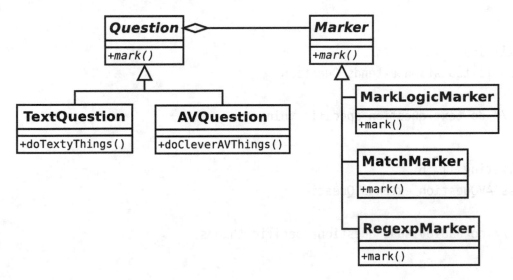

Figure 11-5. *Extracting algorithms into their own type*

Remember the Gang of Four principle, "Favor composition over inheritance"? This is an excellent example. By defining and encapsulating the marking algorithms, you reduce subclassing and increase flexibility. You can add new marking strategies at any time without the need to change the Question classes at all. All Question classes know is that they have an instance of a Marker at their disposal and that it is guaranteed by its interface to support a mark() method. The details of implementation are entirely somebody else's problem.

Here are the Question classes rendered as code:

```
// listing 11.14
abstract class Question
{
    public function __construct(protected string $prompt, protected Marker
    $marker)
    {
    }

    public function mark(string $response): bool
    {
        return $this->marker->mark($response);
    }
}
```

```
// listing 11.15
class TextQuestion extends Question
{
    // do text question specific things
}
```

```
// listing 11.16
class AVQuestion extends Question
{
    // do audiovisual question specific things
}
```

As you can see, I have left the exact nature of the difference between TextQuestion and AVQuestion to the imagination. The Question base class provides all the real functionality, storing a prompt property and a Marker object. When Question::mark() is called with a response from the end user, the method simply delegates the problem solving to its Marker object.

Now it's time to define some simple Marker objects:

```
// listing 11.17
abstract class Marker
{
    public function __construct(protected string $test)
```

```
    {
        abstract public function mark(string $response): bool;
}

// listing 11.18
class MarkLogicMarker extends Marker
{
    private MarkParse $engine;

    public function __construct(string $test)
    {
        parent:: __construct($test);
        $this->engine = new MarkParse($test);
    }

    public function mark(string $response): bool
    {
        return $this->engine->evaluate($response);
    }
}

// listing 11.19
class MatchMarker extends Marker
{
    public function mark(string $response): bool
    {
        return ($this->test == $response);
    }
}

// listing 11.20
class RegexpMarker extends Marker
{
    public function mark(string $response): bool
    {
        return (preg_match("$this->test", $response) === 1);
    }
}
```

There should be little, if anything, that is particularly surprising about the Marker classes themselves. Note that the MarkParse object is designed to work with the simple parser developed in Appendix B. The key here is in the structure that I have defined, rather than in the detail of the strategies themselves. I can swap RegexpMarker for MatchMarker, with no impact on the Question class.

Of course, you must still decide what method to use to choose between concrete Marker objects. I have seen two real-world approaches to this problem. In the first, producers used radio buttons to select the preferred marking strategy. In the second, the structure of the marking condition itself was used; that is, a match statement was left plain:

```
five
```

A MarkLogic statement was preceded by a colon:

```
:$input equals 'five'
```

And a regular expression used forward slashes:

```
/f.ve/
```

Here is some code to run the classes through their paces:

```
// listing 11.21
$markers = [
    new RegexpMarker("/f.ve/"),
    new MatchMarker("five"),
    new MarkLogicMarker('$input equals "five"')
];

foreach ($markers as $marker) {
    print get_class($marker) . "\n";
    $question = new TextQuestion("how many beans make five", $marker);

    foreach ([ "five", "four" ] as $response) {
        print " response: $response: ";
        if ($question->mark($response)) {
            print "well done\n";
```

```
    } else {
        print "never mind\n";
    }
  }
}
```

I construct three strategy objects, using each in turn to help construct a TextQuestion object. The TextQuestion object is then tried against two sample responses. Here is the output (including namespaces):

```
popp\ch11\batch02\RegexpMarker
    response: five: well done
    response: four: never mind

popp\ch11\batch02\MatchMarker
    response: five: well done
    response: four: never mind

popp\ch11\batch02\MarkLogicMarker
    response: five: well done
    response: five: never mind
```

In the example, I passed specific data (the $response variable) from the client to the strategy object via the mark() method. Sometimes, you may encounter circumstances in which you don't always know in advance how much information the strategy object will require when its operation is invoked. You can delegate the decision as to what data to acquire by passing the strategy an instance of the client itself. The strategy can then query the client in order to build the data it needs.

The Observer Pattern

Orthogonality is a virtue I have described before. One of our objectives as programmers should be to build components that can be altered or moved with minimal impact on other components. If every change we make to one component necessitates a ripple of changes elsewhere in the codebase, the task of development can quickly become a spiral of bug creation and elimination.

Of course, orthogonality is often just a dream. Elements in a system must have embedded references to other elements. You can, however, deploy various strategies to minimize this. You have seen various examples of polymorphism in which the client understands a component's interface, but the actual component may vary at runtime.

In some circumstances, you may wish to drive an even greater wedge between components than this. Consider a class responsible for handling a user's access to a system:

```
// listing 11.22
classLogin
{
    public const LOGIN_USER_UNKNOWN = 1;
    public const LOGIN_WRONG_PASS = 2;
    public const LOGIN_ACCESS = 3;

    private array $status = [];

    public function handleLogin(string $user, string $pass, string $ip):
    bool
    {
        $isvalid = false;
        switch (rand(1, 3)) {
            case 1:
                $this->setStatus(self::LOGIN_ACCESS, $user, $ip);
                $isvalid = true;
                break;
            case 2:
                $this->setStatus(self::LOGIN_WRONG_PASS, $user, $ip);
                $isvalid = false;
                break;
            case 3:
                $this->setStatus(self::LOGIN_USER_UNKNOWN, $user, $ip);
                $isvalid = false;
                break;
        }
```

```
        print "returning " . (($isvalid) ? "true" : "false") . "\n";

        return $isvalid;
    }

    private function setStatus(int $status, string $user, string $ip): void
    {
        $this->status = [$status, $user, $ip];
    }

    public function getStatus(): array
    {
        return $this->status;
    }
}
```

In a real-world example, of course, the handleLogin() method would validate the user against a storage mechanism. As it is, this class fakes the login process using the rand() function. There are three potential outcomes of a call to handleLogin(). The status flag may be set to LOGIN_ACCESS, LOGIN_WRONG_PASS, or LOGIN_USER_UNKNOWN.

Because the Login class is a gateway guarding the treasures of your business team, it may excite much interest during development and in the months beyond. Marketing might call you up and ask that you keep a log of IP addresses. You can add a call to your system's Logger class:

```
// listing 11.23
public function handleLogin(string $user, string $pass, string $ip): bool
{
    switch (rand(1, 3)) {
        case 1:
            $this->setStatus(self::LOGIN_ACCESS, $user, $ip);
            $isvalid = true;
            break;
        case 2:
            $this->setStatus(self::LOGIN_WRONG_PASS, $user, $ip);
            $isvalid = false;
            break;
```

```
        case 3:
            $this->setStatus(self::LOGIN_USER_UNKNOWN, $user, $ip);
            $isvalid = false;
            break;
    }

    Logger::logIP($user, $ip, $this->getStatus());

    return $isvalid;
}
```

Worried about security, the system administrators might ask for notification of failed logins. Once again, you can return to the login method and add a new call:

```
// listing 11.24
if (! $isvalid) {
    Notifier::mailWarning(
        $user,
        $ip,
        $this->getStatus()
    );
}
```

The business development team might announce a tie-in with a particular ISP, asking that a cookie be set when particular users log in. And so on, and so on.

These are all easy enough requests to fulfill, but addressing them comes at a cost to your design. The Login class soon becomes very tightly embedded into this particular system. You cannot pull it out and drop it into another product without going through the code line by line and removing everything that is specific to the old system. This isn't too hard, of course, but then you are off down the road of cut-and-paste coding. Now that you have two similar but distinct Login classes in your systems, you find that an improvement to one will necessitate the same changes in the other—until, inevitably and gracelessly, they fall out of alignment with one another.

So what can you do to save the Login class? The Observer pattern is a great fit here.

Implementation

At the core of the Observer pattern is the unhooking of client elements (the observers) from a central class (the subject). Observers need to be informed when events occur that the subject knows about. At the same time, you do not want the subject to have a hard-coded relationship with its observer classes.

To achieve this, you can allow observers to register themselves with the subject. You give the Login class three new methods, attach(), detach(), and notify(), and enforce this using an interface called Observable:

```
// listing 11.25
interface Observable
{
    public function attach(Observer $observer): void;
    public function detach(Observer $observer): void;
    public function notify(): void;
}
```

```
// listing 11.26
class Login implements Observable
{
    private array $observers = [];

    public const LOGIN_USER_UNKNOWN = 1;
    public const LOGIN_WRONG_PASS   = 2;
    public const LOGIN_ACCESS       = 3;

    public function attach(Observer $observer): void
    {
        $this->observers[] = $observer;
    }

    public function detach(Observer $observer): void
    {
        $this->observers = array_filter(
            $this->observers,
```

```
                function ($a) use ($observer) {
                    return (! ($a === $observer ));
                }
        );
    }

    public function notify(): void
    {
        foreach ($this->observers as $obs) {
            $obs->update($this);
        }
    }

    // ...
}
```

So the Login class manages a list of observer objects. These can be added by a third party using the attach() method and removed via detach(). The notify() method is called to tell the observers that something of interest has happened. The method simply loops through the list of observers, calling update() on each one.

The Login class itself calls notify() from its handleLogin() method:

```
// listing 11.27
public function handleLogin(string $user, string $pass, string $ip): bool
{
    switch (rand(1, 3)) {
        case 1:
            $this->setStatus(self::LOGIN_ACCESS, $user, $ip);
            $isvalid = true;
            break;
        case 2:
            $this->setStatus(self::LOGIN_WRONG_PASS, $user, $ip);
            $isvalid = false;
            break;
```

```
        case 3:
            $this->setStatus(self::LOGIN_USER_UNKNOWN, $user, $ip);
            $isvalid = false;
            break;
    }

    $this->notify();

    return $isvalid;
}
```

Here's the interface for the Observer class:

```
// listing 11.28
interface Observer
{
    public function update(Observable $observable): void;
}
```

Any object that uses this interface can be added to the Login class via the attach()
method. Here's a concrete instance:

```
// listing 11.29
class LoginAnalytics implements Observer
{
    public function update(Observable $observable): void
    {
        // not type safe!
        $status = $observable->getStatus();
        print __CLASS __ . ": doing something with status info\n";
    }
}
```

Notice how the observer object uses the instance of Observable to get more
information about the event. It is up to the subject class to provide methods that
observers can query to learn about state. In this case, I have defined a method called
getStatus() that observers can call to get a snapshot of the current state of play.

This addition also highlights a problem, though. By calling `Login::getStatus()`, the `LoginAnalytics` class assumes more knowledge than it safely can. It is making this call on an `Observable` object, but there's no guarantee that this will also be a `Login` object. I have a couple of options here. I could extend the `Observable` interface to include a `getStatus()` declaration and perhaps rename it to something like `ObservableLogin` to signal that it is specific to the `Login` type.

Alternatively, I could keep the `Observable` interface generic and make the `Observer` classes responsible for ensuring that their subjects are of the correct type. They could even handle the chore of attaching themselves to their subject. Since there will be more than one type of `Observer`, and since I'm planning to perform some housekeeping that is common to all of them, here's an abstract superclass to handle the donkey work:

```
// listing 11.30
abstract class LoginObserver implements Observer
{
    private Login $login;

    public function __construct(Login $login)
    {
        $this->login = $login;
        $login->attach($this);
    }

    public function update(Observable $observable): void
    {
        if ($observable === $this->login) {
            $this->doUpdate($observable);
        }
    }

    abstract public function doUpdate(Login $login): void;
}
```

The `LoginObserver` class requires a `Login` object in its constructor. It stores a reference and calls `Login::attach()`. When `update()` is called, it checks that the provided `Observable` object is the correct reference. It then calls a Template Method: `doUpdate()`. I can now create a suite of `LoginObserver` objects, all of which can be secure they are working with a `Login` object and not just any old `Observable`:

```
// listing 11.31
class SecurityMonitor extends LoginObserver
{
    public function doUpdate(Login $login): void
    {
        $status = $login->getStatus();
        if ($status[0] == Login::LOGIN_WRONG_PASS) {
            // send mail to sysadmin
            print __CLASS__ . ": sending mail to sysadmin\n";
        }
    }
}

// listing 11.32
class GeneralLogger extends LoginObserver
{
    public function doUpdate(Login $login): void
    {
        $status = $login->getStatus();
        // add login data to log
        print __CLASS__ . ": add login data to log\n";
    }
}

// listing 11.33
class PartnershipTool extends LoginObserver
{
    public function doUpdate(Login $login): void
    {
        $status = $login->getStatus();
        // check $ip address
        // set cookie if it matches a list
        print __CLASS__ . ": set cookie if it matches a list\n";
    }
}
```

Creating and attaching LoginObserver classes is now achieved in one go at the time of instantiation:

```
// listing 11.34
$login = new Login();
new SecurityMonitor($login);
new GeneralLogger($login);
new PartnershipTool($login);
```

So now I have created a flexible association between the subject classes and the observers. You can see the class diagram for the example in Figure 11-6.

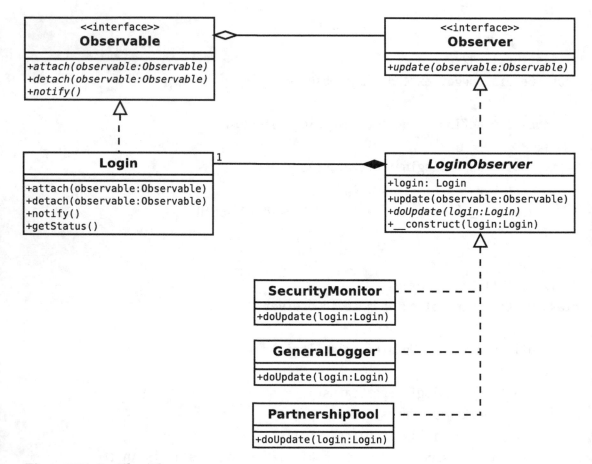

Figure 11-6. *The Observer pattern*

PHP provides built-in support for the Observer pattern through the bundled SPL (Standard PHP Library) extension. The SPL is a set of tools that help with common, largely object-oriented problems. The Observer aspect of this OO Swiss Army knife consists of three elements: SplObserver, SplSubject, and SplObjectStorage. SplObserver and SplSubject are interfaces and exactly parallel the Observer and Observable interfaces shown in this section's example. SplObjectStorage is a utility class designed to provide improved storage and removal of objects. Here's an edited version of the Observer implementation:

```php
// listing 11.35
class Login implements \SplSubject
{
    private \SplObjectStorage $storage;

    // ...
    public function __construct()
    {
        $this->storage = new \SplObjectStorage();
    }

    public function attach(\SplObserver $observer): void
    {
        $this->storage->attach($observer);
    }

    public function detach(\SplObserver $observer): void
    {
        $this->storage->detach($observer);
    }

    public function notify(): void
    {
        foreach ($this->storage as $obs) {
            $obs->update($this);
        }
    }

    // ...
}
```

```
// listing 11.36
abstract class LoginObserver implements \SplObserver
{
    public function __construct(private Login $login)
    {
        $login->attach($this);
    }
    public function update(\SplSubject $subject): void
    {
        if ($subject === $this->login) {
            $this->doUpdate($subject);
        }
    }

    abstract public function doUpdate(Login $login): void;
}
```

There are no real differences, as far as `SplObserver` (which was `Observer`) and `SplSubject` (which was `Observable`) are concerned—except, of course, I no longer need to declare the interfaces, and I must alter my type hinting according to the new names. `SplObjectStorage` provides you with a really useful service, however. You may have noticed that, in my initial example, my implementation of `Login::detach()` applied `array_filter` (together with an anonymous function) to the `$observers` array, in order to find and remove the argument object. The `SplObjectStorage` class does this work for you under the hood. It implements `attach()` and `detach()` methods and can be passed to `foreach` and iterated like an array.

Note   You can read more about SPL in the PHP documentation at `www.php. net/spl`. In particular, you will find many iterator tools there. I cover PHP's built-in Iterator interface in Chapter 13.

Another approach to the problem of communicating between an `Observable` class and its `Observer` could be to pass specific state information via the `update()` method, rather than an instance of the subject class. For a quick-and-dirty solution, this is often the approach I would take initially. So in the example, `update()` would expect a status flag, the username, and IP address (probably in an array for portability), rather than an instance of Login. This saves you from having to write a state method in the Login class. On the other hand, where the subject class stores a lot of state, passing an instance of it to update() allows observers much more flexibility.

You could also lock down type completely, by making the Login class refuse to work with anything other than a specific type of observer class (LoginObserver, perhaps). If you want to do that, then you may consider some kind of runtime check on objects passed to the attach() method; otherwise, you may need to reconsider the Observable interface altogether.

Once again, I have used composition at runtime to build a flexible and extensible model. The Login class can be extracted from its context and dropped into an entirely different project without qualification. There, it might work with a different set of observers.

The Visitor Pattern

As you have seen, many patterns aim to build structures at runtime, following the principle that composition is more flexible than inheritance. The ubiquitous Composite pattern is an excellent example of this. When you work with collections of objects, you may need to apply various operations to the structure that involve working with each individual component. Such operations can be built into the components themselves. After all, components are often best placed to invoke one another.

This approach is not without issues. You do not always know about all the operations you may need to perform on a structure. If you add support for new operations to your classes on a case-by-case basis, you can bloat your interface with responsibilities that don't really fit. As you might guess, the Visitor pattern addresses these issues.

The Problem

Think back to the Composite example from the previous chapter. For a game, I created an army of components such that the whole and its parts can be treated interchangeably. You saw that operations can be built into components. Typically, leaf objects perform an operation, and composite objects call on their children to perform the operation:

```php
// listing 11.37
class Army extends CompositeUnit
{
    public function bombardStrength(): int
    {
        $strength = 0;

        foreach ($this->units() as $unit) {
            $strength += $unit->bombardStrength();
        }

        return $strength;
    }
}

// listing 11.38
class LaserCanonUnit extends Unit
{
    public function bombardStrength(): int
    {
        return 44;
    }
}
```

Where this operation is integral to the responsibility of the composite class, there is no problem. There are more peripheral tasks, however, that may not sit so happily on the interface.

Here's an operation that dumps textual information about leaf nodes. It could be added to the abstract Unit class:

```php
// listing 11.39
abstract class Unit
{
    // ...

    public function textDump($num = 0): string
    {
        $txtout = "";
        $pad = 4 * $num;
```

```
        $txtout .= sprintf("%{$pad}s", "");
        $txtout .= get_class($this) . ": ";
        $txtout .= "bombard: " . $this->bombardStrength() . "\n";

        return $txtout;
    }
    // ...

}
```

This method can then be overridden in the CompositeUnit class:

```
// listing 11.40
abstract class CompositeUnit extends Unit
{
    // ...
    public function textDump($num = 0): string
    {
        $txtout = parent::textDump($num);

        foreach ($this->units as $unit) {
            $txtout .= $unit->textDump($num + 1);
        }

        return $txtout;
    }
}
```

I could go on to create methods for counting the number of units in the tree, for saving components to a database, and for calculating the food units consumed by an army.

Why would I want to include these methods in the composite's interface? There is only one really compelling answer. I include these disparate operations here because this is where an operation can gain easy access to related nodes in the composite structure.

Although it is true that ease of traversal is part of the Composite pattern, it does not follow that every operation that needs to traverse the tree should therefore claim a place in the Composite's interface.

So these are the forces at work: I want to take full advantage of the easy traversal afforded by my object structure, but I want to do this without bloating the interface.

Implementation

I'll begin with the interfaces. In the abstract Unit class, I define an accept() method:

```
// listing 11.41
abstract class Unit
{
    // ...
    public function accept(ArmyVisitor $visitor): void
    {
        $refthis = new \ReflectionClass(get_class($this));
        $method = "visit" . $refthis->getShortName();
        $visitor->$method($this);
    }

    protected function setDepth($depth): void
    {
        $this->depth = $depth;
    }

    public function getDepth(): int
    {
        return $this->depth;
    }
}
```

As you can see, the accept() method expects an ArmyVisitor object to be passed to it. PHP allows you dynamically to define the method on the ArmyVisitor you wish to call, so I construct a method name based on the name of the current class and invoke that method on the provided ArmyVisitor object. If the current class is Army, then I invoke ArmyVisitor::visitArmy(). If the current class is TroopCarrier, then I invoke ArmyVisitor::visitTroopCarrier() and so on. This saves me from implementing accept() on every leaf node in my class hierarchy. While I was in the area, I also added two methods of convenience: getDepth() and setDepth(). These can be used to store and retrieve the depth of a unit in a tree. setDepth() is invoked by the unit's parent when it adds it to the tree from CompositeUnit::addUnit():

```
// listing 11.42
abstract class CompositeUnit extends Unit
{
    // ...

    public function addUnit(Unit $unit): void
    {
        foreach ($this->units as $thisunit) {
            if ($unit === $thisunit) {
                return;
            }
        }

        $unit->setDepth($this->depth + 1);
        $this->units[] = $unit;
    }

    public function accept(ArmyVisitor $visitor): void
    {
        parent::accept($visitor);

        foreach ($this->units as $thisunit) {
            $thisunit->accept($visitor);
        }
    }
}
```

I included an accept() method in this fragment. This calls Unit::accept() to invoke the relevant visit() method on the provided ArmyVisitor object. Then it loops through any child objects calling accept(). In fact, because accept() overrides its parent operation, the accept() method allows me to do two things:

- Invoke the correct visitor method for the current component

- Pass the visitor object to all the current element children via the accept() method (assuming the current component is composite)

I have yet to define the interface for ArmyVisitor. The accept() methods should give you some clue. The visitor class will define accept() methods for each of the concrete classes in the class hierarchy. This allows me to provide different functionality for different objects. In my version of this class, I also define a default visit() method that is automatically called if implementing classes choose not to provide specific handling for particular Unit classes:

```
// listing 11.43
abstract class ArmyVisitor
{
    abstract public function visit(Unit $node);

    public function visitArcher(Archer $node): void
    {
        $this->visit($node);
    }
    public function visitCavalry(Cavalry $node): void
    {
        $this->visit($node);
    }

    public function visitLaserCanonUnit(LaserCanonUnit $node): void
    {
        $this->visit($node);
    }

    public function visitTroopCarrierUnit(TroopCarrierUnit $node): void
    {
        $this->visit($node);
    }

    public function visitArmy(Army $node): void
    {
        $this->visit($node);
    }
}
```

So now it's just a matter of providing implementations of ArmyVisitor, and I am ready to go. Here is the simple text dump code reimplemented as an ArmyVisitor object:

```
// listing 11.44
class TextDumpArmyVisitor extends ArmyVisitor
{
    private string $text = "";

    public function visit(Unit $node): void
    {
        $txt = "";
        $pad = 4 * $node->getDepth();
        $txt .= sprintf("%{$pad}s", "");
        $txt .= get_class($node) . ": ";
        $txt .= "bombard: " . $node->bombardStrength() . "\n";
        $this->text .= $txt;
    }

    public function getText(): string
    {
        return $this->text;
    }
}
```

Let's look at some client code and then walk through the whole process:

```
// listing 11.45
$main_army = new Army();
$main_army->addUnit(new Archer());
$main_army->addUnit(new LaserCanonUnit());
$main_army->addUnit(new Cavalry());

$textdump = new TextDumpArmyVisitor();
$main_army->accept($textdump);
print $textdump->getText();
```

This code yields the following output:

```
popp\ch11\batch08\Army: bombard: 50
    popp\ch11\batch08\Archer: bombard: 4
    popp\ch11\batch08\LaserCanonUnit: bombard: 44
    popp\ch11\batch08\Cavalry: bombard: 2
```

I create an Army object. Because Army is composite, it has an addUnit() method, and I use this to add some more Unit objects. I then create the TextDumpArmyVisitor object, which I pass to Army::accept(). The accept() method constructs a method call and invokes TextDumpArmyVisitor::visitArmy(). In this case, I have provided no special handling for Army objects, so the call is passed on to the generic visit() method. visit() has been passed a reference to the Army object. It invokes its methods (including the newly added getDepth(), which tells anyone who needs to know how far down the composition tree the unit is) in order to generate summary data. The call to visitArmy() is complete, so the Army::accept() operation now calls accept() on its children in turn, passing the visitor along. In this way, the ArmyVisitor class visits every object in the tree.

With the addition of just a couple of methods, I have created a mechanism by which new functionality can be plugged into my composite classes without compromising their interface and without lots of duplicated traversal code.

On certain squares in the game, armies are subject to a tax. The tax collector visits the army and levies a fee for each unit it finds. Different units are taxable at different rates. Here's where I can take advantage of the specialized methods in the visitor class:

```php
// listing 11.46
class TaxCollectionVisitor extends ArmyVisitor
{
    private int $due = 0;
    private string $report = "";

    public function visit(Unit $node): void
    {
        $this->levy($node, 1);
    }

    public function visitArcher(Archer $node): void
    {
        $this->levy($node, 2);
    }
```

402

```
public function visitCavalry(Cavalry $node): void
{
    $this->levy($node, 3);
}

public function visitTroopCarrierUnit(TroopCarrierUnit $node): void
{
    $this->levy($node, 5);
}

private function levy(Unit $unit, int $amount): void
{
    $this->report .= "Tax levied for " . get_class($unit);
    $this->report .= ": $amount\n";
    $this->due += $amount;
}

public function getReport(): string
{
    return $this->report;
}

public function getTax(): int
{
    return $this->due;
}
}
```

In this simple example, I make no direct use of the Unit objects passed to the various visit methods. I do, however, use the specialized nature of these methods, levying different fees according to the specific type of the invoking Unit object.

Here's some client code:

```
// listing 11.47
$main_army = new Army();
$main_army->addUnit(new Archer());
$main_army->addUnit(new LaserCanonUnit());
$main_army->addUnit(new Cavalry());
```

```
$taxcollector = new TaxCollectionVisitor();
$main_army->accept($taxcollector);
print  $taxcollector->getReport();
print "TOTAL: ";
print $taxcollector->getTax() . "\n";
```

The TaxCollectionVisitor object is passed to the Army object's accept() method, as before. Once again, Army passes a reference to itself to the visitArmy() method, before calling accept() on its children. The components are blissfully unaware of the operations performed by their visitor. They simply collaborate with its public interface, each one passing itself dutifully to the correct method for its type.

In addition to the methods defined in the ArmyVisitor class, TaxCollectionVisitor provides two summary methods, getReport() and getTax(). Invoking these provides the data you might expect:

```
Tax levied for popp\ch11\batch08\Army: 1
Tax levied for popp\ch11\batch08\Archer: 2
Tax levied for popp\ch11\batch08\LaserCanonUnit: 1
Tax levied for popp\ch11\batch08\Cavalry:  3

TOTAL: 7
```

Figure 11-7 shows the participants in this example.

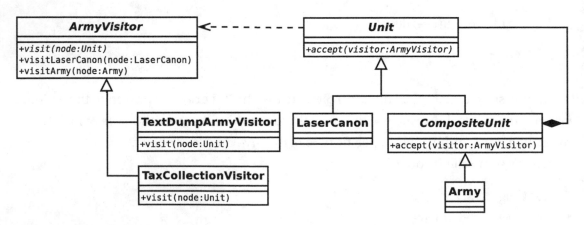

Figure 11-7. *The Visitor pattern*

Visitor Issues

The Visitor pattern, then, is another pattern that combines simplicity and power. There are a few things to bear in mind when deploying this pattern, however.

First, although it is perfectly suited to the Composite pattern, Visitor can, in fact, be used with any collection of objects. So, you might use it with a list of objects where each object stores a reference to its siblings, for example.

By externalizing operations, you may risk compromising encapsulation. That is, you may need to expose the guts of your visited objects in order to let visitors do anything useful with them. You saw, for example, that for the first Visitor example, I was forced to provide an additional method in the Unit interface in order to provide information for TextDumpArmyVisitor objects. You also saw this dilemma previously in the Observer pattern.

Because iteration is separated from the operations that visitor objects perform, you must relinquish a degree of control. For example, you cannot easily create a visit() method that does something both before and after child nodes are iterated. One way around this would be to move responsibility for iteration into the visitor objects. The trouble with this is that you may end up duplicating the traversal code from visitor to visitor.

By default, I prefer to keep traversal internal to the visited classes, but externalizing it provides you with one distinct advantage. You can vary the way that you work through the visited classes on a visitor-by-visitor basis.

The Command Pattern

In recent years, I have rarely completed a web project without deploying this pattern. Originally conceived in the context of graphical user interface design, command objects make for good enterprise application design, encouraging a separation between the controller (request and dispatch handling) and domain model (application logic) tiers. Put more simply, the Command pattern makes for systems that are well organized and easy to extend.

The Problem

All systems must make decisions about what to do in response to a user's request. In PHP, that decision-making process is often handled by a spread of point-of-contact pages. In selecting a page (feedback.php), the user clearly signals the functionality and interface she requires. Increasingly, PHP developers are opting for a single-point-of-contact approach (as I will discuss in the next chapter). In either case, however, the receiver of a request must delegate to a tier more concerned with application logic. This delegation is particularly important in cases where the user can make requests to different pages. Without it, duplication inevitably creeps into the project.

So, imagine you have a project with a range of tasks that need performing. In particular, the system must allow some users to log in and others to submit feedback. You could create login.php and feedback.php pages that handle these tasks, instantiating specialist classes to get the job done. Unfortunately, a user interface in a system rarely maps neatly to the tasks that the system is designed to complete. You may require login and feedback capabilities on every page, for example. If pages must handle many different tasks, then perhaps you should think of tasks as things that can be encapsulated. In doing this, you make it easy to add new tasks to your system, and you build a boundary between your system's tiers. This brings us to the Command pattern.

Implementation

The interface for a command object could not get much simpler. It requires a single method: execute().

In Figure 11-8, I have represented Command as an abstract class. At this level of simplicity, it could be defined instead as an interface. I tend to use abstracts for this purpose because I often find that the base class can also provide useful common functionality for its derived objects.

Figure 11-8. *The Command class*

There are up to three other participants in the Command pattern: the client, which instantiates the command object; the invoker, which deploys the object; and the receiver on which the command operates.

The receiver can be given to the command in its constructor by the client, or it can be acquired from a factory object of some kind. I like the latter approach, keeping the constructor method clear of arguments. All Command objects can then be instantiated in exactly the same way.

Here's the abstract base class:

```
// listing 11.48
abstract class Command
{
    abstract public function execute(CommandContext $context): bool;
}
```

And here's a concrete Command class:

```
// listing 11.49
class LoginCommand extends Command
{

    public function execute(CommandContext $context): bool
    {
        $manager = Registry::getAccessManager();
        $user = $context->get('username');
        $pass = $context->get('pass');
        $user_obj = $manager->login($user, $pass);

        if (is_null($user_obj)) {
            $context->setError($manager->getError());
            return  false;
        }

        $context->addParam("user", $user_obj);

        return true;
    }
}
```

The LoginCommand is designed to work with an AccessManager object. AccessManager is an imaginary class that handles the nuts and bolts of logging users into the system. Notice that the Command::execute() method demands a CommandContext object—this is known as RequestHelper in *Core J2EE Patterns: Best Practices and Design Strategies* (Prentice Hall, 2001) by Alur et al. This is a mechanism by which request data can be passed to Command objects and by which responses can be channeled back to the view layer. Using an object in this way is useful because I can pass different parameters to commands without breaking the interface. The CommandContext is essentially an object wrapper around an associative array variable, though it is frequently extended to perform additional helpful tasks. Here is a simple CommandContext implementation:

```
// listing 11.50
class CommandContext
{
    private array $params = [];
    private string $error = "";

    public function __construct()
    {
        $this->params = $_REQUEST;
    }

    public function addParam(string $key, $val): void
    {
        $this->params[$key] = $val;
    }

    public function get(string $key): string
    {
        if (isset($this->params[$key])) {
            return $this->params[$key];
        }
        return null;
    }
    public function setError($error): string
    {
        $this->error = $error;
    }
```

```
    public function getError(): string
    {
        return  $this->error;
    }
}
```

So, armed with a `CommandContext` object, the `LoginCommand` can access request data: the submitted username and password. I use `Registry`, a simple class with static methods for generating common objects, to return the `AccessManager` object with which `LoginCommand` needs to work. If `AccessManager` reports an error, the command lodges the error message with the `CommandContext` object for use by the presentation layer and returns `false`. If all is well, `LoginCommand` simply returns `true`. Note that `Command` objects do not themselves perform much logic. They check input, handle error conditions, and cache data, as well as calling on other objects to perform operations. If you find that application logic creeps into your command classes, it is often a sign that you should consider refactoring. Such code invites duplication, as it is inevitably copied and pasted between commands. You should at least look at where such functionality belongs. It may be best moved down into your business objects or possibly into a Facade layer. In my example, I am still missing the client, the class that generates command objects, and the invoker, the class that works with the generated command. The easiest way of selecting which command to instantiate in a web project is by using a parameter in the request itself. Here is a simplified client:

```
// listing 11.51
class CommandFactory
{
    private static string $dir = 'commands';

    public static function getCommand(string $action = 'Default'): Command
    {
        if (preg_match('/\W/', $action)) {
            throw new \Exception("illegal characters in action");
        }

        $class = __NAMESPACE__ . "\\commands\\" .
        UCFirst(strtolower($action)) . "Command";
        if (! class_exists($class)) {
            throw new CommandNotFoundException("no '$class' class located");
        }
```

```
        $cmd = new $class();

        return $cmd;
    }
}
```

The CommandFactory class simply looks for a particular class. A fully qualified class name is constructed using the CommandFactory class's own namespace, the string "\commands\", and the CommandContext object's $action parameter. The last item should have been passed to the system from the request. Thanks to Composer's autoload magic, we don't need to worry about explicitly requiring a class. If the class exists, then an object is instantiated and returned to the caller. I could add more error checking here, ensuring that the found class belongs to the Command family and that the constructor expects no arguments; however, this version will do fine for my purposes. The strength of this approach is that you can create a discoverable Command object with the correct namespace at any time, and the system will immediately support it.

The invoker is now simplicity itself:

```
// listing 11.52
class Controller
{
    private CommandContext $context;

    public function __construct()
    {
        $this->context = new CommandContext();
    }

    public function getContext(): CommandContext
    {
        return $this->context;
    }

    public function process(): void
    {
        $action = $this->context->get('action');
        $action = (is_null($action)) ? "default" : $action;
        $cmd = CommandFactory::getCommand($action);
```

```
        if (! $cmd->execute($this->context)) {
            // handle failure
        } else {
            // success
            // dispatch view
        }
    }
}
```

Here is some code to invoke the class:

```
// listing 11.53
$controller = new Controller();
$context = $controller->getContext();

$context->addParam('action', 'login');
$context->addParam('username', 'bob');
$context->addParam('pass','tiddles');
$controller->process();

print $context->getError();
```

Before I call Controller::process(), I fake a web request by setting parameters on the CommandContext object instantiated in the controller's constructor. The process() method acquires the "action" parameter (falling back to the string "default" if no action parameter is present). The method then delegates object instantiation to the CommandFactory object. It invokes execute() on the returned command. Notice how the controller has no idea about the command's internals. It is this independence from the details of command execution that makes it possible for you to add new Command classes with a relatively small impact on this framework.

Here's one more Command class:

```
// listing 11.54
class FeedbackCommand extends Command
{
    public function execute(CommandContext $context): bool
    {
        $msgSystem = Registry::getMessageSystem();
        $email = $context->get('email');
```

411

```
    $msg   = $context->get('msg');
    $topic = $context->get('topic');
    $result = $msgSystem->send($email, $msg, $topic);

    if (! $result) {
        $context->setError($msgSystem->getError());
        return false;
    }

    return true;
    }
}
```

Note   I will return to the Command pattern in Chapter 12, with a fuller implementation of a Command factory class. The framework for running commands presented here is a simplified version of another pattern that you will encounter: the Front Controller.

This class will be run in response to a "feedback" action string, without the need for any changes in the controller or CommandFactory classes.

Figure 11-9 shows the participants of the Command pattern.

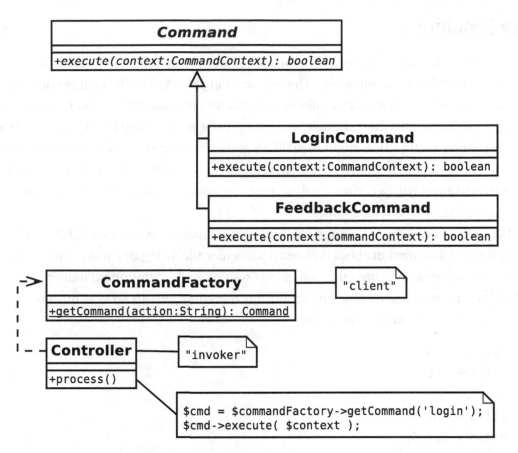

Figure 11-9. *Command pattern participants*

The Null Object Pattern

Half the problems that programmers face seem to be related to type. That's one reason PHP has increasingly supported type checks for method declarations and returns. If dealing with a variable that contains the wrong type is a problem, dealing with one that contains no type at all is at least as bad. This happens all the time, since functions often return null when they fail to generate a useful value. You can avoid inflicting this issue on yourself and others by using the Null Object pattern in your projects. As you will see, while the other patterns in this chapter try to get stuff done, Null Object is designed to do nothing as gracefully as possible.

The Problem

If your method has been charged with the task of finding an object, sometimes there is little to be done but to admit defeat. The information provided by the calling code may be stale or a resource may be unavailable. If the failure is catastrophic, you might choose to throw an exception. Often, though, you'll want to be a little more forgiving. In such a case, returning a null value might seem like a good way of signaling failure to the client.

The problem here is that your method is breaking its contract. If it has committed to return an object with a certain method, then returning null forces the client code to adjust to unexpected circumstances.

Let's return once again to our game. And let's say that a class named TileForces keeps track of information about units on a particular tile. Our game maintains local saved information about the units in the system, and a component named UnitAcquisition is responsible for turning this metadata into an array of objects.

Here is the TileForces constructor:

```
// listing 11.55
class TileForces
{
    private int $x;
    private int $y;
    private array $units = [];

    public function __construct(int $x, int $y, UnitAcquisition $acq)
    {
        $this->x = $x;
        $this->y = $x;
        $this->units = $acq->getUnits($this->x, $this->y);
    }

    // ...
}
```

The TileForces object does little but delegate to the provided UnitAcquisition object to get an array of Unit objects. Let's build a fake UnitAcquisition object:

```
// listing 11.56
class UnitAcquisition
{
    public function getUnits(int $x, int $y): array
    {
        // 1. looks up x and y in local data and gets a list of unit ids
        // 2. goes off to a data source and gets full unit data
        // here's some fake data
        $army = new Army();
        $army->addUnit(new Archer());
        $found = [
            new Cavalry(),
            null,
            new LaserCanonUnit(),
            $army
        ];

        return $found;
    }
}
```

In this class, I hide the process of getting Unit data. Of course, in a real system, some actual lookup would be performed here. I have contented myself with a few direct instantiations. Notice, though, that I embedded a sneaky null value in the $found array. This might happen, for example, if our network game client holds metadata that has fallen out of alignment with the state of data on a server.

Armed with its array of Unit objects, TileForces can provide some functionality:

```
// listing 11.57
// TileForces

public function firepower(): int
{
    $power = 0;

    foreach ($this->units as $unit) {
        $power += $unit->bombardStrength();
    }
```

```
    return $power;
}
```

Let's put the code through its paces:

```
// listing 11.58
$acquirer = new UnitAcquisition();
$tileforces = new TileForces(4, 2, $acquirer);
$power = $tileforces->firepower();

print "power is {$power}\n";
```

Thanks to that lurking null, this code causes an error:

```
Error: Call to a member function bombardStrength() on null
```

TileForces::firepower() cycles through its $units array, calling
bombardStrength() on each Unit. The attempt to invoke a method on a null value, of
course, causes an error.

The most obvious solution is to check each element of the array before working
with it:

```
// listing 11.59

// TileForces

public function firepower(): int
{
    $power = 0;
    foreach ($this->units as $unit) {
        if (! is_null($unit)) {
            $power += $unit->bombardStrength();
        }
    }

    return $power;
}
```

On its own, this isn't too much of a problem. But imagine a version of `TileForces` that performs all sorts of operations on the elements in its $units property. As soon as we begin to replicate the `is_null()` check in multiple places, we are presented once again with a particular code smell. Often, the answer to parallel chunks of client code is to replace multiple conditionals with polymorphism. We can do that here, too.

Implementation

The Null Object pattern allows us to delegate the doing of nothing to a class of an expected type. In this case, I will create a `NullUnit` class.

```
// listing 11.60
class NullUnit extends Unit
{
    public function bombardStrength(): int
    {
        return 0;
    }

    public function getHealth(): int
    {
        return 0;
    }

    public function getDepth(): int
    {
        return 0;
    }
}
```

This implementation of `Unit` respects the interface, but does precisely nothing. Now, I can amend `UnitAcquisition` to create a `NullUnit` rather than use a `null`:

```
// listing 11.61
public function getUnits(int $x, int $y): array
{
    $army = new Army();
    $army->addUnit(new Archer());
```

```
    $found = [
        new Cavalry(),
        new NullUnit(),
        new LaserCanonUnit(),
        $army
    ];

    return $found;
}
```

The client code in TileForces can call any methods it likes on a NullUnit object without problem or error:

```
// listing 11.62

// TileForces

public function firepower(): int
{
    $power = 0;

    foreach ($this->units as $unit) {
        $power += $unit->bombardStrength();
    }

    return $power;
}
```

Take a look at any substantial project and count up the number of inelegant checks that have been forced on its coders by methods that return null values. How many of those checks could be dispensed with if more of us used Null Object?

Of course, sometimes you *will* need to know that you are dealing with a null object. The most obvious way of doing this would be to test an object with the instanceof operator. That is even less elegant than the original is_null() call, however.

Perhaps the neatest solution is to add an isNull() method to both a base class (returning false) and to the Null Object (returning true):

```
// listing 11.63
if (! $unit->isNull()) {
    // do something
```

```
} else {
    print "null - no action\n";
}
```

That gives us the best of both worlds. Any method of a NullUnit object can be safely called. And any Unit object can be queried for null status.

Summary

In this chapter, I wrapped up my examination of the Gang of Four patterns, placing a strong emphasis on how to get things done. I began by showing you how to design a mini-language and build its engine with the Interpreter pattern.

In the Strategy pattern, you encountered another way of using composition to increase flexibility and reduce the need for repetitive subclassing. And with the Observer pattern, you learned how to solve the problem of notifying disparate and varying components about system events. You also revisited the Composite example; and with the Visitor pattern, you learned how to pay a call on, and apply many operations to, every component in a tree. You even saw how the Command pattern can help you to build an extensible tiered system. Finally, you saved yourself a heap of checking for nulls with the Null Object pattern.

In the next chapter, I will step further beyond the Gang of Four to examine some patterns specifically oriented toward enterprise programming.

CHAPTER 12

Enterprise Patterns

PHP is, first and foremost, a language designed for the Web. And, because of its extensive support for objects, we can take advantage of patterns hatched in the context of other object-oriented languages, particularly Java.

I develop a single example in this chapter, using it to illustrate the patterns I cover. Remember, though, that by choosing to use one pattern, you are not committed to using all of the patterns that work well with it. Nor should you feel that the implementations presented here are the only way you might go about deploying these patterns. Rather, you should use the examples here to help you understand the thrust of the patterns described, feeling free to extract what you need for your projects.

Because of the amount of material to cover, this is one of this book's longest and most involved chapters, and it may be a challenge to traverse it in one sitting. It is divided into an introduction and two main parts. These dividing lines might make good break points.

I also describe the individual patterns in the "Architecture Overview" section. Although these are interdependent to some extent, you should be able to jump straight to any particular pattern and work through it independently, moving on to related patterns at your leisure.

This chapter will cover several key topics:

- *Architecture overview*: An introduction to the layers that typically comprise an enterprise application

- *Registry pattern*: Managing application data

- *Presentation layer*: Tools for managing and responding to requests and for presenting data to the user

- *Business logic layer*: Getting to the real purpose of your system, which is addressing business problems

© Matt Zandstra 2021
M. Zandstra, *PHP 8 Objects, Patterns, and Practice*, https://doi.org/10.1007/978-1-4842-6791-2_12

Architecture Overview

With a lot of ground to cover, let's kick off with an overview of the patterns to come, followed by an introduction to building layered, or tiered, applications.

The Patterns

I will explore several patterns in this chapter. You may read from start to finish or dip into those patterns that fit your needs or pique your interest:

- *Registry*: This pattern is useful for making data available to all classes in a process. Through careful use of serialization, it can also be used to store information across a session or even across instances of an application.

- *Front Controller*: Use this for larger systems in which you know that you will need as much flexibility as possible in managing many different views and commands.

- *Application Controller*: Create a class to manage view logic and command selection.

- *Template View*: Create pages that manage display and user interface only, incorporating dynamic information into display markup with as little raw code as possible.

- *Page Controller*: Lighter weight but less flexible than Front Controller, Page Controller addresses the same need. Use this pattern to manage requests and handle view logic if you want fast results and your system is unlikely to grow substantially in complexity.

- *Transaction Script*: When you want to get things done fast, with minimal up-front planning, fall back on procedural library code for your application logic. This pattern does not scale well.

- *Domain Model*: At the opposite pole from Transaction Script, use this pattern to build object-based models of your business participants and processes.

Note   The Command pattern is not described individually here (I wrote about it in Chapter 11); however, it is encountered once again in both the Front Controller and Application Controller patterns.

Applications and Layers

Many (most, in fact) of the patterns in this chapter are designed to promote the independent operation of several distinct tiers in an application. Just as classes represent specializations of responsibilities, so do the tiers of an enterprise system, albeit on a coarser scale. Figure 12-1 shows a typical breakdown of the layers in a system.

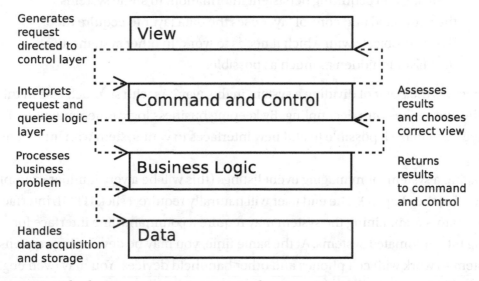

Figure 12-1. *The layers, or tiers, in a typical enterprise system*

The structure shown in Figure 12-1 is not written in stone: some of these tiers may be combined, and different strategies can be used for communication between them, depending on the complexity of your system. Nonetheless, Figure 12-1 illustrates a model that emphasizes flexibility and reuse, and many enterprise applications follow it to a large extent.

- The *view layer* contains the interface that a system's users actually see and interact with. It is responsible for presenting the results of a user's request and providing the mechanism by which the next request can be made to the system.

- The *command and control layer* processes the request from the user. Based on this analysis, it delegates to the business logic layer any processing required in order to fulfill the request. It then chooses which view is best suited to present the results to the user. In practice, this and the view layer are often combined into a single *presentation layer*. Even so, the role of display should be strictly separated from those of request handling and business logic invocation.

- The *business logic layer* is responsible for seeing to the business of a request. It performs any required calculations and marshals the resulting data.

- The *data layer* insulates the rest of the system from the mechanics of saving and acquiring persistent information. In some systems, the command and control layer uses the data layer to acquire the business objects with which it needs to work. In other systems, the data layer is hidden as much as possible.

So what is the point of dividing a system in this way? As with so much else in this book, the answer lies with decoupling. By keeping business logic independent of the view layer, you make it possible to add new interfaces to your system with little or no rewriting.

Imagine a system for managing event listings (this will be a very familiar example by the end of the chapter). The end user will naturally require a slick HTML interface. Administrators maintaining the system may require a command-line interface for building into automated systems. At the same time, you may be developing versions of the system to work with cell phones and other handheld devices. You may even begin to consider SOAP or a RESTful API.

If you originally combined the underlying logic of your system with the HTML view layer (which is still a common strategy), these requirements would trigger an instant rewrite. If, on the other hand, you had created a tiered system, you would be able to bolt on new presentation strategies without the need to reconsider your business logic and data layers.

By the same token, persistence strategies are subject to change. Once again, you should be able to switch between storage models with minimal impact on the other tiers in a system.

Testing is another good reason for creating systems with separate tiers. Web applications are notoriously hard to test. In an insufficiently tiered system, automated tests must negotiate the HTML interface at one end and risk triggering random queries to a database at the other, even when their focus is aimed at neither of these areas. Although any testing is better than none, such tests are necessarily haphazard. In a tiered system, on the other hand, the classes that face other tiers are often written so that they extend an abstract superclass or implement an interface. This supertype can then support polymorphism. In a test context, an entire tier can be replaced by a set of dummy objects (often called "stubs" or "mock" objects). In this way, you can test business logic using a fake data layer, for example. You can read more about testing in Chapter 18.

Layers are useful even if you think that testing is for wimps and your system will only ever have a single interface. By creating tiers with distinct responsibilities, you build a system whose constituent parts are easier to extend and debug. You limit duplication by keeping code with the same kinds of responsibility in one place (rather than lacing a system with database calls, for example, or with display strategies). Adding to such a system is relatively easy because your changes tend to be nicely vertical, as opposed to messily horizontal.

A new feature, in a tiered system, might require a new interface component, additional request handling, some more business logic, and an amendment to your storage mechanism. That's vertical change. In a nontiered system, you might add your feature and then remember that five separate pages reference your amended database table. Or was it six? There may be dozens of places where your new interface may potentially be invoked, so you need to work through your system, adding code for that. This is horizontal amendment.

In reality, of course, you never entirely escape from horizontal dependencies of this sort, especially when it comes to navigation elements in the interface. A tiered system can help to minimize the need for horizontal amendment, however.

Note   While many of these patterns have been around for a while (patterns reflect well-tried practices, after all), the names and boundaries are drawn either from Martin Fowler's key work on enterprise patterns, *Patterns of Enterprise Application Architecture* (Addison-Wesley Professional, 2002), or from the influential *Core J2EE Patterns: Best Practices and Design Strategies* (Prentice Hall, 2001) by Alur et al. For the sake of consistency, I have tended to use Fowler's naming conventions where the two sources diverge.

All the examples in this chapter revolve around a fictional listings system with the whimsical-sounding name, "Woo," which stands for something like "What's On Outside."

Participants of the system include venues (e.g., theaters, clubs, or cinemas), spaces (e.g., screen 1 or the stage upstairs), and events (e.g., *The Long Good Friday* or *The Importance of Being Earnest*).

The operations I will cover include creating a venue, adding a space to a venue, and listing all venues in the system.

Remember that the aim of this chapter is to illustrate key enterprise design patterns and not to build a working system. Reflecting the interdependent nature of design patterns, most of these examples overlap to a large extent with code examples, making good use of ground covered elsewhere in the chapter. As this code is mainly designed to demonstrate enterprise patterns, much of it does not fulfill all the criteria demanded by a production system. In particular, I omit error checking where it might stand in the way of clarity. You should approach the examples as a means of illustrating the patterns they implement, rather than as building blocks in a framework or application.

Cheating Before We Start

Most of the patterns in this book find a natural place in the layers of an enterprise architecture. But some patterns are so basic that they stand outside of this structure. The Registry pattern is a good example of this. In fact, Registry is a powerful way of breaking out of the constraints laid down by layering. It is the exception that allows for the smooth running of the rule.

Registry

The Registry pattern is all about providing system-wide access to objects. These days, it is almost an article of faith that globals are bad. Like other sins, though, global data is fatally attractive. This is so much the case that object-oriented architects have felt it necessary to reinvent globals under a new name. You encountered the Singleton pattern in Chapter 9, although it is true that singleton objects do not suffer from all the ills that beset global variables. In particular, you cannot overwrite a singleton by accident. Singletons, then, are low-fat globals. You should remain suspicious of singleton objects, though, because they invite you to anchor your classes into a system, thereby introducing coupling.

Nevertheless, singletons are so useful at times that many programmers (including me) can't bring themselves to give them up.

The Problem

As you have seen, many enterprise systems are divided into layers, with each layer communicating with its neighbors only through tightly defined conduits. This separation of tiers makes an application flexible. You can replace or otherwise develop each tier with the minimum impact on the rest of the system. What happens, though, when you acquire information in a tier that you later need in another noncontiguous layer?

Let's say that I acquire configuration data in an ApplicationHelper class:

```
// listing 12.01
class ApplicationHelper
{
    public function getOptions(): array
    {
        $optionfile = __DIR__ . "/data/woo_options.xml";

        if (! file_exists($optionfile)) {
            throw new AppException("Could not find options file");
        }

        $options = \simplexml_load_file($optionfile);
        $dsn = (string)$options->dsn;
        // what do we do with this now?
        // ...
    }
}
```

Acquiring the information is easy enough, but how would I get it to the data layer, where it is later used? And what about all the other configuration information I must disseminate throughout my system?

One answer would be to pass this information around the system from object to object: from a controller object responsible for handling requests to objects in the business logic layer and, finally, to an object responsible for talking to the database.

This is entirely feasible. In fact, you could pass the `ApplicationHelper` object itself around or, alternatively, a more specialized `Context` object. Either way, contextual information is transmitted through the layers of your system to the object or objects that need it.

The trade-off is that, in order to do this, you must alter the interface of all the objects that relay the context object, whether they need to use it or not. Clearly, this undermines loose coupling to some extent.

The Registry pattern provides an alternative that is not without its own consequences.

A *registry* is simply a class that provides access to data (usually, but not exclusively, objects) via static methods (or via instance methods on a singleton). Every object in a system, therefore, has access to these objects.

The term "Registry" is drawn from Fowler's *Patterns of Enterprise Application Architecture*; but, as with all patterns, implementations pop up everywhere. In *The Pragmatic Programmer: from Journeyman to Master* (Addison-Wesley Professional, 1999), Andrew Hunt and David Thomas liken a registry class to a police incident notice board. Detectives on one shift leave evidence and sketches on the board, which are then picked up by new detectives on another shift. I have also seen the Registry pattern called Whiteboard and Blackboard.

Implementation

Figure 12-2 shows a `Registry` object that stores and serves `Request` objects.

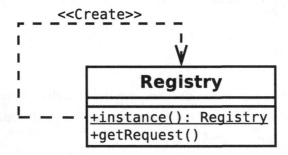

Figure 12-2. *A simple registry*

Here is this class in code form:

```
// listing 12.02
class Registry
{
    private static ?Registry $instance = null;
    private ?Request $request = null;

    private function __construct()
    {
    }

    public static function instance(): self
    {
        if (is_null(self::$instance)) {
            self::$instance = new self();
        }

        return self::$instance;
    }

    public function getRequest(): Request
    {
        if (is_null($this->request)) {
            $this->request = new Request();
        }

        return $this->request;
    }
}

// listing 12.03 class Request
{
}
```

You can then access the same Request from any part of your system:

```
// listing 12.04
$reg = Registry::instance();
print_r($reg->getRequest());
```

As you can see, the Registry is simply a singleton (see Chapter 9 if you need a reminder about singleton classes). The code creates and returns a sole instance of the Registry class via the instance() method. This can then be used to retrieve a Request object.

I have been known to throw caution to the wind and use a key-based system, like this:

```
// listing 12.05
class Registry
{
    private static ?Registry $instance = null;
    private array $values = [];

    private function __construct()
    {
    }

    public static function instance(): self
    {
        if (is_null(self::$instance)) {
            self::$instance = new self();
        }

        return self::$instance;
    }

    public function get(string $key): mixed
    {
        if (isset($this->values[$key])) {
            return $this->values[$key];
        }

        return null;
    }

    public function set(string $key, mixed $value): void
    {
        $this->values[$key] = $value;
    }
}
```

The benefit here is that you don't need to create methods for every object you wish to store and serve. The downside, though, is that you reintroduce global variables by the back door. The use of arbitrary strings as keys for the objects you store means that there is nothing stopping one part of your system from overwriting a key/value pair when adding an object. I have found it useful to use this map-like structure during development and then shift over to explicitly named methods when I'm clear about the data I am going to need to store and retrieve.

Note   The Registry pattern is not the only way of managing the services a system requires. In Chapter 9, we covered a similar strategy named Dependency Injection, which is used in popular frameworks like Symfony.

You can also use registry objects as factories for common objects in your system. Instead of storing a provided object, the `Registry` class creates an instance and then caches the reference. It may do some setup behind the scenes as well, perhaps retrieving data from a configuration file or combining a number of objects:

```
// listing 12.06

// class Registry

private ?TreeBuilder $treeBuilder = null;
private ?Conf $conf = null;

// ...

public function treeBuilder(): TreeBuilder
{
    if (is_null($this->treeBuilder)) {
        $this->treeBuilder = new TreeBuilder($this->conf()->get('treedir'));
    }

    return $this->treeBuilder;
}
```

```
public function conf(): Conf
{
    if (is_null($this->conf)) {
        $this->conf = new Conf();
    }

    return $this->conf;
}
```

TreeBuilder and Conf are just dummy classes, included to demonstrate a point. A client class that needs a TreeBuilder object can simply call Registry::treeBuilder(), without bothering itself with the complexities of initialization. Such complexities may include application-level data such as the dummy Conf object, and most classes in a system should be insulated from them.

Registry objects can be useful for testing, too. The static instance() method can be used to serve up a child of the Registry class, primed with dummy objects. Here's how I might amend instance() to achieve this:

```
// listing 12.07

// class Registry

private static $testmode = false;

// ...

public static function testMode(bool $mode = true): void
{
    self::$instance = null;
    self::$testmode = $mode;
}

public static function instance(): self
{
    if (is_null(self::$instance)) {
        if (self::$testmode) {
            self::$instance = new MockRegistry();
```

```
        } else {
            self::$instance = new self();
        }
    }

    return self::$instance;
}
```

When you need to put your system through its paces, you can use test mode to switch in a fake registry. This can serve up stubs (objects that fake a real environment for testing purposes) or mocks (similar objects that also analyze calls made to them and assess them for correctness):

```
// listing 12.08
Registry::testMode();
$mockreg = Registry::instance();
```

You can read more about mock and stub objects in Chapter 18.

Registry, Scope, and PHP

The term *scope* is often used to describe the visibility of an object or value in the context of code structures. The lifetime of a variable can also be measured over time. There are three levels of scope you might consider in this sense. The standard is the period covered by an HTTP *request*. PHP also provides built-in support for session variables. These are serialized and saved to the file system or the database at the end of a request and then restored at the start of the next. A session ID stored in a cookie or passed around in query strings is used to keep track of the session owner. Because of this, you can think of some variables as having session scope. You can take advantage of this by storing some objects between requests, saving a trip to the database. Clearly, you need to be careful that you don't end up with multiple versions of the same object, so you may need to consider a locking strategy when you check an object that also exists in a database into a session.

In other languages, notably Java and Perl (running on the ModPerl Apache module), there is the concept of application scope. Variables that occupy this space are available across all instances of the application. This is fairly alien to PHP; but in larger applications, it might be considered useful to have access to an application-wide space for accessing configuration variables.

In previous editions of this book, I demonstrated examples of session- and application-scoped registry classes; but in the ten years or so since I first wrote that sample code, I have never had cause to use anything but a request-scoped registry. There is an initialization cost to this per-request approach, but you will typically use caching strategies to manage this.

Consequences

`Registry` objects make their data globally available. This means that any class that acts as a client for a registry will exhibit a dependency that is not declared in its interface. This can become a serious problem if you begin to rely on `Registry` objects for lots of the data in your system. `Registry` objects are best used sparingly, for a well-defined set of data items.

The Presentation Layer

When a request hits your system, you must interpret the requirement it carries, invoke any business logic needed, and finally return a response. For simple scripts, this whole process often takes place entirely inside the view itself, with only the heavyweight logic and persistence code split off into libraries.

Note   A *view* is an individual element in the view layer. It can be a PHP page (or a collection of composed view elements) whose primary responsibility is to display data and provide the mechanism by which new requests can be generated by the user. It could also be a template in a system such as Twig.

As systems grow in size, this default strategy becomes less tenable with request processing, business logic invocation, and view dispatch logic necessarily duplicated from view to view.

In this section, I look at strategies for managing these three key responsibilities of the presentation layer. Because the boundaries between the view layer and the command and control layer are often fairly blurred, it makes sense to treat them together under the common term, "presentation layer."

Front Controller

This pattern is diametrically opposed to the traditional PHP application with its multiple points of entry. The Front Controller pattern presents a central point of access for all incoming requests, ultimately delegating to a view the task of presenting results back to the user. This is a key pattern in the Java enterprise community. It is covered in great detail in *Core J2EE Patterns: Best Practices and Design Strategies*, which remains one of the most influential enterprise pattern resources. The pattern is not universally loved in the PHP community, partly because of the overhead that initialization sometimes incurs.

Most systems I write tend to gravitate toward the Front Controller. That is, I may not deploy the entire pattern to start with, but I will be aware of the steps necessary to evolve my project into a Front Controller implementation should I need the flexibility it affords.

The Problem

Where requests are handled at multiple points throughout a system, it is hard to keep duplication from the code. You may need to authenticate a user, translate terms into different languages, or simply access common data. When a request requires common actions from view to view, you may find yourself copying and pasting operations. This can make alteration difficult, as a simple amendment may need to be deployed across several points in your system. For this reason, it becomes easy for some parts of your code to fall out of alignment with others. Of course, a first step might be to centralize common operations into library code, but you are still left with the calls to the library functions or methods distributed throughout your system.

Difficulty in managing the progression from view to view is another problem that can arise in a system where control is distributed among its views. In a complex system, a submission in one view may lead to any number of result pages, according to the input and the success of any operations performed at the logic layer. Forwarding from view to view can get messy, especially if the same view might be used in different flows.

Implementation

At heart, the Front Controller pattern defines a central point of entry for every request. It processes the request and uses it to select an operation to perform. Operations are often defined in specialized command objects organized according to the Command pattern.

Figure 12-3 shows an overview of a Front Controller implementation.

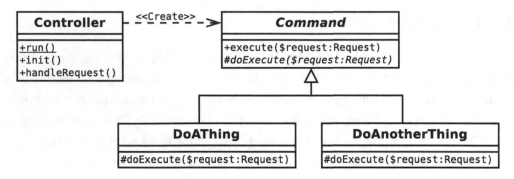

Figure 12-3. *A Controller class and a command hierarchy*

In fact, you are likely to deploy a few helper classes to smooth the process, but let's begin with the core participants. Here is a simple Controller class:

```
// listing 12.09
class Controller
{
    private Registry $reg;

    private function __construct()
    {
        $this->reg = Registry::instance();
    }

    public static function run(): void
    {
        $instance = new self();
        $instance->init();
        $instance->handleRequest();
    }

    private function init(): void
    {
        $this->reg->getApplicationHelper()->init();
    }
```

```
    private function handleRequest(): void
    {
        $request = $this->reg->getRequest();
        $resolver = new CommandResolver();
        $cmd = $resolver->getCommand($request);
        $cmd->execute($request);
    }
}
```

Simplified as this is, and bereft of error handling, there isn't much more to the Controller class. A controller sits at the tip of a system, delegating to other classes. It is these other classes that do most of the work. run() is merely a convenience method that calls init() and handleRequest(). It is static, and the constructor is private, so the only option for client code is to kick off execution of the system. I usually do this in a file called index.php that contains only a few lines of code:

```
// listing 12.10
require_once(__DIR__ . "/../../../vendor/autoload.php");

use  \popp\ch12\batch05\Controller;
Controller::run();
```

Notice that nasty looking require statement. It is really only there so that the rest of the system can live in ignorance of the need for requiring files. The autoload.php script is automatically generated by Composer. It manages the logic for loading class files, as needed. If that meant nothing to you, don't worry; we cover autoloading in much more detail in Chapter 15.

The distinction between the init() and handleRequest() methods is really one of category in PHP. In some languages, init() would be run only at application startup, and handleRequest() or an equivalent would be run for each user request. This class observes the same distinction between setup and request handling, even though init() is called for each request.

The init() method makes a call to a class called ApplicationHelper via the Registry class, which is referenced by the Controller's $reg property. The ApplicationHelper class manages configuration data for the application as a whole. Controller::init() calls a method in ApplicationHelper, also called init(), which, as you will see, initializes data used by the application.

The handleRequest() method uses a CommandResolver to acquire a Command object, which it runs by calling Command::execute().

ApplicationHelper

The ApplicationHelper class is not essential to Front Controller. Most implementations must acquire basic configuration data, though, so I should develop a strategy for this. Here is a simple ApplicationHelper:

```
// listing 12.11
class ApplicationHelper
{
    private string $config = __DIR__ . "/data/woo_options.ini";
    private Registry $reg;

    public function __construct()
    {
        $this->reg = Registry::instance();

    public function init(): void
    {
        $this->setupOptions();
        if (defined('STDIN')) {
            $request = new CliRequest();
        } else {
            $request = new HttpRequest();
        }

        $this->reg->setRequest($request);
    }

    private function setupOptions(): void
    {
        if (! file_exists($this->config)) {
            throw new AppException("Could not find options file");
        }
```

```
    $options = parse_ini_file($this->config, true);

    $this->reg->setConf(new Conf($options['config']));
    $this->reg->setCommands(new Conf($options['commands']));
    }
}
```

This class simply reads a configuration file and adds various objects to a registry, thereby making them available to the wider system. The init() method calls a private method—setupOptions()—which reads an .ini file and passes two arrays (each in an instance of an array wrapper named Conf) to the Registry object. There is nothing to Conf but a get() and a set() method—although more sophisticated configuration classes might manage searching for and parsing files, as well as managing the found data. One of these Conf arrays is intended to hold general configuration values—and that is passed to Registry::setConf(). The other array is for mapping URL paths to Command classes, and I pass that to Registry::setCommands().

The init() method also attempts to discover whether the application is being run in a web context or on the command line (by checking whether or not the constant STDIN is defined). It passes a distinct Request subclass to the Registry object, depending on the result of that test.

Since Registry classes do very little but store and serve up objects, they do not make for exciting source code listings. For the sake of completeness, though, here are the additional Registry methods used or implied by the ApplicationHelper:

```
// listing 12.12
// must be initialized by some smarter component
public function setRequest(Request $request): void
{
    $this->request = $request;
}
public function getRequest(): Request
{
    if (is_null($this->request)) {
        throw new \Exception("No Request set");
    }

    return $this->request;
}
```

```
public function getApplicationHelper(): ApplicationHelper
{
    if (is_null($this->applicationHelper)) {
        $this->applicationHelper = new ApplicationHelper();
    }

    return $this->applicationHelper;
}

public function setConf(Conf $conf): void
{
    $this->conf = $conf;
}

public function getConf(): Conf
{
    if (is_null($this->conf)) {
        $this->conf = new Conf();
    }

    return $this->conf;
}

public function setCommands(Conf $commands): void
{
    $this->commands = $commands;
}

public function getCommands(): Conf
{
    if (is_null($this->commands)) {
        $this->commands = new Conf();
    }

    return $this->commands;
}
```

Here is the simple configuration file:

```
[config]
dsn=sqlite:/var/popp/src/ch12/batch05/data/woo.db

[commands]
/=\popp\ch12\batch05\DefaultCommand
```

CommandResolver

A controller needs a way of deciding how to interpret an HTTP request, so that it can invoke the right code to fulfill that request. You could easily include this logic within the `Controller` class itself, but I prefer to use a specialist class for the purpose. That makes it easy to refactor for polymorphism, if necessary.

A Front Controller often invokes application logic by running a `Command` object (I introduced the Command pattern in Chapter 11). The `Command` is chosen according to the request URL (using either the URL path or, less frequently these days, a GET parameter). Either way, you end up with a token or pattern which can be used for Command selection. There is more than one way of using a URL to select a command. For example, you can test the token against a configuration file or data structure (a *logical* strategy). Or, you can test it directly against class files on the file system (a *physical* strategy).

You saw an example of a command factory that used a physical strategy in the last chapter. This time, I will take the logical approach, mapping URL fragments to Command classes:

```
// listing  12.13
class CommandResolver
{
    private static ?\ReflectionClass $refcmd = null;
    private static string $defaultcmd = DefaultCommand::class;

    public function __construct()
    {
        // could make this configurable
        self::$refcmd = new \ReflectionClass(Command::class);
    }
```

441

```php
    public function getCommand(Request $request): Command
    {
        $reg = Registry::instance();
        $commands = $reg->getCommands();
        $path = $request->getPath();
        $class = $commands->get($path);
        if (is_null($class)) {
            $request->addFeedback("path '$path' not matched");
            return new self::$defaultcmd();
        }

        if (! class_exists($class)) {
            $request->addFeedback("class '$class' not found");
            return new self::$defaultcmd();
        }

        $refclass = new \ReflectionClass($class);

        if (! $refclass->isSubClassOf(self::$refcmd)) {
            $request->addFeedback("command '$refclass' is not a Command");
            return new self::$defaultcmd();
        }

        return $refclass->newInstance();
    }
}
```

This simple class acquires a Conf object from the registry and uses the URL path (provided by the Request::getPath() method) to attempt to get a class name. If the class name is found, and if the class both exists and extends the Command base class, then it is instantiated and returned.

If any of these conditions are not met, the getCommand() method degrades gracefully by serving up a default Command object.

A more sophisticated implementation (e.g., like the ones used by the routing logic in Symfony) would allow for wildcards in these paths.

You may wonder why this code takes it on trust that the Command class it locates does not require parameters:

```php
return $refclass->newInstance();
```

The answer to this lies in the signature of the Command class itself:

```
// listing 12.14
abstract class Command
{
    final public function __construct()
    {
    }

    public function execute(Request $request): void
    {
        $this->doExecute($request);
    }

    abstract protected function doExecute(Request $request): void;
}
```

By declaring the constructor method final, I make it impossible for a child class to override it. No Command class, therefore, will ever require arguments to its constructor.

When creating command classes, you should be careful to keep them as devoid of application logic as you possibly can. As soon as they begin to do application-type stuff, you'll find that they turn into a kind of tangled transaction script and duplication will soon creep in. Commands are a kind of relay station: they should interpret a request, call into the domain to juggle some objects, and then lodge data for the presentation layer. As soon as they begin to do anything more complicated than this, it's probably time to refactor. The good news is that refactoring is relatively easy. It's not hard to spot when a command is trying to do too much, and the solution is usually clear: move that functionality down to a helper or domain class.

Request

Requests are magically handled for us by PHP and neatly packaged up in superglobal arrays. You might have noticed that I still use a class to represent a request. A Request object is passed to CommandResolver and, later on, to Command.

Why do I not let these classes simply query the $_REQUEST, $_POST, or $_GET arrays for themselves? I could do that, of course, but by centralizing request operations in one place, I open up new options.

You could, for example, apply filters to the incoming request. Or, as the next example shows, you could gather request parameters from somewhere other than an HTTP request, allowing the application to be run from the command line or from a test script.

The Request object is also a useful repository for data that needs to be communicated to the view layer. In fact, many systems offer a separate Response object for that purpose, but we will keep things lean here.

Here is a simple Request superclass:

```php
// listing 12.15
abstract class Request
{
    protected array $properties = [];
    protected array $feedback = [];
    protected string $path = "/";
    public function __construct()
    {
        $this->init();
    }

    abstract public function init(): void;

    public function setPath(string $path): void
    {
        $this->path = $path;
    }

    public function getPath(): string
    {
        return $this->path;
    }

    public function getProperty(string $key): mixed
    {
        if (isset($this->properties[$key])) {
            return $this->properties[$key];
        }

        return null;
    }
```

```php
public function setProperty(string $key, mixed $val): void
{
    $this->properties[$key] = $val;
}

public function addFeedback(string $msg): void
{
    array_push($this->feedback, $msg);
}

public function getFeedback(): array
{
    return $this->feedback;
}

public function getFeedbackString($separator = "\n"): string
{
    return implode($separator, $this->feedback);
}

public function clearFeedback(): void
{
    $this->feedback = [];
}
}
```

As you can see, most of this class is taken up with mechanisms for setting and acquiring properties. The init() method is responsible for populating the private $properties array, and it will be handled by child classes. It's important to note that this example implementation ignores request methods—not something you would ever want to do in the real world. A full implementation should manage GET, POST, and PUT arrays, as well as provide a unified query mechanism. Once you have a Request object, you should be able to access a parameter via the getProperty() method, which accepts a key string and returns the corresponding value (as stored in the $properties array). You can also add data via setProperty().

The class also manages a $feedback array. This is a simple conduit through which controller classes can pass messages to the user. In a fuller implementation, we would likely want to differentiate between error and informational messages.

You may remember that ApplicationHelper instantiates one of HttpRequest and CliRequest. Here is the first of these:

```
// listing 12.16
class HttpRequest extends Request
{
    public function init(): void
    {
        // we're conveniently ignoring POST/GET/etc distinctions
        // don't do that in the real world!
        $this->properties = $_REQUEST;
        $this->path = $_SERVER['PATH_INFO'];
        $this->path = (empty($this->path)) ? "/" : $this->path;
    }
}
```

CliRequest takes argument pairs from the command line in the form key=value and breaks them out into properties. It also detects an argument with a path: prefix and assigns the provided value to the object's $path property:

```
// listing 12.17
class CliRequest extends Request
{
    public function init(): void
    {
        $args = $_SERVER['argv'];

        foreach ($args as $arg) {
            if (preg_match("/^path:(\S+)/", $arg, $matches)) {
                $this->path = $matches[1];
            } else {
                if (strpos($arg, '=')) {
                    list($key, $val) = explode("=", $arg);
                    $this->setProperty($key,  $val);
                }
            }
        }
```

```
        $this->path = (empty($this->path)) ? "/" : $this->path;
    }
}
```

A Command

You have already seen the Command base class, and Chapter 11 covered the Command pattern in detail, so there's no need to go too deep into Commands. Let's round things off, though, with a simple, concrete Command object:

```
// listing 12.18
class DefaultCommand extends Command
{
    protected function doExecute(Request $request): void
    {
        $request->addFeedback("Welcome to WOO");
        include(__DIR__ . "/main.php");
    }
}
```

This is the Command object that is served up by CommandResolver if no explicit request for a particular Command is received.

As you may have noticed, the abstract base class implements execute() itself, calling down to the doExecute() implementation of its child class. This allows us to add setup and cleanup code to all commands, simply by altering the base class.

The execute() method is passed a Request object that gives access to user input, as well as to the setFeedback() method. DefaultCommand makes use of this to set a welcome message.

Finally, the command dispatches control to a view, simply by calling include(). Embedding the map from command to view in the Command classes is the simplest dispatch mechanism; but for small systems, it can be perfectly adequate. A more flexible strategy can be seen in the "Application Controller" section.

The file, main.php, contains some HTML and a call into the Request object to check for any feedback (I'll cover views in more detail shortly). I now have all the components in place to run the system. Here's what I see:

```
<html>
<head>
<title>Woo! it's WOO!</title>
</head>
<body>

<table>
<tr>
<td>
Welcome to WOO</td>
</tr>
</table>

</body>
</html>
```

As you can see, the feedback message set by the default command has found its way into the output. Let's review the full process that leads to this outcome.

Overview

It is possible that the detail of the classes covered in this section might disguise the simplicity of the Front Controller pattern. Figure 12-4 shows a sequence diagram that illustrates the life cycle of a request.

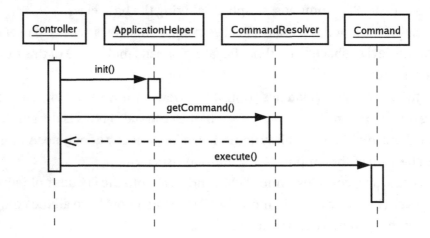

Figure 12-4. *The Front Controller in operation*

As you can see, the Front Controller delegates initialization to the `ApplicationHelper` object (which could use caching to short-circuit any expensive setup). The `Controller` then acquires a `Command` object from the `CommandResolver` object. Finally, it invokes `Command::execute()` to kick off the application logic.

In this implementation of the pattern, the `Command` itself is responsible for delegating to the view layer. You can see a refinement of this in the next section.

Consequences

Front Controller is not for the fainthearted. It does require a lot of up-front development before you begin to see benefits. This is a serious drawback if your project requires fast turnaround or if it is small enough that the Front Controller framework would weigh in heavier than the rest of the system.

Having said that, once you have successfully deployed a Front Controller in one project, you will find that you can reuse it for others with lightning speed. You can abstract much of its functionality into library code, effectively building yourself a reusable framework.

The requirement that all configuration information be loaded up for every request is another drawback. All approaches will suffer from this to some extent, but Front Controller often requires additional information, such as logical maps of commands and views.

This overhead can be eased considerably by caching such data. The most efficient way of doing this is to add the data to your system as native PHP. This is fine if you are the sole maintainer of a system; but if you have nontechnical users, you may need to provide a configuration file. You can still automate the native PHP approach, though, by creating a system that reads a configuration file and then builds PHP data structures, which it writes to a cache file. Once the native PHP cache has been created, the system will use it in preference to the configuration file until a change is made and the cache must be rebuilt.

On the plus side, Front Controller centralizes the presentation logic of your system. This means that you can exert control over the way that requests are processed and views are selected in one place (well, in one set of classes, anyway). This reduces duplication and decreases the likelihood of bugs.

Front Controller is also very extensible. Once you have a core up and running, you can add new `Command` classes and views very easily.

In this example, commands handled their own view dispatch. If you use the Front Controller pattern with an object that helps with view (and possibly command) selection, then the pattern allows for excellent control over navigation, which is harder to maintain elegantly when presentation control is distributed throughout a system. I cover such an object in the next section.

Application Controller

Allowing commands to invoke their own views is acceptable for smaller systems, but it is not ideal. It is preferable to decouple your commands from your view layer as much as possible.

An application controller takes responsibility for mapping requests to commands and commands to views. This decoupling means that it becomes easier to switch in alternative sets of views without changing the codebase. It also allows the system owner to change the flow of the application, again without the need for touching any internals. By allowing for a logical system of Command resolution, the pattern also makes it easier for the same Command to be used in different contexts within a system.

The Problem

Remember the nature of the example problem. An administrator needs to be able to add a venue to the system and to associate a space with it. The system might, therefore, support the AddVenue and AddSpace commands. According to the examples so far, these commands would be selected using a direct map from a path (/addvenue) to a class (AddVenue).

Broadly speaking, a successful call to the AddVenue command should lead to an initial call to the AddSpace command. This relationship might be hard-coded into the classes themselves, with AddVenue invoking AddSpace on success. AddSpace might then include a view that contains the form for adding the space to the venue.

Both commands may be associated with at least two different views, a core view for presenting the input form and an error or "thank you" screen. According to the logic already discussed, the Command classes themselves would include those views (using conditional tests to decide which view to present in which circumstances).

This level of hard-coding is fine, as long as the commands will always be used in the same way. It begins to break down, though, if I want a special view for AddVenue in some circumstances, and if I want to alter the logic by which one command leads to another (perhaps one flow might include an additional screen between a successful venue addition and the start of a space addition). If each of your commands is only used once, in one relationship to other commands and with one view, then you should hard-code your commands' relationship with each other and their views. Otherwise, you should read on.

An application controller class can take over this logic, freeing up Command classes to concentrate on their job, which is to process input, invoke application logic, and handle any results.

Implementation

As always, the key to this pattern is the interface. An application controller is a class (or a set of classes) that the Front Controller can use to acquire commands based on a user request and to find the right view to present after the command has been run. You can see the bare bones of this relationship in Figure 12-5.

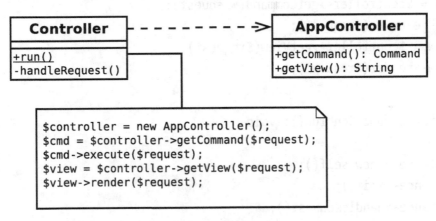

Figure 12-5. *The Application Controller pattern*

As with all patterns in this chapter, the aim is to make things as simple as possible for the client code—hence the spartan Front Controller class. Behind the interface, though, I must deploy an implementation. The approach laid out here is just one way of doing it. As you work through this section, remember that the essence of the pattern lies in the way that the participants (the application controller, the commands, and the views) interact—and not with the specifics of this implementation.

Let's begin with the code that uses the application controller.

The Front Controller

Here is how the FrontController might work with the AppController class (simplified and stripped of error handling):

```
// listing 12.19
// Controller
private function __construct()
{
    $this->reg = Registry::instance();
}

private function handleRequest(): void
{
    $request = $this->reg->getRequest();
    $controller = new AppController();
    $cmd = $controller->getCommand($request);
    $cmd->execute($request);
    $view = $controller->getView($request);
    $view->render($request);
}

public static function run(): void
{
    $instance = new self();
    $instance->init();
    $instance->handleRequest();
}

private function init(): void
{
    $this->reg->getApplicationHelper()->init();
}
```

Moving on from the previous example, the principal difference is that, in addition to changing a class name from CommandResolver to AppController (admittedly a somewhat cosmetic move), we now retrieve a ViewComponent as well as a Command object. Notice that this code uses a registry object to acquire the Request object. We might also store the AppController object in the Registry—even if it isn't used elsewhere by other components. Classes that avoid direct instantiation are generally more flexible and easier to test.

So by what logic does the AppController know which view to associate with which command? As always with object-oriented code, the interface is more important than the implementation. Let's fill in a possible approach, however.

Implementation Overview

A Command class might demand a different view according to different stages of operation. The default view for the AddVenue command might be a data input form. If the user adds the wrong kind of data, the form may be presented again, or an error page may be shown. If all goes well, and the venue is created in the system, then I may wish to forward to another in a chain of Command objects: AddSpace, perhaps.

The Command objects tell the system of their current state by setting a status flag. Here are the flags that this minimal implementation recognizes (set as a property in the Command superclass):

```
// listing 12.20
public const CMD_DEFAULT = 0;
public const CMD_OK = 1;
public const CMD_ERROR = 2;
public const CMD_INSUFFICIENT_DATA = 3;
```

The application controller finds and instantiates the correct Command class using the Request object. Once it has been run, the Command will be associated with a status. This combination of Command and status can be compared against a data structure to determine which command should be run next or—if no more commands should be run—which view to serve up.

The Configuration File

The system's owner can determine the way that commands and views work together by setting a set of configuration directives. Here is an extract:

```
// listing 12.21
<woo-routing>
    <control>

        <command  path="/"  class="\popp\ch12\batch06\DefaultCommand">
            <view name="main" />
            <status value="CMD_ERROR">
                <view name="error" />
            </status>
        </command>

        <command path="/listvenues" class="\popp\ch12\batch06\ListVenues">
            <view  name="listvenues" />
        </command>

        <command path="/quickaddvenue" class="\popp\ch12\batch06\AddVenue">
            <view name="quickadd" />
        </command>

        <command path="/addvenue" class="\popp\ch12\batch06\AddVenue">
            <view name="addvenue" />
            <status value="CMD_OK">
                <forward path="/addspace" />
            </status>
        </command>
        <command path="/addspace" class="\popp\ch12\batch06\AddSpace">
            <view name="addspace" />
            <status value="CMD_OK">
                <forward path="/listvenues" />
            </status>
        </command>

    </control>
</woo-routing>
```

This XML fragment shows one strategy for abstracting the flow of commands and their relationship to views from the Command classes themselves. The directives are all contained within a control element.

Each command element defines path and class attributes which describe basic command mapping. The logic for views is more complex, however. A view element at the top level of a command defines a default relationship. In other words, if no more specific condition is matched, this view will be used for a command. The status elements define these specific conditions. Their value attributes should match one of the command statuses you have seen. When a command's execution renders a CMD_OK status, for example, if an equivalent status has been defined in the XML document, the corresponding view element will be used.

A view element defines a name attribute. This value is used to build a path to a template file which can then be included.

A command or a status element might contain a forward element instead of a view. The Woo system treats a forward as a special kind of view which, instead of rendering a template, reinvokes the application with a new path.

Let's work through a fragment of this XML in the light of that explanation:

```
// listing 12.22
<command path="/addvenue" class="\popp\ch12\batch06\AddVenue">
    <view name="addvenue" />
    <status value="CMD_OK">
        <forward path="/addspace" />
    </status>
</command>
```

When the system is invoked with the /addvenue path, the AddVenue command is called. It then generates a status value—one of CMD_DEFAULT, CMD_OK, CMD_ERROR, or CMD_INSUFFICIENT_DATA. For any status but CMD_OK, the addvenue template will be invoked. If the command returns a CMD_OK status, however, the condition is matched. The status element could simply contain another view that would be included in place of the default. Here, though, the forward element comes into play. By forwarding to another command, the configuration file delegates all responsibility for handling views to the new element. The system will then begin again with the /addspace path in a new request.

Parsing the Configuration File

Thanks to the SimpleXML extension, we don't have to do any actual parsing—that is handled for us. All that is left is to traverse the SimpleXML data structure and build our own data. Here is a class named ViewComponentCompiler that does just that:

```php
// listing 12.23
class ViewComponentCompiler
{
    private static $defaultcmd = DefaultCommand::class;

    public function parseFile(string $file): Conf
    {
        $options = \simplexml_load_file($file);

        return $this->parse($options);
    }

    public function parse(\SimpleXMLElement $options): Conf
    {
        $conf = new Conf();

        foreach ($options->control->command as $command) {
            $path = (string) $command['path'];
            $cmdstr = (string) $command['class'];
            $path = (empty($path)) ? "/" : $path;
            $cmdstr = (empty($cmdstr)) ? self::$defaultcmd : $cmdstr;
            $pathobj = new ComponentDescriptor($path, $cmdstr);

            $this->processView($pathobj, 0, $command);

            if (isset($command->status) &&  isset($command-
>status['value'])) {
                foreach ($command->status as $statusel) {
                    $status = (string)$statusel['value'];
                    $statusval = constant(Command::class . "::" . $status);

                if (is_null($statusval)) {
                    throw new AppException("unknown status: {$status}");
                }
```

```
            $this->processView($pathobj, $statusval, $statusel);
        }
    }

    $conf->set($path, $pathobj);
}

return $conf;
}

public function processView(ComponentDescriptor $pathobj, int
$statusval, \ SimpleXMLElement $el): void
{
    if (isset($el->view) && isset($el->view['name'])) {
        $pathobj->setView($statusval, new TemplateViewComponent((string)
        $el->view['name']));
    }

    if (isset($el->forward) && isset($el->forward['path'])) {
        $pathobj->setView($statusval, new
        ForwardViewComponent((string)$el->forward['path']));
    }
}
}
```

The real action here takes place in the parse() method, which accepts a
SimpleXMLElement object for traversal. I start by instantiating a Conf object (remember,
this is just a wrapper around an array). Then I loop through the command elements in
the XML. For each command, I extract the values of the path and class attributes, and
I pass this data to the constructor of a ComponentDescriptor object. This object will
manage the bundle of information associated with a command element—you'll see the
class soon.

Then I call a private method named processView(), passing it the
ComponentDescriptor, a zero-valued integer (because we're handling the default
status), and a reference to the current XML element (that is command right now).
Depending on what it finds in the XML fragment, processView() either creates a
TemplateViewComponent or a ForwardViewComponent, which it passes along to Compon

457

entDescriptor::setView(). It may match nothing and make no call at all, of course—but that is probably inadvisable. Perhaps we'd make it an error condition in a fuller implementation.

Back in parse(), I begin work on the status attributes. I call processView() once again—but this time with the integer that corresponds to the string in the status element's value attribute. In other words, the string CMD_OK becomes 1, CMD_ERROR becomes 2, and so on. PHP's constant() method provides a neat way of making this conversion. So I pass processView() a nonzero integer this time around, as well as the status XML element.

Once again, processView() populates the ComponentDescriptor with any found ViewComponent objects.

Finally, I store the ComponentDescriptor object in the Conf object, indexed by the command component's path value.

Once the loop is finished, I return the Conf object.

It may take a little re-reading before you can follow this flow; but in essence, the process is very simple: ViewComponentCompiler builds up an array (wrapped, as previously, in a Conf object) of ComponentDescriptor objects. Each ComponentDescriptor object maintains information about a path and a Command class, as well as an array of ViewComponent objects (managing template display or forwarding) indexed by a status value (0 for the default view).

Despite all this busywork, it is important to remember the high-level process is pretty simple. We are constructing the relationships between potential requests on the one hand and commands and views on the other. Figure 12-6 shows this initialization process.

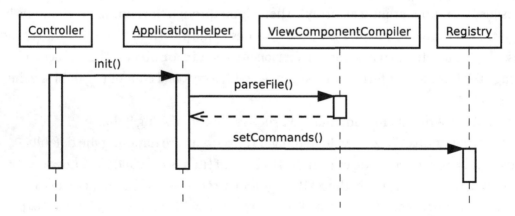

Figure 12-6. *Compiling commands and views*

Managing the Component Data

You have seen that the compiled ComponentDescriptor objects are stored in a Conf object—essentially a getter and setter for an associative array. The keys here are the paths the system recognizes: /, for example, or /addvenue.

So let's take a look at ComponentDescriptor, which manages command, view, and forward information:

```
// listing 12.24
class ComponentDescriptor
{
    private array $views = [];

    public function __construct(private string $path, private string
    $cmdstr)
    {
    }

    public function getCommand(): Command
    {
        $class = $this->cmdstr;
        if (is_null($class)) {
            throw new AppException("unknown class '$class'");
        }

        if (! class_exists($class)) {
            throw new AppException("class '$class' not found");
        }

        $refclass = new \ReflectionClass($class);

        if (! $refclass->isSubClassOf(Command::class)) {
            throw new AppException("command '$class' is not a Command");
        }

        return $refclass->newInstance();
    }
```

```
    public function setView(int $status, ViewComponent $view): void
    {
        $this->views[$status] = $view;
    }

    public function getView(Request $request): ViewComponent
    {
        $status = $request->getCmdStatus();
        $status = (is_null($status)) ? 0 : $status;

        if (isset($this->views[$status])) {
            return $this->views[$status];
        }

        if (isset($this->views[0])) {
            return $this->views[0];
        }

        throw new AppException("no view found");
    }
}
```

So you can see the storage and retrieval here, but there's a little more work going on, too. Command information (the full class name for the Command) is added via the constructor and only lazily converted into a Command object when getCommand() is called. This instantiation and checking takes place in a private method: resolveCommand(). The code here should look familiar—it's actually stolen from (*ahem* ... inspired by) the equivalent functionality in CommandResolver from earlier in the chapter.

Acquiring views is easier. Remember, each view component will have been stored via the setView() method. Behind the scenes, we now see that the ViewComponent objects are managed in an array property, $views, and indexed by an integer, a Command status value. When the getView() method is called by client code, we are passed a Request object in which the Command status may have been cached. We get at this value via a new convenience method, Request::getCmdStatus(). Armed with this, it's simply a matter of checking the $views array for a corresponding ViewComponent element. If there is no match, we return the default, which is indexed by zero.

In this way, this little class provides all of the logic implied by a command element in the XML file.

Because most of the real work is done by helper classes, the application controller itself is relatively thin. Let's take a look:

```
// listing 12.25
class AppController
{
    private static string $defaultcmd = DefaultCommand::class;
    private static string $defaultview = "fallback";

    public function getCommand(Request $request): Command
    {
        try {
            $descriptor = $this->getDescriptor($request);
            $cmd = $descriptor->getCommand();
        } catch (AppException $e) {
            $request->addFeedback($e->getMessage());
            return new self::$defaultcmd();
        }

        return $cmd;
    }

    public function getView(Request $request): ViewComponent
    {
        try {
            $descriptor = $this->getDescriptor($request);
            $view = $descriptor->getView($request);
        } catch (AppException) {
            return new TemplateViewComponent(self::$defaultview);
        }

        return $view;
    }

    private function getDescriptor(Request $request): ComponentDescriptor
    {
        $reg = Registry::instance();
        $commands = $reg->getCommands();
        $path = $request->getPath();
        $descriptor = $commands->get($path);
```

461

```
        if (is_null($descriptor)) {
            throw new AppException("no descriptor for {$path}", 404);
        }

        return $descriptor;
    }
}
```

There is little actual logic in this class since most of the complexity has been pushed down to various helper classes. Both getCommand() and getView() call a private method, getDescriptor(), to acquire a ComponentDescriptor for the current request. The getDescriptor() method gets the current path from the Request object and uses it to extract a ComponentDescriptor object from a Conf object which is also stored by the registry and returned by getCommands(). Remember that this array of ComponentDescriptor objects was previously populated by the ViewComponentCompiler object with potential paths as keys.

Once getCommand() and getView() have a ComponentDescriptor object, each can call its corresponding method. In getCommand(), we call ComponentDescriptor::getCom mand(); in getView(), we call ComponentDescriptor::getView().

Before we move on, there are a few details to wrap up. Now that Command objects no longer invoke views, we need a mechanism for rendering templates. This is handled by TemplateViewComponent objects. These implement an interface, ViewComponent:

```
// listing 12.26
interface ViewComponent
{
    public function render(Request $request): void;
}
```

Here is TemplateViewComponent:

```
// listing 12.27
class TemplateViewComponent implements ViewComponent
{

    public function __construct(private string $name)
    {
    }
```

```
    public function render(Request $request): void
    {
        $reg = Registry::instance();
        $conf = $reg->getConf();
        $path = $conf->get("templatepath");

        if (is_null($path)) {
            throw new AppException("no template directory");
        }
        $fullpath = "{$path}/{$this->name}.php";

        if (! file_exists($fullpath)) {
            throw new AppException("no template at {$fullpath}");
        }

        include($fullpath);
    }
}
```

This class is instantiated with a name—which it then uses at render() time, combined with a path-configuration value, to include a template.

Why is ViewComponent an interface? While TemplateViewComponent handles rendering, we also treat forwarding as a view process in this implementation.

Here is ForwardViewComponent:

```
// listing 12.28
class ForwardViewComponent implements ViewComponent
{
    public function __construct(private ?string $path)
    {
    }

    public function render(Request $request): void
    {
        $request->forward($this->path);
    }
}
```

This class simply calls `forward()` on the provided Request object. The implementation of `forward()` varies depending upon the Request subtype. For HttpRequest, it is a matter of setting the Location header:

```
// listing 12.29

//HttpRequest

public function forward(string $path): void
{
    header("Location: {$path}");
    exit;
}
```

For `CliRequest`, we can't rely on the server to handle forwarding, so we have to take a different approach:

```
// listing 12.30

// CliRequest

public function forward(string $path): void
{
    // tack the new path onto the end the argument list
    // last argument wins
    $_SERVER['argv'][] = "path:{$path}";
    Registry::reset();
    Controller::run();
}
```

We take advantage of the fact that, when the argument array is parsed for a path, the final match found is ultimately set on the Request. All we need to do is add a path argument, clear the Registry, and run the controller from the top.

And that leads us full circle, an excellent moment for an overview!

The strategies an application controller might use to acquire views and commands can vary considerably; the key is that these are hidden away from the wider system. Figure 12-7 shows the high-level process by which a Front Controller class uses an application controller to acquire first a Command object and then a view.

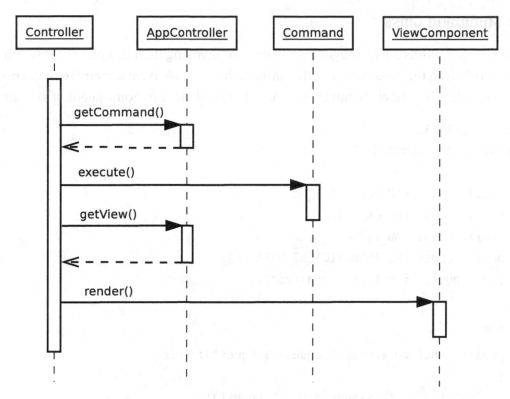

Figure 12-7. *Using an application controller to acquire commands and views*

Note that the view that is rendered in Figure 12-7 could be one of
ForwardViewComponent (which will start the process over again with a new path) or
TemplateViewComponent (which will include a template file).

Remember that the data needed for the process of acquiring Command
and ViewComponent objects in Figure 12-7 was compiled by our old friend,
ApplicationHelper. As a reminder, here is the high-level code that achieved that:

```
// listing 12.31
private function setupOptions(): void
{
    //...
    $vcfile = $conf->get("viewcomponentfile");
    $cparse = new ViewComponentCompiler();

    $commandandviewdata = $cparse->parseFile($vcfile);
    $this->reg->setCommands($commandandviewdata);
}
```

465

The Command Class

Now that commands are no longer responsible for invoking their templates, it's worth looking briefly at the base class and the implementation. We have already seen the new statuses in the Command class, but there is an additional piece of housekeeping to note:

```
// listing 12.32
abstract class Command
{
    public const CMD_DEFAULT = 0;
    public const CMD_OK = 1;
    public const CMD_ERROR = 2;
    public const CMD_INSUFFICIENT_DATA = 3;
    final public function __construct()
    {
    }

    public function execute(Request $request): void
    {
        $status = $this->doExecute($request);
        $request->setCmdStatus($status);
    }

    abstract protected function doExecute(Request $request): int;
}
```

In a good example of the Template Method pattern, the execute() method calls the abstract doExecute() method and caches the return value in the Request object. This will be used a little later by the ComponentDescriptor in selecting the correct view to return.

A Concrete Command

Here is how a simple AddVenue command might look:

```
// listing 12.33
class AddVenue extends Command
{
    protected function doExecute(Request $request): int
```

```
    {
        $name = $request->getProperty("venue_name");

        if (is_null($name)) {
            $request->addFeedback("no name provided");
            return self::CMD_INSUFFICIENT_DATA;
        } else {
            // do some stuff
            $request->addFeedback("'{$name}' added");
            return self::CMD_OK;
        }

        return self::CMD_DEFAULT;
    }
}
```

In fact, this is missing functional code related to building a Venue object and saving it to a database, but we will get to all that. All that's important at this point is the fact that the command returns different statuses, according to the circumstances. As we have already seen, different statuses will cause different views to be selected and returned by the application controller. So, if we're using the example XML, when CMD_OK is returned, the forwarding mechanism will trigger forwarding to /addspace. This is triggered in this way only for /addvenue. If the request that caused this command to be invoked uses the path /quickaddvenue, then no forwarding will take place, and the quickaddvenue view will be displayed. The AddVenue command knows nothing of this, though. It sticks to its core responsibilities.

Consequences

A fully featured instance of the Application Controller pattern can be a pain to set up because of the sheer amount of work that must go into acquiring and applying metadata that describes the relationships between command and request, command and command, and command and view.

For this reason, I tend to implement something like this only when my application tells me it is needed. I usually hear this whisper when I find myself adding conditionals to my commands that invoke different views or invoke other commands, according to the circumstances. It is at about this time that I feel that command flow and display logic are beginning to spiral out of my control.

Of course, an application controller can use all sorts of mechanisms to build its associations among commands and views, not just the approach I have taken here. Even if you're starting off with a fixed relationship among a request string, a command name, and a view in all cases, you could still benefit from building an application controller to encapsulate this. It will give you considerable flexibility when you must refactor in order to accommodate more complexity.

Page Controller

Much as I like the Front Controller pattern, it is not always the right approach to take. The investment in up-front design tends to reward the larger system and penalize simple, need-results-now projects. The Page Controller pattern will probably be familiar to you already as it is a common strategy. Nevertheless, it is worth exploring some of the issues.

The Problem

Once again, the problem is your need to manage the relationship among request, domain logic, and presentation. This is pretty much a constant for enterprise projects. What differs, though, are the constraints placed on you.

If you have a relatively simple project, one in which big up-front design could threaten your deadline without adding huge amounts of value, Page Controller can be a good option for managing requests and views.

Let's say that you want to present a page that displays a list of all venues in the Woo system. Even with the database retrieval code finished, without Front Controller already in place, I have a daunting task to get just this simple result.

The view is a list of venues; the request is for a list of venues. Errors permitting, the request does not lead to a new view, as you might expect in a complex task. The simplest thing that works here is to associate the view and the controller—often in the same page.

Implementation

Although the practical reality of Page Controller projects can become fiendish, the pattern is simple. Control is related to a view or to a set of views. In the simplest case, this means that the control sits in the view itself, although it can be abstracted, especially when a view is closely linked with others (i.e., when you might need to forward to different pages in different circumstances).

Here is the simplest flavor of Page Controller:

```php
// listing 12.34
<?php
namespace popp\ch12\batch07;

try {
    $venuemapper = new VenueMapper();
    $venues = $venuemapper->findAll();
} catch (\Exception) {
    include('error.php');
    exit(0);
}

// default page follows
?>
<html>
<head>
<title>Venues</title>
</head>
<body>
<h1>Venues</h1>

<?php foreach ($venues as $venue) { ?>
    <?php print $venue->getName(); ?><br />
<?php } ?>

</body>
</html>
```

This document has two elements to it. The view element handles display, while the controller element manages the request and invokes application logic. Even though view and controller inhabit the same page, they are rigidly separated.

There is very little to this example (aside from the database work going on behind the scenes, of which you'll find more in the next chapter). The PHP block at the top of the page attempts to get a list of Venue objects, which it stores in the $venues global variable.

If an error occurs, the page delegates to a page called error.php by using include(), followed by exit() to kill any further processing on the current page. I could equally have used an HTTP forward. If no include takes place, then the HTML at the bottom of the page (the view) is shown.

You can see this combination of controllers and views in Figure 12-8.

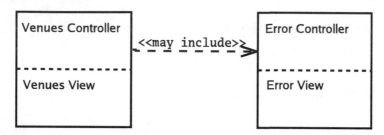

Figure 12-8. *Page Controllers embedded in views*

This will do as a quick test, but a system of any size or complexity will probably need more support than that.

The Page Controller code was previously implicitly separated from the view. Here, I make the break, starting with a rudimentary Page Controller base class:

```
// listing 12.35
abstract class PageController
{
    private Registry $reg;

    abstract public function process(): void;

    public function __construct()
    {
        $this->reg = Registry::instance();
    }

    public function init(): void
    {
        if (isset($_SERVER['REQUEST_METHOD'])) {
            $request = new HttpRequest();
        } else {
            $request = new CliRequest();
        }
```

```
        $this->reg->setRequest($request);
    }

    public function forward(string $resource): void
    {
        $request = $this->getRequest();
        $request->forward($resource);
    }

    public function render(string $resource, Request $request): void
    {
        include($resource);
    }

    public function getRequest(): Request
    {
        return $this->reg->getRequest();
    }
}
```

This class uses some of the tools that you have already looked at—in particular, the Request and Registry classes. The PageController class's main roles are to provide access to a Request object and to manage the inclusion of views. This list of purposes would quickly grow in a real project as more child classes discover a need for common functionality.

A child class could live inside the view and thereby display it by default as before. Or, it could stand separate from the view. The latter approach is cleaner, I think, so that's the path that I take. Here is a PageController that attempts to add a new venue to the system:

```
// listing 12.36
class AddVenueController extends PageController
{
    public function process(): void
    {
        $request = $this->getRequest();
```

```
        try {
            $name = $request->getProperty('venue_name');

            if (is_null($request->getProperty('submitted'))) {
                $request->addFeedback("choose a name for the venue");
                $this->render(__DIR__ . '/view/add_venue.php', $request);
            } elseif (is_null($name)) {
                $request->addFeedback("name is a required field");
                $this->render(__DIR__ . '/view/add_venue.php', $request);

                return;
            } else {
                // add to database
                $this->forward('listvenues.php');
            }
        } catch (Exception) {
            $this->render(__DIR__ . '/view/error.php', $request);
        }
    }
}
```

The AddVenueController class only implements the process() method. process() is responsible for checking the user's submission. If the user has not submitted a form, or has completed the form incorrectly, the default view (add_venue.php) is included, providing feedback and presenting the form. If I successfully add a new venue, then the method invokes forward() to send the user to the ListVenues page controller.

Note the format I used for the view. I tend to differentiate view files from class files by using all lowercase filenames in the former and camel case (running words together and using capital letters to show the boundaries) in the latter.

You may have noticed that there is nothing within the AddVenueController class that causes it to be run. I could place runner code within the same file, but this would make testing difficult (because the very act of including the class would execute its methods). For this reason, I create a runner script for each page. Here is addvenue.php:

```
// listing 12.37
$addvenue = new AddVenueController();
$addvenue->init();
$addvenue->process();
```

Here is the view associated with the AddVenueController class:

```
// listing 12.38
<html>
<head>
<title>Add Venue</title>
</head>
<body>
<h1>Add Venue</h1>

<table>
<tr>
<td>
<?php
print $request->getFeedbackString("</td></tr><tr><td>");
?>
</td>
</tr>
</table>

<form action="/addvenue.php" method="get">
    <input type="hidden" name="submitted" value="yes"/>
    <input type="text" name="venue_name" />
</form>

</body>
</html>
```

As you can see, the view does nothing but display data and provide the mechanism for generating a new request. The request is made to the PageController (via the /addvenue.php runner), not back to the view. Remember, it is the PageController class that is responsible for processing requests.

You can see an overview of this more complicated version of the Page Controller pattern in Figure 12-9.

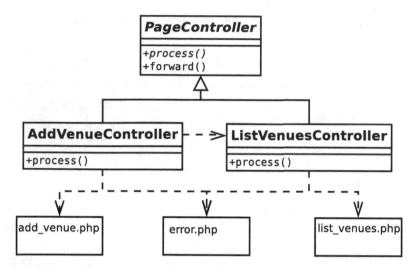

Figure 12-9. *A Page Controller class hierarchy and its include relationships*

Consequences

This approach has the great merit that it immediately makes sense to anyone with any web experience. I make a request for venues.php, and that is precisely what I get. Even an error is within the bounds of expectation, with "server error" and "page not found" pages an everyday reality.

Things get a little more complicated if you separate the view from the page controller class, but the near one-to-one relationship between the participants is clear enough.

A page controller includes its view once it has completed processing. In some circumstances, though, it forwards instead to another page controller. So, for example, when AddVenue successfully adds a venue, it no longer needs to display the addition form. Instead, it delegates to ListVenues.

This is handled within the PageController by the forward() method which, like the ForwardViewComponent we have already seen, simply calls forward() on the Request.

Although a page controller class might delegate to Command objects, the benefit of doing so is not as marked as it is with Front Controller. Front Controller classes need to work out what the purpose of a request is; page controller classes already know this. The light request checking and logic layer calls that you would put in a Command sit just as easily in a page controller class, and you benefit from the fact that you do not need a mechanism to select your Command objects.

Duplication can be a problem, but the use of a common superclass can factor away a lot of that. You can also save on setup time because you can avoid loading data that you won't need in the current context. Of course, you could do that with Front Controller, too, but the process of discovering what is needed, and what is not, would be much more complicated.

The real drawback to the pattern lies in situations where the paths through your views are complex—especially when the same view is used in different ways at different times (add and edit screens are a good example of this). You can find that you get tangled up in conditionals and state checking, and it becomes hard to get an overview of your system.

It is not impossible to start with Page Controller and move toward the Front Controller pattern, however. This is especially true if you are using a `PageController` superclass. As a rule of thumb, if I estimate a system should take me less than a week or so to complete, and that it isn't going to need more phases in the future, I would choose Page Controller and benefit from the fast turnaround. If I were building a large project that needs to grow over time and has complex view logic, I would go for a Front Controller every time.

Template View and View Helper

Template View is pretty much what you get by default in PHP, in that I can commingle presentation markup (HTML) and system code (native PHP). As I have said before, this is both a blessing and a curse because the ease with which these can be brought together represents a temptation to combine application and display logic in the same place—with potentially disastrous consequences.

In PHP then, programming the view is largely a matter of restraint. If it isn't strictly a matter of display, treat any code with the greatest suspicion.

To this end, the View Helper pattern (Alur et al.) provides for a helper class that may be specific to a view or shared between multiple views to help with any tasks that require more than the smallest amount of code.

The Problem

These days it is becoming rarer to find SQL queries and other business logic embedded directly in display pages, but it still happens. I have covered this particular evil in great detail in previous chapters, so I'll keep this brief.

Web pages that contain too much code can be hard for web producers to work with, as presentation components become tangled up in loops and conditionals.

Business logic in the presentation forces you to stick with that interface. You can't switch in a new view easily without porting across a lot of application code, too.

Systems that separate their views from their logic are also easier to test. This is because tests can be applied to the functionality of the logic layer in isolation of the noisy distractions of presentation.

Security issues often appear in systems which embed logic in their presentation layer, too. In such systems, because database queries and code to handle user input tend to be scattered in with tables and forms and lists, it becomes hard to identify potential hazards.

With many operations recurring from view to view, systems that embed application code in their templates tend to fall prey to duplication as the same code structures are pasted from page to page. Where this happens, bugs and maintenance nightmares surely follow.

To prevent this from happening, you should handle application processing elsewhere and allow views to manage presentation only. This is often achieved by making views the passive recipients of data. Where a view does need to interrogate the system, it is a good idea to provide a View Helper object to do any involved work on the view's behalf.

Implementation

Once you have created a wider framework, the view layer is not a massive programming challenge. Of course, it remains a huge design and information architecture issue, but that's another book!

Template View was so named by Fowler. It is a staple pattern used by most enterprise programmers. In some languages, an implementation might involve cooking up a templating system that translates tags to values set by the system. You have that option in PHP, too. You could use a templating engine like the excellent Twig. My preferred option, though, is to use PHP's existing functionality, but to use it with care.

In order for a view to have something to work with, it must be able to acquire data. I like to define a View Helper that views can use.

Here is a simple View Helper class:

```
// listing 12.39
class ViewHelper
{
    public function sponsorList(): string
    {
        // do something complicated to get the sponsor list return "Bob's
        Shoe Emporium";
    }
}
```

All this class does at present is provide a sponsor list string. Let's assume that there is some relatively complex process to acquire or format this data that we should not embed in the template itself. You can extend it to provide additional functionality as your application evolves. If you find yourself doing something in a view that takes up more than a couple of lines, chances are it belongs in the View Helper. In a larger application, you may provide multiple View Helper objects in an inheritance hierarchy in order to provide different tools for different parts of your system.

I might acquire a View Helper from a factory of some kind—perhaps the registry. From the point of view of the template, the simplest approach is to make a helper instance available in the render() method:

```
// listing 12.40
public function render(string $resource, Request $request): void
{
    $vh = new ViewHelper();
    // now the template will have the $vh variable include($resource);
}
```

Here is a simple view that uses the View Helper:

```
// listing 12.41
<html>
<head>
<title>Venues</title>
</head>
```

```
<body>
<h1>Venues</h1>

<div>
Proudly sponsored by: <?php echo $vh->sponsorList(); ?>

</div> Listing venues
</body>
</html>
```

The view (list_venues.php) is granted a ViewHelper instance in the $vh variable. It calls the sponsorList() method and prints the results.

Clearly, this example doesn't banish code from the view, but it does severely limit the amount and kind of coding that needs to be done. The page contains a simple echo statement and will inevitably require other method calls as it grows in complexity, but a designer should be able to work around code of this kind with little or no effort.

Slightly more problematic are if statements and loops. These are difficult to delegate to a View Helper because they are usually bound up with formatted output. I tend to keep both simple conditionals and loops (which are very common in building tables that display rows of data) inside the Template View; but to keep them as simple as possible, I delegate things like test clauses, where possible.

Consequences

There is something slightly disturbing about the way that data is passed to the view layer, in that a view doesn't really have a fixed interface that guarantees its environment. I tend to think of every view as entering into a contract with the system at large. The view effectively says to the application, "If I am invoked, then I have a right to access object This, object That, and object TheOther." It is up to the application to ensure that this is the case.

You could make views stricter by providing accessor methods in the helper classes, but I have always found it easier to register objects dynamically for the view layer through a Request, Response, or Context object.

While templates are often essentially passive, populated with data resulting from the last request, there may be times when the view needs to make an ancillary request. The View Helper is a good place to provide this functionality, keeping any knowledge of the mechanism by which data is required hidden from the view itself. Even the View Helper should do as little work as possible, delegating to a command or contacting the domain layer via a facade.

Note   You saw the Facade pattern in Chapter 10. Alur et al. look at one use of Facades in enterprise programming in the Session Facade pattern (which is designed to limit fine-grained network transactions). Fowler also describes a pattern called Service Layer, which provides a simple point of access to the complexities within a layer.

The Business Logic Layer

If the control layer orchestrates communication with the outside world and marshals a system's response to it, the logic layer gets on with the *business* of an application. This layer should be as free as possible of the noise and trauma generated as query strings are analyzed, HTML tables are constructed, and feedback messages composed. Business logic is about doing the stuff that needs doing—the true purpose of the application. Everything else exists just to support these tasks.

In a classic object-oriented application, the business logic layer is often composed of classes that model the problems that the system aims to address. As you shall see, this is a flexible design decision. It also requires significant up-front planning.

Let's begin, then, with the quickest way of getting a system up and running.

Transaction Script

The Transaction Script pattern (*Patterns of Enterprise Application Architecture*) describes the way that many systems evolve of their own accord. It is simple, intuitive, and effective, although it becomes less so as systems grow. A transaction script handles a request inline, rather than delegating to specialized objects. It is the quintessential quick fix. It is also a hard pattern to categorize because it combines elements from other layers in this chapter. I have chosen to present it as part of the business logic layer because the pattern's motivation is to achieve the business aims of the system.

The Problem

Every request must be handled in some way. As you have seen, many systems provide a layer that assesses and filters incoming data. Ideally, though, this layer should then call on classes that are designed to fulfill the request. These classes could be broken down to represent forces and responsibilities in a system, perhaps with a facade interface.

This approach requires a certain amount of careful design, however. For some projects (typically small in scope and urgent in nature), such development overhead can be unacceptable. In this case, you may need to build your business logic into a set of procedural operations. Each operation will be crafted to handle a particular request.

The problem, then, is the need to provide a fast and effective mechanism for fulfilling a system's objectives without a potentially costly investment in complex design.

The great benefit of this pattern is the speed with which you can get results. Each script takes input and manipulates the database to ensure an outcome. Beyond organizing related methods within the same class and keeping the Transaction Script classes in their own tier (i.e., as independent as possible of the command, control, and view layers), there is little up-front design required.

While business logic layer classes tend to be clearly separated from the presentation layer, they are often more embedded in the data layer. This is because retrieving and storing data is key to the tasks that such classes often perform. You will see mechanisms for decoupling logic objects from the database later in the chapter. Transaction Script classes, though, usually know all about the database (although they can use gateway classes to handle the details of their actual queries).

Implementation

Let's return to my event listing example. In this case, the system supports three relational database tables: venue, space, and event. A venue may have a number of spaces (e.g., a theater can have more than one stage, and a dance club may have different rooms). Each space plays host to many events. Here is the schema:

```
CREATE TABLE 'venue' (
    'id' int(11) NOT NULL auto_increment,
    'name' text,
    PRIMARY KEY  ('id')
)

CREATE TABLE 'space' (
    'id' int(11) NOT NULL auto_increment,
    'venue' int(11) default NULL,
    'name' text,
    PRIMARY KEY ('id')
)
```

```
CREATE TABLE 'event' (
    'id' int(11) NOT NULL auto_increment,
    'space' int(11) default NULL,
    'start' mediumtext,
    'duration' int(11) default NULL,
    'name' text,
    PRIMARY KEY ('id')
)
```

Clearly, the system will need mechanisms for adding both venues and events. Each of these represents a single transaction. I could give each method its own class (and organize my classes according to the Command pattern that you encountered in Chapter 11). In this case, though, I am going to place the methods in a single class, albeit as part of an inheritance hierarchy. You can see the structure in Figure 12-10.

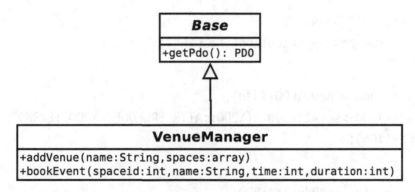

Figure 12-10. *A Transaction Script class with its superclass*

So why does this example include an abstract superclass? In a script of any size, I would be likely to add more concrete classes to this hierarchy. Since most of these will share at least some core functionality, it makes sense to lodge this in a common parent.

In fact, this is a pattern in its own right (Fowler has named it Layer Supertype). Where classes in a layer share characteristics, it makes sense to group them into a single type, locating utility operations in the base class. You will see this a lot in the rest of this chapter.

In this case, the base class acquires a PDO object, which it stores in a property.

```
// listing 12.42
abstract class Base
{
    private \PDO $pdo;
    private string $config = __DIR__ . "/data/woo_options.ini";

    public function __construct()
    {
        $reg = Registry::instance();
        $options = parse_ini_file($this->config, true);
        $conf = new Conf($options['config']);
        $reg->setConf($conf);
        $dsn = $reg->getDSN();

        if (is_null($dsn)) {
            throw new AppException("No DSN");
        }

        $this->pdo = new \PDO($dsn);
        $this->pdo->setAttribute(\PDO::ATTR_ERRMODE, \PDO::ERRMODE_
        EXCEPTION);
    }

    public function getPdo(): \PDO
    {
        return $this->pdo;
    }
}
```

I use the Registry class to acquire a DSN string, which I pass to the PDO constructor. I make the PDO object available via a getter method: getPdo(). In fact, a lot of this work can be pushed back into the Registry object itself—a strategy you'll see that I have adopted elsewhere in this chapter and the next.

Here is the start of the VenueManager class, which sets up my SQL statements:

```
// listing 12.43
class VenueManager extends Base
{
    private string $addvenue = "INSERT INTO venue
                                ( name  )
                                VALUES( ? )";

    private string $addspace = "INSERT INTO space
                                ( name, venue )
                                VALUES( ?, ? )";

    private string $addevent = "INSERT INTO event
                                ( name, space, start, duration )
                                VALUES( ?, ?, ?, ? )";

// ...
```

Not much new here. These are the SQL statements that the transaction scripts will use. They are constructed in a format accepted by the PDO class's prepare() method. The question marks are placeholders for the values that will be passed to execute(). Now it's time to define the first method designed to fulfill a specific business need:

```
// listing 12.44

// VenueManager

public function addVenue(string $name, array $spaces): array
{
    $pdo = $this->getPdo();
    $ret = [];
    $ret['venue'] = [$name];
    $stmt = $pdo->prepare($this->addvenue);
    $stmt->execute($ret['venue']);
    $vid = $pdo->lastInsertId();

    $ret['spaces'] = [];

    $stmt = $pdo->prepare($this->addspace);
```

483

```
    foreach ($spaces as $spacename) {
        $values = [$spacename, $vid];
        $stmt->execute($values);
        $sid = $pdo->lastInsertId();
        array_unshift($values, $sid);
        $ret['spaces'][] = $values;
    }

    return $ret;
}
```

As you can see, addVenue() requires a venue name and an array of space names. It uses these to populate the venue and space tables. It also creates a data structure that contains this information, along with the newly generated ID values for each row.

If there's an error with this, remember, an exception is thrown. I don't catch any exceptions here, so anything thrown by prepare() will also be thrown by this method. This is the result I want, although I should make it clear that this method throws exceptions in my documentation.

Having created the venue row, I loop through $spaces, adding a row in the space table for each element. Notice that I include the venue ID as a foreign key in each of the space rows I create, associating the row with the venue.

The second transaction script is similarly straightforward:

```
// listing 12.45

// VenueManager

public function bookEvent(int $spaceid, string $name, int $time, int
$duration): void
{
    $pdo = $this->getPdo();
    $stmt = $pdo->prepare($this->addevent);
    $stmt->execute([$name, $spaceid, $time, $duration]);
}
```

The purpose of this script is to add an event to the events table, associated with a space.

Consequences

The Transaction Script pattern is an effective way of getting good results fast. It is also one of those patterns many programmers have used for years without imagining it might need a name. With a few good helper methods like those I added to the base class, you can concentrate on application logic without getting too bogged down in database fiddle-faddling.

I have seen Transaction Script appear in a lessc welcome context. I thought I was writing a much more complex and object-heavy application than would usually suit this pattern. As the pressure of deadlines began to tell, I found that I was placing more and more logic in what was intended to be a thin facade onto a Domain Model (see the next section). Although the result was less elegant than I had wanted, I have to admit that the application did not appear to suffer for its implicit redesign.

In most cases, you would choose a Transaction Script approach with a small project when you are certain it isn't going to grow into a large one. The approach does not scale well because duplication often begins to creep in as the scripts inevitably cross one another. You can go some way to factoring this out, of course, but you probably will not be able to excise it completely.

In my example, I decide to embed database code in the transaction script classes themselves. As you saw, though, the code wants to separate the database work from the application logic. I can make that break absolute by pulling it out of the class altogether and creating a gateway class whose role it is to handle database interactions on the system's behalf.

Domain Model

The Domain Model is the pristine logical engine that many of the other patterns in this chapter strive to create, nurture, and protect. It is an abstracted representation of the forces at work in your project. It's a kind of plane of forms, where your business problems play out their nature unencumbered by nasty material issues like databases and web pages.

If that seems a little flowery, let's bring it down to reality. A Domain Model is a representation of the real-world participants of your system. It is in the Domain Model that the object-as-thing rule of thumb is truer than elsewhere. Everywhere else, objects tend to embody responsibilities. In the Domain Model, they often describe a set of attributes, with added agency. They are *things* that do *stuff*.

The Problem

If you have been using Transaction Script, you may find that duplication becomes a problem as different scripts need to perform the same tasks. That can be factored out to a certain extent, but over time it's easy to fall into cut-and-paste coding.

You can use a Domain Model to extract and embody the participants and process of your system. Rather than using a script to add space data to the database, and then associate event data with it, you can create `Space` and `Event` classes. Booking an event in a space can then become as simple as a call to `Space::bookEvent()`. A task like checking for a time clash becomes `Event::intersects()` and so on.

Clearly, with an example as simple as Woo, a Transaction Script is more than adequate. But as domain logic gets more complex, the alternative of a Domain Model becomes increasingly attractive. Complex logic can be handled more easily, and you need less conditional code when you model the application domain.

Implementation

Domain Models can be relatively simple to design. Most of the complexity associated with the subject lies in the patterns that are designed to keep the model pure—that is, to separate it from the other tiers in the application.

Separating the participants of a Domain Model from the presentation layer is largely a matter of ensuring that they keep to themselves. Separating the participants from the data layer is much more problematic. Although the ideal is to consider a Domain Model only in terms of the problems it represents and resolves, the reality of the database is hard to escape.

It is common for Domain Model classes to map fairly directly to tables in a relational database, and this certainly makes life easier. Figure 12-11, for example, shows a class diagram that sketches some of the participants of the Woo system.

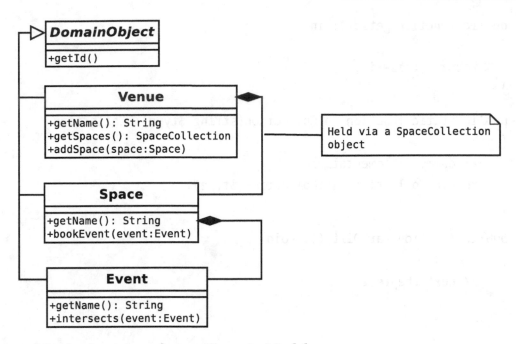

Figure 12-11. *An extract from a Domain Model*

The objects in Figure 12-11 mirror the tables that were set up for the Transaction Script example. This direct association makes a system easier to manage, but it is not always possible, especially if you are working with a database schema that precedes your application. Such an association can itself be the source of problems. If you're not careful, you can end up modeling the database rather than the problems and forces you are attempting to address.

Just because a Domain Model often mirrors the structure of a database does not mean that its classes should have any knowledge of it. By separating the model from the database, you make the entire tier easier to test and less likely to be affected by changes of schema or even changes of storage mechanism. It also focuses the responsibility of each class on its core tasks.

Here is a simplified Venue object, together with its parent class:

```
// listing 12.46
abstract class DomainObject
{

    public function __construct(private int $id)
    {
    }
}
```

```php
    public function getId(): int
    {
        return $this->id;
    }

    public static function getCollection(string $type): Collection
    {
        // dummy implementation
        return Collection::getCollection($type);
    }

    public function markDirty(): void
    {
        // next chapter!
    }
}

// listing 12.47
class Venue extends DomainObject
{
    private SpaceCollection $spaces;

    public function __construct(int $id, private string $name)
    {
        $this->name = $name;
        $this->spaces = self::getCollection(Space::class);
        parent:: __construct($id);
    }

    public function setSpaces(SpaceCollection $spaces): void
    {
        $this->spaces = $spaces;
    }
    public function getSpaces(): SpaceCollection
    {
        return $this->spaces;
    }
```

```
public function addSpace(Space $space): void
{
    $this->spaces->add($space);
    $space->setVenue($this);
}

public function setName(string $name): void
{
    $this->name = $name;
    $this->markDirty();
}

public function getName(): string
{
    return $this->name;
}
}
```

There are a few points that distinguish this class from one intended to run without persistence. Instead of an array, I am using an object of type SpaceCollection to store any Space objects the Venue might contain (though it could be argued that a type-safe array is a bonus whether you are working with a database or not!). Because this class works with a special collection object rather than an array of Space objects, the constructor needs to instantiate an empty collection on startup. It does this by calling a static method on the layer supertype:

```
$this->spaces = self::getCollection(Space::class);
```

I will return to this system's collection objects and how to acquire them in the next chapter. For now, though, the superclass simply returns an empty array.

Note   In this chapter and the next, I will discuss amendments to both the Venue and Space objects. These are simple domain objects, and they share a common functional core. If you're coding along, you should be able to apply concepts I discuss to either class. A Space class may not maintain a collection of Space objects, for example, but it might manage Event objects in exactly the same way.

I expect an $id parameter in the constructor that I pass to the superclass for storage. It should come as no surprise to learn that the $id parameter represents the unique ID of a row in the database. Notice also that I call a method on the superclass called markDirty() (this will be covered when you encounter the Unit of Work pattern).

Consequences

The design of a Domain Model needs to be as simple or complicated as the business processes you need to emulate. The beauty of this is that you can focus on the forces in your problem as you design the model, handling issues like persistence and presentation in other layers—in theory, that is.

In practice, I think that most developers design their domain models with at least one eye on the database. No one wants to design structures that will force you (or, worse, your colleagues) into somersaults of convoluted code when it comes to getting your objects in and out of the database.

This separation between the Domain Model and the data layer comes at a considerable cost in terms of design and planning. It is possible to place database code directly in the model (although you would probably want to design a gateway to handle the actual SQL). For relatively simple models, especially if each class broadly maps to a table, this approach can be a real win, saving you the considerable design overhead of devising an external system for reconciling your objects with the database.

Summary

I have covered an enormous amount of ground here (although I have also left out a lot). You should not feel daunted by the sheer volume of code in this chapter. Patterns are meant to be used in the right circumstances and combined when useful. Use those described in this chapter that you feel meet the needs of your project, and do not feel that you must build an entire framework before embarking on a project. On the other hand, there *is* enough material here to form the basis of a framework or, just as likely, to provide some insight into the architecture of some of the prebuilt frameworks you might choose to deploy.

And there's more! I left you teetering on the edge of persistence, with just a few tantalizing hints about collections and mappers to tease you. In the next chapter, I will look at some patterns for working with databases and for insulating your objects from the details of data storage.

CHAPTER 13

Database Patterns

Most web applications of any complexity handle persistence to a greater or lesser extent. Shops must recall their products and their customer records. Games must remember their players and the state of play. Social networking sites must keep track of your 238 friends and your unaccountable liking for boy bands of the 1980s and 1990s. Whatever the application, the chances are it's keeping score behind the scenes. In this chapter, I look at some patterns that can help.

This chapter will cover the following:

- *The data layer interface*: Patterns that define the points of contact between the storage layer and the rest of the system

- *Object watching*: Keeping track of objects, avoiding duplicates, and automating save and insert operations

- *Flexible queries*: Allowing your client coders to construct queries without thinking about the underlying database

- *Creating lists of found objects*: Building iterable collections

- *Managing your database components*: The welcome return of the Abstract Factory pattern

The Data Layer

In discussions with clients, it's usually the presentation layer that dominates. Fonts, colors, and ease of use are the primary topics of conversation. Among developers, it is often the database that looms large. It's not the database itself that concerns us; we can trust that to do its job unless we're very unlucky. No, it's the mechanisms we use to translate the rows and columns of a database table into data structures that cause the problems. In this chapter, I look at code that can help with this process.

491

© Matt Zandstra 2021
M. Zandstra, *PHP 8 Objects, Patterns, and Practice*, https://doi.org/10.1007/978-1-4842-6791-2_13

Not everything presented here sits in the data layer itself. Rather, I have grouped some of the patterns that help to solve persistence problems. All of these patterns are described by one or more of Clifton Nock, Martin Fowler, and Alur, et al.

Data Mapper

If you thought I glossed over the issue of saving and retrieving Venue objects from the database in the "Domain Model" section of Chapter 12, here is where you might find at least some answers. The Data Mapper pattern is described as a Data Access Object in a couple places. First, it's covered by Alur et al. in *Core J2EE Patterns: Best Practices and Design Strategies* (Prentice Hall, 2001). It's also covered by Martin Fowler in *Patterns of Enterprise Application Architecture* (Addison-Wesley Professional, 2002). Note that a Data Access Object is not an exact match to the Data Mapper pattern, as it generates data transfer objects; but since such objects are designed to become the real thing if you add water, the patterns are close enough.

As you might imagine, a data mapper is a class that is responsible for handling the transition from database to object.

The Problem

Objects are not organized like tables in a relational database. As you know, relational database tables are grids made up of rows and columns. One row may relate to another in a different (or even the same) table by means of a foreign key. Objects, on the other hand, tend to relate to one another more organically. One object may contain another, and different data structures will organize the same objects in different ways, combining and recombining objects in new relationships at runtime. Relational databases are optimized to manage large amounts of tabular data, whereas classes and objects encapsulate smaller focused chunks of information.

This disconnect between classes and relational databases is often described as the object-relational impedance mismatch (or simply impedance mismatch).

So how do you make that transition? One answer is to give a class (or a set of classes) responsibility for just that problem, effectively hiding the database from the domain model and managing the inevitable rough edges of the translation.

Implementation

Although with careful programming, it may be possible to create a single Mapper class to service multiple objects, it is common to see an individual Mapper for a major class in the Domain Model.

Figure 13-1 shows three concrete Mapper classes and an abstract superclass.

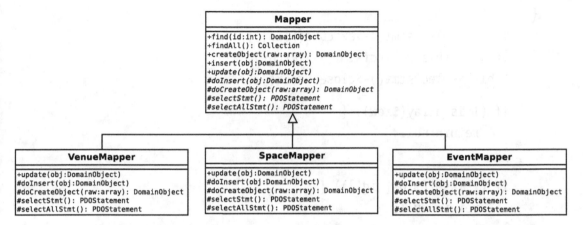

Figure 13-1. *Mapper classes*

In fact, because the Space objects are effectively subordinate to Venue objects, it may be possible to factor the SpaceMapper class into VenueMapper. For the sake of these exercises, I'm going to keep them separate.

As you can see, the classes present common operations for saving and loading data. The base class stores common functionality, delegating responsibility for handling object-specific operations to its children. Typically, these operations include actual object generation and constructing queries for database operations.

The base class often performs housekeeping before or after an operation, which is why the Template Method is used for explicit delegation (e.g., calls from concrete methods like insert() to abstract ones like doInsert(), etc.). Implementation determines which of the base class methods are made concrete in this way, as you will see later in the chapter.

Here is a simplified version of a Mapper base class:

```
// listing 13.01
abstract class Mapper
{
    protected \PDO $pdo;
```

```php
    public function __construct()
    {
        $reg = Registry::instance();
        $this->pdo = $reg->getPdo();
    }

    public function find(int $id): ?DomainObject
    {
        $this->selectstmt()->execute([$id]);
        $row = $this->selectstmt()->fetch();
        $this->selectstmt()->closeCursor();

        if (! is_array($row)) {
            return null;
        }

        if (! isset($row['id'])) {
            return null;
        }

        $object = $this->createObject($row);

        return $object;
    }

    public function createObject(array $raw): DomainObject
    {
        $obj = $this->doCreateObject($raw); return $obj;
    }

    public function insert(DomainObject $obj): void
    {
        $this->doInsert($obj);
    }

    abstract public function update(DomainObject $obj): void;
    abstract protected function doCreateObject(array $raw): DomainObject;
    abstract protected function doInsert(DomainObject $object): void;
```

```
    abstract protected function selectStmt(): \PDOStatement;
    abstract protected function targetClass(): string;
}
```

The constructor method uses a `Registry` to get a PDO object. A registry really shows its worth for classes like this. There isn't always a sensible path from the control layer to a `Mapper` along which data can be passed. Another way of managing mapper creation would be to hand it off to the `Registry` class itself. Rather than instantiate it, the mapper would expect to be *provided* with a PDO object as a constructor argument:

```
// listing 13.02
abstract class Mapper
{
    public function __construct(protected \PDO $pdo)
    {
    }
}
```

Client code would acquire a new `VenueMapper` from `Registry` using a method such as `getVenueMapper()`. This would instantiate a mapper, generating the PDO object too. For subsequent requests, the method would return the cached mapper. Because it allows me to keep mappers ignorant of the complications of configuration (even with a registry as a facade), this latter approach is the one I usually opt for.

Returning to the `Mapper` class, the `insert()` method does nothing but delegate to `doInsert()`. This is something that I would factor out in favor of an abstract `insert()` method, were it not for the fact that I know that the implementation used here will be useful here in due course.

`find()` is responsible for invoking a prepared statement (provided by an implementing child class) and acquiring row data. It finishes up by calling `createObject()`. The details of converting an array to an object will vary from case to case, of course, so the implementation is handled by the abstract `doCreateObject()` method. Once again, `createObject()` seems to do nothing but delegate to the child implementation; and once again, I'll soon add the housekeeping that makes this use of the Template Method pattern worth the trouble.

Child classes will also implement custom methods for finding data according to specific criteria (e.g., I will want to locate `Space` objects that belong to `Venue` objects).

You can take a look at the process from the child's perspective here:

```php
// listing 13.03
class VenueMapper extends Mapper
{
    private \PDOStatement $selectStmt;
    private \PDOStatement $updateStmt;
    private \PDOStatement $insertStmt;

    public function __construct()
    {
        parent:: __construct();
        $this->selectStmt = $this->pdo->prepare(
            "SELECT * FROM venue WHERE id=?"
        );

        $this->updateStmt = $this->pdo->prepare(
            "UPDATE venue SET name=?, id=? WHERE id=?"
        );

        $this->insertStmt = $this->pdo->prepare(
            "INSERT INTO venue ( name ) VALUES( ? )"
        );
    }

    protected function targetClass(): string
    {
        return Venue::class;
    }

    public function getCollection(array $raw): VenueCollection
    {
        return new VenueCollection($raw, $this);
    }
}
```

```
protected function doCreateObject(array $raw): Venue
{
    $obj = new Venue(
        (int)$raw['id'],
        $raw['name']
    );

    return $obj;
}

protected function doInsert(DomainObject $obj): void
{
    $values = [$obj->getName()];
    $this->insertStmt->execute($values);
    $id = $this->pdo->lastInsertId();
    $obj->setId((int)$id);
}

public function update(DomainObject $obj): void
{
    $values = [
        $obj->getName(),
        $obj->getId(),
        $obj->getId()
    ];

    $this->updateStmt->execute($values);
}

public function selectStmt(): \PDOStatement
{
    return $this->selectStmt;
}

}
```

Once again, this class is stripped of some of the goodies that are still to come.
Nonetheless, it does its job. The constructor prepares some SQL statements for use
later on.

Note   Notice that, in VenueMapper, doCreateObject() declares its return type Venue rather than DomainObject as specified in the parent Mapper class. The same is true of getCollection() which here declares VenueCollection rather than the more generic return type of Collection specified in the Mapper class. This is an example of *return type covariance*, introduced in PHP 7.4, which allows you to declare more specialized return types in child classes.

The parent Mapper class implements find(), which invokes selectStmt() to acquire the prepared SELECT statement. Assuming all goes well, Mapper invokes VenueMapper::doCreateObject(). It's here that I use the associative array to generate a Venue object.

From the point of view of the client, this process is simplicity itself:

```
// listing 13.04
$mapper = new VenueMapper();
$venue = $mapper->find(2);
print_r($venue);
```

The call to print_r() is a quick way of confirming that find() was successful. In my system (where there is a row in the venue table with ID 2), the output from this fragment is as follows:

```
popp\ch13\batch01\Venue Object
(
    [name:popp\ch13\batch01\Venue:private] => The Likey Lounge
    [spaces:popp\ch13\batch01\Venue:private] =>
    [id:popp\ch13\batch01\DomainObject:private] => 2
)
```

The doInsert() and update() methods reverse the process established by find(). Each accepts a DomainObject, extracts row data from it, and calls PDOStatement::execute() with the resulting information. Notice that the doInsert() method sets an ID on the provided object. Remember that objects are passed by reference in PHP, so the client code will see this change via its own reference.

Another thing to note is that doInsert() and update() are not really type safe. They will accept any DomainObject subclass without complaint. You should perform an instanceof test and throw an Exception if the wrong object is passed.

Once again, here is a client perspective on inserting and updating:

```
// listing 13.05
$mapper = new VenueMapper();
$venue = new Venue(-1, "The Likey Lounge");
// add the object to the database
$mapper->insert($venue);
// find the object again - just to prove it works!
$venue = $mapper->find($venue->getId());
print_r($venue);
// alter our object
$venue->setName("The Bibble Beer Likey Lounge");
// call update to enter the amended data
$mapper->update($venue);
// once again, go back to the database to prove it worked
$venue = $mapper->find($venue->getId());
print_r($venue);
```

Why have I used a negative value for the id of the Venue object I wish to add to the database? As you will see later in the chapter, I use this convention to distinguish between objects which have already been allocated a database id and those which have not. VenueMapper::doInsert() does not check the id—it simply uses the name of the venue to create a new row and then sets the generated database id on the provided Venue object. Here's that doInsert() method again:

```
// listing 13.06
protected function doInsert(DomainObject $obj): void
{
    $values = [$obj->getName()];
    $this->insertStmt->execute($values);
    $id = $this->pdo->lastInsertId();
    $obj->setId((int)$id);
}
```

Handling Multiple Rows

The find() method is pretty straightforward because it only needs to return a single object. What do you do, though, if you need to pull lots of data from the database? Your first thought may be to return an array of objects. This will work, but there is a major problem with the approach.

If you return an array, each object in the collection will need to be instantiated first, which, if you have a result set of 1000 objects, may be needlessly expensive. An alternative would be to simply return an array and let the calling code sort out object instantiation. This is possible, but it violates the very purpose of the Mapper classes.

There is one way that you can have your cake and eat it. You can use the built-in Iterator interface.

The Iterator interface requires implementing classes to define methods for querying a list. If you do this, your class can be used in foreach loops just like an array.

Table 13-1 shows the methods that the Iterator interface requires.

Table 13-1. *Methods Defined by the Iterator Interface*

Name	Description
rewind()	Send pointer to the start of list
current()	Return element at current pointer position
key()	Return current key (i.e., pointer value)
next()	Advance the pointer
valid()	Confirm that there is an element at the current pointer position

In order to implement an Iterator, you need to implement its methods and keep track of your place within a dataset. How you acquire that data, order it, or otherwise filter it is hidden from the client.

Here is an Iterator implementation that wraps an array but also accepts a Mapper object in its constructor for reasons that will become apparent:

```
// listing 13.07
abstract class Collection implements \Iterator
{
    protected int $total = 0;
```

```php
private int $pointer = 0;
private array $objects = [];

public function __construct(protected array $raw = [], protected
?Mapper $mapper = null)
{
    $this->total = count($raw);
    if (count($raw) &&  is_null($mapper)) {
        throw new AppException("need Mapper to generate objects");
    }
}

public function add(DomainObject $object): void
{
    $class = $this->targetClass();

    if (! ($object instanceof $class)) {
        throw new AppException("This is a {$class} collection");
    }

    $this->notifyAccess();
    $this->objects[$this->total] = $object;
    $this->total++;
}

abstract public function targetClass(): string;

protected function notifyAccess(): void
{
    // deliberately left blank!
}

private function getRow(int $num): ?DomainObject
{
    $this->notifyAccess();

    if ($num >= $this->total || $num < 0) {
        return  null;
    }
```

501

```php
    if (isset($this->objects[$num])) {
        return $this->objects[$num];
    }

    if (isset($this->raw[$num])) {
        $this->objects[$num] = $this->mapper->createObject(
        $this->raw[$num]);

        return $this->objects[$num];
    }

    return null;
}

public function rewind(): void
{
    $this->pointer = 0;
}

public function current(): ?DomainObject
{
    return $this->getRow($this->pointer);
}

public function key(): mixed
{
    return $this->pointer;
}

public function next(): void
{
    $row = $this->getRow($this->pointer);

    if (! is_null($row)) {
        $this->pointer++;
    }
}
```

```
    public function valid(): bool
    {
        return (! is_null($this->current()));
    }
}
```

The constructor expects to be called with no arguments or with two (the raw data that may eventually be transformed into objects and a mapper reference).

Assuming that the client has set the $raw argument (it will be a Mapper object that does this), this is stored in a property together with the size of the provided dataset. If raw data is provided, an instance of the Mapper is also required, as it's this that will convert each row into an object.

If no arguments were passed to the constructor, the class starts out empty; note, however, that the add() method is available for adding to the collection.

The class maintains two arrays: $objects and $raw. If a client requests a particular element, the getRow() method looks first in $objects to see if it has one already instantiated. If so, that gets returned. Otherwise, the method looks in $raw for the row data. $raw data is only present if a Mapper object is also present, so the data for the relevant row can be passed to the Mapper::createObject() method you encountered earlier. This returns a DomainObject object, which is cached in the $objects array with the relevant index. The newly created DomainObject object is returned to the user.

The rest of the class is a simple manipulation of the $pointer property and calls to getRow(). It also includes the notifyAccess() method, which will become important when you encounter the Lazy Load pattern.

You may have noticed that the Collection class is abstract. You need to provide specific implementations for each domain class:

```
// listing 13.08
class VenueCollection extends Collection
{
    public function targetClass(): string
    {
        return Venue::class;
    }
}
```

The VenueCollection class simply extends Collection and implements a targetClass() method. This, in conjunction with the type checking in the superclass's add() method, ensures that only Venue objects can be added to the collection. You could provide additional checking in the constructor as well if you wanted to be even safer.

Note that I used the ::class syntax to get a fully qualified string representation of the class. This feature has only been available since PHP 5.5. Prior to that, I would have had to have been careful to provide the full namespace path myself.

Clearly, this class should only work with a VenueMapper. In practical terms, though, this is a reasonably type-safe collection, especially as far as the Domain Model is concerned.

There are parallel classes for Event and Space objects, of course. Figure 13-2 shows some Collection classes.

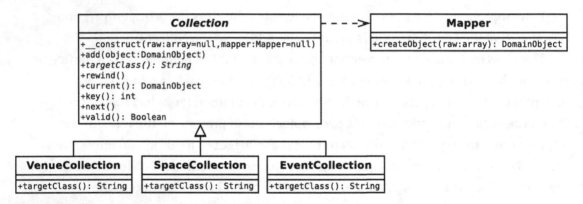

Figure 13-2. *Managing multiple rows with collections*

Because the Domain Model needs to instantiate Collection objects, and because I may need to switch the implementation at some point (especially for testing purposes), I provide convenience getter methods in the Registry to acquire empty collections. As your system grows, you may delegate this to a dedicated factory. During development, though, I tend to begin with the simplest approach and default to using the Registry for most object creation. Here's how I get an empty VenueCollection object:

```
// listing 13.09
$reg = Registry::instance();

$collection = $reg->getVenueCollection();
$collection->add(new  Venue(-1, "Loud  and  Thumping"));
$collection->add(new  Venue(-1, "Eeezy"));
$collection->add(new  Venue(-1, "Duck  and  Badger"));
```

```
foreach ($collection as $venue) {
    print $venue->getName() . "\n";
}
```

Once again, in this example, I have used the convention that I use an id of –1 for an object that has not yet been added to the database. The `Collection` object does not care whether or not its `DomainObject` members have yet been inserted.

With the implementation I have built here, there isn't much else you can do with this collection; however, adding `elementAt()`, `deleteAt()`, `count()`, and similar methods is a trivial exercise. (And fun, too! Enjoy!)

Using a Generator in Place of the Iterator Interface

Although it's not difficult to do, implementing an `Iterator` interface can be a chore. As of PHP 5.5, you can use a simpler (and often more memory efficient) mechanism called a *generator*. A generator is a function that can return multiple values, usually in a loop. Instead of using the `return` keyword, a generator function will use `yield`. When the PHP processor sees `yield` in a function, it will return an `Iterator` of type `Generator` to calling code. This new object can be treated like any `Iterator`. Cleverly, the loop that yielded a value using `yield` will continue to run, but only as the `Generator` is asked for its next() value. Practically speaking, the flow looks like this:

- Client code calls a generator function (a function containing a `yield` keyword).

- The generator function contains a loop or a repetitive process which returns multiple values via yield. On encountering yield, the PHP processor creates a `Generator` object and returns it to client code.

- The repetitive process in the generator function is temporarily frozen at this point.

- Client code takes this `Generator` and treats like any `Iterator`—probably passing it to `foreach`.

- With every iteration of `foreach`, the `Generator` object gets the next value from the generator function.

So I could use this feature for my Collection base class. Because a generator function (or method) returns a Generator, the Collection itself would no longer be iterable—instead, I'll use a generator method as a factory:

```
// listing 13.10
abstract class GenCollection
{
    protected int $total = 0;
    private array $objects = [];

    public function __construct(protected array $raw = [], protected
    ?Mapper $mapper = null)
    {
        $this->total = count($raw);

        if (count($raw) && is_null($mapper)) {
            throw new AppException("need Mapper to generate objects");
        }
    }

    public function add(DomainObject $object): void
    {
        $class = $this->targetClass();

        if (! ($object instanceof $class )) {
            throw new AppException("This is a {$class} collection");
        }

        $this->notifyAccess();
        $this->objects[$this->total] = $object;
        $this->total++;
    }

    public function getGenerator(): \Generator
    {
        for ($x = 0; $x < $this->total; $x++) {
            yield $this->getRow($x);
        }
    }
```

```
abstract public function targetClass(): string;

protected function notifyAccess(): void
{
    // deliberately left blank!
}

private function getRow(int $num): ?DomainObject
{
    $this->notifyAccess();

    if ($num >= $this->total || $num < 0) {
        return null;
    }

    if (isset($this->objects[$num])) {
        return $this->objects[$num];
    }

    if (isset($this->raw[$num])) {
        $this->objects[$num] = $this->mapper->createObject(
        $this->raw[$num]);
        return $this->objects[$num];
    }

    return null;
}
}
```

As you can see, this makes for a more compact base class. I have been able to do away with current() and reset() and so on. The one drawback is that the Collection itself can no longer be iterated directly. Instead, client code must call getGenerator() and iterate the Generator object that yield causes to be returned, like this:

```
// listing 13.11
$genvencoll = new GenVenueCollection();
$genvencoll->add(new Venue(-1, "Loud and Thumping"));
$genvencoll->add(new Venue(-1, "Eeezy"));
$genvencoll->add(new Venue(-1, "Duck and Badger"));
```

```
$gen = $genvencoll->getGenerator();

foreach ($gen as $wrapper) {
    print_r($wrapper);
}
```

Because I'd rather not add this additional layer to my system, I'm going to stick with the implemented Iterator version for this example. However, generators are really the way to go for making lightweight iterators with the minimum of setup.

Acquiring Collection Objects

We have already seen that I have decided to use the Registry as a factory for Collections. I also use it for serving up Mapper objects. Here is the code:

```
// listing 13.12

public function getVenueMapper(): VenueMapper
{
    return new VenueMapper();
}

public function getSpaceMapper(): SpaceMapper
{
    return new SpaceMapper();
}

public function getEventMapper(): EventMapper
{
    return new EventMapper();
}

public function getVenueCollection(): VenueCollection
{
    return new VenueCollection();
}
```

```
public function getSpaceCollection(): SpaceCollection
{
    return new SpaceCollection();
}

public function getEventCollection(): EventCollection
{
    return new EventCollection();
}
```

I'm beginning to push the boundaries of what fits neatly in the Registry. A few more getter methods, and it will be time to refactor this code to use the Abstract Factory pattern instead. I'll leave that to you, though (head back to Chapter 9 if you need a reminder).

Now that accessing Mapper and Collection classes is so easy, the Venue class can be extended to manage the persistence of Space objects. The class provides methods for adding individual Space objects to its SpaceCollection or for switching in an entirely new SpaceCollection:

```
// listing 13.13

// Venue

public function getSpaces(): SpaceCollection
{
    if (is_null($this->spaces)) {
        $reg = Registry::instance();
        $this->spaces = $reg->getSpaceCollection();
    }

    return $this->spaces;
}

public function setSpaces(SpaceCollection $spaces): void
{
    $this->spaces = $spaces;
}
```

```
public function addSpace(Space $space): void
{
    $this->getSpaces()->add($space);
    $space->setVenue($this);
}
```

The setSpaces() operation currently takes it on trust that all Space objects in the collection refer to the current Venue. It would be easy enough to add checking to the method. This version keeps things simple though. Notice that I only instantiate the $spaces property when getSpaces() is called. Later on, I'll demonstrate how you can extend this lazy instantiation to limit database requests.

The VenueMapper needs to set up a SpaceCollection for each Venue object it creates:

```
// listing 13.14

// VenueMapper

protected function doCreateObject(array $raw): Venue
{
    $obj = new  Venue(
        (int)$raw['id'],
        $raw['name']
    );

    $spacemapper = new SpaceMapper();
    $spacecollection = $spacemapper->findByVenue($raw['id']);
    $obj->setSpaces($spacecollection);

    return $obj;
}
```

The VenueMapper::doCreateObject() method creates a SpaceMapper and acquires a SpaceCollection from it. As you can see, the SpaceMapper class implements a findByVenue() method. This brings us to the queries that generate multiple objects. For the sake of brevity, I omitted the Mapper::findAll() method from the original listing for woo\mapper\Mapper. Here, it is restored:

```
// listing 13.15

// Mapper
```

```
public function findAll(): Collection
{
    $this->selectAllStmt()->execute([]);

    return $this->getCollection(
        $this->selectAllStmt()->fetchAll()
    );
}

abstract protected function selectAllStmt(): \PDOStatement;
abstract protected function getCollection(array $raw): Collection;
```

This method calls a child method: selectAllStmt(). Like selectStmt(), this should contain a prepared statement object primed to acquire all rows in the table. Here's the PDOStatement object as created in the SpaceMapper class:

```
// listing 13.16

// SpaceMapper::__construct()

$this->selectAllStmt = $this->pdo->prepare(
    "SELECT * FROM space"
);
$this->findByVenueStmt = $this->pdo->prepare(
    "SELECT * FROM space WHERE venue=?"
);
```

I included another statement here, $findByVenueStmt, which is used to locate Space objects specific to an individual Venue.

The findAll() method calls another new method, getCollection(), passing it its found data. Here is SpaceMapper::getCollection():

```
// listing 13.17
public function getCollection(array $raw): SpaceCollection
{
    return new SpaceCollection($raw, $this);
}
```

A full version of the Mapper class should declare getCollection() and selectAllStmt() as abstract methods, so all mappers are capable of returning a collection containing their persistent domain objects. In order to get the Space objects that belong to a Venue, however, I need a more limited collection. You have already seen the prepared statement for acquiring the data; now, here is the SpaceMapper::findByVenue() method, which generates the collection:

```
// listing 13.18
public function findByVenue($vid): SpaceCollection
{
    $this->findByVenueStmt->execute([$vid]);

    return new SpaceCollection($this->findByVenueStmt->fetchAll(), $this);
}
```

The findByVenue() method is identical to findAll(), except for the SQL statement used. Back in the VenueMapper, the resulting collection is set on the Venue object via Venue::setSpaces().

So Venue objects now arrive fresh from the database, complete with all their Space objects in a neat type-safe list. None of the objects in that list are instantiated before being requested.

Figure 13-3 shows the process by which a client class might acquire a SpaceCollection and how the SpaceCollection class interacts with SpaceMapper::createObject() to convert its raw data into an object for returning to the client.

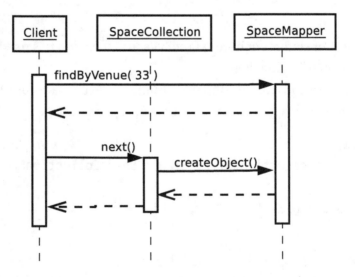

Figure 13-3. *Acquiring a SpaceCollection and using it to get a Space object*

Consequences

The drawback with the approach I took to adding Space objects to Venue ones is that I had to take two trips to the database. In most instances, I think that is a price worth paying. Also, note that the work in VenueMapper::doCreateObject() to acquire a correctly populated SpaceCollection could be moved to Venue::getSpaces(), so that the secondary database connection would only occur on demand. Here's how such a method might look:

```
// listing 13.19

// Venue

public function getSpaces2(): SpaceCollection
{
    if (is_null($this->spaces)) {
        $reg = Registry::instance();
        $finder = $reg->getSpaceMapper();
        $this->spaces = $finder->findByVenue($this->getId());
    }

    return $this->spaces;
}
```

If efficiency becomes an issue, however, it should be easy enough to factor out SpaceMapper altogether and retrieve all the data you need in one go using an SQL join.

Of course, your code may become less portable as a result of that, but efficiency optimization always comes at a price!

Ultimately, the granularity of your Mapper classes will vary. If an object type is stored solely by another, then you may consider only having a Mapper for the container.

The great strength of this pattern is the strong decoupling it effects between the domain layer and the database. The Mapper objects take the strain behind the scenes and can adapt to all sorts of relational twistedness.

Perhaps the biggest drawback with the pattern is the sheer amount of slog involved in creating concrete Mapper classes. However, there is a large amount of boilerplate code that can be automatically generated. A neat way of generating the common methods for Mapper classes is through reflection. You can query a domain object, discover its setter and getter methods (perhaps in tandem with an argument naming convention), and generate basic Mapper classes ready for amendment. This is how all the Mapper classes featured in this chapter were initially produced.

One issue to be aware of with mappers is the danger of loading too many objects at one time. The Iterator implementation helps us here, though. Because a Collection object only holds row data at first, the secondary request (for a Space object) is only made when a particular Venue is accessed and converted from array to object. This form of lazy loading can be enhanced even further, as you shall see.

You should be careful of ripple loading. Be aware as you create your mapper that the use of another one to acquire a property for your object may be the tip of a very large iceberg. This secondary mapper may itself use yet more in constructing its own object. If you are not careful, you could find that what looks on the surface like a simple find operation sets off tens of other similar operations.

You should also be aware of any guidelines your database application lays down for building efficient queries and be prepared to optimize (on a database-by-database basis if necessary). SQL statements that apply well to multiple database applications are nice; fast applications are much nicer. Although introducing conditionals (or strategy classes) to manage different versions of the same queries is a chore, and potentially ugly in the former case, don't forget that all this mucky optimization is neatly hidden away from client code.

Identity Map

Do you remember the nightmare of pass-by-value errors in PHP 4? The sheer confusion that ensued when two variables that you thought pointed to a single object turned out to refer to different but cunningly similar ones? Well, the nightmare has returned.

The Problem

Here's a variation on some test code created to try out the Data Mapper example:

```
// listing 13.20
$mapper = new VenueMapper();

$venue = new Venue(-1, "The Likey Lounge");
$mapper->insert($venue);
```

```
$venue1 = $mapper->find($venue->getId());
$venue2 = $mapper->find($venue->getId());

$venue1->setName("The Something Else");
$venue2->setName("The Bibble Beer Likey Lounge");

print $venue->getName() . "\n";
print $venue1->getName() . "\n";
print $venue2->getName() . "\n";
```

The purpose of the original code was to demonstrate that an object that you add to the database could also be extracted via a Mapper and would be identical. Identical, that is, in every way except for being the *same* object. Here, I make the problem obvious by working with three versions of Venue—an original and two instances extracted from the database. I alter the names of my new instances and output all three names. Here is my output:

```
The Likey Lounge
The Something Else
The Bibble Beer Likey Lounge
```

Remember that I am using the convention that a brand-new DomainObject (i.e., one that does not yet exist in the database) should be instantiated with a –1 id value. Thanks to the VenueMapper::insert() method, my initial Venue object will be updated with the id value autogenerated by the database.

I sidestepped this issue earlier by assigning the new Venue object over the old, so I did not end up with multiple clone-like objects. Unfortunately, you won't always have that kind of control over the situation. The same object may be referenced at several different times within a *single* request. If you alter one version of it and save that to the database, can you be sure that another version of the object (perhaps stored already in a Collection object) won't be written over your changes?

Not only are duplicate objects risky in a system, they also represent a considerable overhead. Some popular objects could be loaded three or four times in a process, with all but one of these trips to the database entirely redundant.

Fortunately, fixing this problem is relatively straightforward.

Implementation

An Identity Map is simply an object whose task it is to keep track of all the objects in a
system and thereby help to ensure that nothing that should be one object becomes two.

```
// listing 13.21
class ObjectWatcher
{
    private array $all = [];
    private static ?ObjectWatcher $instance = null;

    private function __construct()
    {
    }
    public static function instance(): self
    {
        if (is_null(self::$instance)) {
            self::$instance = new ObjectWatcher();
        }

        return self::$instance;
    }

    public function globalKey(DomainObject $obj): string
    {
        return  get_class($obj) . "." . $obj->getId();
    }

    public static function add(DomainObject $obj): void
    {
        $inst = self::instance();
        $inst->all[$inst->globalKey($obj)] = $obj;
    }

    public static function exists(string $classname, int $id):
    ?DomainObject
    {
        $inst = self::instance();
        $key = "{$classname} . {$id}";
```

```
        if (isset($inst->all[$key])) {
            return $inst->all[$key];
        }

        return null;
    }
}
```

Figure 13-4 shows how an Identity Map object might integrate with other classes you have seen.

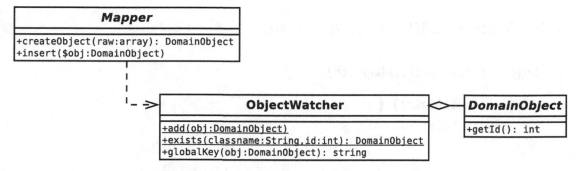

Figure 13-4. *An Identity Map*

The main trick with an Identity Map is, pretty obviously, identifying objects. This means that you need to tag each object in some way. There are a number of different strategies you can take here. The database table key that all objects in the system already use is no good because the ID is not guaranteed to be unique across all tables.

You could also use the database to maintain a global key table. Every time you created an object, you would iterate the key table's running total and associate the global key with the object in its own row. The overhead of this is relatively slight, and it would be easy to do.

As you can see, I have gone for an altogether simpler approach. I concatenate the name of the object's class with its table ID. There cannot be two objects of type popp\ch13\batch03\Event with an ID of 4, so my key of popp\ch13\batch03\Event.4 is safe enough for my purposes.

The globalKey() method handles the details of this. The class provides an add() method for adding new objects. Each object is labeled with its unique key in an array property, $all.

The exists() method accepts a class name and an $id rather than an object. I don't want to have to instantiate an object to see whether or not it already exists! The method builds a key from this data and checks to see if it indexes an element in the $all property. If an object is found, a reference is duly returned.

There is only one class where I work with the ObjectWatcher class in its role as an Identity Map. The Mapper class provides functionality for generating objects, so it makes sense to add the checking there:

```
// listing 13.22

// Mapper

public function find(int $id): ?DomainObject
{
    $old = $this->getFromMap($id);

    if (! is_null($old)) {
        return $old;
    }

    // work with db return $object;
}

abstract protected function targetClass(): string;

private function getFromMap($id): ?DomainObject
{
    return ObjectWatcher::exists(
        $this->targetClass(),
        $id
    );
}

private function addToMap(DomainObject $obj): void
{
    ObjectWatcher::add($obj);
}
```

```
public function createObject($raw): ?DomainObject
{
    $old = $this->getFromMap((int)$raw['id']);

    if (! is_null($old)) {
        return $old;
    }

    $obj = $this->doCreateObject($raw);
    $this->addToMap($obj);

    return $obj;
}

public function insert(DomainObject $obj): void
{
    $this->doInsert($obj);
    $this->addToMap($obj);
}
```

The class provides two convenience methods: addToMap() and getFromMap(). These save me the bother of remembering the full syntax of the static call to ObjectWatcher. More importantly, they call down to the child implementation (e.g., VenueMapper) to get the name of the class currently awaiting instantiation.

This is achieved by calling targetClass(), an abstract method that is implemented by all concrete Mapper classes. It should return the name of the class that the Mapper is designed to generate. Here is the SpaceMapper class's implementation of targetClass():

```
// listing 13.23

// SpaceMapper

protected function targetClass(): string
{
    return Space::class;
}
```

519

Both `find()` and `createObject()` first check for an existing object by passing the object ID to `getFromMap()`. If an object is found, it is returned to the client and method execution ends. If, however, there is no version of this object in existence yet, object instantiation goes ahead. In `createObject()`, the new object is passed to `addToMap()` to prevent any clashes in the future.

So why am I going through part of this process twice, with calls to `getFromMap()` in both `find()` and `createObject()`? The answer lies with `Collections`. When these generate objects, they do so by calling `createObject()`. I need to make sure that the row encapsulated by a `Collection` object is not stale, as well as to ensure that the latest version of the object is returned to the user.

Consequences

As long as you use the Identity Map in all contexts in which objects are generated from or added to the database, the possibility of duplicate objects in your process is practically zero.

Of course, this only works *within* your process. Different processes will inevitably access versions of the same object at the same time. It is important to think through the possibilities for data corruption engendered by concurrent access. If there is a serious issue, you may need to consider a locking strategy. You might also consider storing objects in shared memory or using an external object caching system like Memcached. You can learn about Memcached at `https://memcached.org/` and about PHP support for it at `https://www.php.net/memcache`.

Unit of Work

When do you save your objects? Until I discovered the Unit of Work pattern (written up by David Rice in Martin Fowler's *Patterns of Enterprise Application Architecture*), I sent out save orders from the presentation layer upon completion of a command. This turned out to be an expensive design decision.

The Unit of Work pattern helps you to save only those objects that need saving.

The Problem

One day, I echoed my SQL statements to the browser window to track down a problem and had a shock. I found that I was saving the same data over and over again in the same request. I had a neat system of composite commands, which meant that one command might trigger several others, and each one was cleaning up after itself.

Not only was I saving the same object twice, I was saving objects that didn't need saving.

This problem, then, is similar in some ways to that addressed by Identity Map. That problem involved unnecessary object loading; this problem lies at the other end of the process. Just as these issues are complementary, so are the solutions.

Implementation

To determine what database operations are required, you need to keep track of various events that befall your objects. Probably the best place to do that is in the objects themselves.

You also need to maintain a list of objects scheduled for each database operation (i.e., insert, update, delete). I am only going to cover insert and update operations here. Where might be a good place to store a list of objects? It just so happens that I already have an ObjectWatcher object, so I can develop that further:

```
// listing 13.24
// ObjectWatcher
private array $all = [];
private array $dirty = [];
private array $new = [];
private array $delete = []; // unused in this example
private static ?ObjectWatcher $instance = null;

public static function addDelete(DomainObject $obj): void
{
    $inst = self::instance();
    $inst->delete[$inst->globalKey($obj)] = $obj;
}
```

```php
public static function addDirty(DomainObject $obj): void
{
    $inst = self::instance();

    if (! in_array($obj, $inst->new, true)) {
        $inst->dirty[$inst->globalKey($obj)] = $obj;
    }
}

public static function addNew(DomainObject $obj): void
{
    $inst = self::instance();
    // we don't yet have an id
    $inst->new[] = $obj;
}

public static function addClean(DomainObject $obj): void
{
    $inst = self::instance();
    unset($inst->delete[$inst->globalKey($obj)]);
    unset($inst->dirty[$inst->globalKey($obj)]);
    $inst->new = array_filter(
        $inst->new,
        function ($a) use ($obj) {
            return !($a === $obj);
        }
    );
}

public function performOperations(): void
{
    foreach ($this->dirty as $key => $obj) {
        $obj->getFinder()->update($obj);
    }
```

```
foreach ($this->new as $key => $obj) {
    $obj->getFinder()->insert($obj);
    print "inserting " . $obj->getName() . "\n";
}

$this->dirty = [];
$this->new = [];
}
```

The ObjectWatcher class remains an Identity Map and continues to serve its function of tracking all objects in a system via the $all property. This example simply adds more functionality to the class.

You can see the Unit of Work aspects of the ObjectWatcher class in Figure 13-5.

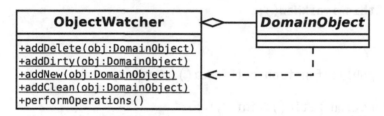

Figure 13-5. *Unit of Work aspects in the ObjectWatcher class*

Objects are described as "dirty" when they have been changed since extraction from the database. A dirty object is stored in the $dirty array property (via the addDirty() method) until the time comes to update the database. Client code may decide that a dirty object should not undergo update for its own reasons. It can ensure this by marking the dirty object as clean (via the addClean() method). As you might expect, a newly created object should be added to the $new array (via the addNew() method). Objects in this array are scheduled for insertion into the database. I am not implementing delete functionality in these examples, but the principle should be clear enough.

The addDirty() and addNew() methods each add an object to their respective array properties. addClean(), however, *removes* the given object from the $dirty array, marking it as no longer pending update.

When the time finally comes to process all objects stored in these arrays, the performOperations() method should be invoked (probably from the controller class or its helper). This method loops through the $dirty and $new arrays, either updating or adding the objects.

The ObjectWatcher class now provides a mechanism for updating and inserting objects. The client code is still missing a means of adding objects to the ObjectWatcher object.

Because it is these objects that are operated upon, they are probably best placed to perform this notification. Here are some utility methods I can add to the DomainObject class—notice the constructor method in particular:

```php
// listing 13.25
abstract class DomainObject
{
    public function __construct(private int $id = -1)
    {
        if ($id < 0) {
            $this->markNew();
        }
    }
    abstract public function getFinder(): Mapper;

    public function getId(): int
    {
        return $this->id;
    }

    public function setId(int $id): void
    {
        $this->id = $id;
    }

    public function markNew(): void
    {
        ObjectWatcher::addNew($this);
    }

    public function markDeleted(): void
    {
        ObjectWatcher::addDelete($this);
    }
```

```
public function markDirty(): void
{
    ObjectWatcher::addDirty($this);
}

public function markClean(): void
{
    ObjectWatcher::addClean($this);
}
}
```

As you can see, the constructor method marks the current object as new (by calling markNew()) if no $id property has been passed to it.

Note   Remember that our convention for an uninserted database row is an id of −1. This allows us to always demand an integer value and then test whether the value is greater than zero in order to determine whether the row data should be treated as fresh. Of course, you might opt to use a null value for new data instead and change the constructor signature in DomainObject to private ?int $id = null.

This qualifies as magic of a sort and should be treated with some caution. As it stands, this code slates a new object for insertion into the database without any intervention from the object creator. Imagine a coder new to your team writing a throwaway script to test some domain behavior. There's no sign of persistence code there, so all should be safe enough, shouldn't it? Now imagine these test objects, perhaps with interesting throwaway names, making their way into persistent storage. Magic is nice, but clarity is nicer. It may be better to require client code to pass some kind of flag into the constructor in order to queue the new object for insertion.

I also need to add some code to the Mapper class:

```
// listing 13.26

// Mapper

public function createObject($raw): DomainObject
{
    $old = $this->getFromMap($raw['id']);

    if (! is_null($old)) {
        return $old;
    }

    $obj = $this->doCreateObject($raw);
    $this->addToMap($obj);

    return $obj;
}
```

The only thing remaining to do is to add markDirty() invocations to methods in the Domain Model classes. Remember, a dirty object is one that has been changed since it was retrieved from the database. This is the one aspect of this pattern that has a slightly fishy odor. Clearly, it's important to ensure that all methods that mess up the state of an object are marked dirty, but the manual nature of this task means that the possibility of human error is all too real.

Here are some methods in the Space object that call markDirty():

```
// listing 13.27

// Space

public function setVenue(Venue $venue): void
{
    $this->venue = $venue;
    $this->markDirty();
}
```

```
public function setName(string $name): void
{
    $this->name = $name;
    $this->markDirty();
}
```

Here is some code for adding a new Venue and Space to the database, taken from a Command class:

```
// listing 13.28

// a -1 id value represents a brand new Venue or Space
$venue = new Venue(-1, "The Green Trees");

$venue->addSpace(
    new Space(-1, 'The Space Upstairs')
);
$venue->addSpace(
    new Space(-1, 'The Bar Stage')
);
// this could be called from the controller or a helper class
ObjectWatcher::instance()->performOperations();
```

I have added some debug code to the ObjectWatcher, so you can see what happens at the end of the request:

```
inserting The Green Trees
inserting The Space Upstairs
inserting The Bar Stage
```

Because my Venue and Space objects were instantiated with ids of –1, they were treated as new by DomainObject. Internally, in each case, the domain object constructor called DomainObject::markNew() which then called ObjectWatcher::addNew(). When ObjectWatcher::performOperations() was eventually called, these objects were inserted into the database (rather than updated there), and my debug output was triggered.

Because a high-level controller object usually calls the performOperations() method, all you need to do in most cases is create or modify an object, and the Unit of Work class (ObjectWatcher) will do its job just once at the end of the request.

Consequences

This pattern is very useful, but there are a few issues to be aware of. You need to be sure that all modify operations actually do mark the object in question as dirty. Failing to do this can result in hard-to-spot bugs.

You may like to look at other ways of testing for modified objects. Reflection sounds like a good option there, but you should look into the performance implications of such testing—the pattern is meant to improve efficiency, not undermine it.

Lazy Load

Lazy Load is one of those core patterns most web programmers learn for themselves very quickly, simply because it's such an essential mechanism for avoiding massive database hits, which is something we all want to do.

The Problem

In the example that has dominated this chapter, I have set up a relationship between Venue, Space, and Event objects. When a Venue object is created, it is automatically given a SpaceCollection object. If I were to list every Space object in a Venue, this would automatically kick off a database request to acquire all the Events associated with each Space. These are stored in an EventCollection object. If I don't wish to view any events, I have nonetheless made several journeys to the database for no reason. With many venues, each with two or three spaces, and with each space managing tens, perhaps hundreds, of events, this is a costly process.

Clearly, we need to throttle back this automatic inclusion of collections in some instances. Here is the code in SpaceMapper that acquires Event data:

```
// listing 13.29

// SpaceMapper
protected function doCreateObject(array $raw): Space
{
    $obj = new Space((int)$raw['id'], $raw['name']);
    $venmapper = new VenueMapper();
```

```
$venue = $venmapper->find((int)$raw['venue']);
$obj->setVenue($venue);

$eventmapper = new EventMapper();
$eventcollection = $eventmapper->findBySpaceId((int)$raw['id']);
$obj->setEvents($eventcollection);

    return $obj;
}
```

The doCreateObject() method first acquires the Venue object with which the space is associated. This is not costly because it is almost certainly already stored in the ObjectWatcher object. Then the method calls the EventMapper::findBySpaceId() method. This is where the system could run into problems.

Implementation

As you may know, a Lazy Load means to defer acquisition of a property until it is actually requested by a client.

The easiest way of doing this is to make the deferral explicit in the containing object. Here's how I might do this in the Space object:

```
// listing 13.30

// Space

public function getEvents2(): EventCollection
{
    if (is_null($this->events)) {
        $reg = Registry::instance();
        $eventmapper = $reg->getEventMapper();
        $this->events = $eventmapper->findBySpaceId($this->getId());
    }

    return $this->events;
}
```

This method checks to see whether or not the $events property is set. If it isn't set, then the method acquires a finder (i.e., a Mapper) and uses its own $id property to get the EventCollection with which it is associated. Clearly, for this method to save us a potentially unnecessary database query, I would also need to amend the SpaceMapper code, so that it does not automatically preload an EventCollection object, as it did in the preceding example!

This approach will work just fine, although it is a little messy. Wouldn't it be nice to tidy the mess away? This brings us back to the Iterator implementation that goes to make the Collection object. I am already hiding one secret behind that interface (the fact that raw data may not yet have been used to instantiate a domain object at the time a client accesses it). Perhaps I can hide still more.

The idea here is to create an EventCollection object that defers its database access until a request is made of it. This means that a client object (such as Space) need never know that it is holding an empty Collection in the first instance. As far as a client is concerned, it is holding a perfectly normal EventCollection.

Here is the DeferredEventCollection object:

```
// listing 13.31
class DeferredEventCollection extends EventCollection
{
    private bool $run = false;

    public function __construct(
        Mapper $mapper,
        private \PDOStatement $stmt,
        private array $valueArray
    ) {
        parent:: construct([], $mapper);
    }

    protected function notifyAccess(): void
    {
        if (! $this->run) {
            $this->stmt->execute($this->valueArray);
            $this->raw = $this->stmt->fetchAll();
            $this->total = count($this->raw);
        }
```

```
        $this->run = true;
    }
}
```

As you can see, this class extends a standard `EventCollection`. Its constructor requires `Mapper` and `PDOStatement` objects and an array of terms that should match the prepared statement. In the first instance, the class does nothing but store its properties and wait. No query has been made of the database.

You may remember that the `Collection` base class defines the empty method called `notifyAccess()` that I mentioned in the "Data Mapper" section. This is called from any method whose invocation is the result of a call from the outside world.

`DeferredEventCollection` overrides this method. Now if someone attempts to access the `Collection`, the class knows it is time to end the pretense and acquire some real data. It does this by calling the `PDOStatement::execute()` method. Together with `PDOStatement::fetch()`, this yields an array of fields suitable for passing along to `Mapper::createObject()`.

Here is the method in `EventMapper` that instantiates a `DeferredEventCollection`:

```
// listing 13.32

// EventMapper

public function findBySpaceId(int $sid): DeferredEventCollection
{
    return new DeferredEventCollection(
        $this,
        $this->selectBySpaceStmt,
        [$sid]
    );
}
```

Consequences

Lazy loading is a good habit to get into, whether or not you explicitly add deferred loading logic to your domain classes.

Over and above type safety, the particular benefit of using a collection rather than an array for your properties is the opportunity this gives you to retrofit lazy loading should you need it.

531

Domain Object Factory

The Data Mapper pattern is neat, but it does have some drawbacks. In particular, a Mapper class takes a lot on board. It composes SQL statements; it converts arrays to objects; and, of course, it converts objects back to arrays, ready to add data to the database. This versatility makes a Mapper class convenient and powerful. It can reduce flexibility to some extent, however. This is especially true when a mapper must handle many different kinds of queries or when other classes need to share a Mapper's functionality. For the remainder of this chapter, I will decompose Data Mapper, breaking it down into a set of more focused patterns. These finer-grained patterns combine to duplicate the overall responsibilities managed in Data Mapper, and some or all can be used in conjunction with that pattern. They are well defined by Clifton Nock in *Data Access Patterns* (Addison-Wesley, 2003), and I have used his names where overlaps occur.

Let's start with a core function: the generation of domain objects.

The Problem

You have already encountered a situation in which the Mapper class displays a natural fault line. The createObject() method is used internally by Mapper, of course, but Collection objects also need it to create domain objects on demand. This requires us to pass along a Mapper reference when creating a Collection object. Although there's nothing wrong with allowing callbacks (as you have seen in the Visitor and Observer patterns), it's neater to move responsibility for domain object creation into its own type. This can then be shared by Mapper and Collection classes alike.

The Domain Object Factory is described in *Data Access Patterns*.

Implementation

Imagine a set of Mapper classes, broadly organized so that each faces its own domain object. The Domain Object Factory pattern simply requires that you extract the createObject() method from each Mapper and place it in its own class in a parallel hierarchy. Figure 13-6 shows these new classes.

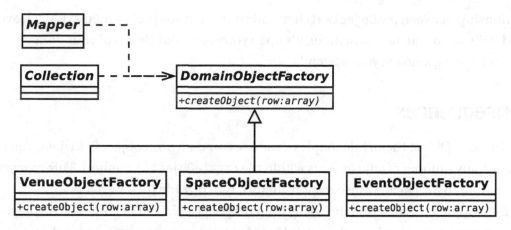

Figure 13-6. *Domain Object Factory classes*

Domain Object Factory classes have a single core responsibility, and as such they tend to be simple:

```
// listing 13.33
abstract class DomainObjectFactory
{
    abstract public function createObject(array $row): DomainObject;

}
```

Here's a concrete implementation:

```
// listing 13.34
class VenueObjectFactory extends DomainObjectFactory
{
    public function createObject(array $row): Venue
    {
        $obj = new Venue((int)$row['id'], $row['name']);

        return $obj;
    }
}
```

Of course, you might also want to cache objects to prevent duplication and prevent unnecessary trips to the database, as I did within the Mapper class. You could move the addToMap() and getFromMap() methods here, or you could build an observer relationship between the ObjectWatcher and your createObject() methods. I'll leave the details up to you. Just remember, it's up to you to prevent clones of your domain objects running amok in your system!

Consequences

The Domain Object Factory decouples database row data from object field data. You can perform any number of adjustments within the createObject() method. This process is transparent to the client, whose responsibility it is to provide the raw data.

By snapping this functionality away from the Mapper class, it becomes available to other components. Here's an altered Collection implementation, for example:

```
// listing 13.35
abstract class Collection implements \Iterator
{
    protected int $total = 0;
    protected array $raw = [];

    private int $pointer = 0;
    private array $objects = [];

    // Collection

    public function __construct(array $raw = [],
    protected  ?DomainObjectFactory $dofact = null)
    {
        if (count($raw) && ! is_null($dofact)) {
            $this->raw = $raw;
            $this->total = count($raw);
        }
        $this->dofact = $dofact;
    }

// ...
```

The DomainObjectFactory can be used to generate objects on demand:

```
// listing 13.36

private function getRow(int $num): ?DomainObject
{
    // ...
    if (isset($this->raw[$num])) {
        $this->objects[$num] = $this->dofact->createObject(
        $this->raw[$num]);

        return $this->objects[$num];
    }
}
```

Because Domain Object Factories are decoupled from the database, they can be used for testing more effectively. I might, for example, create a mock DomainObjectFactory to test the Collection code. It's much easier to do this than it would be to emulate an entire Mapper object (you can read more about mock and stub objects in Chapter 18).

One general effect of breaking down a monolithic component into composable parts is an unavoidable proliferation of classes. The potential for confusion should not be underestimated. Even when every component and its relationship with its peers is logical and clearly defined, I often find it challenging to chart packages containing tens of similarly named components.

This is going to get worse before it gets better. Already, I can see another fault line appearing in Data Mapper. The Mapper::getCollection() method was convenient; but once again, other classes might want to acquire a Collection object for a domain type, without having to go to a database-facing class. So I have two related abstract components: Collection and DomainObjectFactory. According to the domain object I am working with, I will require a different set of concrete implementations: VenueCollection and VenueObjectFactory, for example, or SpaceCollection and SpaceObjectFactory. This problem leads us directly to the Abstract Factory pattern, of course.

Figure 13-7 shows the PersistenceFactory class. I'll be using this to organize the various components that make up the next few patterns.

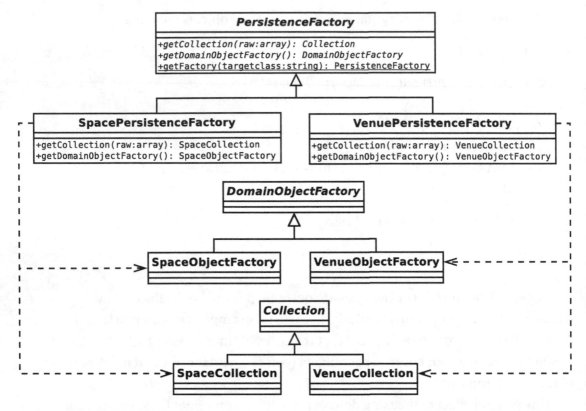

Figure 13-7. *Using the Abstract Factory pattern to organize related components*

The Identity Object

The mapper implementation I have presented here suffers from a certain inflexibility when it comes to locating domain objects. Finding an individual object is no problem. Finding all relevant domain objects is just as easy. Anything in between, though, requires you to add a special method to craft the query (EventMapper::findBySpaceId() is a case in point).

An identity object (also called a Data Transfer Object by Alur et al.) encapsulates query criteria, thereby decoupling the system from database syntax.

The Problem

It's hard to know ahead of time what you or other client coders are going to need to search for in a database. The more complex a domain object, the greater the number of filters you might need in your query. You can address this problem to some extent by adding more methods to your Mapper classes on a case-by-case basis. This is not very flexible, of course, and can involve duplication as you are required to craft many similar but differing queries both within a single Mapper class and across the mappers in your system.

An identity object encapsulates the conditional aspect of a database query in such a way that different combinations can be combined at runtime. Given a domain object called Person, for example, a client might be able to call methods on an identity object in order to specify a male, aged above 30 and below 40, who is less than 6 feet tall. The class should be designed so that conditions can be combined flexibly (perhaps you're not interested in your target's height, or maybe you want to remove the lower age limit). An identity object limits a client coder's options to some extent. If you haven't written code to accommodate an income field, then this cannot be factored into a query without adjustment. The ability to apply different combinations of conditions does provide a step forward in flexibility, however. Let's see how this might work.

Implementation

An identity object will typically consist of a set of methods you can call to build query criteria. Having set the object's state, you can pass it on to a method responsible for constructing the SQL statement.

Figure 13-8 shows a typical set of IdentityObject classes.

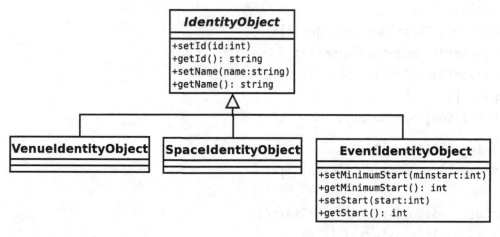

Figure 13-8. *Managing query criteria with identity objects*

You can use a base class to manage common operations and to ensure that your criteria objects share a type. Here's an implementation that is simpler even than the classes shown in Figure 13-8:

```
// listing 13.37
abstract class IdentityObject
{
    private ?string $name = null;

    public function setName(string $name): void
    {
        $this->name = $name;
    }

    public function getName(): ?string
    {
        return $this->name;
    }
}
```

Nothing's too taxing here. The classes simply store the data provided and give it up on request. Here's some code that might use EventIdentityObject to build a WHERE clause:

```
// listing 13.38
$idobj = new EventIdentityObject();
$idobj->setMinimumStart(time());
$idobj->setName("A Fine Show");
$comps = [];
$name = $idobj->getName();

if (! is_null($name)) {
    $comps[] = "name = '{$name}'";
}
$minstart = $idobj->getMinimumStart();
if (! is_null($minstart)) {
    $comps[] = "start > {$minstart}";
}
```

```
$start = $idobj->getStart();
if (! is_null($start)) {
    $comps[] = "start = '{$start}'";
}

$clause = " WHERE " . implode(" and ", $comps);
print "{$clause}\n";
```

This model will work well enough, but it does not suit my lazy soul. For a large domain object, the sheer number of getters and setters you would have to build is daunting. Then, following this model, you'd have to write code to output each condition in the WHERE clause. I couldn't even be bothered to handle all cases in my example code (no setMaximumStart() method for me), so imagine my joy at building identity objects in the real world.

Luckily, there are various strategies you can deploy to automate both the gathering of data and the generation of SQL. In the past, for example, I have populated associative arrays of field names in the base class. These were themselves indexed by comparison types: greater than, equal, less than, or equal to. The child classes provide convenience methods for adding this data to the underlying structure. The SQL builder can then loop through the structure to build its query dynamically. I'm sure implementing such a system is just a matter of coloring in, so I'm going to look at a variation on it here.

I will use a fluent interface. That is a class whose setter methods return object instances, allowing your users to chain objects together in fluid, language-like way. This will satisfy my laziness, but still, I hope, give the client coder a flexible way of defining criteria.

I start by creating woo\mapper\Field, a class designed to hold comparison data for each field that will end up in the WHERE clause:

```
// listing 13.39
class Field
{
    protected array $comps = [];
    protected bool $incomplete = false;

    // sets up the field name (age, for example)
    public function __construct(protected string $name)
    {
    }
```

```
    // add the operator and the value for the test
    // (> 40, for example) and add to the $comps property
    public function addTest(string $operator, $value): void
    {
        $this->comps[] = [
            'name' => $this->name,
            'operator'  =>  $operator,
            'value' => $value
        ];
    }

    // comps is an array so that we can test one field in more than one way
    public function getComps(): array
    {
        return $this->comps;
    }

    // if $comps does not contain elements, then we have
    // comparison data and this field is not ready to be used in
    // a query
    public function isIncomplete(): bool
    {
        return empty($this->comps);
    }
}
```

This simple class accepts and stores a field name. Through the addTest() method, the class builds an array of operator and value elements. This allows us to maintain more than one comparison test for a single field. Now, here's the new IdentityObject class:

```
// listing 13.40
class IdentityObject
{
    protected ?Field $currentfield = null;
    protected array $fields = [];
    private array $enforce = [];
```

```php
// an identity object can start off empty, or with a field
public function __construct(?string $field = null, ?array $enforce = null)
{
    if (! is_null($enforce)) {
        $this->enforce = $enforce;
    }

    if (! is_null($field)) {
        $this->field($field);
    }
}

// field names to which this is constrained
public function getObjectFields(): array
{
    return $this->enforce;
}

// kick off a new field.
// will throw an error if a current field is not complete
// (ie age rather than age > 40)
// this method returns a  reference to the current object
// allowing for fluent syntax
public function field(string $fieldname): self
{
    if (! $this->isVoid() && $this->currentfield->isIncomplete()) {
        throw new \Exception("Incomplete field");
    }

    $this->enforceField($fieldname);

    if (isset($this->fields[$fieldname])) {
        $this->currentfield = $this->fields[$fieldname];
    } else {
        $this->currentfield = new Field($fieldname);
        $this->fields[$fieldname] = $this->currentfield;
    }
```

```
        return $this;
    }

    // does the identity object have any fields yet
    public function isVoid(): bool
    {
        return empty($this->fields);
    }

    // is the given fieldname legal?
    public function enforceField(string $fieldname): void
    {
        if (! in_array($fieldname, $this->enforce) && ! empty(
        $this->enforce)) {
            $forcelist = implode(', ', $this->enforce);
            throw new \Exception("{$fieldname} not a legal field
            ($forcelist)");
        }
    }
    // add an equality operator to the current field
    // ie 'age' becomes age=40
    // returns a reference to the current object (via operator())
    public function eq($value): self
    {
        return $this->operator("=", $value);
    }

    // less than
    public function lt($value): self
    {
        return $this->operator("<", $value);
    }

    // greater than
    public function gt($value): self
    {
        return $this->operator(">", $value);
    }
```

```
// does the work for the operator methods
// gets the current field and adds the operator and test value
// to it
private function operator(string $symbol, $value): self
{
    if ($this->isVoid()) {
        throw new \Exception("no object field defined");
    }

    $this->currentfield->addTest($symbol, $value);

    return $this;
}

// return all comparisons built up so far in an associative array
public function getComps(): array
{
    $ret = [];

    foreach ($this->fields as $field) {
        $ret = array_merge($ret, $field->getComps());
    }

    return $ret;
}
}
```

The easiest way to work out what's going on here is to start with some client code and work backward:

```
// listing 13.41
$idobj = new IdentityObject();
$idobj->field("name")
    ->eq("'The Good Show'")
    ->field("start")
    ->gt(time())
    ->lt(time() + (24 * 60 * 60));
```

I begin by creating the IdentityObject. Calling field() causes a Field object to be created and assigned as the $currentfield property. Notice that field() returns a reference to the identity object. This allows us to hang more method calls off the back of the call to field(). The comparison methods eq(), gt(), and so forth each call operator(). This checks that there is a current Field object to work with; and if so, it passes along the operator symbol and the provided value. Once again, eq() returns an object reference, so that I can add new tests or call add() again to begin work with a new field.

Notice the way that the client code is almost sentence-like: field "name" equals "The Good Show" and field "start" is greater than the current time, but less than a day away.

Of course, by losing those hard-coded methods, I also lose some safety. This is what the $enforce array is designed for. Subclasses can invoke the base class with a set of constraints:

```
// listing 13.42
class EventIdentityObject extends IdentityObject
{
    public function __construct(string $field = null)
    {
        parent:: construct(
            $field,
            ['name', 'id', 'start', 'duration', 'space']
        );
    }
}
```

The EventIdentityObject class now enforces a set of fields. Here's what happens if I try to work with a random field name:

```
// listing 13.43
try {
    $idobj = new EventIdentityObject();
    $idobj->field("banana")
        ->eq("The Good Show")
        ->field("start")
        ->gt(time())
        ->lt(time() + (24 * 60 * 60));
```

```
    print $idobj;
} catch (\Exception $e) {
    print $e->getMessage();
}
```

Here is the output:

```
banana not a legal field (name, id, start, duration, space)
```

Consequences

Identity objects allow client coders to define search criteria without reference to a database query. They also save you from having to build special query methods for the various kinds of find operations your user might need.

Part of the point of an identity object is to shield users from the details of the database. It's important, therefore, that if you build an automated solution like the fluent interface in the preceding example, the labels you use should refer explicitly to your domain objects and not to the underlying column names. Where these differ, you should construct a mechanism for aliasing between them.

Where you use specialized entity objects, one for each domain object, it is useful to use an Abstract Factory (like PersistenceFactory described in the previous section) to serve them up along with other related objects.

Now that I can represent search criteria, I can use this to build the query itself.

The Selection Factory and Update Factory Patterns

I have already pried a few responsibilities from the Mapper classes. With these patterns in place, a Mapper does not need to create objects or collections. With query criteria handled by identity objects, it must no longer manage multiple variations on the find() method. The next stage is to remove responsibility for query creation.

The Problem

Any system that speaks to a database must generate queries, but the system itself is organized around domain objects and business rules rather than the database. Many of the patterns in this chapter can be said to bridge the gap between the tabular database and the more organic, treelike structures of the domain. There is, however, a moment of translation—the point at which domain data is transformed into a form that a database can understand. It is at this point that the true decoupling takes place.

Implementation

Of course, you have seen some of this functionality before in the Data Mapper pattern. In this specialization, though, I can benefit from the additional functionality afforded by the identity object pattern. This will tend to make query generation more dynamic, simply because the potential number of variations is so high.

Figure 13-9 shows my simple selection and update factories.

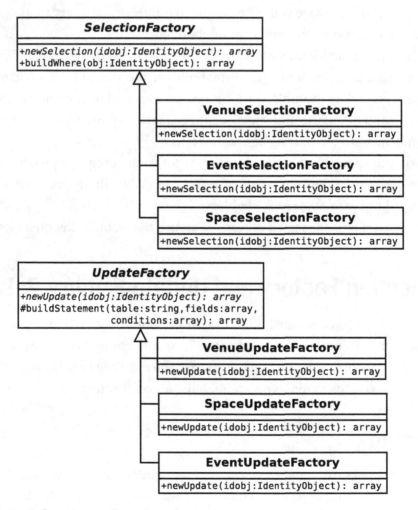

Figure 13-9. *Selection and update factories*

Selection and update factories are, once again, typically organized so that they parallel the domain objects in a system (possibly mediated via identity objects). Because of this, they are also candidates for my `PersistenceFactory`: the Abstract Factory I maintain as a one-stop shop for domain object persistence tools. Here is an implementation of a base class for update factories:

```
// listing 13.44
abstract class UpdateFactory
{
    abstract public function newUpdate(DomainObject $obj): array;

    protected function buildStatement(string $table, array $fields, ?array
    $conditions = null): array
    {
        $terms = array();

        if (! is_null($conditions)) {
            $query = "UPDATE {$table} SET ";
            $query .= implode(" = ?,", array_keys($fields)) . " = ?";
            $terms = array_values($fields);
            $cond = [];
            $query .= " WHERE ";

            foreach ($conditions as $key => $val) {
                $cond[] = "$key = ?";
                $terms[] = $val;
            }

            $query .= implode(" AND ", $cond);
        } else {
            $qs = [];
            $query = "INSERT  INTO {$table} (";
            $query .= implode(",", array_keys($fields));
            $query .= ") VALUES (";

            foreach ($fields as $name => $value) {
                $terms[] = $value;
                $qs[] = '?';
            }
```

```
            $query .= implode(",", $qs);
            $query .= ")";
        }

        return [$query, $terms];
    }
}
```

In interface terms, the only thing that this class does is define the newUpdate()
method. This will return an array containing a query string and a list of terms to apply to
it. The buildStatement() method does the generic work involved in building the update
query, with the work specific to individual domain objects handled by child classes.
buildStatement() accepts a table name, an associative array of fields and their values,
and a similar associative array of conditions. The method combines these to create the
query. Here's a concrete UpdateFactory class:

```
// listing 13.45
class VenueUpdateFactory extends UpdateFactory
{
    public function newUpdate(DomainObject $obj): array
    {
        // note type checking removed
        $id = $obj->getId();
        $cond = null;
        $values['name'] = $obj->getName();

        if ($id > 0) {
            $cond['id'] = $id;
        }

        return $this->buildStatement("venue", $values, $cond);
    }
}
```

In this implementation, I work directly with a DomainObject. In systems where one
might operate on many objects at once in an update, I could use an identity object to
define the set on which I would like to act. This would form the basis of the $cond array,
which here only holds id data.

newUpdate() distills the data required to generate a query. This is the process by which object data is transformed to database information. Notice the check on the value of $id. If the id is set to -1, then this is a new domain object, and we will not provide a conditional value buildStatement(). buildStatement() uses the presence of conditional statements to determine whether or not to generate an INSERT or an UPDATE.

Notice that the newUpdate() method will accept any DomainObject. This is so that all UpdateFactory classes can share an interface. It would be a good idea to add some further type checking to ensure the wrong object is not passed in.

Here's some quick code to try out the VenueUpdateFactory class:

```
// listing 13.46
$vuf = new VenueUpdateFactory();
print_r($vuf->newUpdate(new Venue(334, "The Happy Hairband")));

Array

(

    [0] => UPDATE venue SET name = ? WHERE id = ?
    [1] => Array
    (

        [0] => The Happy Hairband
        [1] => 334
    )
)
```

Now to generate an INSERT statement:

```
// listing 13.47
$vuf = new VenueUpdateFactory();
print_r($vuf->newUpdate(new Venue(-1, "The Lonely Hat Hive")));

Array
(

    [0] => INSERT INTO venue (name) VALUES (?)
    [1] => Array
    (

        [0] => The Lonely Hat Hive
    )

)
```

You can see a similar structure for SelectionFactory classes. Here is the base class:

```
// listing 13.48
abstract class SelectionFactory
{
    abstract public function newSelection(IdentityObject $obj): array;

    public function buildWhere(IdentityObject $obj): array
    {
        if ($obj->isVoid()) {
            return ["", []];
        }

        $compstrings = [];
        $values = [];

        foreach ($obj->getComps() as $comp) {
            $compstrings[] = "{$comp['name']} {$comp['operator']} ?";
            $values[] = $comp['value'];
        }

        $where = "WHERE " . implode(" AND ", $compstrings);

        return [$where, $values];
    }
}
```

Once again, this class defines the public interface in the form of an abstract class. newSelection() expects an IdentityObject. Also requiring an IdentityObject, but local to the type, is the utility method, buildWhere(). This uses the IdentityObject::getComps() method to acquire the information necessary to build a WHERE clause, as well as to construct a list of values, both of which it returns in a two-element array.

Here is a concrete SelectionFactory class:

```
// listing 13.49
class VenueSelectionFactory extends SelectionFactory
{
    public function newSelection(IdentityObject $obj): array
```

```
    {
        $fields = implode(',', $obj->getObjectFields());
        $core = "SELECT $fields FROM venue";
        list($where, $values) = $this->buildWhere($obj);

        return [$core . " " . $where, $values];
    }
}
```

This builds the core of the SQL statement and then calls buildWhere() to
add the conditional clause. In fact, the only thing that differs from one concrete
SelectionFactory to another in my test code is the name of the table. If I don't find that
I require unique specializations soon, I will refactor these subclasses out of existence
and use a single concrete SelectionFactory. This would query the table name from the
PersistenceFactory.

Again, here is some client code:

```
// listing 13.50
$vio = new VenueIdentityObject();
$vio->field("name")->eq("The Happy Hairband");

$vsf = new VenueSelectionFactory();
print_r($vsf->newSelection($vio));

(
    [0] => SELECT name,id FROM venue WHERE name = ?
    [1] => Array
    (
        [0] => The Happy Hairband
    )
)
```

Consequences

The use of a generic identity object implementation makes it easier to use a single
parameterized SelectionFactory class. If you opt for hard-coded identity objects—that
is, identity objects which consist of a list of getter and setter methods—you are more
likely to have to build an individual SelectionFactory per domain object.

One of the great benefits of query factories combined with identity objects is the range of queries you can generate. This can also cause caching headaches. These methods generate queries on the fly, and it's difficult to know when you're duplicating effort. It may be worth building a means of comparing identity objects, so that you can return a cached string without all that work. A similar kind of database statement pooling might be considered at a higher level, too.

Another issue with the combination of patterns I have presented in the latter part of this chapter is the fact that they're flexible, but they're not *that* flexible. By this, I mean they are designed to be extremely adaptable within limits. There is not much room for exceptional cases here, though. Mapper classes, while more cumbersome to create and maintain, are very accommodating of any kind of performance kludge or data juggling you might need to perform behind their clean APIs. These more elegant patterns suffer from the problem that, with their focused responsibilities and emphasis on composition, it can be hard to cut across the cleverness and do something dumb but powerful.

Luckily, I have not lost my higher-level interface—there's still a controller level where I can head cleverness off at the pass if necessary.

What's Left of Data Mapper Now?

So, I have stripped object, query, and collection generation from Data Mapper, to say nothing of the management of conditionals. What could possibly be left of it? Well, something that is very much like a mapper is needed in vestigial form. I still need an object that sits above the others I have created and coordinates their activities. It can help with caching duties and handle database connectivity (although the database-facing work could be delegated still further). Clifton Nock calls these data layer controllers domain object assemblers.

Here is an example:

```
// listing 13.51
class DomainObjectAssembler
{
    protected \PDO $pdo;
```

```
public function __construct(private PersistenceFactory $factory)
{
    $reg = Registry::instance();
    $this->pdo = $reg->getPdo();
}

public function getStatement(string $str): \PDOStatement
{
    if (! isset($this->statements[$str])) {
        $this->statements[$str] = $this->pdo->prepare($str);
    }

    return $this->statements[$str];
}

public function findOne(IdentityObject $idobj): DomainObject
{
    $collection = $this->find($idobj);

    return $collection->next();
}
public function find(IdentityObject $idobj): Collection
{
    $selfact = $this->factory->getSelectionFactory();
    list ($selection, $values) = $selfact->newSelection($idobj);
    $stmt = $this->getStatement($selection);
    $stmt->execute($values);
    $raw = $stmt->fetchAll();

    return $this->factory->getCollection($raw);
}

public function insert(DomainObject $obj): void
{
    $upfact = $this->factory->getUpdateFactory();
    list($update, $values) = $upfact->newUpdate($obj);
    $stmt = $this->getStatement($update);
    $stmt->execute($values);
```

```
        if ($obj->getId() < 0) {
            $obj->setId((int)$this->pdo->lastInsertId());
        }

        $obj->markClean();
    }
}
```

As you can see, this is not an abstract class. Instead of itself breaking down into specializations, it uses the `PersistenceFactory` to ensure that it gets the correct components for the current domain object.

Figure 13-10 shows the high-level participants I built up as I factored out `Mapper`.

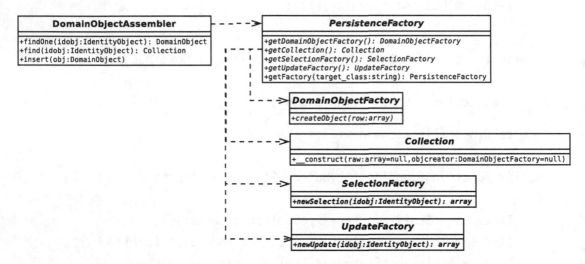

Figure 13-10. *Some of the persistence classes developed in this chapter*

Aside from making the database connection and performing queries, the class manages `SelectionFactory` and `UpdateFactory` objects. In the case of selections, it also works either with a `Collection` class to generate return values.

From a client's point of view, creating a `DomainObjectAssembler` is easy. It's simply a matter of getting the correct concrete `PersistenceFactory` object and passing it to the constructor:

```
// listing 13.52
$factory = PersistenceFactory::getFactory(Venue::class);
$finder = new DomainObjectAssembler($factory);
```

Of course, "client" here is unlikely to mean the end client. We can insulate higher-level classes from even this complexity by adding a getFinder() method to the PersistenceFactory itself and transforming the previous example into a one-liner, like this:

```
$finder = PersistenceFactory::getFinder(Venue::class);
```

I'll leave that to you, however.

A client coder might then go on to acquire a collection of Venue objects:

```
// listing 13.53
$idobj = $factory->getIdentityObject()
    ->field('name')
    ->eq('The Eyeball Inn');
$collection = $finder->find($idobj);
foreach ($collection as $venue) {
    print $venue->getName() . "\n";
}
```

Summary

As always, the patterns you choose to use will depend on the nature of your problem. I naturally gravitate toward a Data Mapper working with an identity object. I like neat automated solutions, but I also need to know I can break out of the system and go manual when I need to, while maintaining a clean interface and a decoupled database layer. I may need to optimize an SQL query, for example, or use a join to acquire data across multiple tables. Even if you're using a complex pattern-based third-party framework, you may find that the fancy object-relational mapping on offer does not do quite what you want. One test of a good framework, and of a good homegrown system, is the ease with which you can plug your own hack into place without degrading the overall integrity of the system as a whole. I love elegant, beautifully composed solutions, but I'm also a pragmatist!

Once again, I have covered a lot in this chapter. Here's a quick rundown of the patterns we looked at and how you use them:

- *Data Mapper*: Create specialist classes for mapping Domain Model objects to and from relational databases

- *Identity Map*: Keep track of all the objects in your system to prevent duplicate instantiations and unnecessary trips to the database

- *Unit of Work*: Automate the process by which objects are saved to the database, ensuring that only objects that have been changed are updated and only those that have been newly created are inserted

- *Lazy Load*: Defer object creation, and even database queries, until they are actually needed

- *Domain Object Factory*: Encapsulate object creation functionality

- *Identity object*: Allow clients to construct query criteria without reference to the underlying database

- *Query (selection and update) factory*: Encapsulate the logic for constructing SQL queries

- *Domain object assembler*: Construct a controller that manages the high-level process of data storage and retrieval

In the next chapter, we take a welcome break from code, and I'll introduce some of the wider practices that can contribute to a successful project.

PART III

Practice

CHAPTER 14

Good (and Bad) Practice

So far in this book, I have focused on coding, concentrating particularly on the role of design in building flexible and reusable tools and applications. Development doesn't end with code, however. It is possible to come away from books and courses with a solid understanding of a language, yet still encounter problems when it comes to running and deploying a project.

In this chapter, I will move beyond code to introduce some of the tools and techniques that form the underpinnings of a successful development process. This chapter will cover the following:

- *Third-party packages*: Where to get them and when to use them

- *Build*: Creating and deploying packages

- *Version control*: Bringing harmony to the development process

- *Documentation*: Writing code that is easy to understand, use, and extend

- *Unit testing*: A tool for automated bug detection and prevention

- *Standards*: Why it's sometimes good to follow the herd

- *Vagrant*: A tool that uses virtualization, so that all developers can work with a system that resembles a production environment, no matter their hardware or OS

- *Continuous integration*: Using this practice and set of tools to automate project builds and tests as well as to be alerted of problems as they occur

© Matt Zandstra 2021
M. Zandstra, *PHP 8 Objects, Patterns, and Practice*, https://doi.org/10.1007/978-1-4842-6791-2_14

Beyond Code

When I first graduated from working on my own and took a place in a development team, I was astonished at how much stuff other developers seemed to have to know. Good-natured arguments simmered endlessly over issues of vital-seeming importance: Which is the best text editor? Should the team standardize on an integrated development environment? Should we impose a coding standard? How should we test our code? Should we document as we develop? Sometimes, these issues seemed more important than the code itself, and my colleagues seemed to have acquired their encyclopedic knowledge of the domain through some strange process of osmosis.

The books I had read on PHP, Perl, and Java certainly didn't stray from the code itself to any great extent. As I have already discussed, most books on programming platforms rarely diverge from their tight focus on functions and syntax to take in code design. If design is off topic, you can be sure that wider issues such as version control and testing are rarely discussed. This is not a criticism—if a book professes to cover the main features of a language, it should be no surprise that this is all it does.

In learning about code, however, I found that I had neglected many of the mechanics of a project's day-to-day life. I discovered that some of these details were critical to the success or failure of projects I helped develop. In this chapter, and in more detail in coming chapters, I will look beyond code to explore some of the tools and techniques on which the success of your projects may depend.

Borrowing a Wheel

When faced with a challenging but discrete requirement in a project (the need to parse a particular format, perhaps, or to use a novel protocol in talking to a remote server), there is a lot to be said for building a component that addresses the need. It can also be one of the best ways to learn your craft. In creating a package, you gain insight into a problem and file away new techniques that might have wider application.

You invest at once in your project and in your own skills. By keeping functionality internal to your system, you can save your users from having to download third-party packages. Occasionally, too, you may sidestep thorny licensing issues. There's nothing like the sense of satisfaction you can get when you test a component you designed yourself and find that, wonder of wonders, it works—it does exactly what you wrote on the tin.

There is a dark side to all this, of course. Many packages represent an investment of thousands of man-hours: a resource that you may not have on hand. You may be able to address this by developing only the functionality needed specifically by your project, whereas a third-party tool might fulfill a myriad of other needs as well. The question remains, however: if a freely available tool exists, why are you squandering your talents in reproducing it? Do you have the time and resources to develop, test, and debug your package? Might not this time be better deployed elsewhere?

I am one of the worst offenders when it comes to wheel reinvention. Picking apart problems and inventing solutions to them is a fundamental part of what we do as coders. Getting down to some serious architecture is a more rewarding prospect than writing some glue to stitch together three or four existing components. When this temptation comes over me, I remind myself of projects past. Although the choice to build from scratch has never killed a project in my experience, I have seen it devour schedules and murder profit margins. There I sit with a manic gleam in my eye, hatching plots and spinning class diagrams, failing to notice as I obsess over the details of my component that the big picture is now a distant memory.

Now, when I map out a project, I try to develop a feel for what belongs inside the codebase and what should be treated as a third-party requirement. For example, your application may generate (or read) an RSS feed; and you may need to validate email addresses and automate mailouts, authenticate users, or read from a standard-format configuration file. All of these needs can be fulfilled by external packages.

In previous versions of this book, I suggested that PEAR (PHP Extension and Application Repository) was the way to go for packages. Times change, though, and the PHP world has very definitely moved to the Composer dependency manager and its default repository, Packagist (`https://packagist.org`). Because Composer manages packages on a per-project basis, it is less prone to the dreaded dependency hell syndrome (where different packages require incompatible versions of the same library). Besides, the fact that all the action has moved to Composer/Packagist means that you're more likely to find what you're looking for there. What's more, many of the PEAR packages are available through Packagist (`https://packagist.org/packages/pear/`).

So, once you have defined your needs, your first stop should be the Packagist site. You can then use Composer to install your package and to manage package dependencies. I will cover Composer in more detail in the next chapter.

To give you some idea of what's available using Composer and Packagist, here are just a few of the things you can do with the packages you'll find there:

- Cache output with `pear/cache_lite`

- Test the efficiency of your code with the `athletic/athletic` benchmark library

- Abstract the details of database access with `doctrine/dbal`

- Extract RSS feeds with `simplepie/simplepie`

- Send mail with attachments with `pear/mail`

- Parse configuration file formats with `symfony/config`

- Parse and manipulate URLs with `league/uri`

The Packagist website provides a powerful search facility. You may find packages that address your needs there, or you may need to cast your net wider using a search engine. Either way, you should always take time to assess existing packages before setting out to potentially reinvent that wheel.

The fact that you have a need—and that a package exists to address it—should not be the start and end of your deliberations. Although it is preferable to use a package where it will save you otherwise unnecessary development, in some cases, it can add overhead without real gain. Your client's need for your application to send mail, for example, does not mean that you should automatically use the pear/mail package. PHP provides a perfectly good `mail()` function, so this would probably be your first stop. As soon as you realize that you have a requirement to validate all email addresses according to the RFC822 standard and that the design team wants to send image attachments with the emails, you may begin to weigh the options differently. As it happens, pear/mail supports both these features (the latter in conjunction with `mail_mime`).

Many programmers, myself included, often place too much emphasis on the creation of original code, sometimes to the detriment of their projects.

Note   The unwillingness to use third-party tools and solutions is often built-in at the institutional level. This tendency to treat external products with suspicion is sometimes known as the *not invented here* syndrome. As a further note, Technical Reviewer and fellow sf fan Paul Tregoing points out that *Not Invented Here* is also the name of a ship in Iain M. Banks' Culture series.

This emphasis on authorship may be one reason that there often seems to be more creation than actual use of reusable code.

Effective programmers see original code as just one of the tools available to aid them in engineering a project's successful outcome. Such programmers look at the resources they have at hand and deploy them effectively. If a package exists to take some strain, then that is a win. To steal and paraphrase an aphorism from the Perl world: good coders are lazy.

Playing Nice

The truth of Sartre's famous dictum that "Hell is other people" is proved on a daily basis in some software projects. This might describe the relationship between clients and developers, symptomized by the many ways that lack of communication leads to creeping features and skewed priorities. But the cap fits, too, for happily communicative and cooperative team members when it comes to sharing code.

As soon as a project has more than one developer, version control becomes an issue. A single coder may work on code in place, saving a copy of her working directory at key points in development. Introduce another programmer to the mix, and this strategy breaks down in minutes. If the new developer works in the same development directory, then there is a real chance that one programmer will overwrite the work of his colleague when saving, unless both are very careful to always work on different files.

Alternatively, our two developers can each take a version of the codebase to work on separately. That works fine until the moment comes to reconcile the two versions. Unless the developers have worked on entirely different sets of files, the task of merging two or more development strands rapidly becomes an enormous headache.

This is where Git, Subversion, and similar tools come in. Using a version control system, you can check out your own version of a codebase and work on it until you are happy with the result. You can then update your version with any changes that your colleagues have been making. The version control software will automatically merge these changes into your files, notifying you of any conflicts it cannot handle. Once you have tested this new hybrid, you can save it to the central repository, making it available to other developers.

Version control systems provide you with other benefits. They keep a complete record of all stages of a project, so you can roll back to, or grab a snapshot of, any point in the project's lifetime. You can also create branches, so that you can maintain a public release at the same time as a bleeding-edge development version.

Once you have used version control on a project, you will not want to attempt another without it. Working simultaneously with multiple branches of a project can be a conceptual challenge, especially at first, but the benefits soon become clear. Version control is just too useful to live without. I cover Git in Chapter 17.

Note   The current edition of this book was written and edited in plain text using Git as a collaboration tool.

Giving Your Code Wings

Have you ever seen your code grounded because it is just too hard to build? This is especially true for projects that are developed in place. Such projects settle into their context, with passwords and directories, databases, and helper application invocations programmed right into the code. Deploying a project of this kind can be a major undertaking, with teams of programmers picking through source code to amend settings, so that they fit the new environment.

This problem can be eased to some degree by providing a centralized configuration file or class so that settings can be changed in one place. But even then, build can be a chore. The difficulty or ease of installation will have a major impact upon the popularity of any application you distribute. It will also impede or encourage multiple and frequent deployments during development.

As with any repetitive and time-consuming task, build should be automated. A build tool can determine default values for install locations, check and change permissions, create databases, and initialize variables, among other tasks. In fact, a build tool can do just about anything you need to get an application from a source directory in a distribution to full deployment.

This doesn't absolve the user from the responsibility for adding information about his environment to the code, of course, but it can make the process as easy as answering a few questions or providing a couple of command-line switches.

Cloud products such as Amazon's AWS Elastic Beanstalk have made it possible to create test and staging environments, as needed. Good build and install solutions are essential in order to take full advantage of these resources. It's no good being able to provision a server on an automated basis if you can't also deploy your system on the fly.

There are various build tools available to the developer. Both PEAR and Composer manage installation (PEAR centrally, and Composer to a local vendor directory). You can create your own packages for either system, which can then be downloaded and installed by users with ease. Build is about much more than the process of placing file A in location B, however.

In Chapter 19, I will look at an application called Phing. This open source project is a port of the popular Ant build tool that is written in and for Java. Phing is written in and for PHP, but it's architecturally similar to Ant and uses the same XML format for its build files.

Composer performs a limited number of tasks extremely well and offers the simplest possible configuration. Phing is more daunting at first, but with the trade-off of immense flexibility. Not only can you use Phing to automate anything from file copying to XSLT transformation, you can easily write and incorporate your own tasks, should you need to extend the tool. Phing is written using PHP's object-oriented features, and its design emphasizes modularity and ease of extension.

Build tools and those designed for package or dependency management are far from mutually exclusive. Typically, a build tool is used during development to run tests, perform project housekeeping, and prepare the packages that are ultimately deployed via PEAR, Composer, or even distribution-based package management systems like RPM and Apt.

Standards

I mentioned previously that this book has shifted its focus from PEAR to Composer. Is this because Composer is much better than PEAR? I do love lots of things about Composer, and these might swing the decision on their own. The principal reason the book is shifting, though, is that everyone else has shifted. Composer has become the standard for dependency management. That is crucial because it means that when I find a package at Packagist, I am also likely to find all its dependencies and related packages. I'll even find many of the PEAR packages there.

Choosing a standard for dependency management, then, ensures availability and interoperability. But standards apply beyond packages and dependencies to the ways that systems work and to the ways that we code. If we agree on protocols, then our systems and teams can integrate seamlessly with one another. And, as more and more components mix across more and more systems, that is increasingly essential.

Where a definitive way of handling, say, logging, is needed, it is obviously ideal that we adopt the best protocol. But the quality of the recommendation (which will dictate formats, log levels, etc.) is possibly less important than the fact that we all comply with it. It's no good implementing the best standard if you're the only person doing it.

In Chapter 15, I discuss standards in more detail with particular reference to a set of recommendations managed by the PHP-FIG group. These PSRs (PHP Standards Recommendations) cover everything from caching to security. In the chapter, I will focus on PSR-1 and PSR-12, recommendations which address the thorny issue of coding style (where do you like to put your braces? And how do you feel about someone else telling you to change the way you do it?). Then I move on to the absolute boon of PSR-4, which covers autoloading (support for PSR-4 is another area in which Composer excels).

Vagrant

What operating system does your team use? Some organizations mandate a particular combination of hardware and software, of course. Often, though, there will be a mix. One developer may have a development machine running Fedora. Another might swear by his MacBook, and a third may stick with his Alienware Windows box (he probably likes it for gaming).

Chances are the production system will run on something else entirely—CentOS, perhaps.

It can be a pain getting a system to work across multiple platforms, and it can be a risk if none of those platforms resemble the production system. You really don't want to discover issues related to the production OS after you've gone live. In practice, of course, you'll likely deploy to a staging environment first. Even so, wouldn't it be better to catch these problems early?

Vagrant is a technology that uses virtualization to give all team members a development environment that is as close as possible to production. Getting up and running should be as simple as invoking a command or two, and, best of all, everyone can stick with their favorite machines and distributions (I'm a Fedora guy, for the record).

I cover Vagrant in Chapter 20.

Testing

When you create a class, you are probably pretty sure that it works. You will, after all, have put it through its paces during development. You'll also have run your system with the component in place, checking that it integrates well and that your new functionality is available and performing as expected.

Can you be sure that your class will carry on working as expected though? That might seem like a silly question. After all, you've checked your code once; why should it stop working arbitrarily? Well, of course, it won't; nothing happens arbitrarily, and if you never add another line of code to your system, you can probably breathe easy. If, on the other hand, your project is active, then it's inevitable that your component's context will change and highly likely that the component itself will be altered in any number of ways.

Let's look at these issues in turn. First, how can changing a component's context introduce errors? Even in a system where components are nicely decoupled from one another, they remain interdependent. Objects used by your class return values, perform actions, and accept data. If any of these behaviors change, the effects on the operation of your class might cause the kind of error that's easy to catch—the kind where your system falls over with a convenient error message that includes a filename and line number. Much more insidious, though, is the kind of change that does not cause an engine-level error, but nonetheless confuses your component. If your class makes an assumption based on another class's data, a change in that data might cause it to make a wrong decision. Your class is now in error and without a change to a line of code.

And it's likely that you will go on altering the class you've just completed. Often, these changes will be minor and obvious—so minor, in fact, that you won't feel the need to run through the careful checks you performed during development. You'll have probably forgotten them all, anyhow, unless you kept them in some way (perhaps commented out at the bottom of your class file as I sometimes do). Small changes, though, have a way of causing large unintended consequences—consequences that might have been caught had you thought to put a test harness in place.

A test harness is a set of automated tests that can be applied to your system as a whole or to its individual classes. Well deployed, a test harness helps you to prevent bugs from occurring and from *recurring*. A single change may cause a cascade of errors, and the test harness can help you to locate and eliminate these. This means you can make changes with some confidence that you are not breaking anything. It is quite satisfying to make an improvement to your system and then see a list of failed tests. These are all errors that might have been propagated within your system, but now it won't have to suffer them.

Continuous Integration

Have you ever made a schedule that made everything okay? You start with an assignment: code maybe or a school project. It's big and scary, and failure lurks. But you get out a sheet of paper, and you slice it up into manageable tasks. You determine the books to read and the components to write. Maybe you highlight the tasks in different colors. Individually, none of the tasks is actually that scary, it turns out. And gradually, as you plan, you conquer the deadline. As long as you do a little bit every day, you'll be fine. You can relax.

Sometimes, though, that schedule takes on a talismanic power. You hold it up like a shield to protect yourself from doubt and from the creeping fear that perhaps this time you'll crash and burn. And it's only after several weeks that you realize the schedule is not magic on its own. You actually have to do the work, too. By then, of course, lulled by the schedule's reassuring power, you have let things slide. There's nothing for it but to make a new schedule. This time, it will be less reassuring.

Testing and building are like that, too. You have to run your tests. You have to build your projects and build them in fresh environments regularly; otherwise, the magic won't work.

And if writing tests is a pain, running them can be a chore, especially as they gain in complexity and failures interrupt your plans. Of course, if you were running them more often, you'd probably have fewer failures, and those you did have would stand a good chance of relating to new code that's fresh in your mind.

It's easy to get comfortable in a sandbox. After all, you've got all your toys there: little scriptlets that make your life easy, development tools, and useful libraries. The trouble is your project may be getting too comfortable in your sandbox, too. It may begin to rely on uncommitted code or dependencies that you have left out of your build files. That means it's broken anywhere else but where you work.

The only answer is to build, build, and build again. And do it in a reasonably virgin environment each time.

Of course, it's all very well to advise this; it's quite another matter to do it. Coders as a breed tend to like to code. They want to keep the meetings and the housekeeping to a minimum. That's where Continuous Integration (CI) comes in. CI is both a practice and a set of tools to make the practice as easy as it possibly can be. Ideally, builds and tests should be entirely automatic or at least launchable from a single command or click. Any problems will be tracked, and you will be notified before an issue becomes too serious. I will talk more about CI in Chapter 21.

Summary

A developer's aim is always to deliver a working system. Writing good code is an essential part of this aim's fulfillment, but it is not the whole story.

In this chapter, I introduced dependency management with Composer and Packagist. I also discussed two great aids to collaboration: Vagrant and version control. I covered why version control requires automated build, and I introduced Phing, a PHP implementation of Ant, a Java build tool. Finally, I discussed software testing and introduced CI, a set of tools to automate build and testing.

## CHAPTER 15

PHP Standards

Unless you are a lawyer or a health inspector, the topic of standards probably does not make your heart race. However, what standards help us achieve is worth getting excited about. Standards promote interoperability, and that gives us access to a vast array of compatible tools and framework components.

This chapter will cover several important aspects of standards:

- Why standards: What are standards and why they matter

- PHP Standards Recommendations: Their origins and purpose

- PSR-1: The Basic Coding Standard

- PSR-12: Extended Coding Style

- PSR-4: Autoloading

Why Standards?

Design patterns interoperate. That is built-in at their core. A problem described in a design pattern suggests a particular solution, which in turn generates architectural consequences. These are then well addressed by new patterns. Patterns also help developers to interoperate because they provide a shared vocabulary. Object-oriented systems tend to privilege the principle of playing nice.

As we increasingly share each other's components though, this informal tendency toward interoperability is not always enough. As we have seen, Composer (or our package management system of choice) allows us to mix and match tools in our projects. These components may be designed as stand-alone libraries, or they may be pieces from a wider framework. Either way, once deployed in our system, they must be capable of working beside and in collaboration with any number of other components. By adhering to core standards, we make it less likely that our work will run into compatibility issues.

© Matt Zandstra 2021
M. Zandstra, *PHP 8 Objects, Patterns, and Practice*, https://doi.org/10.1007/978-1-4842-6791-2_15

In some senses, the nature of a standard is less important than the fact that it is adhered to. Personally, for example, I don't love every aspect of the PSR-12 style guidelines. In most circumstances, including this book, I have adopted the standard. Other developers on my teams will hopefully find my code easier to work with because they will find it in a format that is familiar. For other standards, such as autoloading, failure to observe a common standard will result in components that may not work together at all without additional middleware.

Standards are probably not the most exciting aspect of programming. However, there is an interesting contradiction at their core. It may seem that a standard closes down creativity. After all, standards tell you what you can and can't do. You must comply. You might think that this is hardly the stuff of innovation. And yet we owe the great flowering of creativity that the Internet has ushered into our lives to the fact that every node on this network of networks conforms to open standards. Proprietary systems stuck within walled gardens are necessarily limited in scope and often in longevity—no matter how clever their code or slick their interfaces. The Internet, with its shared protocols, ensures that any site can link to any other site. Most browsers support standard HTML, CSS, and JavaScript. The interfaces we can build within these standards are not always the most impressive we might imagine (though the limitations are much less than they were); still, abiding by them enables us to maximize the reach of our work.

Used well, standards promote openness, cooperation, and, ultimately, creativity. This is true, even if a standard itself enforces some limitations.

What Are PHP Standards Recommendations?

At the 2009 php[tek] conference, a group of framework developers formed an organization they called the PHP Framework Interop Group (PHP-FIG). Since then, developers have come on board from other key components. Their purpose was to build standards, so that their systems could better coexist.

The group vote on standards proposals which progress from Draft through Review and, finally, to Accepted status.

Table 15-1 lists the current standards at the time of this writing.

Table 15-1. *Accepted PHP Standards Recommendations*

PSR Number	Name	Description
1	Basic Coding Standard	Fundamentals such as PHP tags and basic naming conventions
3	Logger Interface	Rules for log levels and logger behaviors
4	Autoloading Standard	Conventions for naming classes and namespaces, as well as their mapping to the file system
6	Caching Interface	Rules for cache management, including data types, cache item lifetime, error handling, etc.
7	HTTP Message Interfaces	Conventions for HTTP requests and responses
11	Container interface	A common interface for dependency injection containers
12	Extended Coding Style Guide	Code formatting, including rules for placement of braces, argument lists, etc.
13	Link definition interfaces	Interfaces for describing hypermedia links
14	Event dispatcher	Definition for event management
15	HTTP Handlers	Common interfaces for HTTP server request handlers
16	Simple Cache	A common interface for caching libraries (a simplification of PSR-6)
17	HTTP Factories	A common standard for factories that create PSR-7-compliant HTTP objects
18	HTTP Client	Interface for sending HTTP requests and receiving HTTP responses

Why PSR in Particular?

So, why choose one standard and not another? It happens that the PHP Framework Interop Group—the originators of PSRs—has a pretty great pedigree, and the standards themselves therefore make sense. But also, these are the standards that the major frameworks and components are adopting. If you are using Composer to add functionality to your projects, you are already consuming code that complies with PSRs. By using its conventions for autoloading and its style guides, you are likely building code that is ready for collaboration with other people and components.

Note   One set of standards is not inherently superior to another. When you choose whether to adopt a standard, your choice may be driven by your judgment of the recommendation's merits. Alternatively, you might make a pragmatic choice based on the context within which you are working. If you're working in the WordPress community, for example, you might want to adopt the style defined in the Core Contributor Handbook at `https://make.wordpress.org/core/handbook/best-practices/coding-standards/php/`. Such a choice is part of the point of standards, which are all about the cooperation of people and software.

PSRs are a good bet because they are supported by key framework and component projects, including Phing, Composer, PEAR, Symfony, and Zend 2. Like patterns, standards are infectious—you're probably already benefiting from them.

Who Are PSRs for?

Ostensibly, PSRs are designed for the creators of frameworks. The fact that the membership of the PHP-FIG group rapidly widened to include the creators of tools as well as frameworks, however, shows that standards have wide relevance. That said, unless you are creating a logger, you may not need to worry too much about the details of PSR-3 (beyond ensuring any logging tool you use is itself compliant). On the other hand, if you've read the rest of this book, chances are you are as likely to be creating tools as you are to be consuming them. So, it's also likely that you'll find something relevant to you either in the present standards or the standards to come.

And then there are the standards that matter to all of us. Unglamorous as style guides are, for example, they are relevant to every programmer. And while the rules that govern autoloading really apply to those who create autoloaders (and the main game in town is probably Composer's), they also fundamentally affect how we organize our classes, our packages, and our files.

For these reasons, I will focus on coding style and autoloading for the rest of this chapter.

Coding with Style

I tend to find pull request comments like "your braces are in the wrong place" disproportionately irritating. Such input often seems nitpicky and perilously close to *bike-shedding*.

Note   In case you have not come across it, the verb "to bike-shed" refers to the tendency in some reviewers to criticize unimportant elements of a project under scrutiny. The implication is that such elements are chosen because they fit within the scope of the commenter's competence. So, given a skyscraper to assess, a particular manager might focus not on the vast and complex tower of glass and steel but on the much easier to comprehend bike shed around the back. Wikipedia has a good history of the term: `https://en.wikipedia.org/wiki/Law_of_triviality`.

And yet I have come to see that conforming to a common style can help improve the quality of code. This is mainly a matter of readability (regardless of the reasoning behind a particular rule). If a team abides by the same rules for indentations, brace placement, argument lists, and so on, then a developer can quickly assess and contribute to a colleague's code.

So, for this edition of the book, I committed to edit all code examples so that they conform to PSR-1 and PSR-12. I have asked my colleague and technical editor Paul Tregoing to hold me to that, too. This was a promise that was so easy to make at the planning stage—and much more effort than I expected. This brings me to the first style guide lesson I learned. If possible, adopt a standard early for your project. Refactoring to a code style will likely tie up resources and make it hard to examine code differences that span The Time of the Great Reformat.

So what changes have I had to apply? Let's start with the basics.

PSR-1 Basic Coding Standard

These are the fundamentals for PHP code. You can find them in detail at `www.php-fig.org/psr/psr-1/`. Let's break them down.

Opening and Closing Tags

First of all, a PHP section should open either with <?php or <?=. In other words, the short opening tag, <?, should not be used, nor should any other variation. A section should close with ?> only (or, as we shall see in the next section, no tag at all).

Note   PSRs follow a set of definitions for words such as *should* and *must* which determine the degree of compliance a directive should command. While this chapter will rely on the plain English meanings of such words, the absolute intended meanings within the context of PSR are defined at www.ietf.org/rfc/ rfc2119.txt.

Side Effects

A PHP file should declare classes, interfaces, functions, and the like, or it should perform an action (such as reading or writing to a file or sending output to the browser); however, it should not do both. If you are accustomed to using require_once() to include other class files, this will trip you up straightaway because the act of including another file is a side effect. Just as patterns beget patterns, so standards tend to require other standards. The correct way to handle class dependencies is through a PSR-4-compliant autoloader.

So, is it legal for a class you declare to write to a file in one of its methods? That is perfectly acceptable because the effect is not kicked off by the file's inclusion. In other words, it's an execution effect, not a side effect.

So what kind of file might perform actions rather than declare classes? Think of the script that kicks off an application.

Here is a listing that performs actions as a direct result of inclusion:

```
// listing 15.01
namespace popp\ch15\batch01;

require_once(__DIR__ . "/../../../vendor/autoload.php");

$tree = new Tree();
print "loaded " . get_class($tree) . "\n";
```

Here is a PHP file that declares a class with no side effects:

```
// listing 15.02
namespace popp\ch15\batch01;

class Tree
{
}
```

Note   In other chapters, I largely omit `namespace` declarations and `use` directives in order to focus on the code. Since this chapter is about the mechanics of formatting class files, I will include `namespace` and `use` statements where appropriate.

Naming

Classes must be declared in upper camel case, also known as studly caps or PascalCase. In other words, a class name should begin with a capital letter. The rest of the name should be lowercase unless it consists of multiple words. In this instance, each word should begin with an uppercase letter, like this:

```
class MyClassName
```

Properties can be named in any way, although consistency is called for. I tend to use camel case, an approach similar to studly caps, but without the leading capital letter:

```
private $myPropertyName
```

Methods must be declared in camel case:

```
public function myMethodName()
```

Class constants must be uppercase, with words separated by underscores:

```
public const MY_NAME_IS = 'matt';
```

More Rules and an Example

Classes, namespaces, and files should be declared in accordance with the PSR-4 autoloading standard. We will come to that later in the chapter, however. PHP documents must be saved as UTF-8 encoded files.

Finally, for PSR-1, let's get it all wrong—and then put it right. Here is a class file that breaks all the rules:

```
// listing 15.03
<?
require_once("conf/ConfFile.ini");

class conf_reader {
    const ModeFile = 1;
    const Mode_DB = 2;

    private $conf_file;
    private $confValues= [];

    function read_conf() {
        // implementation
    }
}
?>
```

Can you spot all the issues? First of all, I used a short opening tag. I also failed to declare a namespace (though we haven't yet covered this requirement in detail). In naming my class, I used underscores and no capitals, rather than studly caps. And I used two formats for my constant names, neither of which are the required one—all capitals with words should be separated by underscores. Although both my property names were legal, I failed to make them consistent; specifically, I used underscores for $conf_ file and camel case for $confValues. In naming my method, read_conf(), I used an underscore rather than camel case.

```
// listing 15.04
<?php
namespace popp\ch15\batch01;

class ConfReader {
    const MODEFILE = 1;
    const MODE_DB = 2;
```

```
    private $conf_file;
    private $confValues= [];

    function readConf() {
        // implementation
    }
}
?>
```

PSR-12 Extended Coding Style

The Extended Coding Style (PSR-12) builds upon PSR-1 and replaces a deprecated standard: PSR-2. Let's jump in and look at some of the rules.

Starting and Ending a PHP Document

We have already seen that PSR-1 requires that PHP blocks open with <``?php. PSR-12 stipulates that pure PHP files should not have an ending ?> tag, but should end with a single blank line. It's all too easy to end a file with a closing tag and then let an extra new line creep in. This can result in formatting bugs as well as errors when you set HTTP headers (you cannot do this after content has already been sent to the browser).

Table 15-2 describes, in order, the statements that might form a valid PHP document.

Table 15-2. *PHP Statements*

Statement	Example
Opening PHP tag	`<?php`
A file-level docblock	`/**`
	`* File doc`
	`*/`
Declare statements	`declare(strict_types=1);`
Namespace declaration	`namespace popp;`
use import statements (classes)	`use other\Service;`
use import statements (functions)	`use function other\{getAll, calculate};`
use import statements (constants)	`use const other\{NAME, VERSION};`

A PHP document should follow the structure in Table 15-2 (though any elements that are not necessary for legal PHP code may be omitted). namespace declarations should be followed by a blank line, and a block of use declarations should be followed by a blank line. Do not put more than one use declaration on the same line:

```
// listing 15.05

namespace popp\ch15\batch01;

use popp\ch10\batch06\PollutionDecorator;
use popp\ch10\batch06\DiamondDecorator;
use popp\ch10\batch06\Plains;

// begin class
```

Starting and Ending a Class

The class keyword, the class name, and extends and implements must all be placed on the same line. Where a class implements multiple interfaces, each interface name can be included on the same line as the class declaration, or it can be placed indented on its own line. If you choose to place your interface names on multiple lines, the first item must be placed on its own line rather than directly after the implements keyword. Class braces should begin on the line *after* the class declaration and end on their own line (directly after the class contents). So, a class declaration might look something like this:

```
// listing 15.06
class EarthGame extends Game implements
    Playable,
    Savable
    {

        // class body
    }
```

However, you could equally place the interface names on a single line:

```
// listing 15.07
class EarthGame extends Game implements Playable, Savable
{

// class body

}
```

Working with Traits

When adding a trait to a class, you must add the use statement to the line directly after the class's opening brace. Although PHP allows you to group your traits onto a single line, PSR-12 requires that you place each use statement on its own line. If your class provides its own elements in addition to the use statements, you must leave a blank line before proceeding with nontrait content. Otherwise, you must close the class block on the line directly after the last use statement.

Here is a class that imports two traits and provides a method of its own:

```
// listing 15.08
namespace popp\ch15\batch01;

class Tree
{
    use GrowTools;
    use TerrainUtil;

    public function draw(): void
    {
        // implementation
    }
}
```

If you declare a block for as or insteadof statements, it should spread over multiple lines. The opening brace should begin on the same line as the use statement. The block should then use one line per statement. Finally, the closing brace should end on its own line, like this:

```
// listing 15.09
namespace popp\ch15\batch01;
class Marsh
{
    use GrowTools {
        GrowTools::dimension as size;
    }
    use TerrainUtil;

    public function draw(): void
    {
        // implementation
    }
}
```

Declaring Properties and Constants

Properties and constants must have a declared visibility (public, private, or protected). The var keyword is not acceptable. We have already covered the format for property and constant names as part of PSR-1.

Starting and Ending a Method

All methods must have a declared visibility (public, private, or protected). The visibility keyword must *follow* abstract or final, but *precede* static. Method arguments with default values should be placed at the end of the argument list.

Single-Line Declarations

Method braces should begin on the line *after* the method name and end on their own line (directly after the method code). A list of method arguments should not begin or end with a space (i.e., they should snuggle in close to the wrapping parentheses). For each argument, the comma should be flush with the preceding argument name (or the default value), but it should then be followed by a space. Let's clarify things with an example:

```
// listing 15.10
final public static function generateTile(int $diamondCount, bool $polluted
= false): array
{
    // implementation
}
```

Multiline Declarations

A single-line method declaration is not practical in cases where there are many arguments. In this situation, you can break the argument list so that each argument (including type, argument variable, default value, and comma) is placed indented on its own line. In this case, the closing parenthesis should be placed on the line after the argument list, flush with the start of the method declaration. The opening brace should follow the closing parenthesis on the same line, separated by a space. The method body should begin on a new line. Once again, that sounds much more complicated than it is. An example should make it clearer:

```
// listing 15.11
public function __construct(
    int $size,
    string $name,
    bool $wraparound = false,
    bool $aliens = false
) {
    // implementation
}
```

Return Types

A return type declaration should be on the same line as the closing parenthesis. The colon should directly follow the closing parenthesis. The colon should be separated from the return type by a single space. For multiline declarations, the return type declaration should precede the opening brace on the same line separated by a space.

```
// listing 15.12
final public static function findTilesMatching(
    int $diamondCount,
    bool $polluted = false
): array {
    // implementation
}
```

PSR-12 does not mandate the use of return type declarations. However, since the introduction of void, mixed, and nullable types, it should be possible to provide a declaration that matches all circumstances.

Lines and Indentation

You should use four spaces rather than tabs for indentation. It's worth checking your editor settings—you can configure good editors to use spaces rather than a tab when you press the Tab key. You should also wrap your text before your line reaches 120 characters (though this is not mandatory). Lines must end with Unix line feed characters and not other platform-specific combinations (such as CR in Macs and CR/LF on Windows). Again, check your editor's settings for this, since it will likely use your operating system's default line ending characters.

Calling Methods and Functions

Do not place a space between the method name and the opening parenthesis. You can apply the same rules to the argument list in a method call as you do to the argument list in a method declaration. In other words, for a single-line call, leave no space after the opening parenthesis or before the closing parenthesis. A comma should follow directly after each argument, with a single space falling before the next one. If you need to use multiple lines for a method call, each argument should sit indented on its own line, and the closing parenthesis should fall on a new line:

```
// listing 15.13
$earthgame = new EarthGame(
    5,
    "earth",
    true,
```

```
    true
);
$earthgame::generateTile(5,  true);
```

Flow of Control

Flow control keywords (if, for, while, etc.) must be followed by a single space.
However, the opening parenthesis must not be followed by a space. Similarly, the closing
parenthesis must not be preceded by a space. So, the contents should be snug in their
brackets. In contrast to class and (single line) function declarations, the opening brace
for the flow control block must begin on the same line as the closing parenthesis. The
closing brace should sit on its own line. Here's a quick example:

```
// listing 15.14
$tile = [];
for ($x = 0; $x < $diamondCount; $x++) {
    if ($polluted) {
        $tile[] = new PollutionDecorator(new DiamondDecorator(new
        Plains()));
    } else {
        $tile[] = new DiamondDecorator(new Plains());
    }
}
```

Notice the space after both for and if. The for and if expressions are flush to the
parentheses that contain them. In both cases, the closing parenthesis is followed by a
space and then the opening brace for the flow control body.

Expressions in parentheses may be split across multiple lines, with each line
indented at least once. Where the expressions are broken, the Boolean operators can go
either at the beginning or end of each line, but your choice must be consistent.

```
// listing 15.15
$ret = [];
for (
    $x = 0;
    $x < count($this->tiles);
    $x++
) {
```

```
    if (
        $this->tiles[$x]->isPolluted() &&
        $this->tiles[$x]->hasDiamonds() &&
        ! ($this->tiles[$x]->isPlains())
    ) {
        $ret[] =  $x;
    }
}
return $ret;
```

Checking and Fixing Your Code

Even if this chapter covered every single directive in PSR-12 (which it does not), it would be hard to keep it all in your mind. After all, we have other things to think about—like the design and implementation of our systems. So, given that we have bought into the value of coding standards, how do we comply without using too much of our time or focus? We use a tool, of course.

PHP_CodeSniffer allows you to detect and even repair standards violations—and not just for PSR. You can get it by following the instructions at https://github.com/squizlabs/PHP_CodeSniffer. There are Composer and PEAR options, but here's how you can download the PHP archive files:

```
curl -OL https://squizlabs.github.io/PHP_CodeSniffer/phpcs.phar
curl -OL https://squizlabs.github.io/PHP_CodeSniffer/phpcbf.phar
```

Why two downloads? The first is for phpcs, which diagnoses and reports on violations. The second is for phpcbf, which can fix a lot of them. Let's put the tools through their paces. First, here is a scrappily formatted piece of code:

```
// listing 15.16

namespace popp\ch15\batch01;
class ebookParser {

    function __construct(string $path , $format=0 ) {
        if ($format>1)
            $this->setFormat( 1 );
    }
```

```
    function setformat(int $format) {
        // do something with $format
    }
}
```

Rather than run through the problems here, let's have PHP_CodeSniffer do it for us:

```
$ php phpcs.phar --standard=PSR12 src/ch15/batch01/phpcsBroken.php

FILE: /var/popp/src/ch15/batch01/phpcsBroken.php
----------------------------------------------------------------------------
FOUND 16 ERRORS AFFECTING 6 LINES
----------------------------------------------------------------------------
 5 | ERROR | [x] Header blocks must be separated by a single blank line
 6 | ERROR | [ ] Class name "ebookParser" is not in PascalCase format
 6 | ERROR | [x] Opening brace of a class must be on the line after the
   |       |     definition
 8 | ERROR | [ ] Visibility must be declared on method " construct"
 8 | ERROR | [x] Expected 0 spaces between argument "$path" and comma; 1
   |       |     found
 8 | ERROR | [x] Incorrect spacing between argument "$format" and equals
   |       |     sign; expected 1 but found 0
 8 | ERROR | [x] Incorrect spacing between default value and equals sign
   |       |     for argument "$format"; expected 1 but found 0
 8 | ERROR | [x] Expected 0 spaces before closing parenthesis; 1 found
 8 | ERROR | [x] Opening brace should be on a new line
 9 | ERROR | [x] Inline control structures are not allowed
 9 | ERROR | [x] Expected at least 1 space before ">"; 0 found
 9 | ERROR | [x] Expected at least 1 space after ">"; 0 found
10 | ERROR | [x] Space after opening parenthesis of function call prohibited
10 | ERROR | [x] Expected 0 spaces before closing parenthesis; 1 found
13 | ERROR | [ ] Visibility must be declared on method "setformat"
13 | ERROR | [x] Opening brace should be on a new line
----------------------------------------------------------------------------
PHPCBF CAN FIX THE 13 MARKED SNIFF VIOLATIONS AUTOMATICALLY
----------------------------------------------------------------------------

Time: 82ms; Memory: 6MB
```

That's an exhausting number of problems for just a few lines of code. Luckily, as the output indicates, we can fix a lot of these with very little effort (applied to a copy so as to keep my formatting errors for another time):

```
$ php phpcbf.phar --standard=PSR12 src/ch15/batch01/EbookParser.php

PHPCBF RESULT SUMMARY
----------------------------------------------------------------------
FILE                                          FIXED       REMAINING
----------------------------------------------------------------------
/var/popp/src/ch15/batch01/EbookParser.php    13          3
----------------------------------------------------------------------
A TOTAL OF 13 ERRORS WERE FIXED IN 1 FILE
----------------------------------------------------------------------

Time: 96ms; Memory: 6MB
```

Now, if we run `phpcs` again, we'll see that the situation is much improved:

```
$ php phpcs.phar --standard=PSR2 src/ch15/batch01/EbookParser.php

FILE: /var/popp/src/ch15/batch01/EbookParser.php
----------------------------------------------------------------------
FOUND 3 ERRORS AFFECTING 3 LINES
----------------------------------------------------------------------
  7 | ERROR | Class name "ebookParser" is not in PascalCase format
 10 | ERROR | Visibility must be declared on method " construct"
 17 | ERROR | Visibility must be declared on method "setformat"
----------------------------------------------------------------------

Time: 76ms; Memory: 6MB
```

I'll go ahead and add the visibility declarations and then change the name of the class—a quick job! And now I have a stylishly compliant code file:

```
// listing 15.17
namespace  popp\ch15\batch01;
class EbookParser
{
```

```
public function __construct(string $path, $format = 0)
{
    if ($format > 1) {
        $this->setFormat(1);
    }
}

private function setformat(int $format): void
{
    // do something with $format
}
}
```

PSR-4 Autoloading

We looked at PHP's support for autoloading in Chapter 5. In that chapter, we saw how we could use the spl_autoload_register() function to automatically require files based on the name of an as yet unloaded class. Although this is powerful, it is also a kind of behind-the-scenes magic. This is fine in a single project, but a recipe for great confusion if multiple components come together and all use different conventions for loading class files.

The Autoloading Standard (PSR-4) requires frameworks to conform to a common set of rules, thereby adding some discipline to the magic.

This is great news for developers. It means that we can more or less ignore the mechanics of requiring files and focus instead on class dependencies.

The Rules That Matter to Us

The main purpose of PSR-4 is to define rules for autoloader developers. However, those rules inevitably determine the way we must declare namespaces and classes. Here are some of the basics.

A fully qualified class name (i.e., the name of a class, including its namespaces) must include an initial "vendor" namespace. So, a class must have at least one namespace.

Let's say that our vendor namespace is popp. We can declare a class in this way:

```
// listing 15.18
namespace popp;

class Services
{
}
```

The fully qualified class name for this class is popp\Services.

The initial namespaces in a path must correspond to one or more base directories. We can use this to map a set of sub-namespaces to a starting directory. If, for example, we want to work with the namespace popp\library (and nothing else under the popp namespace), then we might map that to a top-level directory to spare us from having to maintain an empty popp/ directory.

Let's set up a composer.json file to perform that mapping:

```
{
    "autoload": {
        "psr-4": {
            "popp\\library\\": "mylib"
        }
    }
}
```

Notice that I don't even need to call the base directory, "library". This is an arbitrary mapping of popp\library to the mylib directory. Now I can create a class file under the mylib directory:

```
// listing 15.19
// mylib/LibraryCatalogue.php

namespace popp\library;
use popp\library\inventory\Book;
class LibraryCatalogue
{
    private array $books = [];
```

```
public function addBook(Book $book): void
{
    $this->books[] = $book;
}
```
}

In order to be found, the LibraryCatalogue class must be placed in a file with exactly the same name (with the obvious addition of the .php extension).

After a base directory (mylib) has been associated with initial namespaces (popp\ library), there must then be a direct relation between subsequent directories and sub-namespaces. It happens that I have already referenced a class named popp\library\ inventory\Book in my LibraryCatalogue class. That class file should therefore be placed in the mylib/inventory directory:

```
// listing 15.20
// mylib/library/inventory/Book.php
namespace popp\library\inventory;

class Book
{
    // implementation
}
```

Remember the rule that the initial namespaces in a path must correspond to one *or more* base directories? So far, we have made a one-to-one relationship between popp\ library and mylib. There's actually no reason why we can't map the popp\library namespace to more than one base directory. Let's add a directory named additional to the mapping; here's the amendment to composer.json:

```
{
    "autoload": {
        "psr-4": {
            "popp\\library\\": ["mylib", "additional"]
        }
    }
}
```

Now I can create the additional/inventory directories and a class to go in them:

```
// listing 15.21
// additional/inventory/Ebook.php
namespace popp\library\inventory;
class Ebook extends Book
{
    // implementation
}
```

Next, let's create a top-level runner script, index.php, to instantiate these classes:

```
// listing 15.22
require_once("vendor/autoload.php");

use popp\library\LibraryCatalogue;

// will be found under mylib/
use popp\library\inventory\Book;

// will be found under additional/
use popp\library\inventory\Ebook;

$catalogue = new LibraryCatalogue();
$catalogue->addBook(new Book());
$catalogue->addBook(new Ebook());
```

Note   You must use Composer to generate the autoload file, vendor/autoload. php, and this file must be included in some way before you gain access to the logic you have declared in composer.json. You can do this by running the command composer install (or by running composer dump-autoload if you just want to regenerate the autoload file in an environment that is already installed). You can learn more about Composer in Chapter 16.

Remember the rule about side effects? A PHP file should declare classes, interfaces, functions, and the like; or, it should perform an action. However, it should not do both. This script falls into the taking action category. Crucially, it calls require_once() to include the autoload code generated using the configuration in the `composer.json` file. Thanks to this, all the classes are located, despite the fact that Ebook has been placed in an entirely separate base directory from the rest.

Why would I want to maintain two separate directories for the same core namespace? One possible reason is for unit tests that you want to keep separate from production code. You may also manage plug-ins and extensions that will not ship with every version of your system.

Note   Be sure to keep an eye on all the PSR standards at `www.php-fig.org/ psr/`. This is a fast-moving area, and you'll likely find that standards relevant to you are on their way.

Summary

In this chapter, I wrestled a little with the possibility that standards are less than fantastically exciting—and then made a case for their power. Standards get integration issues out of our way, so that we can get on and do amazing things. I looked at PSR-1 and PSR-12, the standards for basic coding and for wider coding style. Next, I went on to discuss PSR-4, the standard for autoloaders. Finally, I worked through a Composer-based example that showed PSR-4-compliant autoloading in practice.

## CHAPTER 16

PHP Using and Creating Components with Composer

Programmers aspire to produce reusable code. This is one of the great goals in object-oriented coding. We like to abstract useful functionality from the messiness of specific context, turning a particular solution into a tool that can be used again and again. To come at this from another angle, if programmers love the reusable, they hate duplication. By creating libraries that can be reapplied, programmers avoid the need to implement similar solutions across multiple projects.

Even if we avoid duplication in our own code, though, there is a wider issue. For every tool you create, how many other programmers have implemented the same solution? This is wasted effort on an epic scale: wouldn't it be much more sensible for programmers to collaborate and to focus their energies on making a single tool better, rather than producing hundreds of variations on a theme?

In order to do this, we need to get our hands on existing libraries. But then the packages we need will likely require other libraries in order to do their work. So we need a tool which can handle downloading and installing packages, as well as manage their dependencies. That is where Composer comes in; it does all this and more besides.

This chapter will cover several key issues:

- *Installation*: Downloading and setting up Composer
- *Requirements*: Using `composer.json` to get packages
- *Versions*: Specifying versions so as to get the latest code without breaking your system

© Matt Zandstra 2021
M. Zandstra, *PHP 8 Objects, Patterns, and Practice*, https://doi.org/10.1007/978-1-4842-6791-2_16

- *Packagist*: Configuring your code for public access

- *Private repositories*: Leveraging Composer using a private repository

What Is Composer?

Strictly speaking, Composer is a dependency manager rather than a package manager. This, it seems, is because it handles component relationships on a local basis rather than centrally as Yum and Apt do. If you think that this is an overly fine distinction, you could be right. However we define it, Composer allows you to specify packages. It downloads them to a local directory (vendor), finds and downloads all dependencies, and then makes all this code available to your project via an autoloader.

As always, we need to begin by getting the tool.

Installing Composer

You can download Composer at `https://getcomposer.org/download/`. You will find an installer mechanism there. You can also install a stable phar file like this:

```
$ wget https://getcomposer.org/composer-stable.phar
$ chmod 755 composer-stable.phar
$ sudo mv composer-stable.phar ~/bin/composer
```

I download the archive and run `chmod` to ensure that it is executable. Then I copy it into a central location so that I can run it easily from anywhere in my system. Now I can test the command:

```
$ composer --version
```

```
Composer version 2.0.8 2020-12-03 17:20:38
```

Installing a (Set of) Package(s)

Why did I do that funky bit with the brackets? Because packages inevitably beget packages—sometimes a lot of packages.

Let's begin with a library that stands alone, though. Imagine that we're building an application which needs to communicate with Twitter. A little bit of research leads me to the abraham/twitteroauth package. In order to install this, I need to generate a JSON file named composer.json and then define a require element:

```
{
    "require": {
        "abraham/twitteroauth": "2.0.*"
    }
}
```

I begin with a directory that is empty apart from the composer.json file. Once I run a Composer command, though, we'll see a change:

```
$ composer update

Loading composer repositories with package information
Updating dependencies
Lock file operations: 2 installs, 0 updates, 0 removals
  - Locking abraham/twitteroauth (2.0.1)
  - Locking composer/ca-bundle (1.2.8)
Writing lock file
Installing dependencies from lock file (including require-dev)
Package operations: 2 installs, 0 updates, 0 removals
  - Installing composer/ca-bundle (1.2.8): Extracting archive
  - Installing abraham/twitteroauth (2.0.1): Extracting archive
    Generating autoload files
```

So what has been generated? Let's take a look:

```
$ ls

composer.json    composer.lock    vendor
```

Composer installs packages into vendor/. It also generates a file named composer. lock. This specifies the exact versions of all packages installed. If you're using version control, you should commit this file. If another developer runs composer install with a composer.lock file present, package versions will be installed on her system exactly as specified. In this way, the team can stay in sync with one another, and you can be sure that your production environment exactly matches the development and test environments.

You can override the lock file by running `composer update` again. This will generate a new lock file. Typically, you will run this to keep current with new package versions (if you are using wildcards, as I have, or ranges).

Installing a Package from the Command Line

As you have seen, I can create the `composer.json` file using an editor. But you can also have Composer do it for you. This is particularly useful if you need to kick off with a single package. When you invoke `composer require` on the command line, Composer will download the specified package and install it into `vendor/` for you. It will also generate a `composer.json` file, which you can then edit and extend:

```
$ composer require abraham/twitteroauth

Using version ^2.0 for abraham/twitteroauth
./composer.json has been created
Running composer update abraham/twitteroauth
Loading composer repositories with package information Updating dependencies
Lock file operations: 2 installs, 0 updates, 0 removals
  - Locking abraham/twitteroauth (2.0.1)
  - Locking composer/ca-bundle (1.2.8)
Writing lock file
Installing dependencies from lock file (including require-dev)
Package operations: 2 installs, 0 updates, 0 removals
  - Installing composer/ca-bundle (1.2.8): Extracting archive
  - Installing abraham/twitteroauth (2.0.1): Extracting archive
    Generating autoload files
```

Versions

Composer is designed to support semantic versioning. In essence, this involves defining a package's version with three numbers, separated by dots: *major*, *minor*, and *patch*. If you fix a bug, add no functionality, and do not break backward compatibility, you should increment the *patch* number. If you add new functionality, but do not break backward compatibility, you should increment the middle *minor* number. If your new version breaks backward compatibility (in other words, if client code would break if this new version were suddenly switched in), then you should increment the first *major* version number.

Note   You can read more about the semantic versioning convention at `https://semver.org`.

You should bear this in mind when specifying versions in your `composer.json` file: if you are too liberal in your ranges or wildcards, you may find that your system breaks on update.

Table 16-1 shows some of the ways that you can specify versions with Composer.

Table 16-1. *Composer and Package Versions*

Type	Example	Notes
Exact	1.2.2	Only install the given version
Wildcard	1.2.*	Install the exact specified numbers, but find the latest available version matching the wildcard
Range	1.0.0– 1.1.7	Install a version no lower than the first number and no higher than the last number
Comparison	>1.2.0 <=1.2.2	Use <, <=, >, and >= to specify complex ranges. You can combine these directives with a space (equivalent to "and") or with || to specify "or"
Tilde (major version)	~1.3	The given number is the minimum, and the final number specified can increase. So for ~1.3, 1.3 is the minimum and there can be no match at 2.0.0 or above
Caret	^1.3	Will match up to, but not including, the next breaking change. So while ~1.3.1 will not match at 1.4 and above, ^1.3.1 will match from 1.3.1 up to, but not including, 2.0.0. This is generally the most useful shortcut

> **Note**   You can further influence the way that composer selects packages by adding stability suffixes to your version constraint strings. By adding @ followed by one of dev, alpha, beta, and RC (running from least to most stable), you will allow composer to consider nonstable versions in its calculations. Composer can work this out by looking at the git tag names. So 1.2.*@dev can match the tag 1.2.2-dev. You can also use the stability flag stable to signal that you do not want to include bleeding-edge code. This will match version tags which are not defined as dev, beta, and so on.

require-dev

Very often, you need packages during development that are unnecessary in a production context. You will want to run tests locally, for example, but you are unlikely to need PHPUnit available on your public site.

Composer addresses this by supporting a separate require-dev element. You can add packages here, just as you can for the require element:

```
{
    "require-dev": {
        "phpunit/phpunit": "*"
    },
    "require": {
        "abraham/twitteroauth": "^2.0",
        "ext-xml": "*"
    }
}
```

Now, when we run composer update, PHPUnit and all sorts of dependent packages are downloaded and installed:

```
$ composer update

Loading composer repositories with package information Updating dependencies
Lock file operations: 36 installs, 0 updates, 0 removals
  - Locking abraham/twitteroauth (2.0.1)
  - Locking composer/ca-bundle (1.2.8)
  - Locking doctrine/instantiator (1.4.0)
```

...

```
Writing lock file
Installing dependencies from lock file (including require-dev) Package
operations: 36 installs, 0 updates, 0 removals
  - Installing composer/ca-bundle (1.2.8): Extracting archive
  - Installing abraham/twitteroauth (2.0.1): Extracting archive
```

...

```
6 package suggestions were added by new dependencies, use `composer
suggest` to see details.
Generating autoload files
```

If you're installing in a production context, however, you can pass the --no-dev flag to composer install, and Composer will download only those packages specified in the require element:

```
$ composer install --no-dev
```

```
Installing dependencies from lock file
Verifying lock file contents can be installed on current platform.
Package operations: 2 installs, 0 updates, 0 removals
  - Installing composer/ca-bundle (1.2.8): Extracting archive
  - Installing abraham/twitteroauth (2.0.1): Extracting archive Generating
    autoload files
```

Note   When you run the composer install command, Composer creates a file named composer.lock. This records the exact version of every file you installed under vendor/. If you run composer install with a composer.lock file present alongside composer.json, Composer will fetch the package versions it has recorded if they are not present. This is useful because you can commit a composer.lock file to your version control repository and be sure that your team will download the same versions of all the packages you have installed. If you need to override composer.lock, either to get the latest versions of packages or because you have changed composer.json, you should run composer update to override the lock file.

Composer and Autoload

We covered autoloading in some detail in Chapter 15. For the sake of completeness, however, it is worth looking at it briefly. Composer generates a file named autoload. php, which handles class loading for the packages it downloads. You can also leverage this functionality for your own code by including autoload.php (usually with require_ once()). Once you have done this, any class you declare in your system will be found automatically when accessed in your code, so long as your directories and filenames mirror your namespaces and class names.

In other words, a class named poppbook\megaquiz\command\CommandContext must be placed in a file named CommandContext.php in the poppbook/megaquiz/command/ directory.

If you want to mix things up (perhaps by omitting a redundant leading directory or two or by adding a test directory to the search path), then you can use the autoload element to map a namespace to your file structure, like this:

```
"autoload": {
    "psr-4": {
        "poppbook\\megaquiz\\": ["src", "test"]
    }
}
```

In order to generate the latest autoload.php file, I need to run one of composer install (will also install anything specified in the lock file) or composer update (will also install the latest packages that match the specification in composer.json). If you do not want to install or update any packages, you can use composer dump-autoload which will only generate autoload files.

Now, so long as autoload.php is included, my classes are easily discoverable. Thanks to my autoload configuration, the poppbook\megaquiz\command\CommandContext class will now be found in src/command/CommandContext.php. Not only that, but because I have referenced more than one target (test as well as src), I can also create test classes that belong to the poppbook\megaquiz\ namespace under the test/ directory.

Turn to the "PSR-4 Autoloading" section in Chapter 15 to follow a more in-depth example.

Creating Your Own Package

If you have worked with PEAR in the past, you might expect a section on creating a package here to involve an entirely new package file. In fact, we've already been creating a package throughout this chapter. We just have to add some more information and then find a way to make our code available to others.

Adding Package Information

You really do not have to add that much information to make a viable package, but you absolutely need a name, so that your package can be found. I'm also going to include the description and authors elements, as well as to create a fake product named megaquiz which you will find popping up in other chapters occasionally:

```
"name": "poppbook/megaquiz",
"description": "a truly mega quiz",
"authors": [
    {
        "name": "matt zandstra",
        "email": "matt@getinstance.com"
    }
],
```

These fields should be mostly self-explanatory. The exception might be that leading namespace—poppbook, in this case—which is separated from the actual package name by a forward slash. This is known as the *vendor name*. As you might expect, the vendor name becomes a top-level directory under vendor/ when your package is installed. This is often the organization name used by the package owner in GitHub or Bitbucket.

With all that in place, you are ready to commit your package to your version control host of choice. If you're not sure what that involves, you can learn a lot more about this subject in Chapter 17.

Note   Composer supports a version field, but it is considered better practice to use a tag in Git to track your package's version. Composer will automatically recognize this.

Remember that you should not push the `vendor` directory (at least not usually—there are some arguable exceptions to that rule). However, it is a good idea to track the generated `composer.lock` file alongside `composer.json`.

Platform Packages

Although you cannot use Composer to install system-wide packages, you *can* specify system-wide requirements, so that your package will only install in a system which is ready for it.

A platform package is specified with a single key, though in a couple of cases the key is further broken down by type, using a dash. I list the available types in Table 16-2.

Table 16-2. *Platform Packages*

Type	Example	Description
PHP	`"php": "8.*"`	The PHP version
Extension	`"ext-xml": ">2"`	The PHP extension
Library	`"lib-iconv": "~2"`	A system library used by PHP
HHVM	`"hhvm": "~2"`	An HHVM version (HHVM is a virtual machine that supports an extended version of PHP)

Let's try it out:

```
{
    "require": {
        "abraham/twitteroauth": "2.0.*",
        "ext-xml": "*",
        "ext-gd": "*"
    }
}
```

In the preceding code, I specify that my package requires the xml and gd extensions. Now it's time to run update:

```
$ composer update

Loading composer repositories with package information
Updating dependencies
Your requirements could not be resolved to an installable set of packages.

  Problem  1
    - Root composer.json requires PHP extension ext-gd * but it is missing
      from your system. Install or enable PHP's gd extension.
```

It looks as though I was set up for XML; however, GD, an image manipulation package, is not installed on my system, so Composer throws an error.

Distribution Through Packagist

If you've been working through this chapter, you might have wondered where the packages we have been installing actually come from. It feels a lot like magic, but (as you might expect) there is a package repository behind the scenes. It is called Packagist, and it can be found at https://packagist.org. So long as your code can be found in a public git repository, it can be made available through Packagist.

Let's give it a shot. I have pushed my megaquiz project to GitHub, so now I need to tell Packagist about my repository. Once I have signed up, I simply add the URL of my repository. You can see this in Figure 16-1.

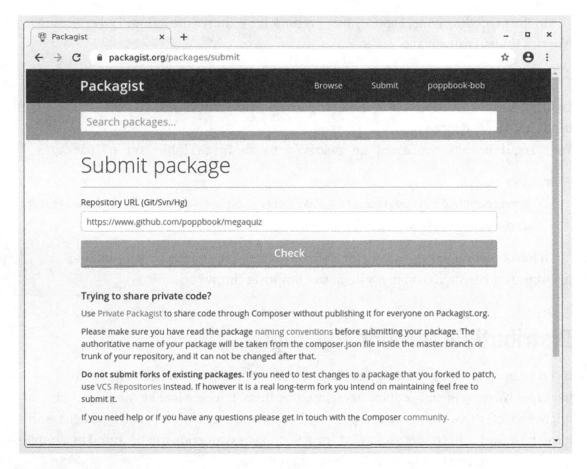

Figure 16-1. *Adding a package to Packagist*

Once I've added `megaquiz`, Packagist locates the repository, checks the `composer.json` file, and displays a control panel. You can see that in Figure 16-2.

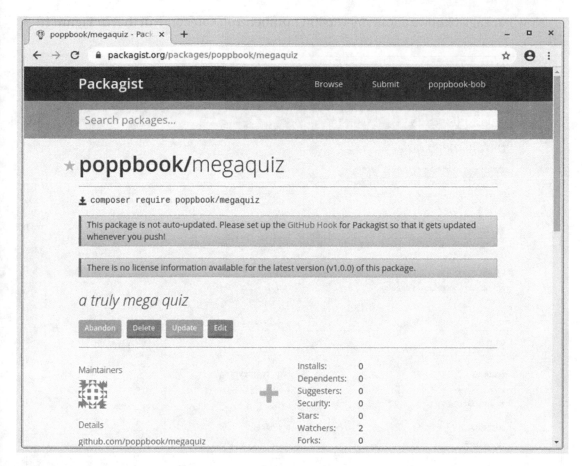

Figure 16-2.   *The package control panel*

Packagist tells me that I have not set license information. I can fix this at any time by adding a `license` element to the `composer.json` file:

```
"license": "Apache-2.0",
```

Packagist has also failed to find any version information. I'll fix this by adding a tag to the GitHub repository:

```
$ git tag -a 'v1.0.0' -m 'v1.0.0'
$ git push --tags
```

Note   If you think I'm cheating by skimming over this Git stuff, you're right. I cover both Git and GitHub in some detail in Chapter 17.

Now Packagist knows about my version number. You can confirm that in Figure 16-3.

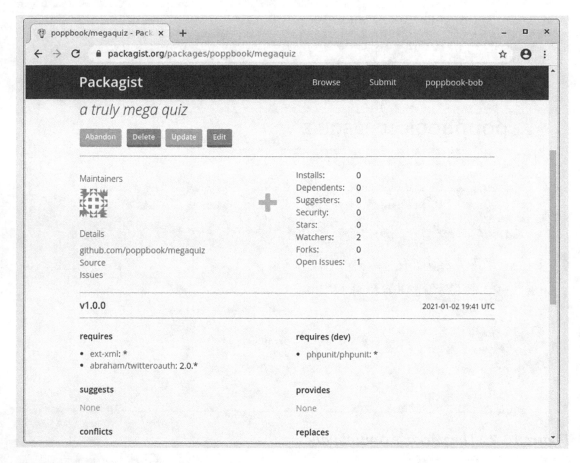

Figure 16-3. *Packagist knows the version*

Now, anyone can include `megaquiz` from another package. Here is a minimal `composer.json` file:

```
{
    "require": {
        "poppbook/megaquiz": "*"
    }
}
```

I specify the vendor name and the package name. Riskily, I am happy to accept any version at all. Let's go ahead and install:

```
$ composer update

Loading composer repositories with package information
Updating dependencies
Lock file operations: 3 installs, 0 updates, 0 removals
  - Locking abraham/twitteroauth (2.0.1)
  - Locking composer/ca-bundle (1.2.8)
  - Locking poppbook/megaquiz (v1.0.0)
Writing lock file
Installing dependencies from lock file (including require-dev)
Package operations: 3 installs, 0 updates, 0 removals
  - Installing composer/ca-bundle (1.2.8): Extracting archive
  - Installing abraham/twitteroauth (2.0.1): Extracting archive
  - Installing poppbook/megaquiz (v1.0.0): Extracting archive
  Generating autoload files
```

Notice that the dependencies I specified when I set up megaquiz are also downloaded.

Keeping It Private

Of course, you don't always want to publish your code to the world. Sometimes, you need to share only with a smaller set of authorized users.

Here is a private package named getinstance/wtnlang-php which contains a library for a scripting language:

```
{
    "name": "getinstance/wtnlang-php",
    "description": "it's a wtn language",
    "license": "private",
    "authors": [
        {
            "name": "matt zandstra",
            "email": "matt@getinstance.com"
        }
    ],
```

```
    "autoload":  {
        "psr-4": {
            "getinstance\\wtnlang\\": ["src/", "test/unit"]
        }
    },
    "require": {
        "abraham/twitteroauth": "*",
        "aura/cli": "~2.1.0",
        "monolog/monolog": "^1.23"
    },
    "require-dev": {
        "phpunit/phpunit": "^7"
    }
}
```

This is hosted in a private Bitbucket repository, so it's not available via Packagist. So how would I include it in a project? I simply need to tell Composer where to look. I can do this by creating or adding to the repositories element:

```
{
    "repositories": [
        {
            "type": "vcs",
            "url": "git@bitbucket.org:getinstance/wtnlang-php.git"
        }
    ],
    "require": {
        "poppbook/megaquiz": "*",
        "getinstance/wtnlang-php": "dev-develop"
    }
}
```

I could have specified a version for getinstance/wtnlang-php in the require block and that would correspond to a tag in the git repository, but, by using the dev- prefix, I can call for a branch. This is very useful during development. So now, so long as I have access to getinstance/wtnlang-php, I can install both my private package and megaquiz at once:

```
$ composer update

Loading composer repositories with package information
Updating dependencies
Nothing to modify in lock file
Installing dependencies from lock file (including require-dev)
Package operations: 7 installs, 0 updates, 0 removals
  - Installing composer/ca-bundle (1.2.8): Extracting archive
  - Installing psr/log (1.1.3): Extracting archive
  - Installing monolog/monolog (1.26.0): Extracting archive
  - Installing aura/cli (2.1.2): Extracting archive
  - Installing abraham/twitteroauth (2.0.1): Extracting archive
  - Installing getinstance/wtnlang-php (dev-develop de3bf14): Cloning
    de3bf1456c
  - Installing poppbook/megaquiz (v1.0.0): Extracting archive Generating
    autoload files
```

Summary

You should leave this chapter with a sense of how easy it is to leverage Composer packages to add power to your projects. Through the composer.json file, you can also make your code accessible to other users, whether publicly by using Packagist or by specifying your own repository. This approach automates dependency downloads for your users and allows third-party packages to use yours without the need for bundling.

CHAPTER 17

Version Control with Git

All disasters have their tipping point, the moment at which order finally breaks down and events simply spiral out of control. Do you ever find yourself in projects like that? Are you able to spot that crucial moment?

Perhaps it's when you make "just a couple of changes" and find that you have brought everything crashing down around you (and, even worse, you're not quite sure how to get back to the point of stability you have just destroyed). It could be when you realize that three members of your team have been working on the same set of classes and merrily saving over each other's work. Or perhaps it's when you discover that a bug fix that you have implemented twice has somehow disappeared from the codebase yet again. Wouldn't it be nice if there were a tool to help you manage collaborative working, allowing you to take snapshots of your projects, roll them back if necessary, and then merge multiple strands of development? In this chapter, we look at Git, a tool that does all that, and more.

This chapter will cover the following aspects of working with Git:

- *Basic configuration*: Exploring some tips for setting up Git

- *Importing*: Starting a new project

- *Committing changes*: Saving your work to the repository

- *Updating*: Merging other people's work with your own

- *Branching*: Maintaining parallel strands of development

Why Use Version Control?

If it hasn't already, version control will change your life (if only your life as a developer). How many times have you reached a stable moment in a project, drawn a breath, and plunged onward into development chaos once again? How easy was it to revert to the

© Matt Zandstra 2021
M. Zandstra, *PHP 8 Objects, Patterns, and Practice*, https://doi.org/10.1007/978-1-4842-6791-2_17

stable version when it came time to demonstrate your work in progress? Of course, you may have saved a snapshot of your project when it reached a stable moment, probably by duplicating your development directory. Now imagine that your colleague is working on the same codebase. Perhaps he has saved a stable copy of the code as you have. The difference is that his copy is a snapshot of his work, not yours. Of course, he has a messy development directory, too. So you have four versions of your project to coordinate. Now imagine a project with four programmers and a web UI developer. You're looking pale. Perhaps you would like to lie down?

Git exists exclusively to address this problem. Using Git, all of your developers can clone their own copies of the codebase from a central repository. Whenever they reach a stable point in their code, they can pull the latest code from the server and merge it with their own recent work. When they are ready, and after they have fixed any conflicts and run all tests, they can push their new stable synthesis back into the shared repository.

Git is a distributed version control system. This means that, once they have acquired a branch, users commit to their own local repository without the need for a network connection. There are a number of benefits to this. It means that day-to-day operations are faster and that you can work easily on planes and trains and in automobiles. Ultimately, however, you can share an authoritative repository with your teammates.

The fact that each developer can merge her work into a central repository means that reconciling multiple strands of development is made vastly easier. Even better, you can check out versions of your codebase based on a date or a label. So when your code reaches a stable point, suitable for showing to a client as work in progress, for example, you can tag that with an arbitrary label. You can then use that tag to check out the correct codebase when your client swoops into your office looking to impress an investor.

Wait! There's more! You can also manage multiple strands of development at the same time. If this sounds needlessly complicated, imagine a mature project. You have already shipped the first version, and you're well into development of version 2. Does version 1._n_ go away in the meantime? Of course not. Your users are spotting bugs and requesting enhancements all the time. You may be months away from shipping version 2, so where do you make and test the changes? Git lets you maintain distinct branches of the codebase. So you might create a bug fix branch of your version 1._n_ for development on the current production code. At key points, this branch can be merged back into the version 2 code (the trunk), so that your new release can benefit from improvements to version 1._n_.

Note   Git is not the only version control system available. You might also like to look into Subversion (`http://subversion.apache.org/`) or Mercurial (`http://mercurial.selenic.com/`). This chapter is necessarily a brief introduction to a large topic. Luckily, however, *Pro Git* by Scott Chacon (Apress, 2014) covers the topic with depth and clarity. Not only that, but a web version is available online at `https://git-scm.com/book/en/v2`.

Let's get on and look at some of these features in practice.

Getting Git

If you are working with a Unix-like operating system (such as Linux or FreeBSD), you may already have Git installed and ready to use.

Note   I show commands that are input at the command line with a leading dollar sign ($) to represent the command prompt to distinguish them from any output they may produce.

Try typing this from the command line:

```
$ git help
```

You should see some usage information that will confirm that you are ready to get started. If you do not already have Git, you should consult your distribution's documentation. You will almost certainly have access to a simple installation mechanism such as Yum or Apt, or you can acquire Git directly from `http://git-scm.com/downloads`.

Note   Technical editor Paul Tregoing also recommends Git for Windows (`https://gitforwindows.org/`) which comes with Git, naturally, but also a set of useful open source tools.

Using an Online Git Repository

You may have noticed by now that this book often goes it alone. I almost never argue that you should reinvent the wheel; rather, you should at least get a sense of what goes into wheel construction before buying one ready-made. For this reason, I'll be covering the mechanics of setting up and maintaining your own central git repository in the next section. Let's get real, though. You'll almost certainly use a specialized host to manage your repositories. There are a number of these to choose from, though the biggest players are probably Bitbucket (`https://bitbucket.org`), GitHub (`https://github.org`), and GitLab (`https://about.gitlab.com/`).

So, which should you choose? As a rule of thumb, GitHub is probably the standard for open source products. So, I'll sign up with GitHub for my project. Figure 17-1 shows my next decision, which is between a public and a private repository. I'll opt for a public project (because I'm creating an open source project).

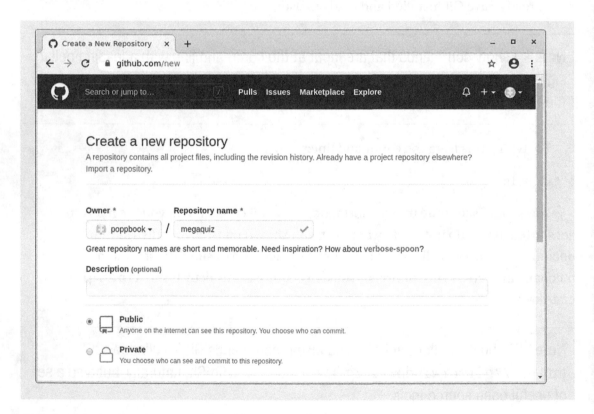

Figure 17-1. *Getting started with a GitHub project*

As you can see, in Figure 17-1, I have not quite finished typing megaquiz. At this point, GitHub offers some helpful instructions for importing my project. You can see those in Figure 17-2.

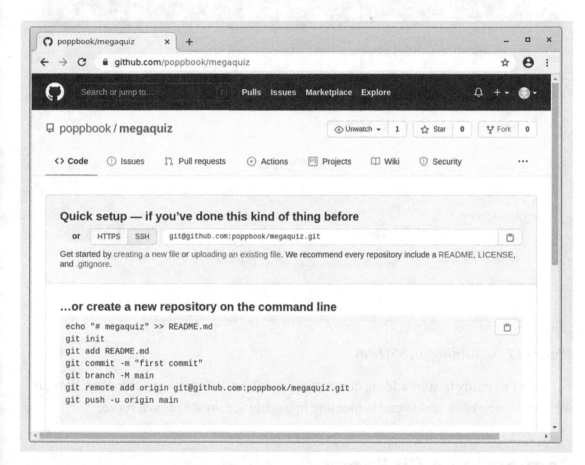

Figure 17-2. *GitHub's import instructions*

I'm not ready to run those commands yet, though. GitHub needs to be able to validate me when I push files to the server. In order to do that, it requires my public key. I describe one way of generating such a key in the next section, "Configuring a Git Server." Once I have a public key, I can add it from the SSH and GPG keys link in GitHub's User Settings screen.

You can see GitHub's settings screen for SSH and GPG keys in Figure 17-3.

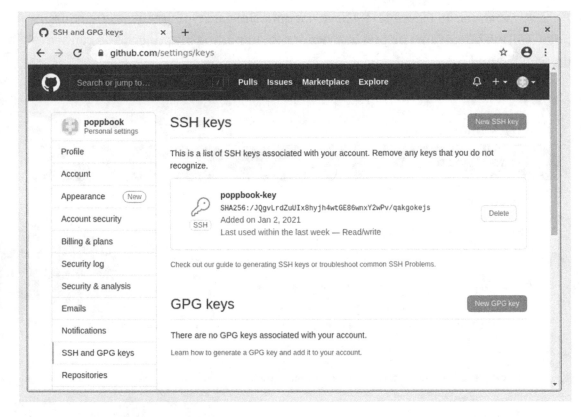

Figure 17-3. *Adding an SSH key*

Now I'm ready to start adding files to my repository. Before we get into that, though, we should step back and spend some time following the do-it-yourself route.

Configuring a Git Server

Git is different from traditional version control systems in two key ways. First, under the hood, it stores snapshots of files rather than the changes made to files between commits. Second, and more obviously to the user, it operates locally to your system until you choose to push to or pull from a remote repository. This means that you are not dependent on an Internet connection to get on with your work.

You do not need a single remote repository in order to work with Git; but in practice, it almost always makes sense to have a shared source of authority if you are working with a team.

In this section, I look at the steps needed to get a remote Git server up and running. I assume root access to a Linux machine.

Creating the Remote Repository

In order to create a Git repository, I must first create a containing directory. I log in to a freshly provisioned remote server via SSH. I am going to create my repository under /var/git. Generally speaking, only the root user can create and modify directories there, so I run the following command using sudo:

```
$ sudo mkdir -p /var/git/megaquiz
$ cd /var/git/megaquiz/
```

I create /var/git, a parent directory for my repositories and a subdirectory for a sample project called megaquiz. Now I can prepare the directory itself:

```
$ sudo git init --bare
```

```
Initialized empty Git repository in /var/git/megaquiz/
```

The --bare flag tells Git to initialize a repository without a working directory. Git will complain if you try to push to a repository that has not been created in this way.

At the moment, only the root user can mess around under /var/git. I can change this by creating a user and a group named git and making it the directory's owner:

```
$ sudo adduser git
$ sudo chown -R git:git /var/git
```

Preparing the Repository for Local Users

Although this is a designated remote server, I should also ensure that local users can commit to the repository. If you're not careful, this can cause ownership and permissions issues (especially if users with sudo privileges push code).

```
$ sudo chmod -R g+rws /var/git
```

This gives members of the git group write access to /var/git and causes all files and directories created here to take on the git group. Now, as long as I ensure that they are members of the git group, local users will be able to write to the repository. Not only that, any files created will be writable by other members of the group.

You can add a local user to the git group like this:

```
$ sudo usermod -aG git bob
```

Now user bob is a member of the git group.

619

Providing Access to Users

The owner of the bob user mentioned in the previous section can log in to the server and interact with the repository from his shell. Generally, though, you won't want to provide shell access to all your users. In any case, most users will prefer to take advantage of Git's distributed nature and to work locally with their cloned data.

One way to grant a user SSH access is via public key authentication. To do this, you first need to acquire the user's public SSH key. The user may already have this—on a Linux machine, he will probably find the key in the configuration directory, .ssh, in a file named id_rsa.pub. Otherwise, he can easily generate a new key. On a Unix-like machine, this is a matter of running the ssh-keygen command and copying the value that it generates:

```
$ ssh-keygen
$ cat .ssh/id_rsa.pub
```

As the repository administrator, I will have asked you for a copy of this key. Once I have it, I must add it to the git user's SSH setup on the repository server. This is merely a matter of pasting the public key into the .ssh/authorized_keys file. I may need to create the .ssh configuration directory for the first key I set up (I am running these commands from the git user's home directory):

```
$ mkdir .ssh
$ chmod 0700 .ssh
# create authorized_keys file and paste in the user's key:
$ vi .ssh/authorized_keys
$ chmod 0700 .ssh/authorized_keys
```

Note   A common cause of SSH access failure is the creation of configuration files with overly liberal permissions. The SSH configuration environment should be readable and writable to the account's owner only. *Pro OpenSSH* by Michael Stahnke (Apress, 2005) covers SSH comprehensively.

Closing Down Shell Access for the git User

No server should be any more open than it needs to be. You may want to enable your user to access Git commands, but probably not much more.

You can see the shell associated with a user on a Linux server by looking at the file, /etc/passwd. Here is the relevant line for the git account on my remote server:

```
git:x:1001:1001::/home/git:/bin/bash
```

Git provides a special shell, named git-shell, that restricts the user to selected commands only. I can enable this program for logins by editing /etc/passwd:

```
git:x:1001:1001::/home/git:/usr/bin/git-shell
```

Now, if I attempt to log in via SSH, I'm told the score and logged out:

```
$ ssh git@poppch17.vagrant.internal
```

```
Last login: Thu Dec 31 14:25:05 2020 from 192.168.33.1
fatal: Interactive git shell is not enabled.
hint: ~/git-shell-commands should exist and have read and execute access.
Connection to 192.168.33.71 closed.
```

Beginning a Project

Now that I have a remote Git server and access to it from my local account, it's time to add my work in progress to the repository at /var/git/megaquiz.

Before I start, I take a good look at my files and directories and remove any temporary items I might find.

Failure to do this is a common annoyance. Temporary items to watch for include automatically generated files such as composer packages, build directories, installer logs, and so on.

Note   You can specify files and patterns to ignore by placing a file named
`.gitignore` in your repository. On a Linux system, the `man gitignore`
command should provide examples of filename wildcarding that you can amend
to exclude the various lock files and temporary directories created by your build
processes, editors, and IDEs. This text is also available online at `http://git-`
`scm.com/docs/gitignore`.

Before I go any further, I should register my identity with Git—this makes it easier to
track who did what in the repository:

```
$ git config --global user.name "poppbook"
$ git config --global user.email "poppbook@getinstance.com"
```

Now that I have established my personal details and ensured that my project is clean,
I can set it up and push its code to the server:

```
$ cd /home/mattz/work/megaquiz
$ git init
```

```
Initialized empty Git repository in /home/mattz/work/megaquiz/.git/
```

Now it's time to add my files:

```
$ git add .
```

Git is now tracking all the files and directories under `megaquiz`. Tracked files can
be in three states: *unmodified, modified,* or *staged.* You can check this by running the
command `git status`:

```
$ git status
```

```
# On branch master
#
# Initial commit
#
# Changes to be committed:
#   (use "git rm --cached <file>..." to unstage)
#
```

```
#      new file:    composer.json
#      new file:    composer.lock
#      new file:    main.php
#      new file:    src/command/Command.php
#      new file:    src/command/CommandContext.php
#      new file:    src/command/FeedbackCommand.php
#      new file:    src/command/LoginCommand.php
#      new file:    src/quizobjects/User.php
#      new file:    src/quiztools/AccessManager.php
#      new file:    src/quiztools/ReceiverFactory.php
#
```

Thanks to my previous `git add` command, all my files are staged for commit. I can go ahead now and execute the `commit` command:

```
$ git commit -m'my first commit'

[master (root-commit) a5ca2d4] my first commit
 10 files changed, 1638 insertions(+)
 create mode 100644 composer.json
 create mode 100644 composer.lock
 create mode 100755 main.php
 create mode 100755 src/command/Command.php
 create mode 100755 src/command/CommandContext.php
 create mode 100755 src/command/FeedbackCommand.php
 create mode 100755 src/command/LoginCommand.php
 create mode 100755 src/quizobjects/User.php
 create mode 100755 src/quiztools/AccessManager.php
 create mode 100644 src/quiztools/ReceiverFactory.php
```

I add a message via the -m flag. If I omitted this, then Git would launch an editor that I can use to add my check-in message.

If you are accustomed to version control systems such as CVS and Subversion, you might think that we're done. And although I could happily continue editing, adding, committing, and branching from here, there is an additional stage I need to consider if I want to share this code using a central repository. As we will see later on in the chapter, Git allows us to manage multiple project branches. Thanks to this feature, I can maintain a branch for each release, but also keep my bleeding-edge risky development safely out of my production code. When we start out, Git sets up a single branch named master. I can confirm the state of my branches with the command git branch:

```
$ git branch -a
```

```
* master
```

The -a flag specifies that Git should show us all branches (the default is to omit the remote ones). And the output shows the master branch.

In fact, I have done nothing yet to associate my local repository with the remote server. It's time to put that right:

```
$ git remote add origin git@poppch17.vagrant.internal:/var/git/megaquiz
```

This command is disappointingly quiet, given the work that it has done. In fact, it is the equivalent of telling Git to "associate the nickname origin with the given server location. Furthermore, set up a tracking relationship between the local branch master and a remote equivalent."

To confirm all of this, I check with Git that the remote handle origin has been set up:

```
$ git remote -v
```

```
origin git@poppch17.vagrant.internal:/var/git/megaquiz (fetch)
origin git@poppch17.vagrant.internal:/var/git/megaquiz (push)
```

Of course, if you used a service like GitHub, you would use your equivalent of the git remote add step shown in Figure 17-2. In my case, that looks like this:

```
$ git remote add origin git@github.com:poppbook/megaquiz.git
```

Do not run the preceding command, though, unless you really want to push to my GitHub repo! I am sticking to my self-hosted Git repository for now.

I still haven't sent any actual files to my Git server, however, so that's my next step:

```
$ git push origin master
Counting objects: 16, done.
Delta compression using up to 2 threads.
Compressing objects: 100% (15/15), done.
Writing objects: 100% (16/16), 8.87 KiB | 0 bytes/s, done.
```

```
Total 16 (delta 2), reused 0 (delta 0)
remote: Resolving deltas: 100% (2/2), done.
To git@github.com:poppbook/megaquiz.git
* [new branch] master -> master
```

Now I can run the git branch command again to confirm that the remote version of the master branch has appeared:

```
$ git branch -a
```

```
* master
  remotes/origin/master
```

Or, to see only the remote branches:

```
$ git branch -r
```

```
  origin/master
```

Note   I have established what is called a *tracking branch*. This is a local branch that is associated with a remote twin.

Cloning the Repository

For the purposes of this chapter, I have invented a team member named Bob. Bob is working with me on the MegaQuiz project. Naturally, he wants his own version of the code. I have already added his public key to the Git server, so he is good to go. In the parallel world of GitHub, I have invited Bob to join my project, and he has added his own public key to his account. The effect is the same; Bob can acquire the repository using the command git clone:

```
$ git clone git@github.com:poppbook/megaquiz.git
```

```
Cloning into 'megaquiz'...
remote: Enumerating objects: 16, done.
remote: Counting objects: 100% (16/16), done.
remote: Compressing objects: 100% (13/13), done.
```

```
remote: Total 16 (delta 2), reused 16 (delta 2), pack-reused 0
Receiving objects: 100% (16/16), 8.87 KiB | 0 bytes/s, done.
Resolving deltas: 100% (2/2), done.
```

Now both of us can develop locally and, when we're ready, share our code with one another.

Updating and Committing

Bob is, of course, a fine and talented fellow—except, that is, for one common and highly annoying trait: he cannot leave other people's code alone.

Bob is smart and inquisitive, easily excited by shiny new avenues of development, and he's keen to help optimize new code. As a result, everywhere I turn, I seem to see the hand of Bob. Bob has added to my documentation, and he has implemented an idea I mentioned over coffee. I may have to kill Bob. In the meantime, however, I must handle the fact that the code on which I am working needs to be merged with Bob's input.

Here's a file called `quizobjects/User.php`. At the moment, it contains nothing but the barest of bones:

```php
namespace poppbook\megaquiz\quizobjects;
class User
{
}
```

I have decided to add some documentation. I begin by adding a file comment to my version of the file:

```php
namespace popp\ch17\megaquiz\quizobjects;

/**
 * @license http://www.example.com Borsetshire Open License
 * @package quizobjects
 */

class User
{
}
```

Remember that a file can have three states: *unmodified, modified,* and *staged.* The User.php file has now moved from *unmodified* to *modified.* I can see this with the git status command:

```
$ git status

# On branch master
# Changes not staged for commit:
#   (use "git add <file>..." to update what will be committed)
#   (use "git checkout -- <file>..." to discard changes in working directory)
#
#       modified: src/quizobjects/User.php
#
no changes added to commit (use "git add" and/or "git commit -a")
```

User.php has been modified, but not yet staged for commit. I can change this state using the command git add:

```
$ git add src/quizobjects/User.php
$ git status

# On branch master
# Changes to be committed:
#   (use "git reset HEAD <file>..." to unstage)
#
#       modified: src/quizobjects/User.php
#
```

Now I am ready to commit:

```
$ git commit -m'added documentation' src/quizobjects/User.php

[master 997622c] added documentation
1 file changed, 5 insertions(+)
```

A Git commit only affects my local repository. If I am sure that the world is ready for my change, I must push my code to the remote repository:

```
$ git push origin master
Counting objects: 9, done.
Delta compression using up to 2 threads.
Compressing objects: 100% (4/4), done.
Writing objects: 100% (5/5), 537 bytes | 0 bytes/s, done.
Total 5 (delta 1), reused 0 (delta 0)
remote: Resolving deltas: 100% (1/1), completed with 1 local object.
To git@github.com:poppbook/megaquiz.git
   ce5a604..997622c master -> master
```

Meanwhile, working in his own sandbox, Bob is keen as ever, and he has created a class comment:

```
namespace popp\ch17\megaquiz\quizobjects;

/**
 * @package quizobjects
 */

class User
{
}
```

Now it's Bob's turn to add, commit, and push. Because the adding and committing parts of this are so commonly run together, Git allows you to combine them into a single command:

```
$ git commit -a -m'my great documentation'

[master 13de456] my great documentation
 1 file changed, 4 insertions(+)
```

So we now have two distinct versions of User.php. There's the version I just pushed to the remote repository, and there is Bob's version, committed, but not yet pushed. Let's see what happens when Bob tries to push his local version to the remote repository:

```
$ git push origin master

To git@github.com:poppbook/megaquiz.git
 ! [rejected]        master -> master (fetch first)
error: failed to push some refs to 'git@github.com:poppbook/megaquiz.git'
```

```
hint: Updates were rejected because the remote contains work that you do
hint: not have locally. This is usually caused by another repository pushing
hint: to the same ref. You may want to first merge the remote changes (e.g.,
hint: 'git pull') before pushing again.
hint: See the 'Note about fast-forwards' in 'git push --help' for details.
```

As you can see, Git won't let you push if there's an update to apply. Bob must first pull down my version of the User.php file:

```
$ git pull origin master
```

```
remote: Enumerating objects: 9, done.
remote: Counting objects: 100% (9/9), done.
remote: Compressing objects: 100% (3/3), done.
remote: Total 5 (delta 1), reused 5 (delta 1), pack-reused 0 Unpacking
objects: 100% (5/5), done.
From github.com:poppbook/megaquiz
 * branch               master        -> FETCH_HEAD
Auto-merging src/quizobjects/User.php
CONFLICT (content): Merge conflict in src/quizobjects/User.php
Automatic merge failed; fix conflicts and then commit the result.
```

Git will happily merge data from two sources into the same file, so long as the changes don't overlap. Git has no means of handling changes that affect the same lines. How can it decide what is to have priority? Should the repository overwrite Bob's changes, or the other way around? Should both changes coexist? Which should go first? Git has no choice but to report a conflict and let Bob sort out the problem.

Here's what Bob sees when he opens the file:

```
/**
<<<<<<< HEAD
 * @package quizobjects
 */
=======
 * @license http://www.example.com Borsetshire Open License
 * @package quizobjects
 */
>>>>>>> f36c6244521dbd137b37b76414e3cea2071958d2
```

```
namespace poppbook\megaquiz\quizobjects;

class User
{
}
```

Git includes both Bob's comment and the conflicting changes, together with metadata that tells him which part originates where. The conflicting information is separated by a line of equals signs. Bob's input is signaled by a line of less than symbols followed by "HEAD". The remote changes are included on the other side of the divide.

Now that Bob has identified the conflict, he can edit the file to fix the collision:

```
/**
 * @package quizobjects
 * @license http://www.example.com Borsetshire Open License
 * @package quizobjects
 */

namespace poppbook\megaquiz\quizobjects;

class User
{
}
```

Next, Bob resolves the conflict by staging the file:

```
$ git add src/quizobjects/User.php
$ git commit -m'documentation merged'

[master c99d3f5] documentation merged
```

And now, finally, he can push to the remote repository:

```
$ git push origin master
```

Adding and Removing Files and Directories

Projects change shape as they develop. Version control software must take account of this, allowing users to add new files and remove deadwood that would otherwise get in the way.

Adding a File

You have seen the add subcommand many times already. I used it during my project setup to add my code to the empty megaquiz repository and, subsequently, to stage files for commit. By running git add on an untracked file or directory, you ask Git to track it—and stage it for commit. Here, I add a document called CompositeQuestion.php to the project:

```
$ touch src/quizobjects/CompositeQuestion.php
$ git add src/quizobjects/CompositeQuestion.php
```

In a real-world situation, I would probably start out by adding some content to CompositeQuestion.php. Here, I confine myself to creating an empty file using the standard touch command. Once I have added a document, I must still invoke the commit subcommand to complete the addition:

```
$ git commit -m'initial check in'

[master 323bec3] initial check in
 1 file changed, 0 insertions(+), 0 deletions(-)
 create mode 100644 src/quizobjects/CompositeQuestion.php
```

CompositeQuestion.php is now in the local repository.

Removing a File

Should I discover that I have been too hasty and need to remove the document, it should come as no surprise to learn that I can use a subcommand called rm:

```
$ git rm src/quizobjects/CompositeQuestion.php
rm 'src/quizobjects/CompositeQuestion.php'
```

Once again, a commit is required to finish the job. As usual, I can confirm this by running git status:

```
$ git status

# On branch master
# Your branch is ahead of 'origin/master' by 1 commit.
#   (use "git push" to publish your local commits)
```

```
#
# Changes to be committed:
#   (use "git reset HEAD <file>..." to unstage)
#
#        deleted:    src/quizobjects/CompositeQuestion.php
#

$ git commit -m'removed Question'

[master 5bf88aa] removed CompositeQuestion
 1 file changed, 0 insertions(+), 0 deletions(-)
 delete mode 100644 src/quizobjects/CompositeQuestion.php
```

Adding a Directory

You can also add and remove directories with add and rm. Let's say Bob wants to make a new directory available:

```
$ mkdir resources
$ touch resources/blah.gif
$ git add resources/
$ git status

# On branch master
# Changes to be committed:
#   (use "git reset HEAD <file>..." to unstage)
#
#        new file: resources/blah.gif
#
```

Notice how the contents of resources are added automatically to the repository. Now Bob can commit and then push the whole lot to the remote repository in the usual way.

Note   Be careful of using git add with directories; it is greedy! The command will pick up any files and directories beneath the given directory. It is always a good idea to check the operation with git status.

Removing Directories

As you might expect, you can remove directories with the rm subcommand. In this situation, however, I must tell Git that I wish it to remove the directory's contents by passing an -r flag to the subcommand. Here, I profoundly disagree with Bob's decision to add a resources directory:

```
$ git rm -r resources/
rm 'resources/blah.gif'
```

Tagging a Release

All being well, a project will eventually reach a state of readiness, and you will want to ship it or deploy it. Whenever you make a release, you should leave a bookmark in your repository, so that you can always revisit the code at that point. As you might expect, you can create a tag in your code with the git tag command:

```
git tag -a 'v1.0.0' -m'release 1.0.0'
```

You can see the tags associated with your repository by running git tag with no arguments:

```
$ git tag
v1.0.0
```

We have been working locally up until this point. In order to get the tag onto the remote repository, we must use the --tags flag with the git push subcommand:

```
$ git push origin --tags

Counting objects: 1, done.
Writing objects: 100% (1/1), 159 bytes | 0 bytes/s, done.
Total 1 (delta 0), reused 0 (delta 0)
To git@github.com:poppbook/megaquiz.git
 * [new tag]         v1.0.0 -> v1.0.0
```

Using the --tags flag causes all local tags to be pushed to the remote repository.

Of course, any action you take on a GitHub repo can be tracked on the site. You can see my release tag in Figure 17-4.

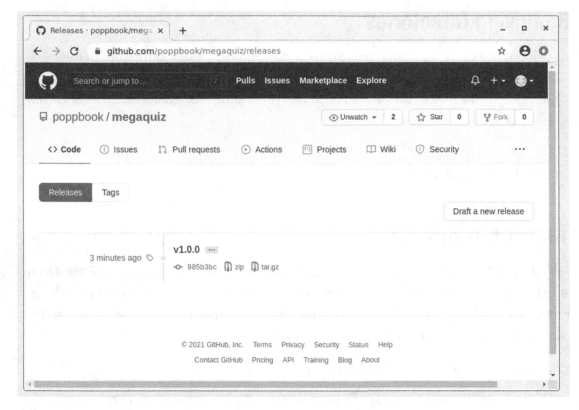

Figure 17-4. *Viewing a tag on GitHub*

Once you can bookmark your code with a tag, it makes sense to wonder how you might go about revisiting old releases. For this, however, you should first spend some time looking at branching—something at which Git is particularly good.

Branching a Project

Once my project has been released, I can pack it away and wander off to do something new, right? After all, it was so elegantly written that bugs are an impossibility, not to mention so thoroughly specified that no user could possibly require any new features!

Meanwhile, back in the real world, I must continue to work with the codebase on at least two levels. Bug reports should be trickling in right about now, and the wish list for version 1.2.0 will be swelling with demands for fantastic new features. How do I reconcile these forces? I need to fix the bugs as they are reported, and I need to push on with primary development. I could fix the bugs as part of development and release everything in one go, when the next version is stable. But then users may have a long wait before they see any problems addressed. This is plainly unacceptable. On the other hand, I could release as I go. In that scenario, I risk shipping broken code. Clearly, I need two strands to my development. I will continue to add new and risky features to the project's main branch (often called the trunk), but I should now create a branch for my new release on which I can add only bug fixes.

Note   This way of managing branches is by no means the only game in town. Developers argue constantly about the best way of organizing branches and managing releases and bug fixes. One of the most popular approaches is git-flow (neatly described at `https://danielkummer.github.io/git-flow-cheatsheet/`). Under this practice, `master` is the release branch. New code goes on a `develop` branch, and it's merged to `master` at release time. Each unit of active development has its own feature branch, which gets merged into `develop` when stable.

I can both create and switch to a new branch using the `git checkout` command. First, let's take a quick look at the state of my branches:

```
$ git branch -a
```

```
* master
  remotes/origin/master
```

As you can see, I have a single branch, `master`, and its remote equivalent. Now, I will create and switch to a new branch:

```
$ git checkout -b megaquiz-branch1.0
Switched to a new branch 'megaquiz-branch1.0'
```

To track my use of branches, I will use a particular file as an example, `src/command/FeedbackCommand.php`. It seems that I created my bug fix branch just in time. Users have started to report that they are unable to use the feedback mechanism in the system. I locate the bug:

```
//...
$result = $msgSystem->despatch($email, $msg, $topic);
if (! $user) {
    $this->context->setError($msgSystem->getError());
//...
```

I should, in fact, be testing $result and not $user. Here is my edit:

```
//...
$result = $msgSystem->dispatch($email, $msg, $topic);
if (! $result)  {
    $this->context->setError($msgSystem->getError());
//...
```

Because I am working on the branch megaquiz-branch1.0, I can commit this change:

```
$ git add src/command/FeedbackCommand.php
$ git commit -m'bugfix'
```

```
[megaquiz-branch1.0 6e56ade] bugfix
 1 file changed, 1 insertion(+), 1 deletion(-)
```

Of course, this commit is local. I need to use the git push command to get the branch onto the remote repository:

```
$ git push origin megaquiz-branch1.0
```

```
Counting objects: 9, done.
Delta compression using up to 2 threads.
Compressing objects: 100% (5/5), done.
Writing objects: 100% (5/5), 456 bytes | 0 bytes/s, done.
Total 5 (delta 3), reused 0 (delta 0)
remote: Resolving deltas: 100% (3/3), completed with 3 local objects. remote:
remote: Create a pull request for 'megaquiz-branch1.0' on GitHub by visiting:
remote: https://github.com/poppbook/megaquiz/pull/new/megaquiz-branch1.0
remote:
To git@github.com:poppbook/megaquiz.git
 * [new branch]     megaquiz-branch1.0 -> megaquiz-branch1.0
```

Now, what about Bob? He will inevitably want to pitch in and fix some bugs. First, he invokes git fetch, which acquires any new information from the server. Then he can look at all available branches with git branch -a.

```
$ git fetch
$ git branch -a
```

```
* master
  remotes/origin/HEAD -> origin/master
  remotes/origin/master
  remotes/origin/megaquiz-branch1.0
```

Now Bob can switch to a local branch which will track the remote one:

```
$ git checkout megaquiz-branch1.0
```

```
Branch megaquiz-branch1.0 set up to track remote branch megaquiz-branch1.0
from origin.
Switched to a new branch 'megaquiz-branch1.0'
```

Bob is good to go now. He can add and commit his own fixes; and when he pushes, they will end up on the remote branch.

Meanwhile, I would like to add some bleeding-edge enhancements on the trunk—that is, my master branch. Let's look again at the state of my branches from the perspective of my local repository:

```
$ git branch -a
```

```
  master
* megaquiz-branch1.0
  remotes/origin/master
  remotes/origin/megaquiz-branch1.0
```

I can switch to an existing branch by invoking git checkout:

```
$ git checkout master
```

```
Switched to branch 'master'
Your branch is up-to-date with 'origin/master'.
```

When I look now at command/FeedbackCommand.php, I see that my bug fix has magically disappeared. Of course, it's still stored under megaquiz-branch1.0. Later, I can merge the fix into the master branch, so there's no need to worry. Instead, I can focus on adding new code:

```
class FeedbackCommand extends Command
{

    public function execute(CommandContext $context): bool
    {

        // new and risky development
        // goes here

        $msgSystem = ReceiverFactory::getMessageSystem();
        $email = $context->get('email');

        // ...
```

All I have done here is to add a comment to simulate an addition to the code. I can now commit and push this:

```
$ git commit -am'new development on master'
$ git push origin master
```

So I now have parallel branches. Of course, sooner or later, I will want my master branch to benefit from the bug fixes that I have committed on `megaquiz-branch1.0`.

I can do this on the command line, but first let's pause to look at a feature supported by GitHub and similar services like Bitbucket. The pull request (often abbreviated to PR) allows me to request a code review before merging a branch. So before megaquiz-branch1.0 hits master, I can ask Bob to check my work. As you can see in Figure 17-5, GitHub detects the branch and gives me the opportunity to issue my pull request.

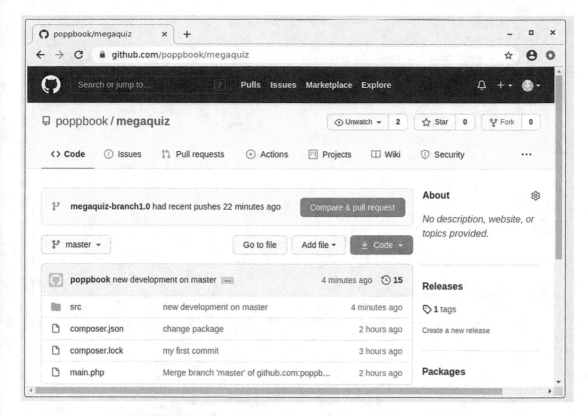

Figure 17-5. *GitHub makes issuing pull requests easy*

I hit the button and add a comment before submitting the pull request. You can see the result of that in Figure 17-6.

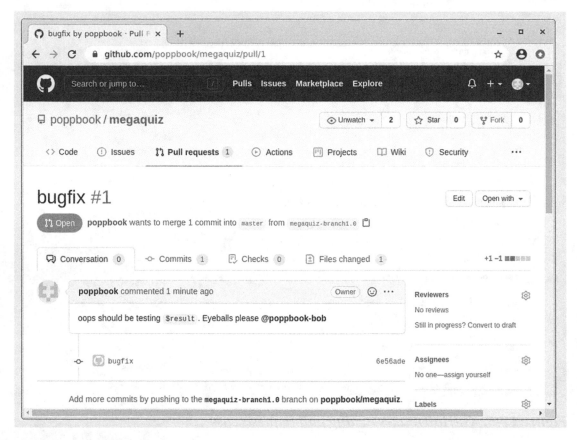

Figure 17-6. *Issuing the pull request*

Now Bob can examine my changes and add any comments he may have. GitHub shows him exactly what has changed. You can see Bob's comment in Figure 17-7.

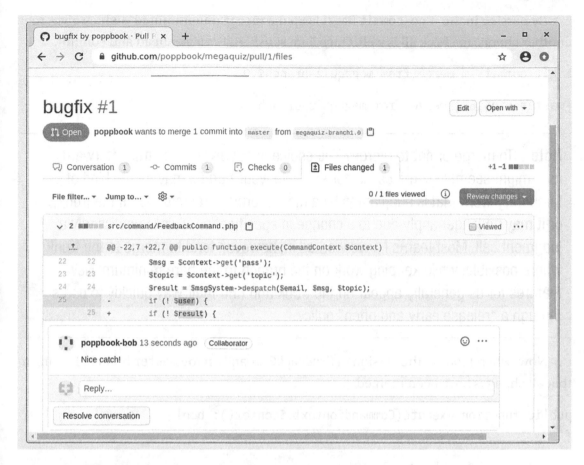

Figure 17-7. *The changes covered by a pull request*

Once Bob approves my pull request, I can merge directly from the browser, or I can return to the command line. This is pretty easy. Git provides a subcommand named merge:

```
$ git checkout master

Already on 'master'
```

In fact, I'm already on the master branch—but it can't hurt to be sure. Now I perform the actual merge:

```
$ git merge --no-commit megaquiz-branch1.0
Auto-merging src/command/FeedbackCommand.php
Automatic merge went well; stopped before committing as requested
```

By passing in the --no-commit flag, I keep the merge uncommitted—which gives me another chance to check all is well. Once I am satisfied, I can go ahead and commit.

```
$ git commit -m'merge from megaquiz-branch1.0'
```

```
[master e1b5169] merge from megaquiz-branch1.0
```

Note   To merge or not to merge? The choice is not always as straightforward as it might seem. In some cases, for example, your bug fix may be the kind of temporary work that is supplanted by a more thorough refactoring on the trunk, or it may no longer apply due to a change in specification. This is necessarily a judgment call. Most teams I have worked in, however, tend to merge to the trunk where possible, while keeping work on the branch to the bare minimum. New features for us generally appear on the trunk and find their way quickly to users through a "release early and often" policy.

Now, when I look at the version of FeedbackCommand on the master branch, I confirm that all changes have been merged:

```
public function execute(CommandContext $context): bool
{

    // new and risky development
    // goes here

    $msgSystem = ReceiverFactory::getMessageSystem();
    $email = $context->get('email');
    $msg = $context->get('pass');
    $topic = $context->get('topic');
    $result = $msgSystem->despatch($email, $msg, $topic);
    if (! $result) {
        $this->context->setError($msgSystem->getError());
        return false;
    }
```

The execute() method now includes both my simulated master development and the bug fix.

I created a branch when I first "released" MegaQuiz version 1.0 and that's what we have been working with. Remember, however, that I also created a tag at that stage. I promised at the time that I would show you how to access the tag. In fact, you've already seen how. You can create a local branch based on the tag in just the same way that Bob set up his local version of our bug fix branch. The difference is that this new branch is entirely fresh. It does not track an existing remote branch:

```
$ git checkout -b v1.0.0-branch v1.0.0

Switched to a new branch 'v1.0.0-branch'
```

However, now that I have this new branch, I can push it and share it just as you have seen.

Note   Git is an amazingly versatile and useful tool. Like all powerful tools, its use can occasionally lead to unintended consequences. For those moments that you have backed yourself into a corner and need to reset things fast, tech editor Paul Tregoing recommends `https://dangitgit.com/en` (actually, he recommended the swearier version!). The site is full of recipes that might just save your sanity, so it is well worth bookmarking if you work seriously with Git.

Two other git commands that are worth having in your arsenal are `git stash` and `git stash apply`. When you are up to your ears in local edits but are called to switch branches, your first option is to commit your work in progress. You may not want to commit rough code, though. You might think that your only choice then is to throw away your local changes or copy them to temporary files. If you run `git stash`, however, all local changes are tucked away for you behind the scenes, and your branch is returned to its state at the last commit. You can go off and do your urgent work and, when you are ready, run `git stash apply` to get your uncommitted work back. It's like magic!

Summary

Git comprises an enormous number of tools, each with a daunting range of options and capabilities. I can only hope to provide a brief introduction in the space available. Nonetheless, if you only use the features that I have covered in this chapter, you should see the benefit in your own work, whether through protection against data loss or improvements in collaborative working.

In this chapter, we took a tour through the basics of Git. I looked briefly at configuration before importing a project. I checked out, committed, and updated code and then showed you how to tag and export a release. I ended the chapter with a brief look at branches, demonstrating their usefulness in maintaining concurrent development and bug fix strands in a project.

There is one issue that I have glossed over here, to some extent. We established the principle that developers should check out their own versions of a project. On the whole, however, projects will not run in place. In order to test their changes, developers need to deploy code locally. Sometimes, this is as simple as copying over a few directories. More often, however, deployment must address a whole range of configuration issues. In the next chapter, we will look at some techniques for automating this process.

CHAPTER 18

Testing with PHPUnit

Every component in a system depends for its continued smooth running on the consistency of operation and interface of its peers. By definition, then, development breaks systems. As you improve your classes and packages, you must remember to amend any code that works with them. For some changes, this can create a ripple effect, affecting components far away from the code you originally changed. Eagle-eyed vigilance and an encyclopedic knowledge of a system's dependencies can help to address this problem. Of course, while these are excellent virtues, systems soon grow too complex for every unwanted effect to be easily predicted, not least because systems often combine the work of many developers. To address this problem, it is a good idea to test every component regularly. This, of course, is a repetitive and complex task; and as such, it lends itself well to automation.

Among the test solutions available to PHP programmers, PHPUnit is perhaps the most ubiquitous and certainly the most fully featured tool. In this chapter, you will learn the following about PHPUnit:

- *Installation*: Using Composer to install PHPUnit

- *Writing tests*: Creating test cases and using assertion methods

- *Handling exceptions*: Strategies for confirming failure

- *Running multiple tests*: Collecting tests into suites

- *Constructing assertion logic*: Using constraints

- *Faking components*: Mocks and stubs

- *Testing web applications*: Testing with and without additional tools

© Matt Zandstra 2021
M. Zandstra, *PHP 8 Objects, Patterns, and Practice*, https://doi.org/10.1007/978-1-4842-6791-2_18

Functional Tests and Unit Tests

Testing is essential in any project. Even if you don't formalize the process, you must have found yourself developing informal lists of actions that put your system through its paces. This process soon becomes wearisome, and that can lead to a fingers-crossed attitude to your projects.

One approach to testing starts at the interface of a project, modeling the various ways in which a user might negotiate the system. This is probably the way you would go when testing by hand, although there are various frameworks for automating the process. These functional tests are sometimes called acceptance tests because a list of actions performed successfully can be used as criteria for signing off a project phase. Using this approach, you typically treat the system as a black box—your tests remain willfully ignorant of the hidden components that collaborate to form the system under test.

Whereas functional tests operate from without, unit tests work from the inside out. Unit testing tends to focus on classes, with test methods grouped together in test cases. Each test case puts one class through a rigorous workout, checking that each method performs as advertised and fails as it should. The objective, as far as possible, is to test each component in isolation from its wider context. This often supplies you with a sobering verdict on the success of your mission to decouple the parts of your system.

Tests can be run as part of the build process, directly from the command line, or even via a web page. In this chapter, I'll concentrate on the command line.

Unit testing is a good way of ensuring the quality of design in a system. Tests reveal the responsibilities of classes and functions. Some programmers even advocate a test-first approach. You should, they say, write the tests before you even begin work on a class. This lays down a class's purpose, ensuring a clean interface and short, focused methods. Personally, I have never aspired to this level of purity—it just doesn't suit my style of coding. Nevertheless, I attempt to write tests as I go. Maintaining a test harness provides me with the security I need to refactor my code. I can pull down and replace entire packages with the knowledge that I have a good chance of catching unexpected errors elsewhere in the system.

Testing by Hand

In the last section, I said that testing was essential in every project. I could have said instead that testing is *inevitable* in every project. We all test. The tragedy is that we often throw away this good work.

So, let's create some classes to test. Here is a class that stores and retrieves user information. For the sake of demonstration, it generates arrays rather than the User objects you'd normally expect to use:

```
// listing 18.01
class UserStore
{
    private array $users = [];

    public function addUser(string $name, string $mail, string $pass): bool
    {
        if (isset($this->users[$mail])) {
            throw new \Exception(
                "User {$mail} already in the system"
            );
        }

        if (strlen($pass) <  5) {
            throw new \Exception(
                "Password must have 5 or more letters"
            );
        }

        $this->users[$mail] = [
            'pass' => $pass,
            'mail' => $mail,
            'name' => $name
        ];

        return true;
    }

    public function notifyPasswordFailure(string $mail): void
    {
        if (isset($this->users[$mail])) {
            $this->users[$mail]['failed'] = time();
        }
    }
```

```
    public function getUser(string $mail): array
    {
        return ($this->users[$mail]);
    }
}
```

This class accepts user data with the addUser() method and retrieves it via getUser(). The user's email address is used as the key for retrieval. If you're like me, you'll write some sample implementation as you develop, just to check that things are behaving as you designed them:

```
// listing 18.02
$store = new UserStore();
$store->addUser(
    "bob williams",
    "bob@example.com",
    "12345"
);
$store->notifyPasswordFailure("bob@example.com");
$user = $store->getUser("bob@example.com");
print_r($user);
```

Here is the output:

```
Array
(
    [pass] => 12345
    [mail] => bob@example.com
    [name] => bob williams
    [failed] => 1609766967
)
```

This is the sort of thing that I might add to the foot of a file as I work on the class it contains. The test validation is performed manually, of course; it's up to me to eyeball the results and confirm that the data returned by UserStore::getUser() corresponds with the information I added initially. It's a test of sorts, nevertheless.

Here is a client class that uses UserStore to confirm that a user has provided the correct authentication information:

```
// listing 18.03
class Validator
{

    public function __construct(private UserStore $store)
    {
    }

    public function validateUser(string $mail, string $pass): bool
    {
        if (! is_array($user = $this->store->getUser($mail))) {
            return false;
        }

        if ($user['pass'] == $pass) {
            return  true;
        }

        $this->store->notifyPasswordFailure($mail);

        return false;
    }
}
```

The class requires a UserStore object, which it saves in the $store property. This property is used by the validateUser() method to ensure, first of all, that the user referenced by the given email address exists in the store and, second, that the user's password matches the provided argument. If both these conditions are fulfilled, the method returns true. Once again, I might test this as I go along:

```
// listing 18.04
$store = new UserStore();
$store->addUser("bob williams", "bob@example.com", "12345");
$validator = new Validator($store);
if ($validator->validateUser("bob@example.com", "12345")) {
    print "pass, friend!\n";
}
```

I instantiate a `UserStore` object, which I prime with data and pass to a newly instantiated `Validator` object. I can then confirm a username and password combination.

Once I'm finally satisfied with my work, I could delete these sanity checks altogether or comment them out. This is a terrible waste of a valuable resource. These tests could form the basis of a harness to scrutinize the system as I develop. One of the tools that might help me to do this is PHPUnit.

Introducing PHPUnit

PHPUnit is a member of the xUnit family of testing tools. The ancestor of these is SUnit, a framework invented by Kent Beck to test systems built with the Smalltalk language. The xUnit framework was probably established as a popular tool, however, by the Java implementation, jUnit, and by the rise to prominence of agile methodologies like Extreme Programming (XP) and Scrum, all of which place great emphasis on testing.

You can get PHPUnit with Composer:

```
{
    "require-dev": {
        "phpunit/phpunit":  "^9"
    }
}
```

Once you have run composer install, you will find the phpunit script at `vendor/bin/phpunit`. Or, you can download a PHP archive (.phar) file. You can then make the archive executable:

```
$ wget https://phar.phpunit.de/phpunit.phar
$ chmod 755 phpunit.phar
$ sudo mv phpunit.phar /usr/local/bin/phpunit
```

Note   I show commands that are input at the command line with a leading $ to represent a command prompt and distinguish them from any output they may produce.

Creating a Test Case

Armed with PHPUnit, I can write tests for the UserStore class. Tests for each target component should be collected in a single class that extends PHPUnit\Framework\ TestCase, one of the classes made available by the PHPUnit package. Here's how to create a minimal test case class:

```
// listing 18.05
namespace popp\ch18\batch01;
use PHPUnit\Framework\TestCase;
class UserStoreTest extends TestCase
{

    protected function setUp(): void
    {
    }

    protected function tearDown(): void
    {
    }

}
```

I named the test case class UserStoreTest. It is often useful to place your test in the same namespace as the class under test. This will give you easy access to the class under test and its peers, and the structure of your test files will likely mirror that of your system. Remember that, thanks to Composer's support for PSR-4, you can maintain separate directory structures for class files in the same package.

Here's how we might do this in Composer:

```
"autoload": {
    "psr-4": {
        "popp\\": ["myproductioncode/", "mytestcode/"]
    }
}
```

In this code, I have nominated two directories that map to the popp namespace. I can now maintain these in parallel, making it easy to keep my test and production code separate.

The setUp() method is automatically invoked for each test method, allowing us to set up a stable and suitably primed environment for the test. tearDown() is invoked after each test method is run. If your tests change the wider environment of your system, you can use this method to reset state. The common platform managed by setUp() and tearDown() is known as a *fixture*.

In order to test the UserStore class, I need an instance of it. I can instantiate this in setUp() and assign it to a property. Let's create a test method as well:

```
// listing 18.06
namespace popp\ch18\batch01;
use PHPUnit\Framework\TestCase;
class UserStoreTest extends TestCase
{
    private UserStore $store;

    protected function setUp(): void
    {
        $this->store = new UserStore();
    }

    protected function tearDown(): void
    {
    }

    public function testGetUser(): void
    {
        $this->store->addUser("bob williams", "a@b.com", "12345");
        $user = $this->store->getUser("a@b.com");
        $this->assertEquals("a@b.com", $user['mail']);
        $this->assertEquals("bob williams", $user['name']);
        $this->assertEquals("12345", $user['pass']);
    }
}
```

Note   Remember that setUp() and tearDown() are called once for every test method in your class. If you want to include code that will be run once before all the test methods in a class, you can implement the setUpBeforeClass() method. Conversely, for code that should be run after all the test methods in a class, implement tearDownAfterClass().

Test methods should be named to begin with the word "test" and should require no arguments. This is because the test case class is manipulated using reflection.

Note   Reflection is covered in detail in Chapter 5.

The object that runs the tests looks at all the methods in the class and invokes only those that match this pattern (i.e., methods that begin with "test").

In the example, I tested the retrieval of user information. I don't need to instantiate UserStore for each test because I handled that in setUp(). Because setUp() is invoked for each test, the $store property is guaranteed to contain a newly instantiated object.

Within the testgetUser() method, I first provide UserStore::addUser() with dummy data, and then I retrieve that data and test each of its elements.

There is one additional issue to be aware of here before we can run our test. I am using use statements without require or require_once. In other words, I am relying on autoloading. Finding and including the autoload file is handled automatically if you installed phpunit with Composer and if the autoload file for your project was generated in the same context. This may not always be the case, however. I may be running a global PHPUnit command which knows nothing of my local autoload, for example, or I may have downloaded a phar file. In this case, how do I tell my tests how to locate the generated autoload.php file? I could put a require_once statement in the test class (or a superclass), but that would break the PSR-1 rule that class files should not have side effects. The simplest thing to do is to tell PHPUnit about the autoload.php file from the command line:

```
$ phpunit src/ch18/batch01/UserStoreTest.php --bootstrap vendor/autoload.php
PHPUnit 9.5.0 by Sebastian Bergmann and contributors.
.                                  1 / 1 (100%)

Time: 00:00.012, Memory: 4.00 MB

OK (1 test, 3 assertions)
```

Assertion Methods

An assertion in programming is a statement or method that allows you to check your assumptions about an aspect of your system. In using an assertion, you typically define an expectation that something is the case, that $cheese is "blue" or $pie is "apple". If your expectation is confounded, a warning of some kind will be generated. Assertions are such a good way of adding safety to a system that PHP supports them natively inline and allows you to turn them off in a production context.

Note   See the manual page at https://php.net/assert for more information on PHP's support for assertions.

PHPUnit supports assertions through a set of methods that can be called either statically or on an instance of a class that extends PHPUnit\Framework\TestCase.

In the previous example, I used a TestCase method, assertEquals(). This method compares its two provided arguments and checks them for equivalence. If they do not match, the test method will be chalked up as a failed test. Having subclassed PHPUnit\Framework\TestCase, I have access to a set of assertion methods. Some of these methods are listed in Table 18-1.

Table 18-1. *PHPUnit\Framework\TestCase Assert Methods*

Method	Description
assertEquals($val1, $val2, $message)	Fail if $val1 is not equivalent to $val2
assertFalse($expression, $message)	Evaluate $expression; fail if it does *not* resolve to false
assertTrue($expression, $message)	Evaluate $expression; fail if it does *not* resolve to true
assertNotNull($val, $message)	Fail if $val is null
assertNull($val, $message)	Fail if $val is anything other than null
assertSame($val1, $val2, $message)	Fail if $val1 and $val2 are not references to the same object, or if they are variables of different types or values

(continued)

Table 18-1. (*continued*)

Method	Description
assertNotSame($val1, $val2, $message)	Fail if $val1 and $val2 are references to the same object or variables of the same type and value
assertMatchesRegularExpression ($regexp, $val, $message)	Fail if $val is not matched by the regular expression, $regexp

Testing Exceptions

Your focus as a coder is usually to make stuff *work* and work well. Often, that mentality carries through to testing, especially if you are testing your own code. The temptation is to test that a method behaves as advertised. It's easy to forget how important it is to test for failure. How good is a method's error checking? Does it throw an exception when it should? Does it throw the right exception? Does it clean up after an error if, for example, an operation is half complete before the problem occurs? It is your role as a tester to check all of this. Luckily, PHPUnit can help.

Here is a test that checks the behavior of the UserStore class when an operation fails:

```
// listing 18.07
public function testAddUserShortPass(): void
{
    try {
        $this->store->addUser("bob williams", "bob@example.com", "ff");
    } catch (\Exception $e) {
        $this->assertEquals("Password must have 5 or more letters",
        $e->getMessage());
        return;
    }

    $this->fail("Short password exception expected");
}
```

If you look back at the UserStore::addUser() method, you will see that I throw an exception if the user's password is less than five characters long. My test attempts to confirm this. I add a user with an illegal password in a try clause. If the expected

exception is thrown, then flow skips to the catch clause, and all is well. If the addUser()
method does not throw an exception as expected, the execution flow reaches the fail()
method call.

Another way to test that an exception is thrown is to use an assertion method called
expectException(), which requires the name of the exception type you expect to be
thrown (either Exception or a subclass). If the test method exits without the correct
exception having been thrown, the test will fail.

Note   The expectException() method was added in PHP 5.2.0.

Here's a quick reimplementation of the previous test:

```
// listing 18.08
public function testAddUserShortPassNew(): void
{
    $this->expectException(\Exception::class);
    $this->store->addUser("bob williams", "bob@example.com", "ff");
}
```

So, given that there is a neat way of testing for exceptions, why did I show
the older approach at all? In most circumstances, the simplest approach—using
expectException()—will be the best. However, occasionally, you may want to perform
further tests on the exception, on the state of the object under test, or you may want to
clean up some side effect. In such cases, it may still make sense to go old school.

Running Test Suites

If I am testing the UserStore class, I should also test Validator. Here is a cut-down
version of a class called ValidateTest that tests the Validator::validateUser()
method:

```
// listing 18.09
namespace popp\ch18\batch02;
use PHPUnit\Framework\TestCase;
class ValidatorTest extends TestCase
{
    private Validator $validator;
```

```
protected function setUp(): void
{
    $store = new UserStore();
    $store->addUser("bob williams", "bob@example.com", "12345");
    $this->validator = new Validator($store);
}

public function testValidateCorrectPass(): void
{
    $this->assertTrue(
        $this->validator->validateUser("bob@example.com", "12345"),
        "Expecting successful validation"
    );
}

}
```

So now that I have more than one test case, how do I go about running them together? The best way is to place your test classes in a common root directory. You can then specify this directory, and PHPUnit will run all the tests beneath it:

```
$ phpunit src/ch18/batch02/

PHPUnit 9.5.0 by Sebastian Bergmann and contributors.
........                     8 / 8 (100%)

Time: 00:00.026, Memory: 6.00 MB

OK (8 tests, 11 assertions)
```

Constraints

In most circumstances, you will use off-the-peg assertions in your tests. In fact, at a stretch, you can achieve an awful lot with AssertTrue() alone. As of PHPUnit 3.0, however, PHPUnit\Framework\ TestCase included a set of factory methods that return PHPUnit\Framework\Constraint objects. You can combine these and pass them to TestCase::AssertThat() in order to construct your own assertions.

It's time for a quick example. The UserStore object should not allow duplicate email addresses to be added. Here's a test that confirms this:

```
// listing 18.10

// UserStoreTest

public function testAddUserDuplicate()
{
    try {
        $ret = $this->store->addUser("bob williams", "a@b.com", "123456");
        $ret = $this->store->addUser("bob stevens", "a@b.com", "123456");
        $this->fail("Exception should have been thrown");
    } catch (\Exception $e) {
        $const = $this->logicalAnd(
            $this->logicalNot($this->containsEqual("bob stevens")),
            $this->isType('array'),
        );
        $this->AssertThat($this->store->getUser("a@b.com"), $const);
    }
}
```

This test adds a user to the UserStore object and then adds a second user with the same email address. The test thereby confirms that an exception is thrown with the second call to addUser(). In the catch clause, I build a constraint object using the convenience methods available to us. These return corresponding instances of PHPUnit\ Framework\Constraint. Let's break down the composite constraint in the previous example:

```
$this->logicalNot($this->containsEqual("bob stevens"))
```

This returns a PHPUnit\Framework\Constraint\Traversable\ TraversableContainsEqual object. When passed to AssertThat, this object will generate an error if the test subject does not contain an element matching the given value ("bob stevens"). I negate this, though, by passing this constraint to another: PHPUnit\Framework\Constraint\Not. Once again, I use a convenience method, available through the TestCase class (actually through a superclass, Assert):

```
$this->logicalNot( $this->contains("bob stevens"))
```

Now, the AssertThat assertion will fail if the test value (which must be traversable) contains an element that matches the string, "bob stevens". In this way, you can build up quite complex logical structures. By the time I have finished, my constraint can be summarized as follows: "Do not fail if the test value is an array and does not contain the string "bob stevens"." You could build much more involved constraints in this way. The constraint is run against a value by passing both to AssertThat().

You could achieve all this with standard assertion methods, of course, but constraints have a couple of virtues. First, they form nice logical blocks with clear relationships among components (although good use of formatting may be necessary to support clarity). Second, and more important, a constraint is reusable. You can set up a library of complex constraints and use them in different tests. You can even combine complex constraints with one another:

```
$const = $this->logicalAnd(
    $a_complex_constraint,
    $another_complex_constraint
);
```

Table 18-2 shows some of the constraint methods available in a TestCase class.

Table 18-2. *Some Constraint Methods*

TestCase Method	Constraint Fails Unless ...
greaterThan($num)	Test value is greater than $num
containsEqual($val)	Test value (traversable) contains an element that matches $val
identicalTo($val)	Test value is a reference to the same object as $val or, for nonobjects, is of the same type and value
greaterThanOrEqual($num)	Test value is greater than or equal to $num
lessThan($num)	Test value is less than $num
lessThanOrEqual($num)	Test value is less than or equal to $num
equalTo($value)	Test value equals $value

(continued)

Table 18-2. (*continued*)

TestCase Method	Constraint Fails Unless ...
equalTo($value, $delta)	Test value equals $value. $delta defines a margin of error for numeric comparisons
stringContains($str, $casesensitive=true)	Test value contains $str. This is case sensitive by default
matchesRegularExpression($pattern)	Test value matches the regular expression in $pattern
logicalAnd(PHPUnit_Framework_Constraint $const, [, $const..])	All provided constraints pass
logicalOr(PHPUnit_Framework_Constraint $const, [, $const..])	At least one of the provided constraints matches
logicalNot(PHPUnit_Framework_Constraint $const)	The provided constraint does not pass

Mocks and Stubs

Unit tests aim to test a component in isolation of the system that contains it to the greatest possible extent. Few components exist in a vacuum, however. Even nicely decoupled classes require access to other objects as method arguments. Many classes also work directly with databases or the file system.

You have already seen one way of dealing with this. The setUp() and tearDown() methods can be used to manage a fixture (i.e., a common set of resources for your tests, which might include database connections, configured objects, a scratch area on the file system, etc.).

Another approach is to fake the context of the class you are testing. This involves creating objects that pretend to be the objects that do real stuff. For example, you might pass a fake database mapper to your test object's constructor. Because this fake object shares a type with the real mapper class (extends from a common abstract base or even overrides the genuine class itself), your subject is none the wiser. You can prime the fake object with valid data. Objects that provide a sandbox of this sort for unit tests are known as *stubs*. They can be useful because they allow you to focus in on the class you want to test without inadvertently testing the entire edifice of your system at the same time.

Fake objects can be taken a stage further than this, however. Because the object you are testing is likely to call a fake object in some way, you can prime it to confirm the invocations you are expecting. Using a fake object as a spy in this way is known as *behavior verification*, and it is what distinguishes a mock object from a stub.

You can build mocks yourself by creating classes hard-coded to return certain values and to report on method invocations. This is a simple process, but it can be time-consuming.

PHPUnit provides access to an easier and more dynamic solution. It will generate mock objects on the fly for you. It does this by examining the class you wish to mock and building a child class that overrides its methods. Once you have this mock instance, you can call methods on it to prime it with data and to set the conditions for success.

Let's build an example. The UserStore class contains a method called notifyPasswordFailure(), which sets a field for a given user. This should be called by Validator when an attempt to set a password fails. Here, I mock up the UserStore class so that it both provides data to the Validator object and confirms that its notifyPasswordFailure() method was called as expected:

```
// listing 18.11

// ValidatorTest

    public function testValidateFalsePass(): void
    {
        $store = $this->createMock(UserStore::class);
        $this->validator = new Validator($store);

        $store->expects($this->once())
            ->method('notifyPasswordFailure')
            ->with($this->equalTo('bob@example.com'));

        $store->expects($this->any())
            ->method("getUser")
            ->will($this->returnValue([
                "name" => "bob williams",
                "mail" => "bob@example.com",
                "pass" => "right"
            ]));

        $this->validator->validateUser("bob@example.com", "wrong");
    }
```

Mock objects use a *fluent interface*; that is, they have a language-like structure. These are much easier to use than to describe. Such constructs work from left to right, each invocation returning an object reference, which can then be invoked with a further modifying method call (itself returning an object). This can make for easy use, but painful debugging.

In the previous example, I called the TestCase method, createMock(), passing it "UserStore", the name of the class I wish to mock. This dynamically generates a class and instantiates an object from it. I store this mock object in $store and pass it to Validator. This causes no error because the object's newly minted class extends UserStore. I have fooled Validator into accepting a spy into its midst.

Mock objects generated by PHPUnit have an expects() method. This method requires a matcher object (actually it's of type PHPUnit\Framework\MockObject\Matcher\Invocation, but don't worry; you can use the convenience methods in TestCase to generate your matcher). The matcher defines the cardinality of the expectation; that is, it dictates the number of times a method should be called.

Table 18-3 shows the matcher methods available in a TestCase class.

Table 18-3. *Some Matcher Methods*

TestCase Method	Match Fails Unless …
any()	Zero or more calls are made to the corresponding method (useful for stub objects that return values, but don't test invocations)
never()	No calls are made to the corresponding method
atLeastOnce()	One or more calls are made to the corresponding method
once()	A single call is made to the corresponding method
exactly($num)	$num calls are made to the corresponding method
at($num)	A call to the corresponding method made at $num index (each method call to a mock is recorded and indexed)

Having set up the match requirement, I need to specify a method to which it applies. For instance, expects() returns an object (PHPUnit\Framework\MockObject\Builder\InvocationMocker, if you must know) that has a method called method(). I can simply call that with a method name. This is enough to get some real mocking done:

```
// listing 18.12
$store->expects($this->once())
    ->method('notifyPasswordFailure');
```

I need to go further, however, and check the parameters that are passed to notifyPasswordFailure(). The InvocationMocker::method() returns an instance of the object it was called on. InvocationMocker includes a method name, with(), which accepts a variable list of parameters to match. It also accepts constraint objects, so you can test ranges and so on. Armed with this, you can complete the statement and ensure that the expected parameter is passed to notifyPasswordFailure():

```
// listing 18.13
$store->expects($this->once())
    ->method('notifyPasswordFailure')
    ->with($this->equalTo('bob@example.com'));
```

You can see why this is known as a fluent interface. It reads a bit like a sentence: "The $store object *expects* a single call to the notifyPasswordFailure() method with parameter bob@example.com."

Notice that I passed a constraint to with(). Actually, that's redundant; any bare arguments are converted to constraints internally, so I could write the statement like this:

```
// listing 18.14
$store->expects($this->once())
    ->method('notifyPasswordFailure')
    ->with('bob@example.com');
```

Sometimes, you only want to use PHPUnit's mocks as stubs, that is, as objects that return values to allow your tests to run. In such cases, you can invoke InvocationMocker::will() from the call to method(). The will() method requires the return value (or values if the method is to be called repeatedly) that the associated method should be primed to return. You can pass in this return value with TestCase::returnValue() or TestCase::onConsecutiveCalls(). Once again, this is much easier to do than to describe. Here's the fragment from my earlier example in which I prime UserStore to return a value:

Note   `TestCase::returnValue()` and `TestCase::onConsecutiveCal ls()` are not the only methods you can use to set up return values with stubs. There is also `returnValueMap()`, `returnArguments()`, `returnCallback()`, and `returnSelf()`.

```
// listing 18.15
$store->expects($this->any())
    ->method("getUser")
    ->will($this->returnValue([
        "name" => "bob@example.com",
        "pass" => "right"
    ]));
```

I prime the `UserStore` mock to expect any number of calls to `getUser()`. Right now, I'm concerned with providing data, not with testing calls. Next, I call `will()` with the result of invoking `TestCase::returnValue()` with the data I want returned (this happens to be a `PHPUnit\ Framework\MockObject\Stub\ReturnStub` object, although if I were you, I'd just remember the convenience method you use to get it).

You can alternatively pass the result of a call to `TestCase::onConsecutiveCalls()` to `will()`. This accepts any number of parameters, each one of which will be returned by your mocked method as it is called repeatedly.

Tests Succeed When They Fail

Although most agree that testing is a fine thing, you grow to really love it generally only after it has saved your bacon a few times. Let's simulate a situation where a change in one part of a system has an unexpected effect elsewhere.

The `UserStore` class has been running for a while when, during a code review, it is agreed that it would be neater for the class to generate `User` objects rather than associative arrays. Here is the new version:

```php
// listing 18.16
namespace popp\ch18\batch03;

class UserStore
{
    private array $users = [];

    public function addUser(string $name, string $mail, string $pass): bool
    {
        if (isset($this->users[$mail]))   {
            throw new \Exception(
                "User {$mail} already in the system"
            );
        }
        $this->users[$mail] = new User($name, $mail, $pass);

        return true;
    }

    public function notifyPasswordFailure(string $mail): void
    {
        if (isset($this->users[$mail])) {
            $this->users[$mail]->failed(time());
        }
    }

    public function getUser(string $mail): ?User
    {
        if (isset($this->users[$mail])) {
            return ( $this->users[$mail] );
        }

        return null;
    }
}
```

Here is the simple User class:

```
// listing 18.17
namespace popp\ch18\batch03;

class User
{
    private string $pass; private ?string $failed;

    public function __construct(private string $name, private string $mail,
    string $pass)
    {
        if (strlen($pass) <  5) {
            throw new \Exception(
                "Password must have 5 or more letters"
            );
        }

        $this->pass = $pass;
    }

    public function getMail(): string
    {
        return $this->mail;
    }

    public function getPass(): string
    {
        return $this->pass;
    }

    public function failed(string $time): void
    {
        $this->failed = $time;
    }
}
```

Of course, I amend the UserStoreTest class to account for these changes. Consider this code designed to work with an array:

```
// listing 18.18
public function testGetUser()
{
    $this->store->addUser("bob williams", "a@b.com", "12345");
    $user = $this->store->getUser("a@b.com");
    $this->assertEquals($user['mail'], "a@b.com");
    $this->assertEquals($user['name'], "bob williams");
    $this->assertEquals($user['pass'], "12345");
}
```

It is now converted into code designed to work with an object, like this:

```
// listing 18.19
public function testGetUser(): void
{
    $this->store->addUser("bob williams", "a@b.com", "12345");
    $user = $this->store->getUser("a@b.com");
    $this->assertEquals($user->getMail(), "a@b.com");
}
```

When I come to run my test suite, however, I am rewarded with a warning that my work is not yet done:

```
$ phpunit src/ch18/batch03/

PHPUnit 9.5.0 by Sebastian Bergmann and contributors.

....F                              5 / 5 (100%)

Time: 00:00.019, Memory: 6.00 MB

There was 1 failure:

1) popp\ch18\batch03\ValidatorTest::testValidateCorrectPass Expecting
successful validation
Failed asserting that false is true.
/var/popp/src/ch18/batch03/ValidatorTest.php:26

FAILURES!
Tests: 5, Assertions: 5, Failures: 1.
```

Although my tests relating to User pass, my ValidatorTest class has caught the fact that I have not updated the Validator to account for the new return value. Here is the test that is failing:

```
// listing 18.20
public function testValidateCorrectPass(): void
{
    $this->assertTrue(
        $this->validator->validateUser("bob@example.com", "12345"),
        "Expecting successful validation"
    );
}
```

And here is the Validator::validateUser() method that has let me down:

```
// listing 18.21
public function validateUser($mail, $pass): bool
{
    if (! is_array($user = $this->store->getUser($mail))) {
        return false;
    }

    if ($user['pass'] == $pass) {
        return  true;
    }

    $this->store->notifyPasswordFailure($mail);

    return false;
}
```

So User::getUser() now returns an object and not an array. getUser() originally returned an array containing user data on success or null on failure. I validated users by checking for an array using the is_array() function. Now, of course, this condition is never met and the validateUser() method will always return false. Without the test framework, the Validator would have simply rejected all users as invalid without fuss or warning.

It is a relatively quick fix to bring validateUser() method into line.

```
// listing 18.22
public function validateUser($mail, $pass): bool
{
    $user = $this->store->getUser($mail);
    if (is_null($user))  {
        return false;
    }
    $testpass = $user->getPass();
    if ($testpass == $pass) {
        return true;
    }

    $this->store->notifyPasswordFailure($mail);
    return false;
}
```

Now, imagine making the neat little change to `UserStore::getUser()` on a Friday night without a test framework in place. Think about the frantic text messages that would drag you out of your pub, armchair, or restaurant: "What have you done? All our customers are locked out!"

The most insidious bugs don't cause the interpreter to report that something is wrong. They hide in perfectly legal code, and they silently break the logic of your system. Many bugs don't manifest themselves where you are working; they are caused there, but the effects pop up elsewhere, days or even weeks later. A test framework can help you catch at least some of these, preventing rather than discovering problems in your systems.

Write tests as you code, and run them often. If someone reports a bug, first add a test to your framework to confirm it. Next, fix the bug so that the test is passed. Bugs have a funny habit of recurring in the same area. Writing tests to prove bugs and then to guard the fix against subsequent problems is known as *regression testing*. Incidentally, if you keep a separate directory of regression tests, remember to name your files descriptively. On one project, our team decided to name our regression tests after Bugzilla ticket numbers. We ended up with a directory containing 400 test files, each with a name like `test_973892.php`. Finding an individual test became a tedious chore!

Writing Web Tests

You should engineer your web systems in such a way that they can be invoked easily from the command line or an API call. In Chapter 12, you saw some tricks that might help you with this. In particular, if you create a `Request` class to encapsulate an HTTP request, you can just as easily populate an instance from the command line or method argument lists as from request parameters. The system can then run in ignorance of its context.

If you find a system hard to run in different contexts, that may indicate a design issue. If, for example, you have numerous file paths hard-coded into components, it's likely you are suffering from tight coupling. You should consider moving elements that tie your components to their context into encapsulating objects that can be acquired from a central repository. The registry pattern, also covered in Chapter 12, will likely help you with this.

Once your system can be run directly from a method call, you'll find that high-level web tests are relatively easy to write without any additional tools.

You may find, however, that even the most well-thought-out project will need some refactoring to get things ready for testing. In my experience, this almost always results in design improvements. I'm going to demonstrate this by retrofitting one aspect of the Woo example from Chapters 12 and 13 for unit testing.

Refactoring a Web Application for Testing

We actually left the Woo example in a reasonable state from a tester's point of view. Because the system uses a single Front Controller, there's a simple API interface. Here is a simple script in a file I have named `Runner.php`:

```
// listing 18.23
require_once("vendor/autoload.php");

use popp\ch18\batch04\woo\controller\Controller;

Controller::run();
```

That would be easy enough to add to a unit test, right? But what about command-line arguments? To some extent, this is already handled in the `Request` class:

```
// listing 18.24
public function init()
{
    if (isset($_SERVER['REQUEST_METHOD'])) {
        if ($_SERVER['REQUEST_METHOD']) {
            $this->properties = $_REQUEST;
                return;
        }
    }

    foreach ($_SERVER['argv'] as $arg) {
        if (strpos($arg, '=')) {
            list($key, $val) = explode("=", $arg);
                $this->setProperty($key,  $val);
        }
    }
}
```

Note   Just a reminder that, if you do implement your own Request class, you should capture and store GET, POST, and even PUT properties separately, rather than dumping them into a single $request property.

The init() method detects whether the process is running in a server context and populates the $properties array accordingly (either directly or via setProperty()). This works fine for command-line invocation. For example, it means I can run something like this:

```
$ php src/ch18/batch04/Runner.php cmd=AddVenue venue_name=bob
```

The preceding line generates this response:

```
<html>
<head>
<title>Add a Space for venue bob</title>
</head>
<body>
<h1>Add a Space for Venue 'bob'</h1>
```

671

```
<table>
<tr>
<td>
'bob' added (22)</td></tr><tr><td>please add name for the space</td>
</tr>
</table> [add space]
<form method="post">
    <input type="text" value="" name="space_name"/>
    <input type="hidden" name="cmd" value="AddSpace" />
    <input type="hidden" name="venue_id" value="22" />
    <input type="submit" value="submit" />
</form>

</body>
</html>
```

Although this works for the command line, it remains a little tricky to pass in arguments via a method call. One inelegant solution would be to manually set the $argv array before calling the controller's run() method. I don't much like this, though. Playing directly with magic arrays feels plain wrong, and the string manipulation involved at each end would compound the sin. Looking at the Controller class more closely, however, reveals a design decision that can help us:

```
// listing 18.25

// Controller

public function handleRequest()
{
    $request = ApplicationRegistry::getRequest();
    $app_c = ApplicationRegistry::appController();

    while ($cmd = $app_c->getCommand($request)) {
        $cmd->execute($request);
    }

    $this->invokeView($app_c->getView($request));
}
```

This method is designed to be invoked by the static run() method. Note how the Request object is not directly instantiated. Instead, I acquire it from the ApplicationRegistry. When the Registry holds a single instance of an object like Request, I can acquire a reference to it and load it with data from within my test before I start the system running by invoking the controller. In this way, I can simulate a web request. Because my system uses a Request object as its only interface to a web request, it is decoupled from the data source. As long as Request is sane, the system will not care whether its data originates ultimately from a test or from a web server. As a general principle, I prefer to push instantiations back to a registry, where possible.

If all my objects are created by a single ApplicationRegistry, I can overload the static registry factory method (ApplicationRegistry::instance) and have full control over all of the data my application uses during testing. This approach returns a mock registry populated with fake components if a flag is set, thereby creating an entirely mocked environment. I love to fool my systems.

Here, however, I will demonstrate the first, more conservative trick by preloading my Request object with test data.

Simple Web Testing

Here's a test case that performs a very basic test on the Woo system:

```
// listing 18.26
namespace popp\ch18\batch04;

use popp\ch18\batch04\woo\base\ApplicationRegistry;
use popp\ch18\batch04\woo\controller\ApplicationHelper;
use PHPUnit\Framework\TestCase;

class AddVenueTest extends TestCase
{
    public function testAddVenueVanilla(): void
    {
        $this->runCommand("AddVenue", ["venue_name" => "bob"]);
    }
```

```
    private function runCommand($command = null, array $args = null): void
    {
        $reg = ApplicationRegistry::instance();
        $applicationHelper = ApplicationHelper::instance();
        $applicationHelper->init();
        $request = ApplicationRegistry::getRequest();

        if (! is_null($args)) {
            foreach ($args as $key => $val) {
                $request->setProperty($key, $val);
            }
        }

        if (! is_null($command)) {
            $request->setProperty('cmd', $command);
        }

        woo\controller\Controller::run();
    }
}
```

In fact, it does not so much test anything as prove that the system can be invoked.
The real work is done in the runCommand() method. There is nothing terribly clever here.
I get a Request object from the ApplicationRegistry, and I populate it with the keys
and values provided in the method call. Because the Controller will go to the same
source for its Request object, I know that it will work with the values that I have set.

Running this test confirms that all is well. I see the output I expect. The problem is
that this output is printed by the view, so it's hard to test. I can fix that quite easily by
buffering the output:

```
// listing 18.27
namespace popp\ch18\batch04;

use popp\ch18\batch04\woo\base\ApplicationRegistry;
use popp\ch18\batch04\woo\controller\ApplicationHelper;
use PHPUnit\Framework\TestCase;
```

```php
class AddVenueTest2 extends TestCase
{

    public function testAddVenueVanilla(): void
    {
        $output = $this->runCommand("AddVenue", ["venue_name" => "bob"]);
        self::AssertMatchesRegularExpression("/added/", $output);
    }

    private function runCommand($command = null, array $args = null):
    string
    {
        $applicationHelper = ApplicationHelper::instance();
        $applicationHelper->init(); ob_start();
        $request = ApplicationRegistry::getRequest();

        if (! is_null($args)) {
            foreach ($args as $key => $val) {
                $request->setProperty($key, $val);
            }
        }

        if (! is_null($command)) {
            $request->setProperty('cmd', $command);
        }

        woo\controller\Controller::run();
        $ret = ob_get_contents();
        ob_end_clean();

        return $ret;
    }
}
```

By catching the system's output in a buffer, I'm able to return it from the runCommand() method. Next, I apply a simple assertion to the return value to examine. Of course, there are multiple problems with this approach.

Here is the view from the command line:

```
$ phpunit src/ch18/batch04/AddVenueTest2.php

PHPUnit 9.5.0 by Sebastian Bergmann and contributors.

.                                      1 / 1 (100%)

Time: 00:00.029, Memory: 6.00 MB

OK (1 test, 1 assertion)
```

If you are going to be running lots of tests on a system in this way, it would make sense to create a web UI superclass to hold runCommand().

I am glossing over some details here that you will face in your own tests. You will need to ensure that the system works with configurable storage locations. You don't want your tests going to the same datastore that you use for your development environment. This is another opportunity for design improvement. Look for hard-coded file paths and DSN values, and push them back to the Registry. Next, ensure your tests work within a sandbox, but set these values in your test case's setUp() method. Finally, look into swapping in a MockRequestRegistry, which you can charge up with stubs, mocks, and various other sneaky fakes.

Approaches like this are great for testing the inputs and output of a web application. There are some distinct limitations, however. This method won't capture the browser experience. Where a web application uses JavaScript, and other client-side cleverness, testing the text generated by your system won't tell you whether the user is seeing a sane interface.

Luckily, there is a solution.

Introducing Selenium

Selenium (www.selenium.dev/) consists of a set of commands for automating web tests. It also provides tools and APIs for authoring and running browser tests.

In this brief introduction, I'll create a quick test for the Woo system that I created in Chapter 12. The test will work in conjunction with the Selenium Server via an API called php-webdriver.

Getting Selenium

You can download Selenium components at `www.selenium.dev/downloads/`. For the purposes of this example, you will need the Selenium Standalone Server.

Once you've downloaded the package, you should find a file named `selenium-server-standalone-3.141.59.jar` (although, of course, your version number will probably be different). Copy this file somewhere central. To proceed further, you'll need Java installed on your system. Once you've confirmed this, you can start the Selenium Server.

Here, I copy the server to the `/usr/local/lib` directory. Then I start the server:

```
$ sudo cp selenium-server-standalone-3.141.59.jar  /usr/local/lib/
$ java -jar /usr/local/lib/selenium-server-standalone-3.141.59.jar

17:58:20.098 INFO [GridLauncherV3.parse] - Selenium server version:
3.141.59, revision: e82be7d358
17:58:20.200 INFO [GridLauncherV3.lambda$buildLaunchers$3] - Launching a
standalone
Selenium Server on port 4444
2020-09-13 17:58:20.254:INFO::main: Logging initialized @678ms to org.
seleniumhq.jetty9.util.log.StdErrLog
17:58:20.459 INFO [WebDriverServlet.<init>] - Initialising WebDriverServlet
17:58:20.541 INFO [SeleniumServer.boot] - Selenium Server is up and running
on port 4444
```

Note that the startup output tells us the port we should use in order to communicate with the server. This will come in handy later.

We are likely only partway there, however. To lessen the chance of obscure errors, I have found it best to download the correct version of ChromeDriver, the library that conveys UI commands to the browser. At present, Chrome seems to be the best choice of browser for testing with Selenium. Begin by installing Chrome on your local system if you have not yet done this. Determine the version of your browser by looking at the `Help :: About Google Chrome` menu. Then download the version of ChromeDriver that corresponds to your browser version at `https://sites.google.com/a/chromium.org/chromedriver/downloads`. Armed with that library, you can launch Selenium again:

```
$ java -jar -Dwebdriver.chrome.driver="./chromedriver" /usr/local/lib/
selenium-server- standalone-3.141.59.jar
```

Now I'm ready to proceed.

PHPUnit and Selenium

Although PHPUnit has provided APIs for working with Selenium in the past, its support has been patchy, and its documentation has been even more so. In order to access as many of Selenium's features as possible, therefore, it makes sense to use PHPUnit in conjunction with a tool that is designed to provide the bindings that we need.

Introducing php-webdriver

WebDriver is the mechanism by which Selenium controls browsers, and it was introduced with Selenium 2. Selenium developers provide Java, Python, and C# APIs for WebDriver. There are a few PHP APIs available. I have chosen to use php-webdriver, which was created by Facebook developers. It is under active development and mirrors the official APIs. This is very handy when you want to look up a technique, since many examples you'll find online will be offered in Java, which means they will apply readily to php-webdriver with a little porting of code.

You can add php-webdriver to your project with Composer:

```
{
    "require-dev": {
        "phpunit/phpunit": "9.*",
        "php-webdriver/webdriver" : "*"
    }
}
```

Update your `composer.json` file, run `composer update`, and you should be ready to go.

Creating the Test Skeleton

I will be working with an instance of the Woo application, which will run on my system at the URL: `http://popp.vagrant.internal/webwoo/`.

I'll start off with a boilerplate test class:

```
// listing 18.28
namespace popp\ch18\batch04;

use Facebook\WebDriver\Chrome\ChromeOptions;
use Facebook\WebDriver\Remote\DesiredCapabilities;
use Facebook\WebDriver\Remote\RemoteWebDriver;
```

```
use Facebook\WebDriver\Remote\WebDriverCapabilityType;
use PHPUnit\Framework\TestCase;

class SeleniumTest1 extends TestCase
{
    protected function setUp(): void
    {
    }

    public function testAddVenue(): void
    {
    }
}
```

I specify some of the php-webdriver classes I will be using and then create a bare-bones test class. Now it's time to make this test do something.

Connecting to Selenium

Remember that, on startup, the server outputs its connection URL. In order to make the connection to Selenium, I need to pass this URL and a capabilities array to a class named RemoteWebDriver:

```
// listing 18.29
namespace popp\ch18\batch04;

use Facebook\WebDriver\Chrome\ChromeOptions;
use Facebook\WebDriver\Remote\DesiredCapabilities;
use Facebook\WebDriver\Remote\RemoteWebDriver;
use Facebook\WebDriver\Remote\WebDriverCapabilityType;
use PHPUnit\Framework\TestCase;
class SeleniumTest2 extends TestCase
{
    private $driver;

    protected function setUp(): void
    {
        $options = new ChromeOptions();
```

```
        $capabilities = DesiredCapabilities::chrome();
        $capabilities->setCapability(ChromeOptions::CAPABILITY, $options);

        $this->driver = RemoteWebDriver::create(
            "http://127.0.0.1:4444/wd/hub",
            $capabilities
        );

    }

    public function testAddVenue(): void
    {
    }
}
```

If you installed php-webdriver with Composer, you can see a full list of capabilities in the class file at vendor/php-webdriver/webdriver/lib/Remote/ WebDriverCapabilityType.php. For my present purposes, however, I really only need to specify the browser name. I pass the host string and the $capabilities array to the static RemoteWebDriver::create() method and store the resulting object reference in the $driver property. When I run this test, I should see that Selenium launches a fresh browser window in preparation for my tests.

Writing the Test

I would like to test a simple workflow. I will navigate to the AddVenue page, add a venue, and then add a space. This involves interacting with three web pages.

Here is my test:

```
// listing 18.30
namespace    popp\ch18\batch04;

use Facebook\WebDriver\Chrome\ChromeOptions;
use Facebook\WebDriver\Remote\DesiredCapabilities;
use Facebook\WebDriver\Remote\RemoteWebDriver;
use Facebook\WebDriver\Remote\WebDriverCapabilityType;
use Facebook\WebDriver\WebDriverBy;
use PHPUnit\Framework\TestCase;
```

```php
class SeleniumTest3 extends TestCase
{

    protected function setUp(): void
    {
        $options = new ChromeOptions();

        // uncomment this line to run in 'headless' mode
        // $options->addArguments(['--headless', '--no-sandbox']);

        $capabilities = DesiredCapabilities::chrome();
        $capabilities->setCapability(ChromeOptions::CAPABILITY, $options);

        $this->driver = RemoteWebDriver::create(
            "http://127.0.0.1:4444/wd/hub",
            $capabilities
        );
    }

    public function testAddVenue(): void
    {
        $this->driver->get("http://popp.vagrant.internal/webwoo/AddVenue.php");
        $venel = $this->driver->findElement(WebDriverBy::name("venue_name"));
        $venel->sendKeys("my_test_venue");

        $venel->submit();

        $tdel = $this->driver->findElement(WebDriverBy::xpath("//td[1]"));
        $this->assertMatchesRegularExpression("/'my_test_venue' added/",
        $tdel->getText());

        $spacel = $this->driver->findElement(WebDriverBy::name("space_name"));
        $spacel->sendKeys("my_test_space");
        $spacel->submit();

        $el = $this->driver->findElement(WebDriverBy::xpath("//td[1]"));
        $this->assertMatchesRegularExpression("/'my_test_space' added/",
        $el->getText());
    }
}
```

Here's what happens when I run this test on the command line:

```
$ phpunitsrc/ch18/batch04/SeleniumTest3.php

PHPUnit 9.5.0 by Sebastian Bergmann and contributors.

..                                1 / 1 (100%)

Time: 00:00.029, Memory: 6.00 MB
OK (1 test, 2 assertion)
```

Of course, it's not all that happens. Selenium also launches a browser window and performs my specified operations upon it. I have to admit, I find this effect a little eerie!

Let's run through the code. First, I invoke WebDriver::get(), which acquires my starting page. Note that this method expects a full URL (which does not need to be local to the Selenium Server host). In this case, I configured an Apache server on a Vagrant virtual machine to serve up a mocked up AddVenue.php script. Selenium will load the specified document into the browser it has launched. You can see this page in Figure 18-1.

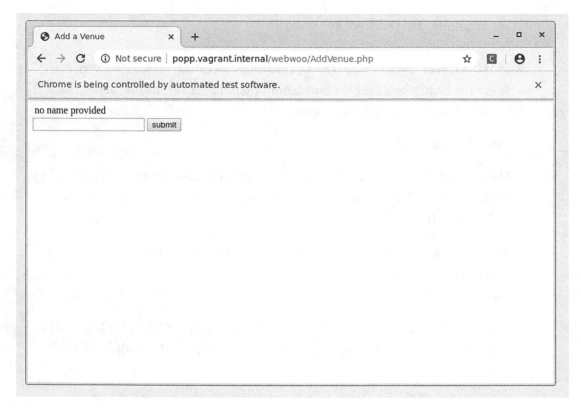

Figure 18-1. *The AddVenue page loaded by Selenium*

Once the page has loaded, I have access to it via the WebDriver API. I can acquire a reference to a page element using the RemoteWebDriver::findElement() method. This requires an object of type WebDriverBy. The WebDriverBy class provides a set of factory methods, each of which returns a WebDriverBy object configured to specify a particular means of locating an element. My form element has a name attribute set to "venue_name", so I use the WebDriverBy::name() method to tell findElement() to look for an element this way. Table 18-4 lists all of the available factory methods.

Table 18-4. *WebDriverBy Factory Methods*

Method	Description
className()	Find elements by CSS class name
cssSelector()	Find elements by CSS selector
id()	Find an element by its id
name()	Find elements by name attribute
linkText()	Find elements by their link text
partialLinkText()	Find elements by a fragment of link text
tagName()	Find elements by their tag
xpath()	Find elements that match an Xpath expression

Once I have a reference to the venue_name form element, an object of type RemoteWebElement, I can use its sendKeys() method to set a value. It's important to note that sendKeys() does more than just set a value. It also simulates the act of typing into an element. This is useful for testing systems that use JavaScript to capture keyboard events.

With my new value set, I submit the form. The API is smart about this. When I call submit() on an element, Selenium locates the containing form and submits it.

Submitting the form, of course, causes a new page to be loaded. So, next I check that all is as I expect. Once again, I use WebDriver::findElement(), although this time I pass it a WebDriverBy object configured for Xpath. If my search is successful, findElement() will return a new RemoteWebElement object. If my search fails, on the other hand, the resulting exception will bring down my test. Assuming that all is well, I acquire the element's value using the RemoteWebElement::getText() method.

At this stage, I have submitted the form and checked the state of the returned web page. You can see the page in Figure 18-2.

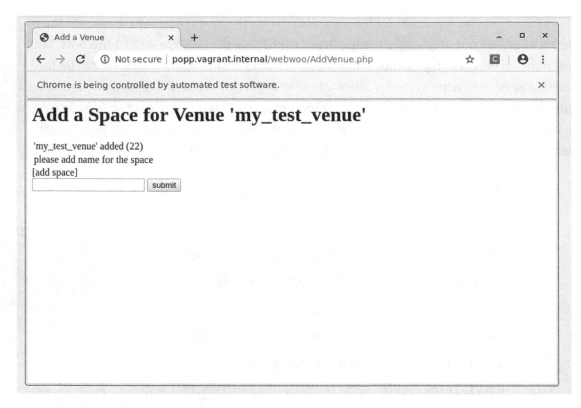

Figure 18-2. *The AddSpace page*

Now all that remains is to populate the form once again, submit, and check the new page. I use techniques that you have already encountered to achieve this.

Of course, I've only just scratched the surface of Selenium here. But I hope this discussion has been enough to give you an idea of the possibilities. If you want to learn more, there is a complete Selenium manual at www.selenium.dev/documentation/en/.

A Note of Caution

It's easy to get carried away with the benefits that automated tests can offer. I add unit tests to my projects, and I use PHPUnit for functional tests, as well. That is, I test at the level of the system, as well as that of the class. I have seen real and observable benefits, but I believe that these come at a price.

Tests add a number of costs to your development. As you build safety into the project, for example, you are also adding a time penalty into the build process that can impact releases. The time it takes to write tests is part of this, but so is the time it takes to run them. On one system, we may have suites of functional tests that run against more than one database and more than one version control system. Add a few more contextual variables like that, and we face a real barrier to running the test suite. Of course, tests that aren't run aren't useful. One answer to this is to fully automate your tests, so runs are kicked off by a scheduling application like cron. Another is to maintain a subset of your tests that can be easily run by developers as they commit code. These should sit alongside your longer, slower test run.

Another issue to consider is the brittle nature of many test harnesses. Your tests may give you confidence to make changes, but as your test coverage increases along with the complexity of your system, it becomes easier to break multiple tests. Of course, this is often what you want. You want to know when expected behavior does not occur or when unexpected behavior does.

Oftentimes, however, a test harness can break because of a relatively trivial change, such as the wording of a feedback string. Every broken test is an urgent matter, but it can be frustrating to have to change 30 test cases to address a minor alteration in architecture or output. Unit tests are less prone to problems of this sort because, by and large, they focus on each component in isolation.

The cost involved in keeping tests in step with an evolving system is a trade-off that you simply have to factor in. On the whole, I believe the benefits justify the costs.

You can also do some things to reduce the fragility of a test harness. It's a good idea to write tests with the expectation of change built in, to some extent. I tend to use regular expressions to test output rather than direct equality tests, for example. Testing for a few keywords is less likely to make my test fail when I remove a newline character from an output string. Of course, making your tests too forgiving is also a danger, so it is a matter of using your judgment.

Another issue is the extent to which you should use mocks and stubs to fake the system beyond the component you wish to test. Some insist that you should isolate your component as much as possible and mock everything around it. This works for me in some projects. In others, however, I have found that maintaining a system of mocks can become a time sink. Not only do you have the cost of keeping your tests in line with your system, but you must keep your mocks up to date. Imagine changing the return type of a method. If you fail to update the method of the corresponding stub object to return the new type, client tests may pass in error. With a complex fake system, there is a real danger of bugs creeping into mocks. Debugging tests is frustrating work, especially when the system itself is not at fault.

I tend to play this by ear. I use mocks and stubs by default, but I'm unapologetic about moving to real components if the costs begin to mount up. You may lose some focus on the test subject, but this comes with the bonus that errors originating in the component's context are at least real problems with the system. You can, of course, use a combination of real and fake elements. I routinely use an in-memory database in test mode, for example.

As you may have gathered, I am not an ideologue when it comes to testing. I routinely "cheat" by combining real and mocked components; and because priming data is repetitive, I often centralize test fixtures into what Martin Fowler calls Object Mothers. These classes are simple factories that generate primed objects for the purpose of testing. Shared fixtures of this sort are anathema to some.

Having pointed out some of the problems that testing may force you to confront, it is worth reiterating a few points that, for my money, trump all objections. Testing accomplishes several things:

- It helps you prevent bugs (to the extent that you find them during development and refactoring).

- It helps you discover bugs (as you extend test coverage).

- It encourages you to focus on the design of your system.

- It lets you improve code design with less fear that changes will cause more problems than they solve.

- It gives you confidence when you ship code.

In every project for which I've written tests, I've had occasion to be grateful for that fact sooner or later.

Summary

In this chapter, I revisited the kinds of tests we all write as developers, but all too often thoughtlessly discard. From there, I introduced PHPUnit, which lets you write the same kind of throwaway tests during development, but then keep them and feel the lasting benefit! I created a test case implementation, and I covered the available assertion methods. I also examined constraints and explored the devious world of mock objects. Next, I showed how refactoring for testing can improve design, demonstrating some techniques for testing web applications—first by using just PHPUnit and then by using Selenium. Finally, I risked the ire of some by warning of the costs that tests incur and discussing the trade-offs involved.

## CHAPTER 19

Automated Build with Phing

If version control is one side of the coin, then automated build is the other. Version control allows multiple developers to work collaboratively on a single project. With many coders each deploying a project in their own space, automated build soon becomes essential. One developer may have her web-facing directory in `/usr/local/apache/htdocs`; another might use `/home/bibble/public_html`. Developers may use different database passwords, library directories, or mail mechanisms. A flexible codebase might easily accommodate all of these differences, but the effort of changing settings and manually copying directories around your file system to get things working would soon become tiresome—especially if you need to install code in progress several times a day (or several times an hour).

You have already seen that Composer automates package installation. You'll almost certainly want to deliver a project to an end user via a Composer or PEAR package because that mechanism is straightforward for the user and because package management systems handle dependencies. But there's a lot of work that might need automating before a package has been created. You may need to generate template-generated code, for example. You should run tests and provide mechanisms for creating and updating database tables. Finally, you may want to automate the creation of a production-ready package. In this chapter, I introduce you to Phing, which handles just such jobs. This chapter will cover the following:

- *Getting and installing Phing*: Who builds the builder?

- *Properties*: Setting and getting data

- *Types*: Describing complex parts of a project

- *Targets*: Breaking a build into callable, interdependent sets of > functionality

- *Tasks*: The things that get stuff done

What Is Phing?

Phing is a PHP tool for building projects. It is very closely modeled on the hugely popular (and very powerful) Java tool called Ant. Ant was so named because it is small but capable of constructing things that are very large indeed. Both Phing and Ant use an XML file (usually named `build.xml`) to determine what to do in order to install or otherwise work with a project.

The PHP world *really* needs a good build solution. Serious developers have had a number of options in the past. First, it is possible to use `make`, the ubiquitous Unix build tool that is still used for most C and Perl projects. However, `make` is extremely picky about syntax and requires quite a lot of shell knowledge, up to and including scripting—this can be challenging for some PHP programmers who have not come to programming via the Unix or Linux command line. What's more, `make` provides very few built-in tools for common build operations such as transforming filenames and contents. It is really just a glue for shell commands. This makes it hard to write programs that will install across platforms. Not all environments will have the same version of `make` or even have it at all. Even if you have `make`, you may not have all the commands the makefile (the configuration file that drives `make`) requires.

Phing's relationship with `make` is illustrated in its name: Phing stands for PHing Is Not GNU `make`. This playful recursion is a common coder's joke (e.g., GNU itself stands for GNU is Not Unix).

Phing is a native PHP application that interprets a user-created XML file in order to perform operations on a project. Such operations would typically involve the copying of files from a distribution directory to various destination directories, but there is much more to Phing. Phing can be used to generate documentation, run tests, invoke commands, run arbitrary PHP code, create packages, replace keywords in files, strip comments, and generate tar/gzipped package releases. Even if Phing does not yet do what you need, it is designed to be easily extensible.

Because Phing is itself a PHP application, all you need to run it is a recent PHP engine. As Phing is an application for installing PHP applications, the presence of a PHP executable is a reasonably safe bet.

Getting and Installing Phing

If it is difficult to install an install tool, then something is surely wrong! However, assuming that you have PHP 5 or better on your system (and if you haven't, this isn't the book for you!), installation of Phing could not be easier.

You can acquire and install Phing with Composer. You should add this to your composer.json file:

```
{
    "require-dev":  {
        "phing/phing": "2.*"
    }
}
```

Note   As I write this, Phing version 3 is still in alpha. All the examples in this chapter (and in Chapter 21) work very well with it, but installation requires some unorthodox hacking. Hopefully as you read this, these gremlins have been ironed out. Check the installation instructions at the Phing homepage: www.phing.info/#install.

Composing the Build Document

You should now be ready to get cracking with Phing! Let's test things out:

```
$ phing vendor/bin/phing -v

Phing 2.16.3
```

The -v flag to the phing command causes the script to return version information. By the time you read this, the version number may have changed, but you should see a similar message when you run the command on your system.

Note   If you installed Phing using Composer, the runnable script file will be installed in your local `vendor/bin/` directory. To run Phing, you should either add this directory to your $PATH environment variable or use an explicit path to the executable. In future examples, I will omit the path.

Now I'll run the phing command without arguments:

```
$ phing

Buildfile: build.xml does not exist!
```

As you can see, Phing is lost without instructions. By default, it will look for a file called build.xml. Let's build a minimal document so that we can at least make that error message go away:

```
// listing 19.01
<?xml version="1.0"?>
<!-- build xml -->

<project name="megaquiz" default="main" description="my project"
basedir="/tmp">
    <target name="main"/>
</project>
```

This is the bare minimum you can get away with in a build file. If we save the previous example as build.xml and run phing again, we should get some more interesting output:

```
$ phing

Buildfile: /var/popp/src/ch19/build.xml
Warning: target 'main' has no tasks or dependencies

megaquiz > main:

BUILD FINISHED

Total time: 0.0976 seconds
```

A lot of effort to achieve precisely nothing, you may think, but we have to start somewhere! As you can see, Phing also helpfully points out there's nothing very useful about this build file. Look again at that build file. Because we are dealing with XML, I include an XML declaration. As you probably know, XML comments look like this:

```
<!-- this is an XML comment. OK? -->
```

So, because it's a comment, the second line in my build file is ignored. You can put as many comments as you like in your build files, and as they grow, you should make full use of this fact. Large build files can be hard to follow without suitable comments.

The real start of any build file is the `project` element. The `project` element can include up to five attributes. Of these, `name` and `default` are compulsory. The `name` attribute establishes the project's name; `default` defines a target to run if none are specified on the command line. An optional `description` attribute can provide summary information. You can specify the context directory for the build using a `basedir` attribute. If this is omitted, the current working directory will be assumed. Finally, you can specify the minimum version of the Phing application with which the build file should work using `phingVersion`. You can see these attributes summarized in Table 19-1.

Table 19-1. *The Attributes of the Project Element*

Attribute	Required	Description	Default Value
Name	Yes	The name of the project	None
Description	No	A brief project summary	None
Default	Yes	The default target to run	None
phingVersion	No	The minimum version of Phing to run against	None
Basedir	No	The file system context in which build will run	Current directory (.)
Strict	No	Run in strict mode: treat warnings as errors Once I have defined a `project` element, I must create at least one target—the one I reference in the `default` attribute	false

Targets

Targets are similar, in some senses, to functions. A target is a set of actions grouped together to achieve an objective: to copy a directory from one place to another, for example, or to generate documentation.

In my previous example, I included a bare-minimum implementation for a target:

```
// listing 19.02
<target name="main"/>
```

As you can see, a target must define at least a name attribute. I have made use of this in the project element. Because the default element points to the main target, this target will be invoked whenever Phing is run without command-line arguments. This was confirmed by the output:

```
megaquiz > main:
```

Targets can be organized to depend on one another. By setting up a dependency between one target and another, you tell Phing that the first target should not run before the target it depends on has been run. Now, I'll add a dependency to my build file:

```
// listing 19.03
<?xml version="1.0"?>
<!-- build xml -->

<project name="megaquiz"
         default="main">

    <target name="runfirst" />
    <target name="runsecond" depends="runfirst"/>
    <target name="main" depends="runsecond"/>
</project>
```

As you can see, I have introduced a new attribute for the target element. depends tells Phing that the referenced target should be executed before the current one, so I might want a target that copies certain files to a directory to be invoked before one that runs a transformation on all files in that directory. I added two new targets in the example: runsecond, on which main depends, and runfirst, on which runsecond depends. Here's what happens when I run Phing with this build file:

```
$ phing
```

```
Buildfile: /var/popp/src/ch19/build.xml
Warning: target 'runfirst' has no tasks or dependencies
```

```
megaquiz > runfirst:
```

```
megaquiz > runsecond:
```

```
megaquiz > main:
```

```
BUILD FINISHED
```

```
Total time: 0.1250 seconds
```

As you can see, the dependencies are honored. Phing encounters the main target, sees its dependency, and moves back to runsecond. runsecond has its own dependency, and Phing invokes runfirst.

Having satisfied its dependency, Phing can invoke runsecond. Finally, main is invoked. The depends attribute can reference more than one target at a time. A comma-separated list of dependencies can be provided, and each will be honored in turn.

Now that I have more than one target to play with, I can override the project element's default attribute from the command line:

```
$ phing runsecond
```

```
Buildfile: /var/popp/src/ch19/build.xml
Warning: target 'runfirst' has no tasks or dependencies
```

```
megaquiz > runfirst:
```

```
megaquiz > runsecond:
```

```
BUILD FINISHED
```

```
Total time: 0.1043 seconds
```

By passing in a target name, I cause the default attribute to be ignored. The target matching my argument is invoked instead (as well as the target on which it depends). This is useful for invoking specialized tasks, such as cleaning up a build directory or running post-install scripts.

The target element also supports an optional description attribute, to which you can assign a brief description of the target's purpose:

```
// listing 19.04
<?xml version="1.0"?>
<!-- build xml -->

<project name="megaquiz"
        default="main"
        description="A quiz engine">
    <target name="runfirst"
            description="The first target" />
    <target name="runsecond"
            depends="runfirst, housekeeping"
            description="The second target" />
    <target name="main"
            depends="runsecond"
            description="The main target" />
</project>
```

Adding a description to your targets makes no difference to the normal build process. If the user runs Phing with a -projecthelp flag, however, the descriptions will be used to summarize the project:

```
$ phing -projecthelp

Buildfile: /var/popp/src/ch19/build.xml
Warning: target 'runfirst' has no tasks or dependencies
A quiz engine
Default target:
-------------------------------------------------------------------
Main        The main target

Main targets:
-------------------------------------------------------------------
Main        The main target
Runfirst    The first target
Runsecond   The second target
```

Notice that I added the `description` attribute to the `project` element, too. If you want to hide a target from a listing like this, you can add a hidden attribute. This is useful for targets that provide housekeeping functionality, but which should not be invoked directly from the command line:

```
// listing 19.05
<target name="housekeeping" hidden="true">
    <!-- useful things that should not be called directly -->
</target>
```

Properties

Phing allows you to set such values using the `property` element.

Properties are similar to global variables in a script. As such, they are often declared toward the top of a project to make it easy for developers to work out what's what in the build file. Here, I create a build file that works with database information:

```
// listing 19.06
<?xml version="1.0"?>
<!-- build xml -->

<project name="megaquiz"
        default="main">

   <property name="dbname" value="megaquiz" />
   <property name="dbpass" value="default" />
   <property name="dbhost" value="localhost" />

   <target name="main">
      <echo>database: ${dbname}</echo>
      <echo>pass:     ${dbpass}</echo>
      <echo>host:     ${dbhost}</echo>
   </target>
</project>
```

I introduced a new element: `property`. `property` requires `name` and `value` attributes. I have added three instances of `property` to the `main` target.

I also introduced the echo element. This is an example of a task. I will explore tasks more fully in the next section. For now, though, it's enough to know that echo does exactly what you would expect—it causes its contents to be output. Notice the syntax used to reference the value of a property here. By using a dollar sign, and wrapping the property name in curly brackets, you tell Phing to replace the string with the property value:

```
${propertyname}
```

All this build file achieves is to declare three properties and to print them to standard output. Here it is in action:

```
$ phing
```

```
Buildfile: /var/popp/src/ch19/build.xml
megaquiz > main:

    [echo] database: megaquiz
    [echo] pass:     default
    [echo] host:     localhost

BUILD FINISHED

Total time: 0.0989 seconds
```

Now that I have introduced properties, I can wrap up my exploration of targets. The target element accepts two additional attributes: if and unless. Each of these should be set with the name of a property. When you use if with a property name, the target will only be executed if the given property is set. If the property is not set, the target will exit silently. Here, I comment out the dbpass property and make the main task require it using the if attribute:

```
// listing 19.07
<project name="megaquiz"
        default="main">

    <property name="dbname" value="megaquiz" />
    <!--<property name="dbpass" value="default" />-->
    <property name="dbhost" value="localhost" />
```

```
    <target name="main" if="dbpass">
        <echo>database: ${dbname}</echo>
        <echo>pass:     ${dbpass}</echo>
        <echo>host:     ${dbhost}</echo>
    </target>
</project>
```

Let's run phing again:

```
$ phing

Buildfile: /var/popp/src/ch19/build.xml
megaquiz > main:

BUILD FINISHED

Total time: 0.0957 seconds
```

As you can see, I have raised no error, but the main task did not run. Why might I want to do this? There is another way of setting properties in a project. They can be specified on the command line. You tell Phing that you are passing it a property with the -D flag followed by a property assignment. So the argument should look like this:

```
-Dname=value
```

In my example, I want the dbname property to be made available via the command line:

```
$ phing -Ddbpass=userset

Buildfile: /var/popp/src/ch19/build.xml

megaquiz > main:
    [echo] database: megaquiz
    [echo] pass:     userset
    [echo] host:     localhost

BUILD FINISHED

Total time: 0.0978 seconds
```

The if attribute of the main target is satisfied that the dbpass property is present, and the target is allowed to execute.

697

As you might expect, the `unless` attribute is the opposite of `if`. If a property is set and it is referenced in a target's `unless` attribute, then the target will not run. This is useful if you want to make it possible to suppress a particular target from the command line. So I might add something like this to the main target:

```
// listing 19.08
<target name="main" unless="suppressmain">
    <echo>database: ${dbname}</echo>
    <echo>pass:     ${dbpass}</echo>
    <echo>host:     ${dbhost}</echo>
</target>
```

`main` will be executed unless a `suppressmain` property is present:

```
$ phing -Dsuppressmain
```

I have wrapped up the `target` element; Table 19-2 shows a summary of its attributes.

Table 19-2. *The Attributes of the Target Element*

Attribute	Required	Description
name	Yes	The name of the target
depends	No	Targets on which the current depends
if	No	Execute target only if given property is present
unless	No	Execute target only if given property is not present
logskipped	No	If a target is skipped (e.g., because of `if`/`unless`), add a notification to output
hidden	No	Hide target from lists and summaries
description	No	A short summary of the target's purpose

When a property is set on the command line, it overrides any and all property declarations within the build file. There is another condition in which a property value can be overwritten. By default, if a property is declared twice, the original value will have primacy. You can alter this behavior by setting an attribute called `override` in the second `property` element. Here's an example:

```
// listing 19.09
<?xml version="1.0"?>
<!-- build xml -->

<project name="megaquiz"
         default="main">

    <property name="dbpass" value="default" />

    <target name="main">
        <property name="dbpass" override="yes" value="specific" />
        <echo>pass: ${dbpass}</echo>
    </target>

</project>
```

I set a property called dbpass, giving it the initial value "default". In the main target, I set the property once again, adding an override attribute set to "yes" and providing a new value. The new value is reflected in the output:

```
$ phing

Buildfile: /var/popp/src/ch19/build.xml

megaquiz > main:
     [echo] pass: specific

BUILDFINISHED

Total time: 0.0978 seconds
```

If I had not set the override element in the second property element, the original value of "default" would have stayed in place. It is important to note that targets are not functions: there is no concept of local scope. If you override a property within a task, it remains overridden for all other tasks throughout the build file. You could get around this, of course, by storing a property value in a temporary property before overriding and then resetting it when you have finished working locally.

So far, I have dealt with properties that you define yourself. Phing also provides built-in properties. You reference these in exactly the same way that you would reference properties you have declared yourself. Here's an example:

```
// listing 19.10
<?xml version="1.0"?>
<!-- build xml -->

<project name="megaquiz"
          default="main">

    <target name="main">
        <echo>name: ${phing.project.name}</echo>
        <echo>base: ${project.basedir}</echo>
        <echo>home: ${user.home}</echo>
        <echo>pass: ${env.DBPASS}</echo>
    </target>

</project>
```

I reference just a few of the built-in Phing properties. `phing.project.name` resolves to the name of the project as defined in the `name` attribute of the `project` element; `project.basedir` gives the starting directory; and `user.home` provides the executing user's home directory (this is useful for providing default install locations).

Finally, the `env` prefix in a property reference indicates an operating system environment variable. So by specifying $, I am looking for an environment variable called DBPASS. Here, I run Phing on this file:

```
$ phing

Buildfile: /var/popp/src/ch19/build.xml

megaquiz > main:
     [echo] name: megaquiz
     [echo] base: /var/popp/src/ch19
     [echo] home: /home/vagrant
     [echo] pass: ${env.DBPASS}

BUILD FINISHED

Total time: 0.1056 seconds
```

700

Notice that the final property has not been translated. This is the default behavior when a property is not found—the string referencing the property is left untransformed. If I set the DBPASS environment variable and run again, I should see the variable reflected in the output:

```
$ export DBPASS=wooshpoppow
$ phing

Buildfile: /var/popp/src/ch19/build.xml

megaquiz > main:
    [echo] name: megaquiz
    [echo] base: /var/popp/src/ch19
    [echo] home: /home/vagrant
    [echo] pass: wooshpoppow

BUILD FINISHED

Total time: 0.1044 seconds
```

So now you have seen three ways of setting a property: the property element, a command-line argument, and an environment variable.

There is a fourth approach that complements these. You can use a separate file to specify property values. As my projects grow in complexity, I tend to favor this approach. Let's return to a basic build file:

```
// listing 19.11
<?xml version="1.0"?>
<!-- build xml -->

<project name="megaquiz"
        default="main">

    <target name="main">
        <echo>database: ${dbname}</echo>
        <echo>pass:     ${dbpass}</echo>
        <echo>host:     ${dbhost}</echo>
    </target>
</project>
```

As you can see, this build file simply outputs properties without first declaring them or checking that their values exist. This is what I get when I run this with no arguments:

```
$ phing
```

...

```
    [echo] database: ${dbname}
    [echo] pass:     ${dbpass}
    [echo] host:     ${dbhost}
```

...

Now I'll declare my properties in a separate file. I'll call it megaquiz.properties:

```
dbname=filedb
dbpass=filepass
dbhost=filehost
```

Now I can apply this file to my build process with Phing's propertyfile option:

```
$ phing -propertyfile megaquiz.properties
```

...

```
    [echo] database: filedb
    [echo] pass:     filepass
    [echo] host:     filehost
```

...

I find this mechanism much more convenient than managing long lists of command-line options. However, you do need to be careful not to check your property file into your version control system!

You can use targets to ensure that properties are populated. Let's say, for example, that my project requires a dbpass property. I would like the user to set dbpass on the command line (this always has priority over other property assignment methods). Failing that, I should look for an environment variable. Finally, I should give up and go for a default value:

```
// listing 19.12
<?xml version="1.0"?>
<!-- build xml -->
```

```
<project name="megaquiz"
        default="main" basedir=".">

    <target name="setenvpass" if="env.DBPASS" unless="dbpass">
        <property name="dbpass" override="yes" value="${env.DBPASS}" />
    </target>

    <target name="setpass" unless="dbpass" depends="setenvpass">
        <property name="dbpass" override="yes" value="default" />
    </target>

    <target name="main" depends="setpass">
        <echo>pass: ${dbpass}</echo>
    </target>

</project>
```

So, as usual, the default target main is invoked first. This has a dependency set, so Phing goes back to the setpass target. setpass, though, depends on setenvpass, so I start there. setenvpass is configured to run only if dbpass has not been set and if env. DBPASS is present. If these conditions are met, then I set the dbpass property using the property element. At this stage then, dbpass is populated either by a command-line argument or by an environment variable. If neither of these were present, then the property would remain unset at this stage. The setpass target is now executed, but only if dbpass is not yet present. In this case, it sets the property to the default string: "default".

Conditionally Setting Property Values with the Condition Task

The previous example set up quite a complex assignment logic. More often, however, you'll need a simple default value. The condition task allows you to set a property's value based upon configurable conditions. Here is an example:

```
// listing 19.13
<?xml version="1.0"?>
<!-- build xml -->

<project name="megaquiz"
        default="main">
    <condition property="dbpass" value="default">
```

```
        <not>
            <isset property="dbpass" />
        </not>
    </condition>

    <target name="main">
        <echo>pass: ${dbpass}</echo>
    </target>

</project>
```

The `condition` task requires a `property` attribute. It also optionally accepts a `value` attribute, which is assigned to the property if the nested test clause resolves to `true`. If no value attribute is provided, then the property will be set to `true` if the nested test resolves to `true`.

The test clause is one of a number of tags, some of which, like `not` in this example, accept their own nested elements. I used the `isset` element, which returns `true` if the referenced property is set. Because I want to assign a value to the `dbpass` property if it is *not set*, I need to negate this result by wrapping it in the `not` tag. This inverts the resolution of the tag it contains. So, in terms of PHP syntax, the `condition` task in my example is analogous to this:

```
if (! isset($dbpass)) {
    $dbpass = "default";
}
```

Types

You may think that having looked at properties, you are now through with data. In fact, Phing supports a set of special elements called types. These encapsulate different kinds of information useful to the build process.

FileSet

Let's say that you need to represent a directory in your build file. This is a common situation as you might imagine. You could use a property to represent this directory, certainly, but you'd run into problems straightaway if your developers use different platforms that support distinct directory separators. The answer is the FileSet data type.

FileSet is platform independent, so if you represent a directory with forward slashes in the path, they will be automatically translated behind the scenes into backslashes when the build is run on a Windows machine. You can define a minimal fileset element like this:

```
<fileset dir="src/lib" />
```

As you can see, I use the dir attribute to set the directory I wish to represent. You can optionally add an id attribute, so that you can refer to the fileset later on:

```
<fileset dir="src/lib" id="srclib">
```

The FileSet data type is particularly useful in specifying types of documents to include or exclude. When installing a set of files, you may not wish those that match a certain pattern to be included. You can handle conditions like this in an excludes attribute:

```
<fileset dir="src/lib" id="srclib"
    excludes="**/*_test.php **/*Test.php" />
```

Notice the syntax I have used in the excludes attribute. Double asterisks represent any directory or subdirectory within src/lib. A single asterisk represents zero or more characters. So I am specifying that I would like to exclude files that end in _test.php or Test.php in all directories below the starting point defined in the dir attribute. The excludes attribute accepts multiple patterns separated by whitespace.

I can apply the same syntax to an includes attribute. Perhaps my src/lib directories contain many non-PHP files that are useful to developers, but which should not find their way into an installation. I could exclude those files, of course, but it might be simpler just to define the kinds of files I *can* include. In this case, if a file doesn't end in .php, it isn't going to be installed:

```
<fileset dir="src/lib" id="srclib"
    excludes="**/*_test.php **/*Test.php"
    includes="**/*.php" />
```

As you build up include and exclude rules, your fileset element is likely to become overly long. Luckily, you can pull out individual exclude rules and place each one in its own exclude subelement. You can do the same for include rules. I can now rewrite my FileSet like this:

```
<fileset dir="src/lib" id="srclib">
    <exclude name="**/*_test.php" />
    <exclude name="**/*Test.php" />
    <include name="**/*.php" />
</fileset>
```

You can see some of the attributes of the fileset element in Table 19-3.

Table 19-3. *Some Attributes of the Fileset Element*

Attribute	Required	Description
refid	No	Current fileset is a reference to fileset of given ID
dir	No	The starting directory
expandsymboliclinks	No	If set to 'true', follow symbolic links
includes	No	A comma-separated list of patterns—those that match will be included
excludes	No	A comma-separated list of patterns—those that match will be excluded

PatternSet

As you build up patterns in your fileset elements (and in others), there is a danger that you will begin to repeat groups of exclude and include elements. In my previous example, I defined patterns for test files and regular code files. I may add to these over time (perhaps I wish to include .conf and .inc extensions to my definition of code files). If I define other fileset elements that also use these patterns, I will be forced to make any adjustments across all relevant fileset elements.

You can overcome this problem by grouping patterns into patternset elements. The patternset element groups include and exclude elements so that they can be referenced later from within other types. Here, I extract the include and exclude elements from my fileset example and add them to patternset elements:

```
// listing 19.14
<patternset id="inc_code">
    <include name="**/*.php" />
    <include name="**/*.inc" />
    <include name="**/*.conf" />
</patternset>

<patternset id="exc_test">
    <exclude name="**/*_test.php" />
    <exclude name="**/*Test.php" />
</patternset>
```

I create two patternset elements, setting their id attributes to inc_code and exc_test, respectively. inc_code contains the include elements for including code files, and exc_test contains the exclude files for excluding test files. I can now reference these patternset elements within a fileset:

```
// listing 19.15
<fileset dir="src/lib" id="srclib">
    <patternset refid="inc_code" />
    <patternset refid="exc_test" />
</fileset>
```

To reference an existing patternset, you must use another patternset element. The second element must set a single attribute: refid. The refid attribute should refer to the id of the patternset element you wish to use in the current context. In this way, I can reuse patternset elements across different fileset elements:

```
<fileset dir="src/views" id="srcviews">
    <patternset refid="inc_code" />
</fileset>
```

Any changes I make to the inc_code patternset will automatically update any types that use it. As with FileSet, you can place exclude rules either in an excludes attribute or a set of exclude subelements. The same is true of include rules.

Some patternset element attributes are summarized in Table 19-4.

Table 19-4. *Some Attributes of the Patternset Element*

Attribute	Required	Description
id	No	A unique handle for referring to the element
excludes	No	A list of patterns for exclusion
includes	No	A list of patterns for inclusion
refid	No	Current patternset is a reference to patternset of given ID

FilterChain

The types that I have encountered so far have provided mechanisms for selecting sets of files. FilterChain, by contrast, provides a flexible mechanism for transforming the contents of text files.

In common with all types, defining a `filterchain` element does not in itself cause any changes to take place. The element and its children must first be associated with a task—that is, an element that tells Phing to take a course of action. I will return to tasks a little later.

A `filterchain` element groups any number of filters together. Filters operate on files like a pipeline—the first alters its file and passes its results on to the second, which makes its own alterations, and so on. By combining multiple filters in a `filterchain` element, you can effect flexible transformations.

Here, I dive straight in and create a `filterchain` that removes PHP comments from any text passed to it:

```
// listing 19.16
<filterchain>
    <stripphpcomments />
</filterchain>
```

The StripPhpComments task does just what the name suggests. If you have provided detailed API documentation in your source code, you may have made life easy for developers, but you have also added a lot of dead weight to your project. Because all the work that matters takes place within your source directories, there is no reason why you should not strip out comments on installation.

Note   If you use a build tool for your projects, ensure that no one makes changes in the installed code. The installer will copy over any altered files, and the changes will be lost. I have seen it happen.

Let's sneak a peek at the next section and place the `filterchain` element in a task:

```
// listing 19.17
<target name="main">
    <copy todir="build/lib">
        <fileset refid="srclib"/>
        <filterchain>
            <stripphpcomments />
        </filterchain>
    </copy>
</target>
```

The Copy task is probably the one you get most use out of. It copies files from place to place. As you can see, I define the destination directory in the `todir` attribute. The source of the files is defined by the `fileset` element I created in the previous section. Then comes the `filterchain` element. Any file copied by the Copy task will have this transformation applied to it.

Phing supports filters for many operations, including stripping new lines (`StripLineBreaks`) and replacing tabs with spaces (`TabToSpaces`). There is even an XsltFilter for applying XSLT transformations to source files! Perhaps the most commonly used filter, however, is `ReplaceTokens`. This allows you to swap tokens in your source code for properties defined in your build file, whether pulled from environment variables or passed in on the command line. This is very useful for customizing an installation. It's a good idea to centralize your tokens into a central configuration file for easy overview of the variable aspects of your project.

`ReplaceTokens` optionally accepts two attributes, `begintoken` and `endtoken`. You can use these to define the characters that delineate token boundaries. If you omit these, Phing will assume the default character of @. In order to recognize and replace tokens, you must add `token` elements to the `replacetokens` element. Now I'll add a `replacetokens` element to my example:

```
// listing 19.18
<target name="main">
    <copy todir="build/lib">
        <fileset refid="srclib"/>
        <filterchain>
            <stripphpcomments />
            <replacetokens>
                <token key="dbname" value="${dbname}" />
                <token key="dbhost" value="${dbhost}" />
                <token key="dbpass" value="${dbpass}" />
            </replacetokens>
        </filterchain>
    </copy>
</target>
```

As you can see, token elements require key and value attributes. Let's see the effect of running this task with its transformations on a file in my project. The original file lives in a source directory, src/lib/Config.php:

```
// listing 19.19
/*
 * Quick and dirty Conf class
 *
 */
class Config
{
    public string $dbname ="@dbname@";
    public string $dbpass ="@dbpass@";
    public string $dbhost ="@dbhost@";
}
```

Running my main target containing the Copy task defined previously gives the following output:

```
$ phing

Buildfile: /home/bob/working/megaquiz/build.xml

megaquiz > main:
    [copy] Copying 8 files to /home/bob/working/megaquiz/build/lib

BUILD FINISHED

Total time: 0.1413 seconds
```

The original file is untouched, of course, but thanks to the Copy task, it has been reproduced at build/lib/Config.php:

```
class Config {
    public string $dbname ="megaquiz";
    public string $dbpass ="default";
    public string $dbhost ="localhost";
}
```

Not only has the comment been removed, but the tokens have been replaced with their property equivalents.

Tasks

Tasks are the elements in a build file that get things done. You won't achieve much without using a task, which is why I have cheated and used a couple already. I'll reintroduce these.

Echo

The Echo task is perfect for the obligatory "Hello World" example. In the real world, you can use it to tell the user what you are about to do or what you have done. You can also sanity-check your build process by displaying the values of properties. As you have seen, any text placed within the opening and closing tags of an echo element will be printed to the browser:

```
<echo>The pass is '${dbpass}', shhh!</echo>
```

Alternatively, you can add the output message to a `msg` attribute:

```
<echo msg="The pass is '${dbpass}', shhh!" />
```

This will have the identical effect of printing the following to standard output:

```
[echo] The pass is 'default', shhh!
```

Copy

Copying is really what installation is all about. Typically, you will create one target that copies files from your source directories and assembles them in a temporary build directory. You will then have another target that copies the assembled (and transformed) files to their output locations. Breaking the installation into separate build and install phases is not absolutely necessary, but it does mean that you can check the results of the initial build before committing to overwriting production code. You can also change a property and install again to a different location without the need to run a potentially expensive copy/replace phase again.

At its simplest, the Copy task allows you to specify a source file and a destination directory or file:

```
<copy file="src/lib/Config.php" todir="build/conf" />
```

As you can see, I specify the source file using the `file` attribute. You may be familiar already with the `todir` attribute, which is used to specify the target directory. If the target directory does not exist, Phing will create it for you.

If you need to specify a target file, rather than a containing directory, you can use the `tofile` attribute instead of `todir`:

```
<copy file="src/lib/Config.php" tofile="build/conf/myConfig.php" />
```

Once again, the `build/conf` directory is created if necessary, but this time, `Config.php` is renamed to `myConfig.php`.

As you have seen, to copy more than one file at a time, you need to add a `fileset` element to `copy`:

```
// listing 19.20
<copy todir="build/lib">
    <fileset refid="srclib"/>
</copy>
```

The source files are defined by the srclib fileset element, so all you have to set in copy is the todir attribute.

Phing is smart enough to test whether or not your source file has been changed since the target file was created. If no change has been made, then Phing will not copy. This means that you can build many times, and only the files that have changed in the meantime will be installed. This is fine, as long as other things are not likely to change. If a file is transformed according to the configuration of a replacetokens element, for example, you may want to ensure that the file is transformed every time that the Copy task is invoked. You can do this by setting an overwrite attribute:

```
// listing 19.21
<copy todir="build/lib" overwrite="yes">
    <fileset refid="srclib"/>
    <filterchain>
        <stripphpcomments />
        <replacetokens>
            <token key="dbname" value="${dbname}" />
        </replacetokens>
    </filterchain>
</copy>
```

Now whenever copy is run, the files matched by the fileset element are replaced whether or not the source has been recently updated.

You can see the copy element and some of its attributes summarized in Table 19-5.

Table 19-5. *Some Attributes of the Copy Element*

Attribute	Required	Description	Default Value
file	No	File to copy	None
todir	Yes (if tofile not present)	Directory to copy into	None
tofile	Yes (if todir not present)	The file to copy to	None
tstamp or preservelastmodified	No	Match the timestamp of any file overwritten (it will appear unaltered)	false
preservemode or preservepermissions	No	Match the permissions of any file overwritten	false
includeemptydirs	No	Copy empty directories over	false
mode	No	Set the (octal) mode	755
haltonerror	No	Build process will be stopped if an error encountered	true
overwrite	No	Overwrite target if it already exists	no

Input

You have seen that the echo element is used to send output to the user. To gather input *from* the user, I have used separate methods involving the command line and an environment variable. These mechanisms are neither very structured nor interactive, however.

Note   One reason for allowing users to set values at build time is to allow for flexibility from build environment to build environment. In the case of database passwords, another benefit is that this sensitive data is not enshrined in the build file itself. Of course, once the build has been run, the password will be saved into a source file, so it is up to the developer to ensure the security of his system!

The input element allows you to present the user with a prompt message. Phing then awaits input which it assigns it to a property. Here's an example:

```
// listing 19.22
<?xml version="1.0"?>
<!-- build xml -->

<project name="megaquiz"
        default="main" >

    <target name="setpass" unless="dbpass">
        <input message="You don't seem to have set a db password"
            propertyName="dbpass"
            defaultValue="default"
            promptChar=" >" />
    </target>

    <target name="main" depends="setpass">
        <echo>pass: ${dbpass}</echo>
    </target>
</project>
```

Once again, I have a default target: main. This depends on another target, setpass, which is responsible for ensuring that the dbpass property is populated. To this end, I use the target element's unless attribute, which ensures that it will not run if dbpass is already set.

The setpass target consists of a single input task element. An input element requires a message attribute, which should contain a prompt for the user. The propertyName attribute is required and defines the property to be populated by user input. If the user presses Enter at the prompt without setting a value, the property is given a fallback value if the defaultValue attribute is set. Finally, you can customize the prompt character using the promptChar attribute—this provides a visual cue for the user to input data. Let's run Phing using the previous targets:

```
$ phing

Buildfile: /var/popp/src/ch19/build.xml

megaquiz > setpass:

You don't seem to have set a db password [default] > mypass
```

715

```
megaquiz > main:
    [echo] pass: mypass

    BUILD FINISHED

    Total time: 3.8878 seconds
```

The input element is summarized in Table 19-6.

Table 19-6. *The Attributes of the Input Element*

Attribute	Required	Description
propertyName	Yes	The property to populate with user input
message	No	The prompt message
defaultValue	No	A value to assign to the property if the user does not provide input
validArgs	No	A list of acceptable input values separated by commas. If the user inputs a value that is not on this list, Phing will re-present the prompt
promptChar	No	A visual cue that the user should provide input
hidden	No	If set, hide user input

Delete

Installation is generally about creating, copying, and transforming files. Deletion has its place as well, however. This is particularly the case when you wish to perform a clean install. As I have already discussed, files are generally only copied from source to destination for source files that have changed since the last build. By deleting a build directory, you ensure that the full compilation process will take place.

Here, I delete a directory:

```
// listing 19.23
<target name="clean">
    <delete dir="build" />
</target>
```

When I run phing with the argument clean (the name of the target), my delete task element is invoked. Here's Phing's output:

```
$ phing clean

Buildfile: /var/popp/src/ch19/build.xml

megaquiz > clean:

    [delete] Deleting directory /var/popp/src/ch19/build

BUILD FINISHED

Total time: 0.1000 seconds
```

The delete element accepts an attribute, file, which can be used to point to a particular file. Alternatively, you can fine-tune your deletions by adding a fileset subelement to delete.

Summary

Serious development rarely happens all in one place. A codebase needs to be separated from its installation, so that work in progress does not pollute production code that needs to remain functional at all times. Version control allows developers to check out a project and work on it in their own space. This requires that they should be able to configure the project easily for their environments. Finally, and perhaps most importantly, the customer (even if the customer is yourself in a year's time, when you've forgotten the ins and outs of your code) should be able to install your project after a glance at a Read Me file.

In this chapter, I have covered some of the basics of Phing, a fantastic tool, which brings much of the functionality of Apache Ant to the PHP world. I have only scratched the surface of Phing's capabilities. Nevertheless, once you are up and running with the targets, tasks, types, and properties discussed here, you'll find it easy to bolt on new elements for advanced features like creating tar/gzipped distributions, automatically generating PEAR package installations, and running PHP code directly from the build file.

If Phing does not satisfy all your build needs, you will discover that, like Ant, it is designed to be extensible—get out there and build your own tasks! Even if you don't add to Phing, you should take some time to examine the source code. Phing is written entirely in object-oriented PHP, and its code is chock-full of design examples.

717

## CHAPTER 20

Vagrant

Where do you run your code?

Maybe you have a development environment you have honed to perfection with a favorite editor and any number of useful development tools. Of course, your perfect setup for writing code is probably very different from the best system on which to run it. And that's a challenge that Vagrant can help you with. Using Vagrant, you get to work on your local machine and run your code on a system that's all but identical to your production server. In this chapter, I will show you how. We will cover the following:

- *Basic setup*: From installation to choosing your first box

- *Logging in*: Investigating your virtual machine with ssh

- *Mounting host directories*: Editing code on your host machine and having it available transparently in your Vagrant box

- *Provisioning*: Writing a script to install packages and configure Apache and MySQL

- *Set a hostname*: Configuring your box so that you can access it using a custom hostname

The Problem

As always, let's spend a little time defining the problem space. It is relatively easy, these days, to configure a LAMP stack on most desktop or laptop computers. Even so, a personal computer is unlikely to match your production environment. Is it running the same version of PHP? What about Apache and MySQL? If you're using Elasticsearch, you may need to consider Java, too. The list soon grows. Developing against one set of tools on a particular platform can sometimes be problematic if your production stack is significantly different.

© Matt Zandstra 2021
M. Zandstra, *PHP 8 Objects, Patterns, and Practice*, https://doi.org/10.1007/978-1-4842-6791-2_20

You might give up and shift your development to a remote machine—there are plenty of cloud vendors who will allow you to spin up a box quickly. But that's not a free option, and, depending upon your editor of choice, a remote system may not integrate well with the development tools you wish to use.

So it may be worth the effort of matching the packages on your computer as closely as possible with those installed on the production system. The match won't be perfect, but perhaps it will be good enough, and you'll probably catch most issues on the staging server.

What happens, though, when you begin work on a second project with radically different requirements? We have seen that Composer does a great job of keeping dependencies separate, but there are still global packages like PHP, MySQL, and Apache to keep in line.

Note   If you decide to develop on remote systems, I recommend making the effort to learn how to use the vim editor. Despite its quirks, it is extremely powerful, and you can be 99% certain that either vim or its more basic ancestor vi will be available on any Unix-like system you encounter.

Virtualization is a potential solution and a good one. It can be a pain installing an operating system, though, and there can be considerable configuration hassles.

If only there were a tool that made creating a production-like development environment on a local machine really simple. OK, it's obvious that now I'm going to say that just such a tool exists. Well, one does. It's called Vagrant, and it is truly amazing.

A Little Setup

It is tempting to say that Vagrant gives you a development environment with a single command. That *can* be true—but you do have to install the requisite software first. Given that, and a configuration file that you can check out from your project's version control repository, launching a new environment truly can involve a single command.

Let's get started with the setup first. Vagrant requires a virtualization platform. It supports several, but I will use VirtualBox. My host machine runs Fedora, but you can install VirtualBox on any Linux distribution and on OSX or Windows. You can find the download page at `www.virtualbox.org/wiki/Downloads`, together with instructions for your platform.

Once you have VirtualBox installed, you'll need Vagrant, of course. The download page is at www.vagrantup.com/downloads.html. Once we have installed these applications, our next task will be to choose the box we'll run our code on.

Choosing and Installing a Vagrant Box

Probably the easiest way to acquire a Vagrant box is to use the search interface at https://app.vagrantup.com/boxes/search. Since many production systems run CentOS, that's what I will look for. You can see the fruits of my research in Figure 20-1.

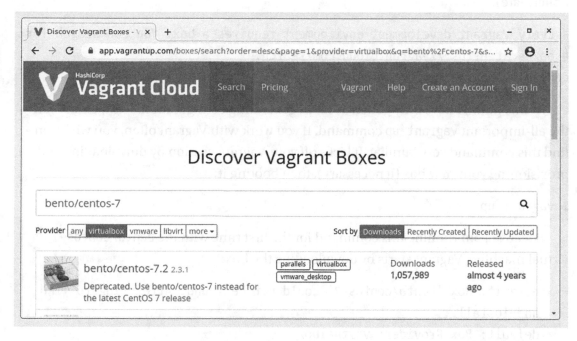

Figure 20-1. *Searching for a Vagrant box*

CentOS 7 looks about right for my needs. I can click the listing for the box that interests me to get setup instructions. This gives me enough information to get a Vagrant environment running. Usually when you run Vagrant, it will read a configuration file named Vagrantfile—but since I am starting from scratch, I need to ask Vagrant to generate one:

```
$ vagrant init bento/centos-7
```

A `Vagrantfile` has been placed in this directory. You are now
ready to `vagrant up` your first virtual environment! Please read
the comments in the Vagrantfile as well as documentation on
`vagrantup.com` for more information on using Vagrant.

As you can see, I pass Vagrant the name of the box I want to work with, and it uses
this information to generate some minimal configuration.

If I open up the generated Vagrantfile document, I can see this (among much other
boilerplate):

```
# Every Vagrant development environment requires a box. You can search for
# boxes at https://vagrantcloud.com/search.
config.vm.box = "bento/centos-7"
```

At this point, I have only gotten as far as generating configuration. Next, I must run
the all-important vagrant up command. If you work with Vagrant often, you will soon
find this command very familiar. It kicks off your Vagrant session by downloading and
provisioning your new box (if necessary), then booting it:

```
$ vagrant up
```

Because I am running this command for the first time with the bento/centos-7
virtual machine, Vagrant starts by downloading the box:

```
==> default: Box 'bento/centos-7' could not be found. Attempting to find
    and install...
    default: Box Provider: virtualbox
    default: Box Version: >= 0
==> default: Loading metadata for box 'bento/centos-7'
    default: URL: https://vagrantcloud.com/bento/centos-7
==> default: Adding box 'bento/centos-7' (v202008.16.0) for provider:
    virtualbox
    default: Downloading:
https://vagrantcloud.com/bento/boxes/centos-7/versions/202008.16.0/
providers/ virtualbox.box
```

```
    default: Download redirected to host: vagrantcloud-files-production.
    s3.amazonaws.com
==> default: Successfully added box 'bento/centos-7' (v202008.16.0) for
    'virtualbox'!
...
```

Vagrant stores the box (under ~/.vagrant.d/boxes/ if you are running Linux) so that you won't have to download it again on your system—even if you run multiple virtual machines. Then it configures and boots the machine (it provides lots of detail as it does so). Once it has finished running, I can test it out by logging in to my new machine:

```
$ vagrant ssh
$ pwd

/home/vagrant

$ cat /etc/redhat-release

CentOS Linux release 7.8.2009 (Core)
```

We're in! So what have we won? Well, we have access to a machine that somewhat resembles our production environment. Anything else? Quite a lot, in fact. I said earlier that I would like to edit files on my local machine but run them in a production-like space. Let's set that up.

Time to leave the box again and get back to the host machine:

```
$ exit
```

Mounting Local Directories on the Vagrant Box

Let's put some sample files together. I ran my first vagrant init and vagrant up commands in a directory I named infrastructure. I will resurrect the webwoo project I used in Chapter 18 (a cut-down version of the system I developed for Chapter 12). Putting all that together, my development environment looks a little like this:

```
ch20/
    infrastructure/
        Vagrantfile
    webwoo/
```

```
AddVenue.php
index.php
Main.php
AddSpace.php
```

Our challenge is to set up the environment so that we can work with webwoo files locally, but run them transparently using a stack installed on the CentOS box. Depending upon our configuration, Vagrant will attempt to mount directories on the host machine within the guest box. In fact, Vagrant has *already* mounted one directory for us. Let's check it out:

```
$ vagrant ssh

Last login: Wed Sep 23 16:46:53 2020 from 10.0.2.2

$ ls -a /vagrant

.  ..    .vagrant    Vagrantfile
```

So Vagrant has mounted the infrastructure directory as /vagrant on the box. That will come in handy when we write a script to provision the box. For now, though, let's focus on mounting the webwoo directory. We can do this by editing Vagrantfile. First, though, now might be a good time to exit again from the virtual machine. Once I have done that, I open up Vagrantfile and add this line:

```
config.vm.synced_folder "../webwoo", "/var/www/poppch20"
```

I can find the best place to put this line by searching the commented boilerplate for the string synced_folder. I find a sample configuration line that looks very like my own. With this directive, I am telling Vagrant to mount the webwoo directory on the guest box at /var/www/poppch20. In order to see that in effect, I need to reboot the box. There's a new command for this (which should be run on the host system and not within the virtual machine):

```
$ vagrant reload
```

The virtual machine shuts down and reboots cleanly. Vagrant mounts the infrastructure (/vagrant) and webwoo (/var/www/poppch20) directories. Here's an extract from the command's output:

```
==> default: Mounting shared folders...
    default: /vagrant => /home/mattz/localwork/popp/ch20-vagrant/
    infrastructure
    default: /var/www/poppch20 => /home/mattz/localwork/popp/ch20-vagrant/
    webwoo
```

I can log in quickly to confirm that /var/www/poppch20 is in place:

```
$ vagrant ssh
$ ls /var/www/poppch20/
```

```
AddSpace.php  AddVenue.php   index.php   Main.php
```

So now I can run a sexy IDE on my local machine and have the changes it makes transparently available on the guest box!

Note   A note from Technical Reviewer and Windows user Paul Tregoing: Don't use a VirtualBox shared file system (which underpins Vagrant's synced folder in this example) if running a Windows host. If you do so, you may encounter issues with case sensitivity and lack of symlink support. In this scenario, it's better to run Samba (most distributions install this as smbd) on the guest OS and map a network drive on the host for a more seamless experience. There are lots of online guides out there for this.

Of course, placing files on a CentOS VM is not the same as running the system. A typical Vagrant box comes without too much preinstalled. The assumption is that the developer will want to customize the environment according to need and circumstance.

The next stage is to provision our box.

Provisioning

Once again, provisioning is directed by the Vagrantfile document. Vagrant supports several tools designed for provisioning machines, including Chef (www.chef.io/chef/), Puppet (https://puppet.com), and Ansible (www.ansible.com). They're all worth investigating. For the purposes of this example, though, I'm going to use a good old-fashioned shell script.

Once again, I begin with `Vagrantfile`:

```
config.vm.provision "shell", path: "setup.sh"
```

This should be reasonably clear. I'm telling Vagrant to use a shell script to provision my box, and I specify `setup.sh` as the script which should be executed.

What you put in your shell script depends upon your requirements, of course. I'm going to begin by setting a couple of variables and installing some packages:

```
#!/bin/bash

VAGRANTDIR=/vagrant
SERVERDIR=/var/www/poppch20/

sudo yum -q -y install epel-release yum-utils
sudo yum -q -y install http://rpms.remirepo.net/enterprise/remi-release-7.rpm

yum-config-manager --enable  remi-php80

sudo yum -q -y install mysql-server
sudo yum -q -y install httpd;
sudo yum -q -y install php
sudo yum -q -y install php-common
sudo yum -q -y install php-cli
sudo yum -q -y install php-mbstring
sudo yum -q -y install php-dom
sudo yum -q -y install php-mysql
sudo yum -q -y install php-xml
sudo yum -q -y install php-dom
```

PHP 8 is not available by default on CentOS 7. However, by installing the package `remi-release-7.rpm`, I am able to install newer versions of PHP. I write my script to a file named `setup.sh` which I place in the infrastructure directory alongside `Vagrantfile`.

Now, how do I kick off the provisioning process? If the `config.vm.provision` directive and the `setup.sh` script had both been in place when I ran `vagrant up`, then the provisioning would have been automatic. As it is, I'll now need to run it manually:

```
$ vagrant provision
```

This will spew an awful lot of information onto your terminal as the `setup.sh` script is run within the Vagrant box. Let's see if it worked:

```
$ vagrant ssh
$ php -v

PHP 8.0.0 (cli) (built: Nov 24 2020 17:04:03) ( NTS gcc x86_64 )
Copyright (c) The PHP Group
Zend Engine v4.0.0-dev, Copyright (c) Zend Technologies
```

Setting Up the Web Server

Of course, even with Apache installed, the system is not ready to be run. First of all, we should configure Apache. The easiest way to do this is to create a configuration file that can be copied into Apache's `conf.d` directory. Let's call the file `poppch20.conf` and drop it into the infrastructure directory:

```
<VirtualHost *:80>
    ServerAdmin matt@getinstance.com
    DocumentRoot /var/www/poppch20
    ServerName poppch20.vagrant.internal
    ErrorLog logs/poppch20-error_log
    CustomLog logs/poppch20-access_log common
</VirtualHost>

<Directory /var/popp/wwwch20>
AllowOverride all
</Directory>
```

I'll return to that hostname a little later. Leaving aside that tantalizing detail, this is enough to tell Apache about our `/var/www/poppch20` directory and to set up logging. Of course, I'll also have to update `setup.sh` to copy the configuration file at provision time:

```
sudo cp $VAGRANTDIR/poppch20.conf /etc/httpd/conf.d/
systemctl start httpd
systemctl enable httpd
```

I copy the configuration file into place and restart the web server so that the configuration is picked up. I also run `systemctl enable` to ensure that the server will be started at boot time.

After making this change, I can rerun this script:

```
$ vagrant provision
```

It's important to note that those parts of the setup script we previously covered will also be rerun. When you create a provisioning script, you must design it so it can be executed repeatedly without serious repercussions. Luckily, Yum detects that my specified packages have already been installed and grumbles harmlessly, in part because I take the precaution of passing it -q flag, which keeps the complaints relatively muted.

Setting Up MariaDB

For many applications, you'll need to make sure that a database is available and ready for connections. Here's a simple addition to my setup script:

```
sudo yum -q -y install mariadb-server
systemctl start mariadb
systemctl enable mariadb

/usr/bin/mysqladmin -s -u root password 'vagrant' || echo " -- unable to
create pass - probably already done"
domysqldb vagrant poppch20_vagrant vagrant vagrant

ROOTPASS=vagrant
DBNAME=poppch20_vagrant
DBUSER=vagrant
DBPASS=vagrant
MYSQL=mysql
MYSQLROOTCMD="mysql -uroot    -p$ROOTPASS"

echo "creating database $DBNAME..."
echo "CREATE DATABASE IF NOT EXISTS $DBNAME" | $MYSQLROOTCMD || die "unable
to create db";

echo "grant all on $DBNAME.* to $DBUSER@'localhost' identified by
\"$DBPASS\""   |
$MYSQLROOTCMD || die "unable to grand privs for user $DBUSER"
echo "FLUSH PRIVILEGES" | $MYSQL -uroot -p"$ROOTPASS" || die "unable to
flush privs"
```

I install MariaDB, the modern replacement for MySQL (created by MySQL developers and compatible to the extent that it implements familiar MySQL tools and commands). I run the `mysqladmin` command to create a root password. This will fail after the first run because the password will already be set, so I use the `-s` flag to suppress error messages and print a message of my own if the command fails. Then I create a database, a user, and a password.

With that in place, I can provision again and then test my database:

```
$ vagrant provision

# much output

$ vagrant ssh
$ mysql -uvagrant -pvagrant poppch20_vagrant

Welcome to the MariaDB monitor. Commands end with ; or \g.
Your MariaDB connection id is 8
Server version: 5.5.65-MariaDB MariaDB Server

Copyright (c) 2000, 2018, Oracle, MariaDB Corporation Ab and others.

Type 'help;' or '\h' for help. Type '\c' to clear the current input statement.

MariaDB [poppch20_vagrant]>
```

We now have a running database and a web server. It's time to see the code in action.

Configuring a Hostname

We have logged in to our new production-like development environment several times, so networking is more or less taken care of. Even though I've configured a web server, I've yet to use it. That's because we still need to support a hostname for our VM. So let's add one to `Vagrantfile`:

```
config.vm.hostname = "poppch20.vagrant.internal"
config.vm.network :private_network, ip: "192.168.33.148"
```

I invent a hostname and use the `config.vm.hostname` directive to add it. I also configure private networking with `config.vm.network`, assigning a static IP address. You should use private address space for this—an unused IP address beginning with `192.168` should work.

Because this is an invented hostname, we must configure our operating system to handle the resolution. On a Unix-like system, that means editing a system file, /etc/ hosts. In this case, I would add the following:

```
192.168.33.148    poppch20.vagrant.internal
```

Note   The hosts file on Windows can be found at %windir%\system32\ drivers\etc\hosts.

Not overly onerous, but we are working toward a one-command install for our team, so it would be good to have a way of automating this step. Fortunately, Vagrant supports plug-ins, and the hostmanager plug-in does exactly what we need. To add a plug-in, you simply run the vagrant plugin install command:

```
$ vagrant plugin install vagrant-hostmanager

Installing the 'vagrant-hostmanager' plugin. This can take a few minutes...
Installed the plugin 'vagrant-hostmanager (1.8.9)'!
```

Then you can explicitly tell the plug-in to update /etc/hosts, like this:

```
$ vagrant hostmanager

[default] Updating /etc/hosts file...
```

In order to make this process automatic for our team members, we should explicitly enable hostmanager in Vagrantfile:

```
config.hostmanager.enabled = true
```

With the configuration changes in place, we should run vagrant reload in order to apply them. Then it's the moment of truth! Will our system run in the browser? As you can see in Figure 20-2, the system should work just fine.

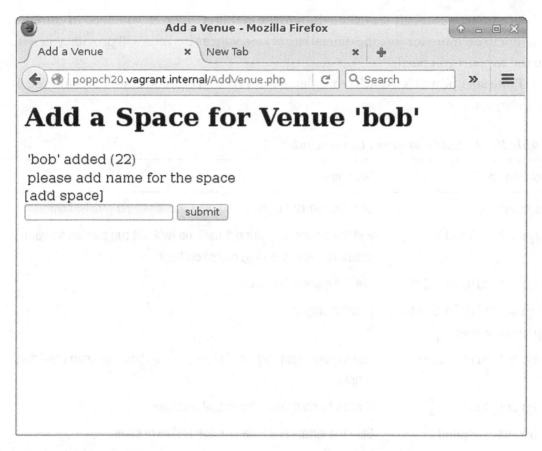

Figure 20-2. *Accessing a configured system on a Vagrant box*

Wrapping It Up

So we have gone from nothing to a fully working development environment. Given that it took a chapter's worth of effort to get here, it might seem like a bit of a cheat to say that Vagrant is quick and easy. There are two answers to that. First, once you have done this a few times, it becomes a pretty simple matter to spin up yet another Vagrant setup—certainly much easier than trying to juggle multiple dependency stacks by hand.

More importantly, though, the real speed and efficiency gain does not lie with the person who sets Vagrant up. Imagine a new developer coming in to your project expecting days' worth of downloads, configuration file edits, and wiki-clicking. Imagine telling her, "Install Vagrant and VirtualBox. Check out the code. From the infrastructure directory, run 'vagrant up'." And that's it! Compare that with some of the painful onboarding processes you have experienced or heard described.

Of course, we've only scratched the surface in this chapter. As you need to configure Vagrant to do more for you, the official site at www.vagrantup.com will provide you with all the support you need.

Table 20-1 provides a quick reminder of the Vagrant commands we encountered in this chapter.

Table 20-1. *Some Vagrant Commands*

Command	Description
vagrant up	Boot the virtual machine and provision if not yet provisioned
vagrant reload	Halt the system and bring it back up (will not run provision again unless run with the --provision flag)
vagrant plugin list	List the installed plug-ins
vagrant plugin install <plugin-name>	Install a plug-in
vagrant provision	Run the provision step again (useful if you have updated provision scripts)
vagrant halt	Gracefully shut down the virtual machine
vagrant suspend	Stop the virtual machine process and save state
vagrant resume	Resume a previously suspended virtual machine process
vagrant init	Create a new Vagrantfile document
vagrant destroy	Destroy the virtual machine. Don't worry, you can always start again with vagrant up!

Summary

In this chapter, I introduced Vagrant, the application that lets you work in a production-like development environment without sacrificing your authoring tools. I covered installation, the choosing of a distribution, and initial setup—including mounting your development directories. Once we had a virtual machine to play with, I moved on to the provisioning process—covering package installation as well as database and web server configuration. Finally, I looked at hostname management, and I showed our system working in the browser!

## CHAPTER 21

Continuous Integration

In previous chapters, you've seen a plethora of tools that are designed to support a well-managed project. Unit testing, documentation, build, and version control are all fantastically useful. But tools, and testing in particular, can be bothersome.

Even if your tests only take a few minutes to run, you're often too focused on coding to bother with them. Not only that, but you have clients and colleagues waiting for new features. The temptation to keep on coding is always there. But bugs are much easier to fix close to the time they are hatched. That's because you're more likely to know which change caused the problem and are better able to come up with a quick fix.

In this chapter, I introduce Continuous Integration, a practice that automates test and build and brings together the tools and techniques you've encountered in recent chapters.

This chapter will cover these topics:

- Defining Continuous Integration
- Preparing a project for CI
- Looking at Jenkins: A CI server
- Customizing Jenkins for PHP projects with specialized plug-ins

What Is Continuous Integration?

In the bad old days, integration was something you did after you'd finished the fun stuff. It was also the stage at which you realized how much work you still had to do. Integration is the process by which all of the parts of your project are bundled up into packages that can be shipped and deployed. It's not glamorous, and it's actually hard.

Integration is tied up also with QA. You can't ship a product if it isn't fit for purpose. That means tests. Lots of tests. If you haven't been testing much prior to the integration stage, it probably also means nasty surprises. Lots of them.

© Matt Zandstra 2021
M. Zandstra, *PHP 8 Objects, Patterns, and Practice*, https://doi.org/10.1007/978-1-4842-6791-2_21

You know from Chapter 18 that it's best practice to test early and often. You know from Chapters 15 and 19 that you should design with deployment in mind right from the start. Most of us accept that this is the ideal, but how often does the reality match up?

If you practice test-oriented development (a term I prefer to test-first development, because it better reflects the reality of most good projects I've seen), then the writing of tests is less hard than you might think. After all, you write tests as you code anyway. Every time you develop a component, you create code fragments, perhaps at the bottom of the class file, that instantiate objects and call their methods. If you gather up those throwaway scraps of code, written to put your component through its paces during development, you've got yourself a test case. Stick them into a class and add them to your suite.

Oddly, it's often the *running* of tests that people avoid. Over time, tests take longer to run. Failures related to known issues creep in, making it hard to diagnose new problems. Also, you suspect someone else committed code that broke the tests, and you don't have time to hold up your own work while you fix issues that are someone else's fault. Better to run a couple of tests related to your work than the whole suite.

Failing to run tests, and therefore to fix the problems that they could reveal, makes issues harder and harder to address. The biggest overhead in hunting for bugs is usually the diagnosis and not the cure. Very often, a fix can be applied in a matter of minutes, set against perhaps hours searching for the reason a test failed. If a test fails within minutes or hours of a commit, however, you're more likely to know where to look for the problem.

Software build suffers from a similar problem. If you don't install your project often, you're likely to find that, although everything runs fine on your development box, an installed instance falls over with an obscure error message. The longer you've gone between builds, the more obscure the reason for the failure will likely be to you.

It's often something simple: an undeclared dependency upon a library on your system or some class files you failed to check in. These are easy to fix if you're on hand. But what if a build failure occurs when you're out of the office? Whichever unlucky team member gets the job of building and releasing the project won't know about your setup and won't have easy access to those missing files.

Integration issues are magnified by the number of people involved in a project. You may like and respect all of your team members, but we all know that they are much more likely than you are to leave tests unrun. And then they commit a week's work of development at 4 p.m. on Friday, just as you're about to declare the project good to go for a release.

Continuous Integration (CI) reduces some of these problems by automating the build and test process.

CI is both a set of practices and tools. As a practice, it requires frequent commits of project code (at least daily). With each commit, tests should be run and any packages should be built. You've already seen some of the tools required for CI, in particular PHPUnit and Phing. Individual tools aren't enough, however. A higher-level system is required to coordinate and automate the process.

Without the higher system, a CI server, it's likely that the practice of CI will simply succumb to our natural tendency to skip the chores. After all, we'd rather be coding.

Having a system like this in place offers clear benefits. First, your project gets built and tested frequently. That's the ultimate aim and benefit of CI. That it's automated, however, adds two further dimensions. The test and build happens in a different thread to that of development. It happens behind the scenes and doesn't require that you stop work to run tests. Also, as with testing, CI encourages good design. In order for it to be possible to automate installation in a remote location, you're forced to consider ease of installation from the start.

I don't know how many times I've come across projects where the installation procedure was an arcane secret known only to a few developers. "You mean you didn't set up the URL rewriting?" asks one old hand with barely concealed contempt. "Honestly, the rewrite rules *are* in the Wiki, you know. Just paste them into the Apache config file." Developing with CI in mind means making systems easier to test and install. This might mean a little more work up front, but it makes our lives easier down the line. Much easier.

So, to start off, I'm going to lay down some of that expensive groundwork. In fact, you'll find that in most of the sections to come, you've encountered these preparatory steps already.

Preparing a Project for CI

First of all, of course, I need a project to integrate continuously. Now, I'm a lazy soul, so I'll look for some code that comes with tests already written. The obvious candidate is the project I created in Chapter 18 to illustrate PHPUnit. I'm going to name it userthing, because it's a *thing*, with a User object in it.

Note   Some of the tools described in this chapter had either been very recently released or were in beta at the time of writing. This resulted in a few quirks and incompatibilities. It is likely that these issues will have been ironed out already by the time you read this. However, in order to build a reliable CI system, I have had to roll back to earlier versions of PHP and PHPUnit for these examples. This should make no difference to the code and configuration shown.

First of all, here is a breakdown of my project directory:

```
$ find src/ test/

src/
src/persist
src/persist/UserStore.php
src/util
src/util/Validator.php
src/domain
src/domain/User.php
test/
test/persist
test/persist/UserStoreTest.php
test/util
test/util/ValidatorTest.php
```

As you can see, I've tidied up the structure a little, adding some package directories. Within the code, I've supported the package structure with the use of namespaces.

Now that I have a project, I should add it to a version control system.

CI and Version Control

Version control is essential for CI. A CI system needs to acquire the most recent version of a project without human intervention (at least once things have been set up).

For this example, I'll use a repository I set up on Bitbucket. I'll configure code on my local development machine, add and commit it, and then push to the remote server:

```
$ cd path/to/userthing
$ git init
$ git remote add origin git@bitbucket.org:getinstance/userthing.git
$ git add build.xml composer.json src/ test/
$ git commit -m 'initial commit'
$ git push -u origin master
```

> **Note** I have created and used a Bitbucket repository in these examples. I could as easily have used GitHub which now supports free private repositories.

I navigated to my development directory and initialized it. Then I added the `origin` remote, to which I pushed the code. I like to confirm that everything is working by performing a fresh clone:

```
$ git clone git@bitbucket.org:getinstance/userthing.git

Cloning into 'userthing'...
X11 forwarding request failed on channel 0
remote: Counting objects: 16, done.
remote: Compressing objects: 100% (11/11), done.
remote: Total 16 (delta 0), reused 0 (delta 0)
Receiving objects: 100% (16/16), done.
Checking connectivity… done.
```

Now I have a `userthing` repository and a local clone. Time to automate build and test.

Phing

We encountered Phing in Chapter 19. I will be using a version installed with composer for this chapter.

```
"require-dev": {
    "phing/phing": "3.*"
},
```

Note   As this chapter was written, Phing 3 was still in alpha testing, and composer installation failed due to dependency issues. There were also issues with the phar version and PHP 8. So, for the purposes of this chapter, we have forked and patched Phing to address the various code and compatibility problems. Hopefully, as you read this, Phing is stable once again! You can find version information and installation instructions for Phing at the homepage: `www.phing. info/#install`.

I will be using this build tool as the glue for my project's CI environment, so I run this install on the server I intend to use for testing (or, of course, you could try this out on a virtual server using Vagrant and VirtualBox). I will define targets for building and testing the code and for running the various other quality assurance tools you will meet in this chapter.

Let's build a sample task:

```
// listing 21.01
<project name="userthing" default="build" basedir=".">
    <property name="build" value="./build" />
    <property name="test" value="./test" />
    <property name="src" value="./src" />
    <property name="version" value="1.1.1" />

    <target name="build">
        <mkdir dir="${build}" />
        <copy todir="${build}/src">
            <fileset dir="${src}">
            </fileset>
        </copy>

        <copy todir="${build}/test">
            <fileset dir="${test}">
            </fileset>
        </copy>

    </target>
```

```
    <target name="clean">
        <delete dir="${build}" />
    </target>
</project>
```

I set up four properties. `build` refers to the directory in which I might assemble my files before generating a package. `test` points to the test directory. `src` refers to the source directory. `version` defines the version number for the package.

The `build` target copies the `src` and `test` directories into the build environment. In a more complex project, I might also perform transformations, generate configuration files, and assemble binary assets at this stage. This target is the project's default.

The `clean` target removes the build directory and anything it contains. Let's run a build:

```
$ ./vendor/bin/phing

Buildfile: /var/popp/src/ch21/build.xml

userthing > build:
    [mkdir] Created dir: /var/popp/src/ch21/build
     [copy] Created 4 empty directories in /var/popp/src/ch21/build/src
     [copy] Copying 3 files to /var/popp/src/ch21/build/src
     [copy] Created 3 empty directories in /var/popp/src/ch21/build/test
     [copy] Copying 2 files to /var/popp/src/ch21/build/test

BUILD FINISHED

Total time: 1.8206 second
```

Unit Tests

Unit tests are the key to continuous integration. It's no good successfully building a project that contains broken code. I covered unit testing with PHPUnit in Chapter 18. If you're reading out of order, however, you'll want to install this invaluable tool before proceeding. Here is one way to install PHPUnit globally:

```
$ wget https://phar.phpunit.de/phpunit.phar
$ chmod 755 phpunit.phar
$ sudo mv phpunit.phar /usr/local/bin/phpunit
```

You can also install PHPUnit with Composer:

```
"require-dev": {
    "phpunit/phpunit": "^9"
}
```

This is the approach I'll take for my example. Because PHPUnit will be installed under the vendor/ directory, my development directory will remain independent of the wider system.

I've separated my test directory from the rest of my source code, so I'll need to set up my autoload rules so that PHP can locate all the system's classes during testing. Here's my complete composer.json:

```
"require-dev": {
    "phpunit/phpunit": "^9"
},
"autoload":  {
    "psr-4": {
        "userthing\\": ["src/", "test/"]
    }
}
```

Don't forget to run composer update after you make any changes to composer.json.

Also in Chapter 18, I wrote tests for a version of the userthing code I'll be working with in this chapter. Here, I run them once again (from within the src directory), to make sure my reorganization has not broken anything new:

```
$ vendor/bin/phpunit test/

PHPUnit 9.5.0 by Sebastian Bergmann and contributors.

.......                        7 / 7 (100%)

Time: 00:00.002, Memory: 18.00 MB

OK (7 tests, 7 assertions)
```

So this confirms that my tests work. However, I would like to invoke them with Phing.

Phing provides an exec task which we might use to invoke the phpunit command. However, it's always best to use a specialized tool if there's one available. There is a built-in task for this job:

```
// listing 21.02
<target name="test" depends="build">
    <phpunit bootstrap="${phing.dir}/vendor/autoload.php" printsummary="true">
        <formatter type="plain" usefile="false"/>
        <batchtest>
            <fileset dir="${test}">
                <include name="**/*Test.php"/>
            </fileset>
        </batchtest>
    </phpunit>
</target>
```

Because these are unit tests and not functional tests, we can run them against the local src/ directory rather than requiring an installed instance (with a functioning database or web server). Among many other attributes, the phpunit task accepts a printsummary attribute, which causes an overview of the test process to be output.

Much of this task's functionality is configured using nested elements. The formatter element manages the way that test information is generated. In this case, I have opted to output basic human-readable data. batchtest lets you define multiple test files using the nested fileset element.

Note   The phpunit task is highly configurable. The Phing manual provides full documentation at www.phing.info/guide/chunkhtml/PHPUnitTask.html.

Here, I run the tests with Phing:

```
$ ./vendor/bin/phing test

Buildfile: /vagrant/poppch21/build.xml

userthing > build:

userthing > test:
```

```
[phpunit] Testsuite: userthing\persist\UserStoreTest
[phpunit] Tests run: 4, Warnings: 0, Failures: 0, Errors: 0, Incomplete:
0, Skipped: 0, Time elapsed: 0.00684 s
[phpunit] Testsuite: userthing\util\ValidatorTest
[phpunit] Tests run: 3, Warnings: 0, Failures: 0, Errors: 0, Incomplete:
0, Skipped: 0, Time elapsed: 0.01188 s
[phpunit] Total tests run: 7, Warnings: 0, Failures: 0, Errors: 0,
Incomplete: 0, Skipped: 0, Time elapsed: 0.02169 s
```

```
BUILD FINISHED
```

```
Total time: 0.1457 seconds
```

Documentation

Transparency is one of the principles of CI. When you're looking at a build in a
Continuous Integration environment, therefore, it's important to be able to check that
the documentation is up to date and covers the most recent classes and methods.
Because the latest version of PHPDocumentor is under active development, composer
installation is not currently encouraged. For the same reason, the PHPDocumentor
GitHub page may be the best place for the most up-to-date information.

```
$ wget -O phpDocumentor https://github.com/phpDocumentor/phpDocumentor/
releases/download/v3.0.0-rc/
phpDocumentor.phar
$ chmod 755 ./phpDocumentor
$ mv phpDocumentor /usr/local/bin/phpDocumentor
```

Running as root, I download phpDocumentor v3, make it executable, and move it to a
central location on my system.

I'd better invoke the tool just to be sure, this time from the build directory:

```
$ cd ./build
$ phpDocumentor --directory=src --target=docs --title=userthing
```

This generates some pretty bare documentation. Once it's published on a CI server,
I'm sure to be shamed into writing some real inline documentation.

Once again, I want to add this to my build.xml document. There is a task named phpdoc2 that is designed to integrate with PHPDocumentor. However, since it does not integrate well with the phar version of PHPDocumentor, I will invoke the tool using the cruder exec task.

```
// listing 21.03
<target name="doc" depends="build">
    <mkdir dir="reports/docs" />
    <exec executable="/usr/local/bin/phpDocumentor" dir="${phing.dir}">
        <arg line=" --directory=build/src --target=reports/docs
        --title=userthing" />
    </exec>
</target>
```

Again, my doc target depends upon the build target. I create the reports/docs output directory and then invoke the PHPDocumentor using the exec task. exec accepts a nested arg element, which I use to specify my command arguments.

Code Coverage

It's no good relying on tests if they don't apply to the code you have written. PHPUnit includes the ability to report on code coverage. Here's an extract from PHPUnit's usage information:

```
--coverage-clover <file>   Generate code coverage report in Clover XML
  format
...
--coverage-html  <dir>     Generate code coverage report in HTML format
```

In order to use this feature, you must have a code coverage extension installed, such as Xdebug or pcov. I will demonstrate how to generate coverage reports with Xdebug. Using pcov is a very similar process. You can find out more about these extensions at http://pecl.php.net/package/Xdebug and https://pecl.php.net/package/pcov (installation information found at http://xdebug.org/docs/install and https://github.com/krakjoe/pcov/blob/develop/INSTALL.md). You may also be able to install these packages directly using your Linux distribution's package management system. This should work for you in Fedora, for example:

```
$  sudo yum install php-xdebug
```

Here, I run PHPUnit from the `src/` directory with code coverage enabled:

```
$ export XDEBUG_MODE=coverage
$ ./vendor/bin/phpunit --whitelist src/ --coverage-html coverage test

PHPUnit 9.5.0 by Sebastian Bergmann and contributors.

.......                              7 / 7 (100%)

Time: 00:00.121, Memory: 12.00 MB

OK (7 tests, 7 assertions)

Generating code coverage report in HTML format ... done [00:00.047]
```

Now you can see the report in your browser (see Figure 21-1).

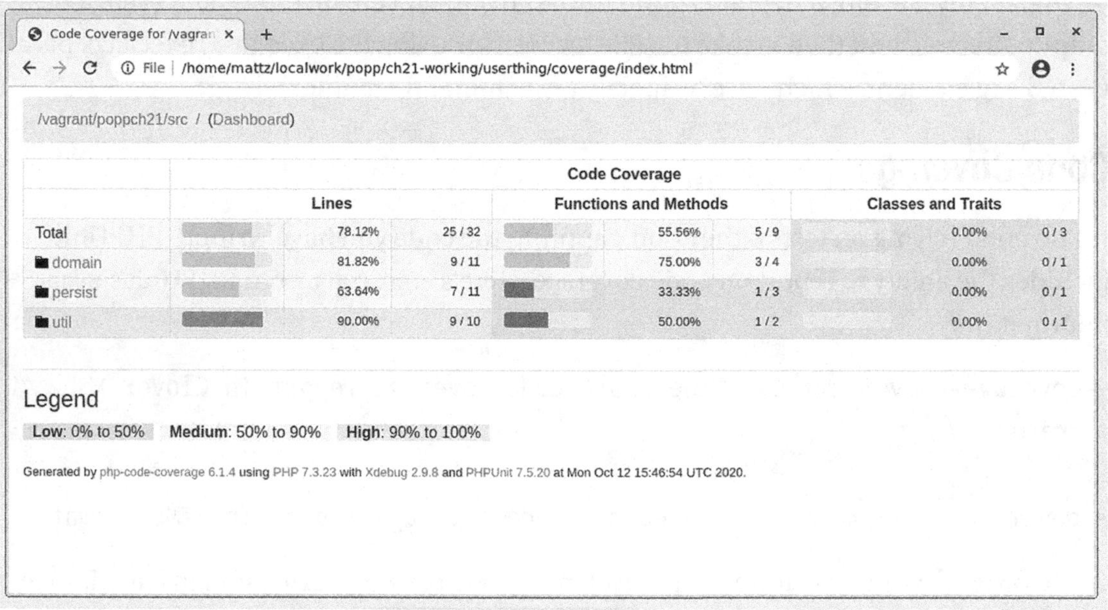

Figure 21-1. *The code coverage report*

It's important to note that achieving full coverage is not the same as adequately testing a system. On the other hand, it's good to know about any gaps in your tests. As you can see, I've still got some work to do.

Having confirmed that I can check coverage from the command line, I need to add this functionality to my build document:

```
// listing 21.04
<target name="citest" depends="build">
    <mkdir dir="reports/coverage" />
    <coverage-setup database="reports/coverage.db">
        <fileset dir="${src}">
            <include name="**/*.php"/>
        </fileset>
    </coverage-setup>

    <phpunit haltonfailure="true" codecoverage="true" bootstrap="${phing.
    dir}/vendor/autoload.php" printsummary="true">
        <formatter type="plain" usefile="false"/>
        <formatter type="xml" outfile="testreport.xml" todir="reports" />
        <formatter type="clover" outfile="cloverreport.xml" todir="reports" />
        <batchtest>
            <fileset dir="${test}">
                <include name="**/*Test.php"/>
            </fileset>
        </batchtest>
    </phpunit>

    <coverage-report outfile="reports/coverage.xml">
        <report todir="reports/coverage" />
    </coverage-report>
</target>
```

I have created a new task named citest. Much of it is a reproduction of the test task you have already seen.

I start by creating a reports directory and a coverage subdirectory.

I use the coverage-setup task to provide configuration information for the coverage feature. I specify where raw coverage data should be stored using the database attribute. The nested fileset element defines the files that should be subject to coverage analysis.

I have added two formatter elements to the phpunit task. The formatter of type xml will generate a file named testreport.xml, which will contain the test results. The clover formatter will generate coverage information, also in XML format. Finally, in the citest target, I deploy the coverage-report task. This takes existing coverage information, generates a new XML file, and then outputs an HTML report.

745

> **Note** The `CoverageReportTask` element is documented at `www.phing.info/guide/chunkhtml/CoverageReportTask.html`.

Coding Standards

I discussed coding standards at length in Chapter 15. Although it can be annoying to have your individual style cramped by a shared standard, it can make a project easier to work with for the wider team. For that reason, many teams enforce a standard. It's hard to enforce this by eye, however, so it makes sense to automate the process.

Once again, I will use Composer. This time, I'll be configuring it to install PHP_CodeSniffer:

```
"require-dev": {
    "phpunit/phpunit": "^9",
    "squizlabs/php_codesniffer": "3.*"
},
```

Now I will apply the PSR-12 coding standard to my code:

```
$ vendor/bin/phpcs --standard=PSR12 src/util/Validator.php

FILE: /vagrant/poppch21/src/util/Validator.php
--------------------------------------------------------------------
FOUND 8 ERRORS AFFECTING 2 LINES
--------------------------------------------------------------------
  7 | ERROR | [x] Header blocks must be separated by a single blank line
 22 | ERROR | [ ] Visibility must be declared on method "validateUser"
 22 | ERROR | [ ] Expected "function abc(...)"; found "function abc (...)"
 22 | ERROR | [x] Expected 1 space after FUNCTION keyword; 4 found
 22 | ERROR | [x] Expected 0 spaces after opening parenthesis; 1 found
 22 | ERROR | [x] Expected 0 spaces before opening parenthesis; 3 found
 22 | ERROR | [x] Expected 1 space between comma and argument "$pass"; 0 found
 22 | ERROR | [x] Opening brace should be on a new line
--------------------------------------------------------------------
PHPCBF CAN FIX THE 6 MARKED SNIFF VIOLATIONS AUTOMATICALLY
--------------------------------------------------------------------
```

Clearly, I need to clean up my code a little!

One benefit of an automated tool is its impersonal nature. If your team does decide to impose a set of coding conventions, it's arguably better having a humorless script correcting your style than a humorless coworker doing the same thing.

As you might expect by now, I would like to add a `CodeSniffer` target to my build file.

```
// listing 21.05
<target name="sniff" depends="build">
    <exec executable="vendor/bin/phpcs" passthru="true" dir="${phing.dir}">
        <arg line="--report-checkstyle=reports/checkstyle.xml
        --standard=PSR12  build/src"
/>
    </exec>
</target>
```

Although Phing provides a `phpcodesniffer` task, it is not compatible with recent versions of PHP_CodeSniffer. Once again, therefore, I use `exec` to run the tool. I invoke `phpcs` with the `--report-checkstyle` flag so that it will generate an XML file in the `reports` directory.

So I have a lot of useful tools that I can use to monitor my project. Of course, left to myself I'd soon lose interest in running them, even with my useful Phing build file. In fact, I'd probably revert to the old idea of an integration phase and pull out the tools only when I'm close to a release, by which time their effectiveness as early-warning systems will be irrelevant. What I need is a CI server to run the tools for me.

Jenkins (formerly named Hudson) is an open source continuous integration server. Although it is written in Java, Jenkins is easy to use with PHP tools. That's because the continuous integration server stands outside of the projects it builds, kicking off and monitoring the results of various commands. Jenkins also integrates well with PHP because it is designed to support plug-ins, and there is a highly active developer community working to extend the server's core functionality.

Note   Why Jenkins? Jenkins is very easy to use and extend. It is well established, and it has an active user community. It's free and open source. Plug-ins that support integration with PHP (and that includes most build and test tools you might think of) are available. There are many CI server solutions out there, however. A previous version of this book focused on CruiseControl (`http://cruisecontrol.sourceforge.net/`), and this remains a good option.

Installing Jenkins

Jenkins is a Java system, so you will need to have Java installed. How you go about this will vary from system to system. The Jenkins site provides good installation instructions at www.jenkins.io/doc/book/installing/.

Thanks to Vagrant I am installing on a CentOS 7 system—so these are my installation steps:

```
$ sudo wget -O /etc/yum.repos.d/jenkins.repo \
    https://pkg.jenkins.io/redhat-stable/jenkins.repo
$ sudo rpm --import https://pkg.jenkins.io/redhat-stable/jenkins.io.key
$ sudo yum update
$ sudo yum install jenkins java-1.8.0-openjdk-devel
$ sudo systemctl daemon-reload
```

You can start Jenkins like this:

```
$ sudo systemctl start jenkins
```

By default, Jenkins runs on port 8080, so you can find out whether you're ready to proceed by firing up your browser and visiting http://yourhost:8080/. You should see something like the screen in Figure 21-2.

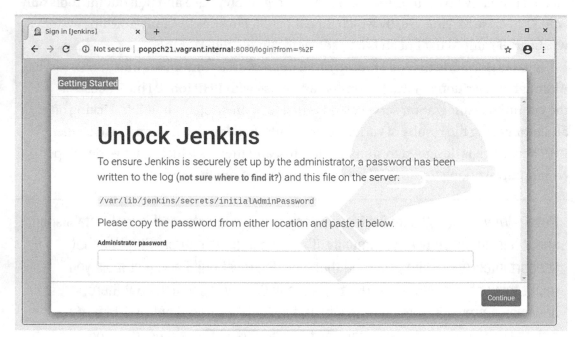

Figure 21-2. *The install screen*

The instructions in Figure 21-2 are pretty self-explanatory. I grab the password from /var/lib/jenkins/secrets/initialAdminPassword (using sudo because of restricted read permissions) and enter it into the box provided. Then I'm presented with a choice: install with popular plug-ins or pick my own? I opt for the most popular plug-ins, which I know will get me support for Git, among other things. If you want a slim system, you might choose to select only those plug-ins you need. After that, it's time to create a username and password before finishing up installation.

Installing Jenkins Plug-ins

Jenkins is highly customizable, and I will need quite a few plug-ins to integrate with the features I have described so far in this chapter. From within the Jenkins web interface, I click Manage Jenkins and then Manage Plugins. Beneath the Available tab, I find a long list. I select the checkboxes in the Install column for all plug-ins that I wish to add to Jenkins.

Table 21-1 describes the plug-ins that I will be using.

Table 21-1. *Some Jenkins Plug-ins*

Plug-in	Description
Git Plug-in	Allows interaction with Git repositories
jUnit Plug-in	Integration with the xUnit family of tools including PHPUnit
Phing Plug-in	Invokes Phing targets
Clover PHP Plug-in	Accesses clover XML file and HTML files generated by PHPUnit and generates report
HTML Publisher Plug-in	Integrates HTML reports. Used for PHPDocumentor output
Warnings Next Generation Plugin	Accesses the XML file generated by PHPCodeSniffer and generates report

You can see the Jenkins plug-in page in Figure 21-3.

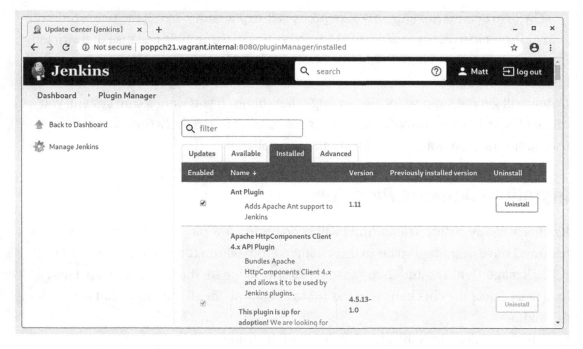

Figure 21-3.   *The Jenkins plug-in screen*

Having installed these plug-ins, I'm almost ready to create and configure my project.

Setting Up the Git Public Key

Before I can use the Git plug-in, I need to ensure that I have access to a Git repository. In Chapter 17, I described the process of generating a public key in order to access a remote Git repository. We need to repeat this process here. But where does Jenkins call home?

This location is configurable, but naturally Jenkins will clue you in. I click Manage Jenkins and then Configure System. I find Jenkins' home directory listed there. Of course, I could also check the /etc/ passwd file for information relating to the jenkins user. In my case, the directory is /var/lib/jenkins.

Now I need to configure an SSH directory:

```
$ sudo su jenkins -s /bin/bash
$ cd ~
$ mkdir .ssh
$ chmod 0700 .ssh
$ ssh-keygen
```

I switch to the jenkins user, specifying the shell to use (because shell access may be deactivated by default). I change to this user's home directory. The ssh-keygen command generates the SSH keys. When prompted for a password, I just hit Return, so Jenkins will be authenticated by its key only. I make sure that the file generated at .ssh/id_rsa is neither world- nor group-readable:

```
$ chmod 0600 .ssh/id_rsa
```

I can acquire the public key from .ssh/id_rsa.pub and add it to my remote Git repository. See Chapter 17 for more on that.

I'm not quite there yet. I need to ensure that my Git server is a known SSH host. I can combine setting this up with a command-line test of my Git configuration. I make sure I'm still logged in as the jenkins user when I do this:

```
$ cd /tmp
$ git clone git@bitbucket.org:getinstance/userthing.git
```

I am prompted to confirm my Git host, and it's then added to the jenkins user's .ssh/known_hosts file. This prevents Jenkins from tripping over later when it makes its Git connection.

Note   There are also various plug-ins you can use to manage Git credentials including *SSH Agent*, *OAuth Credentials*, and *Kubernetes Credentials*.

Installing a Project

From the Jenkins dashboard page, I click New Item. From this new screen, I can, at last, create my userthing project. You can see the setup screen in Figure 21-4.

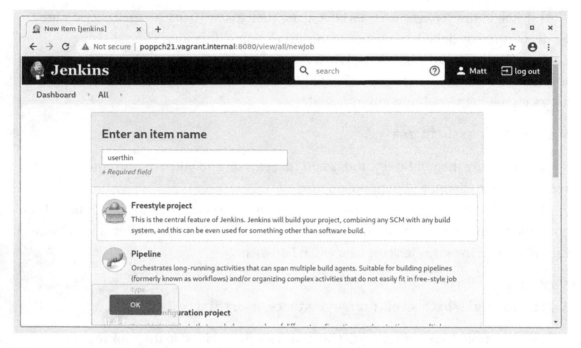

Figure 21-4. *The project setup screen*

I chose Freestyle project and hit OK. That leads me to the project configuration screen. My first order of business is to link up with the remote Git repository. I choose the Git radio button in the Source Code Manager section and add my repository. You can see this in Figure 21-5.

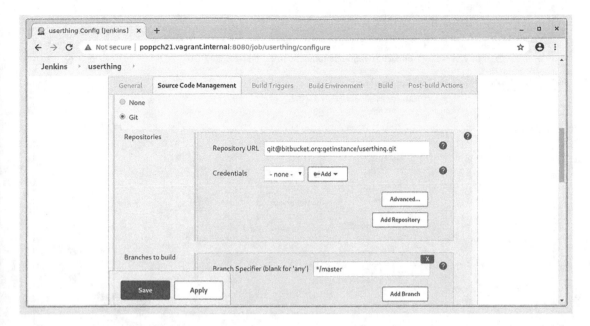

Figure 21-5. *Setting up the version control repository*

If all has gone well, I should be able to access my source code. I can check that by saving and choosing `Build Now` from the dashboard page. In order to see some meaningful action, however, I should also set up Phing. This is simple, because I have installed Phing centrally. If, like me, you're using Composer, however, things are just a little more complicated. You must tell Jenkins where to find the Phing executable. You can do this by choosing `Manage Jenkins` from the main menu and then `Global Tool Configuration`. Because I have installed the Phing plug-in, I will find a configuration area for the tool there. I click `Add Phing` to get access to the form. In Figure 21-6, I show the configuration area you would use to reference a local version of Phing.

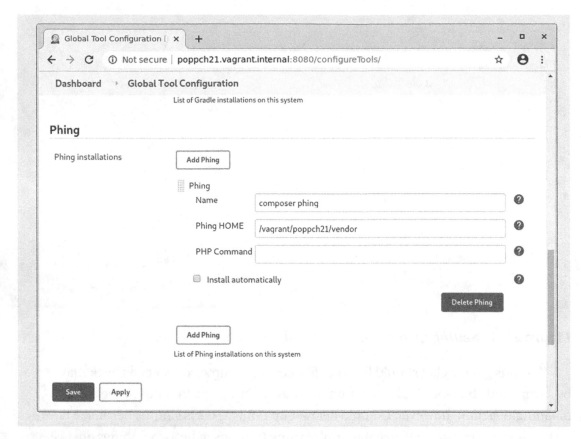

Figure 21-6. *Specifying Phing's location*

I give the configuration a name and add the path to the vendor directory in my project where Phing is to be found.

Once I am confident that Jenkins can find Phing, I can configure it for my project. I return to the userthing project area and the Configure menu. I scroll to the Build section and choose two items from the Add build step pulldown. First, I choose Execute shell. I need to make sure that Jenkins runs composer install, or none of the tools my project depends upon will be installed. Figure 21-7 shows the configuration.

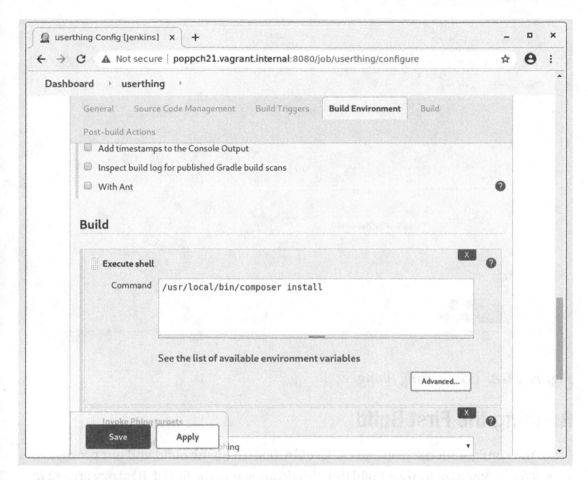

Figure 21-7. Setting up shell execution

The next item I choose from the Add build step pulldown is Invoke Phing targets. I choose the Phing instance I configured earlier (composer phing) from the pulldown and add my targets to the text field. You can see this step in Figure 21-8.

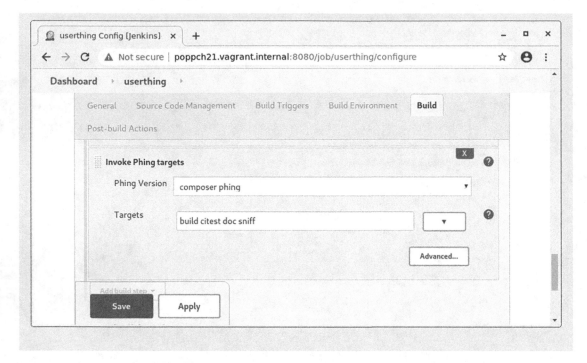

Figure 21-8. *Configuring Phing*

Running the First Build

I save the configuration screen and click `Build Now` to run the build and test process. This is the moment of truth! A build link should appear in the `Build History` area of the screen. I click that and then `Console Output` to confirm that the build went ahead as hoped. You can see the output in Figure 21-9.

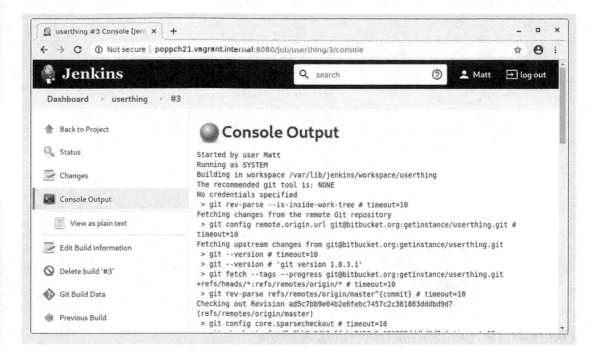

Figure 21-9. *Console output*

Jenkins checks the userthing code out from the Git server and runs all the build and test targets.

Configuring the Reports

Thanks to my build file, Phing saves reports into the build/reports directory and documentation into build/docs. The plug-ins that I activated can be configured from the Add post-build action pulldown in the project configuration screen.

Figure 21-10 shows some of these configuration items.

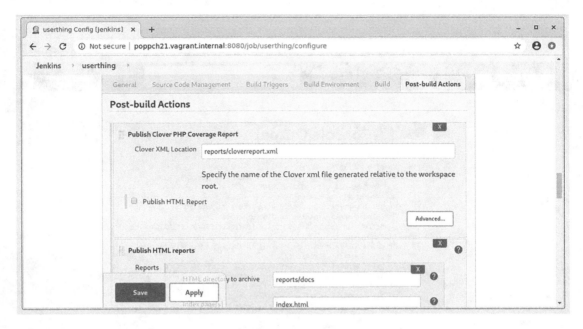

Figure 21-10. *Configuring report plug-in items*

Rather than subject you to screenshot after screenshot, it will be clearer to compress the configuration items into a table. Table 21-2 shows some post-build action fields and the corresponding targets from my Phing build file.

Table 21-2. *Report Configuration*

Configuration Item	Phing Target	Field	Value
Record compiler warning and static analysis results	`sniff`	Tool	`PHP_CodeSniffer`
		Report File Pattern	`reports/checkstyle.xml`
Publish Clover PHP Coverage Report	`citest`	Clover XML Location	`reports/cloverreport.xml`
		Clover HTML report directory	`reports/clovercoverage/`
Publish HTML reports	`doc`	HTML directory to archive Index page[s]	`reports/docs` `index.html`
Publish Junit test result report	`citest`	Test report XMLs	`reports/testreport.xml`
E-mail Notification		Recipients	`someone@somemail.com`

You encountered all of the configuration values in Table 21-2 as I constructed the project's build file. All, that is, apart from the last. The E-mail Notification field allows you to define a list of developers who will all receive notifications when a build fails.

Before I can check coverage, I must create an environment variable named XDEBUG_ MODE with the value coverage. I can do that by heading to Manage Jenkins and then on to the Configure System screen. As you can see in Figure 21-11, I can set environment variables in the Global Properties section.

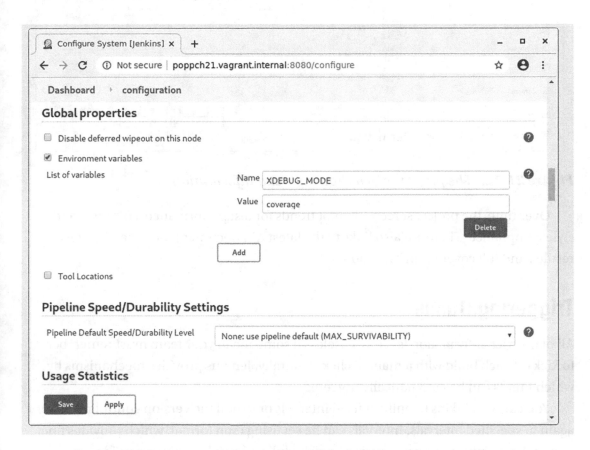

Figure 21-11. *Setting an environment variable*

With all that setup, I can return to the project screen and run another build. Figure 21-12 shows my newly enhanced output.

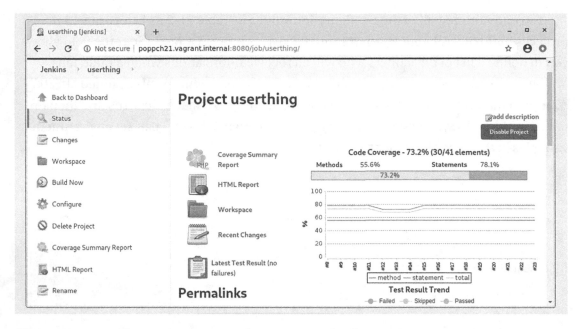

Figure 21-12. *The project screen showing trend information*

Over time, the project screen will plot trends for test performance, coverage, and style compliance. There are also links to the latest API documentation, detailed test results, and full coverage information.

Triggering Builds

All of this rich information is almost useless if someone in your team must remember to kick off each build with a manual click. Naturally, Jenkins provides mechanisms by which builds can be automatically triggered.

You can set Jenkins to build at fixed intervals or to poll the version control repository, again at specified intervals. Intervals can be set using cron format, which provides fine, although somewhat arcane, control over scheduling. Luckily, Jenkins provides good online help for the format, and there are simple aliases if you don't require precision scheduling. The aliases include @hourly, @midnight, @daily, @weekly, and @monthly. In Figure 21-13, I configure the build to run once daily, or every time the repository changes, based upon a poll for changes that should take place once an hour.

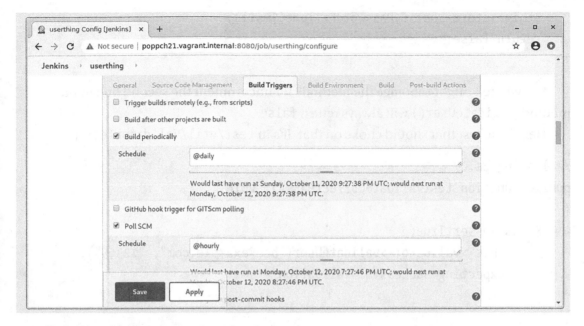

Figure 21-13. *Scheduling builds*

Test Failures

So far, everything seems to be going well, even if userthing won't be winning any code compliance badges any time soon. But tests succeed when they fail, so I'd better break something to make sure that Jenkins reports on it.

Here is a part of a class named Validate in the namespace userthing\util:

```
// listing 21.06
public function validateUser(string $mail, string $pass): bool
{
    // make it always fail
    // return false;
    $user = $this->store->getUser($mail);
    if (is_null($user)) {
        return false;
    }
    $testpass = $user->getPass();
    if ($testpass == $pass) {
        return true;
    }
}
```

```
    $this->store->notifyPasswordFailure($mail);
    return false;
}
```

See where I might sabotage the method? If I uncomment the second line in the method, `validateUser()` will always return `false`.

Here's the test that should choke on that. It's in `test/util/ValidatorTest.php`:

```
// listing 21.07
public function testValidateCorrectPass(): void
{
    $this->assertTrue(
        $this->validator->validateUser("bob@example.com", "12345"),
        "Expecting successful validation"
    );
}
```

Having made my change, all I need to do is commit and wait. Sure enough, before long, the project status shows a build marked by a yellow icon (to indicate that overall project health has taken a ding). Once I click the build link, I find more details. You can see the screen in Figure 21-14.

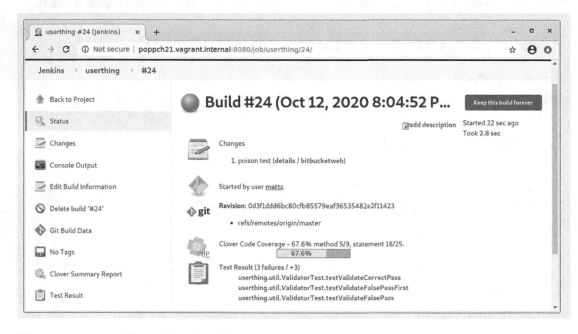

Figure 21-14. *The failing build*

Remember, if you need more information about where a build went wrong, you can always follow the `Console Output` link in the build screen. You will often find more useful information there than on the build summary screen itself.

Summary

In this chapter, I brought together many of the tools that you have seen in previous chapters and glued them in place with Jenkins. I prepared a small project for CI, applying a range of tools including PHPUnit (both for testing and code coverage), PHP_ CodeSniffer, phpDocumentor, and Git. Then I set up Jenkins and showed you how to add a project to the system. I put the system through its paces and, finally, showed you how to extend Jenkins so that it can bug you with emails and test both build and installation.

CHAPTER 22

Objects, Patterns, Practice

From object basics through design pattern principles, and on to tools and techniques, this book has focused on a single objective: the successful PHP project.

In this chapter, I recap some of the topics I have covered and points made throughout the book:

- *PHP and objects*: How PHP continues to increase its support for object-oriented programming and how to leverage these features

- *Objects and design*: Summarizing some OO design principles

- *Patterns*: What makes them cool

- *Pattern principles*: A recap of the guiding object-oriented principles that underlie many patterns

- *The tools for the job*: Revisiting the tools I have described and checking out a few I haven't

Objects

As you saw in Chapter 2, for a long time, objects were something of an afterthought in the PHP world. Support was rudimentary, to say the least, in PHP 3, with objects barely more than associative arrays in fancy dress. Although things improved radically for the object enthusiast with PHP 4, there were still significant problems. Not the least of these was that, by default, objects were assigned and passed by reference.

The introduction of PHP 5 finally dragged objects center stage. You could still program in PHP without ever declaring a class, but the language was finally optimized for object-oriented design. PHP 7 rounded this out, introducing long-awaited features such as scalar and return type declarations. Probably for reasons of backward compatibility, a few popular frameworks remain essentially procedural in nature (notably WordPress); by and large, however, most new PHP projects today are object oriented.

765

© Matt Zandstra 2021
M. Zandstra, *PHP 8 Objects, Patterns, and Practice*, https://doi.org/10.1007/978-1-4842-6791-2_22

In Chapters 3, 4, and 5, I looked at PHP's object-oriented support in detail. Here are some of the new features PHP has introduced since version 5: reflection, exceptions, private and protected methods and properties, the __toString() method, the static modifier, abstract classes and methods, final methods and properties, interfaces, iterators, interceptor methods, type declarations, the const modifier, passing by reference, __clone(), the __construct() method, late static binding, namespaces, and anonymous classes. The extensive length of this incomplete list reveals the degree to which the future of PHP is bound up with object-oriented programming.

The Zend Engine 2 and PHP 5 have made object-oriented design central to the PHP project, opening up the language to a new set of developers and opening up new possibilities for existing devotees.

In Chapter 6, I looked at the benefits that objects can bring to the design of your projects. Because objects and design are one of the central themes of this book, it is worth recapping some conclusions in detail.

Choice

There is no law that says you have to develop with classes and objects only. Well-designed object-oriented code provides a clean interface that can be accessed from any client code, whether procedural or object oriented. Even if you have no interest in writing objects (unlikely if you are still reading this book), you will probably find yourself using them, if only as a client of Composer packages.

Encapsulation and Delegation

Objects mind their own business and get on with their allotted tasks behind closed doors. They provide an interface through which requests and results can be passed. Any data that need not be exposed, and the dirty details of implementation, are hidden behind this front.

This gives object-oriented and procedural projects different shapes. The controller in an object-oriented project is often surprisingly sparse, consisting of a handful of instantiations that acquire objects and invocations that call up data from one set and pass it on to another.

A procedural project, on the other hand, tends to be much more interventionist. The controlling logic descends into implementation to a greater extent, referring to variables, measuring return values, and taking turns along different pathways of operation according to circumstance.

Decoupling

To decouple is to remove interdependence between components, so that making a change to one component does not necessitate changes to others. Well-designed objects are self-enclosed. That is, they do not need to refer outside of themselves to recall a detail they learned in a previous invocation.

By maintaining an internal representation of state, objects reduce the need for global variables—a notorious cause of tight coupling. In using a global variable, you bind one part of a system to another. If a component (whether a function, a class, or a block of code) refers to a global variable, there is a risk that another component will accidentally use the same variable name and substitute its value for the first. There is a chance that a third component will come to rely on the value in the variable as set by the first. Change the way that the first component works, and you may cause the third to stop working. The aim of object-oriented design is to reduce such interdependence, making each component as self-sufficient as possible.

Another cause of tight coupling is code duplication. When you must repeat an algorithm in different parts of your project, you will find tight coupling. What happens when you come to change the algorithm? Clearly, you must remember to change it everywhere it occurs. Forget to do this, and your system is in trouble.

A common cause of code duplication is the parallel conditional. If your project needs to do things in one way according to a particular circumstance (e.g., running on Linux), and another according to an alternative circumstance (e.g., running on Windows), you will often find the same if/else clauses popping up in different parts of your system. If you add a new circumstance together with strategies for handling it (MacOS), you must ensure that all conditionals are updated.

Object-oriented programming provides a technique for handling this problem. You can replace conditionals with *polymorphism*. Polymorphism, also known as *class switching*, is the transparent use of different subclasses according to circumstance. Because each subclass supports the same interface as the common superclass, the client code neither knows nor cares which particular implementation it is using.

Conditional code is not banished from object-oriented systems; it is merely minimized and centralized. Conditional code of some kind must be used to determine which particular subtypes are to be served up to clients. This test, though, generally takes place once, and in one place, thus reducing coupling.

Reusability

Encapsulation promotes decoupling, which promotes reuse. Components that are self-sufficient and communicate with wider systems only through their public interface can often be moved from one system and used in another without change.

In fact, this is rarer than you might think. Even nicely orthogonal code can be project specific. When creating a set of classes for managing the content of a particular website, for example, it is worth taking some time in the planning stage to look at those features that are specific to your client and those that might form the foundation for future projects with content management at their heart.

Another tip for reuse: Centralize those classes that might be used in multiple projects. Do not, in other words, copy a nicely reusable class into a new project. This will cause tight coupling on a macro level, as you will inevitably end up changing the class in one project and forgetting to do so in another. You would do better to manage common classes in a central repository that can be shared by your projects.

Aesthetics

This is not going to convince anyone who is not already convinced, but to me object-oriented code is aesthetically pleasing. The messiness of implementation is hidden away behind clean interfaces, making an object a thing of apparent simplicity to its client.

I love the neatness and elegance of polymorphism, so that an API allows you to manipulate vastly different objects that nonetheless perform interchangeably and transparently—the way that objects can be stacked up neatly or slotted into one another like children's blocks.

Of course, there are those who argue that the converse is true. Object-oriented code can manifest itself as an explosion of classes all so decoupled from one another that piecing together their relationships can be a headache. This is a code smell in its own right. It is often tempting to build factories that produce factories that produce factories, until your code resembles a hall of mirrors. Sometimes it makes sense to do the simplest thing that works and then refactor in just enough elegance for testing and flexibility. Let the problem space determine your solution rather than a list of best practices.

Note   The rigid application of so-called best practice is also often an issue in project management. Whenever the use of a technique or a process begins to resemble ritual, applied automatically and inflexibly, it's worth taking a moment to investigate the reasoning behind your current approach. It could be you're drifting from the realm of tools to that of the cargo cult.

It is also worth mentioning that a beautiful solution is not always the best or most efficient. It is tempting to use a full-blown object-oriented solution where a quick script or a few system calls might have gotten the job done.

Patterns

Recently, a Java programmer applied for a job in a company with which I have some involvement. In his cover letter, he apologized for only having used patterns for a couple of years. This assumption that design patterns are a recent discovery—a transformative advance—is testament to the excitement they have generated. In fact, it is likely that this experienced coder has been using patterns for a lot longer than he thinks.

Patterns describe common problems and tested solutions. Patterns name, codify, and organize real-world best practice. They are not components of an invention or clauses in a doctrine. A pattern would not be valid if it did not describe practices that are already common at the time of hatching.

Remember that the concept of a pattern language originated in the field of architecture. People were building courtyards and arches for thousands of years before patterns were proposed as a means of describing solutions to problems of space and function.

Having said that, it is true that design patterns often provoke the kind of emotions associated with religious or political disputes. Devotees roam the corridors with an evangelistic gleam in their eye and a copy of the Gang of Four book under their arm. They accost the uninitiated and reel off pattern names like articles of faith. It is little wonder that some critics see design patterns as hype.

In languages such as Perl and PHP, patterns are also controversial because of their firm association with object-oriented programming. In a context in which objects are a design decision and not a given, associating oneself with design patterns amounts to a declaration of preference, not least because patterns beget more patterns, and objects beget more objects.

What Patterns Buy Us

I introduced patterns in Chapter 7. Let's reiterate some of the benefits that patterns can buy us.

Tried and Tested

First of all, as I've noted, patterns are proven solutions to particular problems. Drawing an analogy between patterns and recipes is dangerous: recipes can be followed blindly, whereas patterns are "half-baked" (Martin Fowler) by nature and need more thoughtful handling. Nevertheless, both recipes and patterns share one important characteristic: they have been tried out and tested thoroughly before inscription.

Patterns Suggest Other Patterns

Patterns have grooves and curves that fit one another. Certain patterns slot together with a satisfying click. Solving a problem using a pattern will inevitably have ramifications. These consequences can become the conditions that suggest complementary patterns. It is important, of course, to be careful that you are addressing real needs and problems when you choose related patterns, and not just building elegant but useless towers of interlocking code. It is tempting to build the programming equivalent of an architectural folly.

A Common Vocabulary

Patterns are a means of developing a common vocabulary for describing problems and solutions. Naming is important—it stands in for describing and therefore lets us cover lots of ground very quickly. Naming, of course, also obscures meaning for those who do not yet share the vocabulary, which is one reason why patterns can be so infuriating at times.

Patterns Promote Design

As discussed in the next section, patterns can encourage good design when used properly. There is an important caveat, of course. Patterns are not fairy dust.

Patterns and Principles of Design

Design patterns are, by their nature, concerned with good design. Used well, they can help you build loosely coupled and flexible code. Pattern critics have a point, though, when they say that patterns can be overused by the newly infected. Because pattern implementations form pretty and elegant structures, it can be tempting to forget that good design always lies in fitness for purpose. Remember that patterns exist to address problems.

When I first started working with patterns, I found myself creating Abstract Factories all over my code. I needed to generate objects, and Abstract Factory certainly helped me to do that.

In fact, though, I was thinking lazily and making unnecessary work for myself. The sets of objects I needed to produce were indeed related, but they did not yet have alternative implementations. The classic Abstract Factory pattern is ideal for situations in which you have alternative sets of objects to generate according to circumstance. To make Abstract Factory work, you need to create factory classes for each type of object and a class to serve up the factory class. It's exhausting just describing the process.

My code would have been much cleaner had I created a basic factory class, only refactoring to implement Abstract Factory if I found myself needing to generate a parallel set of objects.

The fact that you are using patterns does not guarantee good design. When developing, it is a good idea to bear in mind two expressions of the same principle: KISS ("Keep it simple, stupid") and "Do the simplest thing that works." Extreme programmers also give us another, related, acronym: YAGNI. "You aren't going to need it," meaning that you should not implement a feature unless it is truly required.

With the warnings out of the way, I can resume my tone of breathless enthusiasm. As I laid out in Chapter 9, patterns tend to embody a set of principles that can be generalized and applied to all code.

Favor Composition over Inheritance

Inheritance relationships are powerful. We use inheritance to support runtime class switching (polymorphism), which lies at the heart of many of the patterns and techniques I explored in this book. By relying solely on inheritance in design, though, you can produce inflexible structures that are prone to duplication.

Avoid Tight Coupling

I have already talked about this issue in this chapter, but it is worth mentioning here for the sake of completeness. You can never escape the fact that change in one component may require changes in other parts of your project. You can, however, minimize this by avoiding both duplication (typified in our examples by parallel conditionals) and the overuse of global variables (or Singletons). You should also minimize the use of concrete subclasses when abstract types can be used to promote polymorphism. This last point leads us to another principle.

Code to an Interface, Not an Implementation

Design your software components with clearly defined public interfaces that make the responsibility of each transparent. If you define your interface in an abstract superclass and have client classes demand and work with this abstract type, you then decouple clients from specific implementations.

Having said that, remember the YAGNI principle. If you start out with the need for only one implementation for a type, there is no immediate reason to create an abstract superclass. You can just as well define a clear interface in a single concrete class. As soon as you find that your single implementation is trying to do more than one thing at the same time, you can redesignate your concrete class as the abstract parent of two subclasses. Client code will be none the wiser, as it continues to work with a single type.

A classic sign that you may need to split an implementation and hide the resultant classes behind an abstract parent is the emergence of conditional statements in the implementation.

Encapsulate the Concept That Varies

If you find that you are drowning in subclasses, it may be that you should be extracting the reason for all this subclassing into its own type. This is particularly the case if the reason is to achieve an end that is incidental to your type's main purpose.

Given a type UpdatableThing, for example, you may find yourself creating FtpUpdatableThing, HttpUpdatableThing, and FileSystemUpdatableThing subtypes. The responsibility of your type, though, is to be a *thing* that is *updatable*—the mechanism for storage and retrieval is incidental to this purpose. Ftp, Http, and FileSystem are the things that vary here, and they belong in their own type—let's call it UpdateMechanism. UpdateMechanism will have subclasses for the different implementations. You can then add as many update mechanisms as you want without disturbing the UpdatableThing type, which remains focused on its core responsibility. Incidentally, note that UpdateMechanism might alternatively be named UpdateStrategy. I have described an implementation of the Strategy pattern. For more on that, see Chapter 11.

Notice also that I have replaced a static compile-time structure with a dynamic runtime arrangement here, bringing us (as if by accident) back to our first principle: "Favor composition over inheritance."

Practice

The issues that I covered in this part of the book (and introduced in Chapter 14) are often ignored by texts and coders alike. In my own life as a programmer, I discovered that these tools and techniques were at least as relevant to the success of a project as design. There is little doubt that issues such as documentation and automated build are less revelatory in nature than wonders such as the Composite pattern.

Note   Let's just remind ourselves of the beauty of Composite: a simple inheritance tree whose objects can be joined at runtime to form structures that are also trees, but are orders of magnitude more flexible and complex. Multiple objects share a single interface by which they are presented to the outside world. The interplay between simple and complex, multiple and singular, has got to get your pulse racing—that's not just software design, it's poetry.

Even if issues such as documentation and build, testing, and version control are more prosaic than patterns, they are no less important. In the real world, a fantastic design will not survive if multiple developers cannot easily contribute to it or understand the source. Systems become hard to maintain and extend without automated testing. Without build tools, no one is going to bother to deploy your work. As PHP's user base widens, so does our responsibility as developers to ensure quality and ease of deployment.

A project exists in two modes. A project is its structures of code and functionality, and it is also a set of files and directories, a ground for cooperation, a set of sources and targets, and a subject for transformation. In this sense, a project is a system from the outside as much as it is within its code. Mechanisms for build, testing, documentation, and version control require the same attention to detail as the code such mechanisms support. Focus on the metasystem with as much fervor as you do on the system itself.

Testing

Although testing is part of the framework that one applies to a project from the outside, it is intimately integrated into the code itself. Because total decoupling is not possible, or even desirable, test frameworks are a powerful way of monitoring the ramifications of change. Altering the return type of a method could influence client code elsewhere, causing bugs to emerge weeks or months after the change is made. A test framework gives you half a chance of catching errors of this kind (the better the tests, the better the odds here).

Testing is also a tool for improving object-oriented design. Testing first (or at least concurrently) helps you to focus on a class's interface and think carefully about the responsibility and behavior of every method. I introduced PHPUnit, which is used for testing, in Chapter 18.

Standards

I am a contrarian by nature. I hate being told what to do. Words like *compliance* instantly invoke a fight-or-flight response in me. But, counterintuitive as it may seem, standards drive innovation. That is because they drive interoperability. The rise of the Internet was fueled in part by the fact that open standards are built into its core. Websites can link to one another, and web servers can be reused in any domain because protocols are well known and respected. A solution in a silo may be better than a widely accepted and applied standard, but what if the silo burns down? What if it is bought, and the new owner decides to charge for access? What happens when some people decide that the silo next door is better? In Chapter 15, I discussed PSR, PHP Standard Recommendations. I focused in particular on standards for autoloading, which have done much to clean up the way that PHP developers include classes. I also looked at PSR-12, the standard for coding style. Programmers have strong feelings about the placement of braces and the deployment of argument lists, but agreeing to abide by a common set of rules makes for readable and consistent code and allows us to use tools to check and reformat our source files. In that spirit, I have reformatted all code examples in this edition to *comply* with PSR-12.

Version Control

Collaboration is hard. Let's face it: people are awkward. Programmers are even worse. Once you've sorted out the roles and tasks on your team, the last thing you want to deal with is clashes in the source code itself. As you saw in Chapter 17, Git (and similar tools such as CVS and Subversion) enables you to merge the work of multiple programmers into a single repository. Where clashes are unavoidable, Git flags the fact and points you to the source to fix the problem.

Even if you are a solo programmer, version control is a necessity. Git supports branching, so that you can maintain a software release and develop the next version at the same time, merging bug fixes from the stable release to the development branch.

Git also provides a record of every commit ever made on your project. This means that you can roll back by date or tag to any moment. This will save your project someday—believe me.

Automated Build

Version control without automated build is of limited use. A project of any complexity takes work to deploy. Various files need to be moved to different places on a system, configuration files need to be transformed to have the right values for the current platform and database, and database tables need to be set up or transformed. I covered two tools designed for installation. The first, Composer (see Chapter 16), is ideal for stand-alone packages and small applications. The second build tool I covered was Phing (see Chapter 19), which is a tool with enough power and flexibility to automate the installation of the largest and most labyrinthine project.

Automated build transforms deployment from a chore to a matter of a line or two at the command line. With little effort, you can invoke your test framework and your documentation output from your build tool. If the needs of your developers do not sway you, bear in mind the pathetically grateful cries of your users as they discover that they need no longer spend an entire afternoon copying files and changing configuration fields every time you release a new version of your project.

Continuous Integration

It is not enough to be able to test and build a project; you have to do it *all the time*. This becomes increasingly important as a project grows in complexity and you manage multiple branches. You should build and test the stable branch from which you make minor bug fix releases, an experimental development branch or two, and your main trunk. If you were to try to do all that manually, even with the aid of build and test tools, you'd never get around to any coding. Of course, all coders hate that, so build and testing inevitably get skimped on.

In Chapter 21, I looked at Continuous Integration, a practice and a set of tools that automate the build and test processes as much as possible.

What I Missed

A few tool categories I have had to omit from this book due to time and space constraints are, nonetheless, supremely useful for any project. In most cases, there is more than one good tool for the job at hand, so, although I'll suggest one or two, you may want to spend some time talking with other developers and digging around with your favorite search engine before you make your choice.

If your project has more than one developer or even just an active client, then you will need a tool to track bugs and tasks. Like version control, a bug tracker is one of those productivity tools that, once you have tried it on a project, you cannot imagine not using. Trackers allow users to report problems with a project, but they are just as often used as a means of describing required features and allocating their implementation to team members.

You can get a snapshot of open tasks at any time, narrowing the search according to product, task owner, version number, and priority. Each task has its own page, in which you can discuss any ongoing issues. Discussion entries and changes in task status can be copied by mail to team members, so it's easy to keep an eye on things without going to the tracker URL all the time.

There are many tools out there. Even after all this time, though, I usually return to the venerable Bugzilla (`www.bugzilla.org`). Bugzilla is free and open source and has all the features most developers could need. It is a downloadable product, so you will have to run it on your own server. It still looks a little Web 1.0, but it's none the worse for that.

If you do not want to host your own tracker, and you have or prefer your interfaces a little prettier (and have deeper pockets), you might look at the Atlassian's SAAS solution, Jira (`www.atlassian.com/software/jira`).

For high-level task tracking and project planning (especially if you're interested in using a Kanban system), you might also look at Trello (`www.trello.com`).

A tracker is generally just one of a suite of collaboration tools you will want to use to share information around a project. At a price, you can use an integrated solution such as Basecamp (`https://basecamp.com/`) or Atlassian tools (`www.atlassian.com/`). Or you may choose to stitch together a tools ecosystem using a variety of tools. To facilitate communication within your team, for example, you will probably need a mechanism for chat or messaging. Perhaps the most popular tool for this at the time of this writing is Slack (`www.slack.com`). Slack is a multiroomed web-based chat environment. If you're old school like me, you might instantly think of IRC (Internet Relay Chat)—and you'd be right: there's little you can do with Slack that you couldn't do with IRC, except that Slack is browser based, easy to use, and has integration with other services already built-in. Slack is free unless you need premium features.

Speaking of old school, you might also consider using a mailing list for your project. My favorite mailing list software is Mailman (`www.gnu.org/software/mailman/`), which is free, relatively easy to install, and highly configurable.

For cooperatively editable text documents and spreadsheets, Google Docs (`https://docs.google.com/`) is probably the easiest solution.

Your code is not as clear as you think it is. A stranger visiting a codebase for the first time can be faced with a daunting task. Even you, as author of the code, will eventually forget how it all hangs together. For inline documentation, you should look at phpDocumentor (`www.phpdoc.org/`) which allows you to document as you go and automatically generates hyperlinked output. The output from phpDocumentor is particularly useful in an object-oriented context, as it allows the user to click around from class to class. As classes are often contained in their own files, reading the source directly can involve following complex trails from source file to source file.

Although inline documentation is important, projects also generate a broiling heap of written material. This includes usage instructions, consultation on future directions, client assets, meeting minutes, and party announcements. During the lifetime of a project, such materials are very fluid, and a mechanism is often needed to allow people to collaborate in their evolution.

A wiki (wiki is apparently derived from the Hawaiian word *wikiwiki* meaning "very fast") is the perfect tool for creating collaborative webs of hyperlinked documents. Pages can be created or edited at the click of a button, and hyperlinks are automatically generated for words that match page names. A wiki is another one of those tools that seems so simple, essential, and obvious that you are sure you probably had the idea first, but just didn't get around to doing anything about it. There are a number of wikis to choose from. I have had good experience with PhpWiki, which can be downloaded from `https://phpwiki.sourceforge.io/`, and DokuWiki, which you can find at `www.dokuwiki.org/dokuwiki`.

For documentation (and for writing in general), though, I have tended, increasingly, to pare back to simple text documents and version control. For formatting, I use Markdown, a lightweight markup language. It is easy to read before rendering and usually is clean and well balanced afterward (though, as with all rendering, you are at the mercy of the renderer). The best starting place for Markdown is `https://commonmark.org/`. After years of struggling with Word and Word-compatible word processors, I am very grateful that Apress let me use Markdown for this edition of the book!

Note   Although I did not omit this tool (see Chapter 17), it is worth mentioning that shifting to a plain text format made it possible for us to make extensive use of Git in the development of this book.

The tech reviewer for this edition (Paul Tregoing) would have liked to see Docker (`https://docs.docker.com/`) added to the chapter on Continuous Integration, but time constraints prevented this. Jenkins build jobs running inside Docker containers mean that you have complete freedom to adjust the build environment without constraints imposed by the system hosting Jenkins. You can build using different versions of packages or even a different Linux distribution.

Summary

In this chapter, I wrapped things up, revisiting the core topics that make up the book. Although I haven't tackled any concrete issues such as individual patterns or object functions here, this chapter should serve as a reasonable summary of this book's concerns.

There is never enough room or time to cover all the material that one would like. Nevertheless, I hope that this book has served to make one argument: PHP is all grown up. It is now one of the most popular programming languages in the world. I hope that PHP remains the hobbyist's favorite language and that many new PHP programmers are delighted to discover how far they can get with just a little code. At the same time, though, more and more professional teams are building large systems with PHP. Such projects deserve more than a just-do-it approach. Through its extension layer, PHP has always been a versatile language, providing a gateway to hundreds of applications and libraries. Its object-oriented support, on the other hand, gains you access to a different set of tools. Once you begin to think in objects, you can chart the hard-won experience of other programmers. You can navigate and deploy pattern languages developed with reference not just to PHP but to Smalltalk, C++, C#, or Java, too. It is our responsibility to meet this challenge with careful design and good practice. The future is reusable.

APPENDIX A

Bibliography

Books

Alexander, Christopher, Sara Ishikawa, Murray Silverstein, Max Jacobson, Ingrid Fiksdahl-King, and Shlomo Angel. *A Pattern Language: Towns, Buildings, Construction.* Oxford, UK: Oxford University Press, 1977.

Alur, Deepak, John Crupi, and Dan Malks. *Core J2EE Patterns: Best Practices and Design Strategies.* Englewood Cliffs, NJ: Prentice Hall PTR, 2001.

Beck, Kent. *Extreme Programming Explained: Embrace Change.* Reading, MA: Addison-Wesley, 1999.

Chacon, Scott. *Pro Git.* New York, NY: Apress, 2009.

Fogel, Karl, and Moshe Bar. *Open Source Development with CVS, Third Edition.* Scottsdale, AZ: Paraglyph Press, 2003.

Fowler, Martin, and Kendall Scott. *UML Distilled, Second Edition: A Brief Guide to the Standard Object Modeling Language.* Reading, MA: Addison-Wesley Professional, 1999.

Fowler, Martin, Kent Beck, John Brant, William Opdyke, and Don Roberts. *Refactoring: Improving the Design of Existing Code.* Reading, MA: Addison-Wesley Professional, 1999.

Fowler, Martin. *Patterns of Enterprise Application Architecture.* Reading, MA: Addison-Wesley Professional, 2002.

Gamma, Erich, Richard Helm, Ralph Johnson, and John Vlissides. *Design Patterns: Elements of Reusable Object-Oriented Software.* Reading, MA: Addison-Wesley Professional, 1995.

Hunt, Andrew, and David Thomas. *The Pragmatic Programmer: From Journeyman to Master.* Reading, MA: Addison-Wesley Professional, 2000.

Kerievsky, Joshua. *Refactoring to Patterns.* Reading, MA: Addison-Wesley Professional, 2004. Metsker, Steven John. *Building Parsers with Java.* Reading, MA: Addison-Wesley Professional, 2001.

Nock, Clifton. *Data Access Patterns: Database Interactions in Object-Oriented Applications*. Reading, MA: Addison-Wesley Professional, 2003.

Shalloway, Alan, and James R. Trott. *Design Patterns Explained: A New Perspective on Object-Oriented Design*. Reading, MA: Addison-Wesley, 2001.

Stelting, Stephen, and Olav Maassen. *Applied Java Patterns*. Palo Alto, CA: Sun Microsystems Press, 2002.

Articles

Beck, Kent, and Erich Gamma. "Test Infected: Programmers Love Writing Tests." `http://junit.sourceforge.net/doc/testinfected/testing.htm`

Collins-Sussman, Ben, Brian W. Fitzpatrick, C. Michael Pilato. "Version Control with Subversion." `http://svnbook.red-bean.com/`

Lerdorf, Rasmus. "PHP/FI Brief History." `www.php.net//manual/phpfi2.php#history`

Suraski, Zeev. "The Object-Oriented Evolution of PHP." `www.devx.com/webdev/Article/10007/0/page/1`

Wikipedia. "Law of Triviality." `https://en.wikipedia.org/wiki/Law_of_triviality`

Sites

Ansible: `www.ansible.com`

Basecamp: `https://basecamp.com/`

Bitbucket: `https://bitbucket.org`

Bugzilla: `www.bugzilla.org`

CVS: `www.nongnu.org/cvs/`

Chef: `www.chef.io/chef/`

ChromeDriver: `https://sites.google.com/a/chromium.org/chromedriver`

CommonMark: `https://commonmark.org/`

Composer: `https://getcomposer.org/download/`

CruiseControl: `http://cruisecontrol.sourceforge.net/`

Dang It Git: `https://dangitgit.com/en`

Docker: `https://docs.docker.com/`

DokuWiki: `www.dokuwiki.org/dokuwiki`

Foswiki: `https://foswiki.org/`

GNU: www.gnu.org/

Git: https://git-scm.com/

Git Flow Cheat Sheet: https://danielkummer.github.io/git-flow-cheatsheet/

Git For Windows: https://gitforwindows.org/

GitHub: https://github.com/

GitLab: https://about.gitlab.com/

Google Code: https://code.google.com

Google Docs: https://docs.google.com/

Java: www.java.com

Jenkins: https://jenkins-ci.org/

Jira: www.atlassian.com/software/jira

Magic Methods in PHP: www.php.net/manual/en/language.oop5.magic.php

Mailman: www.gnu.org/software/mailman/

Martin Fowler: www.martinfowler.com/

Memcached: https://memcached.org/

Mercurial: www.mercurial-scm.org/

Openpear: https://openpear.org/

PCOV: https://pecl.php.net/package/pcov

PEAR: https://pear.php.net

PEAR2: https://pear2.php.net/

PECL: https://pecl.php.net/

PHP: www.php.net

PHP Memcached support: www.php.net/memcache

PHPDocumentor: www.phpdoc.org/

PHPUnit: https://phpunit.de

PHP_CodeSniffer: https://github.com/squizlabs/PHP_CodeSniffer

PSR: www.php-fig.org/psr/

Packagist: https://packagist.org

Phing: www.phing.info

PhpWiki: https://phpwiki.sourceforge.net

Pimple: https://pimple.sensiolabs.org/

Portland Pattern Repository's Wiki (Ward Cunningham): www.c2.com/cgi/wiki

Pro Git: https://git-scm.com/book/en/v2

Puppet: https://puppet.com

QDB: www.bash.org

RapidSVN: https://rapidsvn.org/

SPL: www.php.net/spl

Selenium: www.selenium.dev/

Semantic Versioning: https://semver.org

Slack: www.slack.com

Subversion: https://subversion.apache.org/

Symfony Dependency Injection: https://symfony.com/doc/current/components/dependency_injection/introduction.html

Trello: www.trello.com

Vagrant: www.vagrantup.com/downloads.html

Vagrant Box Search: https://app.vagrantup.com/boxes/search

VirtualBox: www.virtualbox.org/wiki/Downloads

WordPress standards: https://make.wordpress.org/core/handbook/best-practices/coding-standards/php/

Xdebug: https://xdebug.org/

Zend: www.zend.com

A Simple Parser

The Interpreter pattern discussed in Chapter 11 does not cover parsing. An interpreter without a parser is pretty incomplete, unless you persuade your users to write PHP code to invoke the interpreter! Third-party parsers are available that could be deployed to work with the Interpreter pattern, and that would probably be the best choice in a real-world project. This appendix, however, presents a simple object-oriented parser designed to work with the MarkLogic interpreter built in Chapter 11. Be aware that these examples are no more than a proof of concept. They are not designed for use in real-world situations.

Note The interface and broad structure of this parser code are based on Steven Metsker's *Building Parsers with Java* (Addison-Wesley Professional, 2001). The brutally simplified implementation is my fault, however, and any mistakes should be laid at my door. Steven has given kind permission for the use of his original concept.

The Scanner

In order to parse a statement, you must first break it down into a set of words and characters (known as *tokens*). The following class uses a number of regular expressions to define tokens. It also provides a convenient result stack that I will be using later in this section. Here is the Scanner class:

```
// listing 24.01
class Scanner
{
    // token types
    public const WORD       = 1;
    public const QUOTE      = 2;
```

```php
    public const APOS        = 3;
    public const WHITESPACE  = 6;
    public const EOL         = 8;
    public const CHAR        = 9;
    public const EOF         = 0;
    public const SOF         = -1;

    protected int $line_no    = 1;
    protected int $char_no    = 0;
    protected ?string $token  = null;
    protected int $token_type = -1;

    // Reader provides access to the raw character data. Context stores
    // result data
    public function __construct(private Reader $r, private Context $context)
    {
    }

    public function getContext(): Context
    {
        return $this->context;
    }

    // read through all whitespace characters
    public function eatWhiteSpace(): int
    {

        $ret = 0;

        if (
            $this->token_type != self::WHITESPACE &&
            $this->token_type != self::EOL
        ) {
            return $ret;
        }
```

```
    while (
        $this->nextToken() == self::WHITESPACE ||
        $this->token_type == self::EOL
    ) {
        $ret++;
    }

    return $ret;
}

// get a string representation of a token
// either the current token, or that represented
// by the $int arg
public function getTypeString(int $int = -1): ?string
{
    if ($int < 0) {
        $int = $this->tokenType();
    }

    if ($int < 0) {
        return null;
    }

    $resolve = [
        self::WORD =>       'WORD',
        self::QUOTE =>      'QUOTE',
        self::APOS =>       'APOS',
        self::WHITESPACE => 'WHITESPACE',
        self::EOL =>        'EOL',
        self::CHAR =>       'CHAR',
        self::EOF =>        'EOF'
    ];

    return $resolve[$int];
}
```

```php
    // the current token type (represented by an integer)
    public function tokenType(): int
    {
        return $this->token_type;
    }

    // get the contents of the current token
    public function token(): ?string
    {
        return $this->token;
    }

    // return true if the current token is a word
    public function isWord(): bool
    {
        return ($this->token_type == self::WORD);
    }

    // return true if the current token is a quote character
    public function isQuote(): bool
    {
        return ($this->token_type == self::APOS || $this->token_type ==
        self::QUOTE);
    }

    // current line number in source
    public function lineNo(): int
    {
        return $this->line_no;
    }

    // current character number in source
    public function charNo(): int
    {
        return $this->char_no;
    }
```

```
// clone this object
public function __clone(): void
{
    $this->r = clone($this->r);
}

// move on to the next token in the source. Set the current
// token and track the line and character numbers
public function nextToken(): int
{
    $this->token = null;
    $type = -1;

    while (! is_bool($char = $this->getChar())) {
        if ($this->isEolChar($char)) {
            $this->token = $this->manageEolChars($char);
            $this->line_no++;
            $this->char_no = 0;

            return ($this->token_type = self::EOL);
        } elseif ($this->isWordChar($char)) {
            $this->token = $this->eatWordChars($char);
            $type = self::WORD;
        } elseif ($this->isSpaceChar($char)) {
            $this->token = $char;
            $type = self::WHITESPACE;
        } elseif ($char == "'") {
            $this->token = $char;
            $type = self::APOS;
        } elseif ($char == '"') {
            $this->token = $char;
            $type = self::QUOTE;
        } else {
            $type = self::CHAR;
            $this->token = $char;
        }
```

```php
        $this->char_no += strlen($this->token());

        return ($this->token_type = $type);
    }

    return ($this->token_type = self::EOF);
}

// return an array of token type and token content for the NEXT token
public function peekToken(): array
{
    $state = $this->getState();
    $type = $this->nextToken();
    $token = $this->token();
    $this->setState($state);
    return [$type, $token];
}

// get a ScannerState object that stores the parser's current
// position in the source, and data about the current token
public function getState(): ScannerState
{
    $state = new ScannerState();
    $state->line_no      = $this->line_no;
    $state->char_no      = $this->char_no;
    $state->token        = $this->token;
    $state->token_type   = $this->token_type;
    $state->r            = clone($this->r);
    $state->context      = clone($this->context);

    return $state;
}

// use a ScannerState object to restore the scanner's
// state
public function setState(ScannerState $state): void
{
    $this->line_no       = $state->line_no;
```

```
    $this->char_no        = $state->char_no;
    $this->token          = $state->token;
    $this->token_type     = $state->token_type;
    $this->r              = $state->r;
    $this->context        = $state->context;
}

// get the next character from source
// returns boolean when none left
private function getChar(): string|bool
{
    return $this->r->getChar();
}

// get all characters until they stop being
// word characters
private function eatWordChars(string $char): string
{
    $val = $char;

    while ($this->isWordChar($char = $this->getChar())) {
        $val .= $char;
    }

    if ($char) {
        $this->pushBackChar();
    }

    return $val;
}

// move back one character in source
private function pushBackChar(): void
{
    $this->r->pushBackChar();
}
```

```php
// argument is a word character
private function isWordChar($char): bool
{
    if (is_bool($char)) {
        return false;
    }

    return (preg_match("/[A-Za-z0-9_\-]/", $char) === 1);
}

// argument is a space character
private function isSpaceChar($char): bool
{
    return (preg_match("/\t| /", $char) === 1);
}

// argument is an end of line character
private function isEolChar($char): bool
{
    $check = preg_match("/\n|\r/",  $char);

    return ($check === 1);
}

// swallow either \n, \r or \r\n
private function manageEolChars(string $char): string
{
    if ($char == "\r") {
        $next_char = $this->getChar();

        if ($next_char == "\n") {
            return "{$char}{$next_char}";
        } else {
            $this->pushBackChar();
        }
    }

    return $char;
}
```

```
    public function getPos(): int
    {
        return $this->r->getPos();
    }
}

// listing 24.02
class ScannerState
{
    public int $line_no;
    public int $char_no;
    public ?string $token;
    public int $token_type;
    public Context $context;
    public Reader $r;
}
```

First, I set up constants for the tokens that interest me. I am going to match characters, words, whitespace, and quote characters. I test for these types in methods dedicated to each token: isWordChar(), isSpaceChar(), and so on. The heart of the class is the nextToken() method. This attempts to match the next token in a given string. The Scanner stores a Context object. Parser objects use this to share results as they work through the target text.

Note that there is a second class: ScannerState. The Scanner is designed so that Parser objects can save state, try stuff out, and restore if they've gone down a blind alley. The getState() method populates and returns a ScannerState object. setState() uses a ScannerState object to revert state if required.

Here is the Context class:

```
// listing 24.03
class Context
{
    public array $resultstack = [];

    public function pushResult($mixed): void
    {
        array_push($this->resultstack, $mixed);
    }
```

```
    public function popResult(): mixed
    {
        return array_pop($this->resultstack);
    }

    public function resultCount(): int
    {
        return count($this->resultstack);
    }

    public function peekResult(): mixed
    {
        if (empty($this->resultstack)) {
            throw new Exception("empty resultstack");
        }

        return $this->resultstack[count($this->resultstack) - 1];
    }
}
```

As you can see, this is just a simple stack, a convenient noticeboard for parsers to work with. It performs a similar job to that of the context class used in the Interpreter pattern, but it is not the same class.

Notice that the Scanner does not itself work with a file or string. Instead, it requires a Reader object. This would allow me to easily swap in different sources of data. Here is the Reader interface and an implementation, StringReader:

```
// listing 24.04 interface Reader
{
    public function getChar(): string|bool;
    public function getPos(): int;
    public function pushBackChar(): void;
}

// listing 24.05
class StringReader implements Reader
{
    private int $pos; private int $len;
```

```
    public function __construct(private string $in)
    {
        $this->pos = 0;
        $this->len = strlen($in);
    }

    public function getChar(): string|bool
    {
        if ($this->pos >= $this->len) {
            return  false;
        }

        $char = substr($this->in, $this->pos, 1);
        $this->pos++;

        return $char;
    }

    public function getPos(): int
    {
        return $this->pos;
    }

    public function pushBackChar(): void
    {
        $this->pos--;
    }

    public function string(): string
    {
        return $this->in;
    }
}
```

This simply reads from a string one character at a time. I could easily provide a file-based version, of course.

Perhaps the best way to see how the Scanner might be used is to use it. Here is some code to break up the example statement into tokens:

```
// listing 24.06
$context = new Context();
$user_in = "\$input equals '4' or \$input equals 'four'";
$reader = new StringReader($user_in);
$scanner = new Scanner($reader, $context);

while ($scanner->nextToken() != Scanner::EOF) {
    print $scanner->token();
    print "    {$scanner->charNo()}";
    print "    {$scanner->getTypeString()}\n";
}
```

I initialize a Scanner object and then loop through the tokens in the given string by repeatedly calling nextToken(). The token() method returns the current portion of the input matched. char_no() tells me where I am in the string, and getTypeString() returns a string version of the constant flag representing the current token. This is what the output should look like:

```
$        1     CHAR
input    6     WORD
         7     WHITESPACE
equals   13    WORD
         14    WHITESPACE
'        15    APOS
4        16    WORD
'        17    APOS
         18    WHITESPACE
or       20    WORD
         21    WHITESPACE
$        22    CHAR
input    27    WORD
         28    WHITESPACE
equals   34    WORD
         35    WHITESPACE
'        36    APOS
four     40    WORD
'        41    APOS
```

I could, of course, match finer-grained tokens than this, but this is good enough for my purposes. Breaking up the string is the easy part. How do I build up a grammar in code?

The Parser

One approach is to build a tree of Parser objects. Here is the abstract Parser class that I will be using:

```
// listing 24.07
abstract class Parser
{
     public const GIP_RESPECTSPACE = 1;

    protected bool $respectSpace = false;
    protected static bool $debug = false;
    protected bool  $discard = false;
    protected string $name;
    private static int $count = 0;

    public function __construct(string $name = null, array $options = [])
    {
        if (is_null($name)) {
            self::$count++;
            $this->name = get_class($this) . " (" . self::$count . ")";
        } else {
            $this->name = $name;
        }

        if (isset($options[self::GIP_RESPECTSPACE])) {
            $this->respectSpace = true;
        }
    }

    protected function next(Scanner $scanner): void
    {
        $scanner->nextToken();
```

```php
        if (! $this->respectSpace) {
            $scanner->eatWhiteSpace();
        }
    }

    public function spaceSignificant(bool $bool): bool
    {
        $this->respectSpace = $bool;
    }

    public static function setDebug(bool $bool): void
    {
        self::$debug = $bool;
    }

    public function setHandler(Handler $handler): void
    {
        $this->handler = $handler;
    }

    final public function scan(Scanner $scanner): bool
    {
        if ($scanner->tokenType() == Scanner::SOF) {
            $scanner->nextToken();
        }

        $ret = $this->doScan($scanner);

        if ($ret && ! $this->discard && $this->term()) {
            $this->push($scanner);
        }

        if ($ret) {
            $this->invokeHandler($scanner);
        }

        if ($this->term() && $ret) {
            $this->next($scanner);
        }

        $this->report("::scan returning $ret");
```

```php
        return $ret;
    }

    public function discard(): void
    {
        $this->discard = true;
    }

    abstract public function trigger(Scanner $scanner): bool;

    public function term(): bool
    {
        return true;
    }

    // private/protected

    protected function invokeHandler(Scanner $scanner): void
    {
        if (! empty($this->handler)) {
            $this->report("calling handler: " . get_class($this->handler));
            $this->handler->handleMatch($this, $scanner);
        }
    }

    protected function report($msg): void
    {
        if (self::$debug) {
            print "<{$this->name}> " . get_class($this) . ": $msg\n";
        }
    }
    protected function push(Scanner $scanner): void
    {
        $context = $scanner->getContext();
        $context->pushResult($scanner->token());
    }

    abstract protected function doScan(Scanner $scanner): bool;
}
```

The place to start with this class is the scan() method. It is here that most of the logic resides. scan() is given a Scanner object to work with. The first thing that the Parser does is defer to a concrete child class, calling the abstract doScan() method. doScan() returns true or false; you will see a concrete example later in this section.

If doScan() reports success, and a couple of other conditions are fulfilled, then the results of the parse are pushed to the Context object's result stack. The Scanner object holds the Context that is used by Parser objects to communicate results. The actual pushing of the successful parse takes place in the Parser::push() method:

```
// listing 24.08
protected function push(Scanner $scanner): void
{
    $context = $scanner->getContext();
    $context->pushResult($scanner->token());
}
```

In addition to a parse failure, there are two conditions that might prevent the result from being pushed to the scanner's stack. First, client code can ask a parser to discard a successful match by calling the discard() method. This toggles a property called $discard to true. Second, only terminal parsers (i.e., parsers that are not composed of other parsers) should push their result to the stack. Composite parsers (instances of CollectionParser, often referred to in the following text as *collection parsers*) will instead let their successful children push their results. I test whether or not a parser is terminal using the term() method, which is overridden to return false by collection parsers.

If the concrete parser has been successful in its matching, then I call another method: invokeHandler(). This is passed the Scanner object. If a Handler (i.e., an object that implements the Handler interface) has been attached to Parser (using the setHandler() method), then its handleMatch() method is invoked here. I use handlers to make a successful grammar actually do something, as you will see shortly.

Back in the scan() method, I call on the Scanner object (via the next() method) to advance its position by calling its nextToken() and eatWhiteSpace() methods. Finally, I return the value that was provided by doScan().

In addition to doScan(), notice the abstract trigger() method. This is used to determine whether a parser should bother to attempt a match. If trigger() returns false, then the conditions are not right for parsing. Let's take a look at a concrete terminal. CharacterParse is designed to match a particular character:

```
// listing 24.09
class CharacterParse extends Parser
{

    public function __construct(private string $char, string $name = null,
    array $options = [])
    {
        parent:: construct($name, $options);
    }

    public function trigger(Scanner $scanner): bool
    {
        return ( $scanner->token() == $this->char );
    }

    protected function doScan(Scanner $scanner): bool
    {
        return ( $this->trigger($scanner) );
    }
}
```

The constructor accepts a character to match and an optional parser name for debugging purposes. The trigger() method simply checks whether the scanner is pointing to a character token that matches the sought character. Because no further scanning than this is required, the doScan() method simply invokes trigger().

Terminal matching is a reasonably simple affair, as you can see. Let's look now at a collection parser. First, I'll define a common superclass and then go on to create a concrete example:

```
// listing 24.10
abstract class CollectionParse extends Parser
{
    protected array $parsers = [];

    public function add(Parser $p): Parser
    {
        if (is_null($p)) {
            throw new Exception("argument is null");
        }
```

```
        $this->parsers[] = $p;

        return $p;
    }

    public function term(): bool
    {
        return false;
    }
}

// listing 24.11
class SequenceParse extends CollectionParse
{
    public function trigger(Scanner $scanner): bool
    {
        if (empty($this->parsers)) {
            return false;
        }

        return $this->parsers[0]->trigger($scanner);
    }

    protected function doScan(Scanner $scanner): bool
    {
        $start_state = $scanner->getState();

        foreach ($this->parsers as $parser) {
            if (! ($parser->trigger($scanner) && $parser->scan($scanner))) {
                $scanner->setState($start_state);

                return false;
            }
        }

        return true;
    }
}
```

The abstract `CollectionParse` class simply implements an `add()` method that aggregates `Parsers` and overrides `term()` to return `false`.

The `SequenceParse::trigger()` method tests only the first child `Parser` it contains, invoking its `trigger()` method. The calling `Parser` will first call `CollectionParse::trigger()` to see if it is worth calling `CollectionParse::scan()`. If `CollectionParse::scan()` is called, then `doScan()` is invoked, and the `trigger()` and `scan()` methods of all `Parser` children are called in turn. A single failure results in `CollectionParse::doScan()` reporting failure.

One of the problems with parsing is the need to try stuff out. A `SequenceParse` object may contain an entire tree of parsers within each of its aggregated parsers. These will push the `Scanner` on by a token or more and cause results to be registered with the `Context` object. If the final child in the `Parser` list returns `false`, what should `SequenceParse` do about the results lodged in `Context` by the child's more successful siblings? A sequence is all or nothing, so I have no choice but to roll back both the `Context` object and the `Scanner`. I do this by saving state at the start of `doScan()` and calling `setState()` just before returning `false` on failure. Of course, if I return `true`, then there's no need to roll back.

For the sake of completeness, here are all the remaining `Parser` classes:

```
// listing 24.12
class RepetitionParse extends CollectionParse
{
    public function __construct(private int $min = 0, private int $max = 0,
    ?string $name = null, array $options = [])
    {
        parent:: __construct($name, $options);

        if ($max < $min && $max > 0) {
            throw new Exception(
                "maximum ( $max ) larger than minimum ( $min )"
            );
        }
    }
```

```php
    public function trigger(Scanner $scanner): bool
    {
        return true;
    }

    protected function doScan(Scanner $scanner): bool
    {
        $start_state = $scanner->getState();

        if (empty($this->parsers)) {
            return true;
        }

        $parser = $this->parsers[0];
        $count = 0;
        while (true) {
            if ($this->max > 0 && $count >= $this->max) {
                return  true;
            }

            if (! $parser->trigger($scanner)) {
                if ($this->min == 0 || $count >= $this->min) {
                    return true;
                } else {
                    $scanner->setState($start_state);

                    return false;
                }
            }
        }

        if (! $parser->scan($scanner)) {
            if ($this->min == 0 || $count >= $this->min) {
                return true;
            } else {
                $scanner->setState($start_state);
```

```
                return false;
            }
        }

        $count++;

        }
    }
}

// listing 24.13
// This matches if one or other of two subparsers match
class AlternationParse extends CollectionParse
{
    public function trigger(Scanner $scanner): bool
    {
        foreach ($this->parsers as $parser) {
            if ($parser->trigger($scanner)) {
                return true;
            }
        }

        return false;
    }

    protected function doScan(Scanner $scanner): bool
    {
        $type = $scanner->tokenType();
        $start_state = $scanner->getState();

        foreach ($this->parsers as $parser) {
            if ($type == $parser->trigger($scanner) && $parser->
            scan($scanner)) {
                return true;
            }
        }
```

```
        $scanner->setState($start_state);

        return false;
    }
}

// listing 24.14
// this terminal parser matches a string literal
class StringLiteralParse extends Parser
{
    public function trigger(Scanner $scanner): bool
    {
        return (
            $scanner->tokenType() == Scanner::APOS ||
            $scanner->tokenType() == Scanner::QUOTE
        );
    }

    protected function push(Scanner $scanner): void
    {
    }

    protected function doScan(Scanner $scanner): bool
    {
        $quotechar = $scanner->tokenType();
        $ret = false;
        $string = "";

        while ($token = $scanner->nextToken()) {
            if ($token == $quotechar) {
            $ret = true;
            break;
        }

        $string .= $scanner->token();
        }
```

```
        if ($string && ! $this->discard) {
            $scanner->getContext()->pushResult($string);
        }

        return $ret;
    }
}

// listing 24.15
// this terminal parser matches a word token
class WordParse extends Parser
{
    public function __construct(private $word = null, $name = null,
    $options = [])
    {
        parent::__construct($name, $options);
    }

    public function trigger(Scanner $scanner): bool
    {
        if ($scanner->tokenType() != Scanner::WORD) {
            return false;
        }

        if (is_null($this->word)) {
            return true;
        }

        return ($this->word == $scanner->token());
    }
    protected function doScan(Scanner $scanner): bool
    {
        return ($this->trigger($scanner));
    }
}
```

By combining terminal and nonterminal Parser objects, I can build a reasonably sophisticated parser. You can see all the Parser classes I use for this example in Figure B-1.

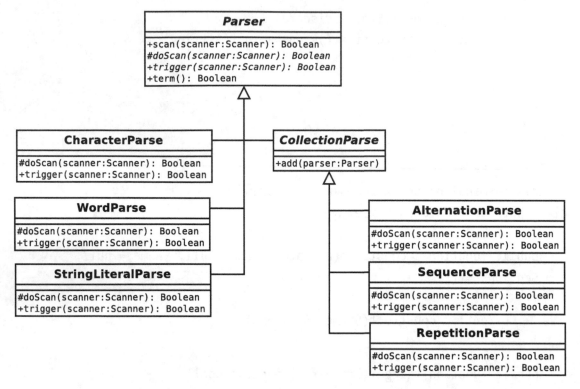

Figure B-1. *The Parser classes*

The idea behind this use of the Composite pattern is that a client can build up a grammar in code that closely matches EBNF notation. Table B-1 shows the parallels between these classes and EBNF fragments.

Table B-1. *Composite Parsers and EBNF*

Class	EBNF Example	Description
AlternationParse	orExpr | andExpr	Either one or another
SequenceParse	'and' operand	A list (all required in order)
RepetitionParse	(eqExpr)*	Zero or more required

Now it's time to build some client code to implement the mini-language. As a reminder, here is the EBNF fragment I presented in Chapter 11:

```
Expr      = operand { orExpr | andExpr }
Operand   = ( '(' expr ')' | ? string literal ? | variable ) { eqExpr }
orExpr    = 'or' operand
andExpr   = 'and' operand
eqExpr    = 'equals' operand
variable = '$' , ? word ?
```

This simple class builds up a grammar based on this fragment and runs it:

```
// listing  24.16
class MarkParse
{
    private Parser $expression;
    private Parser $operand;
    private Expression $interpreter;

    public function __construct($statement)
    {
        $this->compile($statement);
    }

    public function evaluate($input): mixed
    {
        $icontext = new InterpreterContext();
        $prefab = new VariableExpression('input', $input);
        // add the input variable to Context
        $prefab->interpret($icontext);

        $this->interpreter->interpret($icontext);
        return $icontext->lookup($this->interpreter);
    }

    public function compile($statementStr): void
    {
        // build parse tree
        $context = new Context();
        $scanner = new Scanner(new StringReader($statementStr), $context);
        $statement = $this->expression();
```

```
        $scanresult = $statement->scan($scanner);
        if (! $scanresult || $scanner->tokenType() != Scanner::EOF) {
            $msg  = "";
            $msg .= " line: {$scanner->lineNo()} ";
            $msg .= " char: {$scanner->charNo()}";
            $msg .= "  token:  {$scanner->token()}\n";
            throw new \Exception($msg);
        }

        $this->interpreter = $scanner->getContext()->popResult();
    }

    public function expression(): Parser
    {
        if (! isset($this->expression)) {
            $this->expression = new SequenceParse();
            $this->expression->add($this->operand());
            $bools = new RepetitionParse();
            $whichbool = new AlternationParse();
            $whichbool->add($this->orExpr());
            $whichbool->add($this->andExpr());
            $bools->add($whichbool);
            $this->expression->add($bools);
        }

        return $this->expression;
    }
    public function orExpr(): Parser
    {
        $or = new SequenceParse();
        $or->add(new WordParse('or'))->discard();
        $or->add($this->operand());
        $or->setHandler(new BooleanOrHandler());

        return $or;
    }
```

```php
public function andExpr(): Parser
{
    $and = new SequenceParse();
    $and->add(new WordParse('and'))->discard();
    $and->add($this->operand());
    $and->setHandler(new BooleanAndHandler());

    return $and;
}

public function operand(): Parser
{
    if (! isset($this->operand)) {
        $this->operand = new SequenceParse();
        $comp = new AlternationParse();
        $exp = new SequenceParse();
        $exp->add(new CharacterParse('('))->discard();
        $exp->add($this->expression());
        $exp->add(new CharacterParse(')'))->discard();
        $comp->add($exp);
        $comp->add(new StringLiteralParse()
            ->setHandler(new  StringLiteralHandler());
        $comp->add($this->variable());
        $this->operand->add($comp);
        $this->operand->add(new RepetitionParse())->add($this->eqExpr());
    }

    return $this->operand;
}

public function eqExpr(): Parser
{
    $equals = new SequenceParse();
    $equals->add(new WordParse('equals'))->discard();
    $equals->add($this->operand());
    $equals->setHandler(new  EqualsHandler());

    return $equals;
}
```

811

```
    public function variable(): Parser
    {
        $variable = new SequenceParse();
        $variable->add(new CharacterParse('$'))->discard();
        $variable->add(new WordParse());
        $variable->setHandler(new VariableHandler());

        return $variable;
    }
}
```

This may seem like a complicated class, but all it is doing is building up the grammar I have already defined. Most of the methods are analogous to production names (i.e., the names that begin each production line in EBNF, such as eqExpr and andExpr). If you look at the expression() method, you should see that I am building up the same rule as I defined in EBNF earlier:

```
// listing 24.17
// expr = operand { orExpr | andExpr }
public function expression(): Parser
{
    if (! isset($this->expression)) {
        $this->expression = new SequenceParse();
        $this->expression->add($this->operand());
        $bools = new RepetitionParse();
        $whichbool = new AlternationParse();
        $whichbool->add($this->orExpr());
        $whichbool->add($this->andExpr());
        $bools->add($whichbool);
        $this->expression->add($bools);
    }

    return $this->expression;
}
```

In both the code and the EBNF notation, I define a sequence that consists of a reference to an operand, followed by zero or more instances of an alternation between orExpr and andExpr. Notice that I am storing the Parser returned by this method in a property variable. This is to prevent infinite loops, as methods invoked from expression() themselves reference expression().

The only methods that are doing more than just building the grammar are compile() and evaluate(). compile() can be called directly or automatically via the constructor, which accepts a statement string and uses it to create a Scanner object. It calls the expression() method, which returns a tree of Parser objects that make up the grammar. It then calls Parser::scan(), passing it the Scanner object. If the raw code does not parse, the compile() method throws an exception. Otherwise, it retrieves the result of compilation as left on the Scanner object's Context. As you will see shortly, this should be an Expression object. This result is stored in a property called $interpreter.

The evaluate() method makes a value available to the Expression tree. It does this by predefining a VariableExpression object named input and registering it with the Context object that is then passed to the main Expression object. As with variables such as $_REQUEST in PHP, this $input variable is always available to MarkLogic coders.

Note   See Chapter 11 for more about the VariableExpression class that is part of the Interpreter pattern example.

The evaluate() method calls the Expression::interpret() method to generate a final result. Remember, you need to retrieve interpreter results from the Context object.

So far, you have seen how to parse text and how to build a grammar. You also saw in Chapter 11 how to use the Interpreter pattern to combine Expression objects and process a query. You have not yet seen, however, how to relate the two processes. How do you get from a parse tree to the interpreter? The answer lies in the Handler objects that can be associated with Parser objects using Parser::setHandler(). Let's take a look at the way to manage variables. I associate a VariableHandler with the Parser in the MarkParse::variable() method:

```
// listing 24.18
$variable->setHandler(new VariableHandler());
```

Here is the Handler interface:

```
// listing 24.19
interface Handler
{
    public function handleMatch(
        Parser $parser,
        Scanner $scanner
    ): void;
}
```

And here is VariableHandler:

```
// listing 24.20
class VariableHandler implements Handler
{
    public function handleMatch(Parser $parser, Scanner $scanner): void
    {
        $varname = $scanner->getContext()->popResult();
        $scanner->getContext()->pushResult(new VariableExpression($varname));
    }
}
```

If the Parser with which VariableHandler is associated matches on a scan operation, then handleMatch() is called. By definition, the last item on the stack will be the name of the variable. I remove this and replace it with a new VariableExpression object with the correct name. Similar principles are used to create EqualsExpression objects, LiteralExpression objects, and so on.

Here are the remaining handlers:

```
// listing 24.21
class StringLiteralHandler implements Handler
{
    public function handleMatch(Parser $parser, Scanner $scanner): void
    {
        $value = $scanner->getContext()->popResult();
        $scanner->getContext()->pushResult(new LiteralExpression($value));
    }
}
```

```
// listing 24.22

class EqualsHandler implements Handler
{
    public function handleMatch(Parser $parser, Scanner $scanner): void
    {
        $comp1 = $scanner->getContext()->popResult();
        $comp2 = $scanner->getContext()->popResult();
        $scanner->getContext()->pushResult(new
        BooleanEqualsExpression($comp1, $comp2));
    }
}

// listing 24.23

class BooleanOrHandler implements Handler
{
    public function handleMatch(Parser $parser, Scanner $scanner): void
    {
        $comp1 = $scanner->getContext()->popResult();
        $comp2 = $scanner->getContext()->popResult();
        $scanner->getContext()->pushResult(new BooleanOrExpression($comp1,
        $comp2));
    }
}

// listing 24.24

class BooleanAndHandler implements Handler
{
    public function handleMatch(Parser $parser, Scanner $scanner): void
    {
        $comp1 = $scanner->getContext()->popResult();
        $comp2 = $scanner->getContext()->popResult();
        $scanner->getContext()->pushResult
        (new  BooleanAndExpression($comp1, $comp2));
    }
}
```

Bearing in mind that you also need the Interpreter example from Chapter 11 at hand, you can work with the MarkParse class like this:

```
// listing 24.25
$input = 'five';
$statement = "( \$input equals 'five')";
$engine = new MarkParse($statement);
$result = $engine->evaluate($input);
print "input: $input evaluating: $statement\n";

if ($result) {
    print "true!\n";
} else {
    print "false!\n";
}
```

This should produce the following results:

```
input: five evaluating: ( $input equals 'five')
true!
```

Index

A, B

Abstract classes
    error message, 86, 87
    implementations, 87
    ShopProductWriter class, 86
    ShopProductWriter method, 87
    TextProductWriter, 88
    write() method, 87, 88
    XmlProductWriter, 87, 88
Abstract factory pattern, 293
    abstract products, 294, 295
    BloggsCal classes, 294
    consequences, 298–300
    implementation
        CommsManager/
            BloggsCommsManager, 296, 297
        concrete products, 295, 296, 298
        getContactEncoder() method, 297
    make() method, 298, 300
    product families, 293, 294
Anonymous classes, 150–152
Anonymous function, 145, 146, 148, 313,
        322, 394
Application controller pattern
    AddVenue and AddSpace
            commands, 450
    command classes, 450
    component data
        AppController class, 461
        CliRequest class, 464

commands and views, 465
ComponentDescriptor class, 459
forward() method, 464
ForwardViewComponent
    class, 463
getCommand(), 462
getView() method, 460
ViewComponent objects, 465
ViewComponent class, 462
consequences, 467
decoupling, 450
implementation
    class diagram, 451
    command class, 453, 466
    commands and views, 458
    component data, 459–465
    ComponentDescriptor class, 457
    concrete command, 466
    configuration file, 453–455
    FrontController class, 452, 453
    parsing, 456–458
    processView() method, 458
Architecture overview
    applications/layers
        design patterns, 426
        enterprise system, 423, 424
        participants, 426
        persistence strategies, 424
        requirements, 424
        stubs/mock objects, 425

Printed in the United States
by Baker & Taylor Publisher Services

Printed in the United States
by Baker & Taylor Publisher Services